Communication
for Business
and the Professions

MALRA TREECE

Memphis State University

Communication for Business and the Professions

ALLYN AND BACON, INC.
Boston • London • Sydney • Toronto

To Guy

IMPORTANT NOTE

Most of the names of individuals and organizations used in examples and problems are fictitious. For all actual names, the individual and/or organization has furnished written permission that these names, as well as the written work concerned, be used in this book. Street addresses are fictitious; zip codes are intentionally inexact. With these stated exceptions, when actual names of individuals or organizations occur, it is strictly by coincidence.

Fourth printing . . . August, 1979

Copyright © 1978 by Allyn and Bacon, Inc. 470 Atlantic Avenue, Boston, Massachusetts 02210.

Library of Congress Cataloging in Publication Data

Treece, Malra.
  Communication for business and the professions.

  Includes bibliographies and index.
  1. Communication in management. 2. Commercial correspondence. 3. Business report writing.
I. Title.
HF5718.T73   658.4'5   77-18745
ISBN 0-205-05956-2

Contents

VI
COMMUNICATION AND EFFECTIVE BUSINESS MANAGEMENT   493

APPENDIX C

APPENDIX D

Preface

Communication for Business and the Professions is based on the premise that all aspects of communication are interrelated. Principles of effective writing also apply to effective speech. Nonverbal communication enters into both oral and written communication. Communication in any form is affected by the many and varied influences that enter into human behavior.

APPROACH

The approach is a unified one—a combination of theory, techniques, and application, all for the purpose of solving business, professional, and personal communication problems. Basically, the study of communication, as well as the content of this book, is the study of meaning and behavior and of how the transmission and reception of meaning affects behavior.

The study of communication for business and the professions is interdisciplinary. Thus this book contains instruction in aspects of speech, journalism, language, research sources and methods, individual and organizational behavior, general business management, office management, personnel management, marketing, persuasion, and business ethics. Emphasis throughout is upon writing and speaking for effective business management.

Although highly professional in content and organization, all chapters are especially planned for easy and interesting reading. Readability and interest are considered important from three major standpoints: to enable the reader to *enjoy* the book; to illustrate techniques of readable and interesting business writing; and to exemplify by the textbook itself one of the most important attributes of human communication—consideration for the receiver of the message.

Successful communicators are far more than skilled technicians; they must have an understanding of the process of communication and of the effect of varying perceptions and emotions upon the reception of meaning. In addition, they are knowledgeable in the subject matter about which they communicate, and their messages are sincere. Sincerity, perhaps the most essential element of all communication, is stressed throughout the book.

ORGANIZATION OF CONTENT

Part I, Chapters 1 through 5, provides the foundation for the study of communication. Chapter 7 is an introduction to the study of business messages and to basic reference and reading sources. Remaining chapters in Part I summarize organizational communication; general communication theory; interpersonal communication, including listening; general semantics and other aspects of language; and nonverbal communication.

Part II, Chapters 6, 7, and 8, presents additional theory as it relates to business and professional communication and stresses the principles and techniques of effective written messages.

Part III, Chapters 9 through 12, applies the theory and techniques presented in Parts I and II to the study of frequently written business letters.

Part IV, Chapters 13 and 14, is on the subject of communicating about employment, particularly through the use of the data sheet and application letter.

Part V, Chapters 15 through 18, is the study of business research and the preparation of written and oral reports.

Part VI, Chapters 19 and 20, presents further aspects of oral communication—including speaking to groups—and principles of management through communication and the economical management of communication systems.

The four appendix sections include a summary of the characteristics of effective business communication, letter format and appearance, report format and bibliographical references, and a brief guide to English usage.

Each chapter concludes with problems in both oral and written communication. These problems provide for the application of principles and techniques presented in the chapter, as well as in preceding chapters.

ACKNOWLEDGMENTS

Utmost gratitude is expressed to the many persons, including teachers and dozens of students at Memphis State University, who contributed their ideas and words of encouragement during the preparation of this book.

Special appreciation goes to the following firms and individuals for the use of their material:

- The Royal Bank of Canada
- Ford Motor Company
- The New York Life Insurance Company
- *Southern Living* Magazine
- Allyn and Bacon, Inc. and James N. Holm for excerpts from *Productive Speaking for Business and the Professions* (Boston, 1967)
- Francis Weeks, Executive Director, American Business Communication Association
- Sanford Howard, partner, Harris, Kerr, Forster & Company, Atlanta
- Bruce Mitchell and Union Planters National Bank, Memphis
- Lydel Sims, columnist, *Commercial Appeal*, Memphis
- Karen English CaPece and Theatre Memphis
- Binford Peeples, Professor, Memphis State University
- Debra Allen, Sherry Aldridge, and John Robinson, students, Memphis State University

At various stages in the development of the manuscript a number of dedicated teachers and scholars provided their advice and criticism: Violet Thomas, The University of Arizona; Alton V. Finch, The University of Mississippi; Donald J. Caley, Cerritos College; Courtland L. Bovee, Grossmont College; Richard A. Hatch, San Diego State University; Dorothy Dehr, American River College; Arno F. Knapper, University of Kansas; and Kathryn Baughan, Dayton University. Their valuable contributions, which influenced the content and approach of the book, are sincerely appreciated.

A special word of thanks goes to Mary Toombs, Jeanette White, May Henson, and Diana Watson, who assisted in transcribing and typewriting the copy.

Further appreciation goes to the members of the American Business Communication Association who through the years have said that they want a book exactly like this one.

Malra Treece

AN OVERVIEW OF COMMUNICATION

An Introduction to Your Study of Business Communication

You have been communicating since your first baby smile.

Communication is an integral part of daily life. Unless you are a hermit or spend long hours working alone in an occupation that does not include speaking, writing, reading, or listening, communication makes up the major part of your life, both in actual time spent and in importance. Even when you are completely alone, you are communicating with yourself (thinking, or intracommunication) and, in a way, with other persons. Your memory and reasoning power are sorting out, organizing, and accepting or rejecting previous bits of conversations, lectures, movies, or written materials. As long as your mind is alive, it will send messages to be received by other minds, and you will receive messages from everyone and everything around you.

Communication is interaction. If there is no reception of the message, or if the message has no effect, successful communication has not occurred. The lack of reception is similar to the old question of whether, if a tree falls in a forest where there is no ear to hear, does it make a sound? Whether or not there is sound, there is no reception, and thus no communication.

"Communication" is a word heard almost everywhere now, as it has been for a number of years. "A lack of communication," "a communication gap," and a "breakdown in communication" have become popular, trite phrases to describe trouble of any kind, anywhere, with the possible exceptions of bad weather and the inevitable process of growing old. Like most other clichés, though, these are based on truth. Many of the problems of the world are caused by poor communication.

Your success in business, regardless of your specialization or your employing company, will depend to a great extent upon your success in communicating; perhaps more so than upon any other ability. You will spend far more time in communicating than in all other aspects of your job.   As you move up the ladder of responsibility, communication will become even more important.   Your lack of skill in communicating can keep your employment responsibilities at a lower level than they would be otherwise.

In addition to the vocational and professional benefits to be derived from excellent written and oral communication, your personal and social life is vitally affected, for better or for worse, by your relationships with other persons, and these relationships are built by communication.

Effective management is effective communication.   The business manager must read, listen, speak, write, and think, as well as send and receive messages through the various forms of nonverbal communication. Can you think of any business management duties that do not include communication?

Consider the planning responsibilities of managers at any level. Planning consists of the communication process of thinking.   In addition to thinking, other aspects of communication enter into planning: jotting down ideas and outlines; discussing our thinking with other persons; reading in business journals or from company records of the experiences of other persons with similar problems; reading the reports that have been prepared in order to provide information on which to base decisions; making such reports for others to read; listening to the ideas and opinions of others; putting our completed plans into written form for the approval or the direction of others; oral presentation of the plans, which must be approved and accepted.

Effective communication in business is achieved by applying the basic principles that apply to all human communication to the interchange of business messages, in business situations, usually for the purpose of solving business problems.   The word "communication" is also used to mean a medium of communication — as a letter, memorandum, report, or telephone call.

We communicate almost constantly and have been doing so all our lives.   Then why do we study communication?   That it is so continuous an activity is exactly *why* we should strive to improve our ability — our knowledge of the subject and our skills in applying this knowledge.   None of us communicates as effectively as we might, and, according to many studies and surveys of business persons, communication skills are sadly lacking.   These surveys include young college graduates and even those with graduate degrees.   On the whole, ability in oral communication seems to surpass that of written communication.

For a generation or so, business and government organizations have established training courses of their own or have subsidized classes in communication for their employees at nearby colleges and universities. Some companies have conducted continuing training courses and provided special publications for improving their employees' ability in writing, listening, reading, and speaking, with emphasis upon written communication.

The New York Life Insurance Company has maintained such a program for many years and regularly sends to its personnel the booklet "Effective Letters." The Prudential Life Insurance Company, The Royal Bank of Canada, and many other organizations have made a long and continued effort to improve correspondence. Government agencies have also provided such courses, but writing coming from many government offices is still considered to be hard to read and filled with stilted, unnecessary phrases.

Many, if not most, of the persons receiving this special on-the-job training are college graduates. In response to the obviously felt need, courses such as the one in which you now may be enrolled have been offered in colleges and universities throughout the nation, often as one of the requirements for a degree in any field of business administration.

SUGGESTED OBJECTIVES OF YOUR STUDY

Often we believe that we are communicating efficiently and effectively when in fact we are not doing so. We believe that we are competent receivers of information and ideas when in effect we are not.

Effective communication is far more than the knowledge of "correct" English and the expected pronunciation of words; it is more than the ability to speak confidently and audibly from a public platform or to participate in engaging conversation. All these abilities are important, but even more important are other aspects of our relationships with others and our own self-concept. Effective communication requires a knowledge of psychology, of semantics, of logic, of persuasion and conviction. It also requires a workable knowledge of language, including the dictionary meanings of words and their connotations and special uses.

To communicate, we must have meaningful messages to send forth; that is, we must know what we are talking about. Our employment responsibilities must be completely clear in our minds — the company products, policies, services, and procedures. Most important of all, the successful communicator has a healthy self-respect and a corresponding respect for the receiver of the message.

In which aspect of communication knowledge and skills do you feel that you are now the strongest? The weakest? If you already have the answers to these questions, you are well on your way to determining your goals for this course and for your continued study. If you are like most college students or business persons, you will need to concentrate on several areas, with some attention to all major aspects. And you will not be a perfect communicator when you complete your study of this book, or of many courses, but your communication ability will be improved.

You are working for excellence, not merely for adequacy.

At the beginning of your study, as of any endeavor, it is good to determine goals and to decide upon methods of reaching these goals. If you are enrolled in a class, no doubt your instructor's course outline includes specific objectives to be attained during the term or semester. But to be worthwhile, the objectives must also be truly your own. You may wish to set goals for yourself that are higher than the required ones.

Perhaps the following list of objectives will help you think more clearly about what you wish to accomplish.

1. To understand the theory and concepts of the communication process, especially as they apply to business situations and behavior.
2. To strengthen ability in listening, reading, thinking, and speaking.
3. To develop a logical, ethical approach to solving business problems through communication.
4. To increase the ability to inform and convince others through the use of language.
5. To learn the forms and purposes of the more commonly used business reports, letters, and other kinds of business writing.
6. To improve the ability to make decisions involving the selection and organization of content and the choice of media and format.
7. To learn to communicate information and ideas in written form by:
   a. Developing a clear, concise, convincing, and correct writing style that is adapted to the readers of the message.
   b. Learning and applying high standards of physical presentation in preparing business messages.
8. To learn the basic techniques of report preparation, including how to collect, evaluate, analyze, organize, interpret, and present data in written and oral messages.
9. To strengthen the ability to analyze written and oral communication.

Do you have other objectives of your own? Which of these that are given are most important to you? In reality, regardless of your particular goals, to which you will give special emphasis, you will need to work on all aspects of communication, for the attributes of excellent communication do not occur separately but are parts of the whole. The old maxim that a chain is no stronger than its weakest link is true of your ability to communicate.

READING FOR PROFESSIONAL AND PERSONAL GROWTH

Reading is one of the five basic processes of verbal communication, along with listening, speaking, writing, and thinking. Thinking can be considered verbal communication from the standpoint that we think at least partially in words, or "talk to ourselves." In addition to verbal communication, much communication is nonverbal.

Reading is vitally important, for by no other way can we learn and develop in our personal and professional life as by wide and wise reading. Reading also helps us to become better writers, thinkers, listeners, and speakers. We obtain a background of knowledge upon which to shape our ideas, as well as becoming more adept in expressing these ideas as we read the words of others.

Efficient Reading of Textbooks

When you begin the study of any book used as a basic text in a course you are beginning, or when you look over a similar book that you plan to study alone, first notice the organization and the format. Read the preface and any other preliminary parts. A well-planned table of contents summarizes the entire book. If each chapter is summarized, read the summaries, in the order that they are given, before you begin the detailed reading of the chapters. Although some of the information may not be completely clear to you, especially if the book is about a new and unfamiliar subject, you will know basically what the book is about and how to proceed with your study.

In any course it is a good idea to read the book through, even though hurriedly, during the first week or two of the semester. This may sound like absurd advice, especially if you are so busy that you find it difficult to keep up with the reading of assigned chapters and other outside work. Indeed, in books of a highly technical nature, such as statistics, chemistry, or mathematics, this procedure would be difficult and perhaps of little advantage.

But your early reading of some entire books, including this one, is not an impossible or difficult task. It is a desirable practice because you are better able to understand the material as you read it again throughout the semester. Because of your early reading, the day-to-day study will be more efficient and less time consuming than it would be otherwise. The early reading of this textbook, or of any text, is especially beneficial if you are to be assigned a major report or other major project that should be started early in the semester.

In your preview study, notice the appendix sections and how they relate to the chapters themselves. Use the index to find subjects of particular interest to you and read those sections. Few books must be read in an uninterrupted order from the first page to the last.

Growing through Selective Reading

In this course, as in most others, you will find it more beneficial and enjoyable not to confine your reading to the assigned textbook or textbooks, but to read many others in the field and in related fields. Yes, time is limited, and perhaps your effort will be less than you would like. But for the greatest growth, read widely from similar textbooks and from many related books and magazine articles.

Many areas of knowledge relate to your study of business communications, probably more so than in any other business class. A basic course in communication, including one in business communication, is interdisciplinary, regardless of the school or department in which it is offered. Fundamentally, instruction in business communication is instruction in business management. The study of business communication also includes aspects of psychology, philosophy, sociology, speech, journalism, drama, and the structure and use of the English language. In addition, there is a mathematical approach to communication, and communication through the use of computers and other machines and equipment. (Computers and other sophisticated equipment are only the means of effecting human communication.)

Business fields that consist mostly of aspects of communication are public relations, marketing, advertising, personnel management, supervision, credit and collections, and business research and report writing. In fact, practically everything that pertains to business in any way involves some form of communication.

Many kinds of reading material relate in some way to your study of communication, but selected reading is likely to be more beneficial than reading at random. Use the suggested readings at the end of each chapter as a basic guide, but expand your reading to communication as it pertains to your own special area of business study. For example, if you are majoring in accounting, you will be interested in learning the kinds of materials accountants write and their frequently occurring difficulties. If you are majoring in advertising, you will be especially interested in persuasive communication, along with objective, factual writing and speaking. (Persuasive communication is basically a factual presentation, slanted to the needs and desires of the receiver of the message.) If you are majoring in economics, you may be especially interested in research methods and in the graphic presentation of data. Regardless of your major field of specialization, you should be vitally interested in improving your ability to express your ideas and to be receptive to the messages of other persons.

As you read, don't just put aside your own judgment and critical ability and accept unquestioningly anything and everything that you find in print. Errors of all kinds sometimes occur, even in books and journals from the most highly regarded publishers. Remember that words are written by fallible human beings, all of whom have their own particular perception of reality, their whims, and their biases. (See Chapter 3 on the communication process, especially as to how communication can and does go astray.) That this imperfection occurs is another reason for reading widely in order that you can form your own opinions by reading the words of many persons and evaluating differing views.

This book contains quotations and opinions from several other authors in the field and in related fields. These references are included in order to help insure impartiality and a presentation of differing points of view. In addition to these included passages, a reading list is given at the end of each chapter or each section.

Reading requires active, creative effort. Reading skills are essential for your personal and professional growth. Perhaps even more important, reading can give much pleasure. For many people, reading is one of the most enjoyable and important activities of their lives. You are indeed fortunate if you live in a community with excellent public libraries. If you are not taking advantage of these libraries, as well as those of your college or university, you are missing a great portion of your educational opportunities — perhaps the greatest portion. The joy of learning through entering the minds of others, as you do when you read their words, is so enjoyable and beneficial that it is sad to know that some people read only what they must.

Many persons greatly enjoy browsing from book to book, of being led by the ideas of one author to the works of another, of acquiring knowledge from all — of analyzing and comparing ideas and viewpoints and of deciding upon their particular outlook at the moment. These people enjoy finding an interest in fields they have never before explored, of being entertained, amused, enlightened, educated, and sometimes even inspired.

Reading can improve all the other communication skills. Wide reading of professionally written material will carry over to improve your own writing and speaking. Although this process is more or less an unconscious one, your knowledge and vocabulary are increased through reading, as is your ability to express ideas in oral and written form.

In addition to improving your ability to communicate, the acquisition of knowledge through reading provides material for your mind so that you will have something to communicate. This is perhaps the most important attribute of all — for it doesn't matter how well you say it, if you don't have anything to say!

Finding Specialized Reading Material

Do you know how to find specialized information? Suppose, for example, that you want to read recently written articles on communication as it pertains to personnel management. Where would you look first? Then where would you go? Suppose you want to find the books on business communication that have been published in the past two years. Or the books by Stuart Chase that are currently available? Or suppose that you set out to find what has been written about communication in magazines planned for the general reading public, such as *Reader's Digest*. Do you know the leading periodicals in your particular business field? What kind of journal, for example, is *Management Review?* What is the *Journal of Business Communication,* as far as its purposes and readers are concerned? What is meant by *Moody's Manuals?* By *Roget's Thesaurus?* Where is the reference room in your university library? In addition to printed material, what library resources are available, such as cassettes, films, film strips, and transparencies?

Did you immediately know the answers to these questions? Do you know a great deal more than the answers to these particular questions about finding information and reading material? Further and more detailed discussion of library sources will be given later in this textbook with the chapters on report writing. You need the ability to use your libraries, however, aside from finding information for business reporting.

As a partial explanation of these few questions about finding information in libraries, see the following paragraphs. Ask your librarian if you need further assistance.

To find recently published articles on communication as it relates to personnel management, look in the *Business Periodicals Index* under "Personnel Management," "Communication in Management," and other topics that may be referred to under these listings. *The Business Periodicals Index* is the most comprehensive and complete index of periodicals in all fields of business. It is issued monthly, except for July, and cumulated yearly. Business areas indexed include accounting, advertising, banking, finance, credit management, general business, insurance, retailing, real estate, personnel management, office management, public administration, and taxation, as well as special business communication areas, such as letter and report writing. The *Index,* under its present name, goes back to 1958. From 1913, the year it was begun, until 1958, it was known as the *Industrial Arts Index.* These volumes of the *Industrial Arts Index* are still available in most libraries for use in referring to articles written many years ago.

Suppose that you find, through your use of the *Business Periodicals Index,* that several articles have been written within the last year on the subject of communication as it pertains to personnel management. Then find out whether your library subscribes to the journals in which they appear, and whether back issues are on microfilm or in bound volumes. Usually issues that have appeared during the past few months will be kept on the shelves near the current issue.

To find books on business communication that have appeared in the last two years, look in the "Subject Index" of *Books in Print*. This information is also given in the *Cumulative Book Index*. To find the books by Stuart Chase (who is a well-known writer in the field of general semantics and several other fields), look in the "Author Index" of *Books in Print* or in the *Cumulative Book Index*.

To find articles that have appeared in general periodicals, look in the *Reader's Guide to Periodical Literature*. Some business magazines that are also read by large numbers of the general reading public are included in both the *Business Periodicals Index* and the *Reader's Guide to Periodical Literature*.

Management Review, as its name implies, is a publication for business managers. It is one of the publications of the American Management Society. *Supervisory Management* is another.

The Journal of Business Communication is one of the two periodicals published by the American Business Communication Association. Its readers are primarily college teachers of business communication, business writers, and managers of communication.

Moody's Manuals,[1] published by Moody's Investment Service, summarize financial data and operating facts of all major American companies.

Roget's Thesaurus[2] is a word book that gives synonyms, near-synonyms, and words related in meaning. It is a most valuable addition to any writer's bookshelf. Similar word books are also helpful, but *Roget's* is one of the oldest and best known.

Further discussion of the many available reference sources, especially for business information, is given in Chapter 15, which is one of the chapters in Part V on business research and report writing.

Reading for Professional Advancement

Reading will continue to be important to you as you move ahead in your career. Even if it were possible to learn everything you need to know while you are in college (and, as you know, this is far from possible), in a few years you would find that much of what you need to know was not even within the scope of available knowledge when you were in college. A truism often heard but still vitally important to consider is that to stay abreast of any field of knowledge we must continually read and study. No

---

1. *Moody's Investor Service* (New York: Moody's). Annual bound volumes supplemented by loose-leaf services.
2. *Roget's International Thesaurus*, 3d ed. (New York: Thomas Y. Crowell Company, 1962.)

doubt this will be even more true in the years ahead than it has been in the past.

In addition to library sources, home and office reading material and reference sources are helpful to you in school and on the job. A good dictionary is essential for any home or office. English handbooks and a thesaurus (such as *Roget's*, mentioned previously) are also helpful. Handbooks are available in many fields; for example, handbooks of accounting, office management, personnel management, and purchasing. There is even a handbook on how to find handbooks, as well as other business reference sources, in *How to Use the Business Library*, by H. W. Johnson.[3] Another source that provides information on library research is *How and Where to Look It Up*, by Robert W. Murphy.[4]

In your major field of study, and in your continuing education after you complete your formal education, reading professional journals will add to your interest and knowledge. Journals are available in company libraries, or perhaps they will be in your own office. Your own personal subscription to magazines in your field will be well worthwhile.

In addition to professional journals published for broad business fields, such as accounting, economics, and office management, many publications are planned especially for various trades and industries. For example, if you should be employed as an accountant for a shoe manufacturing company, your professional reading might include (in addition to accounting journals) several publications prepared for the shoe manufacturing business, or for those persons engaged in the retailing of shoes.

This discussion has pertained mostly to reading in business fields. For your success in business, however, reading outside your field may be even more helpful. A criticism of some business students and of those already working in business organizations is that they do not have a wide background of general knowledge — that their liberal education is more limited than it should be. Your liberal arts and humanities courses help you to become more thoroughly educated, but education is a continuing process. As the world becomes more complex and more challenging, a broad background of knowledge and understanding is not only desirable, but absolutely essential.

SUMMARY ◆ 1

Communication is interaction. If there is no reception of the message, or if the message has no effect, successful communication has not occurred.

3. H. W. Johnson, ed., *How to Use the Business Library — With Sources of Business Information*, 4th ed. (Cincinnati: South-Western Publishing Company, 1973.)
4. Robert W. Murphy, *How and Where to Look It Up — A Guide to Standard Sources of Information* (New York: McGraw-Hill Book Company, 1958).

Your success in business, regardless of your specialization or employing organization, will depend to a great extent upon your ability to communicate, perhaps more so than upon any other ability. You will spend far more time in communicating than in all other aspects of your job.

Effective management is effective communication.

At the beginning of your study of this or any other course, it is good to determine goals and to decide upon methods of reaching these goals.

Reading, one of the five basic processes of verbal communication, is vitally important to your personal and professional growth. As you read, however, don't put aside your own judgment and critical ability and accept unquestioningly all that you find in print. Reading can improve all your other communication skills, in addition to increasing your store of knowledge.

A great number of reference sources are available in modern, comprehensive libraries. The reader should learn to use these sources.

QUESTIONS AND PROBLEMS ◆ 1

1. Look back at the list of objectives for this course. Which ones interest you the most? The least? Why? In which areas referred to by these various objectives do you feel that you are now the strongest? The weakest?

   Express the answers to these questions in a letter addressed to your instructor. From Appendix B, choose either the "Official" or "Simplified" style in which to arrange your letter, or follow the direction of your instructor.

   In addition to the answer to these questions, perhaps your instructor will want you to include the following information:

   a. Your major and expected date of graduation.
   b. The kind of work you hope to enter or continue after you complete your college work.
   c. Whether you have a part-time job, and, if so, what you do, especially as your work relates to business communication.
   d. Your previous work experience, particularly your communication responsibilities.

2. In the library, look in the *Business Periodicals Index* under "Communication in Management" to find two articles that have been published within the past two years. Try to find articles that are related to your field of specialization; for example, if you are majoring in personnel management, find articles about communication in the field of personnel management. Give the complete bibliographical reference to these articles, as shown in Appendix C. (*Note:* If you are majoring in secretarial administration or business education, use the *Business Education Index* in order to find articles about communication that pertain especially to your field of specialization.)

3. Write a one-page summary of one or both of these articles. Be prepared to present this summary, or these summaries, orally to the class.

4. Look in *Books in Print* to find the names of two books on business communication that have been published within the past two years. Give the complete bibliographical reference to these books, as shown in Appendix C.

5. Check the card catalog of your college library in order to determine the availability of the books listed in the "Further Reading" section of this chapter. Are later editions now available for one or more of these books? (Or, as your instructor directs, different students can determine the availability of library material listed in the "Further Reading" sections of all chapters in this book, in order to draw up a bibliography to use throughout the term or semester.)

6. "Comments and Bits of Information" assignment. The purpose of this assignment is to start you thinking about the wide field of communication and to give you an opportunity to present a bit of information to the class. To find this comment or bit of any information, look in any printed source — one of those given in this chapter, elsewhere in the book, or in newspaper or journal articles. (Do not use your present textbook.) Try to find recent sources, and, as much as possible, make the comment understandable to other students who, like you, are perhaps beginning their first course in business communication.

    Your comment or bit of information should be about communication, preferably business communication. For example, you might say something like this: "Time is a factor in nonverbal communication, and not all persons view tardiness in the way we do in the United States. In many countries, time is treated much more casually than it is here." Give your source for your particular bit of information; you may use the exact words of the author, but if you do so, include a statement to that effect. You might obtain your comment by simply glancing at a newspaper and noting, as an example, that postage rates are expected to rise again soon.

    This assignment has resulted in most interesting and stimulating class sessions; at times, however, all students seem to find about the same kinds of information. Your instructor will determine whether there is time to devote to spending a class session in this way. It can result in giving a quick, although somewhat disorganized, overview of the study of business communication.

FURTHER READING ◆ 1

NOTE: The books listed here pertain not only to Chapter 1 but to sections of the entire course. These books are additional sources that will be helpful to you throughout your study — and you can find others through your library card catalog, most likely indexed under "Communication in Management."

None of the books listed here covers all the subjects included in your present text, but some are especially good in some areas. In all courses, you benefit most by reading widely.   In this particular course, you will benefit by examining the writing examples given in different textbooks; for example, when you are studying sales letters, read the section on sales writing in several books and note the varying examples.

Additional reference sources that pertain to particular aspects of communication are listed at the ends of following chapters.

WARNING: *Never* use sample letters or other kinds of writing as models from which to compose your own letters by lifting words and phrases or by relying on the exact order of presentation.   Model letters are not given to be copied — write your own!

Bonner, William H. *Better Business Writing.* Homewood, Ill.: Richard D. Irwin, 1974.

Brown, Leland. *Communicating Facts and Ideas in Business.* 2d ed. Englewood Cliffs, N.J.: Prentice-Hall, 1970.

Dawe, Jessamon, and Lord, William Jackson, Jr. *Functional Business Communication.* 2d ed. Englewood Cliffs, N.J.: Prentice-Hall, 1974.

Himstreet, William C., and Baty, Wayne Murlin. *Business Communications.* 5th ed. Belmont, Calif.: Wadsworth Publishing Company, 1976.

Janis, J. Harold. *Writing and Communicating in Business.* 2d ed. New York: Macmillan Publishing Co., 1973.

Lesikar, Raymond V. *Business Communication: Theory and Application.* 3d ed. Homewood, Ill.: Richard D. Irwin, 1976.

Menning, J. H.; Wilkenson, C. W.; and Clarke, Peter B. *Communicating through Letters and Reports.* 6th ed. Homewood, Ill.: Richard D. Irwin, 1976.

Murphy, Herta A., and Peck, Charles E. *Effective Business Communications.* 2d ed. New York: McGraw-Hill Book Company, 1976.

Sigband, Norman B. *Communication for Management and Business.* 2d ed. Glenview, Ill.: Scott, Foresman and Company, 1975.

Wolf, Morris Philip, and Aurner, Robert R. *Effective Communication in Business.* Cincinnati: South-Western Publishing Company, 1974.

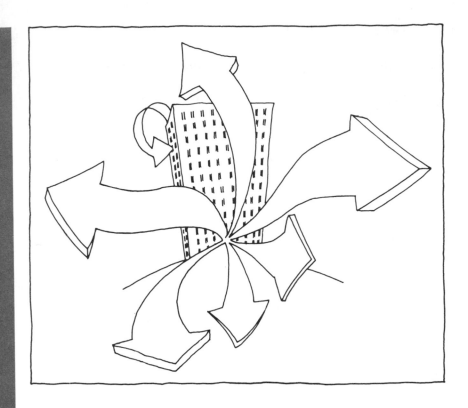

Communication within and from the Organization

2

"Organization" or "organizational," as used in this book, applies to any goal-oriented group, profit or nonprofit, such as businesses, government agencies, educational institutions, charitable foundations, and labor unions. Our major interest is in business organizations, however, and most references to organizations apply to business establishments.

Regardless of the type of organization, the basic principles of communication are the same; purposes, methods, media, and formats may differ somewhat. In addition, many persons who are educated for business obtain employment in government, educational institutions, and other similar organizations.

Successful communication is vital to the functioning of any organization. It cannot be considered as a separate part of organizational activity, for it permeates every facet, especially on the management level, and is an almost continuous activity. Clerical jobs, supervisory work, sales and advertising — all these functions are made up almost altogether of communication activities. Accountants communicate with figures, graphic presentations, and oral and written words. All other personnel in any occupation, with the possible exception of production workers and manual laborers, communicate throughout most of their working day.

Just as communication is an almost continuous process in the personal life of the individual, it is the most vital and continuous force within any organization. Effective communication in a business organization involves, in addition to human processes, the efficient management of mechanical tools of communication — the computer, the typewriter, the telephone, dictating and duplicating machines, and specialized audio and video equipment.

Efficient management requires a choice of the method and media for transmitting information, especially in terms of the ever-increasing costs.

(See Chapter 19, "Efficient and Economical Communication Systems and Procedures.")   A telephone call across the continent may be less expensive than an individually dictated letter, but in some situations the letter will be the better choice.

Regardless of the method used or how the message is sent, the most important tool of communication is language, as it always has been.   The most sophisticated machines cannot be operated without the use of human communication, and, most especially, the application of human thought.

In organizational communication, just as in individual and personal interchange of thoughts and ideas, we must keep in mind that we are socially and morally responsible for the content and effect of our messages. Examples of social responsibility, or the lack of it, have been widely discussed in relation to advertising and mass communication, and laws have been passed to prevent deceptive methods of communication. Legal restrictions apply to many phases of communication within and from the organization — for example, in credit policies and practices, and in the field of employee rights.

In addition to judging messages sent in the light of social and moral responsibility, we should use reason and good judgment in analyzing messages received.   A knowledge of the processes of communication will help you to carefully construct your own messages as well as to analyze the messages of other people.

PURPOSEFUL COMMUNICATION WITHIN THE ORGANIZATION

Internal communication moves upward, downward, or horizontally, using the broad terms to indicate levels of responsibility.   The number of messages that move downward exceeds the number that move upward. These messages, often in the form of memorandums, are used to coordinate efforts and activities, to instruct, to direct, or to explain company decisions or policies.   Upward communication is often in the form of reports, oral or written.

Management must have adequate and correct information in order to make intelligent decisions.   Reports also travel horizontally, as from one department to another.   Reports can be said to move downward in the sense that results of research studies are reported to personnel below the level of the report writer, but they seldom move downward for the purpose of using the report information in decision making.

Insufficient, ineffective, or inefficient communication or communication systems constitute major problems of organizational management. Excellent communication among departments — which does not exist in many organizations — can decrease departmental rivalries and tensions. Within organizations, especially large ones, there exists a large variety of specialists and nonspecialists, supposedly working together toward the same goals for the organization, and for themselves as part of the organization. In some instances, however, each group works with insufficient knowledge and understanding of the purposes and procedures of other groups — or individuals work alone toward their own goals, seeming to disregard everyone else around them. All workers could benefit through sharing in the experiences and problems of their co-workers, although in all instances the opportunity for creativity and individual productivity should prevail.

One factor that hinders the free flow of communications within an organization is that each specialty — for example, marketing, accounting, data processing, engineering, finance, research — has its own language, its own specialized terminology. These specialists must work together if the organization as a whole is to progress as it should.

As much as possible, employees should be given the opportunity to participate in the decision-making processes, for whatever affects the organization also affects personnel. From a practical standpoint, however, every decision will not and cannot be exactly as every employee would desire it to be. At the very least, all persons can be kept informed of the decisions and of the reasons behind them.

The Communication Environment and Atmosphere

Workers at all levels are motivated by communication that assures them of the company's interest in them, as well as by sincere efforts to inform and instruct them about organizational plans, benefits, policies, and newsworthy events.

Fred T. Allen, Chairman of the Board and President of Pitney-Bowes, Inc., makes this statement:

> A basic tenet of our company policy is simply stated: When an individual or institution invests in our stock, he deserves a regular and complete accounting; the employee who invests his working life in our company deserves no less and conceivably more.[1]

If such an open and nonsecretive policy of communication is to exist and flourish, it must be established by top management; it must be sincerely accepted by the employees.

Pitney-Bowes officials have been credited with pioneering in that they have departed from the traditional concepts of employee-

1. Fred T. Allen, "Ways to Improve Employee Communication," *Nation's Business* (September 1975), pp. 54–56.

management communications.   The internal communication system is two-way, from management to employee and from employee to management.   This organization would not describe the communications within the company as being divided into discrete "downward" or "upward" categories, although basically some communication must move either upward or downward.

The opportunity for feedback helps prevent downward communication from being merely informational or instructional, and upward communication from being merely reporting.   The primary elements of the Pitney-Bowes program are the council of personnel relations and the annual jobholders' report and jobholders' meeting.   The council is a monthly forum where representatives of management and representatives of the group of employees sit down to discuss mutual problems and plans. This forum is held at the sectional, departmental, and divisional levels.

Communication from management to employees, as well as from employees to management, must be sincere and built on trust if it is to be conducive to morale building, productivity, or company progress. William V. Haney is one of the authorities in the field of organizational communication who describe the ideal communication environment as being one of trust.   In his words:

> When the organizational climate can be characterized as trusting and supportive, communication practice is generally good.   There are a number of reasons for this.
>
> First of all the members of such an organization, relatively speaking, have no ax to grind, nothing to be gained by miscommunicating deliberately. The aura of openness makes possible candid expressions of feelings and ideas.   Even faulty communication does not lead immediately to retaliation, for others are not prone to presume malice on the offender's part, but instead "carry him"; compensate for his errors. . . .   Obviously, effective communication will do much to reinforce and enhance an existing trusting climate.   But if communication performance begins to falter repeatedly the trusting relationship may be jeopardized. . . .   When self-fulfilling prophecies of intrigue and suspicion emerge the organization may be in for trouble.
>
> Conversely, when the climate is hostile and threatening communication tends to suffer — not only is there a tendency toward miscommunication with malice aforethought but in such an atmosphere true feelings are suppressed lest one be punished for revealing them.   By and large one's communication (as well as his behavior in general) is dominated by the need to protect himself rather than the desire to serve the interests of the organization.   Unfortunately, when the climate is unhealthy even letter-perfect communication practice can be inadequate. . . .[2]

Such a policy of open communication systems built on trust not only builds morale but encourages the flow of vital information, opinions, and

2. William V. Haney, *Communication and Organizational Behavior*, 3d ed.   (Homewood, Ill.: Richard D. Irwin, 1973), pp. 15–16.

criticisms. Honest, open downward communication encourages the same kind of communication to flow upward. Good intent, however, is not enough. This discussion by Haney, as well as similar viewpoints expressed by other leaders in the fields of business communication and business management, should not lead to the conclusion that all will go well "if our heart is in the right place." Poor skills and techniques can also lead to poor communication and poor communication systems.

Employees want and need information, not only for use in carrying out their own duties but also so that they can understand the overall company strategy and purposes. They need to feel proud of their organization, and they can do so even when they realize that it has faults, problems, and weaknesses if they feel that management is sincere and is keeping them informed. Employees at any level want to know what is going on and why.

The organization should keep employees informed of company programs, problems, proposed changes, or any other matters that affect their interest, as well as to encourage free discussion between employees and their supervisors and among the employees themselves. Informed employees, who are more likely to feel that they are valued and trusted by top management, are more likely to be cooperative and to devote their efforts to organizational goals.

Communication Networks

Communication networks, both formal and informal, exist within all sizable organizations. For example, you as an employee will ordinarily be under the direct supervision of one person, to whom you should bring any problems or grievances. This person, in turn, is responsible to someone at a higher level. It is only good manners not to go "over the head" of your immediate supervisor, although in rare and extreme cases it may be necessary.

Reports will ordinarily go to your immediate supervisor, although it is quite possible that they will be assigned by someone higher in the organization or you may be "borrowed" by a department other than your own.

The ever-continuing flow of communication within the organization moves through complex channels which should be carefully planned and supervised. These channels should be varied from time to time in order to meet changing problems and conditions. Procedures often need to be simplified and the actual number and frequency of communications reduced. The vast number of memorandums used in some organizations has become so commonplace that it is the subject of satire and cartoons to the effect that management trainees and executives measure their effectiveness and importance by the number of memorandums flowing from their desks each day.

Reports of various kinds are sometimes prepared unnecessarily. Because of the ease of obtaining detailed data by the use of the computer, or of making multiple copies with duplicating and copying machines, over-communication may occur.   Such a practice wastes time and money and may result in confusion to readers who receive information with which they are not really concerned, although perhaps it is better to overcommunicate than to undercommunicate.   The lack of desirable and needed information decreases efficiency and employee morale — but neither of the extremes, overcommunication or undercommunication, is necessary if communications networks are wisely planned and managed.

Robert Townsend, in *Up the Organization,* advises that decision reports on computers should be kept at the highest level.   "Otherwise . . . your managers will be drowning in ho-hum reports they've been conned into asking for and are ashamed to admit are of no value."[3]   (*Up the Organization* has been described as the funniest, most outrageous, but most constructive book ever written about how to run things.)

Townsend would not agree with the terminology we have used in this discussion of "upward" and "downward" communication, although he emphasizes throughout the book the necessity for strong leadership.   In speaking of organization charts, he states:

> A chart demoralizes people.   Nobody thinks of himself as *below* other people.   And in a good company he isn't.   Yet on paper there it is. . . .   In the best organizations people see themselves working in a circle as if around one table.   One of the positions is designated chief executive officer, because somebody has to make all the technical decisions that enable an organization to keep working.   In this circular organization, leadership passes from one to another depending upon the particular task being attacked — without any hangups.[4]

Up the Organization is an example of clear, direct, concise, emphatic, and entertaining writing, but the extremely informal style of some of the passages would be frowned upon by many traditional-minded business persons, even though the book became a best seller.   Townsend's style would be inappropriate for many kinds of business writing, and no doubt he could never be described as a literary great, but much business communication goes too far in the other direction and becomes stiff, pretentious, and stuffy.

As in all forms of communication, much of the interchange of ideas and information that occurs in any organization seems to have no definite, specific purpose in relation to the formal purposes of the organization. The routine, daily conversation of employees, however, is often a morale builder.   Pleasant personal contacts with co-workers, as well as with management, is a major source of job satisfaction.   Lack of such contact, especially if there is a restrictive atmosphere as to the flow of ideas,

3. Robert Townsend, *Up the Organization* (New York: Alfred A. Knopf, 1970), p. 36.
4. Townsend, *Up the Organization,* p. 134.

information, or casual conversation, can be a most discouraging aspect of employment and certainly not conducive to pleasant and effective human relationships.

The informal communication network in an organization is known as the grapevine. It may carry far more information than formal networks, and the message moves faster. Much of this "information," however, consists of gossip, rumors, and half-truths. Managers recognize the existence of the grapevine, and some try to use it in order to advance the overall effectiveness of company policies and procedures — to spread information that they wish to circulate. They determine the leaders of the grapevine and communicate to them the material that is to be sent through the company via the grapevine. This use of the grapevine has obvious dangers, however, not only because the message is likely to be garbled into many versions (usually incorrect ones), but because the procedure may give the appearance of favoritism.

The best way to eliminate or decrease undesirable effects of the grapevine is for management to maintain an open policy of communication so that employees feel that they are being kept informed — and even better, that they have a part in making decisions that affect their company and themselves. Complete information cannot be released to all employees at all times; some must be kept secret until a public announcement is made, for various reasons.

But all personnel should be made to feel that they are trusted employees and that management and the overall organization can be trusted. Without this atmosphere of confidence, the most highly structured and carefully supervised communication networks within an organization are far less effective, as well as less conducive to pleasant employee-management relationships, than they would be otherwise.

An effective communication network provides for feedback. Without feedback there can be no "open management" policy, for employees receive the downward communication and have no opportunity for response. Some feedback comes through the grapevine, but, like all messages that travel via the grapevine, the feedback is often garbled before it reaches the sender of the original message.

Some companies are making efforts to decrease the formality of communication networks without the use of the more or less "underground" grapevine. According to the article, "Organizing the Kaffe Klatsch" in *Psychology Today*, methods being used to improve employee communication, especially with one another, include:

- providing doorways between work areas in order to encourage more face-to-face communication and decrease the number of memorandums;
- moving individuals or departments that need to communicate with one another so that they are closer together;
- identifying the people who are the communicators within the company and making more information available to them;

- providing a central coffee area where persons of all different units can meet and talk;
- arranging for field people to visit company offices and research departments.[5]

One of these methods, "identifying the communicators," is a restatement of the idea of Keith Davis[6] and others that the grapevine should be used in order to further organizational objectives and not left to grow and branch on its own. (Keith Davis has done research and written widely about the different aspects of the grapevine.)

The channels of internal communication, their appropriateness and their efficiency, must be recognized as being essential to good organizational management. Communication is an important motivating force; it is also necessary that every person have the necessary information and instructions that he or she needs in order to perform assigned and related duties. Much greater emphasis should be placed on the planning and supervision of communication channels in many organizations — perhaps the one in which you will be employed.

To the beginning worker, the initial orientation to company policies and procedures is a necessary form of communication that may vitally affect the success of the employee. The employee, if not adequately informed, should find out as completely and as tactfully as possible the sources of reliable information and instruction. In most organizations, one will find a professional complainer or two for whom no news is ever pleasant. These people can cause a great deal of dissatisfaction among other workers, although most of their co-workers soon learn to "consider the source."

You as a beginning worker will be wise to listen to everyone, reply politely but noncommittally, and go about doing a good job in all your areas of responsibility. But when you need information — ask! Many people hesitate to ask for information or help because they believe it to be a sign of weakness. To do otherwise is a sign of weakness. But you should ask your supervisor, or the person who is in charge of training you. And you should make sure that you have read and understood company manuals, memorandums, and other materials planned and written for your instruction.

Effective Downward Communication

In order to clarify and classify the kinds of downward communication according to purpose, the following distinctions are made.

5. Albert Shapero, Albert Chammah, and Maitland Huffman, "Organizing the Kaffee Klatsch," *Psychology Today* (October 1975), pp. 24–25.
6. Keith Davis, "Management Communication and the Grapevine," *Harvard Business Review* (September-October 1953), pp. 31, 43–49.

1. *Internal downward communication is used to instruct the workers.*   Information and instructions must flow downward so that employees will know exactly what is expected of them and what they can expect from the company.   They must know their duties, responsibilities, rights, and opportunities as they are a part of the organization.

For the new employee, extensive training periods, consisting of on-the-job training and perhaps of classroom instruction, are necessary for orientation into company policies and procedures and the employment responsibilities of the particular position.   Many companies hire individuals from the standpoint of their potential value, not for their present skills, education, or ability.   This potential value may never be reached without sufficient effort to communicate to these employees exactly what is expected of them, how they should go about their work, and organizational goals, plans, and philosophy.

The communication efforts of management toward the new employee during this period will perhaps be a vital factor in his or her contributions to the organization, as well as to job satisfaction and career growth and development.   Effective communication must continue throughout the employee's career, regardless of the level of position.   The employee in turn must communicate effectively with subordinates, as well as with those persons higher in authority.

Like all effective instruction, communication to new employees must be well planned, with definite goals and, perhaps, predetermined time schedules.   The instruction should be done by persons who understand the material being presented and who are adept in the presentation of information.

Instructional methods and material consist of many forms: memorandums; handbooks and manuals, some of which are changed periodically by the addition or deletion of loose-leaf pages; bulletin board announcements or other written messages; meetings, conferences, and workshops; and formal classroom instruction.   Often workers are sent at company expense to community colleges and universities to enroll in classes related to their employment responsibilities.

Perhaps the most important form of communication to employees at any level, or at any time in their career, is the daily face-to-face communication between the employee and the supervisor, as well as with other management personnel.   Employees also receive much instruction from co-workers at their own level, or from those below their level of responsibility.   Many executives, when coming into an organization from the outside or when changing jobs within the organization, rely heavily upon an experienced secretary to orient them into the detailed responsibilities and problems of their new position.

2. *Another purpose of downward communication is to build and maintain employee morale and goodwill toward the organization and toward management personnel.*   Employees have questions about promotion, salary

increases, working conditions, and the goals and plans of the organization as a whole. They need to feel that they are a part of a worthwhile, progressive organization to which they are contributing, and of an organization in which their value as individuals is appreciated and paid for.

Some of the media used for the purpose of building and maintaining goodwill are company magazines and newsletters, bulletin board announcements, annual reports to employees, meetings, family days, and various individual communications, such as interviews, letters, and face-to-face communication between management personnel and workers. To repeat a principle that has already been stated — but that is perhaps the single most important principle of employee communication, or of communication of any kind — messages must be sincere.

3. *Another purpose of downward communication is to keep the routine and special activities of the organization moving smoothly and efficiently.* This purpose is accomplished through the use of many methods and media, both written and oral. In many instances, this purpose is also an instructional one, although at times the organization is kept moving through a seeking of information and opinions, not merely by sending messages.

To meet all goals of downward communication, messages must be understood and accepted. For the sender of the message to achieve understanding and acceptance, he or she must have adequate knowledge, proficient communication skills, and an understanding of the receiver's point of view.

Effective Upward Communication

One basic purpose of upward communication is to provide information for management decisions. The upward flow of communication, often in the form of reports, furnishes information and recommendations upon which intelligent decisions can be made. Such reports also flow horizontally, from one department to another. Much of this information is tabulated and analyzed with the aid of computers.

The effectiveness of upward communication can exist only in the presence of effective downward communication. Some information that is to be reported will be of a negative nature because of the obvious reason that not every operation will be a complete success. Management needs this unpleasant information for wise planning and in order to avoid the continuation of any operation that is unprofitable or unsatisfactory. Yet many persons in business hesitate to report unpleasant information, possibly from the standpoint that it reflects unfavorably upon themselves, their competence, and their positive outlook. Only in an atmosphere of open and honest communication will employees report fully and frankly to management.

When we think of the term "reports," we usually think of rather formal written documents. A report, however, can be a simple oral report, or merely the reply to the question, "How's everything going?" If the organization is to progress as it should, the report, regardless of its form, must "tell it like it is."

The employee who is skillful in communicating has a definite advantage over co-workers who do not possess this skill. Your reporting to management may be the key to your success and job satisfaction. Everything that you can do while you are in college to increase your communication ability will have a most practical value when you begin work in a business organization — or when you begin any career.

Communication Media within the Organization

Oral communication is more important — as far as actual time spent — than is written communication, in almost all business organizations, and in almost all departments. And as the cost of written communication continues to increase, even more emphasis is expected to be given to the many forms of oral communication, although this can also be expensive. The public-address system, intracompany telephone systems, closed circuit television, radio communication systems, and many other arrangements are used in business organizations to facilitate oral communication.

Much reporting is done orally, and in some instances the same report may be presented in both oral and written forms. Meetings and conferences are often used throughout the business organization, as well as in professional organizations. Many of the presentations at these meetings and conferences could be classified as oral reports.

Employee councils and forums, interviews, routine face-to-face communication, casual conversation in the halls or in the coffee room — all these forms of oral communication affect employee performance, morale, and the smooth, efficient, profitable functioning of the employing company.

Written communication within an organization is most likely to be in the form of a memorandum. The memorandum is by far the most widely used type of written communication between members of an organization, and at times it is also sent to persons outside the organization. The memorandum format serves as a medium for various kinds of messages. (See Appendix C for an example of a complete memorandum.)

In addition to memorandums, many prepared forms are used for communication within the organization, as well as for external communication. These standardized presentations of information must be used to decrease costs, if for no other reason. In addition, clarity is more likely to be achieved if the same kinds of information are presented in the same way and on the same form.

This uniformity should not be considered as a means of stifling creative thought or individuality. In some cases, the expected forms and arrangements will need improvement. Suggestions for changes should be made; but until they are adopted, the individual writer should follow the expected arrangement. To do otherwise is distracting and confusing, for the hurried reader learns to look for particular kinds of data in a certain place on the form; to find it elsewhere is not only confusing but annoying and time wasting.

In writing situations for which no standard form or arrangement is available, simplicity and directness are usually the best guides to the method of presentation.

A partial listing of some of the media of internal written communication is given below. Some of these have already been mentioned; some of these messages are also used in external communication.

abstracts, summaries, synopses, etc., especially of research reports

agenda (plans for conferences and meetings)

agreements

announcements (bulletin board, memorandum, letter, paycheck insertion, other forms)

annual reports (prepared for employees, stockholders, and the general public)

booklets and brochures

bulletins

business articles and news releases, especially for employee publications but also for outside publication

catalogs

circulars

citations

collection and credit notices, letters, forms, especially through employee credit union

contracts

data sheets

directories

dividend notices

educational material

employee magazines, newspapers, newsletters

financial reports and analyses

form messages of many kinds

goodwill letters, memorandums, forms, other messages

handbooks and manuals

inquiries

instructions

introductions

invitations

job descriptions

laws and bylaws

leaflets

legal documents of many kinds (may be written in attorney's office, although many organizations employ attorneys)

letters of various kinds, including letter reports

market surveys

memorandums

minutes of meetings

notices inserted with
paychecks or sent in other
forms

orders and order forms

organizational charts, flow
charts, etc.

policy and procedure
statements

proposals

programs

questionnaires and other
research instruments

reading rack literature

recruitment literature

reports of many kinds

requisitions

research studies, reports,
summaries of published
research studies

resolutions

resumes

specifications

speeches

suggestions

tags and labels

telegrams

training films and other
material for presentation to
employees

This list, although long, is incomplete in that it could not include the many and varying kinds of special material and methods used in differing types of organizations.

In addition to the types of communication listed here, according to purpose and format, such things as computer programs and specifications for technical and mechanical communication activities are forms of communication within the organization.

PURPOSEFUL COMMUNICATION FROM THE ORGANIZATION

External communication takes many of the same forms and has some of the same purposes as does internal communication. The organization must build and maintain goodwill with customers and with the public, as it must do with employees. Customers and the public receive directions and instructions about the use of the company's products or services. The organization receives and sends information from customers, stockholders, the public, and government agencies in order to plan and to proceed with manufacturing, selling, and promotional activities.

Customer or potential customer communication includes retail and wholesale selling by personal contact, telephone conversations, written messages, and various kinds of advertising and public relations releases. Other purposes of customer communication are instructions about credit, collection messages, and the adjustment of claims and complaints. A major part of external communication efforts are directed toward building and maintaining goodwill.

The telephone is becoming even more widely used than it has been in the past because of the rapidly increasing costs of business correspondence, although word processing centers and equipment are reducing some of these costs by decreasing labor expense.

The business letter is the most widely used form of external communication. A study of Certified Professional Secretaries,[7] whose responsibilities are assumed to be typical of general business writing, shows that the kinds of letters most frequently written, according to purpose, are:

- inquiry and request letters
- general administrative letters
- replies to requests and inquiries
- "executive" correspondence, including goodwill messages
- miscellaneous letters of other kinds

Other types of letters, although not written so frequently, include:

- letters about employment
- claim and adjustment
- credit and collection
- sales and sales promotion

The particular kinds of letters or other forms of communication will depend upon the kind of organization or department. For example, credit departments naturally deal mostly with credit letters, but these letters are also written by individuals in small business firms with no official credit department.

It would be impracticable, if not impossible, to approach each type of letter as a differing unit, for in addition to the most commonly written types listed here, there are many others. In your business career you may be called upon to compose any or all of those kinds listed, as well as others, but all of the varying kinds of letters or other written messages are much more similar in content and approach than they are dissimilar.

In some of the chapters that follow, you will find illustrations and discussions of the most frequently written letters, and you will have practice in composing them. But most important in your study is a mastery of the communication principles and techniques that apply to all speaking and writing, regardless of its particular purpose and format, and

7. Result of research done by Malra Clifft Treece, "Written Communication Responsibilities and Related Difficulties Experienced by Selected Certified Professional Secretaries" (Doctoral dissertation, The University of Mississippi, 1971), pp. 47–49.

the acquiring of an understanding of business methods, policies, and procedures as they relate to communication.

Form letters are used widely for many purposes. They must be used in order to prevent the costs of communication from zooming to unaffordable heights. Form letters are based on the same principles of effective communication as is an individually dictated letter. Because a copy of a form letter goes to many persons, it is even more important that the letter be well written in order to accomplish its particular purpose. (Form letters are discussed further in Chapter 19.)

DIFFICULTIES MOST OFTEN ENCOUNTERED IN BUSINESS WRITING

According to the study completed in 1971 of the writing of Certified Professional Secretaries,[8] the following difficulties are most likely to be encountered when composing business messages. These difficulties, which are assumed to be typical of all experienced business writers, are listed in order of importance according to the number of respondents reporting difficulties:

1. Being able to compose without wasting time.
2. Avoiding trite expressions.
3. Writing concisely.
4. Achieving the proper psychological approach.
5. Planning the appropriate report form (for reports for use within and from the company).
6. Making meaning clear.
7. Planning different types of letters.
8. Building goodwill.
9. Finding library information (research sources for reports).
10. Making message accomplish its intended purpose.

Keep in mind these often-occurring difficulties and work to eliminate them from your own writing efforts. Becoming proficient in business writing will make you a much more valuable employee, regardless of your occupation. Your skill will also be a source of personal and professional pride and accomplishment.

8. Treece, "Written Communication," p. 130.

SUMMARY ♦ 2

Communication cannot be considered as a separate function of organizational activity; it is an integral part and an almost continuous activity. Successful communication, both internal and external, is vital to the functioning of any organization.

Internal communication moves upward, downward, or horizontally, using the broad terms to indicate levels of responsibility.

Communication from management to employees, as well as from employees to management, must be sincere and built on trust if it is to be conducive to morale building, productivity, or company progress.

In many organizations, communication systems should be simplified and the actual number of messages reduced. In all organizations, however, communication should be sufficient to keep employees informed and motivated.

The informal communication network in an organization is called the grapevine. Much of the information that travels via the grapevine becomes distorted or completely inaccurate. Some managers have tried to "feed" the grapevine; if this method is used, it should be used with extreme caution and discretion, not only from the standpoint that messages may change in meaning but that the method of telling news to only a few employees may lead to an appearance of favoritism. To prevent undesirable effects of the grapevine, the organization must provide information, as needed, through official channels.

Major purposes of downward communication are for instruction, motivation, goodwill, and the smooth and efficient operation of routine organizational activities. A basic purpose of upward communication is to provide information for management decisions; the upward flow of communication is often in the form of reports.

Oral communication is more important within organizations than is written communication as far as in actual time spent.

Written communication within the organization is most likely to be in the form of a memorandum, but it can consist of many other forms.

External communication is used for the purposes of building and maintaining goodwill; selling goods and services; and sending and receiving various other kinds of information from customers, stockholders, the public, and government agencies.

The format of written messages most widely used in external communication is the letter. Some of the most frequently written kinds of letters are inquiries and requests; general administrative letters; replies to requests and inquiries; "executive" correspondence, including goodwill messages; and, in decreasing frequency, letters about employment; claims and adjustments; credit and collection letters; and sales and sales promotion letters.

Three of the difficulties in writing most often encountered, according to one study, are being able to write without wasting time; avoiding trite expressions; and writing concisely.

Proficiency in business communication will greatly increase an employee's value to the employing organization.

QUESTIONS AND PROBLEMS ◆ 2

1. Look in *Business Periodicals Index* or in one of the books of readings listed at the end of this chapter. Select an article that, according to the title, seems to apply to some aspect of communication as discussed in Chapter 2. Summarize this article in a memorandum addressed to your instructor. Include the complete bibliographical reference according to the form shown in Appendix C.

2. Be prepared to present this summary to the class according to the method that your instructor directs.

3. Consider some organization with which you are familiar — a business, club, church, or professional group. What are the strengths and weaknesses of the internal communication system? What media are used in internal communication?

4. Select a letter from a business or other organization. Classify it according to purpose, using the types mentioned in this chapter. If it does not fall into one of these classifications, what seems to be the purpose of the letter?

5. Compare this letter with the letter arrangements shown in Appendix B. Is it arranged in one of these styles?

6. Compare this letter with the characteristics of effective communication as shown in Appendix A. Prepare a summary of your evaluation in the manner suggested by your instructor. You will not be able to judge this letter as quickly and accurately now as you can after you complete the study of this textbook through Chapter 8. Keep a copy of the letter and your analysis of it until that time and check your first evaluation against your later opinion of the letter. You may be surprised at what you have learned.

7. Select a business memorandum. Classify it according to purpose, using the three major ones shown in this chapter: to instruct, to motivate, and to keep the routine and special activities of the organization moving smoothly and efficiently. Your memorandum may accomplish more than one of these purposes.

8. Evaluate this memorandum by the use of Appendix A. Keep a copy of your memorandum and of your evaluation for further consideration later in the course.

9. Assume that you are the personnel manager of a business organization located near the college campus. Write a memo to your employees telling them of

the availability of the course in business communication in which you are presently enrolled. Assume that the company will pay all expenses and that the employees will be excused from work. Give all necessary details. You hope that all who receive the memorandum will attend during this semester or the following one, when the course will be offered at the same place and time. (You do not want them all away from the office during the same period of time.) Ask for their choice of semester.

10. If you have access to a company magazine, bring it to class. Discuss.

11. What is your opinion upon the wisdom of "feeding the grapevine"? Why?

12. Expand upon this statement, agreeing or disagreeing according to your beliefs. Justify your position. "As much as possible, employees should be given the opportunity to participate in the decision-making process."

13. "Comments and Bits of Information" assignment: (See instructions in the "Questions and Problems" section of Chapter 1.) Be prepared to step to the front of the classroom and present in one minute a comment or bit of information about any topic discussed in Chapter 2. Your source can be published material, radio or television, an interview with a business person, or your own personal experience or observation. Do not use your present textbook except in relation to information received from some other source.

14. Interview a person who regularly writes or dictates business letters or memorandums. Ask for his or her opinion about often-occurring difficulties as shown by the research study discussed in Chapter 2. Does the writer believe that these difficulties are the most usual ones? Write a summary of this interview and/or report your findings to the class. Or record the interview and play it to the class.

15. Evaluate the memorandum on page 35 according to Appendix A. Rewrite the memorandum.

TO: All salesmen

FROM: J. X. Taylor, Sales Manager

SUBJECT: Negligence in Turning in Weekly Reports

DATE: January 13, 19__

All weekly sales reports must be received in this
office not later than 2 p.m. on Wednesday of the
week following the week that they cover. You have
all been far too careless in submitting the reports
on time. Toney and Smith have twice been almost
a week late. Don't blame it on your secretaries.
Your delay is putting everybody behind here in this
office. You may not believe it, but it is actually
slowing down the preparation of your paychecks.
Maybe you don't need your check but other people
do.

Don't forget!

FURTHER READING ◆ 2

Campbell, James H., and Helper, Hal W., eds. *Dimensions in Communication.*
    Belmont, Calif.: Wadsworth Publishing Company, 1965.

Davis, Keith. "Making Constructive Use of the Office Grapevine." In *Human
    Relations in Management,* edited by I. L. Heckman, Jr. and S. G. Huneryager,
    pp. 334–46. Cincinnati: South-Western Publishing Company, 1960.

———. "Management Communication and the Grapevine," *Harvard Business
    Review* (September–October 1953), pp. 31, 43–49.

Drucker, Peter. *Technology, Management, and Society.* New York: Harper and
    Row, 1970.

Gieselman, Robert D., ed. *Readings in Business Communication.* Champaign, Ill.: Stipes Publishing Company, 1974.

Haney, William V. *Communication and Organizational Behavior.* 3d ed. Homewood, Ill.: Richard D. Irwin, 1973.

Huseman, Richard C.; Logue, Carl M.; and Freshley, Dwight L., eds. 2d ed. *Readings in Interpersonal and Organizational Communication.* Boston: Holbrook Press, 1973.

Janis, Jack Harold, ed. *Business Communication Reader.* New York: Harper & Row, 1959.

Merrihue, Willard V. *Managing by Communication.* New York: McGraw-Hill Book Company, 1960.

Redding, Charles W., and Sanborn, George A., eds. *Business and Industrial Communication: A Source Book.* New York: Harper & Row, 1964.

Redfield, Charles E. *Communication in Management.* Rev. ed. Chicago: University of Chicago Press, 1958.

Schneider, Arnold E.; Donaghy, William C.; and Newman, Pamela Jane. *Organizational Communication.* New York: McGraw-Hill Book Company, 1975.

Thayer, Lee O. *Administrative Communication.* Homewood, Ill.: Richard D. Irwin, 1970.

———. *Communication and Communication Systems: in Organization, Management and Interpersonal Relations.* Homewood, Ill.: Richard D. Irwin, 1970.

Townsend, Robert. *Up the Organization.* New York: Alfred A. Knopf, 1970.

Whyte, William F. *Organizational Behavior: Theory and Applications.* Homewood, Ill.: Richard D. Irwin, 1969.

——— and the editors of *Fortune. Is Anybody Listening?* New York: Simon and Schuster, 1952.

Yukl, Gary A., and Wexley, Kenneth N., eds. *Readings in Organizational and Industrial Psychology.* New York and London: Oxford University Press, 1971.

The Communication
Process

3

Communication is a behavioral process. The process is complex and complicated even for the most simple and direct message. It involves all our senses, our background, our emotions, our intelligence.

In simple and general terms, the communication process consists of the movement of a message through a channel from the source to the receiver. Before the message is sent, it must be encoded, which is the selecting and organizing of bits of information into a form that can be transmitted by a given means of communication. Before the message is finally received, it must be decoded, or interpreted. The message received is seldom the exact message sent because of interfering factors in the encoder, in the channel, or in the decoder.

DEFINITIONS OF COMMUNICATION

The word "communication" comes from the Latin word *communis*, meaning common. Thus, for successful communication we are trying to meet on common ground, at least momentarily, with the receivers of our messages. We are trying to establish a "commonness" or a sharing — of information, attitudes, ideas, and understanding.

Dictionary definitions of communication include such phrases as "to impart information or knowledge," "to make known," "to impart or to transmit," "to give or interchange thoughts, feelings, information or the like by writing, speaking, etc." Other definitions are limited to stimulus-response situations in which messages are deliberately transmitted in order to invoke a response, as when asking a question and expecting an answer; when giving instructions that are expected to be followed; when telling a story to make other persons laugh or cry; or when writing advertising copy to stimulate people to buy.

A broader definition of communication includes situations in which there is no intention of transmitting messages, as in much of nonverbal communication, such as an unplanned facial expression, body movement, or a blush.

We also communicate unintentionally by our choice of words that carry meanings other than those stated; such meanings are known as metacommunications. For example, the compliment "I've never seen you look so lovely" could imply that the listener's usual appearance should be greatly improved.

Many of the definitions of communication seem to exclude thinking, for in thinking there is no interaction between persons except as we consider another's ideas. But we do "talk to ourselves," literally and figuratively. (It is also a good idea to employ thinking in the other processes of communication, such as listening, reading, speaking, and writing — but it is not at all certain that everyone does.)

Another definition of communication is that it is a process by which one mind influences another. Henry Lingren defines the term in this way: "Communication, viewed psychologically, is a process which is concerned with all situations involving meaning."[1] And another definition, given by Sereno and Mortensen, is "a process by which senders and receivers of messages interact in social contacts."[2]

One of the definitions given in the *Random House Dictionary of the English Language* includes these words: "To have or form a connecting passage, as in 'the rooms communicated by means of halls.'"[3] This description of nonhuman communication is an excellent description of human communication. We cannot give or exchange thoughts without a connecting passage. At times, for many reasons, these passages do not exist or they have become blocked, by language barriers, emotional barriers, intelligence barriers, or actual physical obstructions such as the inability to see or hear.

A simplified definition of communication is that it is a transfer of meaning. Another is that it is the process by which messages affect response.

Communication occurs not only between humans, but from machines to humans and from humans to machines, although perhaps it could be argued that these machines are activated only by human thought. Once

1. Henry Lingren, *The Art of Human Relationship* (New York: Hermitage House, 1953), p. 135.
2. Kenneth K. Sereno and C. David Mortensen, *Foundations of Communication Theory* (New York; Harper & Row, 1970), p. 5.
3. *Random House Dictionary of the English Language* (New York: Random House, 1957), p. 298.

these machines have been set into motion, they can communicate with one another.   Animals communicate with one another and with humans, and humans communicate with animals.

Communication can be classified according to the number of persons to whom it is addressed.   Intrapersonal communication is within the mind of the individual.   Interpersonal is one-to-one contact, as conversation between two persons (although other persons may be present and also interacting).   Interpersonal communication can also be contact from writer to reader, as in letters.   Group communication includes large or small groups, in which a person is said to retain his own identity, as in a classroom, office organization, or club.   Mass communication is sent to very large groups of people, especially by radio, television, or newspapers; each person as an individual has little opportunity for identification or feedback.

As you will learn later in the course, however, all communication should be approached much as if it were on a one-to-one basis.   For example, an effective advertisement sells one person at a time — the wording sounds as if the reader or hearer were being individually addressed.   (This is called the you-approach.)

Communication is either verbal or nonverbal.   Verbal communication consists of written or spoken symbols, usually words, but these symbols can also be such things as groans or punctuation marks.   Nonverbal communication consists of all other methods, of which there are many.

EXAMPLES OF COMMUNICATION

To illustrate the forms of communication, as well as its almost constantly occurring process during our waking hours, let's consider the early part of a day in the life of a business student, Henry Commons, who works part-time in an accounting office.

His first message of the day, apart from his dreams, is the sound of the clock radio.   Although the voice from the radio is intoning the news of the day, it is also telling him that it is time to get up.   This message is an unpleasant one, although it is the one that Henry intended when he set the clock the night before.   Henry groans, a sound that communicates to his wife that he really isn't ready and willing to begin his day.   He groans again at a news item and communicates to his wife, without speaking, that he is unhappy with the state of the world.   He goes back to sleep.

His wife punches him with her elbow — a signal that expresses, without a word being spoken, that if he doesn't get up this minute he will be late for the scheduled examination and then perhaps late at his office, and that if he is late again he may not receive the promised raise, and that if he doesn't get the raise they can't trade in the old car or even have it repaired, and that she has to arise, too, even though she is tired, and that if he hadn't watched the late show the night before he wouldn't be so sleepy, and . . . her second punch with her elbow signifies stronger language.

Several other forms of communication occur as Henry eats breakfast, dresses, and drives to class. In addition to short bits of conversation with his wife, he glances hurriedly at the newspaper and at his class notes. From the notes he is in effect again receiving communication from his professor, as the notes bring into mind the details of the professor's lectures. He drinks his coffee and notices that it is too strong. He wisely refrains from mentioning this to his wife because he had filled the percolator the evening before. The cat rubs against his legs; he strokes her and she purrs. Then the cat goes to the door and meows, saying that she wants to go into the backyard. Henry opens the door.

As he drives to work, a red light communicates to him that he should stop. A singer's voice comes to him from the car radio. So does the voice of an announcer, who asks him to buy a particular kind of soap. The hunched, hurrying figures of pedestrians indicate that it is a cold morning.

As he enters the classroom, he is vaguely disturbed that the chairs have been rearranged and that another student is sitting in his customary place in the room, by the back window. (Have you ever noticed that students tend to sit in the same place from the first class meeting to the last, even though seats are unassigned? According to a theory of nonverbal communication, we seek to preserve our "domain" of established space and feel threatened when this space is not available, especially if it is occupied by others.)[4] Henry receives another message to the effect that the professor does not completely trust the students or he would not have moved the chairs so that they are farther apart than during the regular class meetings.

The professor enters the room and distributes copies of the examination. At the top of page one, the words "name" and "section" appear. Students immediately write their names and the section number on the blanks indicated. This simple action illustrates an example of successful communication; the professor has definitely transmitted to the students a request for an action that in turn transmits information, and the students have complied.

Suppose that the notation on the paper had been "Name and number" and some students had listed their Social Security numbers. Complete communication would not have occurred, in this instance primarily because of an error as the first communication was being sent, in that the kind of number was not specified. If the instructions had been specific

4. Edward T. Hall, *The Hidden Dimension* (New York: Doubleday and Company, 1966).

and the students had misinterpreted them as to show the Social Security number, then the miscommunication would have been in the receiver. At times both the sender and the receiver are at fault.

The teacher stands silently before the roomful of students. Instead of his usual attire, a conservative business suit, he wears crumpled corduroy slacks, a baggy sweater, and worn, casual boots. He does not explain his change of dress, but Henry surmises that he is leaving the campus immediately after the class.

As Henry writes the answers to the examination questions, he tries to express to the reader of the paper his ideas and some of the information that he has obtained during the semester. His ability in written communication will vitally affect his success, although the course is not described as being a course in communication.

The professor seems hurried and asks twice if everyone is nearly finished, although he assures the class that there is still plenty of time. He says that he wishes them well in the completion of the examination. A student raises her hand; he does not seem to see. He looks at his watch.

The examination has not been neatly typewritten and reproduced. Several words are so dim that they are almost impossible to read, and parts of sentences have been omitted. These weaknesses evoke responses of hesitation, confusion, misunderstanding, and irritation, although the students say nothing. Henry notes mentally that he must be more careful in his own written communications that he sends from his office, and that he will insist that the part-time secretary who types his letters and memorandums improve the appearance of the messages he signs.

When the bell rings, signifying the end of the period, Henry has not completed the last discussion question. He folds the paper, places it on the teacher's desk, and hurries from the room without meeting the teacher's eyes. In the hall he meets a friend; he slaps him on the back in a gesture of affection. He meets another professor, smiles, and says good morning. He stops to read a notice on a bulletin board. He hears the next bell, which indicates that it is ten-thirty. He carries his coat on his arm in response to the overheated building. He smells the newly waxed floors of the building and the perfume of a girl who rides with him on the elevator. In the student lounge he puts 20 cents into the coffee machine, which responds to his instructions to deliver black coffee; he had punched the wrong button, for he wanted coffee with cream.

Then it is time for Henry to go to work. When he reaches his office, the receptionist smiles, says good morning, and comments that it is miserable outside today. Henry agrees, although he had found the cold air invigorating. The receptionist goes back to reading the newspaper.

Two memorandums are on Henry's desk. He reads them, makes a note on one and puts it in the out basket and crumples the other and throws it at the wastebasket. He sits at his small desk, in the uncomfortable chair, in the dark corner of the room, reflecting that his employer does not really value his services or he would provide a better working environment.

The employer comes into the room. He does not smile or say good morning, but asks immediately about a report that Henry completed the day before. Henry hands him the report and begins to explain some of the details that are important for the proper interpretation of the report. His employer nods impatiently, frowns, and walks back into his office. Henry wonders whether he should have been more emphatic about the importance of what he had tried to say. He sighs and begins work on another report that he plans to revise.

Was there any time in Henry's morning when he was not sending messages or receiving messages from others? What were the forms of written messages? Of oral messages? Of nonverbal communication? Which messages were received by sight? By hearing? By touch? By smell? By taste? By other forms of sensory reception? Which attempts to communicate were successful? Unsuccessful? Did the intended messages include unintentional messages?

HOW WE COMMUNICATE

We communicate by sending meaningful messages. The message transmitted, even though it is meaningful when it leaves the mind of the sender, is often less so when it reaches the mind of the receiver. The process of communication consists of four factors, or elements: 1) The sender, 2) The message, 3) The medium, or channel, and 4) The receiver.

Noise often, if not always, hinders the process of communication and prevents or alters the reception of the intended message. Noise is any distraction that interferes with the exact transmission of the intended message; it can occur in the encoding, sending, or receiving process, or in all of these. Basic types of noise are described later in this chapter.

Feedback is the return message from the receiver of the original message.

Various models of the communication process have been devised during the past twenty-five years. C. E. Shannon constructed one of the first. Although his model was planned to apply to mathematical or mechanical communication problems, it also applies, basically, to all forms of communication. The model was first published in the Bell System Technical Journal and later included in *The Mathematical Theory of Communication,* co-authored with Warren Weaver.[5] It is now known as

5. Claude Shannon and Warren Weaver, *The Mathematical Theory of Communication* (Urbana, Ill.: University of Illinois Press, 1949), p. 7.

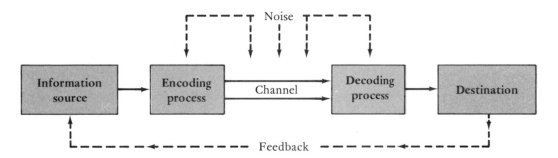

Figure 3-1. *A Communication Model*

the Shannon-Weaver model. The general assumption is that the message must move from the source to its destination through a channel, but that its reception may be blocked or altered by noise.

A modified version of the Shannon-Weaver communication model is shown in Figure 3-1. The Shannon-Weaver model does not include feedback — an essential element of communication, especially of human communication. Perhaps the reason it was omitted is that feedback is actually another act of communication, with the role of the original sender of the message reversed to that of the receiver of the return message.

Verbal encoding processes are speaking and writing; other encoding processes are touching, smiling, gesturing, or, as when transmitting music, playing the piano. Verbal decoding processes are the receiving processes of reading and listening. Other decoding processes include seeing, tasting, smelling, and touching.

David Berlo describes a communication model as consisting of Source-Message-Channel-Receiver ingredients,[6] as follows:

Source	*Message*	*Channel*	*Receiver*
communication skills	content	seeing	communication skills
attitudes	treatment	hearing	attitudes
knowledge	code	touching	knowledge
social system		smelling	social system
culture		tasting	culture

In Berlo's model the source and the receiver are shown as having the same ingredients. As we all know, though, the communication skills, attitudes, knowledge, social system, and culture of any two persons are far from being the same.

6. David Berlo, *The Process of Communication* (New York: Holt, Rinehart & Winston, 1960), p. 72.

The most important idea illustrated by both of these models is that communication is incomplete until it is received; and that, ideally, the message that is sent is received in the exact form.   Realistically, however, we must usually be satisfied with an inexact reproduction of the message, although the received message must be reasonably similar to the transmitted one or communication has not occurred.

WHY WE COMMUNICATE

Three often stated purposes of communication are to inform, to persuade, and to entertain.   These three purposes, however, cannot really be separated.   The intellect does not function separately from the emotions, and the imparting of seemingly routine information is influenced by the emotions of the sender and the receiver of the message — hence persuasion has entered into the process.   Entertainment often acts to change opinions as well as to give information.   Communication planned mainly to be persuasive can also inform and entertain, as illustrated by some television commercials.

All intentional communication is persuasive in the sense that the sender wishes the receiver to understand the message and to accept or be influenced by the message.   David K. Berlo states: "In short, we communicate to influence — to affect with intent."[7]

Lee Thayer says that there are but three generic purposes in human communication:

1.   To affect one's own or another's knowledge of or thinking about something in some way — by attempting to alter a present conception, to add to it, to establish a new conception, etc.

2.   To affect one's own or another's attitudes or orientation toward himself, others, or some aspect of his (or one's own) environment in some way; or

3.   To affect or influence one's own or another's behavior in some way.[8]

According to Thayer's statements, the same communication could accomplish all three purposes.   For example, advertisements or sales messages inform potential customers about a product (Purpose 1); they affect the buyers' attitudes about their environment in relation to the product (Purpose 2); and they influence the receivers of the message to buy the product (Purpose 3).

7. Berlo, *The Process of Communication*, p. 12.
8. Lee Thayer, *Communication and Communication Systems* (Homewood, Ill.: Richard D. Irwin, 1968), p. 145.

A report planned for the purpose of gathering information from which to make a decision (1) affects the reader's knowledge of the situation; (2) affects the reader's attitudes or orientation toward the employment environment from the standpoint of how the information shown in the report affects the company's sales, location, personnel, publicity, or other aspect of the organization, in regard to wise decisions; and (3) motivates the reader to take the steps necessary to implement the recommendations given in the report.

In simple terms, successful communication has occurred when

1. The message received is approximately the same as the one that is sent.
2. The message obtains a favorable response, although this response is not always apparent, and what is considered favorable differs according to the sender, the receiver, the message, and the environment.
3. The sender and the receiver of the message maintain favorable relationships.

Notice that in all of these words about the purposes of communication, emphasis is upon the receiver of the message. When sending messages, we must keep the receiver constantly in mind. This is a restatement of the you-attitude.

Recall briefly a few of the messages sent and received by Henry Commons. The punch from his wife's elbow meets the three factors of successful communication as listed above. He got the message; he arose, eventually; and he and his wife maintained favorable relationships, as shown by the kiss. (This result does not necessarily occur in all marriages; evidently the wife was able to predict the attitude of the receiver of her message.)

The purpose of the cat's meow was to affect Henry's behavior — to effect the opening of the door. (If you are one of the many persons who confuse "affect" and "effect," notice the preceding sentence.)

These purposes apply to intentional communication; much is unintentional. Often our facial expressions, body motions or tone of voice convey messages entirely different from our spoken words. In addition, much conversation is casual, with no definite purpose of being informative, persuasive, or entertaining. We communicate simply because we must. We have a normal, demanding urge to smile when we are happy, to laugh when we are amused, to shout when we are angry, to weep when we are sad. We want to express our emotions and opinions and have them received, understood, and accepted by other persons. This urge is one reason, perhaps the most important one, that some people write poetry or novels, compose music, paint, or communicate through photography. It is why we want to talk with those we love, as well as to converse with strangers we meet on the bus or in a waiting room.

To inform, to persuade, to entertain, or a combination of these purposes — these broad categories describe much casual communication, but not all. The remark, "Isn't it a lovely day?" does not actually present unknown information about the weather. It does impart information about the speaker. It tells the listener: "I accept you, at least to a limited extent. You and I share together this lovely day." At least this is the usual message sent to psychologically mature, secure individuals. Like all other messages, though, even this simple one can become distorted by the time it reaches the mind of the receiver, as will be illustrated in the following section.

WHY THE MESSAGE GOES ASTRAY

Suppose that the person who makes the comment, "Isn't it a lovely day?" is the president of a company and the listener is a new employee. The listener may attach far more significance to the casual, routine remark than the speaker intended. "Ah, he's noticing me already; soon he'll ask me to lunch." Or, if the employee has a weak self-concept or a suspicious nature, or if he has not been having a good day, he may feel that the president is testing him to determine whether he can converse with important persons. As a result, his stammering reply indicates that he is not able to converse with anyone.

A young lady may think, on hearing the words from a man, that he is making a pass. If she is not interested, her reply may sound curt; and the weather commentator will think that somehow he has offended her — or that she does not approve of him.

An unhappy person has not noticed the lovely day. He agrees that it is nice, since that is the expected answer, but he is not really convinced because his own world is less than fair.

An unfavorable reception can occur because of many reasons: because the listener does not like the speaker's appearance, voice, foreign or regional accent, or the magazine he is holding in his hand; because the speaker resembles someone that the listener dislikes; because he distrusts all strangers who speak to him.

Some persons will not even hear the remark because they are engrossed in their own thoughts. Some will not hear because the speaker mumbles. Some will not hear because an automobile horn or other sound drowns out the speaker's words.

The listener may not agree (although he may not say so) because he has already made up his mind that he doesn't like the climate of the particular city — there can be no such thing as a lovely day.

If the speaker and the listener meet each day and the speaker usually comments on the foulness of the weather, he will be expected to do so again, and the listener may actually believe that he said, "Isn't it a rotten day?" We often receive the meaning that we expect to receive.

If the listener has no understanding of the English language, he will not understand the meaning of the words in the remark; but a pleasant look on the face of the speaker may make him nod and smile. He has not understood the code system of the language, but rather the nonverbal symbols.

If so many things can go wrong in the reception of the simple comment, "Isn't it a lovely day?" is it any surprise that the intended message does not always reach the mind of the reader or listener; or, if it does, that it does not achieve its intended purpose? Even less surprising, written messages are often unread, misunderstood, and unaccepted; sales messages do not always sell; newspaper stories do not convey to all readers the same understanding of the printed word; instructions are not always understood or followed.

These varying reactions to a simple comment about the weather show how preconceived opinions, attitudes, and beliefs of the receiver affect the message. The receiver's emotions also affect understanding and acceptance. And the mind of the sender of the message affects the process of communication as the message is prepared (encoded) and in the transmission of thought.

The intended message is often drastically changed by the time it is sent from one mind to another and interpreted according to the receiver's knowledge, perception, and emotions (decoded). Outside sources prevent the passage of an idea from one mind to another, as did the automobile horn in the example above. A poor television picture or sound interferes with whatever bits of information, entertainment, or persuasion are being presented.

As shown in the preceding section on communication models, the term "noise" is used to mean any interference with the reception of the intended message. Noise occurs in the sending of the message: The speaker mumbles or the letter writer uses words or phrases not familiar to the reader. In written communication, noise (distraction) occurs because of any of many reasons: poor writing, unusual letter styles, poor typewriting, incorrect spelling, or an inappropriate letterhead.

A speaker may inject noise into a presentation by confusing gestures, an unpleasant voice, unusual choice of clothing, or visible lack of confidence. Even factors that are usually considered desirable can create noise. For example, a student stated that his French teacher was so beautiful and charming that he couldn't concentrate on learning French. (Could this have been a rationalization?)

Perception and Reality

A major source of noise, or miscommunication, is the differing perception in the mind of the receiver from that in the mind of the sender.

St. Paul said that we see through a glass darkly. Philosophers since the time of Aristotle and Plato have tried to define the meaning of reality. Plato's theory of the cave was that we see only images, as shadows on the wall of a cave; we cannot see the real persons or things that are making the shadows. Some philosophers have said that there is no reality, that reality exists only as the mind perceives it to be, that Plato's shadows are all that really exist.

Whatever your particular philosophy, you will most likely agree that the world contains at least a kind of reality, if not a "real" reality. An automobile, for instance, is thought to be of some particular color; and a red car looks different, to most people, from a tan car. (The most determined skeptics would insist that color exists only in the eye of the beholder.) In darkness, you cannot tell the red car from the tan car; you are unable, because of your environment, to perceive the difference. If the red car is covered with dust, it may seem to be tan — or is it now really tan?

We have all heard or said the remark: "I'll sleep on it. Maybe I'll see things more clearly in the morning." Perhaps we will — or, unfortunately, we may be even more confused. The old admonition never to mail a letter written in anger is based on the knowledge that often our emotions have control over our perception of the situation, and thus of our words and actions.

Even if we were in perfect control of our emotions, our perception would be limited because we cannot perfectly see, hear, taste, feel, or smell. As you look out your window, you cannot see and your mind cannot recognize all the minute details of what is before your eyes. You cannot listen to several conversations at the same time, although all are within hearing distance. You do not see everything that happens in a football game, a play, or an automobile accident.

Your perception and remembrance of a happening or a situation will differ from that of those around you. This difference has been illustrated many times by the varying descriptions you can get of an accident, an individual involved in a crime, or even of a television program. We have all seen "optical illusions" — pictures that can be two completely different pictures, depending upon the way we look at them. We have seen the bridge or railroad track that seems to narrow in the distance so that it is impassable.

The old story of blind men and the elephant illustrates the fact that we often perceive a portion of reality, not the whole. One blind man described the elephant to be like a rope because he had felt only its tail.

Others described the elephant based upon the feel of its side, its legs, or its trunk. All adequately described the parts of the elephant, but none the whole. This story illustrates differences in perception according to individual experience; it also illustrates the danger of generalizing, or assuming the whole truth to be the same as the perceived reality of part of the truth.

Another cause of inaccurate perception is that we tend to see what we expect to see, or what we want to see. Research studies in education have indicated that teachers tend to perceive students as they expect them to be, based on information shown by school records of intelligence test scores and behavior patterns. Because the teacher expects certain children to be slow, or to have problems with the expected classroom behavior, they are treated as such; and they will often live up to the teacher's expectations, even if their school records are incorrect.

We don't need research studies to illustrate the assumption that we see what we want to see. We have all noticed examples of the person who is sure that his next wild scheme will bring him fame and fortune, of the person who cannot begin to see his own faults, of the mother who is sure that her average child is a genius.

Notice the words "wild scheme" in the paragraph above. This is a description of a plan as perceived by an individual other than the planner. The planner may describe the same situation as "a glorious opportunity." If a speaker wishes to maintain favorable relationships, he will not use "wild scheme" or similar words when conversing with the planner. This situation is an illustration of how perception shapes our language.

Our language also affects our perception. These concepts are illustrated in the following passage written by Rothwell and Costigan:

> Our perceptions are based upon interests and backgrounds. Frequently, we "see" only what we want to. Our language reflects this process of perception. The American Civil War (a perception in itself) was referred to in Massachusetts as the "Rebellion of the Southern States." In Pennsylvania, it was a "civil war," in Virginia the "War between the States," and in Texas the "War to Repel Yankee Aggression." Each name for the same event obviously reflects the view of the people in that region of the country. Their interest in the war helped shape the terminology used to describe it. Other examples can be cited to demonstrate this process. For instance, to a child playing in the sand, the results of his meticulous efforts represent a sand castle, to his playmate it may look more like a house, and to a mother it may bear a striking resemblance to a pile of sand. Here again, what one "sees" and calls something is determined by one's experience. The political leader I dislike is a "politician," the one I agree with is a "statesman." New emerging nations are "backward" if they disagree with our policies, "underdeveloped" if they are essentially neutral, and "developing" if they support our policies. Such labels reflect our perceptions of persons or events. . . .

Once a person points out what he sees, however, the other person frequently sees the very same thing. Similarly, one sees the Big Dipper after it
is described to him. Language thus shapes our perceptions.[9]

Errors in perception, and thus barriers to communication, are caused
by the lack of knowledge or observation on the part of the sender or of the
receiver. If the speaker who says "Isn't it a lovely day?" is in the midst of
a blizzard and an earthquake, the words would have an entirely different
meaning than if the sun were shining. The implication that it is a lovely
day could be understood to mean the exact opposite of the literal meaning
of the words, a not unusual interpretation. If the speaker actually
thought, however, that it was a lovely day (the diversity of opinion is
infinite), then, although the listener might agree to the reversed meaning,
there would be no actual meeting of minds.

If the speaker seemed happy about the situation, this emotion would
not be likely in the mind of the receiver. If the speaker or writer is
obviously mistaken, there can be no effective communication — unless the
passing along of misinformation or untruths is to be considered a positive
solution. (It isn't.) The listener who has just come from a grocery store
is not convinced by the words of an economist who says, in a raging
inflation, that prices have come down. Faulty perception is not limited to
facts and circumstances; it is influenced by the way we see ourselves, other
people, and the world about us.

Types of Noise

Basically, there are five types of noise, although these "types" cannot be
considered as being distinct from one another. Like many other aspects
of communication, elements of one enter into another. In broad, general
terms, these kinds of noise are physical, physiological, psychological,
perceptual, and semantic.[10]

Notice, though, that perceptual noises, as discussed in the preceding
section, are essentially psychological. Semantic noise concerns the meanings of words, but our perception and our emotions affect word meanings,
as illustrated in the discussion of the terms applied to the major war in this
nation that occurred more than one hundred years ago.

Physical noise consists of actual sounds and disturbances, such as an
automobile horn, a windstorm, an inaudible voice. It also includes such
things as darkness, an illegible page, static or interference in the sound of a
radio or television set. Other external factors prevent the reception of the

---

9. J. Dan Rothwell and James I. Costigan, *Interpersonal Communication* (Columbus, Ohio:
Charles E. Merrill Publishing Company, 1975), pp. 115–16.
10. Rothwell and Costigan, *Interpersonal Communication,* pp. 15–16.

message.   Traffic congestion may interfere with your listening to the message being sent to you from the automobile radio.

As you read or study, elements of your environment may prevent your concentrating on the writer's meaning — the view from the window, the picture on the wall, a page torn from your book.   If a letter is not delivered by the post office, then certainly there has been a blockage of communication.

Physiological noise is caused by the way we feel physically.   For example, a headache can cause lack of concentration on the part of either the sender or the receiver, resulting in errors in the encoding or the decoding process.   How we feel physically also affects our psychological well-being.

Psychological noise is caused by negative feelings of many kinds in the minds of either the sender, the receiver, or both.   Resentment, fear, boredom, discouragement, anger — all interfere with pleasant relationships and effective communication.   (These attitudes themselves are often effectively transmitted so that they are understood by another person.)   A barrier to communication can be the lack of motivation öf either or both the sender or the receiver.   None are so blind as those who will not see, and none are so deaf as those who will not hear.

In addition, talkers often outnumber listeners.   The world is noisy with monologues about the speaker, with only an occasional interruption by the listener, who also wants to talk.   Another example of lack of motivation is that we may not want to understand the message because it disagrees with our already established beliefs or with our personal desires. We also are not motivated to accept the sender's message if we dislike the sender.

Perceptual noise, as discussed earlier in this chapter, is caused by varying knowledges, values, backgrounds, attitudes, and beliefs.   It is caused by the varying "roles" of the persons who communicate.

Semantic noise occurs in relation to the meaning of words.   Many of the factors that affect the reception of the meaning of words, or the sending of words, are perceptual and psychological.   Other barriers arise because persons trying to communicate do not use the same code, or set of symbols.   We cannot express ourselves well to someone who doesn't understand our language.   We may have difficulty with a person of our own country, or even city, because of differing educational, cultural, or ethnic backgrounds.

Less than perfect communication occurs because of weaknesses on the part of the sender or of the receiver (or of both) and because of influences along the way.   The sender of the message cannot be held completely responsible for the lack of communication; but the sender is the one who can do most about the processes of preparing and sending the message, and, in some cases, in preparing the receiver to accept it.   The responsibility of effective communication is that of both the sender and the receiver, as well as all persons between the two who assist in the transmission of the message. (The telephone company, the mail service, the radio and broadcasting personnel, and so forth.) But most of all, the responsibility is with the sender.

FEEDBACK

Feedback occurs after a communication is received and is an indication to the sender of acceptance and understanding, or the lack of it. Most persons will pleasantly agree that it is a lovely day. Others will ignore the comment and turn away, not wanting to get involved in a conversation or a possible friendship. The foreigner may smile and nod pleasantly; although he does not understand the words, he has understood by nonverbal means.

One person will state emphatically that it is a miserable day, for no weather is like that in San Diego and he has already made up his mind that he wants to return. Another person will say that the day would be all right if he didn't have this horrible cold. (Personal problems have interfered with his perception of reality.)

Feedback is received by the letter writer when he learns that the letter has accomplished its purpose, or that it hasn't. Feedback is obtained by the speaker when his listeners react, if only by going to sleep. The effectiveness of sales campaigns is measured by the amount of sales. The basketball coach receives feedback as to the quality of his coaching through the results of his team's performance. The teacher receives feedback, either positive or negative, through students' test scores.

The results of communication are obtainable only through feedback, which in turn exerts control over future messages. Successful communication often involves an interdependence between the original source and the receiver, and the receiver becomes the source of a subsequent message.

NONVERBAL COMMUNICATION

Nonverbal communication, in its broadest sense, includes all transmission of meaning except that which is expressed in oral or written words. It is described in *Handbook of Communication* in this way:

> The term "nonverbal communication" has been applied to a broad range of phenomena: everything from facial expression and gesture to fashion and

status symbols, from dance and drama to music and mime, from flow of affect to flow of traffic, from the territoriality of animals to the protocol of diplomats, from extrasensory perception to analog computers, from the rhetoric of violence to the rhetoric of topless dancers.[11]

Although all these methods of the transmission of meaning are forms of nonverbal communication, we are concerned here mostly with human nonverbal communication, especially communication between humans and humans, not between humans and machines, humans and animals, machines and machines, and animals and animals. This type of communication will take the form of sign language, action language, or object language, according to Ruesch and Kees, leading researchers and writers in the field. They state:

> In broad terms, nonverbal forms of codification fall into three distinct categories:
>
> *Sign language* includes all those forms of codification in which words, numbers, and punctuation signs have been supplanted by gestures; these vary from the "monosyllabic" gesture of the hitchhiker to such complete systems as the language of the deaf.
>
> *Action language* embraces all movements that are not used exclusively as signals. Such acts as walking and drinking, for example, have a dual function: on one hand they serve personal needs, and on the other they constitute statements to those who may perceive them.
>
> *Object language* comprises all intentional and non-intentional display of material things, such as implements, machines, art objects, architectural structures, and — last but not least — the human body and whatever clothes or covers it. The embodiment of letters as they occur in books and on signs has a material substance, and this aspect of words also has to be considered as object language.[12]

Communication by Time and Space

The use of time and space communicates nonverbally and consists of action language, object language, or both. Like all other forms of nonverbal communication, it often occurs in conjunction with spoken words.

Edward T. Hall says of time:

> Time talks. It speaks more plainly than words. The message it conveys comes through loud and clear. Because it is manipulated less consciously, it

11. Ithiel de Sola Pool et al., eds., *Handbook of Communication* (Chicago: Rand McNally Publishing Company, 1973), p. 93.
12. Jurgen Ruesch and Weldon Kees, *Nonverbal Communication* (Berkeley: University of California Press, 1970), p. 189.

is subject to less distortion than the spoken language. It can shout the truth where words lie.[13]

Edward T. Hall is well known for his theories about the use of time and space to effect nonverbal communication. Dr. Hall, a professor of anthropology, is especially concerned with the ways in which persons of different cultures respond to nonverbal communication. For example, he found that people from Arab and Latin American countries stand closer to other persons, when they are conversing, than we do in America, and persons of some other cultures are much more casual than Americans about the use of time.

Hall uses the word "proxemics" to describe his theories and observations about zones of territory and how they are used and defended by persons of differing cultures. According to Hall, there are four kinds of interpersonal distance: the intimate distance, personal distance, social distance, and public distance.

The intimate distance, close phase, is the distance of lovemaking and wrestling; the intimate distance, far phase, is six to eighteen inches. The personal distance, close phase, is one and a half to two and a half feet; far phase, two and a half to four feet. The social distance, close phase, is four to seven feet, and the far phase is seven to twelve feet. The public distance is twelve to twenty-five feet or more.

Impersonal business occurs at the close social distance, and it is also a very common distance for persons at a casual social gathering. Desks in the offices of some people, especially executives, are large enough to hold visitors at the far phase of social distance. (Some executives come from behind their desks and sit closer to the person being interviewed, or about the same distance away but without the desk to act as a "barrier.")

Hall says:

> The ability to recognize these various zones of involvement and the activities, relationships and emotions associated with each has now become extremely important. The world's populations are crowding into cities, and builders and speculators are packing people into vertical filing boxes — both offices and dwellings. If one looks at human beings in the way that the early slave traders did, conceiving of their space requirements simply in terms of the limits of the body, one pays very little attention to the effects of crowding. If, however, one sees man surrounded by a series of invisible bubbles which have measurable dimensions, architecture can be seen in a new light. It is then possible to conceive that people can be cramped by the spaces in which they have to live and work. They may even find themselves forced into behavior, relationships, or emotional outlets that are overly stressful. . . . When stress increases, sensitivity to crowding rises — people

13. Edward T. Hall, *The Silent Language* (New York: Doubleday and Company, 1959), p. 23.

get more on edge — so that more and more space is required as less and less is available.[14]

Kinesics

The popular name for kinesics is "body language." A pioneer in this field is Ray L. Birdwhistell, who states that there is no particular gesture or body motion that has the same social meaning in all societies. (In some societies, our nod to mean "yes" would mean "no.") Even the smile is not universal, according to Birdwhistell, although it has long been thought to be so. He states:

> Insofar as we know, there is no body motion or gesture than can be regarded as a universal symbol. That is, we have been unable to discover any single facial expression, stance, or body position which conveys an identical meaning to all societies.[15]

The field of kinesics, or body language, is still inexact and nonscientific compared to many other areas of knowledge. Our judgments, for example, of the psychological meaning of the way a person sits in a chair or how one's hands touch the face, hair, or other parts of the body cannot be viewed as an exact interpretation or, in some cases, even an approximate estimate. Even researchers experienced in the field realize this fact — and emphasize it — but many people continue to regard body language as an exact one, if only they could learn to read it.

As an example of this attitude, at a recent regional meeting of the American Business Communication Association, the dinner speaker had as her topic the subject of kinesics — she had recently written a book based on the work of Birdwhistell and other writers and researchers in the field. These were professional communicators in the audience, and teachers of communication, so no doubt they were aware of the inability to exactly interpret body language. Nevertheless, they reacted much as we are all likely to do — with something like "I'd better be careful or I'll give away my innermost thoughts."

Before and during the speech, many of the listeners sat straight and still in their chairs, as if they were afraid of revealing by their posture or mannerisms something that they didn't particularly want other persons to know. (They *were* revealing something about themselves — as we all do.

14. Edward T. Hall, *The Hidden Dimension* (New York: Doubleday and Company, 1959), p. 23.
15. Ray Birdwhistell, *Kinesics and Context* (Philadelphia: University of Pennsylvania Press, 1970), p. 33.

It is impossible *not* to communicate. But even in this "non" communicating state, their body language could not be exactly interpreted.) The
speaker herself, before she was introduced, sat for minutes with her hand
grasped against her throat. This action, although no doubt unconscious
and perhaps impossible to decipher, at least by amateurs, caused comments among the dinner guests, such as "What does *that* mean? Is she
trying to say that she doesn't want to speak?"
    Birdwhistell says:

> Almost as soon as the linguist or the kinesicist meets someone he is asked,
> "What can you tell me from my speech or my body motion?" More fearful
> or more coquettish respondents manifest considerable anxiety that their
> behavior is going to reveal their deepest secrets to the expert. . . . How-
> ever, the specialist cannot determine how distinctively individual any par-
> ticular performance is before he knows his structure and individual range of
> behavior for a particular behavioral area . . . the scientific study of ex-
> pressional behavior must await extensive experimentation before we can test
> productive value and reliability of clinical judgments.[16]

    This discussion should not be interpreted to mean that body motions
are unimportant in nonverbal communication. It is overstatement, however, to describe body motions as a "language." We should avoid hasty
inferences and generalizations in our receiving of nonverbal communication, but these assumptions are dangerous in all forms of communication.
If we had never heard the terms "body language," "kinesics," or "nonverbal communication," we would interpret — often correctly — the
emotions of other persons according to their body movements. We are
more likely to be able to analyze the movements of persons we know well.
    You can recognize in yourself the effect of your emotions upon your
body. The expression "walking on air" would certainly not apply to your
steps when you are discouraged and depressed. You do not clench your
fists when you are happy and relaxed. Your hands sometimes shake a little
when you are anxious or suffering from stage fright. You may put your
hands on your hips when you are "laying down the law."
    Keeping in mind the dangers of overgeneralizations, let's look at the
results of some of the research into the meaning of body motions. The
findings shown were published in *Advances in Communication Research,*
which was published in 1973.
    Albert Mehrabian reports upon the significance of posture and posi-
tion in the communication of attitude and status relationships.

> Mehrabian . . . reviewed experimental findings relating to the communi-
> cation of attitudes (evaluation and liking) and status (potency or social
> control) via posture and position cues. Liking for an addressee is conveyed

16. Birdwhistell, *Kinesics and Context,* pp. 81–82.

by physical proximity, increased eye contact, forward lean toward him rather than a reclining position, and an orientation of the torso toward rather than away from him. Postural relaxation is indexed by the degree of asymmetrical placement of the limbs, the degree of sideways lean or reclining positions while seated, and specific relaxation measures of the hands or neck. This second set of cues has been found to relate primarily to status differences between a speaker and his addressee, a speaker being more relaxed with an addressee of lower status relative to himself than with one of higher status. . . . It is interesting to note that less relaxation, which denotes a relatively higher status of the addressee, also indicates a more positive attitude to an addressee.[17]

Mehrabian further states, in another chapter in the same book:

People of equal status sat closer than people of unequal status. . . . A higher percentage of eye contact between communicators is typically associated with more positive attitudes between the communicators. . . . There was a greater tendency for a communicator to use the arms-akimbo position with disliked addressees than with liked addressees.[18]

These findings are not necessarily the most important ones that have been reported about nonverbal behavior. Also, remember that individuals very often differ from the individuals studied in experiments.

The whole field of nonverbal communication is a fascinating one. You would no doubt enjoy reading further from the books listed at the end of this chapter or from other books on the topic. Like other aspects of communication, nonverbal communication is related to psychology, sociology, anthropology, education, and several other disciplines.

SUMMARY ◆ 3

A simplified definition of communication is that it is the transfer of meaning from the sender to the receiver. Communication involves thinking, reading, listening, speaking, and writing, as well as various nonverbal methods. Communication is received by seeing, hearing, feeling, tasting, and smelling.

The message transmitted, although meaningful in the mind of the sender (or information source) is often less meaningful by the time it

17. Albert Mehrabian, "Introduction: A Semantic Space for Non-Verbal Behavior," in *Advances in Communication Research*, eds. C. David Mortensen and Kenneth K. Sereno (New York: Harper & Row, 1973), pp. 278–87.

18. Mehrabian, "Significance of Posture and Position in the Communication of Attitude and Status Relationships," in *Advances in Communication Research*, pp. 288–303.

reaches its destination.   The message is not exact or complete until it is understood and accepted in the mind of the receiver.

Noise is any distraction that interferes with the exact transmission of the intended message; it can occur in the encoding, sending, or decoding processes.   Noise, or barriers to communication, may be of a physical, physiological, psychological, perceptual, or semantic nature.

Feedback is the return message from the destination to the sender of the original message.

The minds of the sender and of the receiver vitally affect the message. Because the perception of the sender is almost certain to be different from that of the receiver, the message sent is not likely to be exactly the same as the message received.   For effective communication, however, it must be approximately the same.

Three elements of nonverbal communication are sign language, action language, and object language.

Space and time are methods of nonverbal communication.   Edward T. Hall has done research and written books in this field, including *The Silent Language* and *Hidden Dimensions*.   "Proxemics" is a term that Hall uses to describe nonverbal communication through the use of space. Americans do not view time and space, in relation to communication, in the same way as people in some other countries.

"Kinesics" is a term meaning "body language."   Ray Birdwhistell is considered to be an authority in this field.   As he points out, however, this field of study is still far from being an exact science, although many patterns of action emerge from research studies.

Many factors enter into action and object communication: the way we dress; the time we arrive for appointments; our facial expressions, posture, and tone of voice; our eye contact with listeners; our choice of furniture, homes, and automobiles; our gestures as we speak.

QUESTIONS AND PROBLEMS ◆ 3

1. Look in an unabridged dictionary for the definitions of the words "communicate" and "communication."   In addition to the definitions of the words, what other information is given?   Compare these definitions with those from at least one other secondary source.   (Check another dictionary or word book or a book about communication.)

2. In your own words, discuss the meaning of the following terms and concepts as they are used in communication.   As your instructor directs, write or prepare to present orally original examples, based on facts or on your imagination, of any or all of these concepts of communication.   For example, you might describe outstanding examples of nonverbal communication, an inci-

dent in which a person's perception was drastically different from reality, or an illustration of the communication process as shown by a communication model.

a communication model	purposes of communication
barriers to communication	nonverbal communication
reality	intrapersonal communication
perception	communication by actions
feedback	

3. Consider your day. When, how, why, and to whom have you communicated? Has this communication been particularly effective or ineffective? What forms of feedback did you receive? How well have you received the communication of others, and what kind of message did you send in return? What kinds of noise have existed in your communication efforts? How have you and others used nonverbal communication?

4. Find in a magazine or from another source a picture that contains numerous details. Make several photocopies of this picture, distribute them to classmates, let them observe the picture for a short while, and then ask them to write a description of what the picture contains. You can also use an opaque projector to show the picture on a screen. Notice the differences in perception and in the remembering of details.

5. Think of the persons with whom you often communicate. In which ways is their perception likely to differ from that of your own? For example, you perhaps don't "see things" in the same way as your parents in all instances. Is this difference preventing communication about other topics? Do you feel that major difficulties in communicating with others is caused by differing race, age, educational background, sex, or financial status? (This is a "thought" question only and far too personal for written or oral presentation. But it is a very important factor to consider, not only for the understanding of principles discussed in this course but also for the success of your personal communication.)

6. Refer to the experiences of Henry Commons.
   a. What were the forms of written messages?
   b. Oral messages?
   c. Nonverbal communication?
   d. Communication received through machines?
   e. Which messages were received through the process of seeing?
   f. Hearing?
   g. Touch?
   h. Smell?
   i. Taste?
   j. Other forms of sensory reception?
   k. Which attempts at communication were successful?
   l. Unsuccessful?
   m. Did intended messages include unintentional ones?
   n. What types of noise occurred?

o. In which instances was the sending or the receiving of the message, or both, especially affected by previous personal relationships?

p. What forms of feedback occurred?

7. In the Shannon-Weaver model of communication, what element is missing in order for the "process" of communication to be complete?

8. Consider the responses to "Isn't it a lovely day?" in relation to the five general types of noise.

9. What kinds of information do you communicate nonverbally to your instructor? To your classmates? To your employer?

10. How can a business letter communicate "nonverbally"?

11. How can the arrangement of a business office communicate nonverbally?

12. How do business managers communicate nonverbally to employees?

13. Wherever you are at this moment, some types of noise are occurring as you read these words. What are they?

14. Ride a bus, stand at a street corner, or sit on a park bench. Observe the appearance and actions of other persons around you. Without speaking, what are they communicating to you? Whatever your answer, it is only a guess, or an inference, as will be discussed in the next chapter. What is your guess based upon? Consider how you could be wrong. Suppose that a stranger has the same assignment and is observing you. What might this stranger assume about you — and would this assumption be correct? (This problem applies both to Chapter 3 and Chapter 4.)

15. What are some of the meanings that silence can communicate? Discuss and illustrate.

FURTHER READING ◆ 3

Berlo, David K. *The Process of Communication.* New York: Holt, Rinehart & Winston, 1960.

Birdwhistell, Ray L. *Kinesics and Context: Essays on Body Motion Communication.* Philadelphia: University of Pennsylvania Press, 1970.

Campbell, James H., and Hepler, Hal W., eds. *Dimensions in Communication.* Rev. ed. Belmont, Calif.: Wadsworth Publishing Company, 1971.

Hall, Edward T. *The Hidden Dimension.* Garden City, N.Y.: Doubleday and Company, 1966.

————. *The Silent Language.* Garden City, N.Y.: Doubleday and Company, 1959.

Huseman, Richard C.; Logue, Cal M.; and Freshley, Dwight L., eds. *Readings in Interpersonal and Organizational Communication.* 2d ed. Boston: Holbrook Press, 1973.

Lesikar, Raymond V. *Business Communication: Theory and Application.* 3d ed. Homewood, Ill.: Richard D. Irwin, 1976.

Mehrabian, Albert. *Silent Messages.* Belmont, Calif.: Wadsworth Publishing Company, 1971.

Mortensen, C. David. *Basic Readings in Communication Theory.* New York: Harper and Row, 1973.

———. *Communication: The Study of Human Interaction.* New York: McGraw-Hill Book Company, 1972.

Myers, Gail E., and Myers, Michele Tolela. *The Dynamics of Human Communication: A Laboratory Approach.* New York: McGraw-Hill Book Company, 1976.

Rothwell, J. Dan, and Costigan, James I. *Interpersonal Communication.* Columbus, Ohio: Charles E. Merrill Publishing Company, 1975.

Ruesch, Jurgen, and Kees, Weldon. *Nonverbal Communication.* Berkeley: University of California Press, 1970.

Scott, W. E., Jr., and Cummings, L. L., eds. *Readings in Organizational Behavior and Human Performance.* Homewood, Ill.: Richard D. Irwin, 1973.

Words, Meanings, and Common Sense

4

Have you ever thought of the many ways in which words affect lives?

Do you believe that words have definite, exact meanings, which are given in dictionaries, and that we will become effective communicators if only we can learn these definite, exact meanings?

Do you feel that when you know these word meanings, you will be able to handle communications problems logically and sensibly — that is, with the application of common sense?

The answers to these questions is what this chapter is all about. (Yes, this usage of "all about" has become a cliché — but then clichés must also be considered in word meanings and common sense.)

The answers to these beginning questions, with the exception of the first, would be "not necessarily," or "it depends." As discussed in the preceding chapter, word meanings to the individual mind depend upon perception. The logical handling of communication problems depends upon our perception and, especially, upon our maturity.

IN OTHER WORDS . . .

Our world is filled with words. Unless we shut ourselves off from them, they come to us constantly — from television and radio, in newspapers and magazines, from the pulpit, from professors and other lecturers. Sometimes it seems that we are bombarded with words, but we, in turn, add to the total profusion. The problem of too many words is one of the reasons that we sometimes have difficulty in listening to those words we truly wish and need to hear.

The Importance of Words

People have long been aware of the importance of words in our lives, as shown by many maxims and proverbial sayings. For example, "A word fitly spoken is like apples of gold in pictures of silver," is from the Book of Proverbs; from Don Quixote, "An honest man's word is as good as his bond." Mark Twain said, "There is as much difference between the right word and the nearly right word as there is between lightning and the lightning bug." And the common sayings, "I could have bitten off my tongue," and "I really put my foot in my mouth" exemplify our concern with the use and misuse of language.

Words and slogans influence not only our personal and business life, but also the history of nations and of the world. Consider the ways that the following words have affected the thought and action of the American people and the course of American history: "Give me liberty or give me death" (Patrick Henry); "We have nothing to fear but fear itself" (Franklin Roosevelt); "We shall overcome" (song and slogan of civil rights movement); "God bless America" (song made famous by Kate Smith).

Presidential campaigns have been won and lost because of slogans. Advertising campaigns, as we are sometimes too well aware, make extensive use of slogans. Many are so well known that they can be properly described as part of our standard language and vocabulary. Some come into popular usage, and then, like slang, fade away and are forgotten.

The maxim, "sticks and stones can break my bones, but words can never harm me," is far from being accurate. In some cases, words can harm more than sticks and stones: they can lead to frowns, misunderstandings, anger, and the use of sticks and stones, to say nothing of the far more devastating weapons of modern warfare.

Denotative and Connotative Meanings

Words have special characteristics of their own, aside from their dictionary, or denotative, meanings. They have connotative meanings — either general connotative meanings to most persons who see or hear the word, or special meanings to particular individuals because of their specific experiences with the word.

The denotative meaning is the relation between a word and its referent — the thing to which the word refers. For example, you could point to your automobile instead of saying "automobile" or to your house instead of saying "house." As you say or write the word "house," for example, the word stands for the object. The connotative meaning is the suggestion a word acquires through association; it includes qualitative judgment.

Connotative meanings are based on experiences, attitudes, beliefs, and emotions.   Denotative meanings are said to be informative, while connotative meanings have affective results.   To many minds, the word "home" brings thoughts of a fireside, good food, family, friends, comfort, and security; the word "house" has a more neutral meaning.

Words that usually have unpleasant connotations beyond their actual denotative meanings are "criticize," "you claim," and "cheap."   Although the word "criticize" means to evaluate, either positively or negatively, the word connotes a derogatory description, which is one dictionary meaning.   "Cheap" is now considered as a cheap synonym for "inexpensive," but far more derogatory and with an implication of poor quality.   "You claim" indicates that you are lying.

These words and similar ones with unpleasant general connotations should be used with caution, if at all.   Other words to avoid are the negative and unpleasant words of "fail," "reject," "turn down," and "blame."   (Further discussion of positive and negative words is given in Chapter 6 under "A Positive, Pleasant, and Diplomatic Approach.")

We cannot know and control individual connotations based upon the personal experiences of the reader or listener.   For example, if the receiver of the written or spoken message has had an automobile accident on Perkins Road, the name alone will elicit unpleasant memories and feelings.   If a young man is in love with a girl named Linda, another girl with the same name may seem more attractive than a girl named Anna Lou.   If a person has been spurred and bitten by a rooster, the word rooster arouses in his mind a vivid picture, not of an industrious early bird awaking the world, but of a foul fowl that he never wants to see or hear of again.

Aside from their emotional effect, words have their own particular shades of meaning.   Although words are described as being synonyms for other words, there are few real synonyms.   Words are often similar in meaning to other words, but because of their particular connotations or the context in which they are ordinarily used, they cannot be substituted for their near-synonyms without some slight change in meaning.

A real mastery of words consists of far more than the memorization of dictionary meanings or of near-synonyms, although a good dictionary is a vital tool in learning the use of the language.   You will never outgrow your need for a good dictionary, regardless of how knowledgeable or professional you become.   But learning the true nature of words consists of far more than looking them up in a dictionary, as is shown by the humorous misuse of words that sometimes occurs in the translation of passages from one language to another.   As an example, the "body" of an automobile has been translated as the "corpse."   (Oh, you say this describes your particular set of wheels?)

A word is said to have a weak connotation if it has no strong or significant overtones; such a word is also described as being neutral, although in fact no word is completely neutral to all readers and listeners. As mentioned, a "house" has more of a neutral tone than does "home," a word that has favorable and pleasant implications. The word "student" is more neutral than "scholar" or "bookworm."

Words have connotations of high and low status. Garbage collectors are becoming sanitation engineers; janitors are called maintenance engineers, building engineers, or managers. Salesmen are referred to as representatives, special representatives, or registered representatives. Secretaries want to be referred to as "private" secretaries or administrative assistants. (A secretary often acts as an administrative assistant, regardless of his or her title.) In our status-conscious society, perhaps titles are important. The mere change of title can be a morale booster and an asset to a person moving to another department or organization.

In department stores, what was once referred to as the complaint department became the adjustment department and then the customer service department. The credit card is now often called a courtesy card.

Although "the word is not the thing" (a principle of Korzybski's general semantics to be discussed later), at times we should use words as if they really were things — for they represent or call to mind objects, ideas, and emotions. Organizations that we address as "Gentlemen," using the standard salutation of business letters addressed to organizations and not to individuals, are not necessarily made up only of gentlemen. This salutation may be changed eventually, as "chairperson" now often replaces "chairman." The salutation "gentlemen" implies that only males are employed in the organization.

The matter of determining whether the male members of the organization are gentlemen is another problem, semantic or otherwise. Regardless of these questions and the contradiction of terms, as a matter of courtesy we still begin letters with "Gentlemen" or with such endearing terms as "Dear Mr. Jones" or "My dear Ms. Harvey."

Words pertaining to liquor are avoided by some individuals, corporations, and government agencies. Funds for cocktail parties are referred to as "entertainment" or "public relations." The State Department has drawn money for liquor for a "representation fund." Bars are often called lounges, in which you can buy your favorite beverage and become, according to your choice of words and the amount of your favorite beverage consumed (or tippled, guzzled, swizzled, quaffed, sipped, tossed down, swigged, or wet one's whistle with) tipsy, giddy, glorious, dizzy, mellow, merry, fuddled, groggy, high, lit up, tight, high as a kite, three sheets to the wind, inebriated, intoxicated, loaded, plastered, or rip-roaring drunk.

Consider the implications of the following words:

- scheme — plan — program of action
- proposition — proposal — presentation
- gamble — speculation — calculated risk
- scrawny or skinny — slim — slender

- stupid — retarded — exceptional
- stupid — unsound — unadvised
- favoritism — leaning — undetachment

You could make long lists of similar words. Do you recognize that words have differing and definite personalities of their own?

The Changing Language

The English language, like all other languages, is constantly changing. New words are added and others become obsolete. Many words are borrowed from other languages, as they always have been. A changing technological society adds to general usage the specialized words that were first used as the jargon or slang of a particular field or occupation.

These "new" words are not necessarily ones that have never been used before. They may be old words that are used in a new way. For example, "hardware" is used in connection with computers to describe the equipment and machinery with which data are processed, as opposed to "software," which means programs, instruction sheets, or similar materials. "Hardware" used in this way obviously has a connection with the older use of the word, to describe materials sold in hardware stores.

Some slang finds its way into the dictionary and becomes acceptable even for formal usage. Much slang, though, fades away, as "it's the berries" and "the cat's pajamas" of the twenties. The word "cool," so widely used as slang to mean "excellent," is listed in present dictionaries as "slang." This word may someday be used even in formal speech or writing as an ordinary word, or it may disappear and be forgotten. Slang, like more formal language, often makes use of contradictory terms to express the same idea. The person who grew up in the thirties or forties perhaps still uses the term "not so hot" to mean something that is not at all "cool."

Many thousands of words have changed since the time of Chaucer. Spelling has also changed, as well as what is considered to be correct usage. At one time, "you was" was correct; now only "you were" is acceptable. Words change in shades of meaning, as well as completely reversing themselves. At one time, "silly" meant "holy," "fond" meant "foolish," "tree" meant "beam," and "beam" meant "tree."[1] The "charity" of the King James Bible now means "love."

The Story of Language by Mario Pei is a comprehensive, interesting book about the history of language, the elements of language, the social

1. Bergen Evans and Cornelia Evans, *A Dictionary of Contemporary American Usage* (New York: Random House, 1957), p. vi.

function of language, modern spoken tongues, and an international language. In the chapter "Semantics and Semantic Change," Pei states:

> "Infant" was originally "nonspeaking," still partly true in the new connotation, but with a restriction of meaning to the young. The original meaning of "foyer" is "fireplace." A "secretary" was once a "separator," and a "secret" was what is set apart; both words come from *secretus,* the participle of the Latin *secerno* ("to separate"). "Noble" is originally "knowable"; it comes from the Latin root *gno-* ("to know"). A "person" was once a "mask"; *persona,* which can be analyzed into "through-sounding" (the sound of the voice comes through the mask), was the mask worn by Roman actors; but this mask gave them a character and a "personality." "Rival" originally meant "pertaining to a river bank"; its present meaning is due to the concept of two landowners contending for water rights on the bank of a stream. A "comrade" is originally one who shares a room with you; a "companion" one who eats bread with you. "Meat" was once food of any kind, as evidenced by terms like "meat and drink," "sweetmeats," and "flesh meat." "Intoxicated" once meant "poisoned," and "incensed" is etymologically "burned up." "Hose" changed its meaning from "tights," in Shakespeare's times, to "stockings" today. "Typewriter" once meant the typist, not the machine, and "naughty" was "poor," one who had naught. The original application of the term "automobile," in 1883, was to streetcars.[2]

Language is a living thing that will continue to grow and change. It cannot be trapped by dictionaries and English handbooks to remain static so that we can keep up with it. A dictionary, even the best one, is not a supreme authority; it merely reflects usage, supposedly that of "educated" persons.

The Vast and Varied Language

The complete English vocabulary is estimated at about one million words, although this number includes specialized vocabularies of trades, hobbies, and fields of learning, and such terms as names of plants, stars, diseases, and so on. Of the 500 most commonly used words in the English language, it is estimated that there are more than 14,000 dictionary definitions, or an average of 28 per word.

You can think of many words that can be used in numerous ways. The word "break" has 113 definitions or methods of usage listed in *The Random House Dictionary of the English Language.*[3] The word "cast" has

2. Mario Pei, *The Story of Language,* rev. ed. (New York: J. B. Lippincott Company, 1965), p. 44.

3. *The Random House Dictionary of the English Language* (New York: Random House, 1967), pp. 181–82.

75 different descriptions, and the meaning varies according to the accompanying word. "Cast away" and "cast off" mean to discard; "cast off" is also a printing term. "Cast down" means to humble, and "downcast" describes one who is depressed. "Cast on" is a term used in textile manufacture. "Cast out" is to expel. "Cast up" means to add up or to compute, as well as to vomit.[4]

With the many completely different words, and with the many different denotative and connotative meanings of each, it seems to be a miracle that we learn the language as well as we do, whether we are native or foreign born. Much knowledge about the language is gained automatically or subconsciously. To become expert in the use of the language, however, requires long, sustained, and dedicated effort and a sincere interest. Reading the works of writers who use the language expertly and professionally is perhaps the quickest way to learn words, their varieties and shades of meaning, and how they fit together with other words. .Read all kinds of well-written material: business articles, serious and light essays, textbooks, fiction, and poetry. And try your hand at writing material of several kinds — yes, even poetry. In no other medium is the exact word choice so clearly essential.

Many excellent books have been written about words, their history, shades of meaning, and their influence upon our emotions and our lives. One interesting book on the history of the American language is *Our Own Words*, by Mary Helen Dohan. This book "traces the development of language and vocabulary from its dim beginnings in the Indo-European past to medieval and Elizabethan England — then across the Atlantic to contend not only with a whole new world of (unpronounceable) Indian words but a whole new kind of life and terrain."[5]

See the reading list at the end of this chapter for other books about words. Additional ones are listed in the reading lists at the end of other chapters, for a course in communication is basically a course about words.

The Inadequate Language

Our language is extensive, rich, and varied, but it is still not completely adequate for the expression of all emotions and ideas. Louis E. Glorfeld uses the illustration of the paper clip. You know what one looks like, but can you describe it? Can you give someone instructions on how to draw it?[6] Can you accurately describe the taste of a cucumber to someone who has never eaten one? Can you describe the feeling of a snowflake against your cheek? Or the emotion of jealousy?

4. *The Random House Dictionary of the English Language*, p. 230.
5. Mary Helen Dohan, *Our Own Words* (New York: Alfred A. Knopf, 1974), dust jacket.
6. Louis E. Glorfeld, ed., *A Short Unit on General Semantics* (Beverly Hills, Calif.: Glencoe Press, 1969), p. 8.

The English language has no personal pronoun (except for the inappropriate "it") to represent either sex, as in "The accountant decided that (he? she?) would work late. For many years the word "he" was ordinarily used in sentences of this kind, with the understanding that the "he" was serving as a generic word to stand for either a man or a woman. But recently, women's groups have protested this usage, especially in elementary and high school textbooks, and they have valid reasons for doing so. Now the accountant or other professional person is almost as likely to be a woman, and even if he or she is not, by using "he" the implication is that only a man is capable of being, or should be, an accountant.

This problem would not exist if there were a "human" pronoun, instead of the neutral word "it," to mean either he or she. Such a pronoun may someday be added to the language. (The word "he" is likely to slip into sentences in which "she" could also be used. If you find such constructions in this book, you will know that it is not because of male chauvinism: the writer of this book is a woman.)

Words can be chosen, used, and twisted to mean or to imply everything or nothing. President Harry S Truman is quoted in these words as he describes an imaginary Cabinet:

> I have appointed a Secretary of Semantics — a most important post. He is to furnish me with $50 words, and tell me how to say yes and no in the same sentence without contradiction. He is to tell me the combination of words that will put me against inflation in San Francisco and for it in New York.[7]

The books *Strictly Speaking* and *A Civil Tongue* by television commentator Edwin Newman are devoted to the slanted, inexact, exaggerated use of words, especially by politicians. The author includes a former vice president, who used such phrases as "nattering nabobs of negativity," "pampered prodigies," and "vicars of vacillation."[8]

Much misuse of the language, as well as vagueness and inaccuracy, is due to the lack of skill or knowledge on the part of the user of the language, not because of inherent weaknesses in the language itself.

In summary, communication is achieved by the use of symbols, and symbols convey different meanings to different individuals. Words, our most widely used symbols of communication, have no meaning within themselves, even if there is only one dictionary definition. The reader or listener interprets meaning from words according to previous knowledge, background, experience, and attitudes toward the sender of the message, and according to the emotions and physical feelings of the moment. Meaning is in the mind, not in the words themselves.

7. Evans and Evans, *A Dictionary of Contemporary American Usage*, p. 44.
8. Edwin Newman, *Strictly Speaking* (New York: Bobbs-Merrill Company, 1974), p. 2.

THE LANGUAGE OF BUSINESS

The first thing to recognize about the "language of business" is that there is none, except for some specialized terms that exist in particular organizations, industries, offices, or occupations.   The business jargon that some writers use is made up of unnecessary, trite, and wordy phrases, included in business writing because the correspondent has seen them in other letters and memorandums.   Some of these phrases are the following:

- enclosed herewith please find
- we beg to call your kind attention to
- kindly be advised
- in reply to your recent favor we wish to state
- thanking you for your kind attention
- the same being at hand I wish to state

Yes, these ridiculous phrases are still used in many business letters and memorandums, but, fortunately, they are decreasing in number. Some writers seem to think that this special language of business jargon must be included for a businesslike tone; they are sadly mistaken.   Words and sentence structure in business writing or business speech are the same as in any other clear writing or speech.   Business people seem to be more likely to include such unnatural wording than other writers, and they are more likely to use it in writing rather than in speech.

To repeat and emphasize: Words in business writing and speaking are, for the most part, the same words, with the same meanings and implications, as words used in any other kind of writing or speaking. This may sound like a completely unnecessary and obvious statement, but many people in business offices still behave as if business language were of a special category — that it must be stuffy, stiff, and formal, especially when words are put into written form.

The desirability of simple, natural writing is discussed in following chapters in relation to readability and conciseness.   Business usage is mentioned here, in the discussion of language in general, in order to relate the study of word meanings to your overall study of business communication.   Clichés and stereotyped, stale expressions creep into our writing or speech because we do not take the time and trouble to think of our own words instead of using worn-out ones that we have seen and heard in hundreds of business letters and speeches.

Almost always, the wordy phrases and trite business jargon listed below should be omitted or simplified.   Those marked with a star can safely be put into a "never" category for use in business writing.

Most of the others would fit into an "almost never" category, and all should ordinarily be avoided, for they are slow, wordy, and old-fashioned.

- it has come to my attention
- in the amount of (for)
- to the amount of (for)
- for the amount of (for)
- amounting to (for)
- totalling the sum of (for)
- be assured, rest assured
- *be advised, *be informed, *consider yourself informed, *this is to inform you, *this is for your information
- herewith, herein, attached herewith, attached hereto, enclosed herewith, *enclosed please find
- *beg to state, wish to state, regret to state
- *reference to same, *compliance with same, *consideration of same
- *we beg to call your attention to the fact that
- *thank you in advance, *thanking you in advance, *thanking you for your kind attention, *thanking you for your time, *thanking you for your consideration
- *we wish to remain, yours truly
- as of this date, as of this writing, as of the present time
- be kind enough
- due to the fact that, in view of the fact that
- *thank you kindly, *kindly, *we kindly thank you for
- at an early date
- along this line
- *we beg to remain
- pursuant to your request
- *the undersigned (except in legal papers)
- pending receipt of
- for the purpose of, for the reason that, due to the fact that (for, to, because)
- in spite of the fact that (because)
- evident and apparent
- take the liberty of
- regret to advise, regret to inform, regret to state
- your esteemed favor
- AND MANY, MANY MORE

Notice the business jargon and wordy or unnecessary phrases in following paragraph. Although you are unlikely to write a paragraph as terrible as this one, even a few such uses of business jargon weaken the overall effectiveness of your writing:

> We are in receipt of your order of recent date and in
>
> reply wish to state that we thank you kindly for same and
>
> for check in payment that was attached thereto which was in
>
> the amount of $42.50.

An improved version of this sentence is:

> Thank you for your order, and check, for $42.50.

We cannot and should not eliminate all expressions from our language that could possibly be classified as clichés. Although we should work for a fresh, original approach, some phrases because of long usage now have a distinct meaning of their own that is not easily replaced; for example, "the hush of night," "strait-laced," and "gentlemen's agreement."

Some expressions are difficult to classify as to whether they remain clichés or have become idioms, which are particular methods of expression that have unique meanings of their own. Your business communication should be natural and conversational — although one can go too far in the way of informality in certain business messages.

SEMANTICS AND GENERAL SEMANTICS

The study of communication, or at least of the communication that we can hope to control, is basically the study of the *use* of words. We can never know enough about words or have complete skill in their use and application. Consistent care and study, however, will enable the psychologically mature person to use words wisely and effectively. No other study will be of more value to you.

Semantics

Semantics is the study of meaning, especially meaning as expressed in words. "Just a problem in semantics" has become a trite phrase to describe a misunderstanding, but often the difficulty has actually arisen because of different interpretations of the meaning of words.

The word "semantics" first appeared in dictionaries near the beginning of the twentieth century. The word is based on the Greek word *semantikos* meaning "significant." S. I. Hayakawa states:

> Semantics is sometimes defined in dictionaries as "the science of the meaning of words" — which would not be a bad definition if people didn't assume that the search for the meanings of words begins and ends with looking them up in a dictionary.
>
> If one stops to think for a moment, it is clear that to define a word, as a dictionary does, is simply to explain the word with more words. To be thorough about defining, we should have to define the words used in the definition, then define the words used in defining the words used in the definition — and so on. . . . To a person who asked for a definition of jazz, Louis Armstrong is said to have replied, "Man, when you got to ask what it is, you'll never get to know," proving himself to be an intuitive semanticist as well as a great trumpet player.[9]

"Semantics" does not carry the same meaning as the term "general semantics," as discussed below.

General Semantics

The term "general semantics" originated with the works of Alfred Korzybski, the author of *Science and Sanity*, which was published in 1933.[10] General semantics is now described as both a doctrine and an educational discipline, as well as a study into the meaning of words. It is basically concerned with the way in which language affects our thought and behavior.

Science and Sanity is based on the premise that the principles of science can be applied toward the conscious reorientation of the human nervous system for the improvement of the evaluation of language and of human behavior.

Korzybski states: "Since general semantics studies the relationship of language, behavior, and thought, science provides the means to a desired result: sanity."[11] Not all psychologists and scientists in other fields have accepted the premise of conscious reorientation of the nervous system.

The International Society of General Semantics has issued two short, comprehensive definitions, as follows:

9. S. I. Hayakawa, *Symbol, Status, and Personality* (New York: Harcourt, Brace & World, 1963), p. 4.

10. Alfred Korzybski, *Science and Sanity*, 4th ed. (Lakeville, Conn.: The Institute of General Semantics, 1948), p. 387.

11. Korzybski, *Science and Sanity*, p. 387.

- *Semantics:* The systematic study of meaning.
- *General semantics:* The study and improvement of human evaluative processes with special emphasis on the relation of signs and symbols, including
  language.[12]

Francis Weeks describes general semantics in this way:

> It is a theory; it is a philosophy; it is a way of coping with the environ-
> ment; and, to some, it is practically a religious cult. It is too bad that it has
> this cultist aspect, because semantics is very important when taken calmly
> and rationally.[13]

Korzybski believed that the logic of Aristotle has caused much
semantic confusion and distorted our use of reason. He is especially
critical of Aristotle's two-valued thinking — the either-or classification.
Korzybski believed that many things are neither black nor white but
varying shades of gray. He advocated a multivalued logic as being essential to the understanding of the world, including human nature. (Previous skeptics of the wisdom of Aristotle include Roger and Francis Bacon,
Galileo, and William James.)

One important principle of Korzybski's position is that man alone
"binds time" — that is, profits by the experience of past generations.
Although this thought was obvious before Korzybski, he emphasized the
importance of time binding in relation to language. Another statement
attributed to Korzybski is that at the end of all verbal statements are
undefined terms; we cannot say everything about anything. The statement is not the whole story.

One principle of general semantics is that no two events in nature are
truly identical; neither are two persons or two groups. Another is that
events flow into one another in nature by "insensible graduations." In
other words, when we classify or categorize, as we must, we should realize
that these classifications cannot be truly discrete ones with distinct dividing lines. Another principle is that a word is not the thing it represents
but an artificial statement (a map is not the territory). Another principle, although not in Korzybski's words, is that there are no abstract
qualities outside our own heads.

The book *Science and Sanity* has led to several other books in the field
of general semantics, some of which have become best sellers. Writers
who have interpreted Korzybski's ideas and expanded upon them, as well
as expressing them in a more interesting and readable way, are Stuart
Chase, S. I. Hayakawa, and Irving Lee. William V. Haney, a student of
Irving Lee, has written a complete book based on semantic principles that

12. Stuart Chase, *Power of Words* (New York: Harcourt, Brace, 1954), p. 128.
13. Francis Weeks, *Principles of Business Communication* (Champaign, Ill.: Stipes Publishing Company, 1973), p. 25.

go back to Korzybski. Although Haney's book contains some discussion of semantic principles, it is basically made up of business cases that illustrate the difficulties caused by the violation of semantic principles in business situations. (The reading list at the end of this chapter gives complete bibliographical references to the books mentioned here, as well as to other related books.)

"General semantics" is often referred to simply as "semantics," and some writers use the term "general semantics" to include everything that concerns the use, development, or meaning of words. (Korzybski made a lasting contribution to the confusing elements of language.) Because the definitions — even as given in dictionaries — are somewhat overlapping, the term "semantics" seems to be a better choice unless the reference is specifically to Korzybski or his ideas.

APPLYING GENERAL SEMANTICS TO COMMUNICATION ERROR

The principles of general semantics are related to the processes of communication, especially to the causes of miscommunication.

Failure to Discriminate

We tend to interpret two events as if they were identical, or to think in terms of stereotypes. The job we are now doing is not exactly the same as the one we did last year or even last week. Our co-workers are not the same as those we worked with in another organization. The employees we supervise are different from one another and will no doubt require different types of instruction and motivation. An application letter sent to one corporation should not be exactly like one sent to a differing organization. You are not the same person that you were ten years ago, last year, or even last week. The report you submit cannot tell everything you know about the subject; how can you be sure that you have chosen wisely the material to abstract?

We tend to see similarities instead of differences. We may communicate and react in terms of categories, generalizations, and stereotypes, when we should be looking for uniqueness. Although we do and should see similarities and use them for generalizing, categorizing, and arriving at conclusions, we should keep in mind that events are not truly identical and that events have unlimited characteristics.

The statement that an event has unlimited characteristics could be restated as "The statement is never the whole story." Can you tell everything about anything? Could you describe yesterday in complete detail, including all the elements of your environment? Could you completely describe the past hour or the past minute? Could you tell all there is to know about the pencil you hold in your hand or the view from your window?

We fail to discriminate when we do not choose the most fitting things to communicate about a particular event or situation, or when we do not adequately judge the most important points of the communication of others. The missing elements are perhaps the most important ones.

Interpreting Abstractions as Specifics

What, if anything, do superlatives like "finest," "best," and "awful" indicate if they have no specific terms to substantiate them? Or "good," "bad"; "big," "little"; "rich," "poor"? All such terms are relative — as is almost everything else. This principle of relative values applies not only to the use of abstract terms but to the semantic principle that multivalued logic is cardinal in understanding and explaining nature.

We will continue to use and to receive abstract words — as we should. The danger lies in interpreting them as specific ones, and in using them at times when we should be more definite and specific. We should keep in mind Korzybski's idea that there are no abstract qualities outside our own heads. But even if they exist only in our own heads, and the heads of persons with whom we communicate, they still exist. The trouble is that abstract words often do not mean the same thing to different persons, or at best these words have hazy, indefinite meanings.

Word-Thing Confusion

A word is not a thing but an artificial symbol. Some students, when hearing this statement for the first time, comment upon the obviousness of it, as, "Of course the word is not the thing — whoever thought that it is? If you think that the word is the thing, write the word 'horse' and ride it in a horse show!"

Even with the seemingly obvious aspect of this semantic principle, it is true that many people do mistake the word for the thing, an error in judgment that plays havoc with communication as well as with many other aspects of life. Hayakawa states:

> In all civilized societies (and probably in many primitive ones as well) the symbols of piety, civic virtue, and of patriotism are often prized above actual piety, civic virtue, or patriotism. In one way or another, we are all like the brilliant student who cheats in his examination in order to make Phi Beta Kappa; it is so much more important to have the symbol than the things it stands for.[14]

14. S. I. Hayakawa, *Language in Thought and Action* (New York: Harcourt, Brace & World, 1939), p. 30.

Remember that words are symbols, but only symbols. They have no meaning or reality within themselves; their reality is in their interpretation.

The Fact-Inference-Value Judgment Confusion

Facts are verifiable by direct observation. An inference is an assumption, or "an educated guess," based on known facts. A value judgment is a subjective evaluation based on an individual's particular way of looking at the world and at himself.

One illustration of facts, inferences, and value judgments, attributed to Irving Lee when he was a professor at Northwestern University, is based on the statement, "There are seeds in this apple." Is this statement a factual one, or is it an inference? Or perhaps a statement of judgment? You will be making a logical assumption, or inference, if you say that there are seeds in the apple; but the statement is only an inference until you cut the apple open and see the seeds. Your value judgment about the apple could be one or all of these: "This is a good apple." "This apple is sour." "I don't like apples." "This apple is pretty." "This is an inferior apple."

For an excellent discussion of inferences and value judgments (longer than can be included in this textbook), see Chapter 3, "The Language of Reports," in *Language in Thought and Action,* by S. I. Hayakawa.[15] Hayakawa uses the term "reports" instead of the word "facts." He states:

> Reports adhere to the following rules: first, they are capable of verification; second, they exclude, as far as possible, inferences and judgments.[16]

> An inference, as we shall use the term, is a statement about the unknown made on the basis of the known.[17]

> By judgments, we shall mean all expressions of the writer's approval or disapproval of the occurrences, persons, or objects he is describing.[18]

Now let's apply Hayakawa's definitions to illustrations of our own. Suppose you say, "A magnolia tree is in bloom in Overton Park — I saw it on the way to work." Is this a report or an inference? If you are not sure that it is a magnolia tree, it is an inference. Suppose you say, "I saw a tree covered with white blossoms, as I drove by Overton Park on my way to work." Perhaps the tree is really a magnolia; inferences can be correct as well as incorrect. Suppose you say, "The blossoms have a sickening sweet smell." This statement is a value judgment.

15. Hayakawa, *Language in Thought and Action,* pp. 38–53.
16. Hayakawa, *Language in Thought and Action,* p. 38.
17. Hayakawa, *Language in Thought and Action,* p. 41.
18. Hayakawa, *Language in Thought and Action,* p. 43.

Inferences are based upon matters that seem to be correct, based upon what one has observed.   For example, a person who has never seen a magnolia tree looks at a tree blooming in Overton Park in Memphis.   He reaches the conclusion that it is a magnolia tree based upon these known facts: Overton Park is in Memphis, Tennessee, but only a few miles from the state of Mississippi.   Mississippi is known as the Magnolia State.   One variety of magnolia has white blossoms and blooms in late spring and early summer.   It is now May; the tree has white blossoms.   The assumption that the observed tree is a magnolia is a reasonable inference, but it may be absolutely incorrect.   Several other kinds of trees having white blossoms bloom in Memphis and in Mississippi in spring and early summer.

Suppose that you are tailgating and run into the back of a truck ahead of you.   This occurrence, unfortunately, is a fact; when you tell others about it, it is a report — as long as you do not embellish it.   The driver stops and comes toward you.   His face is red, he is frowning, and his fists are clenched.   You infer that he is angry, but you can't really be sure — maybe he looks like that all the time!   You say (to yourself), "Truckers are nasty, mean people."   This is a value judgment.

We cannot live or work without making inferences.   Value judgments will also continue to be part of our lives — if we have a system of values, to say nothing of attitudes and opinions of our own.   We should not try to eliminate inferences and value judgments, only to recognize them in our own minds and in the communication of others.   We cannot limit our conversation to our actual observed experiences; we must make inferences in order to survive.   Inferences and value judgments, however, are a source of human miscommunication.   We confuse them — we interpret facts in the light of our limited experiences or nonobjective mind and arrive at inferences that are far from accurate; then we accept these inferences as facts, and communicate as if they were facts.

You may be paid to make inferences.   When you work as a personnel manager or in any other position in which you hire others, you cannot be sure that you are making the right decision in every hiring situation.   The only way to obtain the "true facts" of how well a particular person will perform is to hire the person; if you guess wrong, you have cost your company money and perhaps done an injustice to the employee.

Because evaluation and interpretation are mental processes, the ability to evaluate and interpret is closely related to mental capacity.   This ability is improved by knowledge gained through experience and by specific and accurate information about the problem being studied.   Most of all, critical ability is strengthened by the recognition that we are likely to think and act on the basis of what we believe and feel — that is, upon our emotions, instead of upon verifiable facts or upon reasonable inferences based upon verifiable and observable facts.

If you do not hire an applicant because he reminds you of your Uncle William, who wouldn't support his college-age children, or another applicant because she has children and you believe that a woman's place is in the home, you are basing your decisions upon your ideas of the world as you believe it should be — upon your value judgments. (If you do not hire the woman on the basis of her children or marital status, you are also breaking the law.) In both cases you have made unsupported inferences.

Even if the applicant were Uncle William, instead of someone who resembles him, you cannot be sure that he is now the same man you remember. He is applying for a job — perhaps in order to send his children to college. Or it is not impossible that he will be extremely valuable to the employing organization even if he does let his children take care of themselves. (According to another person's value judgment, the kids will be better off if they pay for their own education.)

If you do not hire an applicant because he or she seems to be definitely unqualified — for example, a woman who took a high school course in bookkeeping twenty years ago and has been employed as a dental assistant now applies for a position as supervisor of accounting — you are basing your decision upon reasonable inferences. But even a reasonable inference is still an inference; we cannot know with certainty that this particular applicant will not excel as a supervisor of accounting, although it seems extremely unlikely.

Most decisions must be based at least partly upon inferences. The inferences should be based on facts, if they are to be truly objective. And, being human, we will continue to make decisions based only on value judgments — as perhaps we should. The greatest danger lies in letting our value judgments, which can easily become prejudice and bias, close our minds to the truth, or at least to the search for truth. The gag saying "Don't bother me with facts; my mind is already made up" is a wise commentary, unfortunately, on the usual problem-solving approach.

In summary, errors in communication occur because our attitudes, opinions, and emotions influence our interpretation of events, as well as the interpretation of words and other symbols. Poor communication also occurs because of our lack of ability to handle words sanely and skillfully. Many of these errors are basically due to faulty perception, as discussed in Chapter 3.

MEANING: IN THE MIND, NOT IN WORDS THEMSELVES

A basic principle of semantics is that meaning is in the mind, not in words themselves. Fortunately, though, words do have generally accepted meanings, or else we might as well speak in the Japanese or the Arabic language as in English. Differences in perception of commonly used words are usually minor, but minor differences can result in serious malfunctions of the communication process.

Words have no generally accepted meanings except as we as humans have given them these meanings — and, as previously discussed, these generally accepted meanings often change.   As an illustration of how words can mean what we decide they should mean (as stated by Alice in Wonderland), consider the following story, attributed to Alan Walker Read, the noted lexicographer at Columbia University, and published in a book edited by Louis E. Glorfeld:

> . . . about three baseball umpires who were discussing their trade.   One said, "Some's balls and some's strikes and I calls 'em as they is."   The second said, "Some's balls and some's strikes, and I calls 'em as I sees 'em."   The third said, "Some's balls and some's strikes, but they ain't nothin' till I calls 'em."
>
> The question Read asked following the story was which of the baseball umpires was right and for what reason.   His answer was that the third was at least more right than the others because he seemed to have the idea that two semanticists, Ogden and Richards, have explicated.   They said that there was no inherent relationship between the word and the thing except in the human intellect.   We could choose to call the ball anything we want to, but it is a "ball" because we agree to call it that and for no other reason.[19]

Hayakawa states:

> We who speak English have been so trained that, when our nervous systems register the presence of a certain kind of animal, we may make the following noises, "There's a cat."[20]

Why couldn't this animal be called a dog, a tree, an it, or a cinderella? And why is it called an animal?

SUMMARY ◆ 4

Words and slogans influence not only our personal and business life but also the history of nations and of the world.

Words have both denotative and connotative meanings.   The denotation is the "dictionary" meaning; the connotation is the special meaning of the word based on the individual's experiences and perception.   Aside from their emotional effect, words have their own particular shades of meaning.   There are few real synonyms.

Language is constantly changing.   The complete English vocabulary

19. Glorfeld, *A Short Unit on General Semantics*, pp. 10–11.
20. Hayakawa, *Language in Thought and Action*, p. 27.

is estimated at about one million words. Many words have various definitions, in addition to their connotative meanings.

Semantics is the study of meaning, especially as it is expressed in words. "General semantics" is a term first used by Alfred Korzybski. The principles emphasized by Korzybski include such aspects of communication error as failure to discriminate, interpreting abstractions as specifics, word-thing confusion, and the confusion of facts, inferences, and value judgments.

Meaning is in the mind, not in words themselves.

QUESTIONS AND PROBLEMS ◆ 4

1. Draw up a list of words of high and low status, such as sanitation engineer versus garbage collector; administrators versus clerks; maintenance engineer versus janitor.

2. Look in a dictionary of quotations. Find two quotations about words. Present these in a memorandum addressed to your instructor and/or be prepared to read these quotations to the class.

3. Find a word or phrase with a more favorable connotation for each of the following expressions. For some of the words you can think of at least two or more favorable expressions — one or more somewhat neutral and one or more so favorable that it would be considered a euphemism. For example, "scheme" can be replaced by "plan"; even more favorable is "program of action." Another example is "bogus," "artificial," and "simulated."

    In some instances you will change the meaning slightly. As stated in this chapter, there are few real synonyms. For example, as you try to find another word for "bribe," you could use "subsidy" or "gratuity." Although these words are not exactly synonymous, if used in the proper context their meaning would be clear — and unstated.

chore	poor white trash
deal	poverty
cheap	racket
affair	blemish
liar	rule with an iron hand
messed up	blunder
under arrest	You're dead wrong!
stubborn	long-winded
bookworm	informer
smart aleck	ridiculous
the old woman	

4. "Invent" your own word and introduce it into the English language. (Look in an unabridged dictionary to make sure that it does not already exist!) Use it many times during the next few days. Do other persons begin to use it?

Could they now "define" your word? Be prepared to describe to the class the introduction, promotion, and success of this new word.[21]

5. Describe a paper clip so that a person who has never seen one will be able to draw it.

6. Write specific, detailed instructions on how to operate some business machine or equipment with which you are familiar. Be complete and concise.

7. What is your opinion as to the use of the word "he" as a generic word to represent either a man or a woman? If you do not approve, how do you suggest that writing be adapted to avoid the use of "he," "his," or "him"?

8. Analyze three or four business letters. Do they include any of the phrases listed under the topic "Business Language" in this chapter?

9. Rewrite the following letter; eliminate trite, wordy business jargon. Also look for words which should be omitted because of their unfavorable or inexact connotation. You may add an inside address and closing lines, as your instructor directs, and arrange the letter in your choice of the styles shown in Appendix B. (Of *course* you wouldn't write a letter like this. But if you can turn this one into a good one, you're on your way to professionalism.)

Dear Mrs. James:

We are in receipt of your letter of recent date and in reply wish to state that we shall be jubilant to submit to your claim to send cheaper merchandise than the items you previously and heretofore ordered us to send.

Attached please find a new invoice of this cheaper merchandise which you say will sell better in your neighborhood. Your customers must be low class and down and out.

Thanking you in advance for your esteemed favor, please send your check posthaste and immediately, I am

yours truly,

10. S. I. Hayakawa has said: "Dictionaries are not law books, but history books." What did he mean by this statement? Do you agree?

21. Adapted from problem by Louis E. Glorfeld, *A Short Unit on General Semantics* (Beverly Hills, Calif.: Glencoe Press, 1969), p. 90.

11. Some advertising seems to attempt to sell the "word" instead of the "thing." Can you think of any such examples? (Such advertising occurs less often than in previous years because of fairly recent government regulations.)

12. Using an example from your experience, write a short description of an instance of miscommunication. Was this communication error due to a principle or principles of general semantics?

13. Look at the chair in which you are sitting. According to Korzybski, it has unlimited characteristics. What are some of the things you could say about the chair? For example, you could discuss the method of manufacture, the city in which it was made, speculate on the person who made the chair or cut the tree from which it was made, predict the future of the chair — what else? (Hint: don't try this method of conversation as a way to impress your friends or colleagues.)

14. Discuss the advantages and risks of making inferences in business.

15. Look back to Chapter 3 to the description of the communication experiences of Henry Commons. Interpret the activities only from what is stated on those pages. Which of the following statements are facts? Which are inferences? Which are value judgments? (These are to be *your* facts, inferences, and value judgments, not Henry's. Assume that everything on the pages is true — which is itself an inference.)

   a. Henry and his wife own a cat.
   b. The professor has rearranged the chairs.
   c. Henry's wife has a job.
   d. Cats shouldn't be allowed to go outside.
   e. The professor does not enjoy his work.
   f. The professor should enjoy his work.
   g. The receptionist does not have enough to do.
   h. The employer is inconsiderate.
   i. Henry is inefficient.
   j. The temperature is below freezing.

16. From your travels in different sections of the United States, give examples of regional words or phrases. Have you seen instances when these expressions resulted in miscommunication?

17. Do certain words have particularly pleasant or unpleasant connotations to you because of your experiences?

18. Can you think of words, in addition to those mentioned in this chapter, that have been replaced by higher status words?

19. Ask a person or persons of retirement age whether they remember examples of slang that were in vogue when they were teenagers. Determine what has happened to these expressions; have they been almost forgotten or have they become standard language? As your teacher directs, give an oral or written report to the class.

20. Explain in oral or written form how the study of general semantics can help you to become a better business communicator.

FURTHER READING ♦ 4

Chase, Stuart. *Guides to Straight Thinking*. New York: Harper & Brothers, 1956.

———. *Power of Words*. New York: Harcourt, Brace and Company, 1954.

———. *Tyranny of Words*. New York: Harcourt, Brace & World, 1938.

Dohan, Mary Helen. *Our Own Words*. New York: Alfred A. Knopf, 1974.

Gieselman, Robert D., ed. *Readings in Business Communication*. Champaign, Ill.: Stipes Publishing Company, 1974. See especially articles by Wendell Johnson, Irving J. Lee, and William H. Whyte, Jr.

Glorfeld, Louis E., ed. *A Short Unit on General Semantics*. Beverly Hills, Calif.: Glencoe Press, 1967.

Haney, William V. *Communication and Organizational Behavior*. 3d ed. Homewood, Ill.: Richard D. Irwin, 1973.

Hayakawa, S. I. *Language in Thought and Action*. 2d ed. New York: Harcourt, Brace & World, 1964.

———. *Language, Meaning, and Maturity*. New York: Harper & Brothers, 1954.

———, ed. *Our Language and Our World*. Freeport, N.Y.: Books for Libraries Press, 1959.

———. *Symbol, Status, and Personality*. New York: Harcourt, Brace & World, 1953.

———. *The Use and the Misuse of Language*. Greenwich, Conn.: Fawcett Publications, 1962.

Johnson, Wendell. *People in Quandries*. New York: Harper and Row, 1946.

Korzybski, Alfred. *Science and Sanity*. 4th ed. Lakeville, Conn.: Institute of General Semantics, 1948.

Lee, Irving J. *Language Habits in Human Affairs*. New York: Harper & Row, 1941.

Miller, George A. *Language and Communication*. New York: McGraw-Hill Book Company, 1951.

Newman, Edwin. *Strictly Speaking*. New York: Bobbs-Merrill Company, 1974.

———. *A Civil Tongue*. New York: Bobbs-Merrill Company, 1976.

Pei, Mario. *The Story of Language*. Rev. ed. New York: J. B. Lippincott Company, 1965.

Skinner, B. F. *Verbal Behavior*. New York: Appleton-Century-Crofts, 1957.

Sondel, Bess. *The Humanity of Words*. New York: World Publishing Company, 1958.

Ruesch, Jurgen. *Disturbed Communication*. New York: W. W. Norton & Company, 1957.

Ullman, Stephen. *Semantics: An Introduction to the Science of Meaning*. New York: Barnes & Noble, 1962.

Interpersonal Communication and Listening

5

Communication is a complex process; all aspects are part of the whole. We cannot describe the facets of oral communication as being completely distinguishable from those of written communication, for many of the principles are the same. For example, in all kinds of communication we are concerned with understanding and acceptance. To achieve these goals, we must have a proficiency in language and an empathy with the receiver of the message, plus knowledge of the subject matter.

In written communication we are concerned with such things, among many, as spelling and punctuation. The comparable aspects in oral communication are pronunciation and tone of voice — although tone of voice can be much more expressive of emotions than spelling or punctuation could ever be.

In oral communication we can make far more effective use of feedback than in written communication. We can immediately judge our listeners' reactions, at least to a certain extent, especially when we are conversing with one individual. If we become aware of misunderstanding, we can repeat our ideas in different words or ask for questions. The immediate feedback in oral communication is one of its main advantages. A disadvantage, however, is that we do not have an opportunity to revise our remarks *before* they reach the receiver of the message, as we can do when our words are in written form.

INTERPERSONAL COMMUNICATION

The term "interpersonal," in its broadest sense, includes all human communication except "intrapersonal," as "inter" means "between." The term is usually used, however, to distinguish personal, face-to-face communication from other forms and media, including written, mass, or group. Oral communication within small groups is also considered interpersonal if the members of the group have an opportunity to react individually on a one-to-one basis with other individuals.

The illustration used in Chapter 3 on the reaction of various listeners to the comment "Isn't it a lovely day?" is an example of varying successful and unsuccessful interpersonal communication. The remark was interpreted in the light of pre-established relationships between the speaker and the listener; the emotions and physical well-being of the listener; the self-concept of the listener, and the total environment in which the message was sent. These influences also affected the sender of this simple message.

All these and other aspects (which can become barriers) enter into our attempts at interpersonal exchange of ideas and information. In addition to the spoken words, much communication took place that could be noticed only by seeing the speaker's and respondent's facial expressions and bodily movements and by listening to the tone of voice. Silence also entered into the communication process.

I'm OK, You're OK

For successful interpersonal communication, the individual must have a positive self-concept and a sincere respect for the other participant or participants in the sharing of the communication process. This relationship is expressed in the title of a book that was for many months a best-seller, *I'm OK — You're OK*.[1] Basically, the premise of this book is that the individual must "feel good" about himself and about the other person with whom he interacts. For understanding and acceptance, there must be no attitude of inferiority or superiority, no expression or implication of undue humility or condescension.

This assumption of I-acceptance, you-acceptance is crucial to effective interpersonal relationships. Some persons, after reading about and considering the you-attitude, long emphasized in business communication, may feel that this I-you approach is in conflict. It is not. We cannot truly value another person without also respecting ourselves. In addition, as mentioned in the discussion of the you-attitude (Chapter 6) the consideration of the reader or listener does not preclude the concern for our own welfare, or for that of our employing organization. To think otherwise is being disloyal to our employing organization as well as to ourselves.

Interpersonal communication depends not only upon words, nonverbal signals, and the environment, but also upon relationships. What we say to an old friend will be different from what we say to someone we have

1. Thomas A. Harris, *I'm OK — You're OK* (New York: Avon Books, 1973).

just met, even if the words are the same. Some long-married couples seem to know what the other is about to say before the words are uttered. This is a form of sharing, so that past experiences, including past words, carry over to all our present relationships.

Such a mutual understanding may be less than a real understanding, however, in that one or both of the partners assume too much and no longer listen to the other person as of now, but to the person remembered. This is a way of taking the other person for granted. Such relationships can also occur between business and professional associates. Sincere communication, as discussed in relation to organizational communication in Chapter 2, can occur only in an atmosphere of trust.

Communication must be two-way, but we still tend to think too much in terms of ourselves, the sender. When we give most of the attention to ourselves, we concentrate on the means of the transmission of ideas, not upon the back-and-forth exchange that is most conducive to frank and sincere understanding and expression. We try to impress upon our audiences our own importance, our knowledge, or our authority.

When we cut off the opportunity for feedback, we not only fail to receive ideas and information from the other persons, but most likely the listener is not completely understanding our message. Even if the message is clear, being shut out from participation in the oral interchange is certainly not conducive to the acceptance of ideas or instructions. Ask for the other person's opinions; they may be valuable to you, even if you think you don't need them. You do need their opinions.

Many people hesitate to say "I don't know" because they feel that it shows a weakness. Many times there will be instances when you don't or can't know — and you will be wise, usually, to say so, immediately and frankly. Being a "know-it-all" is attempting to put yourself on a higher plane than your listeners, even if you are thoroughly informed on the subject.

We can go too far in the other way — an attitude of timidity and lack of self-confidence will get you nowhere, unless it is to an employment agency to look for another job. But being an expert on every subject, especially an unqualified expert, can be just as bad. Harry Truman commented during his presidency on what he considered to be the attitude of many college graduates of the time. He said, "I always try to tell them that it's what you learn after you know it all that counts."

"Time to Talk Things Over"

The following article, "Time to Talk Things Over," is from a small book entitled *The Communication of Ideas*, published by The Royal Bank of Canada. The book, which is a collection of monthly letters planned especially for employees, was first published in 1950.

Except for a few illustrations, the author of "Time to Talk Things

Over" does not apply his or her discussion especially to business situations. It is not necessary to point out that the personal interchange of ideas is as vital to one's business career as it is to personal life. Much business exchange takes place as it is described here; unfortunately, it is not all of the urbane, democratic nature that is advocated in the article.

Although these words were written in 1950, nothing is dated, with the exception of "dimly lighted television rooms." (In the early days of television, the small black-and-white screens were watched in near darkness.) Universal, timeless observations do not change in value. "Time to Talk Things Over" will be as appropriate many years from now as it was in 1950.

Since 1950, though, the word "dialogue," used as it is in this article, has become much more widely used — probably overused. Like the word "communication" in some of its applications, it has become somewhat of a cliché. But because a word or concept is widely used or discussed does not disprove its value; conversely, if the concept had not been so especially descriptive and appropriate, its use would not have become so widespread. Even the most descriptive, "viable" words can become stale from overuse. ("Viable," like "dialogue," is a word that some speakers and writers have felt should be worked into each message. Another popular expression is "that's what it's all about.")

As you read "Time to Talk Things Over," notice the theme throughout the article of the importance of considering the person with whom we talk; of listening to the other's point of view; and of maintaining a considerate, civilized, democratic attitude. Give special attention to the references or implications as to the importance of listening. Interpersonal communication must include sincere listening, or it is not communication at all, but only "telling."

This article applies to the following section of this chapter, "Effective and Efficient Listening," as aptly as it does to the topic of interpersonal communication. Although listening is an aspect of interpersonal communication, and an important one, it is discussed separately because of its application to other communication experiences — as, for example, when listening to a lecturer.

TIME TO TALK THINGS OVER[2]

Man is the only creature who can talk himself into trouble, but he is also the only creature who by talking things over can find a way out of trouble. The history of any improvement in politics, business or society, is a course of persistent, reasonable, confrontation of facts and differing ideas with one another.

Anyone who unswervingly refuses to submit his ideas to the test of dialogue will be quite unfit to meet the demands of existence in these days.

2. Reprinted from *The Communication of Ideas* (Montreal: The Royal Bank of Canada, 1950), pp. 129–141. With permission of The Royal Bank of Canada. (No author or editor given.)

Everyone, whatever side he supports in discussion of art, religion, government, business or education, must recognize that technological extension of human capacity to do things has worked a radical change upon our environment. This demands new ways of thinking, feeling, valuing and deciding what is to be done. The ideal society in an age of total communication is the civilization of the dialogue.

It would be fatal to the values in our way of life if we were to give in to the technological forces which threaten our personal reception and communication of ideas. We could become so busy tending our time-saving devices that we have no time to marshal and express our innermost thoughts and ideals; we could lazily allow the mass media to deaden our minds with singing commercials and ready-made opinions; we could shush one another in dimly lighted television rooms instead of talking, debating, and expressing ourselves in the joint discovery of exciting and inspiring new facts and ideas.

Discussion takes for granted that everyone has had experiences which may contribute something of value to the group. It recognizes that one does not possess the whole truth, but seeks, pursues, and finds some part of it.

Dialogue is the language of the adventurer, confronting new things, seeking to enlarge his territory, wanting to expand his knowledge, eager to deepen his understanding. Monologue is the language of the primitive-brained man who thinks he is the centre of the universe. Dialogue is constructive because it adds to knowledge; monologue is destructive because it evidences fear that a creed or opinion is in danger of being disproved by question and answer.

Conversation

It is important for most people to talk and to be heard, to voice their problems, to get things off their minds. A really satisfying talk is one of the greatest pleasures there is.

Conversation has four main purposes: to give information, to get information, to persuade, and to show a human interest in other human beings. No measure comes before the high court of Parliament until it has been long prepared by the grand jury of the talkers.

Conversation is the simplest form of dialogue. It was conversation, in this form, in the age of Socrates, an age without pocket books or their latter-day substitutes, which laid the foundation of the civilization we enjoy. It was conversation of which the New Testament was composed. It was conversation among scholars in a bookless world which revived learning at the end of the dark ages.

Good conversation stretches your mind. Even if no usable conclusions are reached through a conversation, there is profit in the exercise, for we have churned up our minds so as to see new views. But to make the best of it, people must realize conversation as a mental occupation, and not merely a dribbling into words of casual thoughts.

Conversation consists of both transmission and reception. One man put it neatly when he said: "I like so much to talk that I am willing to pay my audience by listening in my turn." To speak and to listen brings into the midst of the group masses of experience, anecdote, cross-lights, quotation, historical incidents, the whole range of minds centred upon the topic from all points of the compass.

There can be a lively diversity of views expressed without appeal to any book of rules of order. You do not need an elaboration of formality, just ordinary politeness. For example, a brilliant conversationalist is not one who holds a group spellbound, but one who draws everyone else in.

Intelligent conversation is only fit for intelligent society. It is downright abhorrent to narrow-minded people who are fixed on a plane of the commonplace and dull. Nothing can be more deadly boring than this: two persons saying words about something in which neither is interested. Ragbag conversation about threadbare things is unprofitable, depressing and futile. You would die of shame if you heard it played back on a tape recorder.

The mistake that many earnest and persistent talkers make is to suppose that to be engrossed in a subject is the same thing as being engrossing. The self-centred person talks without reference to his listeners' interests. If he has been reading about dinosaurs or water pollution or the state of unrest in mid-Africa, he brings out all that is in his mind on the topic.

Story-telling is not conversation, but parlour entertaining. The person is a bore who, on the sidewalk or in a café, on the train or in an office, buttonholes you to listen to anecdotes and jokes pulled out of the air. As Ernest Dimnet wrote in *What We Live By:* "Stories are the stupid man's wit."

Dialogue

Dialogue is conversation with a purpose. It is reason's only weapon. It is a civilized operation, democratic and constructive, and those who refuse dialogue are playing a game with some serious overtones. There was no dialogue in the primitive medicineman's manipulation of people's passions. There was no dialogue for Stalin, who refrained from debating his views in favour of exterminating his opponents physically or compromising them personally.

Democratic institutions and political freedom cannot survive without discussion, criticism, and deliberation. Are we too busy enjoying life to engage in a dialogue designed to make possible the continuation of life? Or too ignorant? Or too lethargic? Or too parasitical? All these entered into the decline of the Roman Empire.

To take useful part in reaching decisions is to seek understanding through consideration of alternatives. In this debate, traditions and dogmas rub each other down. We attain insight and understanding.

A dialogue is not a bargain-basement transaction with haggling and bickering, a low form of negotiation. Neither is it a situation in which A confronts B in a contest, but a conversation in which each presents facts and each considers the other's facts. It is a reasonable exchange of ideas, bringing into being a new body of knowledge. It takes you out of the doldrums of fiddling with good intentions into the region where you act with knowledge and understanding.

Monopoly of the conversation has no place in dialogue. The ball must be thrown back and forth. There is give and take. Participants expect to find things out by examining ideas and facts from several points of view.

This exercise reveals the true personality of those taking part in it. It dissolves the solemn humbug and punctures the know-it-all; it unveils the person who speaks in malice or in self-interest. It reduces prejudice and builds up mutual confidence, the hallmark of social intercourse among equals.

See from Other Viewpoints

Impartiality in listening to points of view is a great aid to the making of good judgments about what is being discussed, and this requires that we try honestly to see things through the other person's eyes.

Many irritations in society are due to the fact that some people do not recognize problems which others think are important. Two cultures may have institutions that look very much alike to the outside observer, and words in their languages which are so alike as to suggest the same meanings, but the realities are different.

When we go abroad we are accustomed to accommodating ourselves to evident differences, such as those of dress, language and architecture. Where we run into trouble is in the little differences: the taste of coffee in England, the siesta hour in Italy, the sounds in the narrow streets of Paris, the rosary of devotion formed by the 24,000 bell-ringing shrines in Benares. These things, nevertheless, are an essential part of the everyday life of people living in those places.

This is not to say that we must be pleased by all sights and sounds. It is quite possible to form and hold a strong opinion of our own and yet to realize that it is after all only one point of view.

In praiseworthy dialogue we show respect for the other man's opinions, and try to push the right button to open him up so that we learn his real thoughts. It is easy and immature to recognize only the spurious and mistaken in a man's contentions: it requires more effort and intelligence to recognize and admit the excellence of some of his ideas.

There are certain simple rules associated with effective dialogue. Much that passes for dialogue is not that at all, but merely the noise made by contending propagandists. Such a debate is governed by the rules of the prize-fight: "Shake hands . . . ready . . . gong!"

Good dialogue requires common substance, a topic about which the participants are informed and to which all can make a contribution by original thinking. It requires a large measure of goodwill. It begins in an act of faith: the assumption that those who converse will speak in honesty for the purpose of reaching understanding, and with generosity toward one another.

The ground rules for dialogue do not call for that glowering acquaintance with Bourinot or Robert's *Rules of Order* so insisted upon by militant chairmen. Dialogue requires only observance of the niceties appropriate in participants who seek mutual enlightenment and growth of knowledge: "Use reason; be fair and gracious."

A good way to start a dialogue is by asking questions and listening to the answers. When Napoleon noticed that his councillors were simply echoing whatever he said he was quick to call them to order. "You are not here," he told them, "to agree with me, but to express your own views."

It is by comparison of views that we reason our way toward truth. We increase the odds of finding the best solution to a problem by considering alternatives.

Do Some Homework

The man who believes in dialogue does not come to the conference table with a fistful of fast deals but with a head full of constructive ideas. He has studied the subject so that he does not need to waste time in quibbles about trifles or to indulge in off-the-cuff masterminding. He has something to contribute that is relevant to the topic.

If the dialogue is to be about an important matter, it is beneficial if all who will participate prepare a sort of "white paper" or preliminary brief, and circulate it. Then everyone will come to the table with an over-all view of the problems, prepared to discuss the way in which the varying ideas or proposals may be reconciled.

"Facts" are worse than useless unless they are accurate. Inaccuracy does not necessarily mean deceitfulness, but may take the form of not being particular to be exact.

Facts are different from opinion. Look at the confusion caused in many conversations when people apply differing opinions to the same body of facts. They confuse belief with evidence, and insist upon the truth of a statement because they believe it to be so. Truly, it is not things, but people's opinions about things, that trouble mankind.

Mutual understanding is helped by clear definition. Make sure that everyone knows exactly what your language means. It helps, often, to define conflicting arguments with clarity, so as to arrive at the critical point free of non-essentials. To do this honestly you need to understand not only the technicalities but the nature of what is proposed. If the point is not clear to you, say: "Well, if my view of this is not acceptable, could you make some proposals?" This leaves you free to modify your view if given convincing reasons.

Make sure that the real problem is brought out into the open. There are no solutions to unknown problems. Einstein is quoted as saying: "The formulation of a problem is often more essential than its solution." And John Dewey summarizes the procedure well in his *How We Think:* first there is awareness of the problem, resulting in perplexity; then definition of the problem by analysis and observation; then consideration of different solutions; selection of the most effective solution; verification of its fitness to attain the desired result.

Sweeping generalities must be broken down if they are to be digested into something useful. Small problems are more easily solved than large ones, but at the same time the pattern of the whole must be kept in mind.

Keep to the Point

In discussing the small problems within the large picture it is necessary to stick to the point. The truly basic elements in a good pictorial composition are unity and simplicity. No picture can be strong, and no spoken presentation can be effective, if it tries to tell several stories at once.

Most of us, when we get on a subject we think we know, are likely to say too much. The centre of discussion should be the point of the problem, and the circumference no wider than is needed to air the subject fully. Irrelevant particularities slow down conversation and sometimes bring it to a complete stop. Everyone knows the feeling of frustration caused by people who digress from the point in a spate of words and never omit an unnecessary fact.

Dialogue is seeking truth. St. Thomas Aquinas said: "An angel perceives the truth by simple apprehension, whereas man becomes acquainted with a simple truth by a process from manifold data." The search involves having willingness of mind to reach out to that which is not yet understood, or even to something which at first repels you. When one idea supplements another it is surprising how often a joint truth emerges from the dialogue of persons who started with divergent beliefs.

Some solutions to problems may seem harsh, but no true values are destroyed by learning the truth about them. Pontius Pilate stands condemned in history not because he asked a great question: "What is truth?" but because he did not wait for an answer.

The honest person in a dialogue is he who does his best to learn and to tell the truth, confesses to uncertainty when he is uncertain, does not pretend to knowledge he does not have, and is candid and fair.

The Benison of Silence

Sometimes it is well to converse mostly in pauses. Mozart is quoted as saying: "My rests are more important than my notes."

There are, of course, modes of silence: that of listless ignorance and that of intelligent attention. To ask oneself what can be left unsaid is a golden attribute in diplomacy and it plays a big part in that everyday tact that helps people to get along better with one another.

Sometimes it is well, during a dialogue, to remain silent even though it makes you appear eccentric. One man, popular on committees, carried a little card which he set up on the table before him. On it he had written: "Keep quiet." James Simpson, the clerk who became chairman of Marshall Field and Company, smoked cigars so as to be sure he would keep his mouth shut in conferences. Perhaps he was copying the geese migrating over the mountain Taurus, which is full of eagles. The geese took up stones in their bills to restrain their gaggling, thus passing over the eagles without being heard.

Silence is not to be confused with listening. Every participant in a dialogue has the duty to listen. Listening intently and asking pertinent questions provide you with the needed information for orderly mental processing.

Listening that is merely courteous is not good enough: you need to be interested in what is being said, keen to learn what is in the speaker's mind. This has the added advantage of assuring him of your entire fairness and predisposing him to a like attitude.

When you listen attentively you may learn about options that are not at once visible. You listen to the facts, but you concentrate on finding what they all add up to. If you are too busy thinking of what you are going to say next you miss the points and end up in the confusion of a completely unrelated line of talk.

There is little room in dialogue for hot and hasty words. The only downright prohibition in the rules governing dialogue is against losing your temper, even in the face of the most petulant or waspish remarks.

Dialogue should be marked by urbanity. Begin in a friendly way, express your views coolly and without passion. If you assert your ideas with vehemence you will be suspected of wilfully trying to shout down the ideas of others, because the expression of knowledge and conviction is in its nature cool and unimpassioned.

Show respect for other people's knowledge, say what is needful and civil, speak compactly, and emphasize a point by increasing the earnestness of your tone, not the volume of your sound.

You will be called upon sometimes to converse with people who rub you the wrong way. Concentrate, then, upon the topic, whose facts are impersonal. Even if you cannot acquiesce, be sympathetic with the other person's ideas and desires, so that you disagree without being disagreeable.

The dialogue is more an occasion to seek light than an occasion to generate heat. It is more conducive to mature judgment than would be a shouting match between two small boys. The ideal participant in conversation or dialogue is not the man who comes to it with a ready-made theory which he refuses to abandon. He does not say "Yes, yes" or "No, no," but an enlightened "Yes, but" or "No, and yet."

To sit still and be pumped into is not an exhilarating experience. Everyone in a dialogue should contribute; no one should be denied his word; no one person should dominate. There are some, possessed by a sense of mission, who will seek to seize and hold the floor. They have a vast capacity for talk and great cleverness in evading requests to state clearly what all the torrent of words is about. As the Straw Man said in *The Wizard of Oz:* "Some people without brains do an awful lot of talking, don't they?"

In the interests of fair play, those who share in a dialogue should see to it that the zealot is kept within bounds even though he takes it as a personal affront.

The Value of Dialogue

To some people the world is so filled with antagonisms and uncertainties that the resolving of differences of opinion seems to be impossible. To others, life is so complex as to be meaningless.

Neither view is right. By talking together reasonably we may iron out the antagonisms. By exchanging views we may bring meaning into a life which is too complicated for an individual to grasp unaided. Through dialogue we enlarge our minds so as to grasp new ideas and to reconcile the new with what is old. In dialogue we are putting to use those qualities which differentiate human beings from the lower animals: intelligence and the communication of ideas.

Many Canadians have come to believe that dialogue may be a more effective setting for nation building, or social reform, or community revival, than is the battlefield. The heart and soul of dialogue is this: to realize that there is no once-and-for-all answer to a complicated historical or social problem, but only an answer as of now based upon knowledge of what is going on.

People have different ideas even about what is a solution. Some are satisfied with a temporary settlement, and are content to have a continuing dialogue in which every new settlement is a step toward a final solution. Others pursue their purposes with a sense of finality; they want things settled once and for all; they wager for all or nothing.

It seems more rational to take the first course: to seek a philosophy which is adequate for the circumstances of our time. We must recall that ages are no more infallible than individuals. Every age has held many opinions which subsequent ages have deemed not only false but absurd. The way to progress appears to lie in talking things over with one another, exchanging and enlarging our ideas, so that we grow into our future. That is dialogue.

EFFECTIVE AND EFFICIENT LISTENING

Listening, like reading, involves receiving the verbal messages of other persons. Regardless of the excellent quality of the spoken or written message sent to us, we cannot rely solely on the knowledge and skills of the speaker or the writer. We must exert an active effort to receive these messages.

The Importance of Listening

Various studies have indicated that most business persons spend from 40 to 60 percent of their working day in listening. The business manager will usually spend even more. A manager is paid to listen, even though he or she does not charge by the hour, as does a psychoanalyst. Management is basically decision making, and decisions are based on information about problems and possible solutions. Much of this information is presented orally. In order to make intelligent decisions, the manager must listen — completely, exactly, and critically.

In addition to the obvious purpose of receiving information, listening is essential to the morale of the persons we supervise. "Oh, if someone would only listen!" is a cry heard on occasion in occupations of all kinds, a cry that sometimes disappears in despair because individuals have given up the hope that anyone will ever listen. Employees want to feel that they count, that they are a part of the organization, that their words are worth hearing or reading. This is a universal human desire, and being promoted to management status does not change this feeling, for none of us is ever completely secure in our relationships with others. We all want to be heard, but not enough of us want to listen.

Managers and company presidents often proclaim their open-door policies and go so far as to admit everyone who comes to the office. Then they interrupt by anticipating the speaker's words, looking at the clock, or indicating that they are impatient in some way. They are especially likely to do too much of the talking themselves.

Listening, like all other facets of communication, must be sincere to be effective. It must be sincere to be real. Data received through oral words are likely to be far less permanent in the mind of the receiver than written words. Studies show that we usually forget from one-third to one-half of what we hear within eight hours after hearing it.

When considering the trend to decrease the number of memorandums and other written messages, which is a suggestion that is now appearing frequently in business articles and textbooks, we must keep in mind this certain loss of part of the meaning received through oral communication. This loss will continue to occur, at least to an extent, regardless of the improvement in listening ability.

As an aid to remembering, we should make notes about oral instructions. If done wisely, this notetaking can improve listening; if done unwisely, and to excess, it can hinder it. We can become so involved in getting everything down that we fail to listen for the most important points. When oral exchange of ideas and information is convenient for the speaker and hearer, the listener's notes can be just as effective for later use as a memo would be. An added advantage is the back-and-forth flow of ideas and reactions, and the necessity of writing a memorandum is eliminated. But it is absolutely essential that good listening techniques be applied.

Barriers to Listening

Why do we not listen? Think of the reasons you have not listened to others. Why have you not received their messages? Why do persons not listen to you as you engage in conversations or speak to groups? Or why do they not understand you, or remember what you said?

Check your listening habits. Could the quality of your listening have any relationship to:

1. Your actual physical ability to hear?
2. Attention to the speaker's voice, appearance, pronunciation, accent, use of grammar, or mannerisms — to the exclusion of what the speaker is trying to say to you?
3. Discounting and disregarding what the speaker is saying because you do not like his or her physical appearance, voice, pronunciation, accent, use of grammar, or mannerisms?
4. Listening to words only, not to the underlying feeling behind the words, much of which is communicated by nonverbal methods?
5. Listening for details to the exclusion of the overall meaning, or to the exclusion of the ideas and principles upon which the details are based?
6. Allowing preconceived beliefs about the particular subject being discussed to prevent you from receiving the speaker's ideas?
7. Allowing emotional feelings about the subject to "turn you off," especially if the speaker uses emotional-affective words?
8. Concentrating on notetaking to the extent that you lose the train of thought?
9. Interrupting?
10. Being sure that you already know all there is to know about the subject?
11. Inattention because you do not like to consider unpleasant, complicated, or difficult subjects?
12. Inattention because you are tired, sleepy, hungry, and want to go home?
13. Inattention because you know that whatever is said, you could say it better?
14. Inattention because you have more important things to think about?
15. Boredom because you have already heard too many speeches, lectures, discussions, conversations, and people "talking at you"?
16. Inability to keep your mind on the subject?
17. Inattention to the speaker's words because you are trying to think of a reply, or of a question to ask during the discussion period?
18. Confusion because you don't have the faintest idea of what the speaker is talking about because you have never heard the words before?

19. Lack of understanding because you do not look at the speaker
    so as to grasp the full effect of what is being said, as well as to
    notice the gestures, facial expressions, and other nonverbal
    signals?
20. Lack of concentration because your mind moves faster than the
    speaker's voice and wanders into side paths so that you lose the
    train of thought?

What other factors enter into your reception of spoken words?

Barriers, or noise as applied to communication, have already been
discussed in Chapter 3. As listeners we cannot control all the sources of
noise that prevent our receiving the message exactly as the sender intended
it to be. We cannot control the actual physical noise in the room, nor can
we control miscommunication caused by the speaker, such as using inexact or incorrect words. By our careful attention and thought, however,
we can recognize these inconsistencies and adjust our thinking to them.

Perception affects our reception of the message in any form of communication, especially in the listening process. We cannot immediately
remove all the barriers to the accurate and complete perception of the
intended message. For example, we cannot merely resolve that we will
dispense with all our own preconceived notions and prejudices (we all have
them) and find them gone. But our recognition of these particular biases,
probably even our acceptance of them (if it is reasonable to accept a
prejudice), can serve as a warning that they interfere with our reception of
the spoken message, as well as of the written one.

Look back at the twenty reasons as to why you may not be receiving
communications sent orally to you. How many of these have to do with
perception? Perhaps it would be quicker to list those that do not relate to
perception.

Listening, like reading, requires attention and energy. The better
you listen, however, the less demanding it seems to be. Ralph G. Nichols
lists six bad habits that prevent effective listening.[3] These comments are
concerned mostly with listening to a lecturer or a discussion leader, but
they also apply to direct, face-to-face discussion. (Nichols is one of the
best-known authorities in the field of listening. He is also a teacher of
listening.)

1. *Faking attention.* You are deceiving only yourself — for you will not
   deceive other persons for very long. Besides, you are cheating yourself
   out of the opportunity to learn whatever it is that is being said.

---

3. Ralph G. Nichols and Leonard A. Stevens, *Are You Listening?* (New York: McGraw-Hill
Book Company, 1957), pp. 104–111.

2. *"I get the facts" listening.*   Although Nichols does not say that facts are unimportant, he says that memorizing facts is not the way to listen. When persons talk with you, they usually want you to understand the ideas. We should remember facts only long enough to understand the ideas that are built from these facts. Then the understanding of the ideas will help the listener to remember the supporting facts more effectively than does a person who goes after the facts alone.

3. *Avoiding difficult listening.*   Concentration is necessary in order to understand a lecture or a discussion. We should be willing to devote the needed effort in order to grasp the meaning. Nichols states that if we are affected with this listening habit, we should make a planned and periodic effort to listen to difficult material, lectures, and discussion topics that require mental effort, such as radio commentators, panel discussions, and lectures.

4. *Premature dismissal of a subject as uninteresting.*   Nichols quotes G. K. Chesterton, who once said that there is no such thing as an uninteresting subject; there are only uninterested people.

5. *Criticizing delivery and physical appearance.*   The content of the message is always more important than the form of the delivery.

6. *Yielding easily to distractions.*

Another reason that we have difficulty in listening is that our thought processes move much faster than the speed of the spoken word. The average lecturer speaks at about the rate of 125 words a minute; our minds, even on a slow day, move several times faster. Because of this difference, our minds wander, and we anticipate what is coming next, which may or may not be what actually does come next. Or we mentally take a little rest because we think we know what the speaker is going to say. If our thought processes were not faster than the spoken word, we would be even worse listeners. We would not have time to notice the speaker's nonverbal clues, to determine the feeling behind the words, or to notice the speaker's particular use of words and word meanings.

All these functions enter into effective listening, as well as actually hearing the words themselves. But as we do all these things, we should not fail to concentrate on what the speaker is saying at the moment — and often this is exactly what happens. We get so tangled up in our own thoughts, which have perhaps started in relation to something the speaker has said, that we lose the train of thought or miss a great deal of what has been said. This is especially true when we are listening to lectures, but it can also be true when we are in a group or listening to one individual.

We can become better listeners if we actually try to do so. Good listening is not only beneficial to ourselves from the standpoint of knowledge and information — it is a matter of courtesy toward the speaker, and just plain good manners.

Sympathetic versus Critical Listening

We are engaged in sympathetic listening when we are careful about several of the twenty factors previously mentioned — for example, listening mainly for content and not to the speaker's accent, pronunciation, or grammar; recognizing our own particular bias; and giving the speaker our undivided, conscientious attention.

Sympathetic factors that make for good listening include all the aspects of actively being willing to receive the message, insofar as it agrees with our own intelligent observation. Critical listening involves evaluation. We must listen critically, for we cannot and should not accept completely everything we hear, just as we cannot accept or believe everything that we read.

The world is full of propaganda, high-pressure advertising, and public relations experts and speech writers who distort facts to suit their own particular purposes. Or, even if the message is not planned to be deceitful, the speaker may be misinformed. Individuals may be absolutely and completely sincere, and also absolutely and completely mistaken.

Just as we evaluate what we read, we must evaluate what we hear. Many of us, unfortunately, evaluate too soon, before we have given the lecturer or the conversationist an opportunity to present the complete story or to express opinions. We interrupt the flow of thought directed toward our mind, either by mentally interrupting by turning to our own thoughts or by interrupting with our spoken words. Although we should critically evaluate, we cannot honestly and completely evaluate another's words until we have actually listened to those words.

The principles of general semantics, as discussed in Chapter 4, apply to the evaluation of listening. For example, we must consider the reliability of the speaker's words. Are they based upon facts or upon inferences or value judgments?

- Is the speaker up to date — or, according to Korzybski, has the speaker taken into consideration that what was true yesterday is not necessarily true today?
- Is the speaker competent, as well as being nonbiased? Even well-meaning, sincere persons can be misinformed.
- Is the speaker giving complete information? Although "the statement is never the whole story," has the speaker abstracted the most important information?
- If points are omitted, do you believe that this omission was intentional?
- Does the speaker express ideas in abstractions and generalities instead of using specific, concrete language?

• Does the speaker attempt to persuade by relying upon emotional words and phrases instead of by rational, objective language?

The principles of general semantics, which deal with the ways in which language affects behavior and behavior affects language, are essential to your evaluation of all communication, including spoken words. These principles also apply to the evaluation of written words.

In Chapter 16 you are given pointers on the evaluation of data as well as upon the way to interpret information without letting your personal bias or perception distort conclusions. These pointers in Chapter 16 are also facets of the principles of general semantics, and they are also applicable to the evaluation of listening.

SUMMARY ◆ 5

For successful interpersonal communication, the individual must have a positive self-concept and a sincere respect for the other participant or participants in the sharing of the communication process. There must be no attitude of inferiority or superiority.

Interpersonal communication depends not only upon words, nonverbal signals, and the environment, but also upon relationships.

Business persons spend from 40 to 60 percent of their working day in listening. Listening requires attention, energy, sincerity, and empathy. We should listen both sympathetically and critically.

Various barriers prevent effective listening; many of these barriers are related to our perception, attitudes, and opinions. By recognizing these barriers, we can minimize their effect.

To be a better listener:

1. Concentrate. Remain alert.
2. Listen sympathetically, but also critically.
3. Listen for general meaning and for ideas.
4. Take notes as necessary and appropriate, but do not let note taking interfere with reception of the message.
5. Notice the speaker's nonverbal communication.
6. Keep in mind the various barriers to effective listening and try to minimize them.

QUESTIONS AND PROBLEMS ◆ 5

1. How can too much communication be a barrier to effective listening?
2. Think about your role in interpersonal communication during the past week. If you are employed, give special attention to the interpersonal communication at your place of business. How was your communication affected by your relationships with others, your attitudes, your opinions and biases, and your state of mind at the moment?
3. Assemble into discussion groups of five to eight members. Discuss one of the following topics or choose one of your own, preferably one that pertains to communication. If possible, tape record these discussions. Appoint one member to present your conclusions to the class. After class, write a summary of the methods of discussion and of the results.
    a. deceptive advertising
    b. silly TV commercials
    c. intelligent TV commercials
    d. some aspect of nonverbal communication
    e. barriers to listening
    f. some particular problem of your college or university
4. Comments and bits of information assignment: As instructed in Question 6 at the end of Chapter 1, find a comment or bit of information that applies to topics discussed in Chapter 5. As your instructor directs, prepare these in written form and/or present them to the class.
5. To illustrate communication through tone of voice, see how many messages you can communicate with the word "oh." Or two students can illustrate different meanings by the use of each other's name. (John-Marcia, Marcia-John, etc.) Or use a nonsense phrase, such as "Kiss a checkered cat," to express fear, security, anger, approval, joy, self-confidence, depression, and other emotions. Can you use differing tones of voice without also using nonverbal communication? If you wish, add nonverbal communication to these forms of communication.

FURTHER READING ◆ 5

Barker, Larry L. *Listening Behavior.* Englewood Cliffs, N.J.: Prentice-Hall, 1971.

Hamachek, Don E. *Encounters with the Self.* New York: Holt, Rinehart and Winston, 1971.

Harris, Thomas A. *I'm OK — You're OK.* New York: Avon Books, 1973.

Johnson, David. *Reaching Out: Interpersonal Effectiveness and Self Actualization.* Englewood Cliffs, N.J.: Prentice-Hall, 1972.

Keltner, John W. *Elements of Interpersonal Communication.* Belmont, Calif.: Wadsworth Publishing Company, 1973.

Moray, Neville. *Listening and Attention.* Baltimore: Penguin Books, 1969.

Nichols, Ralph G., and Stevens, Leonard A. *Are You Listening?* New York: McGraw-Hill Book Company, 1957.

Rothwell, J. Dan and Costigan, James I. *Interpersonal Communication.* Columbus, O.: Charles E. Merrill Publishing Company, 1975.

Tubbs, Stewart L., and Moss, Sylvia. *Human Communication.* New York: Random House, 1974.

Wilmont, William W., and Wenburg, John R., eds. *Communication Involvement: Personal Perspectives.* New York: John Wiley and Sons, 1974.

BASIC PRINCIPLES OF EFFECTIVE COMMUNICATION

Building Goodwill
Through Communication

6

We find it easy to express goodwill when we actually feel it. If we have pleasant, positive attitudes toward ourselves, other people, and the company for which we work, this outlook will be reflected in our writing or other communication. If we do not have desirable attitudes, our writing and speech, if not blunt and unpleasant, may sound strained and forced. As much as possible, we should put ourselves into the place of our reader or listener. Although we may not agree with the other's viewpoint, we should try to understand it.

Although many of our letters will be to persons we have never met, we know that these persons are likely to be much like ourselves. They respond to fair and courteous treatment. They want to be treated as intelligent adults. They want their ideas and opinions to be taken seriously. They appreciate sincere praise, but they recognize and dislike flattery. They know that they can be wrong, but they do not enjoy being scolded, bossed, or preached to. They realize that other persons make mistakes, too, and they are usually willing to overlook honest mistakes. They expect and deserve an apology when one is due, but they do not like excessive apologizing or undue humility.

A SINCERE YOU-ATTITUDE

The you-attitude, or the you-approach, is looking at a situation from the viewpoint of the reader or the listener. It must be sincere. The opposite concept is the I-attitude or approach, and the writer-attitude.

The you-viewpoint can and should be used in every kind of business writing and business speech. For example, in a "yes-letter," the you-approach is used to indicate that the request is being granted and, in addition, that the writer and the organization represented are happy to comply with the request. In a "no-letter," the you-attitude can show that, although the exact request cannot be granted, there is a reason for the refusal and it is not given as a mere malevolent whim.

In sales material, the you-viewpoint describes the product or service in terms of what it can do for the reader. In collection letters, the reader-approach emphasizes the benefit that the reader will derive from paying his bill — usually the preservation of a good credit reputation. An application letter, although built around the qualifications of the writer, can include the you-viewpoint by showing how these qualifications can benefit the prospective employer.

Even in reports, which are expected to be completely objective and factual, the writer considers the reader, and thus uses the you-attitude, by careful arrangement and wording for quick and easy understanding; by the completeness of the report so that all questions are answered; and by correct usage in order that the reader's attention or confidence in the message will not be weakened by the way the message is presented.

In using this broad interpretation of the meaning of the you-attitude (or the reader-approach or the you-viewpoint), the concept is not only one of the most important aspects of business communication, but it includes almost all of the other desirable attributes of communication. For example, good letters have often been evaluated by their "C" qualities — consideration, courtesy, completeness, conciseness, correctness, concreteness, and clearness. (See Appendix A, "A Summary of Business Communication Terminology and Concepts," for discussion of these "C" qualities, as well as of other "C" qualities and the terms mentioned in the following paragraphs.)

But the you-attitude cannot be considered separately from these qualities, or any one of them, for if the letter is seriously lacking in one or more of these attributes, then the welfare of the reader has not been served, and the you-attitude or service to the reader is not complete.

A letter written entirely in the you-attitude also includes a positive rather than negative approach, a cheerful rather than pessimistic outlook, and a pleasant rather than unpleasant tone. Even the organization of the material and the actual physical appearance of business writing make up part of the you-attitude, for to mail a messy, carelessly typewritten letter is as discourteous as going to a party in dirty clothes.

It is true that the writer can be filled with goodwill and, because of various reasons, not be able to make this feeling apparent in letters and other communications. The desire to serve does not guarantee proficiency in written or oral business communication, although it is an essential element. Certain techniques and skills must be acquired to achieve all of the desirable qualities of communication, or the total you-attitude.

A type of wording that violates the you-approach is shown by excessive use of sentences such as these:

Our company is pleased to announce the opening of our new store.

We are very happy that the Smith Sporting Goods Company is now expanding.

We are very happy to have your order.

The Smith Sporting Goods Company is very happy to have your order.

We at Smith Sporting Goods Company thank you for your order.

Notice that each of these sentences, when read alone, seems only to show pride in the employing company, which is a worthy attitude but is not enough. Letters may be built around the theme that a company is opening a new store or moving to a new neighborhood, but if the reader does not interpret these company changes in the light of personal benefits, the letter has not been written in the complete you-attitude.

When writing about expansion or other company changes, these changes should be presented in a way to show how they will benefit the reader in the way of convenience or economy. The sentence, "We are now located in your neighborhood," is not nearly so effective as the sentence, "You are now only five minutes away from the store that can fill all your sporting goods needs."

The sentence

We are shipping your goods today.

could not be described as negative, for it is telling what is ordinarily considered good news. It is even more effective, though, if it is written this way:

Your goods will be shipped today.

or

You should receive your complete order within a week. It

was shipped today, by parcel post, as you requested.

Even more effective, in most cases, is a specific, descriptive word rather than "goods" or "order." For example:

Your beautiful suit is on its way to you.

This last sentence, in addition to being more exact as to the type of merchandise, implies that the suit was a wise purchase by describing it as beautiful. Such words and phrases can easily be overused, however, so that they detract from the goodwill-building aspects of the message because they sound insincere. (Emphasis upon the value of a purchase already made is referred to as "resale.")

Some business writers, in an attempt to avoid the use of "I" or "we," continually use the company name, as in a sentence like this:

The Smith Sporting Goods Company thanks you for your

order of November 1.

Some writers include the company name in almost every paragraph. This is not a good practice. In the first place, the company name is given in the letterhead. In the second place, unnecessary use of the company name is really the I-attitude, even though the word "I" is not used. Emphasis is away from the reader and back to the company from which the letter comes. Another disadvantage is that the letter sounds stuffy and formal; it does not sound personal, natural, and friendly. The reader knows that the letter comes not from the company (companies can't speak or write letters), but from someone at the company. "I" and "we" should be used when to do otherwise seems stiff and unnatural.

Some writers routinely use "we" instead of "I," even though they obviously mean "I." Such usage is unnatural and unnecessary. If the writer is talking about himself or herself as an individual company representative — as is possible or desirable even though the you-attitude is used throughout — then the word to use is "I," not "we." If the writer is speaking of a group of employees or the company as an organization of individuals, then "we" is appropriate.

Almost all letters are written in what is described as the personal tone, in which first-person pronouns are used as they seem desirable and necessary. (See Chapter 8, "The Personal and the Impersonal Tone.") Remember, though, that a letter filled with "I's" and "we's," especially if all or most of the paragraphs begin with "I," is likely not to be written with the reader uppermost in mind. Even if both the wording of the letter and the content of the message show consideration for the reader, the abundance of "I's" and "we's" will at least give a first impression that the letter does not exemplify the you-approach.

In the sentence

We are glad to receive your order...

there may be a connotation that the company is selfishly grasping for business because of the profit motive. Although the reader realizes that the company must make a profit, this frank reminder is less than diplomatic.

The you-attitude may be contrasted with both the I-attitude and the more or less neutral-attitude, as far as the exact wording is concerned. The I-attitude is conveyed by the usage of the first-person pronoun, as in this sentence:

> We are happy to announce that we have increased the size
>
> of our store building.

Expressed with "you's," the sentence would read like this:

> Now you will find a wider choice of merchandise in the
>
> greatly enlarged building.

A third way of expressing this same idea does not actually bring the reader into the picture, as the preceding sentence does. This objective and "neutral" writing reads something like this:

> The enlarged store building has allowed for a much greater
>
> variety of merchandise.

Some readers will interpret this last sentence to mean that they now have a wider choice and that the company has increased its services to them. This meaning, however, is not so direct and personal as the one that makes use of the word "you." Both the first and the second illustrations are described as being written in the personal tone; the third is in the impersonal tone.

At times the you-attitude is achieved by using the neutral, impersonal approach. If the idea to be expressed is a disappointing one, the neutral, impersonal tone may be the better choice, although this is not necessarily true. For example, the sentence

> You failed the examination.

does not include the you-attitude, even though the word "you" is used. It may be necessary to convey this disappointing information to the reader. Some ideas, because of their nature, cannot be made pleasant or positive regardless of the skill in word choice. In this sentence, too, the very negative word "failed" contributes to the overall undiplomatic effect of the sentence. Probably there is no way to make this information sound like good news, and we shouldn't try to make it appear so; but we can soften it somewhat by saying it like this:

> The minimum passing score is 70.

This statement may be all that is necessary, if the reader already knows his score, or if the graded paper is included.   If he does not already have this information, then the sentence could read like this:

> The minimum passing score is 70; your score was 68.

At times the personal approach may be effectively used even in a disappointing message, instead of the more impersonal, neutral approach. A revised version of this last sentence could be:

> I am sorry that you did not score the necessary 70;
>
> however, you missed it by only two points.

The cost of a product is subordinated by the use of the neutral approach.   You are more diplomatic when you say:

> This product sells for $22.

than when you say:

> This will cost you $22.

Even worse is:

> You must pay $22 for this product.

The words *I, we, us, our, ourselves, our company,* or *my company* do not of themselves convey an I-attitude instead of a you-attitude.   However, if a letter or other message is conspicuous from the overuse of these words, it is doubtful that the you-attitude has been used.   On the other hand, the use of the word "you" alone is not enough to determine whether or not the message is really written with the you-attitude.   What is said, instead of the choice of words, including the *you*'s, is the basic consideration.

However, the word *you* is important and may make a real difference in the reception of the message, even though the reader has no idea of the you-attitude and does not think about the fact that the letter is written with more *I*'s than *you*'s.   The use of the word *I* will stand out unnecessarily if all or most of the paragraphs begin with *I*.   Also, if the word *I* is used to this extent, then most likely the letter is not really written with the reader in mind.

As shown in the examples below, sentences written in the first person can possibly be more pleasant and positive than those written in the second person:

> We are sorry that we cannot grant a further extension
>
> of time on our loan to you.
>
> You must pay the full amount of your loan
>
> immediately.

Notice the wording of the following letter, which is definitely not written in the complete you-attitude:

> As newly elected membership director of the Junior
>
> Chamber of Commerce, I am in charge of recruiting new
>
> members. I would like very much for you to join. I am
>
> working for a record-making membership this year.
>
> I do not know why you are not a member, anyway;
>
> most of the other young business owners in this town are,
>
> you know.
>
> Fill out the enclosed application blank and return with
>
> your check.

First Paragraph.   Notice the definite "I-attitude" in the emphatic first sentence. Throughout the paragraph, writer benefits are stressed, not those of the reader.

Second Paragraph.   Most undiplomatic. Even if the reader had been planning to join, this letter is enough to keep him away forever.

Third Paragraph.   Dictatorial. Discourteous. No reader benefit.

An improved version of this letter could begin with a paragraph like this:

> You are wanted—and needed—by the Whitehaven
>
> Jaycees.

The middle paragraphs could be devoted to describing the advantages of joining the Junior Chamber of Commerce, especially from the standpoint of how the organization helps the community. This letter is actually a sales letter, as the reader is to be sold on the idea of joining the organization. A sales message should ordinarily be longer than the first version of this letter; in order to convince the reader to act, it must present sufficient evidence and motivation.

An improved closing section could be:

So that you can begin now to enjoy the benefits of

membership and to contribute to the welfare of your

community, fill out the enclosed membership blank and

send it in with your check. It will be a small investment

that you will always remember with pride.

Our next meeting is Monday, September 8, at

7:30 p.m. at the Quality Inn. We are looking forward to

seeing you.

In summary, the you-attitude is a genuine consideration for the reader. Although the word "you" may at times appear to be more considerate than an "I," the actual content of the message is more important than the choice of words. If the word "I" is used to a great extent, however, it is quite likely that the emphasis is upon the writer, not the reader. In disappointing or sensitive situations, the neutral approach may be more diplomatic than either the you-approach or the I-approach.

A POSITIVE, PLEASANT, AND DIPLOMATIC APPROACH

A positive approach and the you-attitude are two of the most important elements of effective communication. In effect, we cannot fully achieve one without the other.

The positive approach includes several aspects. One is the pleasant approach, which stresses the pleasant and not the unpleasant elements of a situation. Another aspect is stating what can be done instead of what cannot be done. Another is eliminating as much as possible the actual grammatical negatives, such as *no, cannot, will not,* and *can't,* as well as other negative words and phrases, including *criticize, reject, fail, turn down, must,* and *force.*

An example of the use of the negative approach is given in the first sentence; the positive approach in the second.

> This plastic dinnerware won't scratch or dent, and it won't melt in your dishwasher.

> Because this sturdy dinnerware is highly resistant to heat and pressure, it will still be shining and beautiful many years from now. It is completely safe in your dishwasher.

The first sentence, by telling what the dinnerware does *not* do (scratch, dent, or melt), suggests to some readers that it may. It may lead to the reaction, "How do I know it won't do all these things?" Although the second sentence is not guaranteed to inspire absolute confidence in all readers, it is more likely to do so than a negatively worded statement.

Saying that something is not undesirable is not nearly so effective or positive as stating that it is desirable. Even better is to give specific and definite information as to why it is desirable, in the terms of how it will benefit the reader. The description of the dinnerware would be more convincing than the sentence given above if it included evidence of why the dinnerware will remain beautiful. Such evidence might include a statement of the material it is made of or the method of manufacture.

The sentence

> You will never regret buying this camera...

is not so positive as saying

> You will always be happy you bought this camera

or

> You will enjoy this camera for many years to come.

Instead of saying

> The odor of this cat food is not offensive

say something like this:

> You'll like the fragrance of Kitty Cuisine almost as much as your friend Cat loves the taste.

or like this:

> Kitty Cuisine is made of pure, fresh meats—with the
>
> delightful aroma of supper simmering on the stove.

Stress benefits the readers or listeners will gain from the product, not the difficulties or the misfortunes that they will avoid.   An unpleasant thought tends to make persons turn away from the subject and think of something else.   Notice the following examples of the negative and positive approach:

Negative	Positive
The store will close at 8:30.	The store will remain open until 8:30.
We cannot ship your merchandise until July 1.	Your merchandise will be shipped on July 1.

Notice the first example given above.   Let us see how we can make the sentence even more negative or more positive.   If we should write,

> We close the store every night at 8:30 so that we can
>
> all go home...

we are using not only the negative approach but also the we-attitude instead of the you-attitude because the emphasis is on the store and its employees rather than on the customer.   Few writers would use such an extreme sentence, although the attitude conveyed with an emphasis upon the negative and upon "I" rather than upon "you" is far too common in business writing.

The first example of the more positive sentence can be made even better from the standpoint of the positive approach and you-attitude. Suppose we write:

> The store will remain open until 8:30 in the evening
>
> for the convenience of our customers.

This sentence tells how long it will be open, not when it will close.   It also brings in the you-attitude, provided the letter is being written to a customer.

This sentence, however, can be improved still further.   Suppose we write it this way:

> For your shopping convenience, the store will remain
>
> open until 8:30 in the evening.

Do you see why this sentence better conveys the you-attitude than the preceding one? Here the actual use of the word "you" makes the difference, for the writing is aimed at an individual. To this individual, the word "you" is more direct, more personal, and more friendly than when the general and collective words "our customers" are used.

The word "you" is usually preferred over the term "our customers," even though the message being written will be printed or duplicated in some form and distributed to thousands of customers. That the same letter is being sent to many persons does not change the fact that each customer reading the message is an individual, and that he thinks of himself alone and not necessarily in relation to the thousands of other customers.

"Success oriented" is a description of another aspect of the positive approach; this concept is also referred to as "success consciousness." The opposite approach is called the *doubtful tone.*   Success consciousness implies acceptance or favorable action on the part of the reader. Words to watch are "if," "hope," and "trust," as well as any other words or phrases that suggest doubt.

Notice the doubtful tone in these sentence beginnings:

> If you want to follow these instructions...
>
> If my qualifications meet your requirements...
>
> If you want to order this book...
>
> We hope this meets your approval...
>
> We trust this is a satisfactory arrangement...
>
> I know that this is less than you expected, but...
>
> I know you will be disappointed in us, but...
>
> We hope that this unfortunate occurrence will not

adversely affect our business relationship, for...

All these expressions imply that the reader may not, or probably will not, agree to the suggested opinions or actions or continue to hold the writer in esteem. More persuasive wordings are these:

> When you want to order this book...
>
> I believe you will find these instructions helpful,

for...

I shall be glad to come for an interview to discuss my

qualifications in detail.

Just sign the enclosed card and Effective

Communication will soon be on its way to you.

Perhaps the other doubtfully worded sentences could be omitted entirely. No matter what the situation, a statement such as:

We hope that this unfortunate occurrence will not

adversely affect our business relationship...

is probably more harmful than the occurrence itself.

Sometimes the positive, diplomatic approach is achieved by what we refrain from stating. For example, you do not need to include the following statement in order to obtain the necessary information:

In your recent order, you failed to include your size.

A better wording is:

The sweaters come in these sizes: Small (34-36),

Medium (38-40), and Large (42-44). Please check your

size on the enclosed card.

This improved version omits the very negative and accusing word "failed" and moves directly to the requested action.

The following statement is another example of a fact that is often best left unexpressed:

Unfortunately, I have no business experience.

This statement from an application letter stresses a supposed weakness. You are not misrepresenting your experience by omitting such references. If no experience is described in your letter or on your data sheet, then the reader should suppose that you have none. Stress strong points, not weaknesses, as:

My courses in business administration at Indiana

State University have given me an understanding of the

fundamentals of management and supervision.

This is a negative sentence from a letter requesting a speaker:

```
We have no money to pay you, except for your
expenses.
```

An improved version would be:

```
Even our limited budget will permit full payment of
your expenses.
```

To fully achieve the positive, pleasant, diplomatic tone, we should make use of the techniques of emphasis and subordination. (These are discussed in greater detail in Chapter 7.) An old song, popular during World War II days but heard occasionally since, urges us to "accentuate the positive and eliminate the negative," or to stress the pleasant and subordinate the unpleasant. We stress or subordinate by position and arrangement, sentence construction, and word choice.

In presenting both good news and bad news, ordinarily the good news should be mentioned first. Concrete, specific words should be used to express pleasant or neutral ideas, but more general, abstract terms should be chosen to express unpleasant ideas. For example:

```
I'm sorry you have terminal carcinoma of the
colon...
```

although specific and more accurate than

```
I'm sorry you are ill...
```

is certainly less diplomatic. (Of course you wouldn't write a sentence like this horrible example; it is used only for the purpose of illustration.) Another extreme example is:

```
We have learned of the unfortunate circumstances of
your psychosis, your bankruptcy, your arrest, and your
prison term.
```

In a situation like this, choose to be less than specific and use some generalized word like "problems." (Although "problems" in most cases is a negative word, here, in comparison with the exact words, it is positively cheerful.)

Express pleasant and neutral ideas or statements in specific, forceful words. For example:

Congratulations on being elected president of your

senior class.

I am interested in typewriting paper with 25-percent

cotton content, 20-pound weight.

Another principle of forceful, descriptive, concise writing is reversed at times for the sake of tact and diplomacy: the active versus the passive voice (see Chapter 8 for further discussion). Although we should usually prefer the active verb, at times the passive construction may be more conducive to goodwill. The following sentence is expressed with the verb in the active voice, but it is not diplomatic:

You failed to water the plants.

Expressed in the passive voice, the words are:

The plants have not been watered.

Notice that in the first example "you" is the subject and "failed" is the verb. In the second sentence, "plants," the grammatical subject, is receiving the action. Because the idea to be expressed is essentially negative, the passive construction is less accusing; emphasis is away from "you" and toward "the plants." The word "failed" adds to the overall accusing tone.

Rewording of such sentences, however, does not necessarily require the passive construction, as in this sentence:

The plants seem dry.

In this example, too, emphasis is away from *you* and upon the plants.

This discussion of the positive approach does not mean that you will never use the words "no," "not," or "cannot." Sometimes such words are necessary for your exact meaning, as in the sentence immediately preceding this one. It is better to use a somewhat negative statement than to run the risk of being misunderstood. Inoffensive writing can include such words as "cannot" and "no," provided it is courteous and considerate. Even the word "must" may be necessary in urgent situations, although it should ordinarily be avoided.

Clearness should not be sacrificed for the sake of diplomacy, but good writing should be both clear and diplomatic. It can be, although at times there must be a direct order or an unmistakable refusal. For example, instead of "Stop," suppose that the roadside sign is worded, "Pause, please, if you have time."

In summary, the positive approach is pleasant and diplomatic. It emphasizes what can be done, not what cannot be done; the pleasant, not the unpleasant. It emphasizes the benefits to be gained, not the unpleasant things that could occur, or even those that won't occur. It eliminates words or phrases that are of themselves negative, such as "fail," "reject," "criticize," and many others.

DETERMINING A CODE OF ETHICS FOR COMMUNICATION

A sound and workable system of communication is based upon openness and honesty. The old-fashioned virtues of dependability, sincerity, and loyalty still build a lasting foundation for business organizations, governments, and individuals. Without trust and confidence, there can be no real communication.

The ancient adage, "Honesty is the best policy," is definitely true, overall and in the long run. But look at the meaning of this sentence, or at least the meaning that the words imply. Are we to be honest because it's the best policy — because it will bring more profit for our company and a raise for ourselves? If this motivation is our reason for being "honest," are we necessarily honest at all? Is an admirable course of action "honestly" a virtue if we are following this course of action for personal gain? Probably not. Nevertheless, honest and ethical business practices are essential for an enduring and successful business enterprise.

A two-year study into the problems of communication resulted in the conclusion that the approach to communication should be based on an honest "leveling" by management and employees as to their feelings, attitudes, and motivations. This approach is based on several assumptions, all of which include the precepts of sincere, nonmanipulative relationships. One assumption is quoted as follows:

> The old values of honesty, sincerity, and trust, sometimes dismissed as Sunday school sentimentality, are actually Monday morning business realism in the quest for better communications. They create the climate in which communication grows. Where they do not exist, communication will be faulty, no matter how they are fertilized with methods and techniques. A man's character seems to have more influence than his personality in improving communications.[1]

1. A. W. Lindh, "Plain Talk About Communicating in Business," in *Readings in Impersonal and Organizational Communication*, ed. Richard C. Huseman, Cal M. Logue, and Dwight L. Freshley (Boston: Holbrook Press, 1973), p. 10.

No thinking, ethical person disputes the premise that business communications should be sincere, honest, and truthful. Without sincerity, all the techniques of skillful writing become only cleverness, a quality far less desirable than wisdom or genuine goodwill. This entire book is based on the assumption that you and the organization you represent are worthy of the goodwill of the customers and of the general public and that goods and services are truthfully presented and not unreasonably priced.

Being honest and sincere, however, does not require bluntness and curtness. Certain basic principles of effective communication — diplomacy, the you-attitude, the positive approach, psychological arrangement, and persuasion — are sometimes viewed with skepticism by some persons, as if all these principles should be disregarded in order to avoid hypocrisy. Because of this attitude, their writing and speech becomes unnecessarily direct, blunt, and harsh. This approach, although "honest," actually is a form of discourtesy to the receiver of the message and disloyalty to the employing company of the writer.

The You-Attitude — Can It Be Real?

The interpretation of the you-attitude should not be that it is a manipulation of the readers or listeners, a way of ingratiating ourselves into their favor so that we can sell our goods or convince them to do as we wish. Even if this is the attitude of the communicator (and every person does and must determine his own system of values), it is difficult to simulate a concern that we do not feel. A reader or listener does not need to be completely alert to realize that the wording sounds "fishy" or that the writer or speaker is trying for a "snow job." A message that provokes these reactions is worse than one that is harshly direct, but there is no reason for either of these two extremes.

The you-attitude has been described as being nonexistent, that the individual's concern must be for himself and for his own company. Much of the controversy over the application of the you-attitude stems from an inexact understanding of the meaning that the term should convey. The business communicator, although using the you-approach, must continue to be concerned with the needs of his or her own company. You as a human being are more interested in your own welfare than that of some person to whom you are writing or dictating a letter, likely a person you have never met. The recognition of these realities, however, does not preclude genuine concern for others or the desire to serve, to play fair, and to understand the reader's point of view.

But good intentions are not enough. The writer or speaker can be filled with genuine goodwill and, because of various reasons, not be able to make this feeling apparent in his letters and other communications. The desire to serve does not guarantee proficiency in written or spoken business communication, although it is an essential element. Certain techniques and skills must be acquired in order to achieve all of the desirable qualities of communication. These skills and techniques, as well as background discussion, are presented throughout the remainder of this textbook.

Persuasion or Conviction?

Persuasion is considered to be the approach that is most likely to make the reader act or think in the way that the writer wishes. The word "persuade" has a connotation of urging, coaxing, or "bending the will." "Convince" does not have this implication, but denotes understanding.

In sales writing, the buyer is not persuaded to buy because the writer wants him to do so. He is convinced that the product will fill his needs or desires. This conviction is not necessarily the result of a common-sense, utilitarian purpose; for example, no one actually *needs* beautiful paintings, an expensive stereo set, or handmade boots. These things or similar ones, however, may be worth far more to the buyer than their cost; if so, they are a bargain regardless of the price.

Products and services are sold because the buyer believes that it will be to his advantage to buy, not because the seller by eloquent persuasion or "hard-sell" tactics has caused him to buy. Nevertheless, the skillful sales person has been able to convince the buyer that the product is more valuable to him than the money he pays for it. Ideally, this conviction is accomplished by truthfully and completely presenting the features of the product or service and showing how these features will meet the buyer's needs.

Although the term "persuasive writing" is used in this book, as in other textbooks, to describe sales messages and other material in which the writer asks the reader to take certain actions, the term should not be interpreted as *manipulation* or *coaxing*. *Convincing* the reader that the desired action will be for his own benefit is the key to successful persuasive writing. All effective business writing or speech is persuasive if it convinces the reader to take a certain course of action, or even to believe in the company from which the message comes. (Later chapters deal with persuasive writing.)

The Truth, the Whole Truth, and Nothing but the Truth?

To be ethical in business communication does not necessarily mean that every message must contain a detailed listing of the complete truth. Each message, however, should contain nothing but the truth. (These statements should *not* be understood to mean that communication should be planned to mislead or to misrepresent the facts.) For the sake of diplomacy and tact, as well as to emphasize the positive aspects of a situation, sometimes we communicate best by what we refrain from saying.

We are not completely truthful with our friends, family, or husband or wife. To be completely, absolutely, and harshly truthful is, as we have all witnessed, devastating to the ego. Persons who take pride in plain speaking describe themselves as "not beating around a bush" or "calling a spade a spade." (Sometimes a spade should be described as an instrument used in digging, and *not* called a spade. The spade referred to by overly frank individuals is at times *exactly* an instrument for digging — into another person's pride and dignity.)

The use of general words instead of overly specific ones can soften an unpleasant message. Unpleasant details that are not necessary for the reception of the intended message are often best omitted. For example, if a person was not hired because he scored lower than anyone else had ever scored on a company aptitude test, only a sadistic personnel manager would spell out this unwelcome news.

In sales writing, you need not include the information that the product you are selling can be bought at a lower price from a competing organization. If your company operates as it should, it is giving something for this extra cost — perhaps a guarantee, free delivery, or a convenient location. Or perhaps the competing company is selling the item at a discount for one of many possible reasons. We should stress the real benefits that the customer receives from buying the product from our organization. To stress these benefits instead of price is not being untruthful, and to do otherwise would be disloyal to your employer. In business communication, as in other situations, it is only sensible to put your best foot forward, and to make sure that the foot is covered by a well-polished shoe.

In his book, *I Never Danced at the White House*, Art Buchwald describes (along with many other topics) an overly frank, direct and "honest" method of selling, which he calls "the soft sell." He describes a young lady, Miss Brandon, a psychology major who goes to work as a salesperson in a dress shop in Georgetown. Her first customer is a lady who comes in to buy a suit and is not concerned over the price.

> "Well, let me ask you this question: Do you want the suit because you need it? Or have you just had a fight with your husband and are trying to get even by making a very expensive purchase?" . . .
> "Perhaps you suspect him of some infidelity and you think this is the only way you can get back at him."
> "I have no idea what you're talking about," the customer said.
> "Spending money in anger is a very expensive form of hostility. My advice to you is to think it over for a few days. Try to patch up your differences. Buying a new suit won't save your marriage."
> "Thank you very much," the customer said frostily and left the store.

The conversation with the next customer went this way:

> The lady said: "I need something really exciting. I'm going to the Kennedy Center, and I want a dress that will knock everyone dead."
>
> Miss Brandon said, "We have some lovely evening dresses for insecure people."
>
> "Insecure people?"
>
> "Oh, yes. Didn't you know that clothes are one of the main ways women compensate for insecurity?"
>
> "I'm not insecure," the lady said angrily.
>
> "Then why do you want to knock them dead at the Kennedy Center? Why can't you be accepted for yourself instead of what you wear? . . . I can sell you a new dress that will attract attention, but then you would never know if it were you or the dress that made people stop and stare."[2]

As you can imagine, the customer did not buy a dress — and Miss Brandon was soon looking for another job.

Although this psychology major did not understand what she was doing in her attempt to be completely honest, she was really manipulating other persons instead of being helpful to them. It is beside the point whether or not the first customer needed the suit. She wanted it, the shop had suits for sale, and no doubt she would have been happier to leave with the suit than without it, regardless of her unconscious motivation for the purchase.

The second customer was perhaps more insecure after having this trait pointed out to her than she would have been with the new evening dress. Besides, she was probably no more insecure than Miss Brandon herself or most other persons in the world.

Shakespeare said, "To thine own self be true." He would no doubt apply this maxim to business problems which you attempt to solve by oral or written communication. If you cannot in good conscience act as a representative of your employing company and follow its established policies, then it is time to look for another job.

SPECIAL GOODWILL MESSAGES

Goodwill building is an important purpose of all business writing, but most letters, memorandums, and other written materials have additional purposes. For example, a sales letter is planned to sell a product or service; to accomplish this purpose, the writer must build the buyer's confidence in the product or service and in the seller. A collection letter, to be successful, must collect and also retain the customer's goodwill. A

2. Art Buchwald, *I Never Danced at the White House* (New York: G. P. Putnam's Sons, 1973), pp. 107–108.

memorandum to a fellow employee should accomplish its purpose of presenting information, ideas, or instructions, as well as promoting pleasant working relationships.

Special goodwill letters or memorandums are those with the single purpose of building goodwill. They express appreciation, congratulations, sympathy, welcome, and good wishes.

The you-attitude and the positive approach, essential qualities of all business writing, are especially important in special goodwill messages. *These messages must be sincere.* If they are written only from the profit motive for your company, they are *not* sincere. These messages should also be conversational, natural, and an expression of your own thoughts. Adapting the wording of a model letter is not an acceptable way of expressing sincere goodwill. Such letters will almost always sound forced, unnatural, and nonpersonal.

Promptness in sending goodwill messages is most important. They should be sent as soon after the event as possible. Immediately upon learning of the occasion for congratulations, sympathy, appreciation, good wishes, or appreciation, write and mail a letter.

Conciseness is desirable in special goodwill messages. Usually, there is not a great deal to say. Say it in a pleasant, natural manner, and stop. Do not be wordy or effusive. The following are examples of some occasions for special goodwill messages.

To customers and business associates, letters expressing appreciation for:

- Record of prompt payment of bills
- Special orders
- Long, continued patronage
- Special services
- Patience in trying situations

To customers, business associates, friends, and fellow employees, letters expressing congratulations for:

- Promotions
- Special accomplishments
- Professional appointments or honors
- Growth or expansion of business
- Personal highlights — weddings, anniversaries, birth of children, accomplishments of children, graduations, special recognition for hobbies, church and civic responsibilities.

Letters expressing greetings:

- At Christmas and on other holidays
- For birthdays

- For anniversaries
- For other special occasions

Other occasions:

- Condolences
- Get-well messages
- Best wishes of any kind
- Letters welcoming a person to the community or to the company

Because goodwill messages are personal and applied to many and varying situations, there can be no suggested formula or plan of presentation. Each must be written individually. These messages may be either typewritten or handwritten. Although handwritten notes are more informal and personal, a typewritten letter is to be preferred to a hard-to-read or unattractive handwritten one. Ordinarily, if the firm's letterhead is used, the letter should be typewritten. If you use your own personalized stationery, either typewrite or handwrite the letter.

The letters in Figures 6–1 through 6–7 are examples of special goodwill letters. Remember, though, that no model letters are to be copied or slightly adapted to meet some particular circumstance. Be yourself.

1329 Dearing Road
Blytheville, Arkansas
January 30, 1978

Dear Mrs. Holmes:

You have my deepest sympathy.

You may remember that I worked with your husband several years ago when he was with the Apex Company.   All of us here learned to respect him highly and to value him as a friend.

Try to take comfort from the knowledge that you were married to a wonderful man.

Sincerely,

Jerry Baxter

Jerry Baxter

Figure 6-1. *Example of Letter of Condolence (often handwritten)*

1329 Dearing Road
Blytheville, Arkansas 74211
April 30, 1979

Dear Bill:

Congratulations, Mr. President!

The Capital Company is in good hands.

You have earned this excellent promotion, and I am proud

of you.

Best wishes for your continuing success.

Sincerely,

John

Figure 6-2. *Example of Letter of Congratulations*

THE SMART SHOPPE

2572 Cherry Roadway

Memphis, Tennessee 38117

July 5, 1978

Mr. Harold Williamson
The Clarke Company
2345 Hudson Avenue
Dallas, TX 78456

Dear Mr. Williamson:

   Thank you for your help in making our Fourth of July sales
campaign an outstanding success.

   Your coaching of our salespersons and the posters and
brochures you displayed in our store most certainly increased
our total sales. Several customers commented upon the
attractive window arrangements and said they had been drawn
into the store because of them.

   All of us here at the store enjoyed working with you. We
look forward to continued business relationships that will be
pleasant and profitable for both your firm and ours.

                        Sincerely,

                        John Hardin

                        John Hardin
                        Manager

rt

Figure 6-3. *Example of Letter Expressing Appreciation. (Written to a
wholesaler or manufacturer's representative. Notice that this letter is
arranged in the semiblock style, a widely used form. See Appendix B.)*

October 11, 1978

Dear Bill and Mary:

Congratulations! May you and your new son be very happy. He

picked an excellent set of parents.

Sincerely,

Jim Blake

Figure 6-4. *Another Letter of Congratulation*

THE SMART SHOPPE
2572 Cherry Roadway
Boston, Massachusetts 02210

December 19, 1978

Mrs. E. E. Dishion
1032 Marcia Road
Boston, MA 02212

Dear Mrs. Dishion:

Customers like you are the basis of our firm's success.

We deeply appreciate your years of continued patronage and
look forward to many more. We are determined to make an
even greater effort to serve you well.

As a small token of our esteem, please deduct 10 percent from
the gross amount of your last month's bill, which is enclosed.
This is our way of saying thanks to a highly valued customer,
Mrs. E. E. Dishion.

Let us know when we can help you in any way. Just call
726-5721 for our customer service representative.

Cordially yours,

L. W. Harding

L. W. Harding, President

Enclosure

Figure 6–5. *Another Letter of Appreciation. (Notice that this letter is
arranged in the full-block style, a particularly efficient style for typewriting
ease. See Appendix B.)*

THE CAPITAL COMPANY   411 Perkins Road   Waco, TX 74230

December 20, 1978

Mr. Harold Peyton, Chief Accountant
The Capital Company
411 Perkins Road
Waco, TX 74230

Dear Mr. Peyton:

Today you complete your fifth year with The Capital
Company. You are to be congratulated for your excellent
record here.

I hope that five years from now I will be writing you a
similar letter on your tenth anniversary.

Sincerely,

Harrison Scott

Harrison Scott, President

Figure 6-6. *Example of Letter of Congratulations to an Employee. (This message could have been prepared in memorandum form, since both the writer and the reader are in the same company. A personal letter, however, adds dignity and importance to a personal message such as this.) (The letter is arranged in the semiblock form. See Appendix B.)*

1064 Estate Drive
Memphis, Tennessee 38117

November 30, 1978

Dear Senator Jennings:

   Congratulations on your recent election.

   I believe that you will represent Tennessee fairly and
effectively.

   You have my continued support.

                         Respectfully,

                         Malra Treece
                         Mrs. Guy Treece

The Honorable Howard H. Jennings
The United States Senate
Washington, D. C. 20515

Figure 6-7. *Letter of Congratulations.   (This letter is arranged in the
"official" style.   It is seldom used for ordinary business letters, but is
appropriate for letters of this kind, especially to persons in high positions.)*

SUMMARY ◆ 6

An organization builds and maintains goodwill by ethical business practices and by a sincere interest in the customers and the public it serves. In
addition to giving value for income received, the organization must cheer-
fully and positively present its products and its services, as well as the
organization itself, through the use of the you-attitude and the positive
approach.

Special goodwill letters or memorandums include business messages
planned for the single purpose of building goodwill. For some communications, a better definition is that they are the messages written not for
business purposes, but because we as humans must express our feelings to
other persons, including persons we have known through business relationships.

Goodwill messages express appreciation, congratulations, sympathy,
welcome, and good wishes. They must be sincere. They should be
written promptly or at the appropriate time.

QUESTIONS AND PROBLEMS ◆ 6

1. Have you seen examples of sales or advertising material in which you believe
    the truth was definitely and intentionally distorted? Explain.

2. Have you seen examples of sales or advertising material which seem to
    include some appeal that you do not consider one of the higher motivations of
    mankind, such as envy, prejudice, greed, or arrogance? Illustrate and
    explain.

3. Do you believe that a business organization has any further responsibilities
    than to make a profit, pay taxes, and provide adequate salaries and working
    conditions for its employees? Why or why not? If you believe that an
    organization does have other responsibilities, what are they? Do you believe
    that the business organizations with which you are familiar are adequately
    fulfilling these responsibilities?

4. Improve the following passages from business letters from the standpoint of
    the you-attitude, diplomacy, and the positive approach. Assume any neces-
    sary and reasonable details.

    (a)   The Scott Appliance Company is pleased to announce

    the opening of our new store, to which all our customers

    are invited. (From opening paragraph of letter to customers.)

(b)   It's against company policy, so we must reject your request for sample packages for your customers. You must realize that if we give away our merchandise you will have to pay more for what you buy. (From manufacturer's letter to retailer.)

(c)   This letterhead paper is not the thin, flimsy kind that always comes out looking cheap.

(d)   This scarf won't keep out the wind and the rain, but it's pretty.

(e)   We were sorry to receive your letter in which you claim your lawn mower is unsatisfactory. (First paragraph.)

(f)   You waited two days past the end of the discount period to pay your bill, so you are not entitled to the discount, which you took anyway. You know our terms quite well, 2/10, net 30.

(g)   Do not fail to finish the project by the end of this week

(h)   I have not had any experience except for helping my father in his real estate business.

(i)   We cannot complete your patio while the temperature is below freezing.

(j)   We are flattered that you want to open a credit account with us. (From a credit refusal letter.)

(k)   I am surprised that you say that our merchandise has

not given good service, but if you will bring it in, we will

consider making some kind of adjustment.

(l)   Your memo indicated that you are ignorant of policies

in our credit department.

(m)   I was sorry to hear that you have been fired.

(n)   Too bad that your son John shot himself.   He was

always on the melancholy side, so don't blame yourself.

(o)   If you are interested in our offer, let us know.

(p)   We trust that you will continue buying from us.

(q)   You have neglected to reply to my letter of August 11.

(r)   It will be impossible to open an account for you

without copies of your financial statements.

(s)   If you can manage to pay your account within ten days,

we will allow you a 10 percent discount.

5. Analyze two or more business letters of any kind, except for mass-distributed
    sales letters. Do these letters effectively build goodwill? Why or why not?
6. Find examples of special goodwill letters or memorandums. Analyze these
    messages. Notice any particularly expressive words or phrases. Make
    suggestions for needed improvements.
7. Look through a newspaper for notices or news items that indicate letters of
    appreciation or congratulation are merited for the persons involved. Assume
    that you know these persons and write the letters.

8.   Write a letter of appreciation to a person toward whom you feel real gratitude — for anything.

9.   Write a memorandum expressing holiday greetings to persons you supervise.

10. Write a letter of congratulations to a friend or acquaintance for a recent honor or accomplishment.

11. Write a memorandum to sales employees, expressing Easter greetings and appreciation for extra effort and longer hours during the pre-Easter sale.

12. You are the credit manager of the Magnolia Milk Company. Mrs. Albert Buchman of 212 Center Hill Drive, Paragould, Arkansas 74201, has been a steady customer for 22 years. Milk has been delivered to her home without interruption, except for short vacation periods. Her bill has always been paid within a few days after its receipt. Write a letter of appreciation.

13. Write a letter of welcome to newcomers to your city. Assume that you are the public relations director of a local bank.

14. Write a letter to your mayor or to another city official expressing agreement with his position on some question pertaining to city government.

15. Write a letter to a state representative or senator, or to the governor of your state, expressing agreement with his position on some question pertaining to state government.

16. Write a letter to your congressman or senator in Washington, D.C. expressing agreement with his position on some question pertaining to national government or support for a bill he is sponsoring. (If you do not agree with the opinions of any person from your state representing you in Washington, write to one from any other state.)

17. Write a letter thanking a former teacher, employer, or business associate who recommended you for a job you recently obtained.

18. Write a letter to the editor of your local newspaper, or to the management of a local radio or television station. Express appreciation for special help given during a disaster period (tornado, flood, or other emergency).

FURTHER READING ◆ 6

Boyd, W. P. "Some Psychological Aspects of Business Letter Writing." *Journal of Business Communication* (October 1963): 37–44.

Brock, Luther A. "Business Letters that Aren't All Business." *Supervisory Management* (April 1971): 7–10.

Brown, J. A. "The Reader Centered Letter." *Office Executive* (May 1961): 16.

"Honest Communication," *The Royal Bank of Canada Newsletter* (May 1972). Reprinted in *Readings in Business Communication,* edited by Robert D. Gieselman. Champaign, Ill.: Stipes Publishing Company, 1974.

Morton, Richard K. "Public Relations Writing and The Corporate Image." *The
Journal of Business Communication* (Winter 1967): 31–37. Reprinted in
Readings in Business Communication, edited by Robert D. Gieselman. Cham-
paign, Ill.: Stipes Publishing Company, 1974.

Planning for Readability and the Desired Emphasis

7

Readability, as the word implies, means the ease with which the reader can obtain the desired message. As the term is used in business communication, it means immediate clearness. It is an important quality of all writing, with the possible exception of some literary works; it is absolutely essential in business writing.

When written material is planned to achieve the desired emphasis, it is likely to be readable as well as arranged in the most desirable psychological approach. The reader may have fifty other letters to be considered along with yours. The telephone rings, visitors arrive, or other pressing business matters intrude upon the attention that can be given to your message. If your writing cannot easily be understood after a hurried reading, it may be placed on the bottom of the stack. There it will remain, while other letters, better than yours, are read and acted upon.

Readability and emphasis are influenced by word choice; by sentence length and paragraph length; by the length of the entire message; by the use or omission of subheads, listings, and other aspects of format; by careful organization, planning, and wording to achieve unity and coherence; and by the way the material is typewritten and arranged on the sheet.

The shortest message is not necessarily the most clear. If details or explanations that are necessary for understanding are omitted, or vaguely implied in order to keep the communication short, the message will not be understood, and further communication will be required. Any material that is not sufficiently complete cannot be clear or readable.

Conciseness (which is discussed in more detail in Chapter 8) also contributes to readability, but the lack of conciseness is more likely to be merely a source of annoyance. Wordy phrases, especially timeworn business jargon, are often quite clear, but they detract from a fresh, original, interesting approach.

We should consider the readers, especially their background and probable knowledge of the subject about which we are writing.   If material is technical and specialized, and if the reader works in an area outside this specialization, some words must be defined, or simple words substituted for technical ones.   We should never, however, give the appearance of writing down.   Nothing is more offensive or lacking in the you-attitude than to give the impression that the writer feels superior in knowledge to the reader.   A choice of simple, everyday words and the attitude of the writer that the purpose of communication is to express facts and ideas, not to impress with an extensive vocabulary, will do much to clarify communication in all aspects of writing, as well as of speaking.

An unnecessary but frequent cause of unclearness is simply that the writer does not carefully read the message that is to be answered — just as a speaker does not listen to the other's message before replying.   The writer should take a few more minutes to read carefully the letter that is being answered, rather than to waste the entire message by leaving out important information.

Another factor of communication that results in unclearness is the lack of planning before a message is written or dictated.   Brief notes on the letter to be answered can result in more coherent arrangements and presentation, as well as in a saving of the expensive time of both the dictator and the secretary.   This planning also aids in the use of the desired emphasis in order to achieve an appropriate and effective psychological approach.

A SIMPLE WRITING STYLE

Simple writing is not necessarily juvenile writing; and it most certainly is not poor writing because of its simplicity.   Some of the best literary works are in simple language: consider the Lord's Prayer and the Gettysburg Address.   It is also true that some great fiction writers do not write simply, and some scholarly writers prefer a profound and complex style — for example, William Faulkner used long, rambling sentences, and many other novelists use a vocabulary not suitable for business writing.   (Their vocabulary is inappropriate in aspects other than the use of certain four-letter words.)

Business writing, however, is approached differently from novels, short stories, essays, articles in scholarly journals, and, especially, poetry. That it is different does not mean that it is inferior, although it is perhaps true that most business writing could never be considered "great."   But it is good communication if it effectively accomplishes its purposes — to sell the merchandise, to keep a customer's or employee's goodwill, to collect an account, or to answer the reader's questions.

A widely held idea is that we achieve prestige and status by the display of complex writing and long words. Francis Weeks, Executive Director of the American Business Communication Association and a teacher of business communication, tells this story and makes these comments:

> I had a Korean graduate student at Houston who asked me, "Are you trying to tell me that I should write simply?" I said, "Yes, that's what I've been trying to get across." "Ah, Professor Weeks," he said, "in my country only poets and poor people write that way."
>
> Graduate students are especially susceptible to the impressive writing syndrome. They say, "But how am I going to get an 'A' on this paper if I write it simply?" They may be right. Following the principle of adaptation to the reader, if you can succeed by "snowing" the professor with your language, go right ahead. You have an audience, you have a purpose, you have a method for achieving that purpose. But do not adopt it as a universal style.
>
> Once you get out of college, you will not be writing to professors. You will be writing to people who want you to do something for them as quickly, and simply, and easily as possible. To do that you develop a style of writing which is simple and unpretentious, built on verbs, using construction adapted to your reader.[1]

You should not interpret Professor Weeks's advice to mean that you need no longer be concerned about the method in which you put words, sentences, and paragraphs together, or about your choice of words. He is emphasizing, not de-emphasizing, the importance of the knowledge of our language and practice in using this knowledge for simple, graceful, and unpretentious writing. Far more knowledge and skill are required for this kind of expression than for a complex, involved style. He is probably mistaken, however, if he is implying that most professors can be "snowed" by big words; he is a professor, and obviously the description does not apply to him.

Readable Words

Short words, provided they are the exact words that will best express the desired meaning, should be preferred to long words. Business communication is no medium by which to show off a vocabulary of unusual or "intellectual" words. This statement does not mean that the business writer need not be concerned about the development of an extensive vocabulary. We must know a great many words in order to write well, so that we will know which words to choose.

We cannot know words without recognizing the various shades of

1. Francis W. Weeks, *Principles of Business Communication* (Champaign, Ill.: Stipes Publishing Company, 1973), p. 77.

meaning that they imply. The dictionary definition alone is not enough, for words carry connotations apart from their dictionary meanings. The writer must be skilled in the use of the language in order to produce clear, simple writing that can be easily understood by almost everyone who can read at all. Simple writing does not limit the wise use of the infinite variety of language; it does require adaptation and careful choice of our method of expression. A skillful writing style does not call attention to the style itself, but to the ideas that the writing conveys.

Do you consider the following paragraph to be readable?

> The positive appeal of a visual object depends not so much upon the objective standards against which said object is measured, nor upon the image said object records upon the retina and the optic nerve, as it does upon the cerebral interpretation of the image recorded by the organ of vision of that individual who observes said object.[2]

The preceding passage, taken from material planned for writers at the New York Life Insurance Company, violates the principle of conciseness as well as that of simplicity. So does the next passage, also from the New York Life Insurance Company.

> It has come to our attention that herbage, when observed in that section of enclosed ground being the property of an individual other than oneself, is ever of a more verdant hue.[3]

Can you simplify these passages so that each is a well-known maxim? Check your answers with those given in the footnote.[4]

The following passage, from a letter about insurance, wastes both time and money, but the worst effect is the unfavorable reaction of the policyholder.

> The current dividend notice from you has been received on which was indicated your election of option to have existing and latest dividend under your above policy applied to reduce future premiums under this policy and we are pleased to advise that this, and further future dividends, in accordance with your election will be duly applied to reduce future premiums.[5]

What the writer was trying to say is this:

> We'll be happy to apply your current and future dividends to reduce premiums on your policy, as you asked.[6]

2. *Effective Letters* (New York: New York Life Insurance Company, May-June 1961).
3. *Effective Letters* (New York: New York Life Insurance Company, March-April 1960).
4. Beauty is in the eye of the beholder.
The grass is always greener on the other side of the fence.
5. *Effective Letters* (New York: New York Life Insurance Company, November-December 1960).
6. *Effective Letters* (November-December 1960).

Look at the memorandum in Figure 7-1. Evidently the writer wrote the message — which could have been a simple and direct one — with the aid of a thesaurus.

At this point a co-worker looked over the writer's shoulder and told her that she need not complete the memo, that telephone calls would be quicker. The memo could have looked like that in Figure 7-2.

Short words are not always the words that will best promote readability. An unusual short word that the reader is not likely to understand is not so desirable as a more familiar longer word. Also, when we are writing to persons who are specialists in our own field, the longer, specialized word is more understandable than a shorter one that is substituted with the mistaken purpose of making the writing more simple and readable.

To an accountant, accounting terms are easily and quickly understood; to the person outside the accounting field, some accounting terms may be misunderstood. The same principle is true for persons in the

DATE: December 4, 1977

TO: Friends of Harry B. Garving

FROM: Joan Wilson, Office Manager

SUBJECT: Retirement Luncheon, December 23, 12 noon,

Executive Dining Room

In virtue of the unrefutable requisiteness, Mr. Garving was

apprised that personnel of the organizational institution are

desirous of partaking a light repast with him on December 23,

but he was not enlightened to the factuality that other amicable

personages and those living in proximity to his place of abode

are also being prevailed upon to present themselves.

You may--

Figure 7-1. *Memorandum without Conciseness or Simplicity*

DATE: December 4, 1977

   TO: Friends of Harry B. Garving

FROM: Joan Wilson, Office Manager

SUBJECT: Retirement Luncheon, December 23, 12 noon,

           Executive Dining Room

Because this couldn't be a complete surprise, Mr. Garving was

told that company personnel would like to have lunch with him on

December 23. He doesn't know, though, that other friends and

neighbors are being asked to join us.

Because Mr. Garving has enriched your life, you may want to

take this occasion to say "Thank you" by joining us for this

retirement luncheon.

To make your reservation, complete and return the enclosed

form. Mr. Garving will be honored, and so will all his

colleagues, that you have helped us say, "Thank you, Harry B.

Garving."

Figure 7-2. *Memorandum Showing Conciseness and Simplicity*

medical field or in any other specialization. Almost every profession, occupation, or particular kind of business enterprise soon develops its own vocabulary, which comes automatically to the writer in each specialization. The writer or speaker may easily forget that these terms are not understood by the reader.

Short words, appropriately chosen, not only increase readability but also help to form a vivid and forceful writing style. Compare the effectiveness of these words:

Instead of	*Why Not Use*
approbation	approval
approximately	about
ameliorate	improve
incorporate	include
interrogate	ask
promulgate	publish
peruse	read
utilize	use
engrossment	attention
expectancy	hope
utilizable	useful
salience	importance

To repeat a word of warning — *choose words carefully*, even when you are trying, as you should, to simplify. Few words have exact synonyms, long or short. Find the word that is most likely to express your exact meaning to the mind of the reader — but remember that this word is most often a short, familiar one.

Readable Sentences

Sentences need not and should not be the same length. In order to avoid monotony, if for no other reason, both short and fairly long sentences should be used. Most important, sentences should be of the length that best conveys a wise choice of ideas and information so closely related that they belong together in a single sentence.

The average sentence length, however, usually should not exceed seventeen to twenty words, although a skillful writer can use longer sentences and achieve a readable style. A series of short, simple sentences, similar to a first grade reader, is monotonous, juvenile, and un-businesslike. A thorough and automatic knowledge of sentence construction is essential to the expert business writer, not only from the standpoint of readability, but also from the standpoints of emphasis and correctness.

The type of sentence chosen for a particular idea depends upon the idea that is to be expressed. Experienced writers do not consciously think of sentence construction as the material is written or dictated. As they revise, they often change sentence structure. The revision most often necessary is that of cutting sentence length. All writers should check their work to make sure that only complete sentences are used and that there is a variety of sentence construction.

In most business writing, simple sentences should outnumber complex sentences and compound sentences. In almost all writing, compound sentences should be the fewest of the three. Complex sentences are useful to subordinate or emphasize ideas.

Readable Paragraphs

Short paragraphs are useful in achieving readability in all kinds of writing. A paragraph of many lines is hard to read and discouraging to the reader, especially when time is short. At times, paragraphs in a letter, memorandum, or report — especially if the overall work is short — must be broken arbitrarily to increase readability.

Some business writers believe that a paragraph must have more than one sentence. The idea may have originated in a class in English composition, although in all kinds of writing one-sentence paragraphs are quite acceptable. Overall, however, paragraphs tend to be shorter in letters and memorandums than in other types of writing. In business letters, often the first and last paragraph should consist of only one sentence. Any paragraph may be only one sentence in length if that is all that seems to fit into the particular paragraph.

A short, one-sentence paragraph can be used for attention, interest, and emphasis, especially if the sentence is the first one in the communication.

Although no exact rule can be given about maximum paragraph length, you should regard with suspicion any typewritten paragraph more than seven or eight lines long, especially in short messages. Paragraphs should average fewer lines than this when they make up letters, memorandums, and short reports.

READABILITY FORMULAS

Several formulas, or "indexes," have been developed, supposedly to measure readability. Two of these are the Flesch Reading Ease Formula and the Gunning Fog Index. Rudolf Flesch 's formula is presented in his book, *The Art of Readable Writing*,[7] published in 1949. Robert Gunning's formula appears in his book, *The Technique of Clear Writing*.[8] (This book first appeared in 1952; this reference is to a revised edition.)

Both the Flesch formula and the Gunning Fog Index rely heavily on sentence and word lengths to determine reading levels. Although Gun-

7. Rudolph Flesch, *The Art of Readable Wrtiting* (New York: Harper & Row, 1949), pp. 213–216.
8. Robert Gunning, *The Technique of Clear Writing* (New York: McGraw-Hill Book Company, 1968), pp. 30–45.

ning recognizes factors other than sentence and word length in determining readability — such as percentage of verbs expressing forceful action, proportion of familiar words, proportion of abstract words — only sentence and word length are considered in his easy-to-use plan.

The readability score obtained through the use of a formula is expressed in terms of the general educational level of the reader, which may have little relationship to the actual grade completed in school. If, for example, the readability score is 17, this indicates that the material could be read easily by someone who has completed college. A score of 16 is used to mean that a person completing the sixteenth year of schooling, a college senior, could easily read the material.

Most effective writing of all kinds, however, has a lower readability score than 16 or 17, even if the material is planned for graduate students. Material may have a readability score lower than high school level and still be suitable for adults.

An important point to remember is that formulas cannot measure the quality of writing, only its complexity, and that to a limited extent. An expert writer can use long words and sentences and make his work more interesting and readable than can a writer with less ability, although the expert's work has a higher readability score.

The formulas make no distinction between exact, well-chosen words and vague, confusing words, or between familiar words and rare ones. They measure only word length. They also do not distinguish sentences that are constructed wisely in order to exactly express the intended ideas. Excellent writing cannot be measured by any formula, but an average reader can usually recognize its quality and understand its meaning.

These cautions about using readability formulas are not given to disparage their worth, for their admittedly limited purposes are valid ones. They measure sentence and word length and express this measurement in a score that is likely to apply to different groups of readers. The formulas can be dangerous, however, if they are misused. An appropriate readability score should not be accepted without question as an indication that the writing needs no improvement. And writing with a score higher than the expected "norms" should not be automatically classified as lacking in readability, although it should be re-examined.

The Gunning Fog Index is as follows:

1. Select a sample of writing of at least 100 words. Divide the total number of words by the number of sentences. This is the average sentence length. [Using several samples will result in a more reliable score. The independent clauses of a compound sentence are counted as separate sentences.]

2. Count the number of words of three syllables or more. Don't count proper names; combinations of short, easy words, such as bookkeeper or teenager; or verb forms made into three syllables by adding *ed* or *es*. This figure is the number of "hard" words in the passage.

Divide this figure by the total number of words to find the percentage of "hard" words.

3. Add the average sentence length to the percentage of hard words and multiply by .4. The figure obtained through these calculations is the Gunning Fog Index, or readability score, expressed in grade-reading level.[9]

This readability formula is not the method used by writers of material for use in many textbooks, especially those for use at the elementary school level, for in these books the vocabulary, or the actual words to be included, must be considered. In readability formulas for adult use, only the length of words is considered, along with sentence length, although some methods include the consideration of "personal interest" words.

Let's find the readability score for the following paragraph from *The Mature Mind* by H. A. Overstreet, written in 1949. This book is much more readable than many other books on psychological subjects, but the 12.2 score is higher than an ideal score for short, nontechnical business communications. The example paragraph is well written: even with a higher percentage of long words, provided they were no more unusual than those actually used, the passage would be easily understandable. Another passage with a similar score could be much less understandable, according to the skill in sentence construction and word choice. (Overstreet does not mention television because in the year in which this paragraph was written, television was in its infancy.)

Newspapers, radio, movies, and advertising — these might be called the "big four" of communication. These are the four great money-making enterprises of mind-making. It would be pleasant to report that they all make for the fine maturing of human character. But the report must be otherwise. In spite of what each has contributed to our growth, each has, through its own formula, found it profitable to keep us from full psychological maturing. Or, to put the best possible face upon the matter, each has found in us some immaturity that waited to be tapped. Engaged in the tapping process, each of these powerful forces has been too busy to think about the long-range consequences of its formula.[10]

The paragraph contains 120 words and 7 sentences. The words of three or more syllables (those not excluded by the formula) total 16. "Newspapers" and "otherwise" are considered to be excluded because they are combinations of short, easy words, like "bookkeeper," mentioned in the formula.

To find the sentence length, divide 120 by 7, which gives an average sentence length of 17.1. To find the percentage of hard words, divide 16

9. Gunning, *The Technique of Clear Writing*, p. 39.
10. H. A. Overstreet, *The Mature Mind* (New York: W. W. Norton & Company, 1949), pp. 225–226.

by 120; the percentage is 13.3. Add 17.1 to 13.3; the result is 30.4. Multiply by .4 to obtain the readability score of 12.16 or 12.2.

This reading-level score means that the material should be easily read by someone in the twelfth grade, or approximately so. This is similar to the reading level of such magazines as *Atlantic Monthly* and *Harper's*, although articles by different authors vary somewhat in difficulty. Other popular magazines, especially *Reader's Digest*, are written at a level two or three grades below this twelfth-grade score. To obtain an accurate average score of writing of considerable length, we should use far more material than the paragraph we have considered here.

Although you should check passages of your own writing occasionally, most college students do not write in an extremely complex style — unless they are trying to impress their professor. Twenty or thirty years from now, when you are a business executive, a politician, or a high-ranking government official, check your writing by the use of the Gunning Fog Index or a similar formula. If you resemble your present-day counterparts, you will need to simplify.

Robert Gunning and his associates have used the Fog Index in an attempt to simplify writing coming from the Army, Navy, Air Force, and the Department of Agriculture. It has also been used in many industries and with writers for newspapers and magazines. For Gunning's description of the use of this formula, its advantages and disadvantages, see his article, "The Fog Index After Twenty Years," which he wrote in 1968. He states:

> My feelings are mixed about this readability yardstick that I developed back in the 1940's; but they are much more positive than negative. The wide use the Fog Index has received is gratifying. On the other hand, occasional misunderstanding and misuse of it have been disturbing.[11]

READABLE FORMATS

The letter, memorandum, report or other bit of writing should be arranged attractively on the typing sheet or sheets, leaving plenty of white space. A minimum of one-inch side, top, and bottom margins should be left on all work. For short and average length letters, wider margins are better, as explained in Appendix B. The same factors that make for an attractive appearance — an electric typewriter, good quality paper and typewriter ribbon, and neat corrections — promote readability.

Subheads are essential to readability if the written message is long, and usually "long" should be interpreted as any communication of more

---

11. Robert Gunning, "The Fog Index after Twenty Years," *Journal of Business Communication* 6 (Winter 1968): 3.

than one page. Subheads can also be used in material of one page or less. They add readability in several ways.

Subheads also force the writer to organize the material in meaningful units. It the subhead does not include a reference to the information under it, and only to that information, it is not a well-chosen one. Poor subheads are worse than none at all.

Subheads help the reader in that he knows what to expect in each section of the writing, and he immediately sees the organization of the ideas or even a summary of the ideas. The efficient reader will glance over the subheads before he reads the message for detail, so that he has the gist of the message already in mind.

Subheads are often underlined. They may also be shown in all capitals. To add emphasis and to make the subheads easier to see and read, leave a triple space (two blank spaces) before the subhead and at least a double space after it. (Follow the instructions in the handbook you are using for a guide. See Appendix C for a suggested arrangement.) In a report or other long communication, different kinds of subheads will be needed in order to show organization and the importance of the different parts.

Lists and tabulations make ideas stand out; they present ideas in a logical order. The arrangement of each statement, question, or idea on a separate line, with a blank space between the lines, makes each of the items easier to understand than if they were crowded together into a paragraph.

Even in such a listing, the organization of the ideas presented should be considered, although it is not always possible to determine the importance of these listed items. If there is a definite difference, ordinarily the most important ones should be listed first. In any work, unless there is a definite reason for doing otherwise, give the most important information first, followed by material of less importance.

To illustrate the use of a listing, or a tabulation, as well as to summarize, the following information is repeated.

Readable formats should include:

1.   Plenty of white space
2.   An overall attractive appearance
3.   Subheads
4.   Lists and tabulations

BASIC PRINCIPLES OF EMPHASIS

The business writer should know and keep in mind the principles of emphasis, which will contribute to readability, the desired psychological approach, and other attributes of effective communication. The qualities of excellent communication exist only in connection with other qualities.

Emphatic Positions

Position is one of the most important means of achieving emphasis. The beginning section of any kind of writing is the most emphatic position, provided that the writer has used this position advantageously. In most communications, this first position should be used to present the most important idea. This arrangement is referred to as the direct arrangement.

The first paragraph is the most emphatic section of a memorandum, a letter, or any other short written message. In a long report, the first paragraph is still an emphatic one, but because of the comparative length, the first section, often titled the *Introduction*, becomes especially important because of its position, as well as for other reasons. The first sentence in a paragraph is the most emphatic one — hence the use of a topic sentence, as the first sentence, increases readability and emphasizes the principal meaning intended for that paragraph.

The first word of a sentence, along with the last one, is in an emphatic position, except for such sentence beginnings as "a," "an," and "the," which are used as introductory words so that the emphasis shifts to the immediately following words. The emphatic first position of the sentence is one reason why it is best not to start several sentences on the same page with "I"; the "I" becomes overemphasized and does not convey the desired you-attitude, or at least the impression of the you-attitude.

The closing word, sentence, paragraph, or section of a written message is also emphatic, next in importance to the opening word, sentence, paragraph, or section. The last word of a sentence is second in emphasis to the first word of a sentence; or, in periodic sentences, the last words are most emphatic because the preceding words build up to the conclusion. Thus, to de-emphasize an idea or statement, do not place it in the opening or the closing of the written work.

This principle applies throughout business writing; for example, the idea to be de-emphasized should be somewhere within the body of the letter, not in the opening or the closing paragraph. An idea can be subordinated, also, by sentence structure so that it is within a sentence instead of being expressed in the emphatic opening or closing position.

The Direct and the Indirect Arrangements

Basically, the difference between the direct and the indirect arrangement is this: The direct (also described as the deductive) arrangement begins with the main gist of the message and uses the remaining space to expand upon this central message by giving details, examples, or added information of any kind.   The indirect (also described as the inductive) builds up to the gist of the message.   These arrangements can be used in written works of all lengths.   The direct presentation is usually to be preferred unless there is a definite reason for using the indirect.

The direct arrangement is advantageous in that it is easier to read. The reader immediately knows what the message is about.   The emphatic beginning of the message is used as it should be, to emphasize something important.   The direct arrangement, however, has a psychological disadvantage in some instances.   The reader may not be prepared for "the answer," especially if the most important part of the message is a disappointing one or something that the reader is not prepared to readily believe or accept.

In such a situation, the indirect arrangement should be used in order to prepare the reader to accept or to believe the conclusions of the letter or report.   For example, if reasons are given first or if information is included to show how the final conclusions and recommendations were reached, the reader is more likely to accept these conclusions and recommendations.   Also, some explanation of a situation is often necessary in order to make the important part of the message clear, even though the reader is willing to accept the message.

The direct order often increases readability.   News stories and news releases are usually written in the direct order; the main facts of the story are given in the first paragraph, facts of lesser importance are given in the second, and so on.   This plan is used especially in news releases, in order that any necessary cutting be done from the bottom.   Such condensing must sometimes be done because of limited space.   Even when the news article or release appears in its complete and original form, this arrangement of ideas, from the most important to the least, increases reader interest and understanding.   Business letters, like newspapers, are often read hurriedly, and any arrangement that will increase quick and easy understanding should be used.

Not all material can be written in this direct order, even when there is no psychological aspect to consider, for to do so would decrease, not increase, reader understanding.   The reader must have an idea of the subject to be discussed before he can understand the conclusions.   There may be need for introductory paragraphs, or sections, to lead to an understanding of the most important facts.

A paragraph is also arranged in the direct or the indirect order, or perhaps in a chronological order.   A paragraph arranged in the direct order begins with a topic sentence.   A paragraph that builds up to the topic sentence is arranged in the indirect order.   For most business writing, the direct arrangement of paragraphs is preferred, although paragraphs, like sentences, should be varied in order to improve the style, flow of thought, and the exact expression of ideas.

The chronological order can be used not only for paragraphs but for writing of all lengths, although this as-it-happened arrangement is often unnecessarily slow and detailed.   In addition, it does not place emphasis upon what should ordinarily be emphasized.   Although some kinds of business writing should be arranged in this way, usually the direct or the indirect order is preferable.

Emphatic Sentence and Paragraph Construction

The most emphatic way to present an idea is in a paragraph that consists of only one short, simple sentence.   Since the most emphatic position is the first position, then the greatest emphasis is achieved by letting this short, one-sentence paragraph be the first paragraph of the message.   The short, simple sentence emphasizes because it stands alone, with no distracting or cluttering words or phrases to detract from the meaning.

Suppose that, in a sales letter, you state the price this way:

The cost is $15.98.

If this sentence stands alone as a paragraph, you are probably giving too much emphasis to the cost, for ordinarily the price of an article should be subordinated and stated in connection with the benefits the purchase will bring.   An exception is a sales letter in which an unusually favorable price is a favorable selling point; in such a letter the price should be emphasized.

In a complex sentence, the idea to be emphasized should be placed in the main clause and the subordinated idea in the dependent clause.   In addition to the subordinate clause, a phrase can also be used to de-emphasize by placing in the phrase the idea to be subordinated.   The cost is presented in a prepositional phrase in the following sentence:

You will receive for only $15.98 many hours of

listening pleasure.

In addition to the use of the word "only," the price is de-emphasized by placing it in a phrase and by placing it within the sentence, not at the beginning or the end.

Sentences written with the verb in the active voice emphasize the *doer* of the action; the passive construction emphasizes the receiver of the action. (See the section in Chapter 8 entitled "The Active and the Passive Voice.")   Sentences should be constructed according to the desired emphasis.   For more forceful writing, choose the active construction.

Word Choice to Emphasize or to Subordinate

Specific, concrete language is more emphatic, as well as more descriptive and readable, than vague, abstract wording.   Try to emphasize positive, pleasant ideas and to de-emphasize unpleasant ones, as discussed in Chapter 6 in connection with the positive approach. At times the general word, not the specific, is more diplomatic, although less emphatic and forceful.

An abstract word describes ideas or concepts that cannot be easily visualized. Examples of abstract words are *conception*, *democracy*, *abstractness*, *charity*. Examples of concrete words are *blackbird*, *plaid*, *crunch*, *dawn*, *rain*, *saxophone*, *automobile* — particular objects which can be seen, heard, felt, touched, smelled. These words as are more vivid than abstract ones. Specific words are more emphatic than general words. An example of a general word is music; a more specific term is piano solo; a still more descriptive term is Chopin's "Polonaise in A-Flat" played by Artur Rubenstein.

Fresh, natural words are more emphatic than stale, stereotyped expressions. Avoid trite phrases such as "spring is just around the corner" and "last but not least." These trite expressions also violate the principles of conciseness.

Space — Much or Little

Giving more space emphasizes one idea over the remaining parts of the message. Notice that this is just the opposite of the method discussed previously, in which the main idea is quickly and bluntly stated in a sentence alone. Ordinarily the writer does not think — "Well, I will just give this more space because it is important" — but writes the message giving the necessary details, which require more space. Repetition may be used with discretion in order to emphasize, but much repetition is due to carelessness. Repetition, even of the same words, can sometimes be effective, but the writer must be skillful and the message must be carefully planned. Repetition is often used for sales writing or advertising, especially radio and television commercials, but not always to the best advantage.

The main idea of a message often requires more space in order to convey it completely and clearly; this is the reason that using more space is said to be a method of emphasis. You are violating another principle of effective writing if you make the writing longer than it needs to be to convey the intended message.

Mechanical Means of Emphasis

Mechanical means are such methods as underlining; the use of all capitals, dashes, and special or unusual means of letter arrangement or indenting; and lists and tabulations. Different colors of ink, especially red, are often used in sales messages. Setting off lines with plenty of white space calls attention to these lines.   The mechanical means of emphasis are similar to those of readability, except that at times the methods used for emphasis are more unusual and extreme.

Subheads emphasize, as well as help to display the organization of material.   A postscript can be used to emphasize an important idea, but this postscript should not be used, or appear to be used, for something that should have gone into the letter itself.

Mechanical means of emphasis should not be overused, or they lose any emphatic value that they might otherwise possess.   If many points are emphasized, then the final result is that nothing is emphasized.   Also, some persons object to a message filled with underlining, all capitals, or portions typed in red, feeling that such an approach is unbusinesslike, too emotional, or scatterbrained.   The overuse of dashes, especially, contributes to this scatterbrained appearance of a written message.

Summarizing for Emphasis

Summarizing can be used to emphasize important points, especially in longer works.   In some reports or books, each section or chapter is summarized and then the entire work is summarized, perhaps through the use of a synopsis that is attached to the report itself.   Summarizing, like the other means of emphasizing, contributes also to readability.

A listing of points, such as those below, makes the items stand out and imply that they are important.   They are easy to read and quickly understood.

Emphasis is achieved by:

1. Position
2. Sentence and Paragraph Construction
3. Word Choice
4. Space
5. Mechanical Means of Emphasis
6. Summarizing

COHERENT PHRASING AND ORGANIZATION

Coherence is the logical, easy-to-understand flow of thought from the beginning to the end of the message; it is an essential element of readability.   The term comes from the word "cohesion" and literally means a "sticking together" of ideas so that the message is unified, without abrupt shifts in arrangement or subject matter.   To be coherent, writing must also have unity.   Unity and coherence are achieved by overall organization, so that the message flows naturally and smoothly, according to a plan that should be decided upon before the writing or dictation is begun.   (As we proceed with the writing or dictation, we often see needed changes from the original plan.   These changes should be made, and then the organization should stick to this revised plan.)

If the message is truly coherent, the reader's mind grasps the relationships of words, sentences, and paragraphs and recognizes the overall progression of meaning.   Transitional words and phrases, or the repetition of key words, used with discretion, aid in the transfer of thought from one idea to another.

Coherent Sentence Structure

The choice of sentence structure affects the flow of ideas.   For example, if we mistakenly use a compound sentence to express ideas that are of unequal value, instead of using a complex sentence with subordinated clauses or a simple sentence with subordinated phrases or other modifiers, we disturb the sense of continuity.   We also change the emphasis — that is, we decrease the emphasis upon the main idea.

The following sentence is composed of three clauses, each of which could stand alone as a separate sentence.   This compound sentence, which is really three sentences in one, does not emphasize any particular idea as being more important than the other two.   (This type of sentence, in which one or more of the "main" clauses has a "subordinate" clause, is sometimes referred to as a compound-complex sentence.)

> There is an old admonition that we should never mail a letter written in anger; our emotions have control over our perception of the situation; emotions also have control over our words and actions.

Although this sentence is not interrupted by irrelevant words or phrases that would destroy coherence and the flow of thought, the sentence construction does not effectively show the relationship of ideas.   Compare this sentence with the preceding example:

> The old admonition never to mail a letter written in anger is based on the knowledge that our emotions have control over our perception of the situation and thus over our words and actions.

This is a complex sentence.   This particular group of words, or similar ones, could be arranged in several different combinations, but the emphasis and relationships of ideas would be changed.   We affect meaning, at least to a certain extent, each time we rearrange a sentence.

Experiment with rearranging this sentence. For example, the sentence could begin, "Never mail a letter written in anger, for —."

We are being coherent when we emphasize certain ideas and subordinate others. If a sentence begins "Never mail a letter written in anger —" emphasis is placed upon this aspect of the idea because it comes first in the sentence. From the previous versions of this sentence, this rewritten version changes the relationship of ideas and the actual meaning.

Notice that many of the same considerations discussed in the preceding section on emphasis also apply to achieving coherence. We cannot emphasize effectively without being coherent.

We cannot merely revise sentences to make them "sound better" without considering the subtle or major changes in meaning. In some instances, though, this changed meaning is the preferred one. Perhaps the reason the sentence doesn't "sound right" is that the desired meaning is not exactly expressed.

Coherent Paragraph Structure

Coherent paragraphs are composed of sentences that are coherent within themselves, arranged in a meaningful order within the paragraph, and joined as needed by transitional words and phrases.

In business letters, memorandums, and short reports, paragraphs are usually shorter than in longer compositions and may consist of only one sentence. A one-sentence paragraph serves as a transitional link between the preceding and following paragraph or is used as the opening or the closing of the message.

Paragraphs, like longer units of writing, may be arranged in the direct (deductive) or the indirect (inductive) order. The use of a topic sentence at the beginning of a paragraph, followed by explanatory or illustrative details, is the direct order. This arrangement is the one used for most paragraphs. It is the most readable arrangement. Reverse the order for the indirect arrangement. This method or organization builds up to the topic sentence — and in this way the last sentence is emphasized.

After you complete a letter, memorandum, or other communication, look over it for abrupt changes in subject matter or emphasis. The meaning may be perfectly clear to you, the writer, only because you knew from the beginning what you were trying to say; your reader will not have this advantage.

Planning the Order of Ideas

As an aid to attaining coherence, plan each letter, memorandum, report, or other written material before you write or dictate it. By making notes about needed information and the order of arrangement, you not only will save time but also will increase the likelihood that the work will have coherence, readability, and completeness.

If you are an experienced writer or dictator, you probably will use only mental notes for short, simple messages — but even these kinds of messages can quickly become disorganized without adequate thought and planning.

Even when making a telephone call, you often should make brief notes about the questions you want to ask and the points you want to cover. This suggestion was one of those made recently by a group of business executives who were asked by business educators for information about the communication needs of new employees.[12] Although we cannot plan telephone messages with the exactness of written messages — especially as to the order of presentation — we should have before us a list of what we plan to include.

We cannot always follow this list in the planned sequence, for to do so would almost certainly result in poor listening. But if we do not have a written plan, we are most likely to omit some item of importance. Have you ever remembered, just as you replaced the receiver, "Oh, I meant to ask — "?

As an illustration of planning the content of a short written message before it is written or dictated, suppose that a customer moving to your city has asked you to write to the department store in his home city where he has a credit record. Your outline, which could consist of abbreviated notes on his letter, might look something like this:

1. Welcome to Atlanta

2. Let him know that we are complying

   with his request

3. Show interest in being of further

   service—offer information, etc.

4. Goodwill close

The paragraphs in your dictated or individually written letter might look like these:

Dear Mr. Brown:

Welcome to Atlanta! We are sure you will love our

Paragraph 1

rapidly growing city.

12. Anglea D. Hergenroeder, "The Business Communications Program in Ohio Community Colleges," unpublished doctoral dissertation, The Ohio State University, 1973. Reported at the first international meeting of the American Business Communication Association, Toronto, December 28–30, 1975.

As you requested, we are writing to Goldsmith's in Memphis for a verification of your credit standing. We look forward to having you as a customer.   *Paragraph 2*

The enclosed brochures show some of the attractions of Atlanta, and the pamphlet tells you about our store and its services. Use the city map to find your way to The Atlanta Store.   *Paragraph 3*

Whenever you have questions, or if you need help or advice, call Miss Kay Rollings, Customer Service Representative, at 524-3987. She will also act as your personal shopping consultant and select merchandise to be delivered to your home.   *Paragraph 4*

As soon as we hear from Goldsmith's, we will mail you a Chargecard from The Atlanta Store. Use it often for convenient and economical shopping.   *Paragraph 5*

Sincerely,

Notice that as the writer dictated the message, Point 3 on the outline became Paragraphs 3 and 4 of the letter. Although some dictators make separate notes for each paragraph, the need for division into paragraphs often becomes apparent as the composition of the message proceeds.

This letter could have been effectively arranged in other sequences. Seldom will there be an occasion when there is one — and only one — diplomatic, courteous, orderly pattern of arrangement. You should not attempt to memorize formulas for the many and differing kinds of letters, but use your own good judgment and common sense in approaching each situation individually.

You should, however, remember that the three suggestions listed below are usually advisable:

1. In good-news messages, include the good news near the beginning of the communication, often in the first sentence. If the message contains both good news and bad news, ordinarily the good news should be given first, although you should never give

the appearance of misleading. In a neutral routine request or other message, begin with the request or the gist of the information to be conveyed, unless introductory statements are necessary.

2. In bad-news messages, ordinarily do not begin with the bad news. Start with some pleasant aspect of the situation or use a neutral, relevant, diplomatic paragraph.

3. In messages that request action from the reader, end with an "action close" in which you:

   a. State the requested action. Do not assume that it is implied; state it directly, and, if appropriate, in terms of the benefits that the reader will receive from taking the action.

   b. Make action easy. Do not ask the reader to write a letter if he can respond by checking your enclosed card. If you ask for a telephone call, include your telephone number.

   c. When appropriate, motivate prompt action. If there can be no real benefit to the reader, state, without pushiness or bossiness, the time when you need the information, and give the reason for this deadline.

In the letter to the newcomer to Atlanta, in what other sequences could the paragraphs have been arranged? The letter is not exactly a good news message, although if the customer's good credit rating had already been verified, it would be good news. Even if this were the case, the letter could still be appropriately arranged with the opening paragraph of greeting and welcome. It could also open with the information that the card is being sent to the customer, and that she is now a welcomed charge customer of The Atlanta Store.

Notice the arrangement of the letter. Could the paragraphs have been presented in other sequences? By slightly modifying the wording, we could arrange the paragraphs in this order: 2, 5, 3, 4, 1.

Dear Mr. Brown:

As you requested, we are writing to Goldsmith's in Memphis for a verification of your credit standing. We look forward to having you as a customer.

(Lets customer know that we are complying with his request. Implies that credit rating will be good. Includes a word of welcome.)

As soon as we hear from Goldsmith's, we will mail you a Chargecard from The Atlanta Store. Use it often for convenient and economical shopping.

(Continues thought begun in Paragraph 1.   Includes sales promotion sentence.)

The enclosed brochures will give you an idea of the

many attractions of Atlanta.   The pamphlet about our store

and its services, as well as the city map, will show you the

location of The Atlanta Store.

(Service attitude.)

Whenever you have questions, or if you need special

help or advice, call Miss Kay Rollings, Customer Service

Representative, at 524-3987.   She will also act as your

personal shopping consultant and select merchandise to be

delivered to your home.

(More service attitude.   Also a mild action close, although, as in the previous letter, it does not call for immediate action.   The action close is not necessarily in the last paragraph, but it should be near the end of the message, as it is here.   Often the action close is in the last paragraph.)

We wish you much happiness here in your new city.

You are to be congratulated for choosing it.

Sincerely,

(Another expression of welcome, but at the end.   Also "sales promotion" of Atlanta.)

These two illustrations of the arrangement of the letter are examples planned to show that there can be more than one satisfactory arrangement of business communications, even of those as short and simple as this one. Notice, too, that each paragraph, and each sentence within each paragraph, is coherent within itself.

To summarize, coherence is achieved by:

1. A logical pattern of organization in which there is a continuous, meaningful flow of thought.
2. Topic sentences, which should usually be at the beginning of the paragraph.   Topic sentences also serve as transitional sentences.

3. Transitional words, well chosen and placed with discretion.
4. Repetition of key words.
5. Use of pronouns to replace key words. (Make sure that the pronoun has a logical and definite antecedent.)

The most important of these methods of achieving coherence is the one given first, the orderly arrangement of ideas. This arrangement would be difficult, however, without making use of the remaining methods.

BEGINNINGS AND ENDINGS

Beginnings

Since the first position of any material is the most emphatic one, we should make sure that the important first paragraph of our business messages is planned to include material that we want to emphasize, not that which is better subordinated. We are especially concerned with the first sentence of the first paragraph, and with the first word of the first sentence. Often the first sentence of a business message should make up the entire first paragraph. This short sentence, standing alone at the beginning of a letter, is perhaps the most emphatic position possible.

In a good-news letter, the good news ordinarily belongs in the first paragraph, which is *not* the place for bad news. Neither is the last paragraph a good position for the presentation of unfavorable ideas. The bad news should be placed somewhere in the middle of the letter, after you have given reasons or explanations, or, if appropriate, a counterproposal.

Here are some examples of opening sentences from good-news letters:

The enclosed check for $520 is in payment for your excellent article on gardening.

The educational materials you requested are being mailed today.

Here is the instruction sheet that you requested.

Your credit account has been approved, and your first shipment of Happy Days shoes is on its way to you.

The enclosed salary check is larger than last month's because of your $60 raise.

It is especially important that the first paragraph be short.   Nothing is more discouraging to the reader than a long block of type at the beginning of the letter or memorandum.   Additional sentences deduct from the emphasis that a short paragraph would otherwise express.

Avoid slow, wordy, unnecessary beginnings such as

> We have received your letter of October 1.

> We are writing this letter to advise you...

(This phrasing is unnecessary — just go on and say whatever is to be said. "Advise" used in this way is probably misused; this word means "to give advice"; it should not be used in any other way.)

> Referring to your letter of October 1...

(A slow, weak, participial beginning.)

> Replying to your letter of October 1, you will find...

(Another slow, weak, participial beginning.   This is also a dangling participle because "replying" does not modify "you," although it appears to because of the sentence construction.)

> This letter is in reply to your letter of October 1.

(Slow)

> Acknowledging receipt of yours of recent date...

(Terrible!)

Avoid letter or memorandum beginnings that stress the I-approach instead of the you-approach, as in the following sentences:

> Our company has been operating in Miami since 1905.

> We are pleased to announce the introduction of our new product.

> As chairman of the fund-raising committee of the Jaycees, I am writing you...

> The Smith-Wright Company is pleased to announce...

> We at the Smith-Wright Company...

In replies to requests for information, the first paragraph may be part of the requested information:

> John J. Harris, about whom you inquired in your letter of November 30, was employed in our marketing department as a research assistant from 1971 to 1974.

> Yes, we stock the book, The Status Seekers, by Vance Packard. It can be shipped immediately.

> Our dress material #2112 is 100 percent polyester.

If the information requested is lengthy and complicated, it should be arranged in an orderly, easy-to-understand presentation, perhaps through a tabulation or listing. For such a letter, your first paragraph could read:

> We are happy to send you the information you request.

Although this paragraph opens with a "We," it is acceptable because it contains a courteous, service attitude.

The first paragraph of a memorandum often contains the gist of the message, as:

> Beginning December 13, the library will be open each Saturday from 10 a.m. to 6 p.m.

An additional paragraph may read:

> Please announce these hours to your students at the next class meeting so that they can plan to use the library this coming Saturday.

In a memorandum, the subject line may express the most important idea, as:

> SUBJECT: New library hours, Saturdays, 10 a.m. to 6 p.m.

By using the subject line in this way, the former second paragraph becomes the only paragraph necessary for the body of the memorandum.
Inquiries may begin with a specific question, as:

> Do you have the book, The Status Seekers, by Vance Packard?

> Will you please send me information about your dress material #2112, especially as to its fabric content?

Goodwill messages often open with the greeting, as:

Congratulations!

Best wishes for a happy voyage.

Thank you for...

Happy Groundhog Day!

Openings of bad-news letters are less direct than those of good-news or routine letters, but they should not include the slow, unnecessary wording used in some of the examples given above. The first paragraph of a bad-news or a refusal letter is referred to as the "buffer." This term means that the paragraph is used as an introduction. It must be courteous and pleasant; it should not include the refusal; neither should it imply that the answer is to be a favorable one. It must make sense, be tied to the meaning of the letter, and lead coherently to the next paragraph.

A "thank you" opening can be used as a buffer if it makes sense — if there is any conceivable reason for appreciation for the letter. If so, "Thank you for your letter —" is better than "We have received your letter —" or "We have your letter requesting —." Remember, though, that "Thank you for your letter —" is so widely used that it has become rather stale, although sincere appreciation will never become trite. Even if it is overused, "Thank you for —" is still often an acceptable way to open bad-news or refusal letters. (Your instructor may disagree.)

It is also permissible at times to open a bad-news letter with an expression of regret, although this opening seems to violate the principle of the positive approach. It does, in some situations; in others, it is acceptable. Like most other communication situations (or situations of any kind), few rules or formulas should be regarded as absolute and unchanging. Your own judgment and good common sense must prevail in individual applications over any pattern or formula.

The "we are sorry" approach seems acceptable in this example: Suppose that a customer has written to you asking that you repair without charge his eleven-year-old heating system, although your guarantee expired eight years ago. You should *not* open the letter by saying that you are sorry that you cannot repair the equipment without charge, for you would be stating the refusal too early in the letter. In addition, a statement like this one implies that you feel you really should comply with his wishes, but you are not going to do so. You can, however, empathize with the customer to the extent that you can say sincerely, "I'm sorry that your heating system is not working properly."

Let's look at some opening paragraphs that would be definitely worse:

We will not repair your heating system without charge
because your guarantee expired eight years ago.

(This opening gives the answer too soon and is also tactless.)

We are sorry that we cannot repair your heating system.

(Although this is more diplomatic than "we will not," it is still undesirable, as discussed above.)

We will be happy to repair your heating system.

(Although you don't say so, the reader will think that the services will be free. A misleading statement is worse than a blunt refusal.)

Thank you for your letter. . .

(What do you have to thank him for? Nothing, except for the knowledge that your heating systems can break down after eleven years, as you might have guessed. Or you could thank him for the possibility of the amount to be collected for repair, a favor he hasn't meant to grant.)

A more satisfactory opening is:

We will be glad to send a service representative to help you determine the cause of your heating problems.

If you want to be clever, you can add the sentence

He should be able to "warm you up" within a short time.

Be very careful, though, in using such phrasing, especially in letters conveying unpleasant information. This sentence would be especially bad if the tone of the customer's letter was rather cool. The reader of your letter will be in no mood for levity, and he does not want his problems treated lightly.

Another refusal letter could open in this way:

We appreciate your suggestions for the improvement of our product.

A request for photographs used in advertisements could be answered in this way, provided that the request is to be refused:

Thank you for your compliments on our advertising.

or

We are glad you like our advertising program.

Following paragraphs can be devoted to reasons why the photographs cannot be released.

Many letters and memorandums should end with an *action close*.   Messages written to obtain some action from the reader — to buy a product, come into a store, pay a bill, supply the requested information, follow the suggested instructions — should end with a definite statement of this desired action.

The reader should know how, when, why, and where this action is to take place.   The writer should make this action as easy as possible for the reader; for example, do not request a letter, but a check mark on a card that you have enclosed.   If you ask the reader to come into your store, he will need to know the location and the hours it is open.   If you ask him to telephone you, give him your number.

The action close should be definitely worded, but it should not appear to be demanding or dictatorial.   It should include, when appropriate, some motivation for prompt action.   Certain sales letters state that a special discount or bonus will apply to orders received before a deadline. The only motivation appropriate for some messages is a reasonable explanation for the necessity for prompt action, as in the memorandum from the librarian to the group of teachers.

Try to find a valid reason for setting a deadline, preferably of some kind of benefit to the reader.   Most of us tend to procrastinate if we do not have stated times for a task to be completed, or for a letter to be answered.

The doubtful tone, or lack of success consciousness, should not appear in letter endings, although it often does.   Examples of weak, doubtful phrasing are:

> If you want to look at this set of books, just call our representative...

An improved statement is:

> To examine this valuable set of books in your own home, just call...

The following expressions:

> If this plan meets your approval...

> We hope that you won't disapprove of this suggested plan...

are better stated in this way:

> I believe you will find this plan to be helpful to both
> departments.

Some letters and memorandums are not written for the purpose of obtaining immediate action. Examples are letters that give information only and that ask for no further contact; refusal letters that include no counter proposals; and memorandums telling of changes in methods or procedures.

You are considerate and courteous, though, if you keep channels open for further communication if it is desirable or necessary. You may ask the reader to telephone you or write again if he needs further help or instructions. Such statements should not be used routinely, however, for they may have the negative effect of suggesting trouble or misunderstanding. They may also encourage unnecessary continuing correspondence.

The simple statement

> We are glad to be of service.

can be an appropriate ending. Sales promotion material can be used, too, not only to promote sales but to provide a pleasant letter ending that does not apologize or include added emphasis to the refusal or bad news presented earlier in the letter. Such an ending could be:

> We have just received a shipment of new spring raincoats.
> They are especially colorful and attractive this year, and
> they are priced lower than last year's models. Come in
> early so that you will have a wide choice of styles and
> colors.

This paragraph serves as an action close to promote sales, as well as being a diplomatic ending to a refused-adjustment letter that actually required no further contact.

In reports, memorandums, or long letters, the final paragraph or paragraphs can serve as a summary. The concluding section of a report may be headed "Conclusions and Recommendations" or have a more descriptive heading that tells what these conclusions and recommendations have been determined to be.

Decide upon an appropriate ending, and use it as soon as you have said everything else that you need to say. Don't ramble on and on. Don't, even in personal letters, resort to something like, "Well, I'd better sign off now." That's almost as bad as the expression radio performers formerly used, "Well, the old clock on the wall says that we have to go."

SUMMARY ◆ 7

Readability means immediate clearness.   It is influenced by word choice; sentence and paragraph length; the length of the entire message; the use or omission of subheads, listings, and other aspects of arrangement; careful organization; and planning and wording to achieve unity, coherence, and the desired emphasis.

Short words, appropriately chosen, not only increase readability and emphasis but also help to form a vivid and forceful writing style.

Fairly short sentences aid in achieving readability.

Paragraphs in business writing, especially in letters and memorandums, are shorter than in some other kinds of writing.   Paragraphs of only one sentence are acceptable and sometimes desirable.   Often the first and last paragraphs may or should be only one sentence.

Readability formulas cannot measure the quality of writing, only its complexity, and that to a limited extent.   Word and sentence length are used to determine a "readability score," which is expressed at a reading grade level.

Emphasis is achieved by position, overall arrangement, sentence and paragraph construction, word choice, space, mechanical methods, and summarizing.

The first position of a letter or other written material is considered to be the most emphatic; the last position is also emphatic.   Good-news or neutral messages should ordinarily open with the gist of the message; this plan of organization is known as the direct arrangement.   Material that does not open with the gist of the message, such as bad-news letters or memorandums, is said to be arranged in the indirect order.

Written communications, as well as oral ones, should be planned in order to achieve completeness and coherence.   Coherence depends upon a logical pattern of organization; topic sentences; transitional words, phrases, and sentences; repetition of key words; and the use of pronouns to replace key words.

A buffer paragraph should be used to open bad-news messages. Communications that request some action from the reader should end with an action close.   The action close, which should be no earlier than in the next-to-last paragraph, should specifically state the action, make action easy, and, if appropriate, motivate prompt action.

QUESTIONS AND PROBLEMS ◆ 7

1. Discuss these statements.   Explain by giving examples and illustrations, preferably about business subjects.

    a.   Writing should be planned to express, not to impress.

    b.   A short word can be less readable than a long one.

    c.   Readability formulas can be misleading if used in the wrong way.

    d.   It is best not to start several sentences on the same page with the word "I."

    e.   Specific words are more emphatic and more forceful than general words, but at times the general word is the better choice.

    f.   The lack of planning of business messages results in the loss of time, money, effectiveness, and quality of writing.

    g.   A thorough and automatic knowledge of sentence structure is essential to the expert writer.

    h.   The direct arrangement is often more readable and concise than the indirect arrangement, but at times the indirect arrangement is the better choice.

2.   Rewrite the following sentence so that it becomes a five-word maxim.

It has been observed that an enclosing barrier, for the purpose of discouraging and preventing intrusion upon that which it encloses, tends to enhance the amicability of those whose property abuts on said barriers.[13]

3.   Rewrite the following paragraph from a letter about insurance. Work for simplicity and readability.

Inasmuch as dividends are payable on your above-mentioned policy under date of December 6, it is impracticable and impossible for us to issue and send you a check or payment of said dividend until the date upon which it is due and payable, an irrefutable fact that makes it impossible for you to pay your August premium with the dividend to be payable on December 6.

4.   Collect several business letters or add to your collection analyzed for preceding chapters. Compare these letters with all aspects of effective communication studied so far, and their style and appearance, to Appendix B. Consider these features of the business letters, or make any additional comments.

    a.   Appearance, including the choice of letter style and an attractive placement on the sheet.

13. *Effective Letters* (New York: New York Life Insurance Company, November-December 1960).

   b. Order of presentation — direct or indirect? Is the order used for this
       particular letter the most appropriate one for the subject matter pre-
       sented?
   c. Appropriate, concise, and effective beginning and ending.
   d. The you-attitude.
   e. A positive approach.
   f. Fairly short sentences and paragraphs. Notice especially the length of
       the first and last paragraphs.
   g. Mechanical means of emphasis, if any.
   h. Natural, conversational wording, with no trite business jargon such as
       that illustrated in Chapter 4.
5. As your instructor directs, analyze or rewrite the following sentences. Each
    violates one or more of these principles: the you-attitude; a positive approach;
    simplicity and readability; a natural, conversational style. (When writing or
    rewriting, make reasonable assumptions and/or add necessary details.)

   a.   We hope that our mistake will not adversely affect our

         business relationship. (last paragraph)

   b.   If we can be of further assistance, do not hesitate to

         call.

   c.   This letter is for the purpose of advising you that your

         order is being shipped and that credit is being

         extended, as you requested. (first paragraph)

   d.   In reference to your letter of October 21, we are

         advising you that your order is being sent to you on

         credit. Please make sure that you pay within thirty

         days. (first paragraph)

   e.   I am pleased to announce that we have increased our

         inventory by the addition of a large line of household

         appliances. (first paragraph)

   f.   We are sorry that we must reject your request.

         (last paragraph)

g.   I am sorry to take up so much of your valuable time,

but I really need this information. (last paragraph)

h.   Thanking you in advance for your cooperation, I am...

(last paragraph)

i.   We beg to extend to you our humble apologies.

j.   The instructions are plainly stated, as you can see on

page 12.

6. You are the personnel manager. Write a memo to all office and plant employees. Convey the following information. Choose the best order and approach.
    a. Each employee will receive a small increase in take-home pay.
    b. The reason: a small decrease in insurance premiums.
    c. Effective date: October 1.
    d. Amount of increase: 9.09 percent of present insurance premium.
    e. More increases in take-home pay may occur if the excellent safety record continues. (This insurance covers non-employment related accidents and illnesses.)

7. You are the personnel manager. Instead of the information given in Problem 6, you must report an increase in insurance costs and thus a decrease in take-home pay. The amount is 22.2 percent of present insurance premiums. The reason for the increase is the rapid rise in hospital and other medical rates.

8. Write instructions for using an electrical appliance, such as a blender, tape recorder, or clock radio, in easy-to-understand language.

9. Write a letter to your nephew, Charlie, who is in the sixth grade. He is coming to visit you. Give him specific and exact directions on how to reach your house, apartment, or dormitory room from the nearest bus stop.

10. Summarize a lecture from another business course in which you are enrolled. If you are taking no other business courses, summarize a lecture from any other course.

11. Think of some task or area of responsibility in your present or former job. Tell a new employee exactly how to perform this task or how to handle this responsibility. As your instructor directs, put these instructions in written form or be prepared to present them orally to your classmates.

FURTHER READING ◆ 7

Fielden, John S. "What Do You Mean I Can't Write?" *Harvard Business Review*, May-June, 1964, pp. 144–56.

Flesch, Rudolph F. *The Art of Readable Writing*. New York: Harper & Brothers, 1949.

Geiselman, Robert D., ed. *Readings in Business Communication*. Champaign, Ill.: Stipes Publishing Company, 1974. (See especially articles by Robert Gunning, William H. Whythe, Jr., John Fielden, Norman G. Shidle, Monroe C. Beardsley, H. L. Mencken, and Henry E. Francis).

Gowers, Ernest. *Plain Words: Their ABC*. New York: Alfred A. Knopf, 1954.

Gunning, Robert. *How to Take the Fog Out of Writing*. Chicago: The Dartnell Corporation, 1956.

———. *The Technique of Clear Writing*. New York: McGraw-Hill Book Company, 1968.

———. "The Fog Index after Twenty Years." *Journal of Business Communication* 6 (Winter 1968): 3–13.

Lambuth, David. *The Golden Book on Writing*. New York: Viking Press, 1964.

Morris, John O. *Make Yourself Clear!* New York: McGraw-Hill Book Company, 1972.

Perrin, Porter G. *Writer's Guide and Index to English*. 4th ed. Glenview, Ill. Scott, Foresman and Company, 1965.

Ralph, R. G. *Put It Plainly*. New York: Thomas A. Crowell Company, 1952.

Strunk, W. J. and White, E. B. *The Elements of Style*. New York: Macmillan Company, 1959.

Tichy, H. J. *Effective Writing for Engineers, Managers, and Scientists*. New York: John Wiley and Sons, 1967.

Writing Correctly, Appropriately, and Concisely

8

Correctness should be understood not only as the precise and exact use of language, but also as correctness based upon sound knowledge and thorough research.

Appropriate communication is expressed in a style and format suitable to the material and the situation, as well as to the senders and the receivers of the message.

Concise writing and speech save time and money, as compared to unnecessarily wordy messages. But the communicator should not be so concerned with attaining conciseness that the message is less than complete and courteous.

ACCURACY AND KNOWLEDGE: THE VITAL INGREDIENTS

No matter how skillfully we write or speak, this attempt at communication is not effective unless it is based on a sound knowledge of what we are writing about. It has been said that "You can't write writing." Neither can we "communicate communication." We communicate facts, ideas, and opinions. If we are employed in a business organization, we are paid to communicate facts, ideas, and opinions about business subjects — through face-to-face and telephone conversations; written memos, letters, and reports; and formal and informal presentations at meetings and conferences.

The techniques of communication are vastly important, but mere mastery of these techniques does not insure effective communication. If the thoughts we are trying to communicate are not based on a sound background of information and understanding, then expert expression is of little value. A fuzzy and indecisive mind cannot send clear, correct, convincing messages. In addition, the confidence of the writer or speaker is affected by the knowledge, or the lack of it, of company policy and procedures and of the particular situation.

Obtaining the necessary knowledge and understanding upon which to base effective communication can be a tedious process. To a certain extent, it depends on your entire background. If you are knowledgeable in many areas because of a curious and inquiring mind, varied experiences, and wide reading, you are already far better informed about many specialized business problems than you may think. Even without an excellent background of general knowledge, you can become well informed in your field by consistent and dedicated effort.

Regardless of your wealth of general knowledge, you will need to find out all you can about your job, your company, and about your particular duties and responsibilities. You will need this knowledge and understanding in order to succeed in all functions of your employment, but most especially to be able to communicate effectively in both written and oral messages.

As you communicate orally, at meetings and conferences or informally with colleagues, your certainty of the correctness of what you are saying will give you confidence and thus improve your communication techniques. Some people, however, even though they possess reliable information and a thorough knowledge of the subject, do not effectively express their thoughts to others. You can learn to communicate — although it is not always easy — if you have something to say. If you don't have anything to say, why bother?

The comment, "he knows what he is talking about," is one of the highest forms of praise for any communicator. With this knowledge, and with skill in presenting your thoughts and ideas to others — plus a genuine concern for those with whom you communicate — you will be successful in your communication endeavors.

Mark Twain, in one of his cynical moments, did not agree that success is built on real knowledge or ability. He said, "All you need in this life is ignorance and confidence, and then success is sure."

Don't bet on it, Mark Twain.

Every one of us can think back to mistakes we have made because we did not have certain necessary information, or because we were misinformed, or because we remembered details incorrectly. These errors will continue to occur, regardless of our effort, but at least we can minimize them with sufficient thought and effort.

Before you write or dictate business messages, you will often find it necessary to verify facts, dates, amounts, names, and other details that you include in your message. A secretary can and should do much of this checking for you, provided you are so fortunate as to have secretarial help, but if you write, dictate, supervise, or sign the message, you are responsible for its contents.

Suppose, for example, you announce a meeting for Friday, January 20, in a year when January 20 comes on a Saturday. (You were looking at last year's calendar.) This is a small error, as errors go; someone will likely call your attention to the date, and the whole matter will be straightened out with another memo. But if such errors continue to occur, they will convince your fellow workers that you do not give sufficient attention to details.

If you give the wrong date to a person who comes across the country to see you when you are away from the office, the situation becomes more serious. If you state the wrong price — for example, $1,000 instead of $10,000 — your company could be obligated to take a $9,000 loss. If you misspell the reader's name or use the wrong address, he may not receive an important message, or, even if he does, be annoyed at the misspelling of his name.

Because data are reproduced by computers and by other forms of mass reproduction, one error can become thousands of errors. A bit of incorrect information on a letter sent to one individual is bad enough, but a form letter sent to thousands of people greatly multiplies whatever difficulties will be encountered because of the error.

A message can be inaccurate because it is incomplete — and perhaps it is incomplete because the writer or speaker is overly concerned with being brief. A message can have the same effect as being inaccurate if it is misunderstood; that is, the facts may be correct but presented in such a way that the receiver of the message misinterprets them. A message can be inaccurate — actually or in effect — if the chosen words do not mean the same to the receiver as to the sender of the message.

Messages are likely to be incorrect if the communicator is not adept in the use of the language with which he attempts to communicate. Although grammatical errors do not often result in misunderstanding, they are likely to weaken the reader's confidence in the writer's overall competence. At times, also, the wrong word can alter the intended meaning. Misplaced commas or the omission of needed commas can reverse the intended meaning. Notice the difference in meaning in the following sentences:

All salesmen who have exceeded their quotas will receive a 10 percent bonus.

All salesmen, who have exceeded their quotas, will receive a 10 percent bonus.

The old publications which originally sold for $2 or less are to be destroyed.

The old publications, which originally sold for $2 or less, are to be destroyed.

A misplaced apostrophe can also cause misinterpretation.   Like the comma and other marks of punctuation, the apostrophe is sometimes used to convey meaning, not merely to make the meaning expressed by words more readily understood.   In the following sentence

The customers' orders were promptly filled

the meaning is not the same as in the sentence

The customer's orders were promptly filled.

The first sentence indicates that there are at least two customers; the second sentence indicates that there is only one customer.

The misuse of words similar in meaning or spelling can also cause misreading and misrepresentation.   Usually the words "affect" and "effect," although often confused, do not change the intended meaning. They can do so, however, as in these sentences:

Will the increase in total sales affect the expected salary increase?

Will the increase in total sales effect the expected salary increase?

Although these words are similar in spelling and pronunciation, the questions differ in meaning: the first question asks whether the increase will influence (have an effect on) the expected salary increase; the second question asks whether the increase in sales will bring about a salary increase.

Notice the difference in the two sentences that follow:

We are now expecting to make a change in personnel before the first of the year.

We are not expecting to make a change in personnel before the first of the year.

In another letter, the secretary misread her shorthand notes and typed the sentence

We appreciate your hospitality

in this way:

We appreciate your hostility.

All these "errors" perhaps resulted from haste or the lack of attention.   Similar or worse ones occur because the communicator does not have accurate knowledge to communicate.   Acquiring this knowledge and judgment takes constant effort; by the time you have learned one method of procedure or one set of instructions, new ones will be put into effect, and then more and more.

The overall amount of information available in all fields is increasing at an alarming rate; what you learn in school will be at least partially obsolete in a few years.   To be a leader (or even a good follower) you must be aware of change, accept it, and use it to your advantage and to that of your employing company.

THE FORMAL AND THE INFORMAL WRITING STYLES

The formal and the informal styles of writing do not mean exactly the same thing to all writers.   As in the choice of clothing, what seems informal to one person may seem too formal to another.

Regardless of how the writing is described or how formal the situation, the writing should not sound unnatural, stilted, or pretentious.   A scholarly essay will be more formal than a routine memorandum, but both the essay and the memorandum should be interesting, natural, and easy to read.   Both should use correct English, and both should be arranged and worded with the reader in mind.

Strictly formal writing will not include contractions, any expression that could be considered slang, or any abbreviated sentences or sentence fragments.   It is likely to be written in the impersonal tone, with no first- or second-person pronouns.   The informal style will most likely use the personal tone.   It may include contractions and casual conversational phrases or modes of expression.

The informal style may occasionally make use of some kinds of slang. Slang, however, should be used with the utmost discretion, for several reasons.   First, slang is often not nationwide, so it may not be understood by the reader.   Second, even the mildest slang offends some persons; or, if it doesn't offend, it is in questionable taste and unbusinesslike.   Third, slang becomes quickly dated, and what seems fresh and new to the writer may have already been discarded by the reader.   Fourth, the use of unusual or startling words or phrases may be distracting and thus delay the reception of the message.

The passage quoted below is an example of formal writing:

> He who permits himself to tell a lie once, finds it much easier to do it a second and third time, till at length it becomes habitual; he tells lies without attending to it, and truths without the world's believing him.   This falsehood of the tongue leads to that of the heart, and in time depraves all its good dispositions.[1]

1. Quoted by John Bartlett in *Familiar Quotations*, 14th ed.   (Boston: Little, Brown & Co., 1968), p. 471.

The preceding passage is from a letter from Thomas Jefferson to Peter Carr, written in 1785.   The following passage was written by William Sidney Porter (O. Henry) about 1909 in his story, "The Fourth in Salvador."   This writing is definitely informal.

> You can't appreciate home till you've left it, money till it's spent, your wife till she's joined a woman's club, nor Old Glory till you see it hanging on a broomstick on the shanty of a consul in a foreign town.[2]

Most business writing should be less formal than the passage written by Jefferson, but slightly more formal than the passage written by O. Henry.   The informality used by O. Henry, however, and certainly the quality of writing, would be appropriate for some kinds of business writing planned for some audiences.   Sales and advertising materials are often written in this tone.

Since the time of Jefferson, writing in general, not only business writing, has become more simple.   Sentences are shorter.   Less punctuation is used because, for one reason, shorter sentences require less punctuation in order to be immediately clear.   Actually, neither classification of writing, formal or informal, is an exact description of good business writing.   "Semiformal" is better.   Ordinarily, you will not need to worry about degrees of formality but merely write in a correct, businesslike, natural, respectful manner.

Semiformal or even formal writing need not be stiff, stuffy, or unnatural.   If you are not sure of the personality of your readers (and usually you won't be), it is better to lean more toward the formal side than to be overly casual and familiar.   But remember — stock phrases often found in business letters add nothing to any kind of writing, with the possible exception of a few that may be used in extremely formal situations or in legal documents. Trite, stereotyped phrases only take up space, make the letter sound old-fashioned and stilted instead of fresh and conversational, and detract from the immediate reception of the meaning you are trying to convey.

THE PERSONAL AND THE IMPERSONAL TONE

The personal tone uses the pronouns "I," "we," "our," or any other first-person pronouns, and the second-person pronouns of "you," "your," and "yourself."   Material written strictly in the impersonal tone does not include any first- or second-person pronouns.   The impersonal tone is

---

2. *Familiar Quotations*, 14th ed., p. 864.

used for newspaper writing, many magazine articles, and some textbooks and business reports. This style is also referred to as the third-person objective.

Both the personal and the impersonal forms of writing have advantages and disadvantages. The personal is more natural, more vivid, more forceful — and easier to write. Because of the use of the second-person pronouns, the writing seems more directly related to the reader and may be of more interest. The personal tone is used in practically all business letters, in memorandums, and in many essays and magazine articles. The personal tone is not the best choice for some business reports because the report should give emphasis to the facts and to the information being reported. It should not emphasize what the writer did or what he or she thinks about the information.

Although opinions of the writer may be expressed, emphasis should be upon conclusions based upon the findings of the report, not upon the unsupported beliefs of the researcher. The use of "I's" and "we's" in a formal report may lead readers' thoughts away from the information being reported to the person who did the reporting. This undue emphasis is often reason enough for wording some types of writing in the impersonal tone.

Another objection to the personal tone is that it seems to be more biased than the impersonal tone. This description is not necessarily true, for pronouns alone do not make the facts true or untrue; and the use of the impersonal tone does not prevent slanting or interpreting the information in the light of the reporter's desires or beliefs. However, when it is essential that the writing convey the impression of objectivity and unbiased research, the impersonal tone is perhaps the better choice. Opinions can be stated impersonally without the use of "I"; for example:

The results of the study indicate that more denim

slacks could be sold if they were manufactured in a

wider range of colors.

The study indicates that the company should manufacture

denim slacks in a wider range of colors.

That it is the report writer who is recommending the increase in color selection is apparent in most cases, since he or she has done the research and is writing the report.

The preceding paragraphs, if written in the personal tone, might read as follows:

I believe that the results of the study show that we should

include more colors in our line of denim slacks.

The results of the study indicate that we should include

more colors in our line of denim slacks.

Notice that the personal tone results in a more natural and informal approach, but that in the first example the words "I believe," (especially since they are in the emphatic first position of the sentence) emphasize the writer of the report and not the recommendation. The second version uses "we" and "our," but uses the important first position of the sentence for the results.

Even when using the personal tone, "I," "we," or other personal pronouns should not be used unnecessarily, especially first-person pronouns. An overabundance of "I's" and "we's" will weaken the you-approach, as well as take needed emphasis away from the most important meaning of the written message.

You are likely to do much more business writing in the personal tone than in the impersonal. The expert writer, however, can write well in either style and can choose wisely between the two for differing kinds of material and business situations.

If the written material is considered to be in the formal style, often the impersonal tone should be used; and with the informal style, the personal. These combinations are not always necessary, however, or even desirable. Try to judge each bit of writing according to what you have to say and according to who will read it.

THE ACTIVE AND THE PASSIVE VOICE

A disadvantage of the impersonal tone is that it is likely to include more sentences with the verb in the passive voice instead of in the more forceful and vivid active voice. Material written in the impersonal tone is also likely to contain many sentences beginning with words such as "it is" and "there is." Such sentence beginnings are weaker and less concise than sentences that begin with a subject that does the acting.

A skillful writer, however, can put most statements in the active voice even when using the impersonal tone. Notice these examples:

The company should include more colors in its line of

denim slacks.

(Active voice, impersonal tone. *Company* is the subject, and *should include* is the verb.)

We should include more colors in our line of denim slacks.

(Active voice, personal tone. *We* is the subject and *should include* is the verb.)

More colors should be included in the manufacture of denim

slacks.

(Passive voice, impersonal tone. The subject *colors* is not performing an action but is the receiver of the action; thus the verb is said to be in the passive voice.)

It is desirable to include more colors in the line of denim

slacks.

(Impersonal tone. This sentence is not passive in the sense that the subject is receiving the action, but it has the same weak effect as a verb in the passive voice. Here the *it* is not a real subject but a function word described as an "expletive.")

The active voice is more direct, more forceful, and more concise, but at times the passive voice is to be preferred. When emphasis is meant to be upon the receiver of the action, not the actor, then the receiver of the action becomes the subject of the sentence, and the sentence is passive. Another use of the passive construction is to express negative ideas more tactfully, as discussed in Chapter 6.

CONSERVATIVE, BUSINESSLIKE STANDARDS OF CORRECTNESS

Correct writing and speaking, from the standpoint of grammatical correctness and the accuracy of information, is not necessarily effective communication, nor is it necessarily easily understood, interesting, or diplomatic. Correctness is only one of the many components of effective communication. Most business communication, however, cannot be completely effective if it is not basically correct, grammatically as well as in the information it reports.

Some people seem to have the idea that an exact and "correct" use of the English language is somehow unimportant — that they should be concerned about more important matters. This attitude is in some cases a "sour-grapes" approach by those who lack confidence in their knowledge of the language. To say that we need not be concerned with how we express our thoughts is the same as saying that we are willing to neglect a major aspect of general education and literacy, regardless of our occupation.

We send or receive messages through the use of language almost every waking moment. Why should we not give a great deal of effort to sending and receiving these messages exactly and convincingly? If we played tennis every day, or much less often, most of us would not be content to continue incorrect and ineffective techniques. The true artist or craftsman of any kind continually tries to improve his knowledges, skills, and techniques so that he can do a better job today than he did yesterday.

We will continue to use language, for we must; therefore we should exert continued effort in order to use it effectively. Even though you perhaps will not be a professional writer or speaker, you will, and do, use the language in your profession, as well as in your personal life. In this sense it is a professional knowledge and skill, not only desirable but essential, in the perfection of whatever kind of work you do or will do.

Aside from its professional and social benefits, your growth in the use of the language will be a source of personal pride and accomplishment — and perhaps this is the most worthwhile motive.

The idea that correctness doesn't matter has arisen partially in protest of the overemphasis by some "purists" (and some English teachers) upon minor or controversial points of usage. The attitude may have been strengthened by those obnoxious pests who correct others' grammar or pronunciation in public.

As every thinking person knows, the correct use of language is not the be-all and end-all of life. It does not guarantee success, happiness, the pursuit of liberty, or anything else. But the mastery of the tools of communication can only improve our relationships with others, and this improved relationship can affect our lives in many ways.

Will Rogers used to say: "Maybe *ain't* ain't so correct, but I notice that lots of folks who ain't using *ain't*, ain't eating." What he didn't say was that many persons who did say "ain't" also were not eating well, during the years of the Great Depression.

We should learn and use the accepted and expected conventions of grammar, spelling, and sentence structure for several reasons, in addition to the purpose of maintaining the reader's or listener's confidence in our competence and ability. Even more important is our own self-confidence.

We should adhere, for the most part, to established conventions because to do otherwise is distracting; for example, the reader of a letter can be distracted from the intended meaning while he ponders unusual phrasing or punctuation — or the actual meaning may be changed. In addition, we need to be adept in the use of the language for the pragmatic purpose of saving time.   When we *know*, we do not spend time in trying to decide upon grammatical usage or trying to find examples or instructions in an English handbook.

Remember, though, that expert use of the language consists of far more than learning and applying "rules," and that "correctness," like most other terms, is often relative.   As you remember from the discussion of formal and informal styles of writing and speech, some expressions acceptable or even desirable in conversation are not appropriate in written communication, especially in rather formal situations.   Some terms or expressions acceptable in informal writing are not wisely chosen for formal writing or speech.

CONCISENESS AND COMPLETENESS

Conciseness is not a synonym for brevity.   "Brevity," like "long," "short," and other nonspecific words, is relative; but a report of one hundred pages or more is not usually described as being brief.   It will be concise if it is no longer than it needs to be to accomplish its particular purpose.   Conversely, a one-page report, although brief, is not concise if it is longer than it needs to be in order to accomplish its purpose.

Conciseness is always a desirable quality of business communication; brevity is not necessarily desirable.   When working for conciseness, remember that the purpose of the message is not merely the imparting of information but also building and maintaining goodwill.   To build or maintain goodwill — or from the human standpoint of being friendly and courteous — the writer or speaker perhaps will be required to include additional words, paragraphs, or pages.   A "please" or a "thank you" takes little time and space; even if they did, they would be well worth the effort.

A letter or other message that says "no" or relates unpleasant news usually should be longer than one that says "yes" or relates good news.   Suppose, for example, you are refusing a request.   You could convey the necessary information in this way:

Dear Mrs. Baker:

No.

Sincerely,

This letter, although brief, lacks many of the necessary aspects of an effective letter.   Perhaps it relates all the necessary information, but it requires "padding" (although this word in itself usually has an undesirable connotation). The message requires some explanation and a goodwill paragraph or two, unless the writer wishes to be particularly emphatic in his "no," most likely at the expense of future pleasant relationships. (The one-word sentence that makes up the total message dramatically illustrates a method of emphasis — using short, simple sentences standing alone.)

In messages other than "no" letters, some writers omit necessary details and explanations, often because of an overconcern with brevity. The shortest letter is not economical if it necessitates another letter or a telephone call to clear up what should have been clearly stated in the original letter.

Your reader or listener does not want needless and irrelevant details or explanations, but you must include sufficient facts and explanations, as well as courtesy.

Lack of conciseness in either writing or speaking usually results from one or more of the following weaknesses:

1. Rambling — not keeping the presentation in a straight line of thought from beginning to end. Bringing in unnecessary or irrelevant details. Stating facts that should be left unsaid.

2. Unnecessary repetition.

3. Wordy phrases, especially trite phrases of business jargon, as "enclosed please find," "attached hereto you will find," and many others. (See the list in Chapter 4.)

4. Using long, complicated words and phrases instead of simple wording. (See "A Simple Writing Style" in Chapter 7. Many of the factors that improve readability also increase conciseness.)

We cannot, and perhaps should not, eliminate all expressions from our language that could be classified as clichés. Although we should work for a fresh, original approach, some phrases, because of long usage, now have a distinct meaning not easily replaced.

Let's look at some sentences and paragraphs to see how they can be improved by being made more concise, especially through the elimination of stereotyped business jargon. Although it is unlikely that you would ever write material as completely hopeless as some of these examples, even a few trite phrases or redundancies can weaken an otherwise convincing and interesting message.

This paragraph rambles, repeats unnecessarily, and includes redundant words and phrases:

Will you let us know by any means, telephone or letter

or otherwise, sometime soon, in a month or two but

hopefully within a month, just what to do about the situation we conversed about and discussed pursuant to the changing

of the method in which the beneficiary, that is the former

beneficiary, is notified and informed that he or she is no

longer the beneficiary, that the policyholder has named and

designated a new person to become his beneficiary. Or is

this method and procedure mandatory, necessary, or even

desirable?

The following is a big improvement:

Will you let us know within a month whether a former

beneficiary should be notified that he is no longer a

beneficiary, and, if so, the procedure to follow?

The memorandum shown in Figure 8–1 on page 194 can be shortened considerably. It could have been much better written in this way:

The entire factory and all offices will be closed from

4 p.m. December 23 to 8 a.m. January 2.

You will receive full pay for this holiday season

vacation, which is in addition to your yearly annual vacation.

This is your Company's way of saying "thank you" for

a job well done. Have a happy holiday season.

(No, Figure 8–1 is not a real example — memorandums and letters are often wordy but not usually as much so as this one.)

REVISING FOR PROFESSIONAL QUALITY

Good writing is rewriting and then perhaps rewriting again and again. Even skillful professional writers revise their work — that is one reason why they are skillful professional writers.

TO: All Factory and Office Employees

FROM: J. B. Windy, Personnel Manager

SUBJECT: HOLIDAY VACATION

It has come to my attention that many of you have been asking about a vacation during the holiday season. This memorandum is in answer to these questions that you have been asking.

As a matter of fact, you will be happy and glad that according to our company policy established only this year, which may be true for only this year, there will be a holiday break during the Christmas season of eight days, including weekends, when everything is closed for all of the employees in the factory as well as all of those in the offices. These eight days begin at the end of the regular working day on December 23, which is, as you know, at 4 p.m., and extends to January 2 to the regular opening hour of 8 a.m.

As I said, we will all be on vacation then. And the best part of it is that the regular pay will continue, for all the time of the vacation, except of course for the weekends, when you aren't paid anyway, unless you count what you earn during the week as being spread over the weekends. And you still get your regular vacation.

Your company is grateful and appreciative of your work during the preceding and past year. As a kind of thank-you and bonus, we are making this time off available. Have a happy holiday season. Don't hesitate to call me if you have any questions.

Figure 8-1. *An Overlong Memorandum*

In a busy office, however, there is little opportunity for extensive rewriting. Because of this pressure and the fight against time, which seems to be a part of everyone's work day, you should be thoroughly expert in writing skills so that work that is done hurriedly is acceptable and adequate, although perhaps less than outstanding. A good and experienced writer can write or dictate in a few minutes a better letter than can a poor writer, who may take an hour. Regardless of your knowledge and skill, however, and regardless of the pressure of the lack of time, some revision is usually desirable.

The illustration in Figure 8–2 shows that the first version of a letter has been greatly improved in the final version. This material was used in the continuing series "Effective Letters," which was planned to improve the written communication skills of employees of the New York Life Insurance Company. Like many other learning materials, it is rather exaggerated for the purpose of illustration. No letter writer capable of holding a job would write or dictate a letter like the first one, but even experienced writers may find that some of the suggested improvements would help their own letters.

WRITING IS RE-WRITING

Mining a diamond does not produce an engagement ring any more than a random collection of facts produces a good letter. It is rewriting, the writer's refining process, that turns the raw material into the finished product. Let's look at an example of raw material:

Dear Mr. Jones:

We have received your inquiry of November 6. Regarding this inquiry, we would like to state that we are in no position to comply with your request, changing the method of premium payment on your above-numbered policy to the monthly basis, because the monthly premium must amount to at least the sum of $10 per month, inasmuch as the Company has found it impractical to issue policies with a monthly premium of less than this amount.

We might, however, make mention of the fact that your policy contains an Automatic Premium Loan clause and under this clause, unpaid premiums can be taken care of by loan provided there is sufficient cash value in your above policy to warrant doing so, and provided small repayments are made on your loan from time to time.

Figure 8–2. *Effective Rewriting. From* Effective Letters *(New York: New York Life Insurance Company, November–December, 1960). Copyright 1960, New York Life Insurance Company. Used with permission.*

Figure 8-2. *(Continued)*

If it should be your desire to do this, kindly contact us and we shall be pleased to comply with your request.

Sincerely yours,

The raw material is there, but certain refinements seem to be in order. First of all, because the sentences are overloaded, the letter demands a second or even a third reading — hardly fair to the reader. So on the first rewrite, let's take out the linking words — *and, because, since, inasmuch as* — and make separate sentences out of what follows:

Dear Mr. Jones:

We have received your inquiry of November 6. Regarding this inquiry, we would like to state that we are in no position to comply with your request, changing the method of premium payment on your above-numbered policy to the monthly basis. This is because the monthly premium must amount to at least the sum of $10 per month. You see, the Company has found it impractical to issue policies with a monthly premium of less than this amount.

We might, however, make mention of the fact that your policy contains an Automatic Premium Loan clause. Under this clause, unpaid premiums can be taken care of by loan. This can be done provided there is sufficient cash value in your above policy to warrant doing so, and provided small repayments are made on your loan from time to time.

If it should be your desire to do this, kindly contact us. We will be pleased to comply with your request.

Sincerely yours,

This seems to be a lot clearer. At least it can be better understood on first reading. But what about all the gingerbread — "We are in no position to," "We would like to state that," "If it should be your desire,"? A second rewrite could take care of those:

Dear Mr. Jones:

I am sorry to tell you that we cannot change the method of premium payment on your policy to the monthly basis. This is because the monthly premium must amount to at least $10 a month. You see, the Company has found it impractical to issue policies with a monthly premium of less than this amount.

However, your policy contains an Automatic Premium Loan clause. Under this clause, unpaid premiums can be taken care of by loan. This can be done

Figure 8–2.   *(Continued)*

provided there is sufficient cash value in your above policy and provided small repayments are made on your loan from time to time.

Let us know if you want us to do this, won't you?   It will be a pleasure to take care of it for you.

Sincerely yours,

The language sounds more courteous and clear, but what about the order of the letter?   Is the reader seeing first what's most important to him?   What if it read like this:

Dear Mr. Jones:

Since your policy contains an Automatic Premium Loan clause, we can arrange to have your premiums paid by loan provided there is enough cash value in your policy.   Then you can simply make repayments toward your loan and all will be in order.

I'm sorry that we cannot arrange to have you pay premiums on the monthly basis, as you asked, but monthly premiums must amount to at least $10. However, this Automatic Premium Loan arrangement will, in effect, accomplish the same thing.

Let us know if you want us to do this, won't you?   It will be a pleasure to take care of it for you.

Sincerely yours,

Admittedly, such revisions take time, but with practice, rewriting becomes habitual and takes less and less time.   It's part of the correspondent's job to be an editor, too.

Begin by relying, as we did here, on only 3 simple rules of editing:

1. Look for overloaded sentences.   When you find words like *and, because, since, inasmuch as, which, for the reason that,* you can usually begin a new sentence at that point.
2. Look for words and phrases of traditional "Business English."   Delete them and substitute the language of conversation.
3. Look at your reader.   Arrange your material so that he will see first what is apt to interest him most.

Sometimes changes can result in making material even worse than its original version.   For example, at times a word may be correctly repeated several times in a paragraph.   At the very least, we should not accept as a rule the statement that the same word should never be used twice in the same sentence.   To use a different but similar word can result in confusion and unclearness.   Remember that very few words have exactly the same meaning.   Most word repetition, however, especially when it is used to excess, results from haste and the lack of revision.

"Over and Over and Over Again," also from *Effective Letters*, illustrates what happens in an attempt to avoid the repetition of words (see Figure 8–3).

OVER AND OVER, AND OVER AGAIN . . .

How many times have you asked yourself, "How can I avoid using the same word again and again in a letter?"

Many correspondents are tempted to avoid repetition whenever they can. Often it's because they're afraid of creating a nightmare like this:

Dear Mr. Jones:

We are very sorry to learn of your recent illness, and that this illness will prevent you from returning to your work.

As you are aware, your illness is compatible with the definition of total and permanent disability indicated in your policy.   You are therefore eligible to receive disability benefits.   Please fill in the enclosed disability forms with the requested information pertinent to your illness and return them to us.

Sincerely,

By the time Mr. Jones finishes reading this letter, he may feel very ill, indeed.   What *can* you do when you have to use a word several times in a message?   It's a ticklish problem that can be approached in 1 of 4 ways:

1. By using synonyms — those words that have similar meaning — to replace a recurring word.
2. By recasting the sentences so the word doesn't appear so often.
3. By using a pronoun (*he, she, it,* etc.) instead of the recurring word.
4. And finally, by just giving in and repeating the word . . . but more about that later.

First, let's take a closer look at the synonym approach.   These substitute words can be very helpful in controlling repetition.   But they must be used with

Figure 8–3. *Avoiding Repetition.   From* Effective Letters *(New York: New York Life Insurance Company, July-August, 1962).   Copyright 1962, New York Life Insurance Company.   Used with permission.*

Figure 8–3.   *(Continued)*

caution.   Synonyms don't always have exactly the same meaning as the words they replace.   Too many of them can distract the reader's attention from the real purpose of a message.   Used haphazardly, they can make a letter look like this:

Dear Mr. Jones:

We are very sorry to learn of your recent illness, and that this affliction will prevent you from returning to your work.

As you are aware, your infirmity is compatible with the definition of total and permanent disability indicated in your policy.   You are therefore eligible to receive benefits.   Please fill in the enclosed forms with the requested information pertinent to your incapacity and return them to us.

Sincerely,

This letter doesn't repeat the word "illness."   But it certainly does look awkward.   Besides, there are several shades of difference in the meaning of all those synonyms.   And these differences may puzzle the reader.

Recasting the sentences is another way to solve the repetition problem.   In this case, we changed a few of the sentences so that it wasn't necessary to refer to illness so often.   And where we had to refer to that word, we used the pronoun "it" in place of a synonym:

Dear Mr. Jones:

We are very sorry to learn of your recent illness, and that it will prevent you from returning to your work.

Under the terms of your policy, you are eligible for disability benefits.   To assure the fastest possible consideration of your claim, please fill in the enclosed forms and return them to us.

Sincerely,

We did manage to avoid repetition.   At the same time, we kept the meaning of the message clear.

But sometimes it's impossible to do both.   When this happens, it's better to give in and repeat a word than to sacrifice the meaning of a letter.   For one thing, not all repetition is monotonous.   If a recurring word isn't annoying, why bend over backwards to avoid it?   Some repetition is good for emphasis.   It also makes a letter clearer for the reader by driving a point home.   And it can help the writer connect the different ideas he wants to convey.

When revising:

1.   Check organization and the flow of thought.
2.   Notice the length of sentences and paragraphs. Perhaps they will need to be shortened.
3.   Watch for unnecessary repetition of words or ideas.
4.   Make sure that no essential material is omitted.
5.   Check for subject-verb agreement and pronoun-antecedent agreement.
6.   Watch for misplaced or dangling modifiers.
7.   Make sure that necessary transitional phrases or words have been included. Make sure that there is no abrupt change in the flow of thought.
8.   See if the entire writing can be made more concise.

SUMMARY ◆ 8

Effective communication must be based on sound knowledge and understanding of the material being communicated, as well as upon proficiency in language usage.

Strictly formal writing includes no contractions; casual, conversational, or slang expressions; or abbreviated sentences or sentence fragments. Formal writing is likely to be in the impersonal tone, which includes no first- or second-person pronouns. Although formal writing is used in some reports and other forms of business communication, practically all letters are written in a style that is less than completely formal — although it is a mistake, in many situations, to go too far toward informality and familiarity. Most business messages are written in the personal tone.

The active voice, in which the subject of the sentence is the "actor," is more direct, forceful, and concise than is the passive voice, but at times the passive voice is to be preferred: to place emphasis upon the receiver of the action; to express negative ideas more diplomatically; to avoid the appearance of the "I-attitude"; and to avoid monotony in sentence construction.

Conciseness is not a synonym for brevity. Material is concise if it is no longer than it needs to be to accomplish its particular purpose.

Revision is usually necessary for professional quality in written materials.

QUESTIONS AND PROBLEMS ◆ 8

1. Discuss the advantages and the disadvantages of the personal and the impersonal tone; the formal and the informal writing styles; the active and the passive voice.

2. Rewrite the passage by Jefferson so that it is less formal than the original. (You are not likely to improve upon Jefferson's writing; your purpose is to try to express the same ideas in a less formal and perhaps a more modern way, but you should still strive for a good writing style.)

3. Rewrite the passage by O. Henry in a more formal style. You probably can't say it so well in a more formal style, but try to express the ideas completely and concisely in your own words. Your version does not need to be formal, just not quite so informal as O. Henry's.

4. In what kinds of writing may "you" be used, but not "I" or "we"? Explain.

5. Although a written communication, such as a letter or a memo, is written in the personal tone, it is likely to contain sentences or complete paragraphs that contain no first- or second-person pronouns and are thus in the impersonal tone. For example, "Two handbooks are enclosed" is in the impersonal tone. "I am enclosing two handbooks" is written in the personal tone.

    Is the first example written in the active or the passive voice? What about the second sentence? Why may the impersonal tone be the better choice in sentences such as these?

6. Rewrite the following section from the concluding section of an analytical report. Use the impersonal tone instead of the personal tone in which it is now expressed.

    I completed this study for the following reasons:

    a.   I determined the written responsibilities of Certified

          Professional Secretaries. I assume that these duties

          are similar to those of all high level secretaries. You

          can relate these responsibilities to the education and

          experience of the secretaries according to the type

          and size of the employing organization.

    b.   I identified the areas of difficulty in business writing.

    c.   I analyzed and interpreted the results of the study in

          relation to instruction in courses in written business

          communication.

7. To improve the goodwill approach, rewrite the following sentences in the passive voice. (Use any other techniques to increase diplomacy.)

   a.   You delivered the package to the wrong office.

   b.   All of your past employers told me something different about you.

   c.   You knew the instructions that I distributed to all personnel.

8. Improve the following sentences from business messages. Consider correctness, the you-attitude, the positive approach, effective sentence structure, and all the other aspects of communication studied thus far. (See Appendix D for explanation of standards of language usage.)

   a.   As an outstanding businessman, I request your opinion of the new tax regulations.

   b.   The letter, as well as the two reports, were sent to you this morning.

   c.   He was asked to remove the clutter, repair the fence, and that he must build a sidewalk.

   d.   Taking claims and to analyze them is part of the job's responsibilities.

   e.   Company policy does not allow us to comply with your request therefore it must be rejected.

   f.   We hope to receive the check within a week.

   g.   We are in receipt of your order of a recent date and in reply wish to state that we thank you for same and for your check in payment that was attached thereto, which which was in the amount of $42.50.

h.   That is the typewriter that makes the most noise of all those in the room.

i.   Graduates who are the ones with the highest grade point average will be the first ones who will be interviewed.

j.   I hope that this calamity will not adversely effect our future business relationship.

k.   Although it is against our policy, because you have been a profitable customer we are enclosing two complementary tickets.

l.   During the passed year this principal has been in effect.

m.   The reasoning of all our salesmen and supervisors indicate that this product should be discontinued.

n.   Neither the teacher nor the students was concerned about the noise in the hall.

o.   The employer, who we went to Dallas to see, was most courteous to my wife and I.

p.   The secretaries and myself have long been concerned about this matter.

q.   Is it true that Jerry is the one whom is to be considered?

r.   Tennis racquets we carry come in two different types. The beginner and the professional with different prices for each type.

s.   Coming in two different types, I can send you either
      racquet you prefer.

t.   We only sell the two types. Not one for the
      intermediate player.

u.   This letter is in reply to your letter of November 6.
      In reply to this letter I wish to advise that in
      reference to your question about the Anderson account,
      it has now been partially paid $200 of the $350 has
      been collected.

v.   The question you asked is not a question that can be
      easily answered; your question raises another
      question.

w.   Do not hesitate to telephone me if you have questions
      about the policy enclosed herein and attached hereto.

x.   This policy not only must be read and understood it
      must be signed and returned.

y.   The arrival of the merchandise at this time is
      unfortunate, can it be returned?

z.   Meeting at noon, the constitution was completely
      rewritten by four o'clock by the Board of Directors.

9. Continue your study of business letters and memorandums. Analyze them
    from all the standpoints of effective communication studied thus far, with
    special emphasis upon principles presented in Chapter 8. As your instructor
    directs, rewrite one or more of these messages, or tell your classmates of the
    needed improvements.

10. Edit and revise the following letter. (Except for a few minor changes,
    including names, this is an actual letter mailed in 1975.)

To the Engaged Couple,

We are offering a 10 percent discount on any or all of your wedding needs. We would like to advise you that we have a full and complete wedding service, we can order your personalized invitations, napkins, and wedding scrolls. We have our own florist where we do complete flowers for the wedding party and church, we also do the reception. Including the cake, punch, nuts, mints and food, with all the tables decorated in the colors of your choice.

We are proud of our wedding service. Would it be asking too much to ask you to take time to come in and let us give you a price on your complete wedding, or part of your wedding.

Hope to see you soon. Remember that everything about your wedding effects your future happiness. You will have to come in from 9:30 to 4:30 Tuesday thru Saturday or you can come nights by appointment. Call 365-9821 for any information.

Yours very truly,

Pauline Poindexter
Pauline Poindexter
WEDDINGS OF ELEGANCE

FURTHER READING ◆ 8

Bernstein, Theodore M. *Miss Thistlebottom's Hobgoblins*. New York: Farrar, Straus & Giroux, 1971.

————. *Watch Your Language*. Great Neck, N.Y.: Channel Press, 1958.

————. *More Language That Needs Watching*. Manhassett, N.Y.: Channel Press, 1962.

————. *The Careful Writer: A Modern Guide to English Usage*. New York: Atheneum Press, 1965.

Colwell, Carter C., and Know, James H. *What's the Usage? The Writer's Guide to English, Grammar, and Rhetoric*. Englewood Cliffs, N.J.: Prentice-Hall, 1972.

Evans, Bergen. *Comfortable Words*. New York: Random House, 1962.

Evans, Bergen, and Evans, Cornelia. *A Dictionary of Contemporary American Usage*. New York: Random House, 1957.

Hodges, John C., and Whitten, Mary E. *Harbrace College Handbook*. 7th ed. New York: Harcourt, Brace & World, 1975.

Perrin, Porter G. *Writer's Guide and Index to English*. 4th ed. Glenview, Ill.: Scott, Foresman & Company, 1965.

Strunk, William J., and White, E. B. *The Elements of Style*. 2d ed. New York: Macmillan Company, 1971.

FREQUENTLY WRITTEN
BUSINESS MESSAGES

Writing About the Routine and the Favorable

9

The requirements and considerations for favorable, good-news messages and for routine, neutral, or merely informational messages have already been discussed, to a great extent, in preceding chapters, especially in the presentation of the direct and the indirect orders of arrangement.

As you remember, the direct approach is usually the wiser choice unless there is a definite reason for using the indirect. One reason for choosing the indirect is to be able to prepare the reader, with reasons or other explanatory or introductory material, to accept an unpleasant or surprising conclusion or statement. When the gist of the message is favorable or neutral, opening with the gist of the message, as we do when using the direct approach, has a psychological advantage as well as making the communication easier to read.

Routine and favorable messages should ordinarily be arranged in the direct order.

CHOOSING AND PLANNING THE ORDER OF ARRANGEMENT

To determine the most appropriate arrangement of ideas, first consider the nature of the message to be conveyed and the person or persons who will read the communication. Then decide upon the reader's probable reaction to the message.

These reactions will fall into one of the following general responses, or into a combination of these. Some communications contain both good news and bad news. Unless the bad news far outweighs the good news, these communications can be treated basically as good-news messages.

1. The reader will be pleased.
2. The reader will be displeased.
3. The reader will be neither pleased nor displeased but will have at least some degree of interest.
4. The reader will have little initial interest.

After considering these reader reactions (sometimes you will guess wrongly about the reader), consider the following four kinds of arrangement, classified according to the sequence of ideas, purpose, and probable reader reaction.

1. Good-news messages, to be arranged in the direct order.
2. Bad-news messages, to be arranged in the indirect order.
3. Neutral or informational messages in which the reader has some initial interest, to be arranged in the direct order.
4. Persuasive messages in which the reader is assumed to have little initial interest (sales messages, persuasive requests), to be arranged in a modification of the indirect arrangement, which is the "sales" arrangement of attention, interest, conviction, and action. The most important difference between this plan and the usual indirect arrangement is the wording of the first paragraph or two of the letter.

The communications discussed in this chapter fall into the categories of 1 and 3; those discussed in the following chapter, bad-news letters and persuasive requests, fall into the categories of 2 and 4. In the study of coherence (in Chapter 7) you learned the importance of planning the communication before it is written or dictated. You also learned that there is no exact and unvarying way to arrange written or spoken messages — that it is not a matter of following a formula, but of using your own good judgment. For example, two letters, both of which are on the same subject and both of which are arranged in the direct order, can be quite different, and both can be well written and effective (as illustrated in Chapter 7). And at times the complete arrangement can be varied; for example, some late-stage collection messages open with a statement that would be inappropriate for other types of persuasive messages.

Because the first position of any communication is an emphatic one, we use this position to our advantage when we open with a statement telling the good news or summing up the main idea to be conveyed. When writing inquiries or requests, the inquiry or request itself can often be the opening sentence of the letter.   A subject line is especially useful and appropriate in good-news messages, routine and neutral messages, and in direct inquiries and requests.

A well-chosen subject line tells the reader at the beginning what the letter is about.   It will save explanations or references that would otherwise come in the first paragraph, allowing this paragraph to be used to move the discussion more quickly into the remainder of the presentation.

When requesting or imparting bits of information, the questions or statements should be arranged and worded so that they are easy to read and understand.   Listings and tabulations — or statements or questions standing alone as paragraphs — make the material much easier to read than that presented in long, jumbled paragraphs.   Subheads, underlining, numbering, and other arrangements in format promote readability, as discussed in Chapter 7.

Although letters that present favorable or neutral information (or simple, direct requests) are easier to write well than are unfavorable ones, even these types of messages, ordinarily conducive to pleasant human relations, may have the opposite effect.   They are less than pleasant and positive if they are written in a grudging tone.   Sometimes they seem to imply that although you are doing what the reader requested, the action is inconvenient or unnecessary.   You may give the impression that the reader is not justified in the request but that you are complying because he is a good customer.   These approaches can do more to harm pleasant customer relationships than a diplomatic, reasonable refusal letter.

Ordinarily, favorable letters or memorandums will be shorter than unfavorable ones because there is less need for reasons and explanations and for convincing the reader that the action taken is a wise one.   But even favorable messages can be so short that they seem curt and convey less than the complete information.   You should taken the time and space necessary to include all desirable information, explanations, and instructions, as well as to show that the reader is an esteemed individual to you and to your company.

The letter being answered should be carefully read in order to make sure that all questions, stated or implied, have been answered.

In routine and favorable messages, as in all communication, we must be concerned with goodwill, regardless of the remaining purpose or purposes of the communication, and regardless of whether the message is directed to persons outside or within your own organization.   In addition, we must be concerned with all the other aspects of effective communication, including readability, conciseness and completeness, the positive approach (which is also an aspect of the goodwill approach), and correctness.

Good-news messages in the direct approach follow this sequence of ideas:

1. Good news or other pleasant idea.
2. Details, information, instructions, etc.
3. Closing thought — a pleasant "goodwill closeout" or, if some action is requested of the reader, an appropriate, diplomatic action close.

Neutral messages, also in the direct approach, follow this sequence of ideas:

1. The most important idea or bit of information, or a brief summary of the entire message.
2. Details, information, instructions, etc.
3. Closing thought — a pleasant "goodwill closeout" or, if some action is requested of the reader, an appropriate, diplomatic action close.

A direct request or inquiry — one that is likely to meet no reader resistance — is arranged in this way:

1. The request or inquiry.
2. Details, information, instructions, etc.
3. An appropriate, diplomatic action close.

If you are not sure of the factors that constitute an effective action close, look back to Chapter 7 under the topic, "Planning the Order of Ideas." To briefly restate these factors, the action close should specify the desired action, preferably in terms of reader benefit; make the action easy; and motivate prompt action (if appropriate) or give a date, with reasonable explanations, of when the action should be taken.

Examples of letters that fall into these three general categories of direct-arrangement messages — good news, neutral, and routine request or inquiry — are given in the remaining sections of this chapter. Although the examples and discussion pertain to letters, the same principles and considerations apply to memorandums or any other form of written communications, and, basically, to oral presentations as well.

ORDERS, INQUIRIES, AND DIRECT REQUESTS

Orders, inquiries, and direct requests are considered routine because they are frequently written and because they are not likely to result in reader displeasure or resistance.

Order Letters

Although orders for merchandise or services are often placed by methods other than by writing a letter, the order letter still has a place both in business communication and in your personal business transactions. Order letters are simple to plan and arrange, but many are less than effective because they omit necessary information or ordinary courtesy.

Another common weakness is that information about the merchandise ordered is presented in a way that is hard to read and understand immediately, or in a way that can be easily misunderstood. Necessary information includes the quantity; price; catalog number, if any; and such descriptions as color, size, and model number. In addition, information must be included — if it is not already clear from previous transactions — about the plan of payment and shipping instructions.

The order letter is a direct request, and certainly one that the seller of the merchandise or service will not resist, provided the merchandise is available and the buyer can be expected to pay.

The example letter in Figure 9–1 from an office supply company is sent to a manufacturer from which no other merchandise has been ordered. This letter includes an application for credit; from the subordinated way in which the request is presented, the writer seems to have no doubt that the credit will be approved. (Further discussion of credit applications and of credit approvals and disapprovals is presented in Chapter 12.)

The first paragraph opens directly with the request for the paper shredders to be shipped.

The middle section of the letter gives in exact detail and in easily readable form a statement of the desired merchandise.

The next-to-last paragraph makes application for credit and also requests a catalog; the last paragraph serves as the action close. In routine request letters, including order letters, the direct request for action is omitted. The request has already been stated, usually in the opening paragraph, as in this letter.

Direct Inquiries

Inquiries are, in effect, requests for information. Some of these inquiries are about products or services being considered for purchase. (Replies to these letters are referred to as solicited sales messages.) Other requests for information are of various kinds, including information about persons being considered for employment or as credit customers.

The letter shown in Figure 9–2 requests information about convention accommodations. The subject line conveys immediately the basic purpose of the letter. It also is likely to arouse both the attention and the

QUALITY OFFICE SUPPLY COMPANY
4646 Poplar Avenue
Philadelphia, Pennsylvania 19101

April 23, 1979

Mr. John H. Williamson
Electric Wastebasket Corporation
145 W. 45th Street
New York, NY 10036

Dear Mr. Williamson:

The request

Please send the paper shredders listed below to the address shown above. Please send freight prepaid, as stipulated in your sales letter of April 12.

Specific, complete details

1 each	Model JNS-321 paper shredder	$39.95
2 each	Model JNS-331 paper shredder @ $49.95 each	99.90
1 each	Model JNS-341 paper shredder	59.95
		$199.80
	Less 35% dealer discount	69.93
		$129.87

Credit request; additional request

Our credit application has been mailed; upon its approval, please charge these items according to your terms of 2/10, n/30. Also include your complete catalog of office equipment to aid us with future orders.

Modified action close

We are planning a special advertising campaign to begin on June 1. We will appreciate your sending this equipment about a week before this time.

Sincerely,

David Rose

David Rose, Sales Manager

nw

Figure 9-1. *Order and Application for Credit*

January 2, 1979

Mr. Phillip Smith, Director
Sandburg Hotel
Las Vegas, NV 89154

Dear Mr. Smith:

Subject: REQUEST FOR CONVENTION INFORMATION

Will you please help the Federal Criminal Investigators'
Association to decide whether it can meet at the Sandburg
Hotel? FCIA national headquarters has expressed interest
in having its annual convention in Las Vegas on July 23,
24, and 25. In order to make the necessary arrangements,
we shall need the information requested in the following
questions.

The request, with explanations

Can you accommodate a group such as ours on these dates?
Approximately 300 members are expected to attend, and
they will need about 200 rooms.

What are your convention rates? We need assurance of
having available a minimum of 225 rooms, and we would
be willing to guarantee 200. Would you be willing to
reserve for us the rooms we shall require?

What are your charges for conference rooms? We shall
need five for each of the three days, and each should have
a minimum capacity of 40. Also, during the evening of
the 25th, we shall need a large assembly room with a
capacity of 350. Can you meet these requirements?

Questions, with explanations

Finally, will you please send me your menu selections and
prices for group dinners? On the 25th we plan to have our
closing election dinner. Approximately 350 are expected
for this event.

As convention plans must be announced in the next issue of
our monthly bulletin, may we have your responses right
away? We look forward to the possibility of being with you
in July.

Action close

Sincerely,

Dave Staplestown

Dave Staplestown
Committee Chairman

Figure 9-2. *Request for Convention Information*

interest of the reader, who is, or should be, interested in promoting sales activities of the hotel.

Notice the parallel arrangement of this inquiry. A great deal of information is needed, and some explanation of each point is necessary in order for the director of the hotel to be able to supply the desired data. Each paragraph opens with a question; the remaining sentences in each paragraph give the necessary explanations. Also notice the last paragraph, a specific but diplomatic action close.

The letter shown in Figure 9-3 includes a subject line with the introductory word "Re," still often used in many organizations. Also notice that the subject line is shown here above the salutation, not below it. The usual place is below the salutation, but if there is no attention line — and usually there won't be — the subject line may be placed in this position.

Requests for Adjustments or Refunds

Requests for adjustments, refunds, replacement of merchandise, modification of terms, or similar requests concerning merchandise or service, should all be considered as routine, to be arranged in the direct order, unless something about the situation indicates otherwise. Approaching the request directly indicates that you feel that there will be no hesitation in settling the matter.

These communications, like all others, should be pleasant, positive, and confident. Anger, sarcasm, or a demanding tone will be self-defeating, regardless of the extent of the dissatisfaction.

The usual and most desirable outlook of company personnel, when receiving requests for adjustment, should not be one of annoyance, but one of interest in finding out what happened and whether or not the customer is indeed entitled to an adjustment or refund.

They know that even the best products will at times be less than perfect; that accidents and errors occur; that employees, even themselves, can make mistakes. The customer also realizes these things, and the request letter should be approached in an attitude that reflects this outlook.

The next letter (Figure 9-4) requests replacement of boxes of candy — the boxes were empty!

The letter in Figure 9-5 also includes a subject line.

Other Direct Requests

An invitation is a direct request in that the reader's presence is requested. It is also a good-news message if it can be assumed that the reader is pleased to receive the invitation.

April 15, 1979

Mr. Nolan E. Wilson
NEW Enterprises
P. O. Box 3514
Memphis, TN   38103

Re: NEW Program 330

Dear Mr. Wilson:

The Trust Division of Union Planters is presently seeking
to update its EDP capabilities in regard to our accounts
receivable.

Your firm has been mentioned on several occasions as having
a program which would probably suit our needs. In order for
us to evaluate the program in detail, it will be necessary
for us to see a prospectus with pro forma printouts, so that
we may determine whether further discussions would be
appropriate.

Our EDP is processed on an IBM 360/55 and we have "on line-
real time" terminals with CRT capability.

Please submit your prospectus for the NEW Program 330 that
will interface with our existing EDP hardware. If you would
like to present a formal proposal, we would be most happy to
arrange a time convenient with your schedule.

Very truly yours,

Bruce L. Mitchell
Vice President
and Trust Officer
Project Manager

cm

Figure 9–3.   *Request for Computer Program Information. (Letterhead
used with permission of Union Planters National Bank of Memphis.
Letter content is fictitious.)*

December 24, 1978

Mr. William Roscoe
Roscoe's Candy Shop
1622 West Main Street
Little Rock, AR 76056

Dear Mr. Roscoe:

The request   SUBJECT: REQUEST FOR REPLACEMENTS OF EMPTY
                         CANDY BOXES RECEIVED DECEMBER 24

Thirteen of the twenty boxes (assorted variety, 5-pound
size) we purchased for Christmas gifts from Roscoe's
were empty, and thirteen secretaries went home without
Explanation   their usual Christmas gift.

The boxes were not unwrapped when they arrived, so there
must have been some mistake in the packing process. The
other seven boxes were in good condition.

As we think Roscoe's Candy is the best in town, will you
rush us thirteen replacements to arrive by December 29?
Action close   Will you also wrap these boxes with Happy New Year's
greetings?

Goodwill   We appreciate the prompt and courteous service you have
always given us.

Sincerely,

Laura Maxwell

Laura Maxwell
President

bt

Figure 9-4.   *Request for Replacement*

Notice that such a letter (see Figure 9-6) requires no specific and
definite action close because employees are not requested to make reservations.

Some direct requests can be as short as that in Figure 9-7.

April 27, 1979

Business Forms, Inc.
1212 Union Avenue
St. Louis, Missouri 52413

Gentlemen:

SUBJECT: IMPROPERLY PRINTED FORMS,
YOUR INVOICE 13705

Will you please rush more forms to replace these that   *The request*
were delivered yesterday?

At the time of delivery, it was not possible to tell that the
forms were improperly printed. When they were tested in
a trial run on the computer, however, it was evident that
the forms varied considerably.   *Explanation*

Changes that should be made are shown on the enclosed
sheet of specifications, which is a copy of the sheet sent
with the original order.

I am aware that errors like this will happen in spite of
precautions, and I am confident that you will take care of   *Goodwill*
this exchange with your usual efficiency.

Since we need the forms to print grade reports at the end
of next week, will you arrange to have them here by that   *Action close*
time?

Sincerely,

John Cotton

John Cotton, Manager
Computer Center

jj

Enclosure: specification sheet

Figure 9-5. *Request for Replacement*

September 17, 1978

Dear Fellow Employees:

The invitation (request)

You and your family are cordially invited to attend the Open House at our manufacturing laboratories and administrative and research headquarters on Sunday, September 30, from 1:30 to 4:30 p.m.

Explanation

Each family attending the Open House will receive a gift box containing many of the products we make, so be sure to bring this letter with you for your gift.

Refreshments will be served in the cafeteria and there will be drawings for valuable attendance prizes. All employees attending the Open House are eligible to win.

The enclosed Information Sheet contains your numbered ticket for the drawings so you can fill it out and drop in the drawing box when you arrive.

Goodwill and form of action close

We look forward to seeing you and your family and hope you will take this opportunity to meet your fellow employees and their families.

Sincerely,

Figure 9-6. *An Invitation*

FAVORABLE REPLIES AND OTHER GOOD-NEWS MESSAGES

Types of favorable communications discussed in this chapter are acknowledgments of orders, favorable replies to requests, and granted adjustments, plus miscellaneous messages.

Credit approvals are discussed with other writing about credit in Chapter 12. Replies describing products or services are considered as solicited sales messages and are discussed in Chapter 11. Informational letters about prospective employees are discussed in Chapter 14, with other letters about employment.

Gentlemen:

Please send me a copy of your spring and summer

plant catalog. My mailing address is

> Mrs. Harry Baker
> 1411 State Street
> Paradise, Arkansas 76123

Figure 9–7. *Short Request*

Acknowledgments

A letter of acknowledgment is not necessary for every order. In many instances, especially with a regular customer, filling the order exactly as instructed and shipping it immediately is acknowledgment enough, although a goodwill sentence or two or a "thank you" is appropriate on the invoice.

New customers should be sent a letter of acknowledgment and welcome with the first order. If credit is being granted, the terms should be exactly stated.

Sometimes an order cannot be shipped because the buyer has given incomplete information. Such replies, along with others that are not completely favorable, are discussed in Chapter 10.

Figure 9–8 is a simple acknowledgment of merchandise ordered from a company that sells specialty items by direct mail and through their catalogs. This letter is a printed form letter, as it must be if cost is to be considered. Customers realize that money spent for individually typewritten letters must be added to the price that they pay for merchandise. But the courteous tone and attractive appearance, even though the letter is obviously printed, no doubt builds goodwill and further sales for the company.

This letter was mailed separately to new customers, although it could have been included with the merchandise. A similar letter is included with the packaged items in subsequent orders. The letter is changed every few months so that customers receive different letters.

Favorable Replies

The letter in Figure 9–9 relates the good news in a single sentence first paragraph, using this emphatic position in the most advantageous way.

Dear Customer:

Courtesy and the
"good news"
    Thank you for your order. It is being shipped today
by parcel post, as you directed.

Goodwill
    We welcome you to the group of many fine folks who
are our customers. Some of them have been with us for
many years, and we feel that you will be, too.

    Look through the new fall catalog that is enclosed.
You will find many things that you can buy nowhere else in
the world. And of the other items that can be purchased
elsewhere, you will find no lower prices.

Sales promotion
    We guarantee your complete satisfaction. You will
be delighted with almost everything you purchase--we are
sure of this because of the experience of our other
customers--but in case you want to send something back
we'll be glad to take it with no questions asked.

Action close
    If you prefer, use your BankAmericard or Master
Charge. Just show your card number on the enclosed
order blank.

Sales promotion
    We'll bet you find at least five things in this new
catalog that you must have immediately.

                                    Sincerely yours,

Figure 9-8. *An Acknowledgment*

The next paragraph gives necessary details and requests necessary action from the reader, which is a slight variation of the usual pattern given earlier in this chapter in that the requested action is specified in the next-to-last paragraph.

The letter closes with a goodwill paragraph.

The letter in Figure 9-10 opens with the information that the requested brochures are being sent. The second paragraph is a low-pressure sales promotion paragraph; the third is an offer of further assistance, followed by a goodwill close. This letter requires no action close because no action is requested.

Figures 9-11 and 9-12 supply information requested from Ford Motor Company, evidently by persons other than dealers. These two letters are copies of ones actually mailed. The fictional names and ad-

April 26, 1979

Re: Construction Bids
     Project 76-6
     _____

Mr. Wiley Mayer
Mayer Construction Co., Inc.
438 38th Street
Eugene, OR 97601

Dear Mr. Mayer:

You are the successful bidder on Project 76-6.   *The good news*

Here are the original and two copies of the contract, which
have been signed by J. B. Harrington, Vice President.
Please sign the original and one copy and return them to   *Explanation and*
us. The other copy is for your file. With your acceptance   *instructions*
of this contract, you are released to begin construction.

Your time and effort in preparing this bid are appreciated.   *Goodwill*
We look forward to working with you on this project.

                          Sincerely yours, .

                          Mark David

                          Mark David
                          Staff Engineer

rt

Enclosures

Figure 9-9. *Good News*

dresses of the receivers were supplied by the public relations department
of Ford.

The letter in Figure 9–13 was written in response to a request from a
graduate student for information to use in a research study. The subject
line moves the message forward so that the first paragraph can be used to
begin the relaying of information.

April 9, 1979

Dear Mrs. Koleas:

The good news ⎰ We are pleased to send you some brochures on the points
⎱ of interest in and around Sunnyview Beach.

Sales promotion ⎰ The enclosed brochures will give you valuable information
⎱ concerning the names, locations, times, and dates of
operation of various attractions in this area.

Goodwill and ⎰ The Chamber of Commerce is here to serve the people who
offers of assistance ⎱ live and vacation in Sunnyview Beach. We are delighted to
know that you will visit our lovely city. If we can be of any
assistance to you and your family during your stay, just let
us know.

Have a safe and enjoyable vacation.

Sincerely,

Enclosures

Figure 9–10. *Sales Promotion*

Approved Adjustments

Figure 9–14 shows an adjustment letter, written in response to an adjustment request that appeared earlier in this chapter (Figure 9–4) for filled
candy boxes to replace the empty ones.

The approved adjustment letter shown in Figure 9–15 is in answer to
a claim — the chocolate chip ice cream had no chocolate chips.

Ford Motor Company

The American Road
Dearborn, Michigan 48121

July 22, 1976

Mr. John C. Doe
2421 Londonderry
Anyplace, Illinois 60604

Dear Mr. Doe:

We are glad to be of help with your inquiry about use of the Greyhound symbol in Ford Motor Company advertising.

The Greyhound was designed by the famed silversmith, Gorman, in 1925 to be used as a radiator ornament and symbol on the Lincoln car. The Greyhound radiator ornament was offered as an option in 1926 and as standard equipment in 1927.

A variation of the Greyhound ornament was offered as an optional accessory on Ford cars in 1933-34. While the design was used by Lincoln in certain of its advertisements, we can find no evidence that Ford advertising ever did so.

Since the Lincoln and Ford cars were both products of Ford Motor Company, and one used the design as a symbol while the other did not, we suggest that you and your friend submit your argument to impartial arbitration. We hope we have been helpful.

Sincerely,

J. W. Harris

J. W. Harris

Figure 9-11. *Information Supplied.* (*Used by permission of Ford Motor Company.*)

Ford Motor Company   The American Road
                                                      Dearborn, Michigan 48121

                                                      July 22, 1976

Mrs. Jane Doe
1375 Bardstown Trail
Hometown, New York 10024

Dear Mrs. Doe:

        Thank you for your letter expressing interest in the
possibility of owning and driving an electric automobile from
Ford Motor Company. We very much appreciate your enthusiasm for Ford products and your loyalty to them.

        As you have observed, the Company is deeply com-
mitted to giving our customers the kinds of cars they want
to own and use. In pursuit of this aim, we have carried on
for many years a large and ongoing research and development program into alternative means of propulsion. This
includes battery-powered electric motors for automobiles.

        The attached publication explaining some of our
activities in this field, particularly the section beginning
on page 13, might interest you.

        You can be assured that as soon as our engineers can
achieve the kind of durability, dependability, convenience and
economy that the average American motorist would demand of
a new type of engine, our Company will move quickly to put it
into production.

        In the meantime we will continue offering proven pro-
ducts that we hope will satisfy your needs.

                                      Sincerely,

                                      J. W. Harris

                                      J. W. Harris

Enclosure

Figure 9-12. *Product Information Supplied. (Used by permission of
Ford Motor Company.)*

Dear Miss Bell:

SUBJECT: Reply to your inquiry about the impact of
            shoplifting on Econo-Mart

Reasons for shoplifting can range anywhere from economic
need, emotional disturbances, and the lack of parental
supervision to peer pressure in the case of many juveniles.
The motives thus vary for individual shoplifters.

*Answer to one
question*

The prosecution policy at Econo-Mart is to bring charges
against anyone caught stealing merchandise--no matter how
small the goods are in value. A more lenient policy would
invite more pilferage.

Many shoplifters carry large bags and purses or wear
heavy outer clothing out of season in order to conceal
merchandise. Many shoplifters will also look around to
see if they are being followed. Regular shoppers are more
interested in the merchandise itself.

*Further
information*

Professionals account for the majority of stolen goods, or
about 80 percent. Since professionals steal to fence the
merchandise, they take more expensive items. You might
also be interested to know that there are schools located
right here in our city to teach the techniques of shoplifting
to professionals.

Good luck on your research paper, Miss Bell. If you have
any more questions, be sure to contact me or the manager
of one of the Econo-Mart stores.

*Goodwill and offer
of further
assistance*

Sincerely,

John Johnson

John Johnson, Security Officer

Figure 9-13. *Research Information Supplied*

December 26, 1978

Miss Laura Maxwell, President
Executive Suite
Sensuous Cosmetics
2547 East Raines Road
Little Rock, AR 76056

Dear Miss Maxwell:

The good news

The candy you requested is on its way and will arrive in time for your secretaries to enjoy it for the new year. All thirteen boxes have a decorative "Happy New Year" cover.

Explanation, goodwill, and sales promotion

Because your satisfaction is of real concern to us, we have made arrangements today to have all the packing equipment thoroughly inspected. We want to know why the boxes you received were not filled with our luscious and delightful candy. If this equipment needs replacing, it will be done-- long before you order candy next Christmas. (Have you thought of giving each employee a box of candy on his or her birthday?)

As you know, Roscoe's wraps and delivers candy for all occasions. We consider customers like you the main reason for our success.

Happy Holidays!

ROSCOE'S CANDY SHOP

Roscoe

Roscoe

Figure 9 –14. *Adjustment Reply*

July 14, 1978

Mr. Lester R. Childs
Lester's Market
Hwy. 66 West
Eads, TN 38123

Dear Mr. Childs:

The thirty half-gallons of chocolate chip ice cream you
requested are being rushed to your store at no charge.

The good news

Because your satisfaction is important to us, I immediately
contacted our Quality Control Department on this matter.
We found that a freak mechanical breakdown on the
production line caused chocolate chips to be left out of
several hundred half-gallons of chocolate chip ice cream.
Steps have been taken to prevent this situation from
happening again.

Goodwill and
explanation

After the driver delivers your fresh ice cream, he will
remove the ice cream without chips and dispose of it for
you.

Congratulations on the success of your new store.

Goodwill

Sincerely yours,

Robert Wiggins

Robert Wiggins
General Manager

Figure 9–15. *Approved Adjustment*

SUMMARY ◆ 9

The reader can be expected to react in one of these four ways to various business messages: with pleasure; with displeasure; with neither pleasure or displeasure but with interest; with neither pleasure, displeasure, nor a great deal of interest.

Business messages will fall (basically) into one of these categories: good news; bad news; neither good nor bad news, but with information of interest; and persuasive material.

Good-news and neutral messages are usually best arranged in the direct order. Bad-news messages are usually best arranged in the indirect order. Persuasive messages are usually best arranged in a modified indirect order — attention, interest, conviction, and action.

Frequent weaknesses of direct-approach messages are:

1. A grudging tone, especially in the granting of adjustments.
2. A slow opening, such as "We have received your letter" used instead of giving the good news or stating the request.
3. A dictatorial or demanding action close.
4. A doubtful, overly humble tone, as in "We hope this meets your approval."
5. Lack of complete information, a weakness that is especially likely to occur in order letters.
6. Stating the request in vague terms instead of in simple, direct, and specific ones.
7. Use of trite wording, such as "please be advised" and "enclosed please find" — a weakness of letters of all kinds.
8. Ending the letter with an inadequate action close, when action is desired, or without a goodwill close. (Although we don't want to make letters much longer than they need be to convey the necessary information, ending abruptly seems hurried and discourteous.)

QUESTIONS AND PROBLEMS ◆ 9

1. Prepare to dictate a simple request. (Assume situations and topics.) Make notes as to what to include in the first paragraph; the middle paragraph or paragraphs; the closing paragraph.
2. In the way that you have just planned a request, (Question 1) plan a good-news letter; a neutral, informational message. (Assume situations and topics.)

3. Find examples of good-news letters; direct inquiries and requests; and neutral, informational messages. Analyze these communications and make suggestions for needed improvements.

4. Analyze the following letter, which was written by your new correspondence supervisor. It was intended as an adjustment approval.

Dear Mrs. Devine:

   After reciving your telephone call this morning in regards to our shipment of Valentine cards, I can easily appreciate your concern. Recieving Valentine cards two days after Valentine's Day not only does not generate sales it is an inconvenience to you.

   After checking our records, I find that those cards were send to our shipping dock on February 12. I have interviewed our dock foreman who explains to me that your order was apparently set down with your order of Easter cards and shipped after Valentine's day to avoid overloading your store with cards. Please return this order to us freight collect and accept my personal apoligies for your inconvenience. We don't want to lose you as one of our best customers.

   Yours truly,

5. Rewrite the letter analyzed in Problem 4.

Problems — Order Letters

6. While reading *Journal of Retailing*, you see an advertisement by the Jamison Company, 7290 South Florence Road, Chicago, Illinois 34298 for antique bottles. These antique bottles would make the perfect addition to your gift shop. The ad specified the different types of bottles ranging from small Coke bottles to big milk bottles. The price varies, but each bottle is designed to provide the retailer with a 30 percent markup.

   For your first order, you will order a dozen Coke bottles at $1 each and a dozen big milk bottles at $3 each. You want the order sent by parcel post within ten days. Enclose a certified check for the cost of the bottles. You don't know the postage charges. Ask them to prepay the postage and send you a bill — or, if they won't do this, to let you know and you will pay the postage upon arrival.

7. You are in need of several teacher's manuals and tests that accompany texts used in your classroom. You need these items by April 1, so you ask Mr. Walter Greenway, the textbook representative in your area, to send them air express. You have established credit with the company and will pay for the items in the usual manner — payment upon receipt. You will order the following:

- 1 Placement test manual for typewriting placement tests, T-703 and T-704.
- 1 Teacher's manual for *Machine Office Practice Set*, 2nd ed., Cornelia and Agnew.
- 5 sets each of G-133 and G-134 — Tests and Examination for first and second semester, *General Business for Economic Understanding*, 10th ed., DeBrum, Haines, Malsbary, and Crabbe.

The tests are 30 cents a set. There is no charge for the manuals. (You know Mr. Greenway well. His address is 5050 Briarcrest Road, Cincinnati, Ohio 28976.)

8. You want to order six dozen shirts of a new style that you have seen in a direct mail advertisement sent to you by Campus Wear Company, 3140 Kellwood, La Puento, CA 86703. The shirts are offered in three sizes (small, medium, and large) and in two colors (yellow and blue). You need one dozen shirts of each size in each color. Order the shirts (Style No. 2293a) and charge them to your account. You work for Evans and Company, 201 W. 7th Street, Norwood, New Mexico 87421. The price of the shirts is $73.30 a dozen and your firm normally buys on terms of 3/15, n/30.

Problems — Request for Information about a Product or Service

9. Write the manufacturer of some item in which you are interested, such as a camera or skin diving equipment. Think of all the qualities of the item that are important to you — all the information you will need before you make this rather important decision. Request this information. Ask for the names of local dealers.

10. Write to a competitor of the manufacturer you addressed in Problem 9. Ask for the same information.

11. You are the manager of a large office building. You are not satisfied with the appearance of the floors in the building. Write Central Janitor Supplies, at an address in your city, and ask that a representative visit your building to make recommendations for the proper maintenance. The floors are of vinyl tile and hardwood. Some of the offices are carpeted.

12. You are David Rose, Manager of Quality Office Supply Company. You are interested in a new product mentioned to you by one of your regular customers. He has seen a new type of paper shredder, the JNS-331, advertised in *The Wall Street Journal*. His firm is in the market for a shredder and would like more information pertaining to the features of the JNS-331. Write a letter of inquiry to Electric Wastebasket Corporation, 145 W. 45th Street, New York, NY 10036. Inquire about the specifications, features, and qualities of the JNS-331 machine. You should also find out about the availability of the machines, dealer discounts, and the distribution system.

13. You are the office manager of Bertagna Real Estate Company. You want to buy a photocopy machine — a fairly inexpensive one. Find in your local telephone directory the names of organizations that sell photocopiers. Write a letter of inquiry that is to be sent to the potential suppliers. Ask questions

to obtain all the information you will need before you decide upon a particular model.

14.   You are Traffic Supervisor of WOW Industries, Inc. The organization is in need of additional warehouse space. Since sales have been climbing rapidly during the past decade, warehouse space is inadequate to house all component supplies, raw materials, and finished merchandise. Additional space is needed immediately, but several aspects of the problem must be considered.

Management is presently considering a proposal for an automated high-rise warehouse. You must remain flexible with options for space rented now and prefer to rent the space with no longer than a one-year renewable lease. Your products are regulated by the Federal Drug Administration; you must have a warehouse that will comply with all regulations concerning clean and safe storage areas. Price is also critical in the decision. You need a warehouse that has adequate insurance in case of fire or any other type of disaster.

You have been given the job to find the necessary space. Write a letter that can be sent to several public warehouses in the area of your plant. Names and addresses will be shown on the finished letters.

Problems — Requests for Action, Items, or General Information; Instructional Material

15.   As volunteer coordinator of a mental health center, you are requested to suggest a specific training program for your own job. You have been on the job only a few months and realize you need some outside training. You would like to gather information in the following areas: (1) organizing, developing, and monitoring volunteer programs; and (2) recruiting, training, and supervising volunteers. You have met with a volunteer director who has recently attended a volunteer training program in Boulder, Colorado. She highly recommends the program and suggests that you inquire about it. The director of the program is Miss Mary Cannon, Continuing Education, University of Colorado, Boulder, Colorado 56342.

16.   You are chairman of the committee responsible for planning a professional growth meeting for the business education teachers of your city's school system. The meeting is to be held Friday, May 16, from 8 a.m. to 3 p.m. You expect approximately 50 people to attend. You would like a coffee break at 9:45 and luncheon at 12:15. Coffee and doughnuts are to be served during the break.

Write to a hotel in your city requesting accommodations for the meeting. Request suggested menus and prices for the luncheon and coffee break, along with the amount of the fee for use of the rooms. You will need four small conference rooms for section meetings and one large conference room for the general meeting. Ask for a microphone and projection screen for use during the general meeting.

17.   You are a teacher of business communication courses at the University of

Maine. You want an examination copy of this textbook. (Assume that you have seen a copy in a library.) Write the publisher for a complimentary examination copy. State the title of the course or courses in which you could use this book, when and where these courses are offered, and at what level (sophomore level, junior level, senior level, other), the approximate number of students each semester, and the title of your present text. (Assume any necessary and reasonable details.)

18. You are the president of your local chapter of the American Association of University Women. Write a memorandum or notice to members of the organization. The next monthly meeting will be at the home of Mrs. Robert Barry (Ruth) at 211 Cherry Road. Topics to be discussed are suggested changes in the national charter and local support of the city library. A special guest is Miss Rose Tunney, a native of your city, who is now a nationally known poet. She is a graduate of Sarah Lawrence College.

19. Write a memorandum to employees you supervise giving instructions for a change in procedure. This change is not likely to arouse resentment or resistance.

20. Write an announcement to members of an organization to which you belong. Give the gist of the message in the first paragraph. Use real or imaginary details.

21. Write a memorandum to other students. Summarize a lecture from some class other than this one. Use the direct arrangement, with the first paragraph serving as a brief summary of the entire lecture.

22. Write a letter to business education teachers in your city. Tell them about the meeting you planned in Problem 16. Urge them to attend. Assume reasonable details.

Problems — Requests for Adjustments
(Claims)

23. You, Lester R. Childs, have recently opened a new grocery store. You have chosen Sealfresh Foods to supply ice cream to your store. The chocolate chip ice cream in your last delivery had no chocolate chips in it. Your customers who bought this ice cream have complained and demanded their money back. Write to Sealfresh.

24. Several weeks ago you ordered from Thataway Fashions, Inc., 125 Sycamore, New York, NY 10027 a pair of slacks at their special price of $29.95. As they have done in the past, they made prompt delivery and sent the slacks in time for the office picnic. You tried the slacks on when they arrived and found them to be a perfect fit.

On the day of the picnic, you wore the new slacks and received several compliments. You decided to play in a softball game, and then it happened! You stooped over to pick up the ball and your slacks ripped straight down the middle. Write a letter to Thataway Fashions, Inc. explaining the situation and requesting an adjustment.

25. On March 3 you ordered 5,000 multi-form statement forms from PDQ Print

Shop and were promised delivery in 30 days.   April 3 passed without delivery.   You placed a call to PDQ on April 5 requesting information as to when to expect the forms.   The manager promised delivery no later than the 15th.

PDQ delivered 5,000 statement forms to the bank on April 30 with an invoice for $315.   Upon inspection you find the forms to be sheets of carbon paper rather than noncarbon duplicating paper, as specified.   Also, all copies were white instead of the color that you ordered.   Write to Mr. Robert M. Martin, PDQ manager.

26.   You have just received a prepaid order, No. 3201, from Stereo Equipment, 4646 Poplar, your city, for two rolls of recording tape.   Upon opening the package you notice there is only one roll of tape, but the invoice shows two rolls.   Write Mr. H. Owen, Customer Service Representative.   Tell him of the situation and request that he complete the order by mailing you the missing roll of tape.

27.   Are you now using a product that has been less than satisfactory?   Do you feel that you are honestly entitled to a refund or an adjustment?   If so, write the required letter to the retailer or manufacturer, as appropriate.   Mail the letter.

Problems — Order Acknowledgments

28, 29, 30.   Write the acknowledgment letter for each of the orders in Problems 6, 7, and 8.   You have all the merchandise and are filling the orders exactly as requested.   Assume reasonable and necessary details.

Problems — Favorable Replies to Inquiries about a Product or Service

31.   Assume that you are a representative of the publishing company to which you wrote in Problem 17.   Write a letter to the teacher of business communication saying that you are sending the book by parcel post.   Include any sales promotion paragraphs that you feel are appropriate.

32.   Write to a friend who is interested in buying the item or items you investigated in Problems 9 and 10.

Based on the information you have received from both manufacturers, recommend one brand over the other.   Give reasons and detailed information in order that your recommendation will be convincing.   (This problem may be delayed until later in the semester so that you will have time to receive the desired information.   Or, as your teacher directs, assume details and check later with the exact information received from the manufacturers.)

33.   Assume that you are a manufacturer's representative with the responsibility of answering inquiries such as those you wrote in Problems 9 and 10.   Give complete information about some product or service that you know well.   (This does not need to be the same product or service about which you requested information.)

34. You have been asked to serve on the Traffic Appeals Committee of your college or university. Write Mr. Edwin Rommel, Assistant Dean of Students, accepting the appointment.

35. You are the manager of the Central Janitor Supplies Company. Write the manager of the office building (Problem 11) and tell him that you will be glad to send a consultant. Arrange for a convenient time.

36. Assume that you are employed by the Chargecard Company. Write a letter enclosing an application blank for a Chargecard. This card has been requested by telephone by Mr. Samuel Fenner, 211 Blackstone Avenue, Nevada, Iowa 50201. (This is not a credit approval — his credit will be investigated after he fills in and returns the application blank.)

37. Write a memorandum to all employees in your company. (You are the personnel manager.) Beginning on the first of next month, each employee will receive a 10 percent increase in the amount of life insurance provided by the company. (All life insurance is provided at no cost to the employee.)

Problems — Approved Adjustments

38, 39, 40. Reply to the requests for adjustment you wrote in Problems 24, 25, and 26. You are granting all adjustments. Assume reasonable details.

41. If you have received an answer to your request for adjustment (Problem 27), analyze the letter according to what you have learned about effective letters. If your request was refused, compare the letter with the principles (given next, in Chapter 10) for bad-news letters.

Writing About the Unpleasant and the Uncertain

10

The kinds of communications discussed in this chapter should ordinarily be arranged in the indirect order. These letters and memorandums fall into two categories, according to the expected reader reaction:

1. Messages with which the reader will be displeased or will have little initial interest.
2. Messages for which the reader reaction cannot be predicted.

This chapter combines the consideration of unfavorable messages with that of messages that must convince, or "sell," as in persuasive requests. These two types of letters or memorandums are quite similar in overall approach and in the sequence of ideas. Not included in this discussion are more specialized kinds of persuasive writing, which are presented in following chapters: sales letters, applications for employment, and credit and collection letters.

In persuasive requests, we must sell the reader on complying with the request. As in all sales messages, the reader accepts, or "buys," because he believes in the product and in the seller, and, usually, because he believes that the purchase will be to his benefit. Even if there is no tangible benefit to the reader, he may be convinced to comply with the request if he is sufficiently convinced that the writer is sincere and that the cause is a worthy one.

PLANNING DISAPPOINTING OR
UNFAVORABLE MESSAGES

A sincere you-attitude, desirable in all communication, is absolutely essential for diplomatic bad-news messages. Even when the request must be absolutely and completely refused, which may often be the case, you are using the you-attitude when you look at the situation from the other person's point of view and present your message from that standpoint.

Remember — in most unfavorable communications you should use the indirect order of arrangement; do not begin with the negative statement. Open with some pleasant aspect of the situation if you can find one. If there is no aspect that can be considered pleasant, open with a neutral statement or agree with the reader about something.

A suggested outline for unpleasant messages is shown below:

1. Buffer. Usually one paragraph but can be two. Tells what the letter is about but does not state the obvious. Says neither yes nor no. Pleasant and relevant. Leads naturally to the following paragraphs.
2. Explanation and analysis of situation. Reasons for refusal or other decision.
3. Decision, stated diplomatically or (preferably) clearly implied. If indicated, an alternative or counterproposal. Decision presented as much as possible in terms of reader benefit.
4. A friendly, positive close: a related idea that takes the emphasis away from the refusal or bad news. If appropriate, low-pressure sales promotion, resale, or action close based on the counterproposal.

As has been previously stated, you may find exceptions to the patterns of arrangements that are usually desirable. In a few instances you may actually want to emphasize an unpleasant idea by stating it first, as in some late-stage collection letters. In all letters, however, we must continue to be concerned with courtesy.

The Buffer

The buffer paragraph is planned to get in step with the reader. Dangers to avoid are implying that the answer will be *yes*; stating or implying that the answer is to be *no*; beginning too far away from the subject; seeming to "beat around the bush."

Do not apologize, either in the buffer section or elsewhere, for refusing a request; to do so weakens your explanation of why the request cannot be granted.   Although at all times we should apologize when an apology is due, a refusal letter requires not an apology but courtesy — and, for the sake of goodwill, justification.

Consider these openings for a disappointing communication:

1. Some pleasant aspect of the situation.

2. Agreement or understanding: if you agree with some point of the reader's letter to you, say so.   Show an understanding of the reader's needs or problems.

3. Appreciation: say "thank you" for information, a check, application, or whatever applies — but make sure that the expression of thanks makes sense and is sincere.   Do not use such phrases as "We were happy to receive your request —" if the request is to be denied.   (Why are you happy — because you have an opportunity to refuse?)

4. Assurance: show that careful consideration and investigation occurred before the decision was made.

5. Cooperation: show a sincere desire to be as reasonable and helpful as possible.

6. Sympathy: a simple expression of sympathy such as "I'm sorry —" is appropriate in serious situations or in all other instances if the expression is sincere.

7. Resale: use only if appropriate; and use this approach subtly and wisely so as to avoid a glaring I-attitude.

As mentioned in Chapter 6, the term "resale" re-emphasizes the value of goods and services already purchased.   "Sales promotion" usually refers to future purchases.   The term resale, or "resale of the house," is sometimes used to rebuild confidence in the company itself.   Like all sales messages, resale should be sincere,   specific, and worded in terms of reader interest.

Details and Reasons for the Unfavorable Decision

Use a positive, helpful approach, and give pleasant, convincing reasons. In some instances you will be unable or unwise to give exact, specific reasons because of the need for confidentiality or because the explanation would be very long and involved.   Do not appear evasive in these instances, but emphasize that the request has been carefully and sincerely considered.

Do not use such phrases as:

1. "It's against company policy —"   This is a blanket excuse that is usually meaningless to the reader, as well as being somewhat

insulting and arbitrary.   (The reader may think, "Well, why don't they change the stupid policy?") To the reader, you *are* the company, or at least you express the procedures and the outlook of the company.

In addition, do not pass the buck or blame someone else in your company, or do not imply that you would comply except for "company policy."   If you think that company policies should be changed, suggest these changes, after you have been employed long enough to understand the procedures and to make sure that you are right.   But until they are changed, follow them without criticism.   To do otherwise is disloyalty.

2.   "We cannot afford to —"   A statement like this is the I-attitude, not the you-attitude.

3.   "We must reject —" ("turn down," "refuse," "disappoint you," or other negative terms.)   Also avoid, as much as possible, the use of grammatical negatives, such as "no," and "cannot."   In addition, avoid negative words that refer to the problem, such as "failure," "defective," "inferior" and "trouble."

4.   "You surely understand —"   "Please understand —" or other dictatorial or condescending terms.

5.   "We were surprised at your request —" suggests that the customer is unreasonable.   So is the implication that because all other customers are satisfied with the product he must just be a complainer.

6.   "You claim —" "you state —" or other phrases suggesting disbelief.

Perhaps you may feel that all the "don'ts" given above leave little for you to say in giving details and reasons.   As in all communication situations, however, your sincere and accurate reasoning, stated diplomatically and in terms of the reader's interest, is your best guide to an acceptable psychological approach.

The Decision

The reader must understand your decision; this is of first importance.   An implied decision, however, can be completely clear, as you will notice in some of the following examples.

If the decision can be clearly implied, do not use an "I cannot" expression.   For example, if you say "We sell only to retailers," you do not need to add the statement, "therefore, we cannot sell to you, an individual consumer."

If there is a possibility that the decision will be misunderstood, state it plainly and clearly, even if you must use a "cannot" or similar expression. But state it after most of the explanatory material has been given.   Although we wish to subordinate the unpleasant, it is even more important that the reader understand what we are saying.

Remember the principles of emphasis and use the reverse procedures to subordinate the refusal or the other unpleasant news.   You make use of a principle of subordination when you move the statement or implication of the decision away from the opening section of the letter, as well as when you refrain from mentioning the unpleasant news in the emphatic last paragraph.   Also remember that exact, vivid, and specific words emphasize, while more general words are softer in expressing unwelcome news.

As a one-sentence paragraph is emphatic, do not express the bad news in a short sentence standing alone.

Try to include with the expression of the unfavorable news some positive aspect of the situation, or offer a counterproposal.   For instance, if you cannot grant credit, offer a special discount for cash or suggest a layaway plan.   Or, as illustrated in one of the following letters, instead of allowing a group of school children to visit your plant, offer to send a film or to postpone the trip until next year.

Resale can be used, when appropriate, in the decision section of the letter as well as in the remaining sections.

A Courteous, Positive Ending

Do not refer to the unfavorable news in the emphatic closing paragraph.

You may need an action close.   Perhaps you have suggested an alternative and have asked the reader to make some decision.   Such an action close will be similar to those used in other kinds of messages.   As in all letters, avoid a demanding or "hard-sell" tone.

Resale or sales promotion material can be effectively used in the closing section of a disappointing message, but make sure that such material is appropriate and diplomatic for the particular situation.

Don't close with a suggestion of further trouble, as in "If you have this problem again —" Also , don't express doubt that the decision will be accepted, as in "We hope this meets your approval" or "We hope you will not be disappointed."   Even worse, don't imply that you fear you will lose a customer, as in "We hope you will keep on doing business with us."

Don't offer future help if it will give an appearance of insincerity. For example, if you have been able to do absolutely nothing for the reader, don't end with "If we can help further —" or "Call on us again if —."

REFUSING A REQUEST

Requests are made for many purposes. Some seem completely unwarranted, presumptuous, and absolutely ridiculous to the person receiving the request. In most instances, though, the request seems valid and reasonable to the person making it.

You should assume that the person is sincere and plan the reply from this standpoint. Even if the person has in mind "getting something for nothing," a courteous reply will perhaps make him sorry that he tried to hoodwink such a helpful, cooperative organization that had the good sense to refuse his outrageous request.

The example letter shown in Figure 10-1 is a refusal to serve as a guest speaker. Notice that nowhere in the letter is there a direct refusal, such as "I cannot" or "I must refuse." But the answer is obvious — the speaker cannot be in Atlanta on May 21 because he must be in Washington.

The letter in Figure 10-2 is a modification of the preceding one. It is given here to illustrate the principle that the usual patterns of arrangement can be varied somewhat to achieve an equally effective message. In this version of the letter, the "no" is implied in the first paragraph by the "I would not miss it under normal circumstances." The overall tone of the letter is considerate.

You should learn the "patterns" that are usually best — beginning "yes" letters with the "yes," and "no" letters with a well-chosen buffer. You should realize, however, that these patterns are not the only possible arrangement for effective written or oral communications.

The letter in Figure 10-3 also refuses by implication. The refusal is presented in terms of reader benefit — the safety of the children. (You will not always have such a convenient and convincing reason.) This letter offers two counterproposals: the film and the offer of a trip for next year. Perhaps the writer had furnished films previously to the school or he would have asked whether the teacher wanted this particular one. Under all circumstances, this question would probably have been a wiser choice.

The letter to Mrs. Rose La Plume (see Figure 10-4) also refuses by implication, but the meaning is quite clear.

WRITING UNFAVORABLE MESSAGES ABOUT A PRODUCT OR SERVICE

A company will not always be able to provide the merchandise that the customer has requested. The product may be discontinued, temporarily

April 14, 1979

Mr. George W. Montgomery
Atlanta Community Action Agency
149 Tanner Building
Atlanta, Georgia 30603

Dear Mr. Montgomery:

I am delighted to know that you and your agency are hosting
the May 21 meeting of the National Association of CAP
Directors. I am sure it will be a most successful and
informative meeting.

Buffer

As you know, I took this position only a few weeks ago, and
there has been a need for a great deal of reorganization.
In addition to this, I have had to keep several commitments
already made by my predecessor. This is the case for
May 21.

Reasons

At that time, I must appear before the Joint Committee in
Washington regarding the new bill affecting CAP agencies.
As the passage of this bill is important for your agency, as
well as for all others around the country, I am sure you
can understand the importance of my presence there.

*Decision in terms
of reader interest*

From all indications you are doing a superb job in Atlanta.
All of the comments I hear are quite favorable. How about
sharing your secret with me?

Goodwill close

                    Sincerely yours,

                    James D. Phillips

                    James D. Phillips
                    Regional Director

JDP:jmo

Figure 10-1. *Implied Refusal to Serve as Guest Speaker*

April 14, 1979

Mr. George W. Montgomery
Atlanta Community Action Agency
149 Tanner Building
Atlanta, Georgia 30603

Dear Mr. Montgomery:

Goodwill opening, with implied decision

I am delighted to know that you and your agency are hosting the May 21 meeting of the National Association of CAP Directors. I am sure it will be a successful meeting, and I would not miss it under normal circumstances.

Reasons

As you know, however, I took this position only a few weeks ago, and there has been a need for a great deal of reorganization. In addition to this, I have had to keep several commitments already made by my predecessor. This is the case for May 21.

Decision in terms of reader interest

At that time, I must appear before the Joint Committee in Washington regarding the new bill affecting CAP agencies. As the passage of this bill is important for your agency, as well as for all others around the country, I am sure you can understand the importance of my presence there.

Goodwill close

From all indications you are doing a superb job in Atlanta. All of the comments I hear are quite favorable. How about sharing your secret with me?

Sincerely yours,

James D Phillips

James D. Phillips
Regional Director

JDP:jmo

Figure 10-2. *Modification of Implied Refusal to Serve*

out of stock, in short supply and reserved for regular customers, or sold to retailers only and not available to individuals. Or perhaps the merchandise cannot be shipped because the buyer sent incomplete information; these replies must be planned with special consideration in order to avoid an implication of accusation.

April 21, 1979

Miss Emily Harrison
Oakview Elementary School
2112 Oakview Boulevard
Rumney, NH 03266

Dear Miss Harrison:

Your students can certainly benefit from educational field trips. A modern dairy in operation can be a fascinating and educational place for youngsters to visit.

Buffer

For a number of years we have welcomed classes from your school. In addition to providing a tour of the dairy, we have taken precautions to insure that their visits are not only enjoyable but completely safe.

Continuation of buffer and a transition to reasons

To maintain our plant's peak efficiency, we are currently replacing some of our older pasteurizing machines with newer models. I feel that the process of moving this heavy machinery into and out of the plant may pose a safety hazard to any children present at the time. I am sure you will agree, Miss Harrison, that the safety of the children comes first.

Reasons and implied refusal

As the current school year will end before our new equipment is completely installed, I am sending your school a full color film that explains all about the operation of a dairy.

Counteroffer

Our plant will be back to normal by the beginning of the next school year. At that time, we will be happy to arrange a tour for you and your class.

Another counteroffer

Sincerely yours,

Robert Smith

Robert Smith
General Manager

Figure 10-3. *Refusal by Implication*

April 4, 1979

Mrs. Rose La Plume
Clean Air Committee
999 Dawson Avenue
Manitowoc, Wisconsin 54220

Dear Mrs. La Plume:

Buffer

> You are right--pollution is a problem with which all America must be concerned. It is a problem that needs action, such as the action initiated by your organization, which is currently sponsoring the program "Help Us Breathe Fresh Air."

Reasons

> The colored smoke being emitted by the Bright Aluminum Company at our plant located at Novak and Jogodensky streets has been a concern of ours for some time. Your request to correct this situation immediately gives us an opportunity to make our position known.
>
> This particular plant employs 2,575 citizens of our community, people whose livelihood depends on that plant. To correct the problem immediately would mean a temporary dismissal of all those people for five to six months--what would you do, faced with this decision?

Decision

> We have been conducting research which will lead to an eventual solution in two or three years without a shutdown. Since the smoke is no serious danger to the health of our community, according to government scientists, we believe that the financial welfare of 2,575 citizens, as well as that of the entire community, must be given first priority.

Goodwill close

> We do appreciate your concern. You are to be commended for your efforts and leadership in the Clean Air Committee, which is certainly a worthwhile organization.

Sincerely,

George R. Yohanek

George R. Yohanek
President

jn

Figure 10-4. *Another Refusal by Implication*

Regardless of the reason for the refused or delayed shipment, the letter in explanation is basically a bad-news message and should be arranged in the sequence of ideas used for other refused requests.

Avoid such expressions as "you failed to state the color" or "you did not state the color."

Figure 10–5 conveys the information that the order cannot be filled because the customer did not state the desired colors of paint and because the tablets are temporarily out of stock. Notice that the letter opens with the favorable portion of the information. The "next year" in the last paragraph is appropriate because this order had been planned as the last one of the present school year.

The letter shown in Figure 10–6 must tell a customer that a substantial order, already delayed for six months, has been delayed an additional three weeks. In addition, the price has increased.

REFUSING AN ADJUSTMENT

According to the outlook of most business establishments, some requests for adjustments must be refused, or some compromise must be made.

As this refusal or compromise is explained, the writer must be concerned with maintaining goodwill, just as in all comumunications. Outstanding adjustment letters can do more to keep customers and build sales — at least as to the particular customers receiving the letters — than expensive advertising campaigns and extensive sales promotion procedures.

Some companies seem to take the position that the customer is always right, regardless of the particular occurrence. Although some large organizations that follow this policy seem to prosper (no doubt the absolute and unconditional guarantee of satisfaction builds public confidence), to accede to all requests for refunds or adjustments, regardless of merit, is forcing customers who do not make unreasonable demands to subsidize those who do.

In your writing or oral communication about adjustments you will of necessity follow the set and expected procedures of the organization. If the choice is yours, fairness to all customers seems to indicate that you should determine each adjustment situation on its individual merit.

In adjustment letters, whether they are granted or refused, you should subordinate references to the weaknesses of the product or service. Remember to use specific words to emphasize, general ones to subordinate.

For example, you are being too specific in this sentence: "You say that your washing machine runs over every time you use it and floods your

April 7, 1979

Ms. Jan Jarnagin
Southside Elementary School
805 Roan Street
Northville, MI 48167

Dear Ms. Jarnagin:

Good news

You will receive your order of Judy's paint brushes, assorted crayons, colored chalk, poster board, and assorted construction paper early Monday morning, April 19.

Bad news

Your 35 tablets of 18" by 32" art paper will reach you by May 5. The unique finishing of this art paper makes it especially adaptable to the classroom--it has become so popular that we are in short supply. We placed a rush order for art paper today and have reserved 35 tablets.

Action

So that we may be sure of sending the paint colors you need this term, will you check the desired color combination on the enclosed card? We will deliver all 45 cans to your school within two days after we know your choice.

Goodwill close

We are always happy to serve a professional like you in the field of art.

Sincerely,

Jo Williams

Jo Williams
Owner

P.S. Look through the enclosed catalog. Perhaps you can begin to plan your supply order for the fall semester. We will be glad to take your order now and have it delivered whenever you wish.

Figure 10-5. *Order Not Filled — Two Reasons*

April 7, 1978

Dear Mr. Jacobs:

Your order of October 6 for 94,000 cases of steel bearings, Catalog No. 7212, will be shipped to you on April 27. We appreciate your patience in waiting for this shipment of the finest quality bearings.

The good news

Unusual circumstances have caused this delay, and, as you know, we will not compromise on quality. The technical difficulty that caused the shutdown in our plant has now been corrected. All your future orders can be shipped immediately, we feel sure.

Explanation

Since Mirror Ball Bearing Company is very price competitive, it is therefore very sensitive to variable cost increases. The price of $4.51 a case reflects our own inflationary cost increases. This new price is still one of the lowest in the industry, and we believe that this savings will justify this temporary delay.

The bad news

We appreciate the courtesy you have always extended to our representative, John Williams. He is to retire in July. A young man just out of college, Gene Simpson, is to take his place. They will both call on you early in May.

Goodwill close

Sincerely,

Figure 10-6. *Additional Delay in Filling Order*

kitchen floor." This sentence is bad from at least three standpoints. First, the "you say" indicates disbelief. Second, you are wasting both reader and writer time by repeating what the writer told you. Third, you are recalling much too vividly the cause of customer dissatisfaction.

This situation is not one that lends itself to a positive description, regardless of the skill of the writer. (Have you ever mopped a flooded kitchen floor?) Here, though, the words "problem" or "trouble," although negative in themselves in most instances, are preferable to these exact, descriptive words. Even better — make your answer clear without using negative words of any kind.

Use resale, when appropriate, to re-emphasize the value of goods or service, but use discretion. Telling the customer that it is a fine washing machine when the customer is mopping the kitchen floor is not exactly convincing. Neither is the fact that the machine was bought at a reduced rate.

In Figure 10–7, the letter is in reply to a customer who wants to return a pair of slacks bought at closeout sale. The goods were marked as damaged merchandise and sold at up to 75 percent off. Large signs read "All Sales Final." This notation was also shown on the sales ticket. The white slacks had yellow spots on them that could not be removed. This customer had also bought several other items, which she did not return.

A letter in reply to a person who rents equipment to tenants is shown in Figure 10–8. The unit has been submerged, perhaps in the suds and water used for cleaning carpets. The instruction book and warranty both warn that the unit cannot be submerged.

WRITING PERSUASIVE REQUESTS

Persuasive requests are arranged in the indirect order — that is, you do not open with the request, as you do in direct requests and inquiries.

Although the opening paragraph may differ somewhat from the buffer paragraph used for disappointing messages, the plan is basically the same. The first paragraph is planned to include some aspect of the situation in which the reader is likely to be interested in order to attract favorable attention. (Direct requests were discussed in the preceding chapter.)

At times you may not be sure whether a particular request should be classified as one that the reader will be happy to grant, or as one that will require persuasion. And in some instances, requests that require a great deal of explanation and sales approach in order to be convincing can be effectively arranged in the direct order. Opening with the direct request, followed by convincing, you-approach details, is far more effective than leaving the reader wondering through several paragraphs what the letter is all about.

In usual practice, though — and in your problems in this course unless your instructor directs otherwise — do not open a persuasive request with a statement of the request itself. Persuasive requests are most effective when they are arranged like sales letters, which in effect they are. The time-honored arrangement of sales letters is this:

- *Attention*. One line may be enough — or even one word.
- *Interest*. Introduce the product, service, or idea.
- *Desire (or conviction)*. Present evidence in terms of reader benefit.

May 7, 1978

Mrs. R. W. Feller
Route 2, Box 506
Kenbridge, VA 23944

Dear Mrs. Feller:

We are glad you enjoyed our annual spring sale last week. As the city's largest retail sports merchandiser, we take pride in offering you quality as well as the lowest prices in town.

Buffer

Reasonable prices and frequent sales are a major reason you shop with us, we feel sure. At all sales, we invite you to try on the merchandise and thoroughly inspect it before you take it home. These low prices are possible because we grant returns only for regularly priced merchandise.

Reasons and decision

The first week of May we will have on display a new line of clothes--the Doris May Playwear. Come in to see us. When you buy $25 worth of merchandise, you are eligible for a 10 percent discount.

Sales promotion

Sincerely,

Mary Vaughn

Mary Vaughn
Customer Service Representative

Figure 10-7. *Refusal of Adjustment*

- *Action.* The action close is similar to that in other kinds of letters. Specify action, make action easy, motivate prompt action, if appropriate, or set a reasonable and convincing deadline. Bring in reader benefit if possible.

A sales letter is a persuasive request to buy. The same pattern of arrangement is shown in Figure 10-9. The first paragraph attracts attention and leads to the discussion of the idea. The middle paragraphs build interest and conviction, as does the last paragraph, which also includes an action close, but without a specified date.

September 10, 1978

Mr. Edward Simpson
5069 Hopkins Road
Redondo Beach, CA 90277

Dear Mr. Simpson:

Buffer

You have every right to expect nothing but the best possible service from Ezy-Clean products. We take great pride in every cleaner bearing our label and are determined to stand behind the reputation we have established during the past thirty years here in Redondo Beach.

Reasons

Because we are continually striving for better service and finer products, we examined closely the Model 3-A unit you recently sent us. This examination disclosed several deposits of water buildup within the unit, indicating that it had been submerged to some extent.

Reasons

If the cleaner remains on the small roll-about platform that is sold with it, there is no danger of shampoo suds or water entering the unit. We believe that one or more of your tenants who rent your equipment removed the platform and let water and suds enter the unit. As we have known this limitation of all products in the Ezy-Clean line--that they cannot be submerged--we have clearly stated a warning in all advertising and on the metal plate attached to the side of each cleaner.

Decision

Although this unit is beyond repair because of the water, to show our appreciation for the years you have been our customer we will take the cleaner as a trade on a new one, counting it as one-third of the purchase price. And you will be glad to know that this new model is permanently attached to a small, light platform.

Action close

To receive this new cleaner for only $124 (the usual price is $186), return the enclosed card. Our delivery truck will bring it the next day.

Sincerely,

Dave Stapleton

Dave Stapleton
Service Manager

Figure 10-8. *Refusal with Explanation and Offer*

April 15, 1979

Mr. David L. Watson
4891 Scottsdale Avenue
Memphis, TN 38118

Dear David:

The idea has been born, plans are in the making, and we
are about to begin the most innovative business venture
to hit Memphis since Overton Square.

It does not encompass the magnitude of the Square, but
it does have great potential according to all the figures
we can put together. To date I have received commitments for almost half of the $10,000 necessary to get
the business off the ground, and I thought you would want
the chance to buy into AUNT NELL'S KITCHENS.

The premise is to locate in a high-traffic mall in
East Memphis or Germantown and sell homemade pies and
cakes. The pastries will be made on the site and sold
as whole units, for take-out, and by the slice for
pedestrians wanting a snack.

Sound funny? Maybe so, but think about it for a
minute and see if it does not interest you. Think
about walking through a mall and smelling pastries
being cooked. Think about being able to walk in
and buy a slice to eat right now. Think about the
success of the ice cream shops in the malls now.
Think how much money is waiting to be made.

You know it is impossible to put the whole proposal
into a letter like this, so I am not going to attempt
it. Just let me say that the opportunity is waiting
and only those investors who get in initially, with
subscriptions of $1,000 multiples, will ever have the
chance to profit in all future growth of AUNT NELL'S
KITCHENS. Pocket your checkbook and call me at
523-6396 now for a full explanation on the whole
venture.

It is too sweet to pass up.

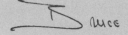

Figure 10-9. *Persuasive Request to Buy*

The letter requesting volunteer workers (shown in Figure 10–10) was written by a coordinator of a mental health center.

In persuasive requests, as in sales writing, the major portion of your letter should be directed toward conviction. By presenting features of the product or facets of the idea in terms of reader interest, you convince the reader to buy, or to accept your request or proposal. In order for the reader to be convinced, you should avoid phrasing or exaggeration that would cause disbelief. And use specific language and vivid description to present favorable aspects.

In the following chapter you will read further about sales writing and the principles of persuasion. Even though you probably won't make a career of writing sales messages (although it is an interesting and profitable career for some talented persons), when you become expert in writing sales letters you will almost surely be able to write all other kinds. The principles of sales writing apply to all kinds of business writing.

SUMMARY ◆ 10

Letters and memorandums that must convey unpleasant information should ordinarily be arranged in the indirect order.

A suggested outline for unpleasant messages is:

1. buffer
2. explanation and analysis
3. decision
4. a friendly, positive close

Persuasive requests are, in effect, sales letters. They are usually handled best in the "sales" arrangement:

1. attention
2. interest
3. desire (conviction)
4. action

The major portion of a persuasive letter should be devoted to conviction.

August 12, 1979

Mrs. R. B. Jones
123 Red Street
Huachuaca, AZ 85635

Dear Mrs. Jones:

Your interest in working with the Widowed Persons Service was indicated by your attendance at the first organizational meeting. This interest is greatly appreciated.

Attention and goodwill

Since that time, various community agencies interested in getting this program started have met, and a Coordinating Board has been formed. The Coordinating Board is in the process of organizing the program and recruiting volunteers. Mr. Leon Batterton, Director of the National Widowed Persons Service, has agreed to provide extensive training for interested volunteers. To utilize Mr. Batterton's professional expertise in training, we must first have a commitment of at least twenty volunteers.

Explanation

You have already experienced the sadness and readjustment of widowhood. Through your experience, you can help other widowed persons cope with the many problems associated with their loss. They need you desperately.

The request

Volunteers are asked to donate an evening a week to this service, plus one Sunday afternoon a month.

Explanation of request

The need for this program is real. Do you remember how you needed help, advice, and comforting words? Every day other persons become widowed and must endure similar experiences.

Your interest as a concerned volunteer can be expressed by completing the enclosed application and returning it to me in the stamped, addressed envelope. If you have any questions about the program, please call me at 327-7391.

Action

Sincerely,

Debra Allen

Mrs. Debra Allen
Acting Volunteer Director
Widowed Persons Services

Figure 10–10. *Letter Requesting Volunteer Workers*

QUESTIONS AND PROBLEMS ◆ 10

1. Prepare to dictate a refused request. (Assume details.) Make notes as to what to include in the first paragraph; the middle paragraph or paragraphs; the closing paragraph.

2. In the way that you have just planned a refused request (Question 1), plan the following:
   a. a letter telling a customer that an order cannot be shipped
   b. a letter telling a customer that an order will be late
   c. a letter telling a customer that you need more information before an order can be shipped
   d. a letter refusing a refund or adjustment
   e. a persuasive request

3. Find examples of bad-news messages of all kinds and of persuasive requests. Analyze these communications and make suggestions for needed improvements.

4. Analyze the following letter, which was written by your new correspondence supervisor. It was intended as a goodwill-building refused request. The reader is a graduate student wanting information for a report.

   Dear Mr. Summer:

   I appreciate the interest you have shown in Ajax

   Company and the pencil industry. However, it is not

   possible for me to release the information you desire

   because this information of Ajax Company and the pencil

   industry is confidential and is not to be released to the

   public.

                                   Sincerely yours,

5. Rewrite the letter analyzed in Problem 4.

6. All these sentences are poor choices for bad-news letters. Why?

   a.   We hope this meets your approval.

   b.   We know that this is not what you requested.

   c.   Your suggestion must be rejected.

   d.   When we can help you again, let us know.

   e.   It's against company policy.

f.   We were flattered to receive your letter.

g.   Read the instructions that came with your toaster.

h.   We are sorry that our paper shredder shredded your $25 tie that was given to you by your ex-fiancee who has now married your boss.

i.   I was surprised at your request for an adjustment.

j.   Please read this letter carefully.

Problems — Refused Requests

7.   You are the sales manager of Quality Office Supply. One of your established accounts, Witt Manufacturing Company, has written you with a request for a sizeable discount on their purchases.
      Witt Manufacturing is located thirty miles out of town.   Your free delivery is limited by policy to within the city limits, but to keep the account you have been giving them free delivery as well as quantity discounts on their orders. The vice president of Witt has been visiting the local plant for the last week, overseeing all operations.   He told Mrs. Johnson, the secretary in charge of ordering office supplies, that in California at the company headquarters they receive a 20 percent discount on all office supplies.   It is now her job to secure this discount.   The answer you must give is no.

8.   You are the coordinator of a mental health center. You frequently receive requests from students who want to schedule individual appointments to learn about the services of your center.   Individual appointments with several students a week can be expensive and time consuming.   You consider that promoting community interest is one of the functions of your office, as well as is the encouraging of students to go into the field or perhaps to work as volunteers.   You have developed a schedule of visiting hours for students and hope that several will come at one time.   These scheduled times are each Tuesday and Thursday from 2:30 to 4:00 p.m.   Write a letter refusing individual appointments.   Invite students to come at scheduled times.

9.   You are manager of Top Resumes, Incorporated.   Your firm specializes in writing resumes for clients who are searching for a job and are in need of an outstanding resume.   You have received a letter from Dr. Wayne Black, professor of business administration at your local college, requesting a number of examples of the resumes you have prepared.   He plans to use them in a book that he hopes to publish.   Since your business depends on writing resumes for its income it is impossible to grant this request.

10. You are responsible for maintaining all patient records that are evaluated at a mental health center.   Recently you received a request form from Mr. H. H. Higgs, an attorney who would like to use a patient evaluation report in a

pending law suit. All your records are strictly confidential, but you suppose that you could release the records with the patient's written permission. You don't want to start a chain of legal actions. Mr. Higgs has been invaluable in providing free consultant services for the center — but now you wonder about his legal expertise. You have in the past referred patients to him that are in need of legal assistance. Refuse the request, but very, very tactfully. You need to keep his goodwill not only because of his consulting work but because he has been active in fund-raising drives for the center.

11.   As owner of a small sporting goods store, you have just received a letter from Bill Riley, who is representing a group of boys interested in organizing a baseball team. He has asked you to sponsor the team and provide the money ($1,000) needed to purchase team uniforms and equipment. Write a letter to Mr. Riley informing him of your decision not to sponsor the baseball team. Do you think that you should offer a counterproposal? If so, what?

12.   You are Area Director for Agricultural Systems, Incorporated. You have received a letter from a former employee, Dick Roberts, who voluntarily left the company two years ago. He is requesting a job he knows you have open. Although you did not know it until after he had resigned, he had seriously violated some rules and regulations of the company. Dick knows many people in the industry, including a number of your present clients, but you do not want a man you do not trust. Write him a letter informing him of your answer. (Always be extremely careful about what you put on paper. Do not leave yourself open to a possible lawsuit.)

13.   Mr. James Watson, a currently enrolled student at Central College, has applied for a loan from the college. As director of financial aid, you are to refuse Mr. Watson's request because the income of his parents is more than adequate to pay his expenses. He has good grades, but the loans that you have available are based on need. Write to Mr. Watson at 1012 Carnes, Memphis, TN 38111.

14.   You are the assistant director of student housing at Central College. You have received a letter from Jimmy Jones, president of the student government association, citing the results of the SGA conducted survey as support for a more liberal visitation policy — an all-night policy. You feel that the survey was statistically invalid and structurally biased. Furthermore, you feel that the real student opinion is just the opposite to that indicated on the SGA survey. Even if it isn't, you have no inclination to support such a policy to a conservative administration. It is important not to discourage organized student involvement, but refuse the request.

15.   You are a nationally known authority in the field of continuing education for metropolitan areas. You have just received a request letter asking you to be the keynote speaker at a continuing education conference. (Assume that the conference is to be held at your local college or university.) You have a prior engagement. (You always play poker on Friday nights.) Write a letter of refusal.

16.   As the manager of the supplies department of the local branch of IBM, you are in charge of maintaining the best line of supplies possible. In an effort to simplify and to economize, you have limited your vendors to three. You normally enter into a contract with these vendors so that shipments will be

made on a constant basis. You have recently been contacted by another vendor about one of their new products. Since you are unable to stock the new items because of your current contracts, you must write the company a letter of refusal. Be sure to include in your letter the fact that you will be interested in talking with them at the end of the current contracts.

17.   As data processing manager for a government agency, you have received a request from Mr. John R. Glipp of Structural Dynamics Company, 928 East Elkhorn Drive, Yazoo, Mississippi. Mr. Glipp would like your agency to perform the computer analysis for a new bridge to be built over the Yazoo River. Your agency is prohibited from doing work for private firms, as such work would place it in competition with private industry. You feel that Computamatics Corporation in Jowkow, Alabama, could possibly perform the analysis.

Problems — Unfavorable Information about a Product or Service

18.   You are manager of the School and College Uniform Company. You have received an order for 7 dozen jackets (2 dozen small and 5 dozen medium) from Campbell Elementary School, 1617 West 37th Street, Topeka, KS 66609. According to the request, the jackets are to be in royal blue and should be accompanied by 7 dozen felt-back letter "C's" in white. The letters come in two different styles, described in your sales literature as "block" and "script." The order does not indicate the style desired.

   You have on hand enough jackets in the small size to fill the order, but your supply of medium jackets has been depleted. You expect to receive a new supply by May 17 and could have them in Topeka by May 24. Decide upon what you should include in your letter to Mrs. Andrea Pilgram, Principal. Write the letter.

19.   As owner of the World Order House, you must write a letter to Mr. Glen Burrows, a new customer, telling him of the status of his recent order. Of the three products he has ordered, one is out of stock, another is in the mail, and the third has been delayed because of insufficient information. He has sent a check in full payment. Assume necessary details and write a letter to Mr. Burrows.

20.   You are the sales manager of Quality Office Supply Company. Three days ago you received a long-distance telephone call from Wellington Construction Company in Carlise, Pennsylvania. Mrs. Rodgers, the secretary who called, has ordered office supplies from you in the past and this time she is in need of a box each of ⅝-inch and ¾-inch GBC bindings. She asks you to send them either by mail or United Parcel Service as soon as possible.

   You have a box of ¾-inch bindings on hand but must call the wholesaler about the ⅝-inch size. The next day you learn that the supplier is out of stock also, but that they are expected within ten days. You decide to go ahead and mail the one box and write a letter explaining the delay of the other box. Remembering her phone call, you realize that she sounded as if she needed the bindings immediately.

21. Miss Gloria Quindle has sent you an order for 10,000 ITS @ 10 cents each and has enclosed a check for $1,000 endorsed "for 10,000 ITS @ 10 cents each, paid in full." The price of an IT is 20 cents, as shown in your catalog. As sales manager of ITS, Incorporated, write to Miss Quindle. She lives at 572 Turnberry Boulevard, Newport News, Virginia 23602. The name of her shop is Stuff and Nonsense.

22. You are the shipping manager of Industrial Distributing Company. Mr. Jack North of Acme Manufacturing Company has placed an initial order with you for 200 five-inch flexible gaskets, 450 twelve-inch idler rods, and 3,000 one-inch fiberglass rollers. You can supply the rollers right away, but the gaskets will not be available until about a month from now. There are three types of idler rods, and Acme's order was not specific. Write to Mr. North.

23. You work for a furniture manufacturer. Through her decorator, Mrs. Janice Rose, Mrs. J. B. Marino of 3450 Maricopa Street, Torrance, California 90317 has ordered a $1,200 sofa. Delivery was promised within three months, but you now find that you are out of the particular fabric with which the sofa is to be covered. The fabric is still being manufactured, but it will not be available to your company for six months. (You have been unable to determine the reason for the delay.) You will not be able to send the sofa to Mrs. Marino until more than a year after she has ordered it. Write to her; suggest that she pick another fabric or wait for the delivery of the sofa as ordered.

Problems — Refused Adjustments

24. You are the manager of the Denver Corporation, a manufacturer of men's and ladies' watches. You receive a package containing a digital watch and a letter from Mr. George McCallen, 6434 Bridgehampton, New Orleans, LA 70126. Mr. McCallen states that the watch is not working properly and asks you to honor the one-year guarantee and replace the watch with a new one.

It is evident that the watch has been used in water. The warranty clearly states that the company will not assume responsibility for failure due to misuse and warns that the watch should not be dipped in water. Your repairman says that the watch can be repaired. The cost will be $22. Write to Mr. McCallen.

25. You are chief accountant at Central College. You receive an irate letter from Miss Margaret Glass, an instructor. Miss Glass believes that the amount she earned last year has been overstated on her W-2 form. She asks, "If I earned that much, how come I don't have any?" She quotes her annual salary, which is $400 less than the amount shown on the W-2 form. You review the accounting records and find that she has forgotten about the amount she earned in a special summer program, a ten-day workshop. Write a letter to Miss Glass to explain the source of additional income.

26. Mrs. Bill Vinson of 7118 Bridlespur Lane, Charlotte, North Carolina 28210 has purchased an Easter coat for her daughter from your department store. In May she visits your store and notices that the same coat is now on sale at one-half the original price. She writes to you, the president, asking that the

$45, one-half the purchase price, be credited to her account. She and her family have been customers for sixty years. You are the boss. Decide what to do and write the letter.

27. You are the manager of a shoe store. Mrs. Timothy Lancelot, 4686 Sunset Drive, Bloomington, Indiana 47401 has returned a pair of shoes purchased for her ten-year-old son. After six weeks' use, the shoes are stiff and badly cracked. Your investigation shows that the shoes seem to have been worn constantly in snow or rain and then dried too near a stove or radiator. Write to Mrs. Lancelot and refuse the adjustment.

28. You are a sales representative for Quality Office Supply. Mr. Gary Watson bought an electric stapler from you more than a year ago for his legal office. He writes you a letter, commenting that he has tried dozens of times to get you on the telephone. The machine has jammed several times in the last week, and he wants his money back. You think that he may have used the wrong size staples, those designed for another model stapler. Even if the stapler is defective, you cannot refund the money because of the elapsed time. Write to Mr. Watson.

29. You are a salesman for Agricultural Systems, Incorporated. You sell an accounting service to farmers. You have just received a letter from Bill Larson, Route 3, Tupelo, Mississippi 38801. He has just signed a two-year contract. At the time of signing the contract, he paid the usual $200 fee to begin the system. You spent almost three days in going over his records and in setting up the system. The monthly fees have not yet started. Mr. Larson has changed his mind and does not want the service. He requests a refund of the $200 and that the signed contract be voided. Write a letter voiding the contract, but do not refund the $200.

30. You are a general paving contractor. You receive a claim letter from Dr. Fred Crain, 9 High Plains Road, Branford, Connecticut 06405. Dr. Crain states that the driveway has cracked after two years of use. When the driveway was paved, he refused the proper foundation of gravel and sand because of the cost factor. The lack of a good foundation was pointed out to him before the concrete was poured. Refuse the claim for a new driveway.

31. You are the customer services representative of Kodo Film Company. You have received from Mr. A. M. Neal of Neal's Photography Shop, 235 Gilmore, Winnipeg, Manitoba, Canada R2G-023, a request for replacement for 213 rolls of film. He states that it is defective. Tests of the film show that it has been exposed to a temperature of over 185 degrees. Each roll of film you sell has a warning label that states that damage to the film will occur if it is exposed to temperatures over 120 degrees F.

Problems — Persuasive Requests

32. As Dean of the College of Business Administration (your college) you are interested in persuading several of the leading businessmen and businesswomen in your city to give informal speeches at the university. One man in particular, Mr. Sam Smith, Jr., is president of one of the largest cotton brokerage firms in the United States.

You know that Mr. Smith graduated from this college. You also know that he is an extremely busy man. His contribution as an entrepreneur would be especially valuable to the students, as the college presently does not offer courses in the commodities exchange market. You will not be able to pay him for his time. You want him to share his experiences, problems, and rewards in building his own business (from the mere six million dollars left him by his father). Ask him to speak to your school. Any week night during the month of March will be satisfactory.

33. Write a fund-raising letter for your church or for your civic or professional organization.

34. You have been appointed chairman of a local "Stop Smoking" committee. Write a letter that is to be published as an advertisement in the local newspaper.

35. Write a letter to secure new members for the Society for the Advancement of Management, or for a similar professional organization. Obtain the information you will need in order to write a convincing letter.

36. You have bought a washing machine that runs over almost every time you use it. You have owned this machine for more than a year. During the one-year warranty period, a representative of the local appliance store that sold you the washer examined it several times and could find nothing wrong with it. (Naturally, it worked perfectly each time he came.)

    You have written the manufacturer three times and have received in reply generalized form letters saying that replacement must be recommended by the local dealer. The last form letter stated that nothing could be done because the warranty has expired. You cannot afford to buy another washer. The washer runs over again. You sit at the kitchen table — with your feet in the water — and write to the manufacturer.

37. You go to your college library to read an article that has appeared in the *Journal of Business Communication*. The library does not have this journal. Write the head librarian and request it. You will need convincing details. Find them.

38. You are an inventor. You have a product that will revolutionize the bedding industry. (Or choose some industry with which you are familiar.) You do not have the capital or expertise to produce, sell, and distribute your product. You have decided to try to sell your idea, and you hope to realize some monetary rewards from the royalties.

    An additional problem is that you cannot fully describe your product. You do not have a patent on it, and to describe the product in detail might relinquish rights to the idea. In your letter you must sell yourself as well as the product. You find the names of the companies and its officers in the library.

Selling a Product
or Service

11

Because you have received a great number of sales messages, some of which were poorly planned and written, or outside your area of interest, selling by mail may not be completely appealing to you.

The term "junk mail," like "just another form letter," has a derogatory connotation because the mails have at times been misused in selling, as well as unwisely used. That sales messages are less than perfect in distribution or approach, however, should not make you distrust the entire industry.

Selling by mail is a completely legitimate, ethical method of selling, and often a profitable one. You as the buyer must use judgment, common sense, and perhaps sales resistance in response to sales letters, but this attitude should apply to all buying situations. And purchases made through the mail may be returned, according to law.

Buying by mail has certain advantages, one of which is the convenience factor. Another aspect is that certain items are sold only by mail. Others are sold directly to the consumer at a lower price than if they were distributed through retail outlets. A disadvantage of buying by mail is that even with the most vivid verbal description and colorful photographs, the imagined product or service sometimes differs drastically from the actual one. This factor is a disadvantage for the seller as well, in terms of dissatisfied customers and returned merchandise.

The sales approach should not be thought of as "the old hard sell," which was never a credible or creditable technique. We sell because the customer is convinced that the purchase will meet his needs and will be more valuable to him than the cost, as well as being more valuable than competing products. To build this conviction, the seller presents the prospective purchase in terms of what it will do for the prospective buyer — which is only a restatement of the you-attitude. In addition, the customer must believe that the organization or organizations that manufacture and sell the product, as well as the salespeople, are sincere and trustworthy.

If you do not honestly believe that your product or service is valuable and worthwhile, you probably will not be able to make a convincing sales presentation. Customers are not easily fooled. (The writer of this textbook is not so naive as to believe that poor and overpriced products are never profitable or that a clever, convincing sales message is necessarily an honest one. The assumption is, however, that all sales messages should be sincere. Another such assumption is that all the world should be bright and beautiful. That it is not does not justify our making it worse.)

The discussion in this chapter pertains mostly to written sales messages presented in letter form. Basic principles of selling, however, pertain to all sales messages, including various kinds of advertising and face-to-face presentation of the product or service.

These principles consist of an application of the basic principles of communication, most especially the you-attitude and the positive approach. Even more important is the ability to establish belief and trust.

CLASSIFICATIONS OF SALES MESSAGES

The term "classifications" is used loosely here, for sales messages cannot be separated into exact and discrete categories. And, as in most situations involving communication, terminology differs. But to bring some semblance of order to the study of selling by mail, a general overview of the field is first presented in terms of the kinds of sales messages according to their purpose, format, and use.

Of the millions of sales messages that are sent through the mails, most are professionally written by experts in the field. In addition, these letters are tested before they are sent out in great numbers. Even under these special circumstances, however, the writers of the letters can never be sure until results come in whether their efforts will be successful.

In addition to the letters and other written messages that are sent nationwide, or throughout wide areas, many sales messages are distributed only within one city or neighborhood.

Many letters are planned for the purpose of selling the product or service (usually a product) on the basis of the letter alone, or on the basis of a series of letters. Others promote sales by soliciting inquiries, asking the readers to come into the store, or requesting that an appointment be made for a representative to call.

The terms "direct mail," "direct selling," "mail order" and "direct-mail advertising" are not always used in exactly the same way.

Because direct-mail advertising is often planned for the purpose of selling directly, without the aid of a salesperson, the term "direct mail" is sometimes used in the limited sense of a letter planned only to obtain the order. In a broader sense, however, the term describes the use of the mails for any advertising, including both mail-order and sales promotion.

"Direct selling" includes any effort to sell without salespersons; for example, a television advertisement that asks that you telephone your order to a stated telephone number. "Mail order" denotes the ordering and shipping of goods by mail, regardless of the type of sales organization.

To avoid further confusion, we shall refer to letters or other written communications that attempt to obtain the order without the aid of a salesperson as "direct-sales messages." Other types of sales writing are referred to as sales promotion if they are to be distinguished from direct-sales. All these kinds — or any other messages planned to promote or sell — are correctly called by the general terms "sales letters," "sales communications," or "sales messages."

Sales messages are either solicited or unsolicited. Solicited messages are replies to requests for information about a product or service, similar to some of the direct requests discussed in Chapter 9. Unsolicited letters are known as prospecting communications. Names and addresses are obtained from mailing lists, which may be compiled from various sources or purchased from organizations that specialize in preparing mailing lists for many and varied sales efforts.

Sales messages are directed to the users of the product as well as to dealers and distributors. Letters are sent from manufacturers to wholesalers, retailers, and consumers; wholesale distributors write to retailers and sometimes to consumers; and retailers write to consumers.

Much sales material is in the form of printed material, including form letters and notes. These mass-produced forms are necessary for economy and prompt response to inquiries. Like all types of written communication, they should be neat in appearance and planned and worded to attain all the desirable characteristics of effective communication.

MAILING LISTS

Selling by mail can be a highly specialized and individualized approach. With the use of an appropriate and up-to-date mailing list, sales material can be sent only to those persons who are likely to be in the market for what we are selling.

If the merchandise to be sold is likely to be of interest only to a specialized group, we cannot afford to advertise by mass media, such as radio, television, general magazines, and newspapers. Although direct-mail advertising is more expensive (compared to advertising by mass media) for each person reached, it is much less expensive per sale — and this is the only cost that can be considered.

The preparation or purchase of a suitable mailing list is expensive, but not so expensive as using a poor one. When mailings are sent to persons who cannot use or who are most unlikely to want the particular product or service, these wasted mailings add greatly to the cost of the sales campaign.

Under the best of circumstances, some letters will be sent to persons who are certain not to be prospects, but these mailings should be kept to the minimum that can be achieved. Mailing lists become quickly outdated because so many people change their address each year. For this and for other reasons, no mailing list will be completely accurate, even if it is frequently revised.

The use of inappropriate mailing lists is one of the reasons that direct-mail advertising is not always highly regarded. If you are a college student wondering how to pay for your next pair of shoes, you will not be interested in a retirement annuity, and you cannot buy an expensive vacation home. A person who has completed a Ph.D. in English is not in the market for a book that will help the reader "speak like a college graduate." A president of a bank is not likely to be interested in a correspondence course in welding.

Mailing lists can be purchased from organizations that specialize in this service. As a general rule, the more difficult the list is to prepare, the more it costs. Thousands of different lists are available. A directory of companies that make, sell, and rent mailing lists is published by the Department of Commerce.

When selling some items, you will be interested in obtaining the names and addresses of persons in a particular occupation. Other classifications to be considered are age groups, hobbies, type of dwelling, special interests, and geographical location. In some sales campaigns you will need a list of persons who fall into more than one of these classifications.

For example, you may want a list of retired persons in a certain locality who own their homes, or a list of retired teachers who like to travel. You could buy these, as well as a list of owners of tropical fish, people who buy books about history and subscribe to historical journals, or the florists in Baltimore. (You could prepare your own list of the florists in Baltimore, even though you live in another city, by looking in a current telephone directory. Out-of-town directories are often available in your local library.)

If you are to sell only in your home town, you may be able to prepare your own mailing list — but to do so can be more expensive than buying a list. Many companies keep a list of their established customers for use in sales and sales promotion writing.

If a product or service is not so specialized that you need a particular mailing list, probably it should be sold by means other than direct-mail advertising, at least on a national basis. Nonspecialized products (in the sense that many persons could use them) can be profitably sold by mail in limited areas, as is the residential cleaning service that is advertised in Figure 11–1, shown later in this chapter.

A CENTRAL SELLING POINT

A good product, even an outstanding one, must be sold. Potential customers do not beat a path to the door of a person who builds a better mousetrap if they do not know about the mousetrap. They must be told.

In the telling process, even with the best mailing list or other method of selection, the message will go to some persons who don't happen to need a mousetrap or who cannot afford to buy one. If the mousetrap maker is to prosper, the sales message must go to people who both need and can buy the product. These persons must be convinced that the product will meet their needs and that it is better than competing ones from the buyer's particular standpoint.

A mousetrap ordinarily will not meet their needs because it is beautiful or because it is made of the finest steel or wood (or whatever mousetraps are made of) but because it will catch mice — and more particularly, because it will catch the specific mouse that is now plaguing the potential buyer or his wife and children. (Although some persons may be looking for a conversation piece for the coffee table, these buyers will no doubt be limited in number.)

The moral of this story is that the product or service must be presented in terms of the readers' most probable interest. To determine this interest, we must know what the product will do and what the buyer is most likely to want. This important principle of selling, regardless of the method, is a further application of the you-approach.

So how is the builder of the better mousetrap to choose a central theme, based on a central selling point, that will best market his merchandise? The first step is to analyze the product.

Analyzing the Product or Service

Is it true that the mousetrap is really better? If so, why? Is it better from all standpoints, or does it need improvement in certain areas? What are its best features in relation to the customers' expected needs? What are other desirable features? Of all possible selling points, which two are the most likely to be effective? Which particular point is likely to be most effective for the largest group of buyers?

To answer these questions, the particular product or service to be sold must be completely studied in detail; and so must competing products. In such a study, the analyst may find that even though the product is the best, overall, of all the rest, some competing items have certain features that excel in comparison. For example, a competitor's mousetrap is painted a bright lemon yellow while ours is painted a dull gray (to match the mouse).

Or perhaps another product lasts longer but is not so effective. In this instance, we should not base our sales approach upon color, or upon our three-year guarantee if the competing model includes a five-year guarantee. These themes would not be the most effective, anyway, based on the customers' probable needs. And, to determine these needs, we must analyze as much as possible the potential buyers.

Analyzing the Potential Buyer

The central selling point should be a feature in which the product excels, provided it is also a feature that is likely to make the customer want to buy. This is the real key to choosing a central selling point: What is it about this particular product that is most likely to make this particular person want to buy?

The central selling point is chosen to give unity and emphasis to the sales message. We can never be sure that we have chosen the best possible approach, or that we have chosen the feature that is most likely to appeal to the particular reader or group of readers. For example, the prospective buyer who wants a mousetrap to serve as a paperholder on an office desk will not be interested in the fact that the product will also catch mice. If a person keeps mice as pets, a letter built around what seems to be a logical selling point will appear ruthless and offensive.

If we were attempting to sell through conversation, we could determine individual interests and adjust our presentation accordingly. When we write letters that are to go to a large group of readers, we must make an educated guess (an inference) and choose the approach that seems to be best fitted to the largest group.

How can you study the prospective buyer? Scientifically and objectively, there is no way, in spite of the many specialized books and journal articles about sales psychology. You can find many lists of psychological drives, differing somewhat from book to book. And even without books, we know that we are are all interested, at least to a certain extent, in self-preservation, food, bodily comfort, sex, financial security, recognition, affection, pleasure, adventure, and the opportunity to grow and learn. We are also interested in communicating with other persons so that we do not feel isolated and alone. Can you think of anything you have willingly purchased that did not help you meet one or more of these drives?

We should make use of such information as we have about our potential customers, such as age group, educational background, national origin, occupation, and hobby. The more we know about our readers or listeners the more likely we are to be able to adapt our message to their particular interests. A carpenter is more likely to buy a hammer than is a kindergarten teacher, or such is a logical assumption, but the kindergarten teacher could be a more likely customer because the carpenter already has a hammer.

A teenager is perhaps more likely to be interested in the styling of a sports car, rather than in the economy, but this is not necessarily the case. His schoolteacher mother, who looks like the typical little old lady in tennis shoes, may be unconcerned with gas mileage and very much interested in the appearance of the car. This little old lady also may be about to purchase a $100,000 life insurance policy, while the well-dressed businessman is wondering how to buy his lunch.

As you learned in Chapters 3 and 4, as you studied the theory of communication, including semantics, you found that putting persons into categories — or stereotyping — is a dangerous practice. Each person is different from every other person. That we sometimes act like sheep — and to the benefit of the seller of merchandise who approaches us as if we were sheep — does not indicate that all members of any certain group are identical to all other members of that group. Such an individual approach, however, is impossible to obtain in sales campaigns in which the same message must be sent to many people because to do otherwise would be prohibitive both in time and expense.

Instead, we must generalize, and all generalizations are likely to be less than exact. For this reason, the central selling point, whatever it is, is not likely to be the one that will be the most appropriate one for all readers, provided that the contemplated purchase has more than one desirable factor.

Some writers of sales messages do not use a central selling point but try to stress equally all major factors of the product or service. Overall, however, a presentation is likely to be less than effective if many points are equally emphasized — an approach that in effect emphasizes nothing.

Presenting the Central Selling Point

Sales letters are longer, as a general rule, than other kinds of business letters. Many sales letters consist of four or more complete pages, plus enclosed leaflets and brochures. Even these longer letters, as well as the complete sales package, are likely to be most effective if they are based around a central selling point. In addition to this major aspect, however, they also present other features of the product or service.

If the message is an attempt to sell directly from the written presentation, all necessary information must be included, either in the letter or in supplementary sales leaflets or brochures. For example, if you are selling a clock radio, you can build around the theme of an excellent tone or that of easy-to-read numerals, provided either of these features is superior to competing brands. If you are able to sell this product at a price considerably less than similar models, the price itself can become the central selling point. Whatever your chosen selling point, you also include all necessary information about size, color, method of operation, source of power, price, and methods of shipment and payment.

Figure 11-1, which shows a sales letter about a residential cleaning service, illustrates the use of a central theme with additional factors also included. This theme is the hours that can be saved for the reader to spend in more enjoyable and valuable ways than in cleaning house. Could the central selling point logically be anything else? In addition to this factor, which other ones are mentioned?

In this lengthy sales letter, the central theme — that the reader will be saved valuable time for more rewarding and enjoyable tasks than housecleaning — is carried from the beginning of the letter to the end. Other features of the service that are presented in the letter are the dependability and trustworthiness of Suzy and her Menfolks, their ability to clean, and their helpful attitude.

This message would probably be prepared as a form letter, perhaps by the use of an automatic typewriter that would insert the name and address of each person, as well as the current date. This type of duplication is too expensive for letters that are sent out by the thousands, but this service being presented would not be sold to a great number of persons, at least in the present stage of development of the business enterprise. This letter could also be individually typewritten or prepared by other means of attractive duplication, such as the offset process. If the individual's name is inserted in each letter, the typewriter ribbon should match the print.

SPECIAL CHARACTERISTICS OF SALES MESSAGES

In addition to the unified theme, the letter about Suzy and her Menfolks illustrates several other characteristics of effective sales letters, which make them differ somewhat from the usual business letter. This particular letter differs from the most effective approach of certain other sales messages. For example, if you were an investment broker describing

Date

Dear Mrs. _____

WHICH DO YOU ENJOY MORE--

    Dusting the furniture--

        or reading to your children?

    Washing the windows--

        or preparing that special dessert your husband loves?

    Cleaning the bathroom--

        or playing tennis with your friends?

    Running the vacuum--

        or attending that planned but postponed class at the university?

    Scrubbing and mopping and sweeping and straightening--

        or sitting on your patio reading a magazine?

WE FEEL PRETTY SURE OF YOUR ANSWER. LET SUZY AND HER
MENFOLKS HELP.

    You don't really like to spend your days and hours and years in washing

and waxing and doing all the other necessary chores, but you like a shining

house, for your family and friends as well as for yourself. So what do you

do? You dust and wash and clean and mop and wipe, to say nothing of all the

other work that you must complete in your busy week? It doesn't leave much

time for living--right?

HAVE YOU HEARD ABOUT SUZY AND HER MENFOLKS?

    Some persons have the idea that with modern-day appliances

Figure 11-1. *Sales Message*

Figure 11-1. *(Continued)*

homemakers have little to do, even if they work outside the home. But even with these appliances, which really can't do much by themselves, as well as with the help of a considerate husband, much work remains--right?

And, regardless of the television advertisements, all those expensive cleaners and polishes and waxes don't make our lives easy and relaxing, fulfilling, and worthwhile.

SUZY AND HER MENFOLKS CAN'T GUARANTEE EVERLASTING HAPPINESS--BUT THEY'LL CLEAN YOUR HOUSE FOR YOU.

Suzy and her Menfolks is a new residential cleaning service. Suzy has four grown sons, all enrolled here in City University. Big strapping fellows--Bob is a graduate student in physical education, with a lovely wife who is an attorney and the treasurer of the organization. Bill is also a graduate student, but he hasn't really made up his mind as to what he wants to study. Joseph and Richard are red-headed twins--they're freshmen this year. And each one of these boys can work like a house afire.

These four boys (they like to be called men) will clean your three-bedroom house in an hour. They come in the door a-running, brandishing their cleaning tools. Bob is the vacuum-cleaner man. He gets over your carpets like a soft-footed tiger running down a basketball court, then stands back and purrs at their gleaming beauty. (You can be working in your flower garden.)

Richard cleans the bathrooms and washes the windows and mirrors.

Figure 11–1. *(Continued)*

Joseph dusts--oh how he dusts! Into every little nook and crevice and even

under the tabletops.

Bill hasn't yet decided on his specialty. If he sees that there is

something to be done, he does it. He is open for special requests. For

example, last week one of our clients asked him to take some boxes to the

attic and to move a piano. Most of the time, though, he helps the other

three men dust and wash and wax and mop and wipe and straighten and pick

up--but then you know the rest of the story.

And Suzy? Suzy keeps everything and everybody going. She is the

administrator and the inspector. If you knew Suzy--

Although they remain only an hour in most houses, they can do more in

the hour than most maids can do in a day. The secret is organization,

planning--and tremendous energy. And Suzy. (Besides, who can find a maid

nowdays?) In the hour they have saved you practically your whole week! (If

a little dust accumulates before they return next week, I would advise you to

forget it.)

Suzy and her Menfolks are bonded, to say nothing of being mighty fine

people and completely trustworthy. Although they would like for you or your

husband to be at home on their first day with you, afterwards you don't need

to be if you have an obliging neighbor to let them in. Or, if you desire, they

will arrange to come to your home on a weekday evening, up to nine o'clock.

Your free week, which Suzy and her Menfolks by their efforts will

Figure 11-1. *(Continued)*

make possible, is priced at only $27, including all costs of equipment and

cleaning materials. As you relax in your spotless living room, you will feel

that this weekly investment is the most enjoyable one you could make. Where

else can you buy time?

Their schedule is filling up in a hurry, so you might want to send them

an invitation to your home as soon as you can. Telephone 685-5624 to

reserve your hour, or to ask any questions that may have popped into your

head. I'll be glad to answer them all for you. (I am the brains of the

organization.)

After you call for them, they'll be right out. And so will you--

out of the house for a change.

                              Sincerely,

                              Martha Martin

                              Martha Martin
                              Suzy's Maid

P.S. Although Suzy and her Menfolks have been in business for only a

    month, they have already established an enthusiastic clientele,

    including some of your neighbors. If you would like to telephone

    these wise and wonderful people to let them tell you how clean your

    house will be, I'll be glad to give you their names and telephone

    numbers.

your firm and services in response to a request for information, your tone
would be much less casual.

Some of the differences between many sales letters and business
letters in general are these:

1. An overall informal tone. You have learned that most business messages are rather informal, but that the degree of formality differs according to the purpose of the communication and according to the reader or readers. Sales messages as a group tend to be more informal than other kinds of letters. As in other communication situations, you should plan the degree of formality to best fit the purpose and readership, both of which will be influenced by the product you are selling.

2. Special emphasis on descriptive, vivid, forceful words and phrases.

3. Special emphasis to the you-approach in that you show the reader enjoying or benefiting from the purchase — putting the object into the reader's hands to solve problems or to increase pleasure. In the preceding letter, the reader worked in her flower garden while the Menfolks cleaned her house. She is also pictured on her patio, playing tennis, and sitting in her living room admiring its cleanliness.

    In the discussion of sales writing in this chapter and in the following questions and problems, we shall refer to this particular application of the you-approach as "psychological description." Psychological description pictures the product or service being sold, in terms of reader benefit. For example, a salesperson's statement that a scarf is blue is description; a statement that it is periwinkle blue is more vivid description; "it is the exact blue of your eyes" is psychological description.

4. Increased use of the mechanical means of emphasis, such as all capitals, underlining, dashes, special arrangements, and color. The preceding letter does not use these devices to the extent that they are often used in sales letters. Although we are concerned with readability in all writing (which is achieved by mechanical as well as by other means), we are especially concerned with this quality in sales material because we must keep the prospective customer reading until he or she is convinced to buy.

Now let's look at the suggested arrangement of ideas of a sales letter.

ATTENTION, INTEREST, DESIRE, ACTION

This arrangement of sales letters — attention, interest, desire, and action — has long been used in the discussion, planning, and writing of sales messages. (This pattern of arrangement has already been presented in Chapter 9 with the discussion of persuasive requests.)

Variations in this pattern, from the standpoint of terminology only, are attention, interest, conviction, and action; attention, interest, desire, conviction, and action; and attention, conviction, and action. All these patterns are basically the same. In the first part of the letter, we must gain the reader's attention. In the middle section of the letter, we present convincing evidence. In the last part of the letter, we ask for action, as we have used the action close in other types of messages.

A description of a sales letter planned in this arrangement was included in a book published in 1919: *Business Correspondence*, by Harrison McJohnston.

1. Will the very first part of the letter get favorable attention and cause the reader to want to read on? (This usually means a direct, concrete, and convincing appeal to one or more of the reader's personal desires, and a forecast of the possible satisfaction of the desire as a result of reading the letter.)

2. Will the reader's interest increase as he reads? (Do you keep him in the letter? Could you add or subtract anything and thereby increase his interest?) Remember, you must make him read, and read with keen interest, or your effort is likely to be wasted. Lead him to a climax of thought and feeling which causes him to be willing to do as you wish.

3. Will the reader believe all the statements you make? Is it all the truth from his point of view? Do you give him facts, and not your own arbitrary opinions or conclusions? Do you avoid telling him what he already knows (as well or even better than you)? Especially, do you avoid telling him what he ought to know, so that he might get the impression that you think he does not know? Do you supplement his knowledge of facts so that he will be likely to conclude for himself that he ought to do as you want him to?

4. Do you cause him to get a vivid impression of the resulting good to him of doing as you want him to?

5. Will your closing sentences be likely to cause him to *act* upon his willingness to do as you want him to? Does he get a *definite* suggeston of just how he may do as you want him to? Have you avoided the hackneyed "do-it-now" close?

6. Is your expression effective? Is it all clear to him? Does it *all* sound natural and sincere to him? Is it free from hackneyed phraseology and lifeless expressions? Is it direct and simple and definite, and free from waste of words and unnecessary statements? Does it attract the eye?[1]

All the suggestions presented by Mr. McJohnston in 1919 are as applicable today as they were at that time. Isn't it ironic that the "do-it-now" close

1. Harrison McJohnston, *Business Correspondence* (New York: Alexander Hamilton Institute, 1918, 1919), pp. 207–208.

(or "Act today!" or "Don't wait!" close), which had already become hackneyed in 1919, is still used in the last quarter of the century.

Obtaining Favorable Attention

The attention section of a solicited sales letter differs somewhat from that of an unsolicited one. In responses to inquiries, you already have the reader's attention, provided you have replied promptly.

In solicited letters you need only to open with favorable information about the prospective purchase, expressed in terms of the reader's interest. In unsolicited messages, you work harder to gain and keep attention and interest — to keep the letter from going into the wastebasket.

The attention section of unsolicited messages may consist of a question, a startling statement, mention of an outstanding feature of the product, a proverb, a news announcement, a gadget or gimmick, or other similar approaches. Whatever you use to attract attention, it must make sense and tie in with the following paragraphs. Preferably it begins with a reference to the chosen theme or leads directly to that theme. It should be reader centered.

The following sentence, used alone as an opening paragraph of a letter planned to sell a barbeque grill, begins with a quotation.

> Harry Truman once said that if you can't stand the
>
> heat you should get out of the kitchen.

This opening paragraph ties in with the central theme of the letter, that the reader will avoid heating the house with the range or oven by cooking outside, as well as enjoying meal preparation and dining on the patio in the cool of the evening. Here, as you no doubt recognize, Truman's analogy was reversed to its original and literal meaning.

A letter from an exterminating company opened in this way:

> Did you hear about the hungry termite who got help
>
> from the welfare board?

The opening paragraph of a letter from a manufacturer to a dealer stresses features of the product in terms of reader benefit.

> When you show a customer a Gardener, a grass
>
> collector that sweeps and combs a lawn in one operation,

you have obtained a a quick sale, a satisfied customer, and

a $30. 81 profit.

From a letter to sell a spray to cleanse and deodorize pets:

You can now wash, deodorize, and protect your pet

from ticks and fleas in the time it takes to push a button.

Does that sound like an economical and convenient way to

care for your pet?

From a letter to sell a calculator, described as a minicomputer, planned to be worn like a wristwatch and sold especially to engineers.

Do you usually wear your calculator on your wrist?

How about a computer?

From a letter from publisher of textbooks to high school teachers:

Have you ever heard the term "It's books" to mean

that school is now in session—that recess or another free

period is over and that it's time to get down to serious

business?

The next paragraph explained that "it's books" is an old-fashioned term that was once widely used, and that it expressed the early concern, appreciation, and awe with which students and teachers viewed the few books that were then available. The central theme of the message was that, to improve education and our society, books must be reliable, interesting, challenging, and appropriate, and that such books just happen to be the exact kind that the publisher is selling.

From a letter to sell a burglar alarm system to persons who have just purchased citizens band radios to be installed in automobiles:

Protect your new investment!

Watch for these weaknesses in opening paragraphs of sales letters:

1. A too-long first paragaraph. Although opening paragraphs should be short in all business letters, overly long ones are

particularly bad in sales letters, in which you must gain and hold attention.

2. Questions with obvious answers such as "Would you like to increase profits?"

3. Obvious statements such as "to make a profit, you have to move merchandise."

4. A writer-centered opening such as "We are proud to announce the opening of our new store."

5. Slow openings such as "We have received your inquiry about our products," "We are writing to give you the information you requested."

6. Openings used only for a surprise or startling effect without regard for relevance or a tie-in with following paragraphs.

7. Obvious flattery, as "A person with your social position, Mrs. Jones —"

8. Openings that mention a negative aspect of the product or service. These are especially likely to occur when replying to inquiries. The potential customer's questions need not be answered in the order they were asked.

9. A reference to the cost of the purchase, unless price is to be used as the central selling point.

Presenting Convincing Evidence in Terms of Reader Interest

We must give specific, objective details about the product or service we are attempting to sell. In addition, we must present these details in terms of the reader's interest. (This is the psychological description mentioned earlier.) Instead of saying that a swimming pool is surrounded by a 12-foot-wide redwood sundeck, word the statement so that the buyer is shown using the sundeck. The statement that it is a 12-foot-wide redwood sundeck is good, as far as it goes, and much better than saying that the pool is surrounded by a wide sundeck. (How wide is wide?) But it is even better if you describe the sundeck in these specific terms and also show the reader enjoying it, as in:

        The redwood sundeck (12 feet wide!) that surrounds

    the pool gives you plenty of room for cookouts and parties

    for many happy summers to come.

Remember, however, that in addition to presenting sales material in emotional terms, you must give solid, tangible evidence as well. In the letter about the residential cleaning service (Fig. 11-1), concrete evidence is given as to why the reader should purchase the service: what is done, who does it, how it is done, when the cleaners come, cost, and other details of arrangement. Also, the reader is asked to telephone present customers for proof that the service is helpful and reliable. In addition to these concrete descriptions, psychological description is used throughout, built around the central theme of saving time for more pleasant and worthwhile activities.

A weakness of many sales letters is a lack of attention to conviction by hurrying through from the attention section to the action close. In the middle paragraphs of the letter, give enough time and space to build conviction. You will not convince with vague generalities, such as saying that the product is fine, nice, beautiful, strong, or "absolutely the finest in the world." Give reasons, details, and specifications to convince the reader that the product is absolutely the finest in the world.

Do not leave questions unanswered, either those that are asked in a letter of inquiry or those that are likely to occur to the reader. Most especially, do not leave unanswered questions in a direct-sales message, in which you attempt to sell on the strength of the letter alone.

Discussions of the you-attitude and the positive approach in Chapter 6 apply especially to the conviction section (or interest, desire, etc.) of a sales letter. Rereading these passages now will aid your writing of the important middle paragraphs of the sales letter, as well as other paragraphs, where you present convincing evidence.

Do not speak in generalities. If it's sturdy, why and how? If it's roomy, how big is it? If it's dependable, how do you know? If it's economical to operate, how many miles to a gallon? How do you know that it gets that many miles to a gallon? How do you know that the tests were reliable?

As you describe the product or service, you will often find that you have a great many features to list or describe in addition to your central selling feature. Items are easier to read if they are set up in a listing instead of crowded together in paragraph form. For example,

In sales letters, use

1.   Listings

2.   Plenty of white space

3.   Capitals, underlining, special arrangements

4.   Any other form of mechanical emphasis, as long as

     it is not used to excess

is easier to read than if presented in this way:

> In sales letters, use listings, plenty of white space,
> capitals, underlining, special arrangements, and any other
> form of mechanical emphasis, as long as it is not used to
> excess.

The cost of an item should be subordinated unless it is being used as a major selling factor. If it is not a good price, or at least somewhat lower than competing products, it should not be used as a major selling factor.

You remember the principles of emphasis presented in Chapter 7. To subordinate the price, reverse the principles of emphasis. Present it only after convincing evidence to justify the price. But do not leave it for the last paragraph, which is one of the most emphatic ones, unless you wish to emphasize the price.

Do not present the price in a sentence standing alone as a paragraph; this is one of the methods of emphasis. You achieve more subordination by presenting the price in a minor clause or phrase than if you put it in the more emphatic main clause. You also subordinate when you show how the reader will benefit by the purchase, with an emphasis upon these benefits, not upon the price.

Notice the methods of subordination in this paragraph from the Suzy letter.

> Your free week, that Suzy and her Menfolks by their
>
> efforts will make possible, is priced at only $27, including
>
> all costs of equipment and cleaning materials.

Although the $27 is presented in the main clause of the sentence, it is tucked into the middle of the sentence and not placed in the emphatic opening or closing position, both of which consist of definite and positive reader benefits. The "only" and "including all costs of equipment and cleaning materials" suggest that the service is a good buy. The remaining sentences in the paragraph reemphasize reader benefit.

Let's look at opening paragraphs from a sales letter planned to sell season tickets to a community theatre.

> "Something for everyone, Tragedy tomorrow, Comedy
>
> tonight"...
>
> These words from A Funny Thing Happened on the Way
>
> to the Forum closed the Rock City Player's 1975-76

season with a look to the year to come. A variety of

productions has been selected to bring something for

everyone--tragedy and comedy, music and history,

Shakespeare and Simon. A theatre membership will give

you advance reservations for more performances of more

shows than ever before.

A portion of the following paragraph illustrates further the presentation of specific details in terms of reader enjoyment.

As you listen to the romantic lyrics of "We Kiss in a

Shadow" and watch the pageantry of the children's march in

the first production, you will relax and look forward to your

other seven evenings at the theatre.

In addition to these and several other convincing paragraphs, a brochure was enclosed that showed a list of plays, dates, and the benefits of membership. These benefits — a saving over the method of buying individual tickets, convenience in obtaining reservations, enjoyment, and making a contribution to the community and to the arts — were stressed in the letter itself.

The following paragraph is from a letter to a dealer. Although the reader will not use the Gardener Grass Sweeper, the specific and objective details are convincing evidence that consumers will like the product — and thus the dealer will benefit by increased sales and satisfied customers.

Your customers will like the Gardener because it

gives them more time to call their own--without leaving

their large lawns and moving into condominiums. The

Gardener sweeps right up to trees, flower beds, fences,

and walls, eliminating the need for hand raking in spots not

reached by ordinary grass collectors. Its rollers fully

adjust to the sweeping and combing height that the users

prefer. With a minimum of care, it's always ready for

use--just empty the grass and it's ready to go.

The following paragraph is from a letter to a farmer:

Settle yourself into a 6600 seat and you'll find all the

controls easy to use and easy to reach. The tractor seat is

contoured for your all-day comfort. Clutch and brake

requirements are low. You'll feel completely at ease, with

full confidence in the quickly mastered controls.

As you write sales letters, don't skimp on your efforts — or on space — in the parts of the letter in which you prove to the reader that the product or service you are selling is exactly the one that should be selected. As in the opening attention paragraph or paragraphs, and as in the action close, carry through with your chosen theme built around the central selling point.

Asking for Action

The action close in sales letters is the same as in other types of communications: Specify the action, preferably in terms of reader interest; make action easy; and, if appropriate, motivate prompt action.

A weakness that still occurs in the action section of sales letters is a pushy and demanding attitude, often displayed by the trite phrases mentioned in the book on business correspondence published in 1919. Even if the reader is prepared to buy, a phrase such as "run down to your nearest drugstore right now!" is enough to send the letter to the nearest wastebasket right now.

Make sure that the reader understands exactly what the necessary action is and how it is to be accomplished. Make this action easy. Don't ask for a letter in return, only a pencil check on a postage-paid card, or perhaps a signature. If you want the reader to telephone, give the telephone number. If you want the reader to come into a store, give the location of the store and the hours it is open.

The paragraph shown below is from a publishing house to a high school teacher:

Just return the enclosed card and we will have our

salesman call on you. He will bring a free copy of <u>Practical</u>

English for Tomorrow's Leaders and discuss with you the benefits of using this book in your classroom.

The following paragraph is from a hotel promoting a bridal suite to a bridegroom-to-be:

Simply fill out the enclosed reservation card, mail it to us, and we will have this beautiful suite waiting for you and your bride--along with fresh flowers and a chilled bottle of champagne.

The following paragraph is from a letter promoting package delivery by a taxicab company:

Give me the opportunity to prove that Yellow Shuttle and Yellow Rush are everything I've said. Paste the enclosed stickers near your telephones and call 536-1214 for your next package delivery.

The closing paragraph shown below is from a letter to a garden equipment dealer:

By filling out and returning the enclosed order blank along with your remittance, you'll be assured that your Gardener Grass Sweepers will be on hand when your customers start asking for them.

The next paragraph is from a letter selling a tractor to a farmer:

You can look at all the different models at our showroom, 1411 Getwell Road, until nine each evening. There you can talk with a helpful salesman and decide upon the exact tractor for your farm.

The following paragraph is from a direct-sales letter selling a purse described as the Everything Bag:

By filling out and returning the enclosed card, you can

have your Everything Bag before your next shopping

excursion.

The most convincing sales letter, up to the action close, is not convincing at all if the reader does not know how to buy the product or service, or if this purchase is not easy to make. No matter how much a prospective buyer wanted the Everything Bag, she would be an unlikely customer unless she were told exactly how to buy it. Or, if the bag were being sold in a store, she would need to know which store and its location.

AN UNSOLICITED DIRECT-SALES LETTER

A complete illustration of a widely distributed direct sales letter is given in Figure 11-2. It was sent to subscribers of *Southern Living* magazine and it is used here by permission of *Southern Living* and the writer of the letter.

This long letter is shown in its entirety to illustrate several aspects of direct-sales letters sent out in great numbers over a wide area. One of these aspects is the length itself; such letters must be long enough to convince. Although some persons may not read all of this letter, the length alone will not lose a sale. If a person becomes interested in this cookbook and then finds that some mental questions are unanswered, he or she is much less likely to buy than if the writer had taken ample space to present convincing details.

Notice these things about this letter:

1. The attention-getting first paragraph is preceded by five attention-getting statements.
2. The second paragraph of the letter itself you may consider negative. How would this affect you, if you were a rather uncertain housewife — or one who was completely sure of her ability as a hostess?
3. Throughout the letter, listings, dashes, questions, and other aspects of format make the letter interesting and readable.
4. Throughout the letter, the reader is brought into the picture as she is pictured as a gracious hostess.
5. The "action close" is the third paragraph from the last, followed by a paragraph about price, another short paragraph, and a postscript. Why do you think the price has been presented in this way, which is different from the more usual earlier position?

Southern Living MAGAZINE OF THE MODERN SOUTH / BOX 2463 / BIRMINGHAM, ALABAMA 35202
PHONE (205) 870-4440

An invitation for Southerners only to ...

Learn how to entertain so confidently,
you never get the pre-party jitters again

Learn how to entertain so gracefully,
people will almost think you have a kitchen
full of servants

Learn how to entertain so economically,
you can afford many, many more of the
wonderful parties you love

Learn the secrets of the South's greatest
ladies and most gracious hostesses in your
home -- free -- for 30 days

Dear Southern Living Subscriber:

    If there's any time you should be the belle of the ball, it's
in your own home, at your own party, surrounded by your admiring
guests.

    But in spite of our fame for Southern hospitality (or because
of it), all too often you're not quite ready when the doorbell rings.
Your makeup's melted from the heat of the oven. Your hair's a mess.
You've forgotten the salad forks. You're not quite sure you picked
the right wine. And you're just a little bit worried about whether
or not folks will like the dinner.

Figure 11–2. *A Widely Distributed Direct-Sales Letter.* (*Used with permission of* Southern Living *Magazine.*)

Figure 11-2. *(Continued)*

Well, now there's a new book to help you bring off all kinds of
parties -- for a few people, dozens, even hundreds! -- with confidence,
ease, economy ... and a Southern flavor.

It's called the Southern Living PARTY COOKBOOK and it's just
incredible, the way it makes you feel like a guest at your own party!

The contents?

   400 pages, lavishly illustrated with full-color
   photographs, drawings, sketches, charts, diagrams,
   table and seating arrangements!

. 100 complete menus for brunches, luncheons,
  cook-outs, cocktail parties and suppers, buffets,
  seated dinner parties, fondue parties, teas
  and receptions, parties with a foreign flavor
  and traditional holiday feasts!

. Hundreds of tips from the South's most experienced party-givers. The fashionable way
  to invite people over. How to plan your party.
  How to set the table and decorate it. What
  time to eat. How to carve. How to serve.
  How to wind up the evening in style.

. Complete recipes for every menu -- plus menus
  and recipes from the South's greatest gourmet
  restaurants that have never been published
  before.

. A complete range of recipes -- from easy to
  rather complicated, from inexpensive on up.
  There's nothing in the Southern Living PARTY
  COOKBOOK that a brand-new bride couldn't
  accomplish on her budget. Yet there's nothing
  in it that wouldn't win praise for the most
  knowledgeable hostess.

For instance, how about this menu next time the ladies come
over for a festive luncheon?

                    Marinated mushrooms
       Carrot strips   Avocado dip with corn chips
                   Chicken with dried beef
         My favorite tomato aspic with vegetables
                   Lemon cream dressing
                      Angel biscuits
                Strawberry jam and butter
                Date-nut meringue squares
           Coffee   Iced tea

Figure 11-2. *(Continued)*

It sounds fancy. It looks fancy. But it couldn't be much easier
or less expensive. Take the chicken recipe, for instance --

<u>Chicken with dried beef</u>

6 chicken breasts, boned	6 strips lean bacon
3/4 pound dried chipped beef	1 (10-1/2 oz.) can mushroom soup

In bottom of shallow casserole arrange dried beef. Wrap
a strip of bacon around each chicken breast; arrange over
beef. Spread undiluted soup over chicken, cover with
aluminum foil, and bake in 300° oven for 2 hours; increase
heat to 350° and bake for another 20 to 30 minutes, basting
several times. Serves six.

As you probably noticed, there's no seasoning mentioned in the
recipe. You may want to add a little black pepper. You may want
to add a little sherry to the sauce for the last few bastings before
serving. But you don't really have to -- the beef and bacon dissolve
completely in the cooking, seasoning the chicken just marvelously.

Just as useful as the wonderful recipes and imaginative menus --
and perhaps even more reassuring to the harried hostess -- are the
pages and pages of answers to questions that come up for every woman:

. How should I invite people to a formal dinner,
  a luncheon, a cook-out? When is it all right to
  use the telephone? When should I write out an
  invitation?

. How do I set the table for a tea, a buffet, a
  luncheon, a Sunday supper party? Is it all right
  to use candles at lunch time? What, besides
  flowers, can I use to decorate the table? How
  should I fold my napkins? Where should I put them?
  What kind of wine glasses go with what? At a
  buffet, where do the coffee cups and dessert plates
  go?

. What time should I serve luncheon, dinner, supper?
  How do I get folks to the table while the food's
  still hot? What can I do about problem drinkers?
  What should I do if the guest of honor is just
  ages late? How can I get people to go home without
  hurting anyone's feelings?

The <u>Southern Living</u> PARTY COOKBOOK is a complete cookbook, menu
book and etiquette book, too. With it, you'll never need worry again
about whether you're doing the "correct thing" or not. You'll know
everything you need to know about wines and how to serve them. Meats
and how to carve them. Interesting and unusual foods and how to serve
and eat them.

Figure 11-2.   *(Continued)*

And you'll learn how to give the kind of parties that could make you famous as a hostess. Hawaiian luaus. Mexican fiestas. Chinese feasts. German, Italian, French, and Spanish dinners. Special kinds of parties from all around the world, especially adapted to our Southern way of entertaining -- and to the foods we Southern women have available from our stores and gardens.

As Southerners, you and I have a great tradition to try to live up to -- a tradition of gentleness, charm and elegance that has made us famous all around the world for the graciousness of our hospitality.

The Southern Living PARTY COOKBOOK is the biggest help I, personally, have ever seen. And it's one of the most beautiful books that's come out in a long, long time! 448 pages, printed on rich, heavy matte finish enamel, with a glorious full-color cover and color plates galore. And scattered all through its handsome pages, you'll find wine charts, glassware charts, table-setting charts, sauce and spice charts. Everything you need to know to entertain in style -- all carefully indexed for your convenience.

You just have to see the Southern Living PARTY COOKBOOK to appreciate how much help it will be to you, in your home, when you entertain your friends, your relations, your husband's business associates.

And now we'd like you to see it -- and use it -- in your own kitchen for the next 30 days absolutely free. To get the extraordinary Southern Living PARTY COOKBOOK, just slip the token on the enclosed order card into the "yes" slot and mail in the postpaid envelope today.

If, after trying it out for 30 days, you decide you want to keep it, do nothing. We will bill you for the low, low price of only $7.95 plus postage and handling -- a savings of $2.00 over the March 1 retail price. (The retail price will be $9.95 on March 1.)

Thank you for your interest.

Sincerely,

Betty Ann Jones

Betty Ann Jones

BAJ/fm

P. S. When your friends start talking about PARTY COOKBOOK, you're inevitably going to try it, so why pay $2.00 more for it after the first of January - without any refund guarantee? Try it now and protect your price and your pleasure.

6. The last paragraph is weak and unnecessary. With the exception of this paragraph, however, the letter as a whole is professionally and expertly written; so is the postscript.

7. If you had received this letter (regardless of where you live) would you have been convinced to buy? Why, or why not?

SOLICITED SALES LETTERS

Letters written in reply to requests for information about a product or service are quite similar to all other sales letters with the exception of the attention-getting paragraph or paragraphs. Because you already have the reader's attention, you can begin directly with favorable information about the contemplated purchase.

You must at times give an answer different from the one that the customer is hoping to receive. Do not be evasive, but present each factor in the most positive way possible. For example, do *not* say that you are sorry that the product requested is not now available but that you have an excellent substitute. From what you have learned about the positive approach and the connotations of words, you recognize that you should omit the "not" in the first part of this sentence, as well as the word "substitute," which implies that the proffered item is only second-best to the one requested. How could you phrase this idea, assuming you knew the outstanding features of the new product?

In the letter from the hotel to the bridegroom-to-be, which was written in response to an inquiry, the writer brought in the information that the dining room is closed during the winter months. In the original version of the letter, a postscript was added: "The dining room is closed during the winter months. Several good restaurants are within walking distance, however."

The writer revised the letter so that less emphasis was placed upon this lack of service in the hotel during the winter months. The information was moved away from the postscript; this portion of a letter is in a particularly emphatic position and should be used only for material that you wish to stress because of its assumed positive effect. How would you word this information about the dining room? Where in the letter would you include it?

The letter in Figure 11–3 was written in response to a letter from a newly established drive-in grocery store.

Date

Mr. Lester R. Childs
Lester's Market
Highway 66 West
Eads, TN 38123

Dear Mr. Childs:

Yes, Fresh and Sweet can supply your ice cream needs on   *Favorable answers*
a year-around basis. We can make deliveries to your new   *to questions*
store on Tuesday and Friday of each week.

Our ice cream flavors presently available are vanilla,
chocolate, strawberry, peach, butter pecan, chocolate   *Specific details,*
chip, and peppermint. In July and August we shall add   *also answers*
three sherbet flavors, orange, lemon, and pineapple. All   *to questions*
flavors are packed in half-gallons, quarts, and pints, as
well as in ten-gallon cans used in ice cream parlors. (Have   *Additional detail,*
you thought of selling ice cream cones? No other ice cream   *plus sales*
store is now operating in Eads.)   *promotion*

Our current prices are as follows:

        Half-gallons---------$1.04

        Quarts-------------- .59

        Pints--------------- .39

A 5 percent discount applies to each order of fifty or more   *Is this completely*
units. And, if you decide to add an ice cream cone counter,   *clear?*
we can make you a special price on the large cans of ice
cream, in all flavors.

To help celebrate the opening of your new store, Mr. Childs,
we are happy to offer you the special price of 84 cents a
half-gallon for a period of two weeks. This special offer,
enabling you to reduce your own prices, should attract
many customers, and the taste and economy of Fresh and
Sweet ice cream will keep them coming.

Our truck will stop at your store next Tuesday afternoon,
April 12. Tell the driver how much Fresh and Sweet you
want. (I'll make sure that he takes plenty for you and all   *Action close*
our other customers.) Or, if you wish, telephone me collect
at 901-333-6001 to place your order or to ask any questions
that occur to you.

Figure 11-3. *Individual Sales Message, in Response to Inquiry*

Figure 11-3. *(Continued)*

Goodwill

All of us at Fresh and Sweet wish you great success in your new business. We look forward to supplying your ice cream needs.

Sincerely,

Leo Bertagna

Leo Bertagna
District Sales Manager

mt

SUMMARY ◆ 11

Effective sales messages convince the reader or listener that the suggested purchase will meet the particular need of the specific individual and that the purchase will be more valuable than the necessary cost or effort necessary to acquire the product or service.

The customer must believe that the company or companies manufacturing and selling the product are trustworthy and reliable. The customer must also believe in the salesperson or salespersons who present the product, service, or idea.

A "direct-sales" letter is understood to mean a letter that attempts to sell on the strength of the written message alone, without the assistance of salespersons.

A well-chosen mailing list can make selling by mail a specialized and economical approach, as messages are sent only to persons who are likely to have an interest in the offered product or service.

Often the most economical way to obtain a mailing list is to purchase it from an organization that specializes in preparing and selling mailing lists, or in leasing these lists.

A central selling point is the factor that is most likely to convince the prospective buyer that the product or service best meets the individual's particular needs.

In order to determine the most effective central selling point, the seller must analyze the product or service and the possible needs of the prospective buyer. Once the central selling point is chosen, the sales letter is built around a theme that presents the central selling point.

Special characteristics of most sales letters are these:

1. An overall informal approach.

2. Special emphasis to descriptive, vivid, forceful words and phrases.

3. Special emphasis to the you-approach, especially from the standpoint of presenting the prospective purchase in terms of reader benefit.

4. Increased used of the mechanical means of emphasis.

A pattern of arrangement long used in planning sales letters is that of attention, interest, desire, and action.

The writer must present detailed, specific, convincing evidence in terms of the reader's interest.

Solicited sales messages are planned and written in much the same way as unsolicited ones, with the exception that less emphasis is given to obtaining the attention of the reader.   The reader is already interested in the product or service, as shown by a preceding inquiry.

QUESTIONS AND PROBLEMS ◆ 11

1. Look at several advertisements of approximate full-page length in magazines and newspapers.   Analyze these advertisements according to these factors:

   a. Is the advertisement built around a central selling point?   If so, what is it?   Is this theme carried from the beginning of the advertisement to the end?   Do you feel that the factor chosen as the central selling point is an appropriate one?   Why, or why not?   Can you think of another factor of the product or service that could be used as a central selling point?   Is this feature also stressed in the advertisement?

   b. Is the product or service described in terms of actual reader benefit? Give examples.

   c. Is humor used in the advertisement?

   d. Would this advertisement make you buy the product, provided it is something you need, want, and can afford?

2. Analyze at least ten sales letters as you did the advertisements in the preceding problem.   In addition to the factors considered for the advertisements, evaluate the letters from these standpoints:

   a. Did the writer make effective use of the mechanical means of emphasis, such as special arrangements, color, unusual spacing, all capitals, or underlining?

   b. Is the attention-getting beginning effective?   Does it illustrate one of the characteristics of securing attention illustrated in this chapter?   Is a theme built around a central selling point used in the attention-getting section of the letter?

    c. Does the action close specify action in terms of reader benefit, make action easy, and motivate prompt action? Does the action close include a reference to the central selling point?

    d. Does the letter answer all questions that might logically occur to the reader?

    e. Would this letter sell the product or service to you? Why or why not?

3. Using the information given in one of the advertisements you analyzed, or in a similar advertisement, construct a direct-sales letter. Choose your advertisement with care; make sure that your product is one that could effectively be sold by mail. If the advertisement does not include all the information that your reader will need, assume reasonable details.

4. Using the information given in an advertisement, construct a sales letter to be sent to retailers. Assume names, addresses, and any needed explanation or details.

5. Look at the advertisements for this year's new cars. Pick the one you would most like to buy. Assume that you are selling this car. Write a sales letter to persons who are likely to be good prospects. Ask them to come to the showroom for a demonstration. You will need to know a great deal about the automobile in order to make your letter convincing. It should do a great deal more than ask the potential customers to come in to look. You must offer proof in your letter that the automobile is the one they should buy.

6. Follow the instructions given in the preceding problem except that you will choose some product other than an automobile — for example, a motorcycle, camera, sailboat, or any other item you would like to buy. Investigate the features of this product, as well as the features of competing products. Write a sales letter to persons who seem to be good prospects. (You may use a direct-sales letter or a sales promotion letter of some kind, depending upon your chosen product.)

7. Write a direct-sales letter, to persons similar to yourself, about one of your favorite possessions that sells for no more than $50. (If it is more than a few months old, a new one probably costs more now.) Choose an object that could be effectively sold by mail. Consider the reasons you particularly like this product; its weaknesses, if any; and the approach that is most likely to sell the same product to other people.

8. Rewrite the following paragraph, an action close of a sales letter promoting paneling sold to builders.

       Presently our new catalog is being printed and will be available to you in the very near future. This will provide detailed information on our products as well as color-matched gutters, downspouts, flashing, and other accessories. In the meantime, we would like very much to hear from you on your present requirements and of course on all of your future requirements, which could result in a

savings to you. If any additional information is needed,

please do not hesitate to call. Simply, but emphatically,

thank you!

9. As a public relations director for a regional professional theater you have been directed to write a sales letter to prospective new members about the theater's next season. Additional shop and rehearsal space has made it possible to extend production lengths from three to four weeks and to increase the number of productions from six to eight. This expansion makes it desirable to add 2,500 members to your list of season ticket holders. The types of memberships, number of tickets for each show, and costs are as follows:

Student	1	$ 16
Regular	1	40
Patron	2	100
Benefactor	4	250
Sponsor	8	500

A brochure is enclosed with dates and descriptions of the shows, a seating chart, directions for making reservations, and a membership application. Sponsors and benefactors are allowed to make reservations for specific seats and dates before other members and are invited to special opening and end-of-the-season parties with the actors and staff of the theater. The theater has operated for 50 years and this season plans to produce *The King and I*, *Crown Matrimonial*, *Taming of the Shrew*, *The Cherry Orchard*, *The Fantastiks*, *After the Fall*, *Prisoner of Second Avenue*, and *Cabaret*. Regular box office tickets to nonmembers are $5 for students and $8.50 for adults, and are available only for those seats not reserved by members four days before a performance.

10. Write a sales letter to high school English and business teachers. You are the educational sales manager for the Excel Publishing Company. Excel is marketing a new business English book for high school students. By returning the enclosed postcard the teacher can request a salesman to call with a free sample copy of the book and a price list for the book, workbook, and teacher's manual. The book, *Practical English for Tomorrow's Leaders*, covers material that will be used by all adults in common business transactions of life, by students going directly into office work after they graduate from high school, and by students who plan on post high school education but will eventually end up in the business world. Topics include interviewing and writing job applications, placing orders, keeping personal records and filling out tax forms, reading and analyzing business news, and writing common types of business letters with an emphasis on reviewing grammar and punctuation rules.

Emphasize that the material is all new, and compare this to other business English books which are updated versions of books in print more than fifteen years. Most of the older books are aimed at below average students, are almost entirely grammar exercises, and make little effort to show practical application of their material to modern, everyday living.

11. You are the general manager of an old hotel in Eureka Springs, Arkansas. (Give the hotel a name.) This is an old Victorian hotel. Eureka Springs is known as the "Little Switzerland of America" — with buildings on mountainsides and narrow, winding streets. (It was a well-known resort city of the last century.) You read announcements of engagements and send sales promotion material to bridegrooms-to-be in Arkansas and surrounding states.

    These are the features of your hotel:

    • Built on mountaintop overlooking the town.
    • Honeymoon suite is spacious with a magnificent view.
    • Lovely dining room, but it is closed November through May (assume that it is now October).
    • Other dining facilities are nearby.
    • Cocktail lounge is located on observation deck.
    • Fresh flowers and a bottle of chilled champagne await honeymoon couple.
    • Heated pool.
    • Tennis courts.
    • Horseback riding.
    • Rates are $32 a day or $200 a week.
    • There are only two honeymoon suites. (First come, first served.)

12. You are the sales manager of a wholesale equipment company that manufactures the Gardener Grass Sweeper. Write a sales letter to be sent to all hardware and gardening equipment shops in your city or state covering the following features:
    a. Its one-step operation saves lawn-sweeping time.
    b. The lightweight Gardener Grass Sweeper weighs only twenty pounds when full.
    c. The Grass Sweeper will hold up to five large lawn bags of grass.
    d. The Grass Sweeper rollers have a lifetime guarantee. The canvas grass container has a fifteen-year guarantee.
    e. The Grass Sweeper sweeps right up to trees, fences, walls, and flower beds — which means no hand raking is necessary! Ordinary sweepers don't do this.
    f. It costs retailer only $34.95. It retails for $65.76 — a profit of $30.81.
    g. The Grass Sweeper's rollers are fully adjustable so that sweeping may be done at the height that the customer prefers.
    h. The Grass Sweeper requires only minimum care.
    i. The full-page advertisement run in *House and Garden*, *Beautiful Lawns*, and *Sports Illustrated* will be seen by many customers of hardware stores. They will be run monthly from April until September. They are three-color ads.

Enclose brochures and copies of magazine advertisements. Ask customers to mail in order (a blank is enclosed) or to telephone your number (901-567-2591) collect.

13. As Director of Sales, Westward-Ho Flying Company, 910 Windwood Road, Denver, Colorado 80218, mail to ranchers information concerning the model TMT 100 Aztec airplane. Stress the convenience, pleasure, and time-saving aspects of the small plane. Ask ranchers to use the toll-free number 1-800-456-3648 to have a regional salesman telephone to arrange for an appointment and demonstration. Give them these facts:

   a. Aztec model TMT 100.
   b. Twin gas-burning engines.
   c. Seating arrangements for six persons.
   d. Maximum speed of 250 mph.
   e. List price of $45,000 plus tax. Terms can be arranged. Depreciation and maintenance are business expenses for income tax purposes.
   f. Gauge panel and instrument controls are easily readable and within reach.
   g. Maximum luggage space for six people.
   h. Latest safety designs inspected and approved by Federal Aviation Agency.

14. Asume that you own a farm equipment company. (Give it a name.) Send to farmers in your section of the state information about the 6600 Workhorse tractor. Stress the work power and comfort of the tractor. If needed, financing can be arranged through Workhorse Motor Credit Company. Here are engine specifications you might need:

Horsepower — mfg's estimated observed PTO	
with 8-speed transmission	70
with 16-speed transmission	68
Number of Cylinders	4
Displacement	256.4 cu. in.
Rated Engine Speed	2100 rpm
Starting — Electric start with safety switch.	
Cold start kits optional for diesels.	

15. You own a taxicab company in your city. You have begun a desk-to-desk scheduled package delivery shuttle between three leading business centers — the airport, downtown, and Easthaven (or use the names of three actual business districts in your city). Features of your shuttle are:

   • Customer can telephone before 9:30 a.m. for delivery to one or both of the other centers by noon. If customer calls by 2:30 p.m., delivery can be made by 5:00 p.m.
   • Rates are $4 for total deliveries to the same address and up to 25 pounds. For customers who sign up for every-day service, the rate is reduced by 20 percent. (This regular service is known as the "Yellow Shuttle.")
   • The *Yellow Rush* service, with higher rates, will deliver to any point within the city in no more than an hour, except for unforeseen emergencies.

You ask reader to telephone you or, if someone else in the company is in charge of package deliveries, to pass the letter along.

16. You are the owner of Lebanon Kennels, Rural Route 2, Lebanon, MO 62275. You raise shetland sheepdogs, which are also known as shelties, shetland collies, and miniature collies. These dogs are about twenty inches high when full grown and weigh about fifty pounds. They are originally from the border country of Scotland and England. These dogs can be used for herding sheep, showing, and merely as pets.

    Because the dogs were quite productive during the spring, you now have a surplus of puppies. Although the price of the dogs won't be any lower because of the surplus, you are anxious to find owners for the dogs while they are still puppies. Do not tell the price ($250) in your original letter; make the potential customers want a puppy and ask them to come to your kennels to look at them. Enclose snapshots of some of the puppies and of full-grown dogs.

17. You are the manager of a new fabric store opening soon in your city. You have a mailing list of women in the neighborhood with school-age children. You have something to offer that you think will be attractive to these women. The store will be conducting sewing classes at no charge other than for the cost of material and supplies. The employees are skilled in sewing and eager to teach these classes. In addition, those who enroll in the sewing classes will be given a 10 percent discount on all items bought from the store during the next six months. Write a letter to be sent to these women. Ask them to come to visit the store and to ask more questions about the program.

18. You are the manager of a tax consulting firm in your city. (Give it a name.) Realizing that the recent changes in the tax laws will cause many individual taxpayers who fill out their own returns to make costly mistakes, you write a sales letter to increase your clients in the middle income group.

    The basic philosophy of your tax consulting service is client satisfaction through able assistance by capable, honest, and courteous tax consultants. By knowing the new tax laws and how they affect your clients, you can save them both time and money. You provide the clients with economical help in the preparation of their income tax returns, confidentiality, year-around income tax service, and audit assistance. Fees are based solely on the complexity of the return. The average fee last year was $24 for each tax return. Your "one-time" fee entitles the client to assistance with tax estimates, audits, and tax questions. Write the letter.

19. You are the sales manager for the Big Bass Boat Company. Your product is one of the best boats on the market. It is constructed of a heavy gauge aluminum, is wider than most boats, has a semi-V hull for a better ride, is modestly priced at $375, and is guaranteed for five years. However, your product is new and few people are aware of its high quality. You have a list of names from a local bass fishing club. Write a letter to these members and promote your superior boat.

20. If you did not write No. 33, Chapter 9, earlier in the semester, do so at this time, using the information you collected from the letters you wrote as directed by Problems 9 and 10, Chapter 9.

21. You are the personnel manager of Countrywide Life Insurance Company. You want employees to pay $2 to join "Activities," a plan sponsored by the Activities Board. (While you are about it, perhaps you can think of a better name for the program than "Activities." If not, use this name.) For the $2, employees receive a 40 percent discount on all film processing for a year plus prizes in a photography contest, discounts on local football and basketball games, a golf tournament, magazines provided for free use in lunchroom, coffee for ten cents a cup, noon craft classes, a Christmas party for employees' children, a bingo party, other activities as suggested by employees. Write this sales message in memo form.

22. Bring a product to class. Give a three-minute sales presentation about this product. As your instructor directs, record this message.

23. Write a one-minute television or radio commercial for any product or service, real or imaginary. Do not modify existing commercials unless your modification is truly original. If you have access to a tape recorder, record your message.

24. Write a sales letter in reply to inquiry from a housewife about the Gardener Grass Sweeper described in Problem 12. She has seen the Sweeper advertised in *House and Garden* and wants to know where to buy it. You are sending her a list of all the dealers in her city. (You have these printed lists already prepared.) The price was not shown in the advertisement.

     The customer has stated, "I don't want to pay more than $40 for this equipment, as I really don't have to buy it." She also asks whether the full bag is too heavy for her husband to lift, since he is not very strong. She also wants to know whether the sweeper will pick up leaves, twigs, and small stones. (The sweeper is designed only for grass clippings; although it may perhaps pick up small leaves, it will not pick up the large magnolia leaves and seed pods that the customer mentioned having on her lawn.) She also asks, "Will I have to use a hand rake around walks, fences, etc.?" Answer all the customer's questions, but present your product in a positive way so that the reader will be convinced to buy.

25. Form into committees of five or six. Elect a sales manager for each group. Think of a new product or service to be put on the market. Analyze your product or service as to its strengths and weaknesses, especially as to how it compares with similar products or services. Is your product or service one that can be effectively sold or promoted by mail? Should you use direct-sales messages, or should the product be sold through retail outlets? Who will be your most likely prospects? How will you determine your mailing list? What will be the central theme of your message? As your instructor directs, hold sales meetings to answer the preceding questions and others that occur to you.

26. Write an appropriate sales message for the product or service studied in the preceding problem.

FURTHER READING ◆ 11

Abelson, Herbert I., and Karlins, Marvin. *Persuasion: How Opinions and Attitudes are Changed*. 2d ed. New York: Springer Publishing Company, 1970.

Anderson, Kenneth E. *Persuasion: Theory and Practice*. Boston: Allyn and Bacon, 1971.

Buckley, Earle A. *How to Increase Sales with Letters*. New York: McGraw-Hill Book Company, 1961.

————. *How to Write Better Letters*. New York: McGraw-Hill Book Company, 1971.

Crane, Edgar. *Marketing Communications*. New York: John Wiley and Sons, 1965.

Dichter, Ernest. *The Strategy of Desire*. Garden City, N.Y.: Doubleday and Company, 1960.

Hodgson, Richard S. *Direct Mail and Mail Order Handbook*. Chicago: Dartnell, 1965.

Keys, Langley Carlton. "Profits in Prose," *Harvard Business Review* (January-February 1961), pp. 105–112.

Royal Bank of Canada. "Letters that Sell." Reprinted in *American Business Communication Bulletin*, September 1974.

Yeck, J. D., and Maguire, J. T. *Planning and Creating Direct Mail*. New York: McGraw-Hill Book Company, 1961.

Writing about Credit and Collections

12

Business messages discussed and illustrated in this chapter include inquiries about credit applicants, replies to these inquiries, credit approval and credit refusal letters, and collection messages.

These inquiries and direct replies are similar to the letters you studied in Chapter 9, with the exception that they are about some aspect of the credit process. Unfavorable responses or persuasive requests about credit are similar to the business messages you studied in Chapter 10, except for the subject matter. Your review now of Chapters 9 and 10 should help you as you plan and write similar letters about credit.

Collection letters are also sales letters; you attempt to persuade the reader to pay the amount owed by providing convincing evidence that the payment will be to the reader's benefit. Like other sales messages, collection letters are most emphatic and convincing when they are built around a theme, or a major selling point. Remember that the central selling point of any product, service, or idea must be presented with the you-approach — that is, the reader must realize the benefits to be derived from paying the bill.

CREDIT POLICIES AND PROCEDURES

Credit policies differ widely; even if they did not, they could not be adequately described in the section of this chapter or in a chapter devoted only to this subject. Some of you probably already know a great deal about credit policies (although perhaps not so much about collection policies) from your personal experience. We need to consider, however, the usual policies as they apply to your communications tasks, especially those of written communications.

Credit is a major function of almost every business organization, and working in some way with credit and collection procedures is likely to be a part of your responsibility sometime during your business or professional career. As a consumer, you are almost sure to be a part of the nationwide system of requesting, receiving, and benefiting from credit transactions.

If you have ever bought anything on credit, rented an apartment, or been involved in various other business transactions, you probably have a credit record. The nation is covered with networks of credit associations that make credit information easily available. The "Credit Bureau" is an association of firms that grant credit: banks, financial companies, stores, credit unions, automobile dealers, and other types of lending institutions.

Credit bureaus make their information available to other bureaus in other cities so that an individual's credit reputation follows even a coast-to-coast move. Credit bureaus do not make recommendations but merely furnish the applicant's record, from which potential lenders make their own decisions.

Desirable Attitudes about Credit

Just as in asking for employment, when you apply for credit you should not take the attitude that the lender is doing you a favor. You are paying for the credit, either through the interest rate or carrying charge or through the cost of the merchandise.

Without you and many other credit customers, most business organizations could not continue to prosper. But you too are benefiting from credit transactions if you are mature and wise enough to manage your financial affairs. Not every person is, regardless of his or her chronological age.

These truisms form the background not only for the consideration of the most desirable attitudes toward credit but also for the most realistic and positive attitudes to be taken by personnel who work with credit in any way. The assumption should be that most persons will pay. This assumption is correct, or the widespread, almost universal system of doing business on credit could not exist. If most persons could not be trusted, even the system of using checking accounts would break down. We all know, however, that some persons do not pay their debts when they become due. And a few persons do not pay them at all unless they are forced to do so.

Credit managers and accountants realize that some debts will be uncollectible even with the best-planned credit procedures and collection policies.   Reserves are regularly set aside for bad debts.

But for every bill that remains uncollected, some other customer pays.   The cost of uncollected debts must of necessity be added to the cost of products or services sold, just as shoplifting penalizes honest customers.

Because of this factor, and because an organization cannot long stay in business if it loses an unreasonable amount through bad debts, credit and collection policies are important to all employees and customers of a business organization.   The organization that does not establish and maintain a firm and definite collection policy is not being fair to anyone concerned, including the debtors, who are deprived (or they deprive themselves) of their self-respect.

In addition to the final loss because a bad debt is written off, the creditor loses interest income because of slow payments.   Also, if an account must be turned over to a collection agency, 50 percent or more of the amount is paid to the agency.

The assumption among credit personnel is that most people mean to pay when they assume an obligation.   That they do not pay is due to a variety of reasons, including simple procrastination.   Sometimes individuals and organizations cannot pay because of such things as illness, loss of jobs, and the other misfortunes that can happen to all of us at any time.

Reasonable credit personnel realize that when a debtor absolutely cannot pay the complete bill, there is no need to push.   (The old saying, "You can't get blood out of a turnip," remains an apt expression for this situation and illustrates the fact that clichés are sometimes more descriptive than any other group of words.)   When a person reaches such a financial impasse, creditors will usually accept smaller installments, extend the time period, or give a grace period when no payment at all is expected.   They do these things not only from a humanitarian standpoint but from a practical businesslike motivation.

Although a credit manager would surely prefer that all bills be paid on the day that they are due, much more money will be lost if the bill is not paid at all.   In addition, the creditor is interested in keeping customers, even those who are now in a poor financial situation.   This condition may be only temporary, and the customer may recover to become a profitable buyer for many years to come.

In the collection process, we must keep in mind two goals: that of getting the money and that of maintaining goodwill.   Although at times the person in charge of collections may feel that the obstinate individual who has ignored all collection attempts is a customer well worth losing, this attitude is a dangerous one.   On the whole, it is not a practical or a businesslike attitude, even though there will be some customers that we do not wish to keep as credit customers, at least in the immediate future.

In addition to driving away customers who may at a later time be extremely profitable to the company, a harsh, demanding, and otherwise undiplomatic attitude in collection letters, at least in the early stages of collection, is not nearly so effective in obtaining payment as are more diplomatic ones. Even if such a letter "works," it is at the expense of goodwill and future pleasant relationships.

When collection letters or other attempts at collection are necessary (other than routine statements and simple reminders), something has gone wrong in the business relationship. If a great many credit customers reach this stage, something is wrong in the credit policies of the lending institution.

As you attempt to collect, either through the use of letters, the telephone, or face-to-face conversations, you can more intelligently approach each individual if you know what has gone wrong — just as we can better approach each communication situation if we know exactly the background and the likely reaction of each individual reader or listener. How much we can know about each individual debtor, however, is limited, so we must make reasonable assumptions upon which to base our collection policies.

Customers differ in both their ability and willingness to pay. Much of this difference is apparent from their previous history of payment. Some credit records are so poor that credit should not have been granted in the first place, although looking back at what should have been done is of little value. The recognition that customers differ in their bill-paying habits should help the writer of collection letters tailor the collection attempts to different groups, provided that information is available about customers' previous records.

Even more important than detecting the "slow" or "uncertain" is the ability to recognize the good customer in order to make absolutely sure that our early letters do not appear urgent and demanding. Early letters should not appear this way to any group of clients, but a personalized, urgent approach should come sooner for slow customers than for those who have in the past met their bills on time.

Depending upon your age, you may not realize that the entire philosophy of credit has changed from the world of your grandparents or great-grandparents. At one time only the "trifling poor" applied for credit. Respectable persons paid cash. Although this thinking was not prevalent among all groups of persons in all regions of the country, buying on time was regarded as a sin by many individuals. This thinking resulted in such actions as couples delaying the purchase of a home until they no longer needed it when the money paid for rent could have bought them that home.

As you can imagine, in those early days collection letters were different from good ones of today. When a person did not pay promptly, letters and other messages sent to the debtor were often rude, blunt, threatening, and sarcastic.   Even then, however, some books on business communication were protesting this attitude in collection letters.

The excerpt below, from a book written in 1919, contains excellent advice even though written at least sixty years ago.[1]

> Collecting money is like selling goods. It involves a knowledge of human nature and ability to select the methods that work best with individual debtors. No matter how carefully you pass upon your credit risks, some are sure to be slow in settling. Misfortune may befall them. Any one of twenty things may cause the customer to fall behind. It naturally follows, then, that the better you are acquainted with your debtors, the more successful will be your collection methods.
>
> A very important essential of the successful collector is firmness. Many a dealer will not press a customer because he is afraid of losing his trade. So he lets the bill get bigger and bigger until finally the customer leaves because the bill has got beyond him. This is a very weak position and a useless one.
>
> At the same time you must know the customer from whom you are trying to collect. What might answer with one will offend another. Understand the circumstances as completely as possible before you do anything.
>
> A grocer who insisted on collecting his bills on the 1st and 15th of each month noticed that one of his new customers was two weeks in arrears. So he wrote the customer reminding him very curtly that his account was running entirely too high and must be settled, as the policy of the store was that bills should be paid promptly on the first and the fifteenth.
>
> The bill was paid. A check came by return mail. But the grocer never sold that family five cents' worth of merchandise again.
>
> The fact was, that this customer's wife had been called away from home by the sickness of a relative. Her departure was sudden. The maid she left in charge of the house was not instructed to pay the grocer's bill — a very natural omission.
>
> Then the grocer made his mistake. He found out afterward that the customer's financial standing was even better than his own — that the customer was good for many, many times the amount of the bill, and that he had a high position among business men. If he had investigated before writing the letter, of course, he would not have written it. He not only could have collected his money in due course, but now would be selling more groceries.
>
> This loss to the grocer seemed unjust in a way. He had asked for nothing more than was due him. He had given the family his goods and was entitled to his money. Probably the aggrieved customer would admit as much. At the same time, the customer had a right to resent the unnecessarily sharp letter the merchant wrote. Anyway, he did resent it and this is what caused the grocer to lose.

1. As quoted by Harrison McJohnston in *Business Correspondence* (New York: Alexander Hamilton Institute, 1919), pp. 172–73. Passages were credited in this way: Quoted by permission, from the "Butler Way System Book," published by Butler Brothers, Chicago [n.d.].

You don't have to be apologetic about collecting your money. It is yours. But you do need to know your customers and to deal with them in accordance with what you know. If you don't you are likely to lose them.

Evaluating Credit Applicants

Credit applicants are evaluated, as they must be. The factors that go into this judgment are based on the four C' s of credit, a long-established basis for evaluating credit applications. These four C's of credit are:

- character
- capital
- capacity
- conditions

Character is judged by a person's reputation of honesty and integrity, especially as shown by past experience in meeting financial obligations in the manner and at the time promised.

Capital describes overall financial worth: assets minus outstanding obligations.

Capacity is the ability to produce capital — the ability to earn in order to repay. Young college graduates often have very little capital. After finding a job, establishing a business, or entering a profession, they often have an excellent capacity to pay and become excellent credit risks. This capacity, along with character, suggests evidence of the ability and willingness to pay.

Conditions, although one of the four C's of credit, are often beyond the control of the credit applicant. This factor includes not only general business conditions and conditions in a specific business or industry but also specific financial circumstances pertaining to a particular individual or organization.

For example, if a clerk has been employed for many years in a factory that is being shut down, this person is adversely affected. The ability to earn, or capacity, is threatened. If this applicant has a large amount of capital, credit may be gladly given. All factors are considered in making the determination. Regardless of the excellent rating on three of the factors, however, an applicant is not a good risk without the first and most important element of all, character.

How Legal Considerations Affect Credit and Collection Policies

The Consumer Credit Protection Act became effective in 1969 and has been amended several times since. As originally passed, Title I of the Act is referred to as the Truth-in-Lending Act.

The main purpose of the original Truth-in-Lending Act was to require a lender to reveal all costs and terms of a loan in writing in advance. The finance charge and the annual percentage rate must be clearly stated. This statement enables the consumer to compare terms and interest rates and thus shop for credit.

The Fair Credit Reporting Act, which became effective in 1971, is Title VI of the Consumer Credit Protection Act. Major provisions as they affect credit and collection correspondence are these:

1. The credit applicant must be made aware that a credit report is being requested.

2. The person, organization, or credit reporting agency that furnishes the credit report must make reasonably sure that the information will be used only for the stated purpose.

3. Consumers have the right, at any time and for any reason, to examine their records as maintained by a credit bureau or any credit reporting agency. This information can be obtained free of charge if the applicant has been denied credit, insurance, or employment within thirty days of the interview with the credit reporting agency. Otherwise, the agency is permitted to charge a reasonable fee. The applicant has the right to have incomplete or incorrect information reinvestigated. If the information is inaccurate or cannot be verified, the information is to be removed from the file. In case of dispute as to the accuracy of the information, the individual has the right to have his or her version of the information placed in the file and included in subsequent consumer reports.

4. Credit reporting agencies must not report adverse information that is over seven years old, with the exception of bankruptcies, which may be reported for fourteen years.

The Depository Institutions Act went into effect in 1975, amending the Truth-in-Lending law by adding the Fair Credit Billing Act and adding the Equal Credit Opportunity Act to the Credit Protection Act of 1969.

Major provisions of these acts are as follows:

1. A retailer must acknowledge within thirty days customer inquiries about a credit account and resolve such inquiries within ninety days after they are made. (In past years, some organizations conveniently "lost" undesirable applications.)

2. A creditor cannot directly or indirectly threaten to report adversely to any person, other than the debtor, on the debtor's credit standing in order to force the debtor to pay.

3. A retailer may not refuse credit on the basis of sex or marital status.

4. A creditor must supply a written statement of reasons for denying or terminating credit when any rejected applicant requests an explanation.

In the illustrations of credit and collection letters shown later in this chapter, you will notice phrasing planned specifically to comply with legal restrictions. Examples are references to the fact that the applicant has given the addressee as a credit reference, cautious wording to avoid implying any kind of threat, and statements to the effect that the requested information is to be kept confidential.

A statement that a credit report is to be kept confidential, which is routinely and wisely used on credit inquiries and replies to these inquiries, should be interpreted to mean that the information will not be released to persons or organizations other than to the applicant. As mentioned above, under the Fair Credit Reporting Act the applicant has the right to know why credit was refused and to examine his or her own record in a credit reporting agency.

ESTABLISHING THE CREDIT RELATIONSHIP

Effective letters about credit applicants and credit procedures greatly decrease the collection letters that will become necessary. These letters about credit include inquiries and replies about credit applicants; credit approval letters that include a specific statement of terms, due dates, interest rates, and other necessary details; and, when necessary, letters refusing credit.

Inquiries about Credit Applicants

A request for information about a credit applicant is similar both to an inquiry about an applicant for employment and to requests and inquiries of any kind (see Chapter 9). Many credit inquiries are made by telephone. When written messages are used, often form messages with fill-in blanks are chosen for convenience, economy, and a prompt response.

Replies to Requests for Credit Information

An example of a letter written to provide information about a credit applicant is shown in Figure 12-1.

Dear Mr. Wilson:

SUBJECT: CONFIDENTIAL CREDIT INFORMATION ABOUT
          PHOENIX LAND CORPORATION, AUSTIN, TEXAS

Phoenix Land Corporation has had an active account with our

company for the last five years. They currently have charges

due within thirty days with no overdue balance.

Their record of payment is excellent. Our terms are 2/10, net

30; Phoenix Land Corporation takes advantage of the discount

on a regular basis. Their credit limit of $10,000 has been

sufficient for their needs. If their needs should increase, we

would gladly increase their credit limit.

We regard Phoenix Land Corporation as a profitable account.

                                        Sincerely,

Figure 12-1. *Letter Providing Credit Information*

Credit Approvals

Credit approvals, like other messages that convey positive information, ordinarily should open with the news that the credit relationship has been established. (Chapter 9, as you remember, includes a discussion and examples of letters arranged in the direct order. Often a credit approval is also the acknowledgment of an order; this type of business message was also presented in Chapter 9.)

So that the debtor will be completely sure of the time when payments are due, how they are to be made, and credit terms, you should include specific statements about these regulations in the credit approval letter. In addition, the customer must be informed in writing, although not necessarily within the letter itself, of the annual interest rate.

As in letters that grant adjustments, the writer should avoid a grudging tone. Even if the decision to grant credit was not easily made, this negative aspect should not be mentioned.   But, as in all communication, do not be insincere, and make sure that all necessary details are included.

In the credit approval letter to Mrs. Zorsybski (see Figure 12-2), the "excellent credit rating" mentioned should be just that or the words should be omitted.

A credit approval letter is an appropriate message in which to use sales promotion sentences and paragraphs, as well as other goodwill building passages.

Dear Mrs. Zorsybski:

The approval

Because of your excellent credit rating, we are happy to provide all your office supply needs on our regular credit terms.

Statement of terms

The full account balance is due not later than thirty days from the date of your monthly statement.   You will receive a 2 percent discount if the full amount is paid within ten days.

Credit limit and other credit plans

Use your credit freely--up to $700 a month.   When you need to make larger purchases, telephone or come in and talk with me.   Perhaps you will want to take advantage of our extended credit terms.

Sales promotion

We look forward to a long and pleasant business relationship.   Harvey Flowers, our sales representative, will drop by within a few days and bring you a complete catalog of our office equipment and supplies.

Sincerely,

Figure 12-2.   *Credit Approval Letter*

Credit Refusals

Credit refusals present all the problems inherent in any refusal or bad-news message, plus other ticklish aspects of dealing with the reader's ego and reputation, both of which must be involved when credit is not allowed. In addition, the writer must make sure to abide by all legal stipulations.

In the next letter, written to a recent college graduate (Figure 12-3), the writer retains a positive approach by the congratulatory opening and the forward-looking, optimistic close. This letter is diplomatic, although it is much shorter than the usual refusal letter of any kind. (The credit applicant had given no credit references, and none were checked.)

In the letter from Herby's Furniture Store shown in Figure 12-4, the credit applicant is told that the decision is based upon the credit references supplied by the applicant. This business message is an example of an implied refusal. The writer does not include words like "we cannot sell to you on credit." The same message is conveyed quite explicitly, but more softly, in "we feel the best way to serve you is on a cash basis."

The credit refusal letter to Charles Maxwell, of Maxwell's Men, ends with a request for a cash order (see Figure 12-5). An ending of this kind, if it is subtly worded to convey a you-attitude, softens the refusal in that it indicates to the applicant that he continues to be a valued customer. In addition, employees in all departments of organizations that sell merchandise or service must promote sales, even though they are not classified as sales representatives.

The offer of a discount shows special consideration, regardless of the fact that credit is not being granted at this time. The last paragraph is also an action close in that it asks specifically for the order, makes action easy, and shows how the action will benefit the reader.

A knowledge of your organization's policies and procedures, in addition to the principles of communication you have previously studied, should enable you to plan and compose the various messages about credit.

THE COLLECTION SERIES

Collection messages are classified here as being in the early, middle, or late stage in the collection series. The early stage consists of reminder messages in the form of notes, obvious form letters, or stamped reminders on duplicate bills.

Middle-stage messages are more individualized; they are individually written and dictated or planned to give the appearance of personally

Dear Mr. Davis:

   Congratulations! A college degree means a lot.

   To us, it means a job. Mr. Davis, just as soon as

you receive that all-important job, we will reconsider your

request for credit.

   We look forward to hearing from you in the very near

future.

                              Yours sincerely,

Figure 12-3. *Diplomatic Credit Refusal*

directed letters. Middle-stage collection letters are longer than either the early or late messages because they must develop an appeal. Late-stage letters are shorter and more direct. They speak firmly of the urgency of the situation and of the importance of immediate payment.

As we speak of stages in the collection series, remember that they differ from organization to organization in time span and in the number of messages in each stage. They also differ in the length of time from the beginning of the series until the end. They may differ according to the particular group of customers of the same organization.

As a general rule, the total time of the collection series is longer for good credit risks than for poor ones. More mailings are included, and more time is allowed to elapse between mailings. A typical series may consist of two to four reminders (the early stage of the series), two or three inquiries and appeals (the middle stage), and two or three urgency letters, the final one of which is an ultimatum.

Intervals between mailings vary from ten to thirty days, with longer intervals at the beginning of the series and shorter ones toward the end.

The series may be lengthened or shortened. It is shortened when readers are considered to be poor credit risks or when conditions indicate that the collection process should be accelerated.

The number of mailings may be reduced and the intervals between the mailings shortened, or some of the steps in the usual series may be omitted altogether. Perhaps there will be no reminders, one appeal, and then an urgency letter, followed by an ultimatum.

Regardless of the length of the series, the tone of the message changes from the beginning to the end.

Dear Mrs. Love:

Welcome to Portland! We are certainly pleased that you
and Mr. Love came by Herby's Furniture Store to see our   *Goodwill buffer*
merchandise.

In order to determine how we could best meet your needs
while you are here in Portland, we made the routine checks
on the references you gave us. From this information, we   *Explanation,*
feel the best way to serve you is on a cash basis. As one   *implied refusal,*
                                                                         and sales
of the largest furniture stores in the city, we invite you to   *promotion*
join the ranks of our many satisfied customers.

Won't you drop by to see us again soon? Our interior
decorator, Mrs. Judy Mosca, will be happy to help you   *Goodwill and sales*
                                                                        promotion
coordinate the furnishings for your new apartment.

                             Yours sincerely,

Figure 12-4.   *Credit Refusal Based on Credit Check*

All collection messages should include a statement of the amount due
and how long it is overdue.

Early-Stage Collection Messages

The first step in the collection series is the statement — usually a monthly
statement — of the amount due.

Reminders may be additional statements with a stamped notation that
the bill is past due. Instead of a second or a third statement, the reminder
or reminders may be short, simple requests presented as form letters,
printed notes, or, occasionally, greeting cards.

April 26, 1978

Mr. Charles Maxwell
Maxwell's Men
702 Canal Street
New Orleans, LA 70126

Dear Mr. Maxwell:

Goodwill buffer

Your order of I & I men's furnishings indicates that your business is rapidly growing. You have our best wishes for your continued success.

Explanation,
implied refusal,
and forward look

We have carefully and thoroughly analyzed the financial statements you provided us. We find it to your best interest to look at these statements from the standpoint of bankers and credit managers--that a 2-to-1 ratio of assets to liabilities is a good indication of a financially sound organization. We feel sure that this ratio will be accomplished in a short time at Maxwell's Men. At that time, we will gladly review your application again and ship your orders on our regular credit basis.

Counter proposal

Our firm offers to many other customers a 10 percent cash discount for orders as large as your present one. This has provided substantial savings to these companies and has also helped to establish the 2-to-1 ratio required for credit.

Action close

Please take advantage of this cash discount as a step toward a sound business relationship between I & I and Maxwell's Men. Your check for the amount of the enclosed invoice, less the 10 percent discount, will send your order on its way.

Sincerely,

Joseph W Sherman

Joseph W. Sherman
Credit Manager

jms

Enclosure

Figure 12–5. *Credit Refusal with Request for Cash Order*

Letters, if used in the early part of the collection series, are quite obviously form letters and are based on the assumption that the obligation has been overlooked. These form letters, as well as any other follow-up reminder messages, are purposely impersonal and routine. This approach is the opposite of what is considered the best approach in many other forms of communications. Used in the early stages of collection, they imply something to this effect:

> Look, we realize that you have merely overlooked this obligation, as you have been prompt in making past payments. But you understand that of course we must remind you, as we do all other customers, when your check does not arrive on time. Your notice that comes in this form letter (or greeting card, stamped message, note, etc.) is the same as we send to everyone. We still like you.

Yes, it is quite a feat to imply all the ideas and attitudes in the preceding paragraph with only the words "just a gentle reminder" or "did you forget?" But, in effect, that is what you are doing in a well-planned reminder message early in the collection series.

In reminder messages we may use humor if we do so with discretion. As in all communication, we must be extremely careful when using a humorous approach because it can very easily appear to be sarcasm.

Resale and sales promotion are also used in reminder messages. You have previously learned that resale and sales promotion can be used to soften a message, as in refusal letters. You are using these passages for the same purpose early in the collection series, as well as for the obvious purpose of promoting sales.

Because of the softening effect, however, we most certainly would not use resale, sales promotion, humor, or any similar approach in the late stage of the collection series. At that time we don't want to soften the approach; we want to emphasize the urgency of the situation and insist that the bill be paid immediately.

Middle-Stage Collection Messages

The use of humor, resale, and sales promotion may or may not be appropriate for the middle stages of the collection series, depending upon the type of merchandise sold, the customer, the particular credit policies of the company, and other considerations.

Remember that these approaches soften the urgency of the message; whether or not they should be included depends upon the most appropriate and effective tone. If you use several messages in the middle stage of the collection series, humor, resale, and sales promotion are more appropriate for the first letters than for later ones.

Be careful with the use of humor in all collection messages. Although we are not always required to be deadly serious, a light touch indicates that the writer is not really concerned — so why should the debtor be concerned? If an individual owes you, he or she probably owes other individuals and organizations — perhaps a great many of them. The reader of a collection letter is likely to pay first the creditor who really cares, provided that the letter is convincing and at the same time courteous and considerate.

In the middle stage, we may begin with an inquiry directed personally toward the applicant (although the letter may not be individually written or dictated), followed by a letter or letters built around an appeal of some kind. In these letters, we bring into use a central theme similar to the central selling theme of sales letters.

Messages throughout the series should become increasingly forceful, but "forceful" does not mean that the letters are rude, sarcastic, demanding, or impolite. We should always refrain from using this tone, regardless of the length of the series. A courteous approach is to be chosen not only from the standpoint of consideration for the reader but also because this approach is more likely to be effective in collecting.

Remember the two main purposes of collection letters — to get the money and to maintain goodwill. In addition to maintaining goodwill, a courteous tone is also more likely to collect. In middle-stage messages, the assumption is no longer that of the reminder stage, that the account has merely been overlooked. This assumption is no longer stated or implied.

An inquiry attempts to obtain a response from the reader. Perhaps the customer is dissatisfied with the merchandise, or perhaps because of unexpected financial difficulties the person cannot pay. We should not, however, state these things in our letter to him or make excuses for the readers. (They are perfectly capable of making excuses for themselves.)

The letter to Mr. Peterson (Figure 12-6) is an inquiry used as the first message to be sent after reminders.

An example of an appeal letter is the one directed to a Certified Public Accountant (see Figure 12-7). This letter is in the discussion stage, but it is still low key and nondemanding. The appeal is to the individual's financial standing, specifically to the preservation of his credit rating. This theme is the one most likely to be effective, as the individual's credit future is directly related to satisfactory payments.

A letter of this kind appears more personal and urgent if it is typewritten and directed personally to the addressee. As you can tell from the wording of the letter to the accountant, the message was individually dictated or handwritten, as it includes bits of information that apply to the particular customer.

If form messages are used in the middle stage of the collection series,

Dear Mr. Peterson:

    How is the new 46-percent urea fertilizer performing for you? The increasing size of your recent orders indicates that this year's crop prospects must be good.

> *Resale and goodwill buffer*

    With your farm operation growing as it is, you'll be needing an assortment of agricultural chemicals. This is simply good farm management. It is equally good farm management to pay for your orders within the thirty-day period following the sale.

> *Implied reminder of value of credit, plus request for payment*

    Won't you send your check for $1,084.59, which is approximately twelve weeks past due, and put your account in good standing again?

> *Action close, with statement of amount and time*

                   Sincerely,

P.S. Is there some reason that we should know for your waiting to pay this bill? If so, won't you come in and talk with me--or telephone collect, 901-685-5624?

> *The inquiry*

Figure 12-6. *Inquiry Sent after Reminder*

they should appear to be individually written to the receiver of the messages. Many organizations, however, continue to use obvious form letters throughout the collection series.

    The letter shown in Figure 12-8 from the advertising chairman of Theatre Memphis also appeals to the reader's economic interest, but more specifically from the aspect of the loss of customers than the loss of a credit rating.

December 7, 1978

Mr. Donald Morgan, C.P.A.
1359 Second Street
Philadelphia, Pennsylvania 19104

Dear Mr. Morgan:

When you started your business, a good credit rating made it
possible for you to benefit from credit purchases.

I'm sure you want to protect your good credit rating so that you
can continue to receive equipment and supplies by the convenient
credit plans you have enjoyed in the past.

Quality Office Supply has continued to honor this privilege
because you have always settled your accounts satisfactorily.
At the present time, however, your account is five months past
due. Invoice #97231, which covers a shipment of three
calculators for a total of $813.75, remains unpaid.

To preserve your good credit rating, send your check for
$813.75 right away. A stamped, addressed envelope is enclosed
for your convenience in making immediate payment.

Sincerely,

QUALITY OFFICE SUPPLY

L. Dianne Osborne

(Miss) L. Dianne Osborne
Branch Administrative Manager

pw
enclosure

Figure 12-7.   *A Letter of Appeal re Credit Rating*

September 20, 1978

Mr. John Johnson
Johnson's Steak House
5555 Poplar
Memphis, TN 38111

Dear Mr. Johnson:

I am sending you a copy of our "Kiss Me Kate" program with
your attractive, full-page advertisement on page 3. The
program has been passed out to 5,600 theater-goers in the first
two weeks of our production. Seven more performances are
scheduled.

Many of our members have commented favorably on your new
"after-the-theater dinner" promoted in the program copy you
furnished us. Your location near the theater makes our audience
a select group of prospective customers for your restaurant.

The programs for our next show are being prepared for the
printer, and we're sure you will want your advertisement in
them and in all programs for our 1978-79 productions, as we
agreed in your contract last June.

Just send your check for the $100 balance due in the enclosed,
addressed envelope, or drop the payment by the theater, and
your program copy will be in for the entire season.

Sincerely,

THEATRE MEMPHIS

Karen J. English

Karen J. English
Advertising Chairman

Figure 12-8. *A Letter of Appeal re Customer Loss*

November 30, 1978

Mr. John Jones
1312 Windom
Memphis, Tennessee 38104

Re: Account No. 72831-12

Dear Mr. Jones:

YOUR CREDIT STANDING IS IN SERIOUS DANGER!

Your account, totaling $2,161, is now seriously delinquent. We
have heard nothing from you in response to our previous notices,
letter, and telephone calls.

THIS AMOUNT WAS DUE ON JULY 3.

Unless arrangements are made within three days for payment,
we shall have no alternative but to declare the entire balance due
and take whatever legal action that may become necessary to
collect.

We trust you will realize the importance of this matter. Get in
touch with me immediately.

Yours very truly,

Jay Williamson

Jay Williamson
Collection Department

JW/ck

Figure 12–9. *Late-Stage Collection Message*

Late-Stage Collection Messages

Late-stage collection efforts are often in the form of telephone calls,
telegrams, or even personal visits. They may also consist of letters.

Regardless of the collection methods, attempts at collecting long
overdue accounts state specifically when the amount must be paid and
what action will be taken if it is not paid. The writer should not mention a

lawsuit if there is actually no possibility of a suit. A late-stage message is illustrated in Figure 12–9.

SUMMARY ◆ 12

Granting and using credit is a necessary and valuable business activity. Credit is beneficial to both the lender and the debtor, but it must be used wisely. Well-planned and administered credit policies and procedures are an important aspect of profitable business management.

A long-standing guide to evaluating credit applicants is expressed as the C's of credit: character, capital, capacity, and conditions.

Certain credit and collection policies are regulated by federal law.

Letters about credit — credit inquiries and replies, credit approvals with specific information, and necessary credit refusals — decrease the number of collection letters that will become necessary.

Collection messages can be divided into those that come in the early, middle, or late stages of the collection series. Although the tone of the message becomes more forceful from the beginning of the series to the end, the writer should never resort to threats, rudeness, or sarcasm.

QUESTIONS AND PROBLEMS ◆ 12

Credit Inquiries

1. You are office manager of a government agency. One of your most capable secretaries has been denied credit at a national retail store. The secretary is young, single, and rather nonassertive. She has performed outstanding work during her three years of employment under your supervision. As a close friend of her family, you are sure that she has had no credit difficulties of any kind. Because she has proved herself a dependable and responsible young lady, you decide to write a letter to the store requesting information about her credit application. She has successfully paid out two loans, one for an automobile and one for cash from the Federal Credit Union of your city. Remind the credit manager that federal law prohibits discrimination in the extension of credit for reasons of sex and/or marital status.

2. As credit manager for Quality Office Supply Company, you check all applications for credit. This morning's mail has brought a completed Quality Office Supply credit application form. The form was obtained earlier in the week when one of the secretaries from Old Bay Restaurant Supply House came into the store and made a $63 cash purchase.

    In reviewing the information on the form, you call two of the listed credit references. The information obtained through the phone calls is not sufficient to establish an open account. You decide to write a letter of inquiry to the third listed reference, Pumps and Piping Sales Company, 575 West Oak Avenue, Brandenburg. (Brandenburg is a small town in your state but some distance away.)

3. You are employed in the credit department of Hensen's Department Store, your city. Mr. Richard R. Rush has recently moved into town and applied for a credit card with your store. He would like a $2,000 limitation on the card; he has had no previous credit transactions with your store. You have checked with his present employer and verified his salary, which is almost $50,000 a year. He has listed Gold's Department Store, 729 East Elm Street, Ft. Collins, Colorado 80521 as a credit reference. You would like the following information from Gold's: length of time Mr. Rush has maintained an account, current status of account, payment record, credit limit, number of persons authorized to use account.

4. As credit manager of Sealfresh, Inc., you receive a letter from Corner Parlor requesting a thirty-day open account instead of their usual C.O.D. deliveries. Among the references furnished with the letter is Sunday Ice Cream Sales, a well-established company in your city. Write to Sunday Ice Cream Sales and request the necessary information.

5. You are the owner of Pumps and Piping Sales Company (Problem 2). You have carried Old Bay Restaurant Supply House on open account for more than three years, but they have made no purchases for the last seven months. The organization has never owed more than $200 at one time, and now they do not owe anything at all. But you have had some difficulty in collecting; last year an invoice of $152 remained unpaid from March until November. You have heard that the company is near bankruptcy but later were told that the rumor was incorrect. You do not care for the owner of Old Bay Restaurant Supply House, as he reminds you of your great uncle who ran away with your girl friend and then abandoned her. Answer the inquiry of Quality Office Supply.

6. You are the owner of Sunday Ice Cream Sales (Problem 4). Corner Parlor has been a regular customer of yours since you began operation of the business in 1975. You remember hearing your grandfather say that they had been customers of his since he began operating Sunday Ice Cream Sales in 1920. Never once have they required so much as a collection reminder. Write to Sealfresh.

Credit Approvals and Refusals

7. You are the credit manager of Sealfresh, Inc. Write a credit approval letter to Corner Parlor (Problems 4 and 6).

8. You are the credit manager of Quality Office Supply. Assume that the owner of Pumps and Piping Sales Company told you everything shown in Problem 5. (Also refer to Problem 2.) Decide what to write to Old Bay Restaurant Supply House. Write it.

9. You are the credit manager of the department store that refused credit to the secretary employed by the government agency (Problem 1). You check the

information furnished by her supervisor and find that everything is as stated in the supervisor's letter. Write a letter to the secretary approving her credit.

10.   Write a letter to the office manager (Problems 1 and 9) stating that the secretary's credit has been approved.

11.   You receive a reply from Gold's Department Store (Problem 3). You are informed that Richard Rush has never had an account at Gold's. In addition, the credit manager has checked telephone directories and the city directory and found no Richard Rush listed. What will you write to Richard Rush? Write it.

12.   As a credit analyst in the personal credit department of Holiday Tours and Travel, Inc., you have the task of refusing the Holiday Touraway Credit Card application of Becky Sue Bird.

Becky's application shows that she is a graduate student at your local university and that she has never held a full-time job. You checked the records at the credit bureau of your city and found no indication of Ms. Bird's either applying for credit previously or purchasing anything on credit. The immediate reason for wanting a Holiday Touraway Credit Card, as stated by Becky in her application, is to tour the Caribbean with friends during the mid-term break.

Holiday Tours and Travel, Inc. refuses credit to applicants not having credit references. Your agency also makes travel arrangements for sporting events; consequently, many of your clients are college students. Since you want Becky and other college students in the community to continue using the services of Holiday Tours and Travel, Inc. (on a cash basis until they have established a credit rating), you must refuse as positively as possible to convince Ms. Bird to travel with Holiday in the future.

13.   You are credit manager at I & I Manufacturers, which makes an exclusive men's line of furnishings. You have just received from Mr. Charles March, owner of Men's Top Drawer (2076 Poplar, your city) a credit request of $16,000 for suits and sport coats. Mr. Marshall opened a men's clothing store about two years ago. He has been doing quite well with a moderately priced line of clothing that he has been selling.

Mr. Marshall's clientele, in your opinion, is not ready for the exclusive line you manufacture. After an investigation, you learn that he is planning to relocate and sell to a wide variety of customers. You also find that with his existing customers, more than 50 percent of his business is done through charge accounts and many are delinquent, causing his assets to liabilities to be below the required 2-to-1 ratio. You will have to refuse his credit request, but you want to make available to him cash-saving options. You believe that sometime soon he will be ready for the exclusive line you manufacture.

Collection Messages

14.   The Raleigh office of Tax Consultants, Inc. has been unable to collect from Mr. Fred Dangerfeld. He operates a hammer handle manufacturing business in his garage. Every year for the past ten years Tax Consultants, Inc. has prepared the income tax return for his small business. This year his

return was prepared in January. Since his return was more complex than in prior years, Tax Consultants, Inc. billed Mr. Dangerfeld $37 for tax-consulting services. Thirty days later you (the manager) sent a duplicate of the original bill with a reminder.

Since your reminder failed to bring in the money, after another thirty days you sent your first collection letter to him. Mr. Dangerfeld has always paid promptly in the past; you are surprised that your reminder letter did not convince him to pay his bill. Now, thirty days later, you will write a second letter. What should be your approach? Write a convincing letter.

15. Thirty additional days have elapsed, and still no answer from Mr. Danger-feld. You try to telephone but cannot get an answer. Write a letter. What will you say?

16. Thirty more days go by. You have telephoned twice, and someone has said that he was unable to come to the phone. Write a letter.

17. You are the credit manager for an appliance store. Mrs. Felix Jones has always been a good customer of yours. She has bought several major appliances from you, as well as small ones occasionally. This is the first time that you have had any difficulty collecting from her. You have already written her once when she missed her first payment because you were sure it was just an oversight on her part. This brought no response. She has missed another payment. You feel you must remind her again and insist on payment. You do not want to lose the goodwill that has built up, but you feel that something is wrong when she misses two payments in succession. Write her a letter attempting to work something out with her and request payment.

18. You are the credit manager of an agricultural chemical company. John Travis, a plantation owner, bought fertilizer for $10,084 in March. He has been buying on open account for more than twenty years. He has always paid in full, but only after one or two collection letters.

At the end of March you mailed him a regular monthly statement but received no reply. At the end of April, you mailed another statement with a past-due notation. At the end of May, you wrote a letter asking for the full amount due; you did not receive an answer. You wrote a stronger letter at the end of June but received no reply. You send a representative by the plantation to see him. The representative is told by the farm manager that Mr. Travis has been in Europe but is expected to return on July 15.

It is now July 20. Write to Mr. Travis. What should be your approach at this time?

19. Your supervisor at Hensen's (Problem 3) has granted credit to Richard Rush, based only on his present salary. (The supervisor either did not see the letter from Gold's in Colorado or he ignored it.) It is now five months later. Mr. Rush, his wife, and two daughters have charged clothing and furniture amounting to $3,115.92. (You don't know why they were allowed to exceed the requested $2,000 limit. You mentally note that something must be done immediately about Hensen's credit policies.) No answers have been received from your two previous letters, the first a reminder and the second an appeal based upon the preservation of his credit rating. Previous reminders were only stamped notations on the monthly bill.

You read in the morning paper that the Rush home, purchased five months ago for more than $100,000, is offered for sale at $89,000. You attempt to talk with your supervisor about the situation; he hurriedly tells you to handle it, that if you know what's good for you you'll get the money in a hurry but that right now he has to go play golf with Mr. Rush. What do you do now? Another question in your mind is what has happened to the reply you received from Gold's Department Store.

20. You are owner-manager of a local dance studio. The three daughters of Dr. and Mrs. Frank Williams have been taking dancing lessons for three years. Write a collection letter to Mrs. Williams, who has always paid for the children's lessons promptly. Now the bill is three months past due. Lessons for the girls cost $40 a month. You are on friendly terms with Mrs. Williams. The girls are excellent students, and you don't want to lose them. A reminder note and a note of inquiry have already gone unheeded. The annual dance recital is coming up next month, with extra expense for yourself and the parents of the young dancers. A newsletter was sent to Mrs. Williams at the beginning of the year explaining tuition payments and when they are due, along with other necessary information. You talked with Mrs. Williams in December at a meeting for all parents to discuss the annual recital.

FURTHER READING ♦ 12

Barzman, Sol. *Everyday Credit Checking*. New York: Thomas Y. Crowell Company, 1973.

Cole, Robert H. *Consumer and Commercial Credit Management*. 5th ed. Homewood, Ill.: Irwin, 1976.

Morris, Richard H. *Credit and Collection Letters: New Techniques to Make Them Work*. Great Neck, N.Y.: Channel Press, 1960.

Murphy, Richard J. "For Fast, Accurate Credit Letters." *Credit and Financial Management*, September 1974, p. 18.

"The Telephone as a Collection Tool." *Credit and Financial Management*, January 1975, p. 27.

COMMUNICATING
ABOUT
EMPLOYMENT

Planning the Search for
Career Employment

13

This chapter and Chapter 14 are planned to help you communicate effectively in order to secure employment. Chapter 13 emphasizes the research phase of the job-seeking process and the preparation of the data sheet, or resume. Chapter 14 presents a consideration of the application letter and other letters about employment, as well as a discussion of the employment interview.

An outstanding letter of application, with a well-organized and complete data sheet, can make the difference as to whether or not you find the kind of employment you are seeking. Although an outstanding written presentation will not get a job for you, it can provide an opportunity for an interview, at which time you continue your sales presentation.

The most important factor in the search for employment is that you are qualified for the job for which you apply. The most creative, attractive, and cleverly written letter and data sheet will not substitute for having something to sell, just as a cleverly worded sales letter must be written about a good product if it is to be truly effective.

METHODS OF OBTAINING EMPLOYMENT

Let's consider the various ways in which employment is obtained. Although some methods are more effective than others, depending upon the applicant's background and goals and upon the job requirements, you should consider the use of all appropriate methods. You should take the initiative instead of waiting for an employer to offer a position, regardless of your outstanding qualifications or of a favorable job market.

Taking the initiative has several advantages. You become aware of differing opportunities and are able to compare prospective employers and job opportunities. You are also more likely to find a better job when you actively seek employment because you learn about more openings. Another obvious advantage is that your effort in the job-seeking process tells the employer a great deal about you, including the fact that you have enough energy and ambition to make a dedicated and organized effort to place yourself.

In addition, as you survey employing organizations, you will no doubt find one or more in which you are especially interested. Your interest in this organization, which will be apparent in your application and interview, is a definite positive factor from the standpoint of the employer. Knowing that one person very much wants a job with that firm is enough to make a difference between two applicants who are otherwise about equal in background and estimated ability.

Solicited Application Letters and Data Sheets

A solicited letter of application, with an accompanying data sheet, is based on an "inquiry about the product." These applications are written in reply to advertisements, announcements, or other requests for applicants.

You may find advertisements in your local newspaper of the kind of work you are seeking, but don't wait for these advertisements, which may be long in appearing. A more likely place to find announcements of openings in your specialized field is in professional journals. Your acceptance of these positions, however, may necessitate moving to another locality.

Writing the solicited application letter differs little from writing the solicited sales letter. You must convince the reader that the product you are selling — yourself — is the one that should be selected. As in solicited sales letters, you are less concerned with getting attention in the first paragraph for, in a sense, you already have the reader's attention. In all instances, however, avoid slow, word-wasting openings, and go immediately to the message you are trying to convey.

As in sales letters, the opening section and all remaining sections should be built around the central selling point. The central theme, based upon the central selling point, tells how your most important qualification, or perhaps a group of related qualifications, can benefit the employing organization. Stress the strength or strengths that you believe will be most applicable to the position for which you apply, but include other positive factors as well. The employer looks at the entire background, personality, ability, and attitude of the applicant.

Unsolicited Application Letters and Data Sheets

Unsolicited application letters can be considered a form of direct-mail advertising, similar to messages planned for direct-mail campaigns to sell a product or service.

Prepare a mailing list of organizations for which you would like to work. This mailing list should consist of the names of the organizations and the names, titles, and addresses of persons responsible for receiving and reviewing applications.

Unless you learn otherwise through your research in preparation for mailing applications, find the name of the personnel director and address the application to this person. Try to avoid using only a title, as "Personnel Director," but if you cannot determine the name of the individual, you will be forced to use only the title. Make absolutely sure that the name is spelled correctly and that the title is accurately used. Preparing your mailing list will require a great deal of research in order to select the organizations to which to send your application.

Some books on the job-seeking process advocate sending out several hundred letters and data sheets. Some students have been known to send as many as 1,000. Most likely, though, you are better advised to be more selective in your choice of organizations to which you mail applications. If you attempt such a broad-scale mailing, you lose any hope of tailoring your approach to the individual companies, to say nothing of the great amount of time and expense involved.

Remember, however, that you are not likely to receive favorable replies from all the applications you mail. Depending upon current employment conditions and upon your background and qualifications, you may receive a request for interviews or for further information from only a small percentage of your total list.

Ordinarily the two-part application, consisting of the letter and the data sheet, should be sent as a unit in your direct-mail job search, although some persons send only a prospecting letter and offer to send the complete resume upon request. This type of approach, however, seems to invite an unfavorable reply or no reply at all.

Each letter should be individually typewritten, no matter how many are mailed. To do otherwise is to suggest that the letter is only one of many. This implication shows that you are looking only for a job, any job, and that you are not particularly interested in the individual organization to which the letter is addressed. Letters that are prepared by the use of an automatic typewriter, of which there are several kinds, retain their individually typewritten appearance.

Data sheets are often printed; employers seem to accept neatly printed data sheets as well as those prepared by some other excellent means of reproduction, such as the offset process. As a practical matter, if you send out many unsolicited applications, the data sheet should be duplicated in some way. If you are applying to organizations that are similar in nature and supposed needs, a data sheet can be made to "fit" all of them, although not so exactly as if each were especially written for each organization.

Other Methods of Obtaining Employment

The college placement office, for graduating college seniors, is usually the best means of securing career employment. The services of these offices are available also to alumni and to students who are dropping out of the college for one reason or another.

Placement offices, in addition to arranging interviews with company representatives, usually maintain a library of brochures and literature about employing organizations, including various government agencies. The number of employing organizations that hire through college placement offices changes from year to year, depending upon the economic situation and upon other varying factors.

In the past decade we have seen, for example, very poor and very good years for engineers and for elementary school teachers. Liberal arts majors have always had a harder time finding lucrative employment than have students with more specialized majors, especially business majors. Some liberal arts majors are hired as management trainees because they are expected to have a broad background of general knowledge.

If you find employment through a college placement office, you may not use an application letter or data sheet as they are discussed in this chapter. You will almost certainly make a written application of some kind, however, even if it consists only of filling in the standard application form of the particular organization. In addition, you will probably write follow-up letters and a thank-you letter after the interview.

Some organizations ask the applicant to prepare a letter of application and a data sheet, similar to those discussed here, after the applicant has been interviewed. This instruction may be given to test the communication ability of the applicant or perhaps in order to determine whether there is a sincere interest in the job. Usually, however, the purpose of an application letter and a data sheet is to obtain an interview.

Private and government employment agencies place thousands of persons each year. Government agencies are free. Placement fees are paid to privately owned employment agencies, either by the individual who is hired or by the employing organization, or the fee may be divided between the employer and the employee. Although these fees to private agencies seem high, if you can find a better job through an agency than you could find on your own, your actual value received exceeds the cost. You are wise, however, to check with your local Better Business Bureau before signing a contract with an employment agency.

Jobs are also obtained through the simple process of going to personnel offices and placing applications or by making telephone calls. Although these methods may constitute a satisfactory approach to some kinds of jobs, including those that college students find as part-time work as they complete their schooling, they are not usually the best approach to full-time career employment.

An unsolicited two-part application, based upon research into the company to which the application is sent, shows more care and preparation and more actual interest in the organization. In addition, it can be read when time is available for it to be given complete attention. A telephone call may come at an inopportune time and result in a hasty "no."

ANALYZING YOUR QUALIFICATIONS

When planning a sales campaign, one of the first steps is to make a product analysis. You look at the product, test it, and compare it with competing brands. Then you decide upon your central theme, or the most important selling feature, also called the central selling point.

As you plan a job-seeking campaign, you make this analysis about yourself. You analyze the "product," compare it with competing ones, and note how the product fits the market for which you are preparing your application. Although this analysis is for your use only, it will be far more beneficial and complete if it is in written form.

You will have several features to stress, but the main theme of your sales material will depend upon the kind of work for which you are applying, as well as upon the type of organization. Because the emphasis will differ according to these factors, an individually tailored application letter, as well as an individually planned resume, is more likely to be effective than using the same two-part application for organizations with varying needs.

Because you will not always be sure of these varying needs, you will not always be exactly correct in your choice of the central selling point, just as you cannot always be sure as you plan to sell a product or service. Usually the central selling feature will be either your education or your experience. For most persons completing a college degree, especially young college graduates with limited experience, the central selling point is some facet of the educational background, ordinarily the major field.

After these persons have been out of school for several years, the experience is likely to become the most important selling feature if it is similar to the kind of work for which they are now making application. For people with diversified experience, that to be stressed should be successful experience in a job similar to the one being sought.

In certain instances, extracurricular work or an avocation will be the most convincing central theme. For example, a football star may be hired as a sporting goods salesman; in this case, the football experience is of more value than is the student's major in, for example, journalism. If the person were applying for a job as a newspaper reporter, the academic major should be stressed to the extent that the application is built around it. The football experience would be mentioned but given only limited coverage.

As when selling a product, however, we do not stress the central selling point to the extent that other selling features are omitted or overly subordinated. This factor is important not only from the standpoint that we cannot be completely sure that we are choosing the most logical central selling point, but also from the standpoint that we are usually hired on the basis of our total qualifications, consisting of education, experience, personality, attitude toward work, and the ability to grow and develop in usefulness to the employing organization.

As you analyze yourself, you will no doubt find that you have weak and strong points. As you present yourself to the prospective employers, you will stress the strong points and subordinate or leave unmentioned those factors that you consider to be weaknesses. But never misrepresent in any way. The positive approach, as in other communications situations, "accentuates the positive and eliminates the negative." What you consider to be a weakness can often be presented in positive terms. For example, instead of saying, "I have no experience except for part-time work in a grocery," say

> My four years' experience as a checker and office employee with A&P Grocery Company were valuable in that they gave me experience in working harmoniously with other employees and in courteously serving the customers. I worked an average of twenty-five hours a week during the entire four years of attending college, yet maintained a grade point average of 3.2, a score that qualified me each semester for the Dean's list.

Other examples of points to emphasize and subordinate will be given later in this chapter as you learn to prepare the application letter and resumé.

Education

If you are completing college, your education to be considered in your self-analysis consists especially of work leading toward a degree. Other educational preparation consists of high school subjects, technical or business courses, and other specialized schooling, as well as educational experience obtained in military service. Consider the courses that apply to the job you are seeking, including those within your major field and any others that especially relate.

Consider also your scholastic standing overall and in your major field. Whether or not you mention your scholastic standing depends upon what it is. According to the principle of the positive approach, you are not obligated to emphasize a negative aspect. If you have an average only equal to that necessary to obtain a degree or very slightly above, emphasize the degree and leave unmentioned the actual grade point average.

The degree is a real accomplishment, even if other persons have surpassed you in A's and B's. But if you are asked for your exact standing, be truthful. By being truthful, according to an old adage, you are not forced to remember what you said. Some organizations immediately disqualify any applicant who is discovered to have misrepresented even the slightest bit of information.

You may wish to give your grade point average only in your major field, not the overall average, as the standing in your major field is likely to be higher. This performance in your major field should be of most concern to the employer. In some instances you should mention research projects or papers that are particularly relevant. After you have completed graduate work, mention of a thesis or dissertation is considered an essential part of your educational preparation.

Remember to include specific skills and abilities developed in your educational program, such as ability to work with computers or various office machines, most especially if you are likely to use these machines in your future work. If you have used these machines in previous employment, the mention of this ability should be listed in the section on experience. If you have not actually used them but have had training in their use, mention of this ability should be placed in the educational section of your data sheet.

As you complete the analysis of your educational preparation, you will probably find that it should be your central selling feature. From the standpoint of emphasis, as you have already learned, a description of this preparation in terms of how it will benefit the reader should be described in more detail than other factors. Also from the standpoint of emphasis, this educational preparation should be presented before other less important factors.

Work Experience

Work experience is ordinarily one of the two most important factors for your career preparation, although a few college students complete degrees with no work experience whatsoever. If you have no work experience, your educational preparation must be stressed to an even greater extent; you should also show how your participation in professional and social organizations has provided experience in leadership positions and in working with other persons.

Some applicants have the idea that only related work experience should be mentioned in the application letter or on the data sheet. This approach is unwise. Work experience of any kind, as long as it is legal and honorable, is better than no experience at all. Any job, even the most menial, indicates that you have the energy and initiative to seek and hold a job, as well as the responsibility of earning some or all of your college expenses.

Remember to include your work experience acquired in military service. In many instances this will be your most important and relevant experience, or even the central theme of your entire application. The fact that you were an officer, in itself alone, is not sufficient to serve as the central selling point, although it does indicate that you have handled responsible duties.

As you continue with your self-analysis, remember to make a note of accomplishments in your work experience, such as exceeding a sales quota, earning a promotion, or receiving certificates of recognition for unusual achievement. Begin to think of the best ways to present these successes to show how you can benefit the prospective employer. You also have the problem of presenting these successful experiences without appearing egotistical.

Activities, Achievements, and Personal Characteristics

In this portion of your analysis, list extracurricular activities in high school and college; social and professional organizations, including membership and offices held; and any other meaningful activity or accomplishment. Include honors, awards, publications, and other recognitions. (Scholastic awards are usually presented in connection with your other educational achievements.) Foreign language abilities, hobbies, personal business ventures, and many other facets of your total experience may have a bearing upon your ability to fit into the particular organization to which you are applying.

Check yourself in these and similar areas:

Ability and willingness to assume responsibility

Ability to adapt to changing situations

Ability to communicate in oral and written form

Ability to make decisions

Ability to persevere

Ability to think logically and creatively

Ability to work with other persons

Leadership	Courtesy and diplomacy
Judgment	Emotional and physical health
Self-confidence and poise	Maturity
Appearance	Dependability
Sense of humor	Promptness
Neatness	Ambition and enthusiasm

Most important, ask yourself if the field of work being considered is in line with your real interest and ability.   What do you want from your career?

To prevent the data sheet from becoming extremely long, as well as from the standpoint of presenting only necessary and relevant information, use discretion as you present this type of somewhat supplementary information.

As you remember from your study of emphasis, when you attempt to emphasize a great many things, you succeed in emphasizing nothing.   On the other hand, you are not presenting the best possible picture of yourself if you omit favorable data that may show your ability to be a good employee.

When you know the answers to these questions, and after you have made this complete and objective self-analysis, you should have a realistic approach to the job-seeking process.   You still have the task of choosing the best method of presenting qualifications, as well as determining which factors to stress and which to subordinate.   In order to answer these questions, you need to know something of your prospective employer.

ANALYZING THE EMPLOYMENT MARKET

The market analysis is the next step in the job-seeking process.   Just as a sales writer must know something about the potential buyer so that the product or service can be presented in terms of the reader's interest, so must you know something of the prospective employer.

You must know your employer and the job requirements in order to best present yourself so as to show how your qualifications meet the employer's needs.   Although there are many items of information that you will not be able to obtain until the interview, or perhaps not until you actually begin work or have worked for a considerable time, much information will be available if you diligently look for it.

First of all, what information will you need?   You will need enough information to indicate that an organization is one that will offer you sufficient opportunity, provided you are hired, to justify your accepting this employment.   Although this statement may seem obvious, this is really the most important answer you are seeking.   As you make this investigation, you will also gain enough information to help you intelligently plan your presentation to the specific organization.

You should not take the attitude that you must accept a job that offers little opportunity for growth or for the kind of work you prefer. Although you may be forced to accept an offer that is less than ideal, at least you should aim high. On the other hand, remember that you are not stuck forever in any job; although frequent changes do not look good on your record, many if not most persons change jobs several times during their lifetime. And it is usually easier to find work if you already have a job than if you do not.

Although you may not stay with your first full-time job, it should be chosen with care. In one way or another, it will affect your entire career. In addition, the employing organization will spend time and money in hiring and training you — perhaps a great deal of time and money. If you do not enter into the employment contract with the sincere desire to succeed and to remain with the organization, you are not being completely fair to the employer or to yourself.

Another purpose of research into potential employing organizations is to obtain information about how to sell yourself intelligently. If you can determine your possible duties, you will have a better idea of which of your qualifications to emphasize in order to show how your abilities will be of the most possible benefit to the reader.

Another advantage (as well as an obvious necessity) of doing research into the job market is to know which organizations have openings for persons like yourself. You can assume that many large organizations will periodically employ persons with widely used specializations, such as accounting or sales. For positions such as these, unsolicited letters of application are appropriate and useful. You can, in fact, use unsolicited letters for all possible openings, but you will be less sure of receiving a favorable reply.

Even if an unplanned "hit-or-miss" approach seems to succeed, it is still far from being the best method. You are not able in this way to fit your qualifications to the particular employer. You are also likely not to find the organizations for which you would most like to work.

Where will you find all this information? Let's consider first certain printed sources that will provide some of the information you seek. Annual reports of the firms in which you are interested include far more information than the financial statement. They also tell something of the product or services, as well as the location of the home office and branch offices. They may give information about management policies.

The *College Placement Annual* (College Placement Council, 35 East Elizabeth Street, Bethlehem, PA) is especially applicable to persons graduating from college. A copy of this book is often available through your college placement office. Employing organizations are listed alphabetically and also by occupational specialities and geographic locations. Other information includes brief notations as to the kinds of openings, the educational background of the applicants being sought, and the proper person in the organization whom you should contact.

A similar book is *Career: The Annual Guide to Business Opportunities* (CAREER Publications, Inc., New York).

Moody's Manuals of Investments (Moody's Investors Service, 99 Church Street, New York), although intended primarily to provide information to potential investors, also provides information essential to the potential employee. (As an employee, you are an investor in the company; from your standpoint, it may be the most important investment you will ever make.)

Information included in these manuals consists of a summary of the history of each organization, method of operation, location, products or services, and the financial structure. These books are available in most libraries. (These sources as well as other printed ones, mentioned here in connection with the job-seeking process, are also discussed in Chapter 15 in relation to securing secondary information for the preparation of reports.)

Standard and Poor's Manuals (Standard and Poor's Corporation, 345 Hudson Street, New York) are also planned primarily for investors. They contain information similar to that contained in *Moody's Manuals.*

Another publication of this corporation is *Poor's Register of Directors and Executives, United States and Canada.* This directory may be useful in finding the name and title of the person to whom you should send your application for employment.

The Business Periodicals Index, as well as other periodical indexes (see Chapters 1 and 15), is useful in locating magazine articles that have been written about particular business organizations in which you are interested.

Many government and professional organizations issue publications of their own planned to describe employment opportunities and the necessary qualifications for employees. Much of this literature is available through college placement offices and public and school libraries. You can also learn about job openings from professional journals in your field.

Perhaps the best way of all to learn about prospective employers is to ask other persons who are employed in these organizations doing work similar to the kind you would be doing. As in any other survey, however, the more people you ask, within limits, the more valid your data are likely to be.

ADVANTAGES OF THE TWO-PART APPLICATION

A two-part application enables you to use the letter to present highlights of the detailed information included on the data sheet. These factors are stated in light of what your qualifications will do for the reader. As in other sales messages, the letter is more coherent and emphatic when it is built around a central theme.

Prepare the data sheet, then choose from it important elements to be included in the letter. The letter can be considered as an interpretation of your most important qualifications of all those shown on the data sheet, in terms of reader interest — much as you present important elements of a product as you write a sales letter to be sent with leaflets and brochures. Both of these parts of the two-part application are prepared after you have made a detailed analysis of your qualifications and after you have done research about the companies in which you are interested.

THE DATA SHEET — A REPORT ON YOURSELF

The data sheet (or resumé) can be the deciding factor in getting the interviewer's attention. It can also continue the sales presentation throughout the interview and the negotiation process.

A well-prepared data sheet should be a truly superior expression of your talents and background. It should be a credit to your creativity and ability to put ideas into convincing words. The most effective data sheets sell ability, talent, and potential, as well as education and past experience.

You should not understate your qualifications, but you also must not misrepresent in any way. Two or three hundred applicants may also want the job for which you are applying; now is no time to be modest.

A data sheet, like the letter that accompanies it, should be striking in appearance. It should be absolutely perfect in typewritten form and arrangement. Use good paper, a good typewriter, and a clear typewriter ribbon. Special paper, such as a heavy bond in a light cream or buff color, may make your application stand out from all the rest. A perfectly typewritten copy, however, with correct punctuation and exact wording and spelling, will be superior to many other data sheets, even if it is on plain white paper of good quality. Why anyone would send out unattractive and incorrect applications is difficult to understand, considering the importance of the message. Make sure that you do not leave in such obvious errors as strikeovers, misspelled words, messy erasures, and uneven margins.

Every data sheet should contain certain basic parts, although the format may and should vary according to the aspect to be emphasized. Each should contain the employment objective (this may be included in the heading); education; work experience; personal data; and references, or a statement that you will send references upon request.

The job objective should not be too specific or so general as to be vague.   Work experience should include all positions held, although at times short periods of work may be summarized without giving specific dates and employers.   Work experience should accent specific positive accomplishments.

An example of a well-planned data sheet is given in Figure 13–1. The comments that follow point out minor ways in which the data sheet could be improved.

Let's look at Miss Aldridge's data sheet.   Although overall it is a good one, perhaps it can be improved in some ways.

The *heading* includes, as it should, the applicant's name, the type of work for which she is applying, and her address and telephone number. This qualification sheet could be described with the words "Data Sheet," "Resume," "Personal Data Sheet," "Qualifications of Sherry Aldridge," "Personal Resume," or other similar wording.   In fact, it need not include any of these headings.   It could merely have the applicant's name centered in all capitals at the top.

The term "accounting work" is too general if the candidate is aware of a particular opening that could be described in more specialized and specific terms.   For an unsolicited application, however, for which no exact job description is available, the applicant could have been so specific that she eliminated herself from consideration for general openings.

The truly qualified candidate should be able — with training and experience — to handle a variety of responsibilities related to her educational background and work experience.   Even if she begins in a specialized area, she must be able to assume additional duties if she is to be truly valuable to the employing organization, to say nothing of reaching a higher level of responsibility for her own benefit.

In this heading, the job objective is included in the title.   Sometimes the job objective is set up as a separate part in this way:

> Objective: Beginning accounting and auditing work, with eventual managerial capacities.

Sherry could have mentioned here, or in the following section on education, that she plans to take the Certified Public Accountant Examination. This information is given in the letter, but it is of such importance that it should also be included on the data sheet, as the data sheet is expected to be a complete summary of outstanding data.

Should Sherry have included a photograph?   Why, or why not?   In former years (ten years ago or more) a photograph was considered a standard and expected part of the data sheet — or, if only the application letter was sent, the picture was attached to the letter.

However, today a photograph is no longer required or expected. Most employers will not ask for one for fear that their request will be considered as being for discriminatory purposes.   Under Title VII of the

SHERRY CLARA ALDRIDGE'S QUALIFICATIONS FOR

ACCOUNTING WORK WITH ARTHUR ANDERSEN CORPORATION

Address: 2305 Scaper Street, Memphis, TN 38114
Telephone: 901-743-1278

Professional Education

Two years and nine months of uninterrupted study summer and winter (Fall, 1974-Spring, 1977) at Memphis State University, majoring in accounting. Bachelor of Business Administration degree, May, 1977, with cum laude honors.

Three years of study (Fall, 1971-Spring, 1974) at Memphis Technical High School, majoring in business; graduated as valedictorian of a class of 259 on May 21, 1974.

College Courses Especially Valuable as Preparation for Corporation and Financial Accounting

Accounting

Principles: Accounting theory; financial transactions.

Advanced: Partnerships, consignments, installment sales, insurance, annuities.

Laboratory. The working of a practice set involving current accounting practice; the electronic computer was utilized in this course.

Auditing: Elementary and advanced; public and internal auditing with emphasis on internal control.

Intermediate: Corporate accounting records and statements, miscellaneous ratios.

Systems: Problems involved in designing systems for various types of businesses, including processing accounting data by electronic computer.

Federal Income Tax: Reporting taxes for corporations, partnerships, and individuals.

Consolidations: Business mergers and foreign exchange; complex statements involved.

Related Courses

Corporation Finance	Data Processing Systems	Business Communication
Money and Banking	Statistics	Personnel Management
Economics	Business Law	

Figure 13-1. *Data Sheet — Application for Accounting Work*

Figure 13-1.   *(Continued)*

2

Sherry Clara Aldridge

Activities and Awards

Beta Alpha Psi
The Honor Society of Phi Kappa Phi
Sweetheart of Phi Sigma Kappa fraternity

Work Experience

Summer of 1976 (part-time)

   Accountant for James M. Johnson, electrician, 1923 Madison Avenue,
      Memphis, Tennessee 38111. Designed and supervised the
      accounting system.

Personal Data

Born October 26, 1957, in Memphis, Tennessee
Unmarried
5 feet, 5 inches; 100 pounds
No absence from school or work because of illness in the past four years.
Hobbies: cooking, bowling, basketball, archery, sewing.

References (by permission)

Mr. Truel D. Hicks   Mr. Lawrence Curbo
Professor of Accounting   Professor of Accounting
Memphis State University   Memphis State University
Memphis, Tennessee 38152   Memphis, TN 38118

Mrs. Loretta Smith, Principal   Mr. James M. Jones, CPA
Memphis Technical High School   Jones and Jones, Accountants
Memphis, Tennessee 38111   4646 Poplar Avenue
                                            Memphis, Tennessee 38111

Civil Rights Act, which was amended in March 1972, an employer must consider all applicants equally, regardless of race, religion, sex, or national origin. You as an applicant, however, are free to include a picture if you feel that it will help, although it is possible that some extra-cautious employers will return it to you instead of keeping it in their files.

One advantage of sending a photograph is that the reader will be better able to visualize you and perhaps distinguish you from the many other applicants. When you send out many applications, using the direct-mail advertising approach, perhaps you are wiser to omit the photograph, at least on the first mailing. Whenever you do use a photograph, make sure that it is a black and white, head-and-shoulders view, never a snapshot.

Education is given a special emphasis in Sherry's data sheet, as it is in her letter of application. This is her only reasonable central selling point because of many courses in accounting and because of her excellent grade point average, especially in the accounting field.

This section on education is longer than similar sections on many other data sheets; perhaps it should have been condensed. Most certainly it should have been shortened if the experience section were longer because of a great deal of related successful employment.

The "cum laude" designation should have been made clear by stating the exact grade point average. Although "cum laude" should logically be based on the same standards in all colleges and universities, it is not. In addition, the grade point average should be explained, for these designations also differ. If she had said, "A 3.45 grade point average based on a 4.0 scale," the description would have been exact.

Work experience, as shown in the data sheet, consists only of a short time spent in an accounting office. Perhaps this is all the work experience she has obtained, although, of necessity, the average graduating senior has worked more. If Sherry has worked elsewhere, this work should have been mentioned and described, even though it was completely unrelated to accounting.

One reason for including all experience, related and unrelated, is that all time since graduation from high school should be accounted for. When you have had many short-time or part-time jobs, it is not absolutely essential to give exact dates, with names and addresses, of all employing organizations, although this arrangement is the better choice if it will not make the data sheet too long. You can perhaps summarize certain work experience, for example, "1975–1977, part-time jobs at service stations, grocery stores, and drugstores." In Sherry's data sheet, the time is accounted for, even without stating employment, because of the statement that her college study was uninterrupted.

Personal references are not always listed on the data sheet. In the reference position you may include a statement similar to this one: "References will be furnished upon request." If you are applying to only a few employers, especially if you know that positions are available, you are probably wiser to include specific references. They can add a great deal of weight to the application and could be the determining factor as to whether or not you will be interviewed.

When you are sending out a great many unsolicited applications, however, you are wiser to omit the exact references and offer to send them later. Although potential employers are not likely to get in touch with the persons you name until after the interview, they may do so. You then run the risk of having the persons who have agreed to recommend you bothered unnecessarily by many inquiries. Although these persons recommend you heartily in reply to the first few inquiries, they may become less enthusiastic after a dozen or so.

Always include a person's full name, title, and business organization or occupation, as well as the address and telephone number. Present and past employers, as well as professors, are persons who are likely to be able to tell the potential employer about you. You may also use one or two other people who have known you for a considerable length of time.

Sherry should have been consistent in the use of the two-letter state abbreviations in the reference section.

You may wish at this time to read the letter of application that Sherry sent with her data sheet. The letter is presented in Chapter 14, with the discussion and illustration of other letters of application. Data sheets are presented first because, for one reason, they are most effectively prepared before the letter is written. In addition, differing data sheets are shown together in order to facilitate comparison between order of arrangement and the kinds of information included in relation to the qualifications of the differing individuals and the requirements of the positions sought.

The data sheet in Figure 13–2 describes the qualifications of a young man who has recently completed college with a preparation for teaching business subjects. He is applying for a teaching position in the high school from which he was graduated. On most data sheets, high school experiences are not given special emphasis; often the high school is not even mentioned by college graduates. Outstanding accomplishments in high school, however, such as being the valedictorian of the senior class, are appropriate and convincing on data sheets of young college graduates. In this particular application the writer uses his high school background as an important element in his preparation for teaching there; thus emphasis is given to his high school education.

In Albert Dunn's data sheet, as well as in Sherry Aldridge's (Figure 13–1), the education section is presented before work experience and the other classifications of qualifications. In both instances, education is the only logical choice as the major qualification. As you recall from your study of the techniques of emphasis, the first position is an emphatic one, more so than any of the following positions. After these young applicants have obtained several years of experience, their data sheets may be more

ALBERT ROBERT DUNN'S QUALIFICATIONS FOR
TEACHING BUSINESS SUBJECTS AT
CHESTER HIGH SCHOOL, CHESTER, FLORIDA

Mailing Address: P. O. Box 2343, Chester, Florida
Telephone: 826-4419

EDUCATION

Bachelor of Science in Education degree, Florida State University,
Tallahassee, December, 1977, with a specialization in business
education; 3.6 grade point average, based on a 4-point scale.
Initiated as a junior into The Honor Society of Phi Kappa Phi.
Selected for Who's Who in Colleges and Universities.

Diploma from Chester High School, Chester, Florida, May, 1974.
Selected to give commencement address. Selected for Who's Who
Among American High School Students, 1973-74. President of
Student Body, 1973-74.

WORK EXPERIENCE

December 20, 1977--Present: Bookkeeper-receptionist for Dunn's
Insurance Agency, Chester, Florida

1974-77: Tutor, part-time, Kingsbury High School, Tallahassee.

1975-76: Waiter-cashier for Across-the-Tracks Restaurant, Tallahassee,
Florida (part-time)

1976, 77 (summers) Lifeguard for Lakeland Beach, Inc., Chester,
Florida

1972-1975 (summers) Lifeguard-Swimming Instructor, Chester Swimming
Pool, Chester, Florida

1971-1974 (part-time) newspaper carrier, stocker in grocery stores,
sales clerk (during Christmas seasons) in department stores.

OTHER ACTIVITIES

Resident Housing Association Senator, Florida State University
Marching Band, Florida State University
Symphonic Band of Florida State University
Boy Scouts of America (Received Eagle award)

Figure 13-2. *Data Sheet — Application for Teaching Position*

Figure 13-2.   (*Continued*)

ALBERT ROBERT DUNN'S QUALIFICATIONS--page 2

PERSONAL DATA

Born April 30, 1956, in Chester, Florida. Unmarried. Height, 5', 10". Weight, 150. Excellent health.

REFERENCES (by permission)

Dr. Robert M. Williams
Chairman, Department of Business Education
Florida State University
Tallahassee, Florida 40715

Mrs. Wilma Moore, Instructor
Department of Business Education
Florida State University
Tallahassee, Florida 40715

Dr. Max Jones, Professor
Department of Management
Florida State University
Tallahassee, Florida 40705

Mr. Harvey Franklin, President
First National Bank
Chester, Florida 42789

Mrs. Ruth Knowles, Principal
Kingsbury High School
4311 South Street
Tallahassee, Florida 40725

effectively arranged with their work experience moved to the more emphatic opening position.

Analyze Mr. Dunn's data sheet in relation to the application letter, which was written after the data sheet was prepared. (His letter is shown in Chapter 14.) Notice that the data sheet is complete in itself — that is, even if the employer did not have the letter, all necessary information would be given. The letter emphasizes the highlights of the information shown on the data sheet and is built around the qualifications that seem most likely to meet the needs of the employing organization.

The data sheet showing Carolyn Harrison's qualifications also has an accompanying letter, which is shown in Chapter 14. Notice the positive

CAROLYN HARRISON

Address: 6235 Rolling Water, Houston, Texas 77069
Telephone: 274-6306

EMPLOYMENT OBJECTIVE:

Merchandising Trainee, preferably in Fashions, Lone Star
Department Store

PROFESSIONAL EDUCATION:

Bachelor of Business Administration with major in marketing,
concentrating on retailing and marketing management, from University of
Houston, June, 1978.

"B" average in the following courses related to merchandising:

Marketing Management   Retail Merchandising
Marketing Promotions   Credit and Collections
Retail Store Management   Advertising Fundamentals

WORK EXPERIENCE:

1977-78   Salesperson for The Dandi Lion, 1481 Gold, Houston, TX 77069
(Summers)   Small specialized dress shop.

1976   General office work, Crump London Underwriters, 7900
(Summer)   Creek Bend, Houston, TX 77071

1975   Receptionist for L. Henning Mayfield, M.D.; 2525 South Voss
(Summer)   Road, Houston, TX 77057; general office work and some
                 work with patients.

PERSONAL DATA:

Birth date and place: Born October 19, 1956, Houston, Texas
Physical condition: 5 feet, 5 inches; 115 pounds; blonde hair; green
                          eyes; good health
Family Status: Unmarried
Hobbies: Reading, needlepointing, playing the piano, tennis

REFERENCES:

References will be furnished upon request.

Figure 13-3. *Data Sheet 3 — Application for Position as Merchandising Trainee*

way that Carolyn presented a near-minimum gradepoint average.   This presentation is in no way misleading.   In addition, the courses mentioned are the ones that seem to relate most directly to the position for which she is applying.

SUMMARY ◆ 13

When looking for employees, most organizations consider these factors: related experience, related education, dependability, the ability to cooperate with others, and a willingness to work.

When looking for employment, the use of an unsolicited application letter and data sheet is an advantage in that you show a special interest in a particular organization, a plus factor in the evaluation process.   This approach also shows that you have the initiative and ambition to research employing organizations and to make an intelligent effort to place yourself.   Another advantage is that you are more likely to find the kind of work for which you are best suited and that offers the opportunity you are seeking.

In addition to the use of solicited or unsolicited application letters and data sheets, other methods of obtaining employment consist of the use of college, government, and private employment agencies; going to personnel offices and placing applications in person; and making telephone calls.

In order to plan an effective search for employment, you analyze your qualifications and the employment market.   After these analyses are completed, the letter and data sheet are planned and written to show how your qualifications meet the needs of the employer.

The application letter is a kind of sales message.   The accompanying data sheet, or resumé, is a report on yourself and is also a form of sales presentation.   Like other sales messages, these materials are most effective, as well as concise, when they are built around a central selling theme.

For most young college graduates, education is the most appropriate central selling point.   Other factors that may be central selling themes are work experience, and, in special circumstances, extracurricular activities, hobbies, or special interests.

Like other business messages, the two-part application should make the most effective use of the you-attitude and the positive approach.

QUESTIONS AND PROBLEMS ◆ 13

1. Prepare a self-analysis, similar to that discussed in this chapter.   Include all aspects of your education, experience, hobbies, personal characteristics, or

anything else that will affect your success throughout a career, as well as your success in obtaining employment. Make this study complete. Ordinarily it will be more detailed than your data sheet, but by making a thorough self-analysis, you will be better able to decide which items to include and which to emphasize on your final data sheet. This analysis is for your own use only, not to be prepared as a classroom assignment, so be complete and objective.

2. From your detailed self-study, make a list of the kinds of employment for which you are qualified and in which you are interested. Approach this study from one of two ways:

   a. Assume that you are near graduation and that you are looking for full-time career employment. This assumption is probably the more valuable one if you expect to graduate within a year or, regardless of your standing in college, if you now have in mind definite career objectives.

   b. Prepare this list of various kinds of work in relation to part-time or summer jobs. If applicable, include only the kind of work in which you are sincerely interested and which offers opportunities for career employment.

3. After you have made your self-analysis and listed the kinds of work that you prefer and for which you are qualified, make a study of employing organizations that seem to offer the opportunities you are seeking. Use the sources described in this chapter and/or any other appropriate and useful ones. Write a short report, in the format that your instructor directs, of how you proceeded in the investigation. List the three organizations toward which you plan to direct your efforts and the reasons for these choices.

   (As you were instructed in previous assignments, you will find examples of the memorandum format and of other short reports in Appendix C. In addition, chapters 15 through 18 include a complete discussion of report preparation. Your instructor may ask that you wait until you complete these chapters to hand in this written presentation. You should do your research now, however, in order to prepare yourself to write your letter of application with its accompanying data sheet.

4, 5, 6. Prepare a data sheet from the detailed studies you have made so far. You are to send the letter and a data sheet to each of the three organizations that you have chosen. Perhaps you should prepare three different data sheets; or, if the organizations are similar, you may be able to use the same data sheet for all three.

FURTHER READING ♦ 13 and 14

Angel, J. L. *Why and How to Prepare an Effective Job Resume.* New York: World Trade Academy Press, 1973.

Blackledge, Walter L., et al. *You and Your Job.* Cincinnati: South-Western Publishing Company, 1967.

Douglas, George H., ed. "Employment, Job Research, Resumes, and Application Letters." *ABCA Bulletin* #38, no. 4 (December 1975).

Miller, Theron F. *How to Write a Job-Getting Resumé.* New York: Vantage Press, 1967.

Resumés That Get Jobs. New York: Arco Publishing Company, 1967.

Worthy, James C. *What Employers Want.* Chicago: Science Research Associates, 1971.

Completing the
Job-Finding Process

14

After you have analyzed your qualifications and the job market, and after you have completed your data sheet, you are ready to write the application letter.

This chapter includes discussions and illustrations of application letters, the employment interview, and related letters you may write as you complete the job search. After you begin work, you may write letters to other persons about aspects of employment; such letters are also illustrated here.

THE APPLICATION LETTER

The application letter that accompanies the data sheet is similar to a sales letter in that you gain attention, develop conviction in the reader's mind that you are the person who can best fill the job, and end with the action close, which is the request for an interview.

The application letter written to go along with Sherry Aldridge's data sheet illustrates the arrangement of an application letter in the sales letter plan of organization (see Figure 14–1). The first paragraph makes clear what the letter is about and attracts attention by alerting the reader that her qualifications are likely to fit the needs of the employing organization.

The middle section of the letter — the paragraphs between the attention section and the action close — presents highlights of the information shown on the data sheet and builds conviction by presenting evidence in specific terms, as related to reader interest. The closing section of the letter, in the next-to-last paragraph, asks for an interview.

2305 Scaper Street
Memphis, TN 38114
July 5, 1977

Mr. Doyle J. Smith, Personnel Manager
Arthur Andersen Corporation
8776 Mount Pilot Avenue
Miami, Florida 98755

Dear Mr. Smith:

My thorough education in accounting, plus willingness to learn, should enable me to succeed as an accountant with your firm.

A comprehensive program of accounting instructions at Memphis State University prepared me to assume responsibility in your organization and to adjust to changing conditions and procedures. All of my college work, leading to a Bachelor of Business Administration degree with cum laude honors, was directly related to the work done by your organization--as described by Mr. Robert Maxwell, your Memphis State University representative.

To increase my usefulness and efficiency, I plan to study for the Certified Public Accountant Examination and to take it next year. Even after passing the examination, however, I shall continue to study and learn--for the benefit of my employer as well as for myself.

Four months as an accounting systems designer and supervisor for James M. Johnson, an electrician in Memphis, forms my foundation of experience. As systems designer, I developed an accounting system for an electrical partnership. As supervisor, I was in charge of two bookkeepers. I also filed all the required tax returns for the business, quarterly and yearly.

Should you need more information at this time than that shown in this letter and on the enclosed data sheet, I shall be glad to supply it.

Will you write or telephone me about the possibility of working for you? Perhaps I could talk with someone in your Memphis office as a preliminary step. Or, if you wish, I will arrange to come for an interview in Miami.

I am ready to begin work immediately.

Sincerely,

Sherry Aldridge

Sherry Aldridge

Enclosure

Figure 14-1. *Sherry Aldridge's Application Letter*

The emphatic last paragraph accomplishes multiple purposes: it conveys the necessary information that Sherry is ready to begin work; it implies an eagerness to work; and it ends the letter on a positive tone — but not an overly aggressive one — by implying confidence that she will be hired.

The letter from Albert Robert Dunn (Figure 14-2) is the covering letter for his data sheet, which was shown in Chapter 13. As you analyze the letter, compare it with the data sheet. What does Mr. Dunn use as his central sales theme? Why? Is this different from the one used by Sherry Aldridge?

The data sheet that accompanied the letter from Carolyn Harrison was shown in Chapter 13. Notice how in her letter (Figure 14-3) Carolyn expresses a positive aspect of her employment at The Dandi Lion. Suppose, instead of mentioning the benefits she derived from its being a small store, she had used words to this effect: "Although The Dandi Lion is only a small store."

The letter from Frank B. Scott (Figure 14-4) is an illustration of a letter sent without a data sheet. It includes information that would ordinarily be placed on the data sheet only, for example, age and other personal details. On the other hand, the letter does not include some information that would ordinarily be stated, such as the name of his present employer. Although this letter does not give complete information, it is convincing and probably the best choice for this individual's particular situation. More details of his background will be given at the interview or before that time.

What does Mr. Scott believe to be his most important qualification for this position?

As you plan your letter of application, keep in mind the following guides:

1. Use the positive approach. Emphasize strengths and subordinate weaknesses, but do not misrepresent.

2. Use the you-attitude in that you stress what you can do for the reader. Do not use a "hard-sell" method, but state your work experience and educational background in specific and positive terms, especially as they relate to the work for which you are applying.

3. Show that you are definitely interested in the position. But don't sound as if this is your last chance.

4. Do not copy a letter written by some other person — or one from this book or any other book. This warning applies to all material, but such copying, even with changed details and paraphrasing, is almost certain to result in stilted, unnatural writing. In addition, sometimes personnel managers (as well as teachers) learn to determine exactly the book in which the letter originally appeared.

P. O. Box 2343
Chester, Florida 42789
January 7, 1978

Mr. J. B. Billingsley, President
School Board, Chester Community Unit
District Number 139
Chester, Florida 42789

Dear Mr. Billingsley:

Because of my familiarity with Chester High School and my love for it, I am
confident that I can do an effective job of teaching business subjects there.
In addition, I offer a college degree, with honors, as well as teaching and
business experience.

I was graduated from Chester High School in May, 1974. I held various
offices during my four years there, and I am presently serving on the
Advisory Board of Chester High School.

During my college preparation at Florida State University, I studied business
subjects and educational techniques. I am qualified to teach any business
course that you offer at Chester High School. In addition to my college
education, I have the experience of a student teaching assignment at
Germantown High School, Germantown, Florida, as well as experience in
tutoring at Kingsbury High School, Tallahassee.

Because of experience as a lifeguard, a cashier-waiter, a salesman, and a
bookkeeper-receptionist, I feel that I am able to work well with persons of
all ages. As I have earned most of my educational and personal expenses
since I entered high school, I realize the value of hard work and the wise use
of time.

The information shown on the enclosed data sheet will provide you with
additional information. After you have reviewed my qualifications, will you
please telephone me at 826-4419 to name a time when I can talk with you?

Sincerely,

Albert Robert Dunn

Albert Robert Dunn

Enclosure

Figure 14-2. *Albert Robert Dunn's Letter*

6235 Rolling Water
Houston, TX 77069
July 3, 1978

Mr. Fred Koch, Personnel Manager
Lone Star Department Store
Houston, TX 77062

Dear Mr. Koch:

Because of my college training in marketing and work experience in retailing, I believe I could do a good job in Lone Star's merchandise training program.

The courses in merchandising listed on the attached data sheet have given me a good background in retailing. This specialized training, along with the knowledge obtained in working for a Bachelor of Business Administration degree, should enable me to adapt to your merchandising procedure.

Working in sales for The Dandi Lion, a small, specialized dress shop, gave me experience in dealing with people. Because it was a small store, I could observe all of the store operations and participate in most of them. I checked the stock, notified the manager when items were needed, and planned window and interior displays.

I grew up in Houston and am acquainted with Lone Star's layout and its reputation for having an excellent merchandise training program. I would really like to be a part of your organization.

Please telephone me at 274-6306 to arrange a time when I can further discuss with you my qualifications for work in your merchandise training program.

Sincerely yours,

Carolyn Harrison

Carolyn Harrison

Figure 14-3. *Carolyn Harrison's Letter*

5. Although you will of necessity use *I*, try not to use the word to excess. Avoid starting several sentences with *I*.

6. Don't ask for sympathy. This is not the you-approach or the positive approach. You will not be hired because your baby needs shoes

1987 East Mexicali Drive
San Diego, CA 92123
February 22, 1979

Mr. Henry C. Cotton
Personnel Manager
First National Bank
8047 West Loma Boulevard
San Diego, CA 92107

Dear Mr. Cotton:

Three years of banking experience and college education in marketing should
enable me to be successful as the Trust Department Officer for whom you
advertised in the San Diego Times.

I am now employed full-time as a teller at a San Diego bank. Past
experience in banking includes two and one-half years at Mercantile Bank
in Long Beach, California. This experience would be helpful to First
National, as the Mercantile Bank is similar in size and organization. In
addition, I spent nine months there in the Trust Department.

In early 1976 I began work at the Mercantile Bank as a clerical employee.
In May of 1977 I was offered a full-time position as a supervisor of three
other persons. Later that year I moved to my present position as a teller
in a bank in San Diego. (My employers will recommend me highly, I feel
sure, and I will give you their names at our interview. In the meantime,
however, I ask that you keep this application confidential.)

As I have always set high goals for myself, I will continue my education after
graduation from San Diego State College in May of this year. While working
full-time and going to college at night, I have also attended four American
Institute of Banking seminars in finance and international investment banking.

Previous experience includes seven years of sales experience (automotive
parts and industrial paper) and four years in the U.S. Navy.

I am 32 years old and single, although I plan to be married in June. I am
6 feet, 3 inches tall and weigh 210 pounds. My health is excellent.

Will you write me at the address shown above--or telephone me at 458-2514--
in order to arrange an interview? I can begin work two weeks after notifying
my present employer.

Sincerely,

Frank B. Scott

Frank B. Scott

Figure 14-4. *Frank B. Scott's Letter*

but because you can do a good job and earn more for the employer than you are paid. (You must earn more, or you are not a profitable investment.) Even if a job should be filled because of sympathy, the applicant begins work at a disadvantage and not on a businesslike basis.

7. Don't be unduly humble, and don't apologize for taking the reader's time. Remember that the employer is not doing you a favor by hiring you. If you are qualified and a hard worker, the employing organization will benefit from the employment.

8. Don't complain about past or present employers. Even if you should have real grievances, your discussion of these things almost always sounds as if you are to blame. If you find it necessary to explain why you are leaving, and this explanation is because of a real dissatisfaction that must be stated, at least do not mention it in the letter or data sheet. Save this discussion for the interview.

9. Don't boast or sound overly aggressive or presumptuous — although it is just as important not to sound unsure of your abilities. A straightforward, businesslike approach will let you take the middle road between egotism and a doubtful, overly humble tone.

10. Don't lecture or waste time stating the obvious.

11. Don't mention salary, fringe benefits, or working conditions in the application. To do so will emphasize the I-approach, not the you-approach. Such information will be given to you during the interview. If it should not be, ask at that time for information you must have before making a decision.

12. Don't try to be overly clever, at least for most jobs. If you are being considered as an advertising copywriter or for similar work, your application letter and data sheet may be in a more original or unconventional form. Regardless of the position, you do have the problem of making your letter stand out from all the others; but you could work so hard for attention that you receive the wrong kind, even to the extent that your application is eliminated from consideration.

13. Work for original phrasing and eliminate trite, unnecessary stereotyped wording. Avoid such phrases as these: "May I present my qualifications?" "This is my application . . . ." An aptly worded letter will make this fact clear without stating it obviously. As in other communications situations, however, you are wiser to be clear than to be completely concise if there must be a choice. The reader should recognize that your letter is an application without having to read halfway through it. To leave a letter in this state is much worse than saying "This is my application," or "I am an applicant," or "Consider me as an applicant for this position," although you can usually find more original wording.

THE EMPLOYMENT INTERVIEW

When your data sheet and application letter accomplish their purpose, you will be asked to come for an interview. As you no doubt realize, a successful interview is crucial to your obtaining the employment you wish.

Only under unusual circumstances is only one person interviewed for a single opening, a fact that means that some interviewees will not be hired. This necessary and desirable competition requires that the successful applicant continue the sales presentation throughout the interview, presenting the superiority of his or her qualifications and potential for service and development.

Much of your life has been spent in preparation for an interview for employment in which you are interested and for which you are qualified, although you may not have been consciously making this preparation. Your educational background, your avocational interests, your work experience — all these have prepared you for the work for which you are now applying, as well as for a favorable presentation of your qualifications during the interview.

Research to enable you to decide upon the organizations to which to submit your written application will also enable you to participate in a pleasant and successful employment interview. Your knowledge of the organization, as well as your interest in it, can favorably impress the person or persons with whom you talk. This knowledge will be even more beneficial in that it adds to your self-confidence and enables you to ask necessary and intelligent questions.

If you have made your detailed self-analysis, as discussed earlier in relation to your beginning a job search, and if you have made a study of the particular organization to which you are applying as well as of related organizations, you have accomplished a major portion of your preparation for a successful interview. Review your self-analysis and a copy of the letter of application and the data sheet before you go for the interview. Make sure that the details are firmly in your mind. Giving conflicting information will cast doubt upon either your integrity or your memory.

You may wish to take with you to the interview two copies of your data sheet, even if you have previously submitted one to the employing organization. The interviewer is not certain to have a copy, although, ideally, the person with whom you talk has recently reviewed a copy of your letter and data sheet. Also, in some cases you will go for an interview with organizations to which you have not submitted a data sheet, especially when the interview has been arranged through college placement offices. In such interviews your bringing along two copies of the data sheet can save a great deal of time that would otherwise be spent in giving information that can be concisely stated in a well-organized data sheet.

Moreover, your additional effort, interest, and consideration for the interviewer are points in your favor as you are compared with other applicants. Your carefully prepared data sheet continues your sales approach in an orderly manner that may not be possible in the half-hour or so of oral interchange of information.

You should not expect the data sheet in the hands of the interviewer to take the place of conversation, or you might as well have stayed home. The interviewer will ask you, perhaps, to expand upon the information you have shown in written form, which is of necessity shown in condensed wording. You may be asked, for example, to give more details about your work experience.

You may be asked to explain why you left a position or positions, to describe the type of work that you liked best and least, to state what you feel you accomplished on each job, and to express your opinions as to whether your supervisor and co-workers were capable and cooperative. (Be careful when commenting on this topic; your interviewer is not really asking about your co-workers and supervisors but about yourself. But, as in all other situations, do not be untruthful. Remember, though, that your own competence and spirit of helpfulness and dedication will usually result in your finding the same qualities in other persons.)

Principles of communication you have studied previously apply to your attitude toward the interviewer and your conduct in conversation. You have learned, as in written communication, to approach all business interpersonal situations on a straightforward basis of equality. Although you may have much to gain or lose according to the outcome of your search for employment, or upon the outcome of a particular interview, the representative of the employing organization also has a purpose essential to the welfare of the organization — that of finding the best person for the job.

If you sincerely believe that you are this person, and can convince the interviewer of this fact without building resentment because of your egotism or an overly aggressive approach, both you and the employing organization will have benefited from the relatively short time spent in talking about your professional future.

What questions will you ask? Don't be in a hurry to shower the interviewer with questions, many of which will be answered in the course of the conversation. But, on the other hand, don't merely sit and wait for information to come your way. And do not answer in monosyllables. Although you should not try to take charge of the interview, seize the opportunity to present yourself in the most favorable light. If you cannot communicate well enough to do so, you may leave the impression — probably an accurate one — that your communication skills will be less than ideal for your career.

At some time you are likely to be asked if you have questions, or if you have further questions. Inexperienced applicants have been known to blurt out rather odd questions or statements at this time, such as

"Where did you get that tie?" (an actual question) and, from a twenty-one-year-old, "Most of all, I am interested in your retirement plan."

What should you ask? If you have done adequate research into this organization, along with other organizations, you already know something about the company, including its offices and branches, products, and services. You can also find its recent growth and earnings. By reading company brochures, you will know a great deal about training programs and employee benefits.

What then is left to ask? One area of vital concern will be your opportunities for growth and responsibility. Are you likely to become "locked in" regardless of your hard work and ability? (Many persons do.) You will also need to know the company policy on promotions, whether higher positions are filled from the outside or whether you will need to count on moving within a few years to an organization that offers greater opportunity.

Most of all, you will want to know whether the work is the kind for which you are especially well prepared. Is it the kind in which you can excel and maintain a sincere interest? Is this an organization in which you can feel that your work matters and of which you can be proud, not only for the benefit of the employing organization but for yourself and your family? If you cannot feel a sincere pride in the organization that you are joining, you as an idealistic person will not be satisfied, regardless of the salary. Conversely, a good income is essential for most persons as a symbol of competence and accomplishment — to say nothing of its being necessary for comfort and security.

Remember that if you are not fitted for the job for which you are being considered, or if it is not a job in which you can be content to spend a portion of your life, the real benefits to be derived from an interview could be the fact that the job is given to someone else.

Careful attention to your appearance, including neat and appropriate dress, favorably impresses most interviewers and adds to your own self-confidence. A neat business suit or a conservative sport coat, with a dress shirt and tie, is appropriate dress for male applicants. Even in these modern times, some personnel managers still prefer a suit. Although applicants are sometimes told to dress according to what their job will be, this is not always good advice. For example, if you are to be a field engineer working in sturdy coveralls, a conservative business suit or sport coat is still desirable when applying for the job. For one thing, care in your appearance shows that you have a sincere interest in both the job and the organization.

Women applicants are appropriately dressed, according to the opinion of most executives, in a conservative dress, suit, or pantsuit. Some interviewers still prefer a dress, or a suit with a skirt. That a pantsuit is accepted at all is a drastic change from opinions of only a few years ago, when anything less than completely "feminine" attire was not appropriate in an office or for an interview. For a number of years a "lady" was advised to wear a hat and white gloves to all employment interviews. Such attire is almost unheard of today.

All applicants should choose conservative, attractive, flattering, and appropriate clothing and then forget about their appearance and concentrate on the conversation.

You are not likely to be offered a job during the interview, although often you can tell whether or not you are being given favorable consideration. Before you leave, you will need some kind of commitment as to when the interviewer will let you know the decision.

Ordinarily you will not need to inquire about salary, but if the interviewer does not tell you, you will be forced to ask.

Some few interviewers try to test applicants with questions such as, "Which parent did you love best?" or with questions about your religious or personal life. Such questions are encountered much less often than in previous years when, with some organizations, applicants were forced to submit to amateur psychoanalysis. If you are asked about matters that you do not wish too discuss, say so. The organization, by law, cannot base employment decisions upon religious preference or personal matters that are not related to occupational ability. (For a discussion of such attitudes, which prevailed twenty years or more ago, at least in some organizations, read *The Organization Man* by William H. Wythe, Jr.)

The basic principles of communication — the you-attitude, the positive approach, consideration, conciseness, completeness, and courtesy — added to your self-confidence and your attractive appearance, will make your interview successful if you apply for a position for which you are qualified and one in which you are interested.

But remember that communication throughout your interview, like all other communication situations, will be less than perfect and complete. Also remember that nonverbal communication, including such things as your arriving and leaving on time, your posture and facial expressions, your dress, and your voice, will tell the interviewer as much or more about you than your words can do.

FOLLOWING THROUGH IN THE EMPLOYMENT SEARCH

Thank-you Letters

Within a day or two after your employment interview, mail a thank-you letter. This letter is a matter of courtesy; you should send it whether or not you feel that you are being favorably considered.

The thank-you letter is ordinarily short because you have little to say.

It follows the pattern of a good-news or neutral message in that it is arranged in the direct order. It is a form of a goodwill message. Sincerity and a natural, conversational tone are the major requirements (see Figure 14–5).

Many applicants do not send thank-you letters after an interview, perhaps because of a mistaken idea that to do so is "pushy," or, more likely, because of simple procrastination or lack of effort. That few persons send these letters is a point in your favor that may make you stand out from other applicants. It serves as a reminder as to who you are. (After a few days of interviewing, many personnel interviewers are not sure who is who. For this reason a picture on the data sheet can be helpful, although it is not likely to be requested and may even be returned.)

At times you will have additional information to convey in the thank-you letter. For example, perhaps you have been asked whether you would move to another city and you have requested time to think it over. If you have made up your mind in the day or two before the thank-you letter should be mailed, your decision may be stated in the letter. Or perhaps you have read the brochures that were provided for you, or you have been asked to submit the names of persons to recommend you, if these names were not included on the data sheet.

Additional information, however, is not a requirement. Send a thank-you letter even if you have no new information to convey.

Follow-up Letters

Follow-up letters, in addition to thank-you letters, may be helpful when you have not heard from the employing organization within a reasonable time after the interview. The exact time varies; some college seniors are interviewed near the beginning of their senior year and notified within a month or two of graduation. Usually, however, the applicant is notified within a few weeks or even within a few days.

Follow-up letters are also used after the submission of the application letter and data sheet if too much time seems to elapse before the applicant is called for an interview.

Follow-up letters, provided they are well written and used at the proper time, accomplish several purposes. They show that you are still interested in the organization and that you are diligent in your efforts to obtain employment. These letters may also report additional information not included in the application letter and data sheet or reported in interviews — for example, the completion of related courses, additional work experience, or special scholastic honors or other accomplishments.

Avoid a demanding or hurt tone, and don't indicate surprise that you have not been asked for an interview. But don't apologize for writing.

Dear Mr. Samuels:

Thank you for a most pleasant and informative
interview.

After your discussion of the opportunities for growth
as a sales representative with the Yohanak Corporation, I
am even more eager to go to work for you.

I will be glad to supply any more information that you
may need in order to make sure that I am the best choice for
the job.

Sincerely,

John Clifft

Figure 14–5.   *Example of a Thank-you Letter*

Job-Acceptance Letters

Job-acceptance letters, like other good-news and routine informational
letters, are usually best arranged in the direct order, with the acceptance in
the first sentence.

Review Chapter 9 for instructions on how to write this kind of letter.
Adapt your job-acceptance letter to include any additional information
that the employing organization may need, or to ask questions of your
own.

Job-Refusal Letters

Job-refusal letters are usually best arranged in the indirect order, like
similar letters illustrated and discussed in Chapter 10.   Remember to
express appreciation for the employment offer.   As in other negative
messages, your letter will be more psychologically convincing and acceptable if reasons are given before the refusal.

Do everything you can to keep the goodwill of the reader and of the
organization as a whole.   Your letter may be put in your file with applica-

tion letter, data sheet, and other information about you.   You may wish to apply again to the organization.

OTHER LETTERS ABOUT EMPLOYMENT

Inquiries about Prospective Employees

Requests for information about prospective employees are frequently written.   Supplying or requesting such information is considered a normal part of business activity.   Company personnel offices or employment supervisors routinely supply information about past employees so that they, in turn, will receive similar information about other prospective employees.

Such a request differs from a request for information about a product or service in that the reader has nothing to gain, at least immediately, from supplying the desired information.   For this reason, as well as for easy readability of the evaluation, the request should be made easy to answer. Often printed forms are used, forms on which the respondent need only check the appropriate square or fill in a few blanks.   Space should be left, whether or not it is used, for additional comments.   A stamped, addressed envelope should be included.

In some instances, a letter from the previous employer may give more specific and applicable information than will a fill-in form, which suggests answers and may lead to the omission of other necessary information.

The letter in Figure 14–6 is an example of a printed form letter.   The example shown in Figure 14–7 requests a letter in reply.

A needed improvement in the form letter in Figure 14–6 is a question pertaining to the kind of work performed with a brief description of the actual duties.   Although such a description may be requested and given in the employee's application letter or resumé, a similar description by the past employer could serve as a double check.   If the two descriptions greatly differ, the prospective employer has gained more knowledge about the employee than was told by words alone.

Personnel Evaluations

The letter shown in Figure 14–8 is a reply to a request for information about a prospective employee.

Figure 14–9 is a letter written in response to an application for employment.   The bad news is clearly stated: "We are unable to offer you further consideration."   The overall tone of the letter, however, makes this statement acceptable, or as acceptable as such a message can be.

October 2, 1977

The Carder Corporation
3104 Pebble Beach Cove
Houston, TX 77036

Gentlemen:

The individual indicated below has made application with Farmer's Bank of Commerce for employment and has listed your firm as a previous employer. Will you please assist us by providing the requested information and returning this form in the enclosed self-addressed stamped envelope. This information will be held in strict confidence.

We shall appreciate your assistance.

Sincerely yours,

Personnel Officer

Name___George W. Walters_____   Position_____
                                         Employed
Social Security No. 412-44-2525_____   From _____

Last Salary _____   Absenteeism: Excessive _____
                                                Moderate _____
                                                Seldom   _____

Quality of Work: Excellent_____Good_____Fair_____Poor_____

Quantity of Work: Excellent_____Good_____Fair_____Poor_____

Reason for Leaving_____

Eligible for Rehire: Yes____No____Reason_____

_____

Signed_____   Title_____

Date_____

Figure 14–6. *A Printed Form Letter*

Union Planters

NATIONAL BANK OF MEMPHIS

April 19, 1979

Mr. Robert M. Martin
Executive Vice President - Trust
River City National Bank
Paducah, KY 42001

Re: Confidential Inquiry about James R. Hart

Dear Mr. Martin:

Mr. James R. Hart has applied for a position as an
Employee Benefits Account Administrator at Union Planters
and has offered your name as a work reference. We are
seeking information from you to assist us in making a
determination as to his abilities and potential.

In his capacity, Mr. Hart will be responsible for the total
administration of approximately 100 pension and profit-sharing
accounts with a total market value of about $10 million. He
will also be the primary contact officer for the customer
relationships associated with the accounts.

Since Mr. Hart worked in a similar capacity for you during
the past two years, we would be most interested in getting
your candid comments about Mr. Hart insofar as to the following:

Capabilities	Initiative
Limitations	Interests
Morals	Cooperativeness
Dependability	Character

Please respond using the enclosed envelope. Or, if you prefer,
call me at 1-800-238-7501, extension 6396. Your answers will
be maintained in strict confidence. We appreciate your time
and consideration in this matter.

Very truly yours,

Bruce L. Mitchell
Vice President
and Trust Officer

cm

enclosure

Figure 14-7. *A Confidential Inquiry*

The middle paragraph of the letter shown in Figure 14–9 is longer than the ideal length of most paragraphs in business letters. This rather long paragraph, however, de-emphasizes the refusal. Notice that the unfavorable decision would receive more emphasis if the middle paragraph were broken before the word "consequently."

Mentally move "we are unable to offer you further consideration" to the first position of the letter as a one-sentence paragraph standing alone. Even if the remainder of the letter stays as it is, the overall effect becomes far more harsh and disappointing.

When you finish college and begin your search for a job, you are likely to receive several letters similar to this one unless you are most unusual. Under the best of circumstances, these messages are disappointing and a slap at the ego, even when they are as courteous and as well written as this one. But you should realize that many other people are applying for jobs and that some must be turned away. If you are qualified and persistent, you will eventually receive a "yes" letter.

Sometime you may be in the position to write such letters, not to receive them. As with all communication problems, put yourself into the other person's shoes. Your receiving several of these letters could possibly cause you to write better ones of your own.

SUMMARY ◆ 14

The application letter, although sometimes sent alone, is ordinarily a covering letter for the data sheet. In addition, it is a sales letter that should be built around the most outstanding qualifications of the applicant in relation to the position sought.

The purpose of the application letter and the data sheet is to obtain an interview. As in other letters requesting action, the request for an interview should be stated specifically, but diplomatically, near the end of the letter.

The tone of the application letter should be straightforward and businesslike; the applicant must show confidence in his or her ability but refrain from appearing egotistical or overly aggressive.

A thank-you letter should be sent after an employment interview. Other letters written in the search for employment are follow-up letters, job acceptance letters, and job refusal letters.

Inquiries about prospective employees and replies to these inquiries, like other routine inquiries and requests, are best arranged in the direct order. Job refusal letters are best arranged in the indirect order.

November 21, 1978

Mr. Charles Chapman
District Sales Manager
Head Ski Division
Phoenix, Arizona 76543

Dear Mr. Chapman:

Mr. Harry Dickensen, about whom you inquired in your March 27 letter, was my most capable sales representative while he was working for Louisville Paper Company.

I was sorry that Harry left our organization. But since one of his primary goals is to become a sales manager, and there is limited growth potential in this area in our company at this time, I respect his reasons for leaving.

Harry has been a leader in the following areas in my sales district:

1) He is a self-starter, having achieved the largest sales volume for my district for three of the four years he has been with us.

2) He was the leader in opening accounts in each of the four years.

3) He is a professional and would do well as a sales representative or manager in any company.

4) He is a personable young man who has great ambition and leadership potential.

I feel that Harry Dickensen could become a valuable asset to your organization.

Sincerely,

William Raucherman

William Raucherman
District Sales Manager

kl

Figure 14–8. *Reply to a Request for Information*

April 23, 1979

Mr. Terrence Mark
1064 Estate Drive
Wilkes Barre, PA   18701

Dear Mr. Mark:

I enjoyed talking with you at Pennsylvania State University.
Thank you for your time and effort in making our meeting
possible.

Our search has produced a number of individuals with
really fine backgrounds such as your own. After evaluating
numerous candidates in light of our job requirements, we
feel that other individuals have backgrounds that seem to be
more commensurate with the requirements of our positions.
Consequently, even though we were impressed with your
record of accomplishment, we are unable to offer you
further consideration. It is with regret that we have come
to this conclusion, but we felt we should make you aware of
our decision so that you could concentrate your efforts on
other possibilities.

Your interest and consideration of the Yohanak Company as
a potential employer are greatly appreciated. We wish you
success in securing the type of career opportunity you are
seeking.

Sincerely,

WLPerkins

W. L. Perkins
Assistant Manager
Industrial Relations

Figure 14-9.   *Letter Refusing Applicant for Position*

QUESTIONS AND PROBLEMS ◆ 14

1. Write a letter of application to accompany the data sheets you prepared for Problems 4, 5, and 6 in Chapter 13.   These letters should vary according to the organization to which you are applying.

2. Mail these letters and data sheets. (Make sure that the envelopes you use are of good quality and of standard business length so that the letter can be folded in approximate thirds.   The envelopes should match the paper in weight and quality.)   Or, if you still have considerable time left before you complete your degree or your occupational preparation, or if there are other reasons that you do not wish to mail your letters and data sheets at this time, complete some or all of the following assignments as your instructor directs.

    If you do mail the application letters and data sheets, follow through with your interview or with follow-up letters, thank-you letters, acceptance letters, or whatever is appropriate to complete your job search.

3. Assume that three weeks have elapsed and that you have not heard from the organization that you considered to be your first choice.   Write a follow-up letter indicating your continued interest and asking again for an interview. Avoid sounding hurt, doubtful, or demanding.

4. Assume that you have received a letter from the second organization asking you to come to their local office to talk with Mrs. Helen Woolner, the district manager.   The time set is 1 p.m. on Wednesday of the following week. (Use exact date.)   You are asked to write to Mrs. Woolner to confirm the suggested time.   Do so.

5. You received a letter from the third organization on the day after you have mailed your reply to Mrs. Woolner.   You are surprised that Mr. Harry B. Hicks and Mr. John Jerry, who are identified only as being from the personnel office, wish to see you at 1:30 p.m. on the same day that you are planning to talk with Mrs. Woolner.   Write an appropriate reply.   Suggest another time for the interview.

6. You receive a letter from the organization that you had considered to be your first choice.   You are told by Miss Rachel Welsh, Personnel Director, that the organization is not now hiring anyone with your particular background but that she will keep your application on file.   Although her letter does not necessitate a response, you decide to write a short letter that will perhaps be placed in your file.   Decide what you want to say in this letter.   Write it.

7. You go for the scheduled interview with Mrs. Helen Woolner.   You are favorably impressed.   You believe that you have a good chance to be hired. Write a thank-you letter for the interview.   Assume reasonable details.

8. You receive a letter from Mr. Harry B. Hicks in response to your letter written for Problem 5.   He wishes to talk with you at 10 a.m. on Monday of the following week.   You have a final examination scheduled at this hour. You talk to your professor, who refuses to give you the examination at any other time.   Because this is the second time you have been unable to come for

the interview, you realize that you must convince Mr. Hicks that you are still sincerely interested. (He has not mentioned the date you suggested in your last letter to him, which is now more than two weeks past.) State that you will complete your final examinations on Thursday of the following week, at which time your college work will be finished.

What should you say in this letter? You wish to make it clear that you are still interested in the organization and that you are not giving him the runaround. It has now been six weeks since you mailed your application letter and data sheet. Should you mention that you have already been interviewed by Mrs. Woolner? Should you write or telephone? If you decide to telephone, make detailed notes as to the information and ideas you intend to convey.

9. You receive from Mrs. Woolner a letter offering employment beginning four weeks from next Monday. The salary is about $100 a month less than you expected, and you are to begin work in a district more than 500 miles from your home. You believe that the company offers growth opportunities and, although you do not want to move, you realize that mobility is often necessary in order to avoid limiting opportunities for success.

What will you say in your reply? Will you want to ask for more time in order to investigate further the possibilities of beginning work with organization number three? Plan or write your letter according to your decision.

10. At last you go for an interview with the third organization on your list and talk with Mr. Harry B. Hicks, Personnel Manager; Mr. John Jerry, District Manager; and Mr. H. D. Blackburn, Assistant Vice-President. You are given a tour of the offices and plant.

Write an appropriate thank-you note to all three of these persons. The actual choice of the person to whom you should send a thank-you letter will depend upon circumstances, including the consideration of the person who seems to be the one most directly responsible for making the decision. When in doubt, write to each person who spends time with you or who helps you in any way.

11. It is now two weeks later. You receive from Mrs. Woolner a letter stating that she must have your decision immediately. (For this assignment, assume that in Problem 9 you ask for more time in which to make your decision.) In the same mail you receive a letter from Mr. Hicks who offers you work in the local office. He has told you that there is a possibility of transfer within a year or two when you are ready for a promotion, but there is also a possibility that you can be promoted and remain in your home city. Your beginning salary is $200 a month greater than that offered by Mrs. Woolner's organization. You decide to accept Mr. Hicks's offer. Write the letter of acceptance.

12. Write to Mrs. Woolner. Keep her goodwill.

13. You receive a letter from the organization which was originally your first choice. They ask you to come for an interview and to telephone and arrange a time that will be convenient for both of you. Plan what you will say in the telephone conversation.

Requests for Information about Prospective Employees; Replies to These Requests

14. You are the personnel director of Countrywide Life Insurance, 420 Madison Avenue, New York, NY 10577. You have interviewed Miss Sally Ann Benson for a responsible secretarial position. She has recently graduated from Ingram University, Ingram, Texas, with a major in English and a minor in office administration. She gave as a reference one of her former teachers, Dr. Rosemary Randall, Associate Professor of Office Administration, Ingram University, Ingram, Texas 78025.

    You are especially interested in a secretary who can handle correspondence on her own without having each letter dictated to her, who is good with figures, and who is capable of supervising other office workers. You would like a person who is likely to remain with Countrywide for some time, as it is expensive to find, hire, and train new persons. You wonder whether Miss Benson will remain in New York or perhaps become homesick and return to her home and family in Texas. You also want to know something of her scholarship ability and accomplishments. Write to Dr. Randall requesting the information you need.

15. Phillip Morgan is your top candidate for the job of Area Director for the three states of Missouri, Iowa, and Illinois. This job requires the supervision of six outside salesmen as well as the day-to-day office management of the St. Louis office. Your company sells accounting services and systems to farmers. The applicant must know about sales, office management, accounting, and farming. He must be a good leader because the salesmen will be working primarily on their own. He must also be a good desk man, as the paperwork is heavy.

    Phillip meets all the academic qualifications (or at least his application indicates so), and he has sales ability. The most important question is whether he has the necessary leadership ability. Write to Mr. Weldon Thomas, his immediate supervisor for the past five years at Production Credit Association, Jonesboro, Arkansas 71201, requesting information on Phillip Morgan.

16. You are sales manager of Quality Office Supply. The head office has asked you to hire an additional sales representative. You have been interviewing prospective employees at the local university. One particular person has attracted your attention: Miss Molly Bell, who is about to graduate with an MBA in marketing. Her grades are excellent, and during the interview she seemed confident and sincerely interested in the position. You are concerned, though, because she has had little work experience and is only twenty-two.

    You know that hiring a woman to join your all-male sales force could present some special problems. The men on the sales force could see her as a threat, or feel that she is not capable of doing a "man's job." (That the law is on her side will not greatly affect their emotions.) She would, therefore, have to cope with these tensions if the team spirit is to prevail. Also, her customers, mostly men, must be confident in her ability to do the job. Some of them might even make a pass, so Miss Bell must be mature enough to handle the situation. The position requires a person with a well-rounded and pleasant personality. Aggressiveness and getting along with people are also important.

Write a letter to Dr. George Yancey, Professor of Marketing, at your local school. Dr. Yancey was one of Miss Bell's professors and was listed as a reference.

17.   As manager of the Golden Circle Public Relations Firm, 100 North Main, Boulder, Colorado 78721, you want to hire a general office supervisor. You have received many applications and interviewed forty-two people for the job. (You now wonder why you interviewed so many.) All seem to be well qualified. (You can't believe it!) You decide to design a form letter with fill-in blanks to be sent to the persons listed as references. When these are returned and analyzed, you will telephone the persons who have recommended the applicants who seem to be top candidates.

Write the letter and design the fill-in form. Try to plan the mailing so that the form can be on the same page as the short letter. You will consider the desirable attributes of the office supervisor so that the candidate can be evaluated accordingly.

18.   You are now Dr. Rosemary Randall. Write to the personnel director of Countrywide Life Insurance (Problem 14). You know Miss Benson well. She has a grade point average of 3.78 based on a 4-point scale. As could be expected with this scholastic record, she is good with both words and figures. She also seems to get along well with other people. During her last two years on the campus, she was an officer of the Student Government Association.

You are not sure that she will remain with the insurance company, but you do believe that she will stay in New York. She really wants to work for a publishing company and do editing and writing. You believe, though, that the insurance company will get more than its money's worth from her, no matter how short her stay, because of her exceptional mind and her excellent secretarial skills. Should you mention her editorial and writing ambitions? You want to be fair to both Sally Ann and to the insurance company.

19.   You are Bob Lewis, Regional Director for Agricultural Systems, Inc. You have just received a letter from the sales manager of Midwestern Chemical Company inquiring about Joe Hastings, one of your salesmen, who is being considered for a sales supervisor. You have known for about six months that Joe was looking for a better job located in another area. You know Joe is a superior salesman and would be effective in any type of sales work. On the matter of his ability behind a desk you are not certain. You question whether Joe can give the attention to details that this new position will apparently require, as Joe has always had difficulty providing his weekly status reports in correct form and is usually late with them. With these details in mind, write a letter to the manager of Midwestern Chemical Company.

20.   You are the coordinator of a mental health center. One of your best volunteers is graduating from college in May. She has held the position of Social Club Volunteer. She has been very dependable, with absolutely no absenteeism. She has been an ideal employee. She has developed activities for the social club, learned to deal effectively with difficult clients, and has

kept accurate records on all activities. She has applied for a job with another mental health center, this time in a paid position like your own, and has used your name as a reference. You are to write a letter and evaluate her work performance.

21. Consider some person whom you have supervised or with whom you have worked. (Use a fictitious name.) Assume that this person has applied for a position similar to the one in which you have been able to observe his or her ability and personality. The prospective employer has written you asking for a written evaluation. Write it.

Letters Informing Applicants of Decisions

22, 23, 24, 25. Assume that you are the personnel director or other person responsible for filling the positions sought through the four application letters illustrated in this chapter (Aldridge, Dunn, Harrison, Scott). Assume that each of these applicants has been interviewed and has furnished all references and other necessary information. Write to two of these persons and tell them that they are being hired for the job they sought. To the other two persons, write job refusal letters.

COMMUNICATING THROUGH REPORTS

OXNARD COLLEGE

BOOKSTORE

Your ability to ~~write~~ ...ques can be an outstanding asse... ...ss. Reports of many kinds are ... ...business activity. Your abili... ...t needed information may be t... ...the lack of such an ability can k...

Perhaps mo... ...dge and skill in communication ... ...r advancement to responsible po... ...her students in colleges of busi... ...cel in business research and rep... ...nd applied this study to the prep...

Even if you ... ...ow to progress within an organi... ...porting will be beneficial in any ... ...g an important part of a liberal e...

Buy-Back: Any texts scheduled for use in the following term will be purchased from students, providing the store is not overstocked, at the close of each semester and each summer session on dates specified.

Refunds: Full refunds will be made during the first three weeks of class, provided the student has the original receipt and an authorized drop slip, and that no marks are made in the book.

...F REPORTS

A report is a writt... ...rmation or to present a solution... ...many letters, memorandums, te... cepted for the amount of pur...s are forms of reports, as are n... chase only. There is a $5 ...envelopes. A report may also b... charge for all returned ...ges, on which many persons have... checks.

Checks: Checks will be accepted for the amount of purchase only. There is a $5 charge for all returned checks.

Reports consist of written and spoken words, columns of figures, charts, computer printouts, or a combination of all these and of other forms. We speak of news reports, weather reports, stock market reports, accounting reports, and the very broad term, business reports. Although any kind of report conveying business information is a "business report," the definition must be narrowed as it pertains to the study and discussion of reports you are likely to prepare for business purposes.

In the definition that follows, the word "effective" has been inserted to describe what reports should be, not necessarily what they are. Even a poor report is still called by the name, and thus the wording of the exact definition of the term is complicated by semantic factors. Thus:

An effective business report is an orderly, objective presentation of factual information and/or analyses planned to serve some business purpose, usually that of making a decision.

Other descriptions of a report are that it

- is a management tool;
- may be described by many names and in varying ways, according to purpose, format, time prepared, subject matter, scope, length, readership, and other factors;
- varies widely in form, length, and content;
- may merely report information, without analysis, or may report information, and in addition, analyze the information and include recommendations;
- may be planned only to analyze existing information;
- is usually written for one reader or for a small group of readers;
- usually moves up the chain of command;
- tends to be written in a more formal style than other types of business communication;
- ordinarily is assigned;
- may be prepared at specified, regular intervals or only for a special need;
- requires careful planning and organization;
- answers a question or solves a problem.

The basic qualities of effective reports are the same, for the most part, as those of effective communication of any kind. The principles previously discussed — clarity and coherence, conciseness, a wise choice of arrangement in order to achieve readability and the desired psychological approach, correctness, neatness, consideration of the reader, exactness — these considerations apply to all types of communication.

When planning reports, however, we must give special attention to organization and to an objective, nonbiased approach. Because reports are often longer than letters or memorandums, they must be especially planned for readability and an orderly progression of thought.

We are especially concerned about "objectivity" in a report; that is, we must complete the research and analyze the data without letting our preconceived opinions or personal bias influence our efforts in finding and presenting truthful and complete information and interpretations. The semantic principles discussed in Chapter 4 apply especially to problem solving.

One such principle is that we tend to see what we expect to see, particularly what we want to see. The recognition of this natural human failing, with an effort to avoid such an approach, is essential to nonbiased research and reporting. We also tend to overgeneralize and to interpret inferences and value judgments as facts. Although such "twisting of the truth," even though unconscious, is harmful in all facets of life, it is obviously a definite barrier to scientific research and impartial interpretation of the data.

Other applications of a logical and ethical approach to gathering and interpreting information are included in Chapter 4. Rereading these sections will be helpful to you as you begin your study of report preparation.

The discussion of reports in this and the following chapters, or that included in other books on report writing or business communication, is not likely to provide the complete information and direction you will need in an actual business situation. This study will, however, lay a foundation of knowledge that will prepare you to plan and tailor specialized reports of many kinds on many subjects.

Although terminology and formats differ from organization to organization, report purposes are basically the same, as is the general plan of procedure. Your study and practice in writing and orally presenting reports in a college course — or through dedicated self-study — will enable you to adapt to specialized and differing forms and techniques. Most important, this knowledge will enable you to ask intelligent questions about a report project to which you are assigned.

Some of the questions that should be directed either to the authorizer of the report or to yourself are as follows:

- What is the purpose of the report?
- Who will read it?
- Am I expected only to supply information, or am I to analyze this information and interpret its meaning?
- Am I expected to make recommendations?
- What has already been done to find the answer to the question or the solution to the problem?

- How complete is this report expected to be? This is a reasonable question, although at first thought you may assume that it must be "completely complete." But, as you learned in Chapter 4, according to Korsybski and other writers in general semantics — as well as according to your own observation — we cannot give all the possible details about anything. "A statement is never the whole story," and a report, regardless of its length, will omit information that could have been included. Because of this fact, we should state early in the report process the scope of our research. The report should be complete in that it accomplishes its stated purpose.
- In what form should the report be prepared?
- Will some or all of this report be published or distributed in some other way to many readers?
- Should this report be written in the personal or the impersonal writing style? (See Chapter 8.)
- Must I be concerned with using a writing style that could be described as "formal" — that is, must I make sure to avoid contractions, colloquial expressions, and other aspects of informal writing? (See Chapter 8.)
- How should I go about finding the needed information?
- Is this report one of a continuing series, made on a regular, periodic basis, or is it planned only for a special time and purpose?
- Should I prepare progress reports to relate my experiences in preparing the report?
- Exactly what is it that I am trying to find out?

This last question is your starting point, and it is the most important question of all.

Before you can intelligently answer the preceding questions or completely understand another's answers, you should know something about the overall classification of reports as they are used in various business, governmental, and professional organizations. You also should be familiar with research sources and methods and with the techniques of report preparation.

CLASSIFICATION OF REPORTS

Reports are classified by varying terms from organization to organization. Not only do the names given to the reports differ, but the format and presentation also differ. You may find reports called by special names, such as the "2001 Report," in which the descriptive term is only the number of the special form on which the report is prepared. Reports may be classified according to product name or according to a company department or division, or described by the purpose for which the report was prepared.

All these classifications you will learn on the job. Like other specialized terms you use in your daily work, they will soon become familiar to you. For example, Social Security claims representatives refer dozens of times a day to the "101" or the "201," which are the numbers given to special forms on which information is recorded. Accountants, as well as many other persons at income-tax time, refer routinely to the "1040," as well as to other numbers that serve as names. In many reports of this kind, the report procedure consists only of filling in blanks, usually with figures.

Although the terminology may differ, basically reports are classified in the following ways.

Classification by Time Intervals

Periodic reports are prepared at regular intervals, such as daily, weekly, monthly, or annually. The annual corporate report is a periodic report; so is the daily sales report that consists of nothing but rows of figures.

Special reports are not prepared at regular intervals, but only as the need arises

Progress reports, as the name indicates, report the past and expected progress of an assigned project, often of a long, analytical report. These progress reports can also be described as periodic if, for example, a weekly progress report is expected until the project is completed.

Classification by Authorization

Assigned reports, either on a continuing basis or as a special assignment, comprise most business reports. Even if the report writer wishes to undertake a project of his own choosing, ordinarily it should be authorized by someone higher in authority, most especially if the project is one that will necessitate company time and expense. This authorization should be in written form and incorporated into the final report.

Justification reports are usually unassigned. Because they are usually (but not always) short and simply prepared, they do not ordinarily require written or oral authorization. As the name implies, they are prepared for the purpose of justifying a purchase, a procedure, or a change in the method of operation.

Classification by Subject Matter

Classification by subject matter is obviously one that will apply to all reports. (As you have no doubt noticed, the same report can be classified in several different ways.)   Reports can be classified according to their particular subject matter or on the basis of a grouping of subjects.

Such a grouping is also described as classification by departments, if, within an organization, we refer to accounting, sales, management, research and development, credit, and other similar subject fields.   To classify more narrowly, each of these broad subject areas could be divided into more specific descriptions; for example, accounting reports may be described as cost, audit, tax, and finance reports.

Classification by Function

Informational reports simply present data, with no attempt to analyze or interpret the meaning of the data nor to make recommendations for action.

Analytical reports also provide information, and, in addition, include analysis and interpretation.

Informational reports tend to be shorter than analytical ones, but this distinction is not applicable to all.   Informational reports can be of any length, depending upon the amount of information to convey.   Conversely, an analytical report can be short.   ("Long" and "short" are relative terms, in reports as well as in everything else.)   We do, however, often hear the term "long analytical report" or "complete analytical report."   "Complete," when used as a descriptive term, may mean that the report contains various preliminary and supplementary parts, which will be discussed later.   The word may also be used to signify that the report and the investigation that preceded it are broad in scope.

Analytical reports are sometimes further classified by such terms as "examination," "recommendation," or "improvement" reports.   These distinctions are usually made between analytical reports that include stated recommendations and those that do not; for example, an "examination" report includes an analysis of the data but no recommendations for improvement.   Whether or not recommendations are definitely stated, however, the presentation of an analysis of the data implies certain recommendations.   If the study of why a certain product is not selling as fast as expected shows that customers do not like the color, obviously the report implies, or "recommends," that the color should be changed.

The distinction between informational and analytical reports will be important to you as you consider a proposed project.   One of your first steps, especially if you are a new employee, will be to find out exactly what is expected, not only from the standpoint of whether to analyze the data, but from all other aspects of the problem.

Another term that is sometimes used in connection with an analytical report is "research report." A definition of research is "to make a diligent and systematic inquiry or investigation into a subject in order to discover or revise facts, theories, applications, etc."[1] Using this definition, we see that an analytical report is not necessarily based on research gathered by the report writer, who may prepare an analytical report from data already accumulated. Also, a research report is not necessarily an analytical one, as research may be done only to gather information and to relay it, not to analyze it and/or to make recommendations.

An analytical report may consist of many combined informational reports from the standpoint that the data from these reports are combined and analyzed, often with the aid of a computer, and from these combined data, analyses and recommendations are made for the solution of an existing problem.

Classification by Degree of Formality

Purpose and readership determine the degree of formality. The words "formal" and "informal," as when used elsewhere, are relative as they describe reports, insofar as there is no exact and distinct dividing line. Reports that are not definitely and conclusively formal are perhaps best described as informal. These words may be used to describe format, writing style, or both.

The more formal presentation includes preliminary and supplementary parts that will be omitted from the more informal arrangement. (Such a report, as mentioned above, may also be described as being a complete report.) Some of the preliminary parts are the letter of transmittal, the letter of acceptance, table of contents, a list of tables, and a synopsis. Supplementary parts include a bibliography, appendix section, and perhaps an index.

Ordinarily, if this complete format is used, the writing style should also be formal. Remember, though, that a formal writing style does not mean that the tone is "bookish," stiff, pretentious, or hard to read.

Reports may be presented in letter or memorandum form; these are considered informal, insofar as format and arrangement are concerned, although the formal writing style may be appropriate. Reports may omit some of the preliminary and supplementary parts — each should be used only as needed — and still have an air and appearance of formality.

As in any writing, even though we are free to use an informal physical presentation and an informal writing style, we should be careful to avoid being overly informal. Such an approach will offend the more conserva-

---

1. *The Random House Dictionary of the English Language* (New York: Random House, 1967), p. 1218.

tive reader and appear unbusinesslike to all readers. The words that we put on paper are at least semipermanent, and we can never be sure how business reports will be used or when or where they will be read.

A long report is likely to be presented in the formal, or complete, format, and a short report to be arranged in a more informal way. This distinction, however, does not always apply. A fairly short report — for example, seven or eight pages of the report proper — can be arranged in the complete, formal way.

Classification by Arrangement of Ideas

Reports, like all other forms of communication, can be arranged in the direct (deductive) order or in the indirect (inductive) order, as described in Chapter 8. They can also be arranged in the chronological order, but this arrangement usually does not give proper emphasis to whatever should be emphasized.

The indirect arrangement begins with the introduction, presents the findings and their interpretation, and ends with conclusions and recommendations. This arrangement is also described as being in the logical order — an inexact and nondescriptive term, in that a well-organized report arranged in the direct order is also logical from the standpoint that it makes sense.

Many analytical reports, especially short ones, present conclusions as the first section of the report. (Conclusions may be only recommendations, or they may present the writer's most important interpretations and also include recommendations, either stated or implied.) This "gist of the message" is followed by purpose, methods, or other necessary explanatory material, followed by supporting facts and interpretations upon which the conclusions and recommendations are based.

Compare the direct and the indirect arrangements:

Indirect Arrangement	*Direct Arrangement*
Purpose, methods, other introductory material	Conclusions (includes recommendations, either stated or implied)
Findings	
Conclusions (includes recommendations, either stated or implied)	Purpose, methods, other necessary explanatory material
	Findings

Even though the report itself is presented in the inductive order (indirect, logical), the use of a synopsis combines the features of both the direct and indirect arrangements in the overall report "package," which consists of the preliminaries, the report itself, and the supplementary parts.

The synopsis is a greatly condensed version of the complete report, including the introduction and the conclusions and recommendations. Because of the placement of the synopsis before the actual report, the report package is arranged in the direct order, in that the gist of the entire report is presented before the supporting details and information.

As when writing bad-news or refusal letters, in some reports we need to prepare the reader to accept or to believe disappointing or startling conclusions. In such instances, the synopsis is better omitted unless to do so would be going against the expected and assigned format.

We realize, of course, that the reader may look first at the conclusions and recommendations section, no matter where it is placed. But even if this is what happens, the reader is not "hit in the face" by our immediate presentation, without explanation or justification, of a message that will be unwelcome.

Classification by Personal or Impersonal Tone

As you have learned previously, most business writing is written in the personal tone — that is, the writer is free to use "I," "we," "you," and other first- and second-person pronouns. The impersonal tone includes no first- or second-person pronouns. This style of writing is also referred to as the "third-person objective." (The use of "I" and "we" can be excessive, even when using the personal tone, because it may give an appearance of expressing the I-attitude, not the you-attitude.)

An advantage of using the impersonal tone in formal reports is that this style of writing seems more objective and nonbiased because the writer is not speaking of himself. The choice of writing style does not affect real objectivity; nevertheless, because it appears to do so, many persons prefer the impersonal tone.

Another more important advantage is that by using no first- or second-person pronouns more emphasis is given to the facts and analyses being presented — and this is where the emphasis should be. You should not emphasize what you did as a researcher or what you believe about the situation, but the results.

The personal tone is used in many reports, but if the report can otherwise be described as formal, the impersonal tone is more appropriate except in unusual situations. Some textbook writers advocate the use of the personal tone in all types of reports. Some of their reasoning is: (1) material in the personal tone is easier to write, more natural, more forceful, more vibrant; (2) it decreases the use of the slow passive construction; and (3) it is more conversational.

This reasoning does not seem valid for all types of business writing, most especially for complete analytical reports. While it is true that an inexperienced writer can more easily avoid passive constructions when using the personal tone, it has other disadvantages. Several sentences constructed with the verbs in the passive voice are preferable to sentences containing pronouns that emphasize the writer of the report instead of the results and the interpretations of the research.

In addition, a good writer can write well in either the personal or the impersonal tone; if the college student cannot use both approaches easily and well, more study and practice are needed — immediately. The proper use of emphasis is reason enough to write some business reports in the impersonal tone.

Many traditionally minded readers of business reports — and there are still many traditionally minded readers — will judge a report written in the impersonal tone to be more professional, more objective, more scientific, and more carefully prepared than one written in the personal tone. If you are likely to encounter this reaction, you are decreasing the likelihood of the acceptance of your ideas by using the personal tone. The use of "I's," "we's" and other first- and second-person pronouns may be a form of noise, distracting the reader's mind from whatever it is that you are trying to say.

Most news reporting is of necessity in the impersonal tone. News writers are proficient in expressing their ideas directly, forcefully, and concisely. Business writers can also learn to write well in the impersonal tone.

Classification by Method of Presentation

Reports may be presented both in oral and in written form. Most reports of considerable length and scope, or those involving extensive research, are prepared first in written form. Then they may be presented in oral form. Often the oral presentation will include only the highlights of the complete report.

The written report is often condensed for distribution or for publication. The synopsis, which is prepared as a preliminary to a formal report, may be used for this purpose.

The Role of Classifications in Report Planning

The conventional classifications given above are useful in planning, evaluating, and describing reports. The list is not all-inclusive, for, as mentioned earlier, terminology differs widely. Basically, though, the principles that apply to effective reports are the same for all types. Your study will not be planned around these differing classifications; instead, emphasis will be given to how to find, evaluate, and present information and ideas.

The general principles of communication, as presented in Chapters 1 through 8 and Appendix A, apply to reports as well as to letters, memorandums, and oral communication.   In addition, the characteristics of effective reports are similar, regardless of the type of report: logical organization; clear, concise, coherent writing; correctness; and all the other attributes of effective communication.

The following factors, which are described in the various classifications given on the preceding pages, seem to fit together as they are used in the same report, although there can be exceptions:

- Formal format, formal writing style, impersonal tone, inductive arrangement
- Informal format, formal or informal writing style, personal tone, inductive or deductive arrangement depending upon type of information

THE BASIS FOR A REPORT

The basis for a report is a problem — or, as described in some books on research methods, a "felt need."   Even if the report is a simple informational one, the problem or felt need is knowing the answer to a question or questions, or of obtaining the desired information.   The report writer is given the task of relaying this information.

Steps to the Solution of a Problem

Steps to a solution and to presenting the solution are as follows:

1. Determine the problem and define it in specific terms.
2. Choose a method of finding information to lead to a solution.
3. Collect and organize the data.
4. Evaluate and interpret the data.
5. Arrive at a solution to the problem.
6. Present the solution, with reasons, explanations, and recommendations, in appropriate report form.
7. Put the recommendations into action.   (This step will not usually be the responsibility of the report writer.)

As you may have guessed, every problem, business or otherwise, is not so immediately and neatly solved as this listing of steps may indicate. For example, you may not be able to arrive at a solution that you are sure will be the complete answer to the question or problem. Sometimes the best we can do is to state that findings indicate that a certain course of action is likely to be the best choice. Recommendations are and must be based on inferences, although they should be reasonable ones and adequately supported by factual evidence.

And, as a note of warning, perhaps some of Murphy's laws should be cited here: If anything can go wrong, it will. Nothing is as easy as it looks. Everything takes longer than you think it will. If everything seems to be going well, you have overlooked something. When mankind builds a more perfect mousetrap, Mother Nature builds a more perfect mouse. (These statements are not exactly the positive approach.)

An additional step could be inserted, in some types of research, between Steps 1 and 2: formulate a hypothesis. A hypothesis is a statement to be proved or disproved as a result of research; for example, "Employee morale will be strengthened and absenteeism decreased by providing career apparel at company expense." A null hypothesis would be worded in this way: "No significant difference in employee morale or absenteeism will occur by providing career apparel at company expense." The use of the null hypothesis is favored by scientific researchers because the positive statement indicates that the researcher has already decided upon what the results will be, an attitude that is not conducive to unbiased research.

Not all research is of the type that can be exactly formulated in terms of hypotheses. Notice that in the illustration given above, judging employee morale is a task difficult to prove or disprove to the extent that the hypothesis can be definitely tested. This business problem can be "solved," however, to the extent that the person or persons responsible for putting the research results into effect are reasonably sure that the recommended course of action is advisable.

We might add a preliminary step before determining the problem — facing it and acknowledging that a problem exists. In many instances, business persons ignore unpleasant situations with the hope that they will go away. If the problem is faced openly, it may not be half the threat that it seems to be while it lurks unchallenged in the bottom of our mind. On the other hand, it may be even worse — but in that case, it is imperative that we face it.

A Problem-solving Situation

The solutions, wise or unwise, to many of the problems we face are reached without extensive research. Routinely and automatically we make decisions that are minor variations of business problems investigated by various research methods.

Suppose, for example, that you are driving to work and find that there is a severe traffic jam on the street you usually travel. Under ordinary conditions this street is the most direct route to your office. You have an important appointment at 9:15, and it is now 8:15. If normal traffic conditions prevailed, you could reach your office in half an hour.

Your problem is — what to do? Should you wait here and hope that the stalled automobiles will move on, or should you detour, provided you can work yourself into a side street? (A comparable business problem would be to decide whether an organization should continue with the present and heretofore successful method of operation or, because of unexpected difficulties, change the method of operation.) Will the more indirect route, which is ordinarily slower because of school zones, residential areas, and stop lights, provide a quicker method of reaching the office?

You do not put this statement into written form, but, on a simple level, this situation compares to a problem you face when you undertake a business research project: You state the problem, choose a method of solution, collect and organize data, evaluate and interpret its meaning, and arrive at a solution to the problem, whether or not this solution is the best one.

Using this example, however, you usually undertake the action and find the data at the same time — that is, you embark on the assumed solution and collect and organize the data in your mind as you move along. Then your report is presented orally to your employer or associates when you arrive at the office. As you meander through the side streets or wait in your automobile in the traffic jam, you are collecting data as you keep track of the time. This may be unfavorable data, but you made your choice when you turned off the main thoroughfare, or decided to wait.

Some business, professional, and government organizations seem to make their decisions in just this way; they go ahead and turn, or remain immobile on a jammed street, and figure out as time passes whether or not they made the right decision.

When you have more time and a serious problem, you cannot afford to operate in this way. Assuming you do have the time — what kind of research could you do? You could study the maps and determine the mileage by both routes. You could turn your automobile radio to the station that reports traffic conditions; perhaps you can learn the extent of the traffic blockage and when the street can be expected to be back to normal. Perhaps the radio voice could tell you something of the traffic conditions on the side streets you are considering. If you have telephone or radio contact with your office, you could find out how important it is that you arrive at the regular time, for perhaps the important appointment you are hurrying to has been cancelled for some reason, or perhaps it could be delayed.

This question, however, is not relevant to your subquestion of which route will provide the quickest trip to the office; it does apply to the question that you started with — what to do. These questions should not be analyzed together, but ones such as these tend to become jumbled as we find ourselves entangled in a problem or, especially, when putting the report into written form.

In the problem-solving situation, you would collect all this information, analyze it for its validity and applicability, and arrive at a conclusion upon which you would make your recommendation of the better choice of the two courses of action.

Your conclusion has been based partly upon inferences. If the radio voice has told you of a three-car accident that is blocking all lanes of traffic, you infer that it will be some time before your regular route is ready for travel. Your calculations of the mileage by both routes can be considered a fact if you are sure that the mapmakers were accurate — but then this assumption is also an inference. (Even though we can never be completely sure of most things, we must treat some inferences as if they were facts, as least until we have time to investigate them further.)

Reasonable inferences supported by sufficient facts may serve as a basis for recommendations, although at times these recommendations will be incorrect. Your value judgments, unsupported by facts, should not be used as a basis for recommendations. From a practical business standpoint, the fact that the side streets that make up the indirect route are more picturesque is not relevant to your question of which way to drive to the office. Your appreciation of flowering trees and clumps of daffodils is a value judgment, although many people would agree with you.

A form of secondary research would be to call to a person in the next car: "Sir, have you ever driven down Flamingo Street to Cherry, then to Rhodes and Barron, and then on Lamar to downtown?" If he has driven this route recently, his advice would be similar to that you might find in a business journal, located through *Business Periodicals Index*, of how another business organization solved a problem similar to the one you are now trying to solve. In all instances, we should use secondary research sources if they are available in order to take advantage of the experiences of other persons. To do otherwise is the same as reinventing the wheel each time we need a new wheelbarrow.

As you may have realized, much of successful business research and report writing is the application of mere common sense. But then common sense cannot be exactly described as "mere."

Determining and Defining the Problem

The first step — determining the problem — is not difficult from the standpoint of knowing that one exists; but deciding specifically and definitely what the problem *is* accomplishes a major step toward its solution.

If the report is assigned, as it ordinarily will be, the report writer must know exactly what is wanted.

The questions that newspaper reporters are taught to ask — who, what, where, when, why, and how — apply to business report writing. Why is the report requested? Who will read it? When is this information needed? How will this information be used? Where can this information be obtained? And, most important of all, exactly what am I trying to find out?

Your answer to this last problem is your starting point, the statement of the problem. This statement of the problem may be broken into subquestions to include aspects of the who, what, why, when, where, or how. All these questions must be considered together when determining and putting into an exactly written statement the problem you are trying to solve.

We face major and minor problems in all aspects of our work and personal life; the difficulty arises in knowing what to include in the particular research study, for problems tend to overlap. If the statement of the problem cannot be put into definite words and stated in question form, it is not yet clearly defined. If the problem remains vague, general, and undetermined, planning helpful research, finding a solution, and reporting the solution will be difficult indeed.

This initial step of defining the problem should be discussed with whoever assigns the report. The exact purpose must be agreed upon by the person or persons who authorize the report and the person who undertakes the completion of the report.

Often the statement of the problem is used as the first sentence of the introductory section of the report itself. Notice the specific wording of the following problem statements:

> The purpose of this report is to examine all costs and revenues in the movement of sugar from the South Coast Sugar Mill in Matthews, Louisiana, and to determine whether it is profitable for the Kroger Company to transport it with its own equipment.[2]

Although this statement is not now worded in question form, notice that it could be: "Is it profitable for the Kroger Company to initiate a self-haul program for sugar from. . . ."

> Should Countrywide Insurance Company purchase career apparel for its women employees?

> Should Marketing Consultants, Inc. move from their present location in Commerce Square to the office building in Dillard Square?[3]

---

2. Stephen A. Wiggs, "Why the Kroger Company Should Initiate a Self-Haul Program for Sugar" (unpublished report, 1973).

3. Keith Lamar, "Why Marketing Consultants Should Move to Dillard Square" (unpublished report, 1974).

Should Countrywide Insurance Company replace presently owned typewriters, on the established three-year trade-in basis, for self-correcting Selectric II's?

Should the Seligman Realty Company continue the present method of door-to-door rent collection or establish a system of collection by mail?

Are the services and purposes of the local Chamber of Commerce well known to the citizens of the city?

Which kinds of books (recent fiction, older fiction, classics, general nonfiction, textbooks) are most widely circulated in the Whitehaven Branch Library?

Should the Advance Business School offer a course to prepare presently employed secretaries to work in the legal profession?

Why are the sales of the Xtra-Ezy lawnmowers 56 percent less in District I, on the average, than in District II?

All the questions given above are overall statements of the problem, which should be broken down into subcategories near the beginning of the report process. For example, the question about career apparel could be detailed in this way:

Should Countrywide Insurance Company purchase career apparel for its women employees?

- What are the benefits
    to the employer?
    to the employees?
    to the customer?
- What are the disadvantages?
- What is the approximate cost?
- Do the benefits to be derived outweigh the cost consideration and any other disadvantages?
- Where can this apparel be purchased?
- If this change in procedure is put into effect, how should it be administered?

As much as possible, think through the complete problem-solving process before you begin. Although the outline you draw up will be a tentative one, it is far better than none at all.

Limiting the Problem

The boundaries of a research problem are referred to as the "scope." Sometimes the term "scope and limitations" is used in this way; in other reports, "limitations" is used to indicate boundaries. The term "limitations" is also used to refer to situations or handicaps — such as the lack of time or money — that prevented a complete research study or a thorough presentation.

These aspects, especially as they are presented in the introductory section of a formal report, are discussed further in Chapter 18. In this book, the term "scope" is used to indicate boundaries; "limitations," at least as the word is used as a description of a part of the final report, indicates limiting or detrimental factors.

However these terms are used as headings of a report, the scope of a report problem must be limited by exact and definite boundaries. We must consider the scope in order to state the problem in definite and specific wording, as well as to plan research procedures.

Look back at some of the preceding problem statements. Notice that these statements also include boundaries. For example, the problem statement about Xtra-Ezy lawnmowers indicates that the study will be concerned only with District I and District II, not with other districts. We are concerned only with sales, not with other aspects of the two districts, unless these other aspects influence sales in some way, as they may. Only the one product is to be considered.

This problem statement would be improved if it also included an indication of the time span; for example, why have sales for the last year been 56 percent less? If this time element is not specified in the general problem statement, it must be included early in the report along with such information as the description of methods and sources of information.

In this report situation, you are trying to find the "why"; you are also looking for the "how," or how the sales can be increased in the slow district. You have the "what" and the "where": the product and the two districts. The "who" consists of the personnel in the two districts, or perhaps in the general management or in the home office. The "when" is the span of time being studied. The problem is not clearly stated until the scope is definitely and specifically defined.

TENTATIVE REPORT PLAN

Before beginning research to find the answer to a predetermined business problem, consider preparing a report plan, even though it must be a tentative one. Such an outline of procedure, although it will perhaps be changed during the research process, provides a far more efficient method of approach than having no plan at all. This preliminary plan, which should be specifically worded and prepared in written form, is referred to as a proposal if it is to be presented to another person or persons for approval.

This preliminary step is referred to here as a report plan, not a proposal, for you will need such a plan whether or not it is presented for the approval of others. When preparing proposals, which may be for business, government, professional, or educational research, you may find that a specified format and arrangement are required, as well as an estimate of cost.

When a specified format is expected, it is most important that you follow it exactly, just as you adhere to a particular and specified format for the reporting itself. Basically though, a report plan or proposal is likely to consist of the types of information discussed here, which are in turn based on the steps to a solution of a research problem.

The report plan should include:

1. A specific statement of the purpose of the report, including, if necessary, subcategories.
(See the report problem used earlier: Should Countrywide Insurance Company provide career apparel for its women employees?) Try to word the statement of purpose so that the scope (or boundaries) of your research is apparent. If you cannot do so, include a separate statement — or paragraphs, as needed — to make clear exactly what you intend to do.

2. Methods of finding information to lead to a solution to the problem. A tentative bibliography may be included in this section.

3. Methods of organizing, evaluating, and interpreting the data in order to reach a solution. Although this step will not be necessary for all report plans and proposals, it is essential in some situations. If the methods consist only of looking at the data, determining what they mean, and putting them into report form, then these duties can logically be assumed without a definite statement in the report plan. If the data are to be analyzed statistically, or in any special or unusual manner, these methods should be stated.

4. A tentative presentation of the report. This step, like the one preceding, will not be required of many proposals or report plans, but it is helpful to you for your own planning and is also useful in class assignments. Although you cannot determine the exact outline until you have completed the research or even later, a beginning outline keeps you from going too far astray in your thinking or in working toward a solution.

This tentative outline is also a tentative table of contents, perhaps, with the headings of the main divisions of the report based upon the subdivisions of the problem statement. In the report about Countrywide Insurance and career apparel, the divisions of the problem statement (benefits, disadvantages, cost, etc.) are logical divisions of the final report.

In addition to the preceding items to be included in the report plan, state specifically in written form (if only for your own use) the answer to these questions:

- Is this report to be analytical or merely informational?
- Is it to be formal or informal, considering both the format and the writing style?
- Is it to be written in the personal or the impersonal tone?

The example shown in Figure 15-1 should not be considered the only possible report plan. In some instances certain of the items shown here may be omitted, or others not shown here may be needed. In all instances, however, include the purpose, as well as the sources and methods of collecting data.

PLAN OF PROPOSED REPORT

a.   Tentative title: WHAT IMPROVEMENTS SHOULD BE MADE IN

THE THEATRE MEMPHIS SOUND SYSTEM?

b.   Author: Karen English CaPece, Technical Assistant.

c.   Statement of Purpose: The purpose of this report is to examine the

characteristics of a theatrical sound system that will best serve

the play-production activities of Theatre Memphis and to

recommend needed improvements in the present system.

d.   Scope: This research is basically concerned with a sound system to

provide background and sound effects for plays. Other uses--

the public-address system, headset-cueing system, and

backstage-monitor system--are considered only to the extent

that no change in the system should interfere with their use.

Amplification of voices during performances is not considered,

as Theatre Memphis does not use amplification for this purpose.

e.   Readers: The business manager and executive board of Theatre

Memphis.

Figure 15-1. *Example of a Tentative Report Plan*

Figure 15-1. *(Continued)*

Sources and/or methods of collecting data:

Published sources listed in attached bibliography.

Original specifications for the theatre's sound system from the

architect's theatre consultant, Ron Jarrit.

Schematics and instruction manuals furnished with equipment installed

by Audio Communications Consultants.

Interviews and group discussion with Director Sherwood Lohrey, with

all members of the technical staff, with the two chairmen of

Volunteer Sound, and with the two volunteer sound operators.

g.   Tentative Table of Contents.   (See attached outline)

This proposed Table of Contents (see Figure 15-2) includes two closing sections — a summary and a recommendations section — instead of the usual combined section, which is often headed "Conclusions and Recommendations." A summary, as such, is not usually required, especially if a synopsis precedes the report. (Perhaps you can find a more descriptive term than "Conclusions and Recommendations." Regardless of what it is called, a section that includes conclusions and recommendations is ordinarily the last section of a formal, analytical report.)

In this particular report, the writer is doing more than "summing up." By summarizing the needed changes in the order of importance, she is stating her "conclusions" of what the data show or imply. She also indicates how her interpretation leads to the next section, in which she states specific recommendations.

A complete report plan facilitates the preparation of the Introduction, which is the first section of a formal report arranged in the inductive (or indirect) order. Although the Introduction may be called by other names, it remains the introductory section. The unimaginative term "Introduction" is to be preferred to a more original one that does not adequately describe the contents of this report division.

As you look at the example of the Introduction (Figure 15-3), you may comment that it is only a repetition of the report plan, with minor deletions and additions. Remember, though, that these parts of the report are not prepared at the same time — although a tentative Introduc-

TENTATIVE TABLE OF CONTENTS

(An Outline of Possible Divisions of Completed Report)

I.   Introduction

    A.   Purpose

    B.   Scope and Limitations

    C.   Methods and Sources of Data

    D.   Basic Plan of Presentation

II.   Better Recording Production

    A.   Improvements to Allow Additional Recording Procedures

    B.   Improvements to Produce Higher Quality Tapes

III.   Better Playback of Records

    A.   Improvements to Provide Operator Ease and Efficiency

    B.   Improvements to Provide a More Satisfactory Playback

IV.   Better Operating and Maintenance Procedures

    A.   Improved System for Purchasing Supplies

    B.   Additional Equipment Needed for Maintenance

    C.   Proposed Manual for Use and Upkeep of Theatre's
        Particular System

V.   Summary of Needed Improvements in a Suggested Order of
     Importance

VI.   Recommendations for Action toward Needed Improvements

Figure 15–2.   *Example of a Tentative Table of Contents*

tion should be prepared, at least for your own use, along with the report plan.

The Introduction should repeat the proposed plan of procedure, as shown in the proposal, unless this procedure was changed during the research and reporting process. The actual research process is, of course, included in the final Introduction, but you may also need to mention the original plans as well as why they were changed. The original report plan or proposal, as well as any subsequent ones, should be attached as an appendix to the completed report.

Although some parts of the report, including preliminary and supplementary parts, are somewhat repetitious, this repetition serves a purpose. The major form of repetition is that the same material is presented in both the synopsis and in the body of the report itself, although the synopsis is in a greatly condensed form. You will study the parts of a complete, formal report in Chapter 18.

Further study of the preparation of the introductory section of the report body (referred to as the Introduction) is included in Chapter 18. The example given in Figure 15–3 will enable you to compare the course plan with the Introduction. Also, your instructor may ask that you include a tentative Introduction with your presentation of a proposed

WHAT IMPROVEMENTS SHOULD BE MADE IN THE

THEATRE MEMPHIS SOUND SYSTEM?

Introduction

Purpose

The purpose of this report is to examine the characteristics of a theatrical sound system that will best serve the play-production activities of Theatre Memphis and to recommend needed improvements in the present system. Inability to achieve desired results with the present equipment has led the director and the technical staff to request additional funding in this area. Changes and improvements are recommended here to provide a guide for expanding the electronic sound facilities.

Figure 15–3. *Example of Tentative Introduction to a Report Plan*

Figure 15-3. *(Continued)*

Scope and Limitations

This research is basically concerned with a sound system to provide background and sound effects for plays. Other uses--the public-address system, headset-cueing system, and backstage-monitor system--are considered only to the extent that no change in the system should interfere with their use. Amplification of voices during performances is not considered, as Theatre Memphis does not use amplification for this purpose.

Description of functions is emphasized more than electronic descriptions or brands of equipment. The Board of Directors can more wisely select specific equipment after considering the amount of money available and after consultation with a sound engineering firm. (Audio Communications Consultants, which installed and services the present system, is recommended in the conclusion of this report.)

The scarcity of published material on sound systems specifically for the legitimate theatre made it necessary to take suggestions primarily from those involved in using the equipment, as well from the architect's theatre consultant.

Methods and Sources of Data

Interviews with persons who have had experience in working with sound in Theatre Memphis productions provided the basic problems to be studied. A tabulation of information from these interviews (included as an appendix

Figure 15-3.   *(Continued)*

with a list of questions asked) was supplemented with related publications

and a study of the existing equipment as compared to the system

recommended by the architect's theatre consultant.

This combined information provided material for a group discussion by

those who had become involved in the study.   Past personal experience and

future interest in using the theatre's equipment provided a productive base

for the use of problem-solving techniques in group discussion.   Sharing

experiences and clarification of particular problems led to a general

agreement of the relative importance of possible improvements.

Basic Plan of Presentation

To describe and justify the needed improvements, this report divides

the basic problems into three groups--tape production, tape playback, and

procedures for operation and maintenance.   The final sections of the report

summarize the most pressing needs and recommend a procedure for action.

research study — that is, with your report plan.   The final copy of the
Introduction, however, is best written after the remainder of the report is
completed.

SUMMARY ◆ 15

The ability to excel in reporting knowledge and techniques can be a
valuable asset to the progress of a business or professional career, as well as
an important part of a liberal education.

A report is a written or oral message planned to convey information or
to present a solution.   An effective business report is an orderly, objective

presentation of factual information and/or analyses planned to serve some business purpose, usually that of making a decision.

Although the basic qualities of effective reports are the same, for the most part, as those of all effective communication, we must give special attention to planned organization for coherence and readability and to an objective tone and nonbiased approach.

Although terminology differs widely, reports are usually classified according to time intervals; authorization; subject matter; function; degree of formality; arrangement of ideas; the personal or impersonal tone; and method of presentation.

The following classifications of reports are often used together:

- Formal format and writing style; impersonal tone; inductive (indirect, logical) arrangement
- Informal in format; formal or informal writing style; personal tone; direct or indirect arrangement, depending upon type of information.

The basis for a report is a problem. The report process consists of steps to a solution. The first and most important step in the report process is determining exactly what the problem is and stating it in specific terms.

Other steps include choosing a method of finding a solution, collecting and organizing data; evaluating and interpreting the data; arriving at a solution to the problem; presenting the solution in appropriate report form; and putting the recommendations into action.

The report writer should think through the complete problem-solving process before beginning the research project, even though the plans will be somewhat tentative.

The report problem is not clearly defined unless the scope of the research is definitely and specifically stated.

QUESTIONS AND PROBLEMS ♦ 15

1. Assume that each of the following paragraphs is the first one of a report planned to determine which magazines, if any, should be added to those currently available in the teachers' reading room. Consider all examples to be the first one in the report body, not from any of the preliminary or supplementary parts.

    Example A: Subscriptions to the *Journal of Business Education*, *Business Education Forum*, and *The Secretary* should be added to the collection currently available in the teachers' reading room.

Example B: I recommend that subscriptions to the *Journal of Business Education*, *Business Education Forum*, and *The Secretary* be added to the collection currently available in the teachers' reading room.

Example C: The purpose of this study is to determine which magazine subscriptions, if any, should be added to the present collection available in the teachers' reading room.

Example D: With the assistance of the members of the Library Committee, I have completed a study of the magazines in the teachers' reading room. Although deciding whether or not we need any more — and which ones — was quite a hassle, you'll find our recommendations at the end of this report.

   a. Which example(s) indicate(s) that the report is arranged in the direct order? The indirect order?

   b. Which example(s) indicate(s) that the report is written in the personal tone? In the impersonal (third-person objective) tone?

   c. Which example(s) indicate(s) that the report is written in the informal writing style?

   d. Which example(s) is(are) most likely to be taken from a complete and formal analytical report?

   e. Each of the four examples was taken from an analytical report. How can you tell?

   f. Can you determine from the four examples whether or not the study was authorized? If it was not authorized, by what special term could it be described?

   g. From the paragraphs given, do you think the report is a periodic one? Why or why not?

2. For each of the following problem situations, state the problem (purpose) either in the form of a question or as an infinitive phrase. For example, a report planned to study the advisability of providing career apparel can be stated as:

Should the Countrywide Insurance Company provide career apparel for its women employees? (*Question*)

Purpose: To determine whether the Countrywide Insurance Company should provide career apparel for its women employees. (*Infinitive phrase*)

Be specific, but omit subcategories of the problem. Assume necessary and reasonable details, including names.

   a. A restaurant manager wants to know how to improve crowded conditions at the midday meal.

   b. A restaurant manager wants to know how to increase profits on the midday meal.

   c. A restaurant manager wants to know the choices most often made from the luncheon menu.

   d. A college professor is trying to decide whether to authorize monthly deductions from his paycheck for deposit in a tax-sheltered annuity fund.

   e. The professor has decided to invest in a tax-sheltered annuity fund, but he does not know which one to choose.

   f. An officer manager must choose a copying machine.

g. A business education teacher must choose typewriters for a classroom to be used for beginning typists.

h. A Chamber of Commerce wants to know what local citizens think of the Chamber's services and purposes.

i. A dean of a college of business administration wants to determine the business course or courses that former students believe to have been most beneficial to them.

j. A discount department store wants to know something of its "image."

k. A large construction company is considering adopting a pension plan.

l. The Park Commission is thinking of installing Muzak in all offices.

m. A manufacturer needs to know how to market a new product, a compact refrigerator-icemaker.

3. For one of the problem situations listed in Question 2, state the problem in the form of a null hypothesis.

4. Choose a question that you wish to investigate in order to report the results in the formal business report. Prepare a tentative report plan, as shown in this chapter. Include a tentative title, statement of purpose, scope (or scope and limitations), readers, and sources and methods of collecting data. (See topics suggested in Problem 10, Chapter 18.)

5. Prepare a tentative table of contents for the research you planned in Question 4.

6. Prepare a tentative introduction to the report based on the problem stated in Question 4. (This tentative introduction, as well as the tentative table of contents and the tentative bibliography assigned in the next chapter, will almost certainly need revision before inclusion in the final copy of the report.)

FURTHER READING ♦ 15

These references apply to all aspects of business research and report writing as discussed in Chapters 15 through 18. Additional references are given at the end of Chapters 16, 17, and 18; these sources apply especially to topics discussed in the individual chapters. In addition, see the chapters on reports in the books on general business communication listed at the end of Chapter 1.

Berenson, Conrad, and Colton, Raymond. *Research and Report Writing for Business and Economics*. New York: Random House, 1971.

Brown, Leland. *Effective Business Report Writing*. 3d ed. Englewood Cliffs, N.J.: Prentice-Hall, 1973.

Comer, David B. III, and Spellman, Ralph R. *Modern Technical and Industrial Reports*. New York: G. P. Putnam's Sons, 1962.

Damerst, William A. *Clear Technical Reports*. New York: Harcourt Brace Jovanovich, 1972.

Dawe, Jessamond. *Writing Business and Economic Papers.* Totowa, N.J.: Littlefield, Adams, 1965.

Graves, Harold F., and Hoffman, Lyne S. S. *Report Writing.* 4th ed. Englewood Cliffs, N.J.: Prentice-Hall, 1965.

Lesikar, Raymond V. *Report Writing for Business.* 4th ed. Homewood, Ill.: Richard D. Irwin, 1973.

Sigband, Norman B. *Effective Report Writing, for Business, Industry, and Government.* New York: Harper & Bros., 1960.

Sklare, Arnold B. *Creative Report Writing.* New York: McGraw-Hill Book Company, 1964.

Gathering Business Information

16

In the preceding chapter, emphasis was upon the first steps of the report process: determining the problem, defining it in specific terms, and deciding upon the methods of finding a solution to the problem. This chapter moves to the next step in the report process, that of gathering business information.

METHODS OF OBTAINING INFORMATION

After you have determined the purpose of the report and made plans for finding a solution to the problem, your next step is gathering information. At times you will already have some of this information, based upon your own experience.

In the example shown in the preceding chapter, the report writer already knew some of the problems involved with the present sound system of Theatre Memphis, as she had used this equipment in her work. The use of such sources is often necessary in reports of all lengths and formality. In many instances, this type of information is the most important. You will need additional data, however, even if only for the purpose of convincing readers of the accuracy of your decisions.

Sources of data are described as being secondary or primary. The word "secondary" is used to mean that the information has already been gathered by someone else. Since most of this information is in published form and available in libraries, secondary research is often referred to as library research. Secondary research may also include unpublished sources, such as reports and dissertations. In addition, secondary information is obtained from such sources as company brochures and operating and procedures manuals.

Information that has not already been gathered and written by someone else is referred to as primary data. Methods of obtaining primary data are through observation, experimentation, and surveys, often called "normative surveys" because they reflect the "norm" or present conditions. Surveys employ the use of questionnaires and formal or informal interviews.

The researcher for Theatre Memphis made use of printed information, although she stated that not a great deal was available that was specific enough to apply to this particular building. She also made use of observation, based on her present and past experiences with the equipment. In addition, she used surveys.

No formal experimentation was done — as is done in scientific experiments — but some of her observation of the performance of the equipment was obtained through experimentation. So were the observations of other persons working with the equipment.

LIBRARY RESEARCH

The term "library research" is used here to mean any secondary data. As explained earlier, however, not all secondary data will be found in libraries.

A large library can be confusing even to experienced researchers. You may find it frustrating to be surrounded by millions of words, all of which seem to have nothing whatsoever to do with the answer to your particular problem.

Library research should ordinarily be your starting point in the data-gathering process. No matter what the problem you are trying to solve, similar problems are likely to have occurred in other organizations or with other individuals, and they may be reported in a business periodical or elsewhere. Although this will not be the complete solution to your own problem, knowing what others have done about a similar situation can help you to solve your own.

We must build on the experience of others; there is no time to do otherwise. (Remember Korsybski's statement that man binds time.) You as a business person should not spend time in completing a research project that has already been done unless you want to check the validity and the reliability of this project, expand upon it in some way, or to update it.

For example, if a construction company wants to know the rate of increase or decrease in homebuilding — or numbers of other questions that might arise in order for the company to plan its operations — the researcher would no doubt find that recent studies have already been made of these questions.   Chambers of Commerce, government agencies, and professional organizations are engaged in such research and in reporting their findings for the benefit of business persons and of the public in general.

Remember — library research is usually the best way to begin your report writing project.   In addition to finding specific information to include in your report, you will obtain a general overview of the entire problem.   This beginning research may also provide ideas of other methods of investigation.   As you examine possible sources, you may be referred to other sources, perhaps better ones.

As you continue with your library research, you may find it necessary to revise somewhat the tentative report plan.   But keep in mind what you have set out to do and stay within your previously planned scope unless you find that you really need to start over and plan another project.   If this is the situation, make sure that it meets the approval of the person who authorized the report.

You may find that you are gathering too much information or that the information does not apply to the main problem.   Finding it hard to tear yourself away from libraries is not a bad sign — it probably indicates that you have an inquiring mind and broad interests, or that you are diligent in looking at all aspects of a situation.   As mentioned in Chapter 1, a library can be a most worthwhile place in which to spend time.   But straying away from a goal, as you can so easily do, may cause you to be pressured later on in order to meet the report deadline.

A comprehensive library contains reference sources of many kinds: books, magazines, newspapers, reports, leaflets and pamphlets, many forms of government documents, directories, and other sources of information.   In addition to printed material, libraries contain nonprint media, such as sound recordings, transparencies, and films.

Some of the information you need will probably be found in books, including those stored in the reference section of the library.   Other information will be available in magazines, particularly in business and professional journals.   Some needed information may be in the form of reports, bulletins, brochures, and nonprint media.

Chapter 1 includes an overview of library resources; this discussion was placed in the first chapter because additional reading is desirable throughout your study of business communication, or of any other subject, not only for the preparation of business reports.

Your rereading of the section of Chapter 1 entitled "Finding Specialized Reading Material" will be helpful to you as you consider the methods of obtaining business data through library research.

The Evaluation of Library Material

You will find that evaluating secondary sources, as well as primary ones, is one of the most important but most difficult aspects of the report process.

Evaluation of the data is discussed in more detail in the following chapter, where emphasis is upon the analysis of data you have previously collected. Some evaluation must be done, however, as you proceed with library research. If you do not evaluate during the collection process, you will gather much information that is irrelevant or redundant, as well as misleading.

Wide research is probably the most dependable method of determining that information gathered through library research is valid and reliable. If, for example, you rely only upon one or a few sources, you do not have complete assurance that you have not by chance picked writers who for one reason or another give incomplete or inaccurate information.

Be careful to use only recent sources, except for general, mostly unchanging principles, or for historical research. If you believe that the information that you are seeking fits into the category for which you can use standard, older works (sometimes referred to as classics), be sure to compare these sources with later ones to make certain that the included information is still current.

Magazine articles generally relay more recent information than that found in books because of the time that is necessary to complete the publication process of books, although this process is shorter now than it was in previous years. Books, however, are often prepared more carefully than magazine articles by obtaining the viewpoints of reviewers and by more careful and thorough editing.

Nevertheless, all books are not carefully written, edited, or researched. Like magazine articles or any other form of written or spoken communication, they may be reliable or unreliable, truthful or untruthful. The quality depends, to a great extent, upon the author and the publisher, although incorrect information can and does come from the best-known authorities and publishing houses.

You will find many books reviewed in *Book Review Digest*. Many good sources, however, are not included in these digests; they could not possibly be because of the multitude of books that are published each year, and because of the lack of space in the journals from which the entries in the digests are taken.

Your reference librarian can be most helpful to you in your search for data, as well as in giving advice as to the probable accuracy of the various sources. You should not hesitate to ask for the assistance of your librarians, but don't ask them to do something that you can easily do for yourself. Their services are available not only for class assignments but also for actual business research. (Ideally, a class assignment is "actual business research," although in some instances it must be at least partially "pretend.")

Basic Reference Sources

Encyclopedias

Encyclopedias are the best known and most widely used sources of general information, although they may remind you of the extremely limited research that you did in elementary school and high school years in order to prepare a term paper.   Comprehensive encyclopedias, however, are useful in all types of research, especially as a starting place.

Although the scope of your research must include much more than information given in encyclopedias, they are a good place to begin because they give an overall view of a particular field or of supplementary aspects of a report project.   Encyclopedias are useful for general background information.   They may also include a list of supplementary reading materials for your particular topic.

The *Encyclopaedia Brittanica* and the *Encyclopedia Americana* are perhaps the most well-known and respected of a number of encyclopedias in general use.   These books are written on the adult level, although they are not difficult to read.   Some of the other encyclopedias are planned especially for use in elementary schools or high schools.   Encyclopedias are supplemented with yearbooks planned to keep the set as up to date as possible.

In addition to general encyclopedias, a number of specialized ones are available for coverage of specialized areas of knowledge.   Some of these are the *Encyclopedia of Social Science, Exporter's Encyclopedia, Accountant's Encyclopedia,* and *Encyclopedia of Banking and Finance.*

Dictionaries

Dictionaries remain an important library source.   Unabridged dictionaries are more exact and complete than smaller ones, as they can be because of extra space.   In addition to general dictionaries, there are many specialized ones, just as there are specialized encyclopedias.   In fact, the terms are overlapping; one book described as an encyclopedia may be similar to another described as a specialized dictionary.   Some books use both terms in their titles, as in the *Encyclopedic Dictionary of Business,* published by Prentice-Hall.   These reference books are especially good for the definition and explanation of specialized terms.

Handbooks and Manuals

Handbooks are similar to specialized encyclopedias and dictionaries. They tend to be more complete, especially more so than a book described as a dictionary. A business handbook presents a condensed picture of an entire field of business.

These handbooks, which are frequently revised in order to retain only presently accurate information, include the *Handbook of Auditing Methods, Industrial Accountant's Handbook, Handbook of Business Administration, Handbook of Insurance, Management Handbook, Marketing Handbook, Sales Executives' Handbook,* and *Real Estate Handbook.* Many other manuals and handbooks are also available, such as the *United States Postal Manual* and the *United States Government Organizations Manual.*

Yearbooks and Almanacs

Yearbooks, in addition to those that supplement encyclopedias, include publications of various countries, trades, and professions, as well as the *Comprehensive Statistical Abstract of the United States.*

Almanacs, such as the widely available *World Almanac* and *Book of Facts,* contain a wealth of information on many and varied subjects.

Biographical Directories

Biographical directories provide information about leaders or well-known persons, living or dead. The best known is *Who's Who in America,* which summarizes the lives of living Americans who have achieved prominence in any field. Specialized directories include *Who's Who in Insurance, Who's Who in Education,* and *American Men of Science,* as well as specialized directories in many other occupational fields.

In addition to directories that are specialized according to profession, directories are also specialized according to the section of the country; for example, *Who's Who in the South.* Some states are represented by their own particular *Who's Who.* Even more specialized is *Who's Who in State Government,* which is issued for many states.

Who's Who in Commerce and Industry is a directory of prominent businessmen. *Poor's Register of Corporations, Directors and Executives* is a similar publication but more exclusive. The *Biography Index,* published quarterly, is a guide to biographical material in books and magazines.

Business Services Publications

Business services publications, such as *Moody's Investor's Service* and *Standard and Poor's Corporation Services*, provide a wide assortment of business information. These particular guides have already been mentioned in Chapter 13 in the discussion of finding information about possible companies with which to seek employment. Although much of the information is planned for the need of practicing businessmen, especially for the investor or for investors' advisors, much is meaningful to the business researcher.

Moody's Manuals summarize data for all major American companies. These manuals are divided in this way: industrials, banks and finance, the public utilities, transportation, municipals, and government. *Corporation Records*, furnished by Standard and Poor's Corporation, provide similar information.

Guides to Books

The following books and indexes may be especially valuable to you:

- *Business Reference Sources* by Lorna M. Daniels.
- *Encyclopedia of Business Information Sources,* two volumes.
- *Books in Print,* an annual guide to books in print in the United States with the exception of poetry, fiction, and bibles.
- *Cumulative Book Index,* a guide to books published in the English language throughout the world. Each yearly volume includes books published during that year.
- *Business Books in Print,* a comprehensive guide to books in most business areas.

The card catalog in your library (as you most likely know) is arranged according to subject, author, and title. The books shown in the card catalog obviously do not make up the same list of books as those shown in *Books in Print, Cumulative Book Index,* or similar indexes.

Even the largest library is not likely to have all books in any area that are currently in print. In addition, the card catalog may show books, particularly old ones, that are not listed in the indexes. (*Cumulative Book Index* is a guide to all books in print in the United States since 1912.)

Guides to Periodicals and Pamphlets

Among other helpful sources for researching data in journals, magazines, and newspapers are the following:

- The *Reader's Guide to Periodical Literature* is a guide to general magazine articles, classified by author and by subject.
- The *Business Periodicals Index* is a guide to articles in business, industrial, and trade magazines. This index is issued monthly and cumulated annually.
- The *Public Affairs Information Service* (PAIS) is an index, classified by subject, of periodicals, government publications, and pamphlets, especially in the area of economics and social conditions, public administration, and international affairs.
- The *Vertical File Index* lists pamphlets and leaflets, classified by subject and title.
- The *New York Times Index,* although an index of news stories that have appeared in the *New York Times,* can be used as a guide to all newspapers. When looking for stories of national interest, you can find the date when they happened by using the *New York Times Index.* When you have the date, you will often find that it is easy to find the news story in other daily newspapers.

The discussion here is of necessity incomplete. Entire books could not describe the various reference sources in a large comprehensive library. In this book, which is devoted to many facets of business communication, only scanty coverage can be given. Textbooks that are devoted exclusively to business research and business report writing have more space to devote to leading research sources, but these books cannot include all the information you may need. Look over the sources available in your library, and, if necessary, ask a reference librarian for assistance.

Steps to Finding Needed Library Information

Suppose that you are authorized to complete the research and to compare the report for the question presented in Chapter 15, "Should Countrywide Insurance Company provide career apparel for women employees?" Subcategories of these problems are given in Chapter 15, with details of the scope of the problem.

We know from the wording of the title that the report is limited to women employees. (Perhaps male employees are already in uniform or they have voted not to wear uniforms — or perhaps this study is to be left until later.) In any event, if we accept the problem statement as shown, we are concerned only with women employees. Any other aspects of scope or limitations, although they may exist, are not apparent from the stated purpose.

You realize that you cannot depend upon library research alone if the study is to be beneficial for a special purpose and for the particular company for which the research is planned. The researcher obtained the opinions of workers who would wear the career apparel by the use of interviews and a questionnaire. She obtained further information by studying professional and sales literature of companies that could supply the apparel and by talking with sales representatives.

Before she took these steps, however, she looked at library sources. Why? No book or magazine article will completely answer her question. She looked at library sources first — as you should do in a project of this type — in order to determine the experience of other companies with career apparel and to learn, if possible, decisions other persons had made in answer to the following questions.

Has this policy been conducive to better employee morale? Have employees objected to this policy or refused to wear the apparel? Does the employing company ordinarily furnish this clothing without charge, or at a reduced charge, or is the employee expected to pay the entire cost? Do policies differ from organization to organization?

Because employees now pay for their clothes, is it reasonable that they should pay at least part of the cost? Can apparel be planned so that the appearance of each employee can be varied from day to day by the use of a change of blouse or accessories? How can each employee be prevented from being identical in appearance to every other employee? Can apparel be purchased that will be flattering to workers of all ages and sizes?

The steps that follow are not necessarily in the order that you should take them. Much could depend upon the arrangement of your particular library, the availability of other libraries in your city, and information given with library sources that lead to additional reference sources.

You realize that it is unlikely that a book will be written on career apparel and that your most likely source of information is in magazines, especially business journals. You are not completely sure, however, that there are no books on career apparel; as you know, books are written on many thousands of subjects. You look in the card catalog and find nothing. You realize, though, that such a book may be in print but not available at this particular library.

A specialized business library, part of the public library system, is located in the downtown area of your city. The main city library contains thousands of books, and many are shelved in the several branches. Several other college and business libraries are within easy driving distance.

You decide to look in *Books in Print* or the *Cumulative Book Index* to determine whether a book has been written about career apparel. You look in one or both of these indexes and find nothing, as you expected. Now what? You consider that your problem is a business area that is a facet of office management, personnel management, and general business management.

You look in *Books in Print* or the *Cumulative Book Index* to find the name of the most recent books in these areas. Then you check the card catalog and find that your library owns these books. You jot down the call number. If your library has open stacks, find not only the books that you have noted but similar ones that because of similar subject matter are shelved in the same location. By checking the indexes of these books you find references to your particular subject. (The availability of open stacks greatly facilitates library research.)

Your next step is to go to the *Business Periodicals Index* to find articles that apply. You check the *Public Affairs Information Service* to find any other relevant articles. You also use the *Vertical File Index* to find pamphlets or leaflets that deal with the subject. You check local newspaper indexes and the *New York Times Index* or the *Wall Street Journal Index*, if it is available, to guide you to newspaper articles.

Because you wish to be completely thorough in your approach, you also look in the *Reader's Guide to Periodical Literature*, although you realize that your subject is a specialized business one and not likely to be reported in magazines of general interest. Some business articles, however, do appear in general magazines that are not listed in the *Business Periodicals Index*. Then you ask the reference librarian to suggest additional sources that you may have overlooked.

You read all of the material you find, even though very little may go into the final report. You will have a better overview of the field and how to approach the problem after a general reading in the field, even though none of the material seems to describe particularly your own problem. Your report, however, will be more convincing if you include a section as to how the career apparel has worked in other companies.

OBSERVATION

Observation, as the term is used to describe a method of data collection, includes both casual and informal observation and planned, controlled, and scientific observation. The term may also be used to describe a search through company records. Many accounting reports and auditing reports are in reality observation reports based on an analysis of financial records.

In the research that was made in an attempt to find the answer to the improvement of sound equipment in Theatre Memphis, the researcher makes recommendations based partly upon her previous observations as to the efficiency of the present equipment. The person who did the study of the advisability of career apparel used casual observation of the present dress of the employees. She could possibly have used a planned, structured form of observation.

For example, she could have kept detailed, daily records of the dress of all the employees to determine something of their choice of color and style, as well as to consider the question of whether career apparel was needed from the standpoint of improving the overall appearance of the employees. This subject would have been a very touchy one if this study had been kept secret from the employees. The information to be gained would probably not have been worth the risk of discovery with the subsequent mistrust. If the employees knew that they were being studied, no doubt their dress would not have been really typical of their usual dress.

The results of information obtained through observation, like that obtained in any other way, can be trustworthy or completely the opposite, depending upon the care and judgment of the researcher as well as upon many other contributing factors. Observation as a method of research has a disadvantage in that we tend to interpret and misinterpret what we see and hear in light of our preconceived conclusions and desires (as discussed in Chapters 3 and 4).

Carefully planned observation for the purpose of research is more likely to provide dependable information than is the casual and informal relating of experiences, although these experiences, even though unscientific, should not be overlooked. As in all other forms of research, accurate and complete records should be kept as the data are collected. Then the data must be accurately analyzed and interpreted.

EXPERIMENTATION

Experimentation, scientifically done, is reliable and accurate—more so than any other research method. But even experimentation is subject to error. In addition, many business problems are not of the type that lend themselves to the experimental type of research.

In business, as in other areas, the purpose of experimental research is to determine the effect of change under a given set of conditions. The conditions must be carefully constructed so that only one variable is tested at a time. For example, an experiment to determine the effect of career apparel upon employee morale would be difficult to conduct in a completely scientific manner because of the element of human behavior.

Suppose that you want to test the effectiveness of two different sales letters. One is mailed to homeowners in one state, and one is mailed to the homeowners in another state. Depending upon the product, the observed difference in effectiveness of the letters could have a great deal more to do with the choice of states than with the wording of the letter. If you try to sell wind-turned attic ventilators through a letter sent to homeowners in Maine and through another letter sent to homeowners in

Alabama, you are adding variables to the one you set out to test — the effectiveness of the differing letters.

If you sell more ventilators to those persons in Alabama, you may consider the warmer climate to be a factor — but then you realize that people in Maine really should buy more because they are not so likely to have central air conditioners — and then you consider that persons in Alabama need ventilators in order to decrease the cost of electricity. With all these unanswered questions, you cannot be sure that differences in the letter had any effect.

This illustration is perhaps a rather extreme example of uncontrolled experimentation. Competent researchers would not attempt an experiment without attempting to control all contributing factors except the one being tested. But, except in scientific laboratories, it is often difficult to control all factors entirely.

The methods of experimentation, as a means of research, are outside the scope of this book. Reading sources that include more detailed information about methods, including experimentation, are listed at the end of this chapter.

SURVEYS

Surveys are widely used in obtaining business information. They are conducted through interviews and conversations, both face-to-face and by the use of the telephone, and by the use of the mail questionnaire.

Sampling

Unless all members of the entire group are to be surveyed, the assumption must be that those who have been picked to be the respondents are representative of the entire group. Reliability can result only from a representative sample. In research terms, reliability is understood to be the assurance that the data are truthful.

To arrive at this truthfulness, surveys must be scientifically administered. In addition, the survey instrument must be valid. This word, in research terminology, means that the research instrument measures what it is intended to measure. For example, you cannot find the weight of an object by using a yardstick, nor can you find its length by using a bathroom scale, because a yardstick is not a valid instrument for measuring weight, and a scale is not a valid instrument for measuring length. The yardstick is not reliable even for measuring length if it expands or shrinks, nor is the scale reliable for measuring weight if it gives varying readings each time an unchanging object is weighed.

An example of data that are not reliable, even though you used a yardstick, are measurements to determine the average height of a group of employees. If you measure three women and find that their average height is 61 inches, this conclusion seems to mean that by chance you have chosen a nonrepresentative sample of the total group. (The total group is known as the population.) What has gone wrong here is that too few employees have been chosen and also, perhaps, that they were not chosen by a truly random selection process. If the total number of women employees in this organization is 100, certainly you should sample more than three.

If you had chosen twenty-five or thirty, the obtained average would ordinarily have been fairly close, provided you had used a method of random sampling, to the average that you would have obtained if you had measured all 100. If you had chosen twenty-five or thirty, however, your average would not be correct, if, for example, you had measured the twenty players on the company basketball team and had included them in the sample.

When beginning the sampling procedure, the researcher must consider the persons who are to be surveyed, the number, and how to be reasonably assured that those surveyed are representative of the whole group.

A general law of sampling is that a sufficiently large number of items (or opinions, etc.) taken at random from a large group will have the characteristics of the larger group. If the group is small, each item should be examined or each person should be asked for an opinion.

In the study we have discussed previously, the researcher seeking to improve the sound equipment at Theater Memphis asked for the opinion of all persons who work or have worked with this equipment. In the study about career apparel, each employee was asked for her opinion. Because of the time and expense required for a large-scale survey, however, we cannot economically question each person in a large group. We must limit our questioning to a number that we believe will give reliable results and that will not be extravagant in the use of time and money. Anyway, according to experts in statistics, a well-chosen and adequately large sample is likely to be as reliable as examining the entire group.

Random Sampling

Random sampling is defined as the sampling method by which every item in the universe has an equal chance of being chosen. In order to insure that every individual has the same opportunity to be chosen, the researcher must have a complete list of all items (persons, etc.) in the universe.

The old "putting names in a barrel" is a true random sample if you can be sure that the names are thoroughly mixed and that no element other than chance enters into the selection. Remember that random sampling, as it is used in statistics, does not mean "hit or miss" as the word "random" does when used in other instances.

Randomness is most often achieved by the use of a table of random numbers. These tables ordinarily consist of many groups of five-digit numbers. Random numbers can be employed by any systematic method since each of the digits has been selected at random, most likely by a computer. To use these tables, the researcher matches the numbers with previously numbered names or items, taken from a list of the complete group.

Stratified Random Sampling

Stratified random sampling is done by conducting a random sample of subgroups within the universe. To sample the opinions of students in your university, you can use subgroups of such things as classification (freshmen, sophomore, etc.), sex, major fields of interest, age, or many other divisions.

Usually the desired number in each division should be the same as the portion of the universe that the group comprises. For example, if you try to find data as it applies to the entire student body, and in your school there are twice as many freshmen as there are seniors, include in your sample twice as many freshmen as you do seniors.

Systematic Sampling

Systematic sampling is the technique of taking selections at definite and unchanging intervals from a list of the members of the universe. If you have a list of all the students in your college, you would do systematic sampling by taking, for example, each fifteenth name on the list.

Although this method is not strictly random sampling, ordinarily the effect will be the same if the sample size is large enough. To insure an even greater degree of randomness, the researcher could take the first number entirely by chance and proceed through the list using the same number.

Various other sampling methods are described in textbooks and handbooks in statistics. If you have not studied statistics, you should read further into the field of sampling theory before undertaking a research project which makes use of this method of investigation.

Ordinarily, 25 to 30 percent of a large group, based on numbers alone, should provide representative data. At times you will not be able to sample this many because of the time and expense involved. In this case you will need to use some method of determining adequate sample size. A simple method is to split the sample into two or more parts and to compare the results from the various parts. A similarity of results from these parts of the total sample indicates that overall results are likely to be acceptable.

Formulas can be used for checking the adequacy of sample size. These formulas can be applied when you have enough returns to estimate the apparent division of answers. These formulas are given in books on statistics and in some books devoted exclusively to business and report writing.

Constructing the Questionnaire

When you plan a questionnaire, consider the aspects of securing a satisfactory rate of return and of securing accurate answers. You must also consider how you will use the completed questionnaires once they are received. This aspect includes the consideration of the ease and accuracy with which the results can be tabulated and analyzed.

You also plan a covering letter, which is a persuasive request. As you learned in Chapter 10, the most effective way to convince readers to respond is to show them benefits to themselves. Even if there is no immediate apparent benefit to the respondent, many persons will respond if you carefully and convincingly explain the purpose of the study and why you need their opinions. To encourage response, however, you must be especially concerned with making it possible for the respondent to complete and return the questionnaire with the minimum amount of time and effort.

The construction of the questionnaire, including its physical appearance, will influence the percentage of returns and the value of the answers. Specific principles of questionnaire construction are listed below. In addition, principles of communication you have studied throughout this course are most important as you plan the survey instruments and the covering letter. Clearness, conciseness, the you-attitude, and all the other attributes of effective communication apply to obtaining business information through the use of questionnaires.

1. Make the questions easy to understand and concerned with one topic only. Avoid ambiguous wording. For example, the question "why did you buy your last car?" could lead to the response that the respondent liked the color, the price, or the design. Another answer could be that he bought the car because he had wrecked his older one, or because his wife

wouldn't let him buy a motorcycle. Avoid broad, relative terms such as "often," "a long time," and "seldom," unless these terms are specifically defined.

2. Make the questionnaire easy to answer. Providing blanks to be checked facilitates response as well as the researcher's tabulation of the answers.

3. Provide for all likely answers. Although some questions can be answered by a "yes" or a "no," many are somewhere in between. (We are back again to a principle of general semantics — that many things are neither black nor white but varying shades of gray.) Provide for categories such as "I don't know," or "no opinion," "disagree," or "strongly disagree." Allowing for shadings of opinions are much more descriptive and accurate than mere "agree" or "disagree" questions.

4. Ask only for information that can be easily remembered.

5. Keep the questionnaire as short as possible by asking only for needed information.

6. Avoid questions that touch on pride or personal bias, or those that give the effect of prying. Such areas include age, income, morals, and personal habits. A question about education may have a prying effect with persons of limited educational background. Information about age, income status, or education may be necessary in order to accomplish the particular purpose of the report. Even if you need this information, however, you will ordinarily not need the exact age, the exact amount of income, or the exact number of years the person has been in school.

   To encourage response, as well as to facilitate evaluation of the answers, provide ranges from which the respondent may show his age and income range. For example, you can show age brackets "under 21," "20 to 25," and set up income brackets in the same way. Age and income brackets can be an important consideration in marketing research when planning products to manufacture or outlets for distribution.

7. Arrange questions in a logical order.

8. If the questionnaire is mailed, enclose a stamped and addressed envelope.

9. Avoid leading questions — those that by their wording suggest an answer.

10. Provide for additional comments, if any, by the respondent by the use of open-ended questions in which comments can be included in the respondent's own words. Although these

questions are more difficult to tabulate than answers that are shown by check mark, these comments may be more helpful than all the other answers. In addition, they may encourage respondents in that the recipient is asked to speak freely.

In addition to mail questionnaires, surveys are done by personal interviews, either face-to-face or by telephone.

The portion of a questionnaire shown in Figure 16–1 is the second of four pages of a mailing sent to Certified Professional Secretaries.[1] The answers received from 565 secretaries were punched into cards so that a computer analysis could be made of all information furnished by the

page 2

6. DEPARTMENT IN WHICH YOU WORK, OR TITLE OF IMMEDIATE SUPERVISOR: (Check only one. If no item exactly describes your department or immediate supervisor, check the one most similar.)

President, director, or other at head of firm or institution _____ (01)
Purchasing . . . . _____ (02)
Production or engineering . . . . _____ (03)
Financial, accounting, credit . . . . _____ (04)
Marketing, sales, advertising, promotion . . . . _____ (05)
Legal . . . . _____ (06)
Research and development . . . . _____ (07)
Personnel . . . . _____ (08)
Public relations, customer service . . . . _____ (09)
Office services . . . . _____ (10)

7. TYPES OF WRITING: (Include all material that you compose. Do <u>not</u> include writing dictated to you, or work on which your only duty is correcting, proofreading, or typewriting. <u>Regularly</u> or <u>often</u> is used to mean writing that is part of your regular responsibilities, regardless of how often these responsibilities occur. For example, if your writing includes work on the annual report as an ordinary or expected task, check the first column, although this work may occur only once a year. <u>Seldom</u> is used to apply to writing that has occurred at least once in your present position, but has not occurred often enough to be considered part of your regular work. <u>Never</u> applies to types of writing that have not been done at all. For all answers, consider only your responsibilities in your present position.

Figure 16–1. *Portion of a Mailed Questionnaire*

1. Malra Clifft Treece, "Written Communication Responsibilities and Related Difficulties Experienced by Selected Certified Professional Secretaries" (unpublished doctoral dissertation, University of Mississippi, 1971), p. 148.

Figure 16-1. *(Continued)*

	Regularly or Often	Seldom	Never
01. LETTERS, OF ANY OR ALL KINDS, including those listed below and/or any other kind	___ (1)	___ (2)	___ (3)
Types of Letters			
02. Requests (for information, instructions, action, cooperation, appointments, favors, merchandise or service, other kinds of requests)	___ (1)	___ (2)	___ (3)
03. Responses to requests	___ (1)	___ (2)	___ (3)
04. General administrative letters (confirmation of telephone and telegraph messages, transmittal, covering, authorization, remittances, others)	___ (1)	___ (2)	___ (3)
05. Executive correspondence (letters of appreciation, congratulation, sympathy, invitation, other similar letters)	___ (1)	___ (2)	___ (3)
06. Sales or sales promotion	___ (1)	___ (2)	___ (3)
07. Claim or adjustment	___ (1)	___ (2)	___ (3)
08. Credit or collection	___ (1)	___ (2)	___ (3)
09. Letters about employment	___ (1)	___ (2)	___ (3)
10. Miscellaneous, or others not listed 02-09	___ (1)	___ (2)	___ (3)

respondents to the questionnaire. After the information was put into the computer, all counting of answers was done automatically, as well as the figuring of percentages, means, standard deviations, and other measures.

The researcher can determine many kinds of information from only a few questions; for example, from the illustrated questionnaire, the kinds of letters written most often by secretaries to presidents of manufacturing companies. (The kind of employing organization was asked on the first page of the questionnaire.) Because of the ease of obtaining many and various items of information by use of the computer, some researchers are tempted to ask for information and comparisons that they don't really need, thus complicating the analysis and reporting steps in the research process.

Notice the exact instructions given before each of the two groups of questions.

When surveys are conducted through face-to-face or telephone interviews, a form of questionnaire should be drawn up as a guide to the interviewer. Questions should be presented to all respondents in a uniform way, and, as in written questionnaires, wording should be objective and specific. Care should be taken to avoid leading questions or statements, or those that seem to pry.

Questionnaires that are sent by mail must be accompanied with a courteous and convincing letter. This message is of course a request — and ordinarily should be planned as a direct request, as illustrated in Chapter 9. In some instances the respondent may be reluctant to comply with your wishes; if you feel that this is the case, the persuasive request letter, as described in Chapter 10, may be the better choice.

Regardless of the letter plan, you must include necessary information about why you are questioning the reader and how the answers will be used. If you can find a reasonable reader benefit, subtly point it out. And, as in other request letters, a statement of when the completed questionnaire is needed will help to prevent procrastination and a delayed or forgotten return.

SUMMARY ◆ 16

Methods of obtaining information include primary and secondary research. The word "secondary" means that the information has already been gathered by someone else and, usually, is available in printed form in libraries. Some secondary research sources are unpublished.

Forms of primary research are observation, experimentation, and surveys. Surveys employ the use of questionnaires and formal and informal interviews.

Library research should often be the starting point in the data-gathering process. The competent researcher is familiar with basic reference sources and can find needed secondary information.

A basic guide to articles that have appeared in business magazines is the *Business Periodicals Index*.

Reliability in sampling can result only from a representative sample. A general law of sampling is that a sufficiently large number of items (opinions, etc.) taken at random from a large group will have the characteristics of the larger group.

Random sampling is defined as a sampling method by which every item in the universe has an equal chance of being chosen. Stratified random sampling is done by conducting a random sampling of subgroups within the universe.

Questionnaires must be constructed with care in order to encourage response, to obtain the needed information, and to facilitate tabulation of the results.

QUESTIONS AND PROBLEMS ◆ 16

1. Prepare a tentative bibliography of at least five recent secondary sources that seem to apply to the problem for which you prepared a report plan. (Question 4, Chapter 15.) Use the form shown in Appendix C.

2. Prepare an annotated bibliography (see explanation and examples in Appendix C) of five or more recent journal articles on one of these topics:

    a. Aspects of communication as applied to one of these fields:
    - accounting
    - business education
    - management of a small business
    - personnel management
    - marketing
    - office management

    b. New developments in one of these fields:
    - accounting
    - business education
    - management of a small business
    - personnel management
    - marketing
    - office management

3. Prepare a list of periodicals that apply especially to your major field of study.

4. Prepare a tentative bibliography of at least five recent journal articles or books that seem to apply to one of the problem situations listed in Question 2, Chapter 15.

5. Prepare a questionnaire to use in the research project for which you prepared a report plan (Question 4, Chapter 15). If an opaque projector is available in your classroom, show your questionnaire to the class. Ask for comments and suggestions for improvement.

6. Prepare a questionnaire to use in solving one of the research problems listed in Question 2, Chapter 15. Assume the type and number of respondents and any other necessary or helpful details. Show your questionnaire to the class (or ask them to fill it out) and ask for comments and suggestions for improvement.

7. Write a covering letter to accompany the questionnaire prepared in answer to Question 5.

8. Write a covering letter for the questionnaire you prepared in answer to Question 6.

9. Does your school library classify books according to the Dewey Decimal System or according to the Library of Congress System? How does the public library system in your city or town classify books? Write a short memorandum report to your instructor in answer to these questions.

10. Use *Moody's Manuals* and *Standard and Poor's Records* to find information about a large national corporation. Write a short memorandum to your instructor in which you describe the kinds of information you found in both sources.

11. Design a questionnaire to help find the answer to this question: Should the Panhandle Furniture Manufacturing Company begin selling scrap materials to employees?

    The president of Panhandle is considering authorizing sale of scrap materials to employees. Several have requested that they be allowed to purchase scrap materials presently being sold to local scrap dealers. The president has asked you to study the question and make recommendations.

Normally, scrap materials consist of various shapes of fabric and foam rubber used in the manufacture of upholstered furniture. Scrap occurs because of machine errors and faulty workmanship. You are aware that there is considerable interest by some employees in the purchase of scrap materials. Several managers have voiced their objections to such a policy, saying that they feel it would increase the rate of scrap production. The union president has commented that such purchases would increase the goodwill between the employees and the company. (Panhandle has 600 employees.) Another possibility is to allow employees to buy small quantities of new material at cost price, which is about one-half the retail value.

You decide to send a questionnaire to each of the eighty-six companies in the upholstered furniture manufacturing field. Since the administration of the sale of scrap materials will be more difficult in a large company than in a small one, you will need to know company size (fewer than 50 employees, 50 to 200, 201 to 500, more than 500). Other information you will need includes the following:

a.   number of companies that sell scrap
b.   why companies sell scrap
c.   why companies do not sell scrap
d.   whether those companies that now sell scrap would prefer to stop
e.   average dollar amount of each sale of scrap to employees (less than $5, $5.01 to $25, $25.01 to $50, more than $50)
f.   average dollar amount of each sale of scrap to persons or organizations other than employees (same price brackets as e)
g.   opinions as to whether scrap production is increased (or would be increased) by a policy of selling scrap to employees

Design a questionnaire to be sent to the eighty-six furniture manufacturing companies.

FURTHER READING ◆ 16

In addition to the reference sources shown at the end of Chapter 15, at the end of Chapter 1, and within this chapter, the following books may be helpful to you in learning to obtain business information.

Ferber, Robert, and Verdoorn, P. J. *Research Methods in Economics and Business.* New York: Macmillan, 1962.

Janis, Jack Harold. *The Business Research Paper.* New York: Hobbs, Dorman, 1967.

Paradis, Adrian A. *The Research Handbook.* New York: Funk & Wagnalls, 1966.

Rummel, J. Francis, and Ballaine, Wesley C. *Research Methodology in Business.* New York: Harper & Row, 1963.

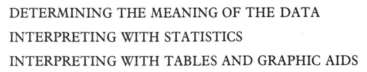

Evaluating, Interpreting, and Organizing the Data

17

After the data have been collected, they must be evaluated, interpreted, and organized for presentation in the most appropriate report form. A systematic method of collecting and recording the data greatly simplifies the remaining steps of the research process.

These steps of evaluating, interpreting, and organizing, as well as the preceding and following steps in the research and report writing process, do not fall into discrete divisions. We do not abruptly begin the evaluation process only after the collection process is completed. Ideally, data are evaluated and organized to a certain extent as they are collected. We must use judgment in the collecting process or we will be swamped with meaningless information and figures.

At some point we must stop formally adding to our collection of data and begin the finishing steps. If additional information or opinions come to light, however, we cannot afford to ignore them merely to end the search, although at times we may be tempted to do so.

DETERMINING THE MEANING OF THE DATA

To interpret the data objectively and impartially, and to evaluate it for accuracy, the researcher should keep in mind the several ways in which communication errors can occur. These errors in the interpretation of data are practically the same as the types of communication errors that occur in the overall process of communications.

You should now reread Chapter 4, especially the section on the causes of miscommunication. The entire chapter — as well as Chapter 3 and sections of the other five chapters at the beginning of the book — are especially applicable to your consideration of evaluation and interpretation of data.

As mentioned in Chapter 4 and elsewhere, in report presentation we must be careful to be completely and thoroughly objective. To do so we must be extremely discerning in our choice of words in order to achieve a matter-of-fact and nonbiased presentation of the facts and to show how this information leads to stated conclusions and recommendations.

In order to make this objective presentation, we must recognize the various connotations as well as the denotations of our chosen words. We should watch for connotative meanings both in our own writing and as we analyze comments received from interviews and questionnaires.

One of the semantic principles that most especially applies to the interpretation of data, as discussed in Chapter 4, is the confusion of facts with inferences and value judgments. We must also make use of multivalued logic — that is, we must keep in mind that we will not always find a definite yes or no answer, that most things are not completely black or white but are varying shades of gray. We should not feel that we must work for a definite yes or no answer when one is obviously not available.

A basic cause of error is that of twisting the facts to obtain definite and specific conclusions, especially preconceived ones. Although we should not hedge with an abundance of indefinite terms such as "it seems," "possibly," and "perhaps" when conclusions or recommendations are based on inferences, these inferences should be clearly understood.

Another principle of general semantics is that events flow into one another by "insensible graduations" — in other words, many so-called classifications are not completely separate entities. From a practical standpoint, we must classify and generalize, for to do otherwise would result only in chaos. We should realize, however, that all classifications will not be completely and perfectly accurate in every respect.

This lack of complete certainty even under the best of conditions is no justification for accepting hasty conclusions. That this lack of perfect classification and judgment is inevitable is only the more reason that we use extreme care in our limited observation so as to present the "true facts" as much as is humanly possible.

We fail to discriminate in our judgment of events as we analyze research findings, as well as in other situations. We tend to think in stereotypes and make false analogies, although in order to reach conclusions of any kind we must generalize. We should avoid making hurried and incomplete generalizations based on insufficient evidence.

For example, the researcher studying the question of career apparel found an article in a business periodical in which the author wrote that the career apparel had been enthusiastically accepted by an organization in New York. If this researcher had assumed that because of this acceptance the apparel was sure to be welcome in her own company, this assumption would not necessarily be correct.   The researcher would have failed to discriminate between conditions from one organization to the next, as well as from one part of the country to another.   If she had justified the cost savings from the fact that the employees invest in a credit union, hence they must have a desire to spend little money on clothing, then the comparison would be even more unconvincing.

Interpreting events as to cause-and-effect relationships may lead to erroneous interpretation.   The observed effect may not be a result of a previous event; it may be that another event occurred previously and, by chance, the observed effect followed.   Or, as often happens, a result can be attributable to more than one cause, perhaps to many.

As was pointed out in Chapter 3, our perception influences our understanding.   The researcher must avoid analyzing the information in light of previously established beliefs and desires.   Being human, the researcher will often foresee the results before beginning the study, although these anticipated results may be incorrect.   The researcher is likely to be affected by these preconceived notions and must guard against them.

These personal considerations, especially the desire to have the data result in desired conclusions, must not be allowed to prevent an objective interpretation.   In his book *Guides to Straight Thinking*,[1] Stuart Chase lists thirteen common fallacies, or barriers to straight thinking.   These statements are subcategories of communication errors and barriers already mentioned in this chapter and discussed at more length in Chapters 3, 4, and 5.   The following fallacies are paraphrased from Chase's words.

1.   Overgeneralizing.
2.   The entering wedge.   (This is another aspect of overgeneralizing — predicting major conclusions on small bits of information.)
3.   Getting personal — judging evidence, not upon the basis of the evidence, but by the judgment of the character or the ability of a person who evaluates the idea.
4.   "You're another."   "If I'm in error, so are you" (or he, she, they), "so that makes it even."
5.   Cause and effect, known as the "post hoc fallacy."   When one event precedes another in time, the first is assumed to be the cause of the second.   An illustration: Because a rooster crows each morning before sunrise, he thinks that his crowing causes the sun to rise.
6.   False analogies.

---

1. Stuart Chase, *Guides to Straight Thinking* (New York: Harper and Row, 1956), pp. 37–38.

7. Wise men can't be wrong. (This is an aspect of "getting personal.")
8. "Figures prove." Statistics can be used to prove almost anything.
9. Appeal to the crowd — an emotional appeal to a popular view or slogan.
10. Arguing in circles — using a conclusion to prove itself. An example is as follows.

    Fortune teller to client: "You'll be famous if you live long enough."
    Client: "What will I be famous for?"
    Fortune teller: "For having lived so long."

11. Self-evident truth — stating an assumption, taking for granted that there is no disagreement. These statements often begin with these words or in similar ways: "Everybody knows —" "Unquestionably —" "You can't deny that —" "It goes without saying —"
12. "Everything is either black or white." This fallacy is a restatement of Korsybski's advice to use multivalued logic.
13. Guilt by association.

Another guide to straight thinking that Chase does not mention specifically is "If ten thousand persons say a foolish thing, it is still a foolish thing." This statement disagrees with another old saying that fifty million Frenchmen can't be wrong. If we are conducting a survey of opinions, however, of the ten thousand persons or the fifty million Frenchmen, their thinking must be reported. This question of correctness may not really matter to the researcher; if the purpose of the study is to report opinions, then the purpose is accomplished, even though the opinions are wrong.

INTERPRETING WITH STATISTICS

Simple statistical terms include the following:

- *Mean.* The arithmetic average obtained by totaling the figures and dividing by the number of cases.
- *Median.* The midpoint, or middle value, in a series of values arranged in the order of magnitude.

- *Mode.* The most frequently occurring value. (The mean, median, and mode are all measures of central tendency.)
- *Range.* The spread between the lowest and the highest values in a series.
- *Standard deviation.* A measure of dispersion in a frequency distribution — a measure of the spread of the normal distribution.

This book cannot cover the study of statistics in a great deal of detail. A basic knowledge of statistics, however, is essential to the analysis of research findings and to their interpretation.

For an interesting and enlightening discussion of how figures can mislead, either intentionally or otherwise, read the book that has now become a classic in its field, *How to Lie with Statistics,* by Darrell Huff.[2] He illustrates how the term "average" or "mean" can mean almost anything or nothing, depending on how it is used.

For example, a statement can be literally true that the average income of a college graduating class of a particular year is $97,000 a year, but it is very unlikely that this figure is the typical income. A few extremely high figures distort the mean. Suppose that the graduating class consisted of only ten members. Each of nine of these persons is now earning about $15,000 annually, and the tenth one earns $835,000 — thus the arithmetic mean is $97,000. But if this figure is used to mean that each of the members is a potential customer for a yacht, you have misinterpreted the data.

INTERPRETING WITH TABLES AND GRAPHIC AIDS

The terms "chart" and "graph" are often used interchangeably. A table, however, is not referred to as a graph or a chart, or vice versa. In some instances, the word "graph" cannot be meaningfully substituted for "chart," as in the terms "flow charts" or "organization charts." We do, however, speak both of "bar charts" and "bar graphs."

Tables and graphic aids are usually labeled and numbered. Charts are often referred to in this way throughout the report: Chart 1, Chart 2, and so on. Or if illustrations of a mixture of types are used, such as maps, charts, photographs, and diagrams, the word "figures" may be used to describe all illustration types.

Traditionally, tables are not grouped with other forms of presenta-

---

2. Darrell Huff, *How to Lie with Statistics* (New York: W. W. Norton & Co., 1954).

tion, but are numbered separately throughout the report as Table 1, Table 2, and so on. This method of numbering, however, is being replaced in some organizations by using the term "figure" to refer to both tables and charts — another trend toward simplification and common sense.

When numerous tables are used throughout the report, a list of tables, used as a prefatory part after the table of contents, is helpful to the reader, as is a list of figures, if applicable.

Tables and the different forms of graphic aids should be considered as supplements to words, not as substitutes for them. Tables present numerical data in column form. Graphic forms make use of visual presentation and are used to show relationships and approximate values. The types of graphic aids most frequently used are line charts, bar charts (also described as column charts), and pie charts (also called circle charts). Graphic aids should be used only as they are needed, not to impress. An irrelevant table or chart is worse than none at all.

Graphic aids are often essential in order to convey information quickly and simply. Tables should be chosen for the presentation of numerous figures. Tables are also the better choice when the reader is interested in the exact amount, not in approximations, trends, and relationships, which are best shown by a chart of some kind. Charts can present in concise form a multitude of details that would take many pages to list and discuss in regular paragraph form. If well made, they facilitate immediate understanding.

Remember that the purpose of graphic aids is to present important trends and relationships more quickly, clearly, and emphatically than can be done in words. Poorly chosen, placed, or designed graphic aids and tables, however, are counterproductive in that they are harder to understand than words would be or may distort the intended meaning. They can also be distracting and confusing, thus becoming noise in the communication process.

In order to use tables and graphic aids to advantage, consider the factors that will make them helpful and useful and those that will have the opposite effect. Pointers for the effective use of visual aids are given below.

1. Use charts, tables, and other visual aids as needed to express meaning quickly and clearly, but do not use them merely to impress.

2. Choose the appropriate type of chart, table, or other visual aid to best convey the desired meaning or comparison. Some information should be shown in more than one way in the same report. For example, the reader may need exact figures, or many figures, instead of trends and relationships; if so, present these figures in tabular form.

3. Ordinarily, a graphic aid should be placed within the text of the report, or as near as possible to the portion of the text that it is used to

illustrate or explain.   If it is not closely related to the material being discussed, it should either be omitted or placed in the appendix section of the report.   Tables and charts, like other information, belong in the appendix if they can be considered supplementary to the report itself.

4. Introduce the graphic device before presenting it, preferably, including a few words of discussion after the device has been presented.

5. Point out the highlights of the visual aid. By pointing out items of major importance, as shown by the table or chart, you are able to refer subordinately to the device, as "The greatest increase in sales occurred in District 1 (72%) and the smallest in District 7 (17%), as shown by Table 3."

6. Make sure that graphic aids are constructed so that relationships are not distorted. Use reasonable proportion. Start at zero or show by broken lines that, because of space limitations, it was impractical to start at zero.

7. Carefully label each graphic device. Provide a key (also called a legend) if it will be helpful to the reader.

8. Keep all tables and charts simple. Do not try to show too much information on one chart.

The table and charts shown on the following pages (called figures in this text) have been adapted, with the exception of a chart showing monthly mean temperatures in Memphis, from originals prepared by the accounting firm, Harris, Kerr, Forster & Company and Pannell-Kerr-Forster & Company.   Illustrations and quoted passages are taken from "Trends in the Hotel-Motel Business."[3]

This long report is an informational one — according to the descriptive terms used in Chapter 15 — in that recommendations for the industry or for a particular organization are not specifically stated.   The report includes sixty-seven tables and charts, all of which are described as "figures," using the simplified labeling system previously mentioned.

The table[4] shown in Figure 17–1 is rather complex. Notice that this table presents all the information shown in the bar chart[5] in Figure 17–2 plus a great deal more. A greater amount of data, as well as exact figures instead of round numbers or approximations, can be shown more easily in a table of this kind than can be included in a chart. A chart, however, presents relationships and trends much more clearly and vividly.

To present all the information shown in the table, the report writer

3. "Trends in the Hotel-Motel Business," 1976 edition, 40th Annual Review (Harris, Kerr, Forster & Company: Pannell, Kerr, Forster & Company, 1976). Used by permission.
4. "Trends in the Hotel-Motel Business," inside front cover.
5. "Trends in the Hotel-Motel Business," inside front cover.

The Trend of Business for the Nation's Hotels and Motels with Payrolls

	1948	1960	1965	1970	1975
Hotels — 25 or More Guest Rooms:					
Number of Establishments	10,425	9,300	7,750	7,435	7,325
Number of Rooms Available per Day	861,000	789,000	707,950	702,800	708,750
Average Number of Rooms per Establishment	82.6	84.8	91.3	94.5	96.8
Average Number of Rooms Occupied per Day	779,350	546,100	467,375	434,250	428,800
Percentage of Occupancy	91%	69%	66%	62%	60.5%
Gross Annual Income — All Establishments ($1,000)	$1,876,874	$2,564,000	$3,292,509	$4,086,929	$ 5,417,968
Average Annual Income per Available Room	$2,180	$3,250	$4,651	$5,815	$7,644
Motels and Motor Hotels — All Sizes:					
Number of Establishments	12,410	27,440	29,800	30,000	30,500
Number of Rooms Available per Day	266,400	742,525	1,030,550	1,178,950	1,317,100
Average Number of Rooms per Establishment	21.5	27.1	34.6	39.3	43.2
Average Number of Rooms Occupied per Day	227,850	508,050	673,850	750,600	786,300
Percentage of Occupancy	86%	68%	65%	64%	59.7%
Gross Annual Income — All Establishments ($1,000)	$ 306,354	$1,301,156	$2,634,922	$4,244,220	$ 6,020,688
Average Annual Income per Available Room	$1,150	$1,752	$2,557	$3,600	$4,571
Combined Totals:					
Number of Establishments	22,835	36,740	37,550	37,435	37,825
Number of Rooms Available per Day	1,127,400	1,531,525	1,738,500	1,881,750	2,025,850
Average Number of Rooms per Establishment	49.4	41.7	46.3	50.3	53.6
Average Number of Rooms Occupied per Day	1,007,200	1,054,150	1,141,225	1,184,850	1,215,100
Percentage of Occupancy	89%	69%	66%	63%	60.0%
Gross Annual Income — All Establishments ($1,000)	$2,183,228	$3,865,156	$5,927,431	$8,331,149	$11,438,656
Average Annual Income per Available Room	$1,937	$2,524	$3,410	$4,427	$5,646

Based on U.S. Census Data and H.K.F. Estimates.

Figure 17–1.   *Example of a Table of Numerical Data in Column Form*

would prepare several charts.   To show trends and relationships of all aspects of the industry, perhaps several kinds of charts should be prepared.

The chart, "The Trend in Available Rooms and Occupancy for the Nation's Hotels and Motels" (Figure 17–2) and the table, "The Trend of

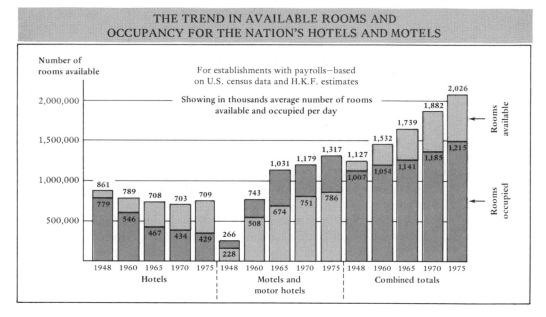

Figure 17-2. *Example of a Bar Chart Showing Relationships and Trends*

Business for the Nation's Hotels and Motels" (Figure 17–1), were placed
on the inside front cover of the report as part of the introductory and
background material to the report itself, which included data only about
1975. These illustrations were not numbered.

Let's look at some of the features of the table and chart. The table
consists of information about three groups of data: hotels, motels and
motor hotels, and combined totals. Under each subheading, the order of
items is the same; to present these items in varied arrangements would be
distracting and make comparisons much more difficult. In the original
table prepared by Harris, Kerr, Forster & Company, sources of data were
shown under the title; a more usual place is at the bottom, as shown here.
Unless you are expected to follow a particular style manual, let clearness
and consistency be your guide to the placement of such bits of information.

In the bar chart (Figure 17–2), columns are drawn to scale. Although a zero is not shown at the bottom of the chart, the height of the
columns shows that "the bottom has not been cut off," an error that
sometimes occurs in chart making. When the amounts to be shown on a
chart are relatively high in value, you may find it necessary to break the
scale somewhere between zero and the lowest value. This break should be
indicated to the reader by broken lines between the zero and the first value
that is shown on the chart.

The widths of the columns are uniform, as they should be. Only the
height should be used to show relationships in a vertical bar chart. Vary-

ing the width of the columns, although such variation would actually show nothing because quantities are shown at the side, is at least momentarily misleading to the reader. In a horizontal bar chart, quantities are shown at the bottom, and only the length of the bars should be varied. The vertical axis is known as the *y*-axis; the horizontal, as the *x*-axis.

This chart is described as a *subdivided bar chart*. It is also a *multiple bar chart* because it combines the three groups of data into one illustration. A *simple bar chart* contains undivided bars and similar data. For example, in the illustrated chart the five columns depicting "hotels" could make up a simple bar chart showing only "rooms available" with no division into "rooms occupied." (If all the information in the illustrated chart had been presented in this way, six simple bar charts would have been necessary.)

The *line chart* is used to show movements or changes of a continuous series over a period of time, as shown in Figure 17–3. The two lines show the mean minimum and maximum temperatures in Memphis from January through December.

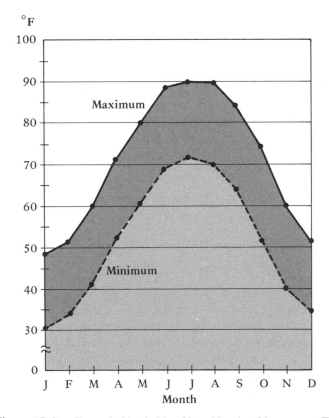

Figure 17–3.   *Example Simple Line Chart Showing Changes over Time*

Now let's compare a line chart from the hotel-motel report (see Figure 17–4) to the simple line chart showing minimum and maximum temperatures. In this *multiple line chart,* the number 100 replaces the usual zero, as shown in the legend, "1955 = 100." In other words, 1955 is used as a base year, and the three lines show decreases as well as increases in room rates, room sales, and occupancy rates for the years following 1955.[6]

Figure 17–5 from the hotel-motel report combines a simple line chart with a simple bar chart.[7] The line depicting the changes in occupancy rate from 1955 through 1975 is superimposed on a simple bar graph showing the yearly expense per available room and ratio to total sales. The 65.5 percent indicates occupancy rate in 1955; the 68.9 percent the occupancy rate in 1975. The "ratio to total sales" refers to the percentage shown at the bottom of each column; that is, in 1975 the cost of heat, light, and power was equal to 5.4 percent of the total "sales" of a resort hotel room.

This type of chart was well chosen and appropriate for the data presented and for the readers of this report. You as a report writer, however, should be extremely careful to avoid making graphic aids so complex that they are not immediately understandable to your particular group of readers.

The pie chart (or circle chart) — also taken from "Trends in the Hotel-Motel Business" — is a simple but expressive form of graphic aid and is used to show component parts of the whole. The slices may be

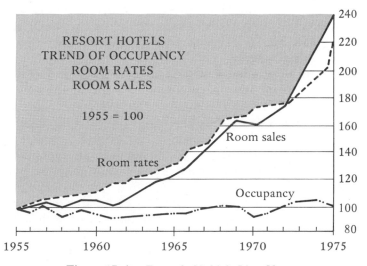

Figure 17–4. *Example Multiple Line Chart*

6. "Trends in the Hotel-Motel Business," p. 10.
7. "Trends in the Hotel-Motel Business," p. 10.

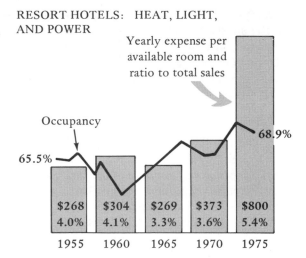

RESORT HOTELS: HEAT, LIGHT,
AND POWER

Figure 17-5. *Example Line Chart and Bar Chart Combined*

labeled, or shading and crossing may be used with an explanatory legend. Slices of the pie should be drawn to scale; in addition, the units of value should be shown within each slice.   Some chart makers prefer to start the largest slice of the pie in the twelve o'clock position and to move clockwise from the largest slice to the smallest.

The kinds of information shown in Figure 17-6 are typical of the usual application of the pie chart — the distribution of income and outgo.[8]

The *bilateral bar chart* shows increases and decreases from a central point of reference.   Bilateral bar charts are especially useful to show changes in percentages, but they may also be used for any series of data that contains minus qualities.

In Figure 17-7, decreases are shown to the left of the central axis; increases to the right.[9]   Another method of constructing the bilateral bar chart is to use vertical columns, with positive values above the line and negative values below.

Maps are another form of graphic aid and are used to present data to be compared by geographic areas.   When these areas are not easily shown on a map by state or regional boundaries, they may be shown by color, shading, or cross-hatching.

Remember that graphic aids should be introduced, often by pointing out major highlights of the chart.   For example, as part of the introductory discussion about the combined line and bar chart shown in Figure 17-5 ("Resort Hotels — Heat, Light, and Power"), the following highlights were mentioned in the report in this way:

8. "Trends in the Hotel-Motel Business," p. 18.
9. "Trends in the Hotel-Motel Business," p. 17.

THE 1975 HOTEL-MOTEL INCOME DOLLAR AND WHERE IT WENT

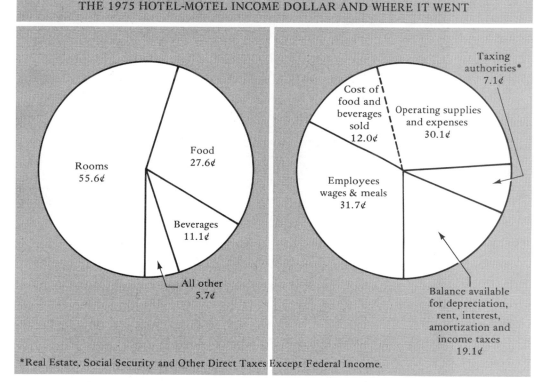

*Real Estate, Social Security and Other Direct Taxes Except Federal Income.

Figure 17-6. *Example Pie (or Circle) Chart Showing Component Parts of a Whole*

The increase of 189% shown for heat, light, and power costs resulted from yearly average rises of 4.7% during the 1956–1973 period and jumps of 33% in 1974 and 21% in 1975. Since 1973, therefore, light and power costs have leaped 60%.[10]

In addition to the most widely used forms of graphic aids already mentioned, pictures and other types of illustrations are used to supplement information presented in verbal form. Pictorial charts can be a form of bar chart in which pictures or drawings of some kind are used, instead of bars, to illustrate quantities. For example, money bags are used to show amounts of money, buildings to show the rate of construction, or barrels to show petroleum production. Although the use of pictorial charts can be interesting and emphatic as well as attention getting, these illustrations can easily be misleading.

As mentioned previously, a principle of construction of the usual bar graph is that columns must measure by the use of only one dimension;

10. "Trends in the Hotel-Motel Business," p. 10.

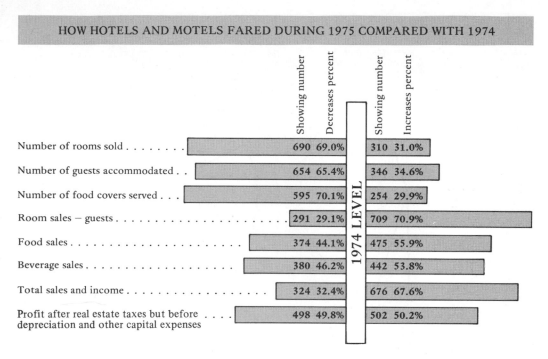

Figure 17-7. *Example Bilateral Bar Chart Showing Increases and Decreases from a Point of Reference*

vertical columns show relationships by their height and horizontal columns by their length.   If one bar (or money bag, petroleum barrel, and so on) is wider than another, the implication is that the "fatter" bar is of much greater magnitude, even though figures are included.

Remember that the purpose of all graphic aids is to show relationships immediately and clearly, not to confuse the issue.   With a ruler you should have no trouble constructing the bars of a regular column chart so that they are of uniform size.   When you decide to use money bags — or sailing ships — or cabbages and kings — your task becomes more difficult.

ORGANIZING THE DATA

Organization of the data, like evaluation, should not be left to a certain time period in the research and reporting process.   Throughout the study, organization should be kept in mind as you decide what to present where.

In addition, the tentative table of contents, prepared at the beginning of this study, helps the final process of arrangement of ideas and prevents the investigation from going astray. Now, perhaps, you will see needed changes in the preliminary organization as shown by the tentative table of contents.

An effective method of organizing material is by use of the card method. Write on separate cards or slips of paper the headings of the report that seem to describe these divisions. Include those shown on the tentative table of contents, as well as additional ones that now occur to you. Be careful not to express the same idea in different words.

After you have noted on the cards the possible divisions, arrange them in the order that seems to be natural, whether or not this sequence agrees with the original outline. As you study and sort the cards, you often find that changes in arrangement will best express your ideas.

This method of organization also helps you to see "holes" in the presentation, as well as redundancy. A logical sequence of topics of the complete report is essential whether the plan of arrangement is to be the direct (deductive) or the indirect (inductive) order. If you are using the traditional and formal report arrangement, you already know that you will start with the introduction, follow with findings and analysis, and end with conclusions and recommendations, as discussed in Chapter 15.

Even though you already have this arrangement in mind, however, you must decide upon the arrangement of topics in the middle section of the report, as well as on the presentation of varying bits of information in the introductory and the concluding sections. The contents of the various preliminary and supplementary portions of the formal report are fairly well standardized. You can safely leave their exact planning until the report itself is completed.

The organization process, when planning reports to be arranged in the direct order, requires the same careful attention to an orderly sequence of ideas. In the direct order, as you remember, you place recommendations at the beginning of the report, as well as any necessary explanatory conclusions, and follow with supporting information. Refer to the tentative table of contents shown in Chapter 15 that was planned for the study on sound equipment. This table of contents shows that the report is arranged in the indirect, or inductive, order.

Choose Appropriate Report Divisions

When the report consists of comparisons, in order to arrive at a recommendation of the choices, you should consider the use of criteria as major divisions instead of the use of the items to be compared. For example, if you were comparing locations 1, 2, and 3 according to cost of land, labor availability, and access to market, the criteria, instead of the locations, would make for a more easily comprehensible format.

You may find instances in which, for one reason or another, such reports are best arranged by possible choices, not by the criteria for these choices. Like other problems in communications, use your own judgment based on an individual approach. Ordinarily, however, criteria will be the better choice.

Use no single subdivisions. If you have no more than one "subdivision," then you have none at all. The main head describes the entire contents of the division. If you have an A you will also need a B. If you have a 1, also a 2, and so forth.

Avoid breaking the report into a great number of main divisions. Although ordinarily you will need from three to five between the introduction and the concluding section or sections, this is no exact guide. If you find that you seem to have too many divisions, consider combining some, perhaps by letting some of the major divisions become subdivisions. You will probably find that this revised arrangement is the better one from the standpoint of emphasis, clarity, and effectiveness.

Word Headings Carefully

Each heading describes the contents of the subdivisions that come under it. "A," "B," "C," and "D" headings combine to equal the heading above them. Watch headings carefully, not only from the standpoint of readability and clarity but also to check the flow of thought and your progression of ideas.

Use parallel grammatical structure for headings of the same degree. For example, all major divisions (I, II, III) should be phrased in the same way, and all A, B, C headings grouped together should be grammatically parallel. Headings may be complete sentences expressed in either question or statement form, noun phrases, or adjectives. (Adjectives are not usually the best choice.)

All headings throughout the report need not be expressed in complete parallel form. That is, every heading does not necessarily need to be parallel in grammatical structure with every other heading in the entire report. For example, headings of main divisions could be worded as questions; subdivisions under one main heading could be complete sentences, expressed in statement form; and subdivisions under another main heading could be expressed as noun phrases.

Try to word the headings so that they give information, not merely indicate the kind of information that is to be included below them. These headings are referred to as "talking headings."

Headings show the organization and the flow of thought, especially in a long report. *In a report or other short work with which you use a table of contents, headings should agree completely and exactly with the divisions and subdivisions as shown in the table of contents.*

No single method of arrangement and format of headings can be said to be the only correct one. A suggested method of showing major and minor headings is shown in Appendix C. These illustrations were placed in Appendix C instead of this chapter or other chapters on report writing because you have referred to them in preceding chapters.

THE LANGUAGE OF REPORTS

The reports shown in the following chapter, with the exception of the complete formal report, are written in the personal tone. All reports are written with a straightforward, courteous business approach. Although they do not sound stiff or formal, they also do not use colloquial phrasing or an overly familiar or a casual tone.

Before you begin your examination of these report examples and read the further discussion about reports, let's review principles you studied in earlier chapters in this book, those applying especially to the writing of the report regardless of the type or format.

1. Write objectively. Base your interpretation and decision upon facts, not upon your personal desires or unsupported beliefs. Although at times you will need to state what you believe about the situation, or what the data seem to mean, make sure that the reader understands that this statement is an opinion and give the details that support your opinion. On the other hand, avoid an appearance of hedging and timidity. Nobody expects you to have positive and definite answers to everything. If you give the impression that you do, nobody will believe you.

2. Write clearly, concisely, and correctly, and give all necessary information convincingly.

3. Write simply. Don't try to impress your readers with an extensive vocabulary of five-syllable words. But don't make it sound like a third-grade textbook.

4. Be specific. Do not state vague generalities.

5. Avoid using an unnecessary number of "I's," even when you are using the personal tone.

6. Write in an interesting and vivid style. Keep sentences fairly short, but vary the sentence length. Avoid using many sentences that begin with a slow expletive opening such as "there are" and "it is." Most business writers use these openings far too often.

7. Use the active voice to emphasize the actor, the passive voice to emphasize the receiver of the action. Do not use the passive voice when

the active voice will more exactly express your idea in more vivid terms, as it often will.

8. Remember techniques of achieving readability through arrangement and format. Use an attractive arrangement with plenty of white space: listings, headings, and summarizing. Use special arrangements, underlining, or other special methods of mechanical emphasis, but do not use them to excess.

9. Remember that the inclusion of additional preliminary and supplementary parts is the greatest distinction between an informal report and a complete, formal report. Another distinction is that the complete, formal report is more likely to be written in the impersonal tone. The shorter report, with its more streamlined format, is most often written in the personal tone. The shorter report can also be written in the impersonal tone, depending upon the subject matter, readership, preferences of the reader and of the writer, and the overall degree of formality. Letter and memorandum reports are almost always written in the personal tone.

SUMMARY ◆ 17

The principles of general semantics are especially applicable to the process of evaluating and interpreting data. In report presentation, as well as in the evaluation of the meaning of the data, we must be careful to be completely and thoroughly objective.

We must use nonbiased evaluation and interpretation in order to present the findings in a matter-of-fact way and to show how these findings lead to the stated conclusions and recommendations.

In a formal report, in which findings are presented as a basis for conclusions, these conclusions should not be stated until all the findings have been presented — except for any needed comments or explanations to make the meaning clear.

Simple statistical measures are useful in the interpretation of data for the usual business report, although they can be used in confusing and misleading ways.

Graphic aids are helpful in conveying information quickly and simply. Well-made charts present trends and relationships more quickly, clearly, and emphatically than can be done with words. Graphic aids should be used only as needed — not to impress. They should be kept simple and constructed so that relationships are not distorted.

The report writer should carefully consider the organization of the material into appropriate report divisions and should use appropriate headings that describe the material under the headings. Parallel grammatical structure should be used for headings of the same degree. Well-chosen and carefully worded headings show the organization and flow of thought throughout the report.

Listings in the table of contents should agree exactly with headings in the text of the report.

QUESTIONS AND PROBLEMS ◆ 17

1. Which form of graphic illustration would you construct to illustrate the following types of information? Support your decision.
    a. Record of the earnings per share of The Local Corporation for the past seven years.
    b. Comparison of sales of The Local Corporation by product line for the past three years.
    c. A comparison of the change in net profit for the seven restaurants of Bigger Burger, Inc.
    d. Comparison of white collar, blue collar, service, and farm workers in the U.S. labor force for each year ending in five or zero from 1955 to the present.
    e. A comparison of the capital structures (deferred taxes, notes payable, equity, and other) of three major real estate development companies.
    f. Breakdown of how the federal government dollar was spent last year.
    g. Mean maximum and minimum temperatures in your city for each month of the year.
    h. Average number of days per year with hail, by geographical area of the United States.
    i. Comparison within the Morano Shoe Corporation to show which subsidiary companies account for different percentages of total sales.
    j. Comparison of the world's ten largest cities to show population changes for the last ten-year period.
    k. Comparison of the consumer price index to the wholesale price index over the last ten years.
    l. Residential buildings permits (single family, multiple family, and total) for Los Angeles County, 1970–1977, January — December.
2. Assume reasonable data and construct appropriate graphic aids to illustrate the comparisons and presentations described in Question 1.
3. Bring to class a photocopy of a graphic presentation as shown in a magazine, newspaper, or recent textbook. Be prepared to show this graphic aid on the opaque projector and to comment on the illustration shown. Is the chart the most appropriate one for the particular data and the desired comparison of relationships? Is the chart correctly and accurately made?
4. Present the information requested in Problem 3 in a memorandum attached to the illustrated chart or other graphic aid.
5. Should the Panhandle Furniture Manufacturing Company begin selling scrap

materials to employees? This problem is a continuation of the one begun with the design of a questionnaire in Chapter 16 (Question 11). Assume that you mailed the questionnaires and received usable ones from sixty of the eighty-six manufacturing companies. Results are as follows:

Company Size:

6 companies, fewer than 50 employees
6 companies, 50–200 employees
12 companies, 201–500 employees
36 companies, more than 500 employees

Companies Selling Scrap Material to Employees:

Fewer than 50 employees	Yes	4	No	2
50–200 employees	Yes	6	No	6
201–500 employees	Yes	2	No	4
Over 500 employees	Yes	2	No	34

Average Amount of Each Sale to Employees:

Less than $10	10
$10–$100	4
Over $100	0

Average Amount of Each Sale Other Than to Employees:

Less than $10	6
$10–$100	12
Over $100	42

Opinions on Whether Scrap Production Is or Would Be Increased with the Selling of Scrap Materials:

| Yes | 42 |
| No | 18 |

Reasons for Selling Scrap
(most important reason):

Employee goodwill	10
Easier administration	2
Best return	2

Reasons for Not Selling Scrap
(most important reason):

Administration too burdensome	29
Increases scrap production	11
Less return for scrap	6

Companies Now Selling Scrap That Would Prefer to Stop:

| Yes | 10 |
| No | 4 |

Draw up tables and charts to present the highlights of the results of your study.

FURTHER READING ◆ 17

In addition to the reference sources shown at the end of Chapters 15, 4, and 1, the following books may be helpful to you as supplements to topics discussed in this chapter.

Chase, Stuart. *Guides to Straight Thinking.* New York: Harper & Row, 1956.

Huff, Darrell. *How to Lie With Statistics.* New York: W. W. Norton & Co., 1954.

Spear, Mary Eleanor. *Practical Charting Techniques.* New York: McGraw-Hill Book Company, 1969.

Presenting the Data in
Appropriate Form

18

The principles of report writing presented in Chapters 15, 16, and 17 are approximately the same for all kinds of reports, regardless of whether they are of minor, limited nature or extensive in coverage.

The researcher must understand the problem and be able to state it exactly. The next steps are to find the necessary information, evaluate and interpret this information, and organize it in the most readable and appropriate form. This procedure remains the same although the finished report may be presented in one of several forms: the complete, formal arrangement, a more informal report arrangement in that some or all of the preliminary and supplementary parts are omitted, a letter, or a memorandum.

In this chapter emphasis is given to the preparation of a complete formal report because, by its very nature, it requires more time, effort, and instruction than shorter, more informal arrangements. You are likely to present reports in this formal arrangement much less frequently than in the shorter and more informal formats. By learning how to prepare a complete formal report, however, you will also be learning to prepare shorter ones, or those with differing formats.

Your ability to do an outstanding job on an extensive report project, which would likely be presented in a rather formal arrangement, could be an aid to the advancement of your business career. Even more important is your increased confidence and sense of accomplishment.

PARTS AND LAYOUT OF A COMPLETE
FORMAL REPORT

Complete formal reports are comprised of three major divisions: preliminaries, the report body (or report proper), and supplementary parts.

The Report Package

This list of report parts is not intended to be used for all formal reports,
regardless of length.   Few reports will need all of these preliminaries, and
parts not shown in this list are desirable for some reports.   All preliminaries, the report proper, and the supplementary parts are considered
as the complete report package.

The preliminary and supplementary parts preceded by a check are the
ones that are most often used.   The others may be included or omitted
depending upon the particular report situation.   The index is likely to be
omitted from all kinds of business reports.   A well-made table of contents
makes an index unnecessary and even undesirable, except in book-length
manuscripts.   In addition, an index is most difficult to construct, and an
incomplete one is worse than none at all.

Preliminaries:
√ Cover
  Title fly
√ Title page
  Letter of authorization
  Letter of acceptance
√ Letter of transmittal
√ Table of contents
  List of charts and tables
√ Synopsis

Body of the report:
Introduction
Text of the report, usually divided into several major sections
Conclusions and recommendations, which are usually combined
into one section

Supplements:
√ Appendix (or appendixes)
√ Bibliography
  Index
(The bibliography may precede appendix sections.)

A preliminary not shown in this list, which may be desirable for some reports, is an acknowledgments section. If you do not use a separate section for acknowledgments, they may be included in the letter of transmittal, unless they are so lengthy as to make the transmittal letter too long.

The letter of transmittal may include the synopsis. These two parts — the letter of transmittal and the synopsis — should not be combined if doing so will make the letter of transmittal longer than one page. Even if the synopsis is short, often it should be a separate part so that it can be duplicated for the use of persons who will not read the entire report, or so that it can be published or otherwise widely distributed.

Preliminary pages are numbered with lower case roman numerals. Preliminary pages are counted beginning with the title page, even if the title fly is included. For example, if all the parts in the preceding list are used in the report package, the letter of authorization would carry the roman numeral ii. (The title page is counted although it is not actually numbered.)

Preliminary Report Parts

The *cover* is used to protect and to hold the report together, as well as to add to its attractive appearance. A cover also shows that you are careful enough about your report to present it in a neat manner. Don't force your reader to open your cover to find the title and author; these should appear on the cover itself or through a cutout section.

The *title fly* is a full page. It shows only the title. This page serves no useful purpose and may be omitted unless the particular handbook you are following tells you to include it.

The *letter of authorization,* as its name indicates, is written by the person who authorizes the report. Some authorizations will not be made in written form. In addition, the authorization may be in the form of a memorandum, not a letter. When a written authorization is given, ordinarily it should be included in the finished report. It not only helps to show the purpose of the report but also adds weight and importance, especially if it was authorized by a person high in the company.

If special instructions as to topics and methods of investigations are given in the letter of authorization, the letter attached to the report acts as a reminder that the report was prepared and presented according to instructions. If the report is to be read by those other than the person or persons who authorized it, the letter of authorization may add a touch of dignity and importance to the work. (You will need all you can get.)

The *title page* includes the title of the report, the name and title of the reader (as "Prepared for Mr. John Harris, Production Manager"), the name and title of the writer ("By Wayne Morrison, Technical Assistant"), and the place and the date. The title page should also include the name of the organization and any other needed or helpful information.

Work for a concise but descriptive title. If you have stated your purpose in a concise, appropriate form, you should have no trouble writing a suitable title. In some instances the statement of purpose may also be a suitable title. A title, unlike the statement of purpose, may be worded to show the results of the investigation. For example, a problem statement worded in this way, "Should Dilliard Enterprises Move to Commerce Square?" may become the title, "Why Dilliard Enterprises Should Move to Commerce Square."

The *letter of transmittal,* also referred to as a covering letter, transmits the finished report. It may be used for helpful and informative comments about the research process, particularly those that do not seem to fit into the report itself. The transmittal letter sometimes suggests follow-up studies or side issues of the problem. It may include mention of special limitations or difficulties encountered in the research or the report-writing process, as well as the highlights of other aspects of the report. Do not include a synopsis, or a statement that sums up findings and recommendations, if you prepare a separate synopsis.

The letter of transmittal is arranged in complete letter form. In some instances a memorandum is used to transmit a report, but a letter is more formal, yet also more personal and friendly. The pronouns "I," "you," and other first- and second-person pronouns are used as necessary and natural, as in all other letters, although the report is written in the impersonal style.

The *table of contents* is the report outline, or the tentative table of contents, in its final and revised form, with the addition of page numbers. A reminder: Items in the table of contents must agree exactly with the report headings.

A *synopsis* is a greatly condensed form of the entire report, including the introduction and the conclusions and recommendations. The synopsis stresses results. To give emphasis to the results, the synopsis is often arranged in the direct order even if the report itself is presented in the indirect order.

The use of the synopsis in effect presents the report package in the direct order, although the report proper (beginning with the introduction and continuing through the conclusions and recommendations) is arranged in the indirect order.

Many synopses that accompany reports arranged in the inductive order are similarly arranged. The synopsis must be brief, no more than one-tenth of the length of the entire report. For a very long report, the proportional length of the synopsis is even shorter. At its longest, the synopsis should fill no more than two typewritten pages, single spaced. Some company and government officials insist that all synopses, regardless of the length of the entire report, be kept to one page.

You may be able to condense the report into an acceptable synopsis by shortening each major division of the report into one paragraph. Thus a report consisting of an introduction (Part I), four sections of findings (Parts II, III, IV, and V), and the conclusions and recommendations (Part VI) would be condensed into a six-paragraph synopsis. If the direct order is used for the synopsis, the first paragraph sums up the conclusions and recommendations section of the report. The second paragraph sums up the introductory section, and the four remaining paragraphs summarize the four middle sections of the report (Parts VI, I, II, III, IV, V).

This neat method of condensing, however, is not always the best choice. Because one of the purposes of the synopsis is to stress results, you may need more than one paragraph to summarize the conclusions and recommendations section — perhaps as much as half the entire synopsis. The synopsis is sometimes reproduced and distributed to persons who do not read the entire report. It is also useful as the basis for a condensed oral presentation.

The Body of the Report

The body of the report, or the "report proper," begins with the introduction and continues through the conclusions and recommendations — if the report is arranged in the indirect (or the inductive) order. In reports arranged in the direct order, which are less likely to have preliminary parts, the report body begins with the gist of the message, which is ordinarily the recommendations.

You considered the makeup of the body of the report as you read Chapter 15, as well as in the preparation of the course plan and tentative table of contents. The introduction of a formal report was also discussed in Chapter 15. To review and summarize, the introduction may include these sections:

1. Authorization. (Not necessary if you use a letter of authorization.)
2. Purpose. (Essential.)
3. Scope. (Essential if it is not obvious from the title; scope may be combined with limitations.)
4. Limitations. (Use only as needed.)
5. Historical background. (Also described as background, background conditions, history, and the like.) This section should be included in your introduction only if it can be kept brief. In some reports this information deserves a complete division, usually as Part II of the report body.
6. Sources and methods of collecting data. (Essential.) In a few long reports for which detailed and complicated methods of collection are used, this section may be too long to include in the

introduction so that this material becomes Part II of the body of the report. If you also need a background or history section, the methods of collecting data may be Part II of the report and historical background Part III, or vice versa, depending upon the particular problem. Ordinarily you will not need both of these special sections, or even one of them.

The *text of a report* is used to mean the divisions of the report that come after the introduction and before the conclusions and recommendations section. This is not a completely descriptive term, for in a sense the entire report is the text. This section of the report is also referred to as the "findings" section. (Terminology as it concerns different sections of reports will differ slightly according to the handbook or textbook you are using as a guide.)

Remember that this part of the report is where you present the data you have gathered, upon which you base your conclusions and recommendations. For the most part, this is the only kind of information you should present in the text of the report, with no analysis or opinions of your own. For clarity and completeness, however, you will at times need to state an analysis of the meaning of some of these facts as they are presented. But remember that your major conclusions and recommendations should be left until the last section.

Conclusions and recommendations are based upon the findings presented in the middle section of the report. Do not bring in new information in these concluding sections. Conclusions and recommendations may be broken into two sections or, occasionally, shown as two separate parts of the report. In your conclusions you state your analysis of what the findings, presented in the earlier sections of the report, mean to you.

Even though these are your conclusions, if you are writing the report in the impersonal tone, do not switch here and include the use of "I." You can present your conclusions and recommendations without the use of "I," as is illustrated in some of the examples shown in this chapter. Avoid using the term "the writer." Since you have collected and analyzed the data, obviously the conclusions are yours unless you state otherwise. Be as objective and impartial as possible in presenting the conclusions and recommendations.

To repeat and emphasize — conclusions and recommendations are made upon the basis of the findings presented in the earlier sections of the report. If you use the conclusions and recommendations section or sections merely as a means of expressing your unsupported beliefs and ideas, then you had no reason to collect and analyze the data upon which these conclusions and recommendations are expected to be based.

Supplementary Report Parts

The *appendix* section is used for supplementary material. ("Appendixes," as well as the Latin term "appendices," is now correctly used as the plural form of "appendix.")

If a questionnaire has been used to gather information, a complete copy of the questionnaire must be included as an appendix; otherwise the reader cannot judge the validity of the reported information. The covering letter, or letters, that accompanied the questionnaire should also be included in the appendix section. Sometimes statistical formulas or computations are appended, as are computer printouts. Extensive tables, large maps, diagrams, or other long materials are placed in the appendix section if they are too bulky for inclusion in the report itself.

The main consideration, however, as to whether materials should go in the report itself or in the appendix section is whether the material relates directly to the text of the report or can be considered as additional and supplementary.

The *bibliography* lists secondary sources used in gathering data and in writing the report. A list of interviews or similar materials may also be included with the secondary sources; to be strictly correct, however, do not include interviews under the heading "bibliography." "Reference sources" is a descriptive term that includes both secondary and primary research. List library sources separately from interviews and other sources.

An *index* is unnecessary in almost all business reports; it is used only for very long, extensive ones. If you do use an index, make sure that you use extreme care in its preparation. An incomplete index is worse than none at all.

AN ILLUSTRATION OF A COMPLETE FORMAL REPORT

The report shown in Figure 18–1 is an example of a report written in the traditional inductive order, with the title page, letter of transmittal, synopsis, and bibliography. This study was completed as a class research project by an individual student, but it is based on conditions in an actual organization. The organizational name shown here, as well as the name of the president, is fictitious. The report is used by permission of the writer. Some of the details have been slightly modified, and other minor changes have been made in the structure and wording of the report.

SHOULD ENVIRONMENTAL SERVICES, INC. CONVERT FROM

GENERALIST SECRETARIES TO A WORD PROCESSING

AND ADMINISTRATIVE SUPPORT CENTER?

Prepared for

Mr. John F. Tatom, President

Environmental Services, Inc.

by

John W. Robinson

Director of Personnel and Training

November 30, 1977

Figure 18–1. *Example of a Complete Formal Report*

Figure 18-1. (*Continued*)

November 30, 1977

Mr. John F. Tatom, President
Environmental Services, Inc.
5100 Poplar Avenue
Merritt Island, Florida 32952

Dear Mr. Tatom:

The accompanying report is the feasibility study you requested on October 12.
The research was planned to determine whether secretarial administrative
costs could be cut by converting from generalist secretaries to a word
processing and administrative support center.

To assist you in deciding whether a word processing and administrative
support system is feasible, I have related the accumulated facts to conditions
in Environmental Services, Inc.

I shall be happy to discuss this report with you. I am ready to provide
additional assistance to you in the planning and implementing of a word
processing conversion by developing career paths, personnel policies, and
training programs.

Sincerely,

John W. Robinson
Director of Personnel and Training

ii

Figure 18-1. *(Continued)*

TABLE OF CONTENTS

Figure 18-1.   (*Continued*)

SYNOPSIS

The purpose of this report is to determine whether a conversion from generalist secretaries to a word processing and administrative support system can cut secretarial administrative costs of Environmental Services, Inc. Information was obtained from secondary sources, interviews with managerial and secretarial staff, and consultation with word processing equipment vendors.

In a word processing system, generalists are replaced by specialists. Correspondence secretaries perform all typewriting and transcription within a word processing center. All other secretarial functions are handled by administrative secretaries. The benefits of word processing are faster turnaround of correspondence, higher quality, reduced costs, improved efficiency, and higher productivity.

Two secretarial positions can be eliminated from the present staff of ten secretaries after conversion to a word processing system. Career paths will permit secretaries to advance from entry-level jobs to supervisory positions. They now have little opportunity for advancement.

Word processing techniques can usually result in savings of from 15 to 30 percent of clerical payroll and overhead. Conversion to a word processing system with administrative support will save $16,632 in salaries each year. In addition, based on the average cost of a letter using the present system and the cost using word processing, $8,610 will be saved each year, based on the present volume of work. Thus the total cost savings a year is $25,242.

Environmental Services Inc. should implement conversion to a word processing and administrative support system with personnel staffing as follows: Word Processing Center--one supervisor and two correspondence secretaries; Administrative Support Center--one supervisor, two secretaries, and one page; Office of the President--one executive assistant; total secretarial staff, eight.

By making use of the existing IBM Magnetic Card Selectric Typewriters and dictation equipment, additional hardware will not be required to install a word processing system.

iv

Figure 18-1. *(Continued)*

SHOULD ENVIRONMENTAL SERVICES, INC. CONVERT FROM
GENERALIST SECRETARIES TO A WORD PROCESSING
AND ADMINISTRATIVE SUPPORT CENTER?

WHY AND HOW THIS REPORT WAS PREPARED

Purpose

The purpose of this report is to explore the possibilities of word processing and administrative support operations for Environmental Services, Inc. and to determine the feasibility of converting to a word processing system. The study is necessary because of rapidly increasing costs in administrative operations, as well as an increased volume of typewriting and related printing.

Scope and Limitations

This study deals primarily with the potential for a word processing system to cut secretarial administrative costs by increasing the productivity of each secretary because of specialization. Not included in this research is a complete analysis of the most desirable equipment, as presently owned equipment will be adequate at the beginning of the operation and possibly for some time to come. Another aspect of the problem not considered is the exact nature of the training to be provided to secretaries and executives. Also excluded is consideration of the increase or decrease in morale because of the conversion to word processing.

1

Figure 18-1. *(Continued)*

2

Sources and Methods of Collecting Data

Secondary sources provided information about the use of data
processing systems by other firms. Interviews with management and the
secretarial staff of Environmental Services, Inc. were conducted to learn
the general functions now being performed and the percentage of time being
spent in each function. The work was broken down into two major categories:
typewriting and administrative functions. IBM sales representatives
provided consultation as to the advisability of establishing a word processing
center. (Professional consultation is not readily available on word
processing needs except from vendors of equipment.)

WHY WORD PROCESSING SHOULD BE CONSIDERED

What Is Word Processing?

No generally accepted definition precisely expresses the meaning of
the term word processing. Kleinschrod stated that "IBM, dominant
manufacturer in the field, says word processing is 'the transition of written,
verbal, or recorded ideas into typewritten or printed form and the
distribution thereof. '"[1] Law and Pereira define word processing as "a
combination of specific procedures, methods, equipment, and people to (1)
accomplish the transition of written or spoken (recorded) messages into
typewritten or printed form and (2) facilitate dissemination of such

---

[1]Walter A. Kleinschrod, Word Processing (New York: AMACOM,
1974), p. 1.

Figure 18–1. (*Continued*)

3

material."[2] Anderson and Trotter define word processing as "a method of producing all types of written communications with optimum speed and accuracy; with the least possible effort; at the lowest possible cost; by means of a correct combination of policies and procedures, automated equipment, and specially trained personnel."[3] The last definition is adopted for use in this report.

The secretaries employed by Environmental Services, Inc. are hired as generalists to perform typewriting tasks and other general office work. A secretary who types 60 words a minute on straight-copy material planned for test purposes probably produces no more than 10 words a minute when errors, telephone interruptions, and other distractions are considered. Through no fault of their own, average secretaries working as generalists are not very productive. A recent study by management consultant Robert Shiff, as reported by Kleinschrod, was conducted to determine how secretaries use their time. Shiff polled 53 secretaries of a large company and obtained the results shown in Chart 1. Shiff says that waiting for work was the greatest duplication of effort that he found among the 53 secretaries.[4] Interviews with the secretaries of Environmental Services, Inc. revealed a similar distribution of time usage. The major variance from Shiff's

---

[2]Donald E. Law and Cesar L. Pereira, "Word Processing: How to Cut Secretarial Administrative Costs," Management Review, March 1976, p. 29.

[3]Thomas J. Anderson and William R. Trotter, Word Processing (New York: AMACOM, 1974), p. 18.

[4]Kleinschrod, p. 7.

Figure 18–1. *(Continued)*

4

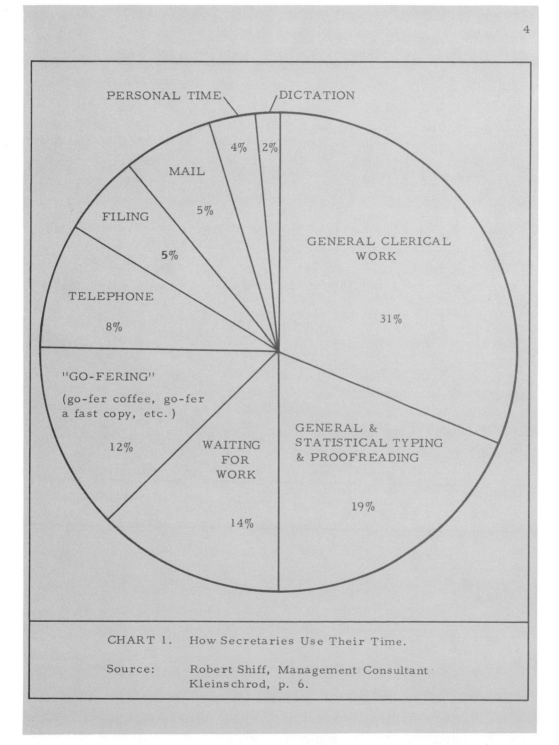

PERSONAL TIME   DICTATION

MAIL

FILING

TELEPHONE

"GO-FERING"
(go-fer coffee, go-fer
a fast copy, etc.)

12%

WAITING
FOR
WORK

14%

GENERAL CLERICAL
WORK

31%

GENERAL &
STATISTICAL TYPING
& PROOFREADING

19%

4% 2%

5%

5%

8%

CHART 1.   How Secretaries Use Their Time.

Source: Robert Shiff, Management Consultant
Kleinschrod, p. 6.

Figure 18–1. (*Continued*)

5

findings was in the percentage of time spent in taking dictation. Only two of the secretaries now employed have been taught to take dictation and only one secretary (the president's) frequently uses this skill.

A secretary doing primarily administrative work rarely needs to use a typewriter. The telephone and copy machine are the major tools. Tasks include answering the telephone, filing, message handling, opening and sorting mail, proofreading and distributing typewritten material, copying, maintaining the calendar, making appointments, arranging meetings, greeting visitors, researching and compiling data for their supervisors' research projects, routing documents, and various other duties, depending upon the needs of the principal and the department.

In word processing, the alternative to the general-purpose secretary is a division-of-work concept. Typewriting duties are taken over by a keyboard specialist (correspondence secretary) in a word processing center. The secretary's other duties are assumed by an assistant in an administrative support center (administrative secretary). Each center, word processing and administrative support, serves the typewriting or administrative needs of the company. Because operators in a word processing center are specialists working with automated equipment, they achieve a far greater output than the traditional secretary whose typewriting and transcribing work is regularly interrupted by other tasks.

Word processing increases the various rates of getting words onto paper. A person can write about 15 words a minute in longhand, but with a

Figure 18-1. *(Continued)*

6

dictating device can record about 60 words a minute. The average secretary using an electric typewriter transcribes from shorthand at a speed of about 15 words a minute, and from machine dictation at about 20 words a minute. Transcription speed from machine dictation can be increased to as high as 30 words a minute with a magnetic media typewriter.

What Has Word Processing Done for Other Firms?

The administrative manager of a large Philadelphia advertising agency reports that word processing techniques have cut secretarial service costs by 45 percent. A small Tennessee manufacturer was able to save $8,000 in equipment costs and $10,000 in annual clerical costs by adopting word processing methods. The office services manager in a manufacturing division of a major United States corporation estimates savings of $40,000 per editing keyboard per year in clerical overhead and executives' time.[5]

Since word processing was introduced by the Richards Manufacturing Company of Memphis (physicians' and surgical supplies) the number of electric typewriters in the office has been reduced from 19 to 9, the clerical/ secretarial staff has been reduced from 20 to 14, efficiency in the production of written work has sharply increased, and the company has realized savings of almost $20,000 a year in overhead costs alone.[6]

The top management of Air Canada has gone on record with the startling estimate that each of its fully productive word processing employees

[5]Kleinschrod, p. 3.

[6]Anderson and Trotter, p. 29

475

Figure 18-1. (*Continued*)

7

provides a tangible yearly savings to the firm of $6,000. One of America's

leading service organizations was able to eliminate 23 secretarial positions,

without reducing the number of principals being served, after converting to

a word processing system with administrative support.[7] The Illinois

National Bank of Springfield reports that typing productivity has increased

340 percent since the installation of a word processing center.[8]

Bruce Payne & Associates, management consultants, estimate that

word processing techniques can usually result in savings of from 15 to 30

percent of clerical payroll and overhead.[9] Retrained as a specialist and

placed in a properly managed word processing system, a secretary can

achieve a realistic net output of from eight to ten times greater than

before.[10]

PROPOSED PERSONNEL CHANGES WITH WORD PROCESSING

Secretarial Staff Can Be Reduced from Ten to Eight

Environmental Services, Inc. currently employs 10 generalist

secretaries to support 33 principals. The functions now being performed

by the secretaries are decentralized. One secretary works in each

---

[7]Kleinschrod, p. 11.

[8]Jeffrey D. O'Neal, "We Increased Typing Productivity 340%," The Office, January 1976, p. 95.

[9]Kleinschrod, p. 3.

[10]Anderson and Trotter, pp. 11-12.

Figure 18-1. *(Continued)*

8

department or division, except for the four who work in administrative

services.

Installation of a word processing system will permit all typing to be

performed in the word processing center and the remaining administrative

tasks to be performed in the administrative support center. The word

processing center will be staffed by one supervisor and two correspondence

secretaries. The administrative support center will be staffed by one

supervisor, two secretaries, and one page. The president's secretary will

become an executive assistant and will remain in the president's office.

After converting to a word processing system, a secretarial staff of eight

can support the same number of principals as before. This conversion will

eliminate two secretarial positions.

This reduction in the number of positions will be accomplished by

attrition. The attrition rate for secretaries employed by Environmental

Services, Inc. is so high that only two of the ten secretaries have been with

the firm longer than one year.

Career Patterns Can Be Established for Secretaries

Word processing helps secretaries to become more valuable and aids

their careers.[11] Instead of being in a dead-end job, secretaries are able

to advance in a word processing system from an entry-level job to a

---

[11] Virginia M. Nardiello, "Word Processing Aids Secretaries'
Careers," The Office, February 1976, p. 87.

Figure 18-1. *(Continued)*

supervisory position. The career path of the personnel in the word processing center would climb from the entry-level job of correspondence secretary (trainee) to correspondence secretary to word processing center supervisor to general manager of word processing and administrative support. In the administrative support center, the career path of personnel would start with the entry-level job of page (messenger) or administrative secretary (trainee) and advance to administrative secretary to administrative support supervisor to general manager of word processing and administrative support.

The training program should include correspondence and administrative secretaries, supervisors and coordinators, methods and standards analysts, and executives. International Business Machines Corporation offers training software to go along with the equipment that Environmental Services, Inc. already owns. Two secretaries are already competent and experienced operators of the current equipment. Other correspondence secretaries can be trained by formal instruction for part of each day for several weeks. This training can be combined with on-the-job experience at progressively more difficult tasks. International Business Machines Corporation provides this training.

Cross-training and cross-utilizing personnel between the word processing center and administrative support center will give secretaries a broader understanding of the company. It will also increase their ability to perform and move up the ladder, based on their attitude toward handling assignments as well as upon actual performance.

Figure 18–1. *(Continued)*

10

ECONOMY AND EFFICIENCY THROUGH WORD PROCESSING

Functions and Costs Prior to Word Processing

Under the present organizational structure, each of the ten secretaries performs all the traditional secretarial functions, including typewriting and all the other administrative tasks that were previously mentioned.

Nearly all typewriting is done from longhand drafts prepared by the principals. The average cost of a 250-word business letter written and typed by this method is estimated to be $8.21.[12]   Based on the amount of correspondence produced during the past twelve months, a total amount of $17,241 is required for this process.

Functions and Costs with Word Processing

All typewriting and dictation functions will be performed in the word processing center after conversion. The other administrative tasks will be provided by personnel in the administrative support center. Telephone calls will be handled in the administrative support center through a call director that is currently installed in the administrative services office but not utilized.

After installation of the word processing center, typing will be performed using the text editor and centralized machine dictation method. The average cost of a 250-word letter using this method is $4.11.[13]

---

[12]Gilbert J. Konkel and Phyllis J. Peck, "Traditional Secretarial Costs Compared to Word Processing," The Office, February 1976, p. 66.

[13]Konkel and Peck, p. 66.

Figure 18-1. *(Continued)*

11

Projecting a constant volume of typewriting for the next twelve months, a total cost of $8,631 will be required for this method.

Two secretarial positions will be eliminated (by attrition) after conversion to a word processing system with administrative support. This decrease in personnel will result in an annual saving of approximately $16,632 in salaries, plus other savings in related costs, such as desks, typewriters, and supplies.

In addition to the economy to be achieved by the use of word processing, the quality of correspondence is expected to improve because of specialized techniques and equipment.

WHY ENVIRONMENTAL SERVICES INC. SHOULD INSTALL A WORD PROCESSING CENTER

Word processing can achieve substantial cost savings for Environmental Services, Inc. Conversion to a word processing system with administrative support will result in an annual saving of $16,632 in salaries, as two secretarial positions can be eliminated. Other savings will be realized through reducing the related costs that occur with any personnel position.

In addition to salaries of the two secretaries, economy will be achieved by decreasing the time spent on each written communication, leaving more time available for other duties. As the volume of typewriting work is increasing, this improved efficiency can enable the eight secretaries who remain in the organization to handle a larger amount of work. Based upon figures of estimated cost of a letter produced by the present method and of a letter produced using word processing, $8,610 will be saved annually. This

Figure 18-1. *(Continued)*

12

amount, plus the savings in salaries, equals $25,242 per year, in addition to other related costs.

Environmental Services, Inc. should convert to a word processing system with personnel staffing as follows:

Word Processing Center

1 word processing center supervisor

2 correspondence secretaries

Administrative Support Center

1 administrative support supervisor

2 administrative secretaries

1 page

Office of the President

1 executive assistant

Training programs are recommended for correspondence and administrative secretaries and for executives.

The IBM Magnetic Card Typewriters and dictation equipment already available in the corporate headquarters are adequate for the installation of a word processing center. This equipment must be relocated to the word processing center. In order to make full use of existing equipment, International Business Machines Corporation is recommended as the vendor of additional hardware options or more efficient hardware, and for any necessary software.

BIBLIOGRAPHY

(Note: The bibliography of this report, which was of course attached to the report, appears in this book in Appendix C, page 567. The bibliography was placed in the appendix so that you could more easily turn to it as you prepared bibliographical notations for assignments earlier in the course, or for reference as you studied report format, as presented in Appendix C.)

INFORMAL REPORTS

A report similar to the one used as an illustration in the preceding example could have been presented with only these parts: the report proper, beginning with the introduction, preceded by the cover and the title page. Or it could have included these parts plus a table of contents. A table of contents should be used in all reports, whether they are considered formal or informal, if the listing of contents is an aid to readability.

In an informal report, if only a few published or other secondary sources are consulted, they may be shown by the use of footnotes only, and the bibliography may be omitted. When the bibliography is omitted, you have no choice in choosing footnote form but must present the complete bibliographical information. If the reader must search for earlier footnotes to previous references, use the complete footnote form throughout. Hence the use of a bibliography may simplify, not complicate, the process of documentation.

Informal reports may be presented in regular manuscript form, as discussed above, with the omission of preliminary and supplementary parts. In addition, they may be presented in memorandum or letter form.

The letters that follow are examples of short reports — information, with recommendations, presented in letter form. They would also be reports (classified as informational) if the recommendations were omitted. Figure 18–2 illustrates a letter report presented in the direct order; recommendations are given first, followed by supporting information. The second example (Figure 18–3) is an illustration of the indirect order; recommendations are given after the supporting details.

Reports similar to those illustrated in letter form could also be presented in the standard memorandum form. If the kind of information shown on the preceding letters had been prepared for an individual within the organization, the reports would have most likely been presented as memorandums.

Short reports are more likely than long ones to be presented as

Dear Mrs. Patterson:

Electric wall heaters seem to be the most practical way to heat your new room addition. We recommend the installation of two Sunny Days heaters in the locations marked on the enclosed room diagram.

Answer to the question

Recommendation

This conclusion was reached after the study of your added floor space, the heating system in the other parts of your house, and comparative fuel costs in your neighborhood.

How conclusion was reached

As you know, in this city gas heat has long been less expensive than electric heat. The price of natural gas, however, is expected to rise considerably during the coming months; the cost of electricity is expected to remain stable, at least for the coming year.

In addition to the consideration of the monthly bill, gas heaters, if installed in the most convenient locations, would require a rather complicated and expensive venting system. The electric heaters are much simpler to install.

Your present heating system will be adequate for the room addition except on the coldest days. If winters continue like our present mild one, most likely you will use the heaters for only a few days each season.

"Findings" of study

Figure 18–2. *Example of Letter Written in Direct Order. (The recommendation of the proposed heating method is considered to be the gist of the message — the question that the letter was written to answer.)*

Figure 18-2.   *(Continued)*

*Action close, also
service attitude and
sales promotion*

A list of Sunny Days dealers is shown on the enclosed

brochure. Any one of them will be glad to show you the

heaters and arrange for installation.

Sincerely,

Dear Mrs. Patterson:

We have completed the study of your heating needs

since the addition of your new room.

*"Introduction" —
and how the study
was made*

We considered the added floor space, the heating

system in the other parts of your house, and comparative

fuel costs in your neighborhood. We also investigated

installation costs and average daily temperature in the city.

Your present heating system will be adequate for the

room addition except on the coldest days. If winters

continue like our present mild one, most likely you will use

the heaters for only a few days each season.

Findings

As you know, in this city gas heat has long been less

expensive than electric heat. The price of natural gas,

however, is expected to rise considerably during the coming

months; the cost of electricity is expected to remain stable,

at least for the coming year.

Figure 18-3.   *Example of Letter Written in Indirect Order. (The
recommendation of the proposed heating method is given after the
explanations for the choice.)*

Figure 18–3. (*Continued*)

In addition to the consideration of the monthly bill, gas heaters, if installed in the most convenient locations, would require a rather complicated and expensive venting system. The electric heaters are much simpler to install. — *Findings*

In view of all these considerations, we recommend the installation of two Sunny Days heaters in the locations marked on the enclosed room diagram. A list of dealers is — *Recommendation*

shown on the enclosed brochure. Any one of them will be glad to show you the heaters and arrange for installation. — *Action close, sales promotion, service attitude*

Sincerely,

memorandums and letters; in addition, short reports are more likely to be written in the direct order. But, as you remember from your study of other written messages, the order of presentation of ideas depends upon what you have to say and who is to read your message. If you wish to refer to an illustration of a memorandum as you prepare a report in this arrangement, see Appendix C.

SUMMARY ♦ 18

Complete formal reports are comprised of preliminary parts, the report body, and supplementary parts.

Informal reports in manuscript form include few if any preliminary or supplementary parts.

Informal reports are also presented in letter and memorandum form.

Informal reports are often presented in the direct order, but the choice of arrangement depends more upon the material to be conveyed than upon the degree of formality desired.

REPORT PROBLEMS ◆ 18

1. Follow through with the report you began with your study of Chapter 15, the project for which you prepared a report plan. Present the results of your investigation in a complete formal report, as discussed and illustrated in this chapter.

2. Plan a report to your instructor of the reading level, according to the Gunning Fox Index (see Chapter 7), of the textbooks you are using this semester. Use at least ten 100-word samples from each book. Use a systematic method of sampling, as described in Chapter 16. Do not include in your samples such passages as questions and problems, reading lists, examples, and so forth. Write a tentative outline of this report. Remember that you will need to explain specifically how you obtained your information. Also, for the benefit of readers who are not familiar with the Gunning Fox Index or other readability formulas, explain exactly. Make sure to explain what such formulas can and cannot do. Write the report.

3. If you collected actual business letters as you studied the principles of letter writing, analyze them from the principles of effective communication presented in Appendix A. Present your findings in a formal analytical report in the format suggested by your instructor.

4. Follow the instructions for Problem 3, but limit your collection, and your analysis, to one of the following kinds of business communications:
    a. Sales
    b. Credit and/or collection
    c. Employment
    d. Good news
    e. Bad news
    f. Memorandums
    g. Your own letters or memorandums completed before beginning this course.

5. Assume that your office has need for one of the following items:
    a. an electric typewriter
    b. a spirit duplicator
    c. a photocopier (some models have both duplicating and photocopy features)
    d. a voice-writing and transcribing machine (or machines) for use in a private office
    e. an intercommunication system or any similar business equipment
    Investigate the brands available and recommend your choice, considering the particular needs of your organization.

6. Assume that you have graduated from college and obtained employment in your field of educational preparation. Your supervisor asks you to examine the national business journals available in your field. You are to recommend that one of these journals be placed in employees' lounges in offices throughout the country. Base your recommendation upon specific, detailed information about your recommended journal. Show that you have thoroughly compared it to others in the same field.

7. Assume that your supervisor (Problem 6) asks you to study these magazines: *Business Week, Newsweek,* and *U.S. News and World Report.* Recommend one of the three to be bought as gift subscriptions to persons similar to yourself.

8. With your instructor's permission and assistance, investigate some problem in your school or community. This research can be planned as a class project with individual class members investigating some phase of the problem and preparing individual reports. The total findings can then be combined for an overall report on the situation. Or the class can be divided into committees with each to assume special responsibilities in regard to researching and reporting aspects of the situation. If your topic has been investigated previously, try to obtain the results of these investigations. Test these results, or use the information to form the basis for further investigation of the problem. Present the results of your study in the form suggested by your instructor.

9. This problem is similar to the one referred to in preceding chapters: "Should Countrywide Insurance Company Provide Career Apparel for Women Employees?" Your study at this time should include information applicable to an organization with which you are familiar, or one that you can study in the research process in order to determine particular needs in regard to career apparel. Include information based on library research, the opinions of persons to wear the apparel, possible suppliers, and costs.

    Present your findings, with recommendations, in a complete formal report.

10. Prepare an analytical report on a subject similar to one of those shown in the list below. These topics have been used by students as topics for major reports. The items shown are *titles;* some are worded in statement form, but the original purpose was, or could have been, stated in the form of a question. In several instances, the topic should have been narrowed in scope. In order to have sufficient time to do well whatever you undertake, severely limit your scope of investigation.

    a. Should the _____ Supermarket Install Automated Checkout Stands?
    b. Should the _____ Company Move to the _____ Industrial Park?
    c. Do Businessmen in _____ Write Letters in the Manner Recommended in Business Communication Textbooks?
    d. Why the _____ Accounting Firm Should Support the Demand for Recognition of General Price-Level Changes
    e. The _____ Department Store: An Image Study
    f. Collection Procedure Errors for _____: A Case Study
    g. The Optimum Location for the Next McDonald's Restaurant in _____
    h. The Doctor's Headache (collection problems of a dentist; not a good title for this type report)
    i. A Study of Whether to Make or Buy an Enlarger Timer
    j. How to Move the Cow (a study of how _____ Supermarket should market cuts of meat; title not good for this type report)
    k. A Study of Business Form Design (Topic is too broad — could be an excellent topic if study of particular department or small company is made in relation to the business forms they should choose)
    l. The Accounting Graduate's Dilemma: Two Years' Experience versus Full-Time Graduate Study

m. Why _____ Academy Should Wait Before Starting a Business Machines
    Class
n. What Are the Employment Opportunities for Accountants in _____
    Corporation?
o. What Are the Employment Opportunities for (sales representatives,
    management trainees, other) at _____?
p. Should _____ Men's Shop Install a Security System?
q. Should Concrete Poles, Inc. Install 16-Inch Octagonal Pile Forms?
r. American Red Cross Volunteer Problems in the City of _____: Recruit-
    ing and Retention
s. How Can the _____ Company Improve the Accuracy of Estimating the
    Cost of Heating Ducts in Commercial Buildings?
t. Recommendations for Improvement of the _____ Reports of the _____
    Accounting Company
u. Recommended Reference Sources for the Account Executive in a
    Stockbroker's Office
v. Recommended Professional Journals for (accountants, high school busi-
    ness teachers, personnel managers, other)
w. What Is the Best Location for a Retail Motorboat Store in the _____
    Standard Metropolitan Statistical Area?

11. Should the Panhandle Furniture Manufacturing Company Begin Selling
    Scrap Materials to Employees? (This problem is a continuation of the one
    begun with Question 11 in Chapter 16 and continued in Question 5 in
    Chapter 17. Present the result of your findings in an informal report
    prepared for Mr. R. C. Tennyson, the president of Panhandle. Include
    specific recommendations.)

12. Assume that the president agrees with your recommendation. Write a
    memorandum to be distributed to all Panhandle employees informing them
    of the new policy.

13. *Investigating problems arising from a truck accident.* You are the Assistant
    Manager of the Car-Wash Division of International Inns, Inc., a diversified
    international motel chain with many subsidiaries in the motel, vacation, and
    recreation field. The division is responsible for a number of car-wash
    facilities located across the country, and some of these are located in the city
    where your office is located.
        The manager of the division has asked you to look into the circumstances
    of an accident involving a company truck from a local car-wash. The truck is
    still carried on the inventory, but someone has noted on the inventory card
    that it has been wrecked, possibly beyond economical repair.
        The truck in question was engaged in the delivery of supplies to the local
    car-wash when the driver skidded on a wet street and struck a telephone pole.
    The truck, a 1971 Ford pickup, received extensive damage that left the
    vehicle inoperative. A wrecker was called to the scene by the company
    vehicle dispatcher, who told the wrecker driver to deliver the truck to the
    nearby Milltown Ford Agency for repairs under the company's vehicle
    insurance policy.
        Milltown Ford, working on the instructions of the vehicle dispatcher, paid
    the wrecker charges and started some preliminary work to determine the

extent of the damages.   The repair mechanics prepared an estimate of the work needed to restore the truck to operation and placed on order the parts needed to effect the repairs.

Immediately upon returning to his office after inspecting the damage, the dispatcher made the necessary notification to the insurance company and asked for a claims adjuster to inspect the wrecked truck.

Subsequently, the claims adjuster notified the dispatcher that the wrecked vehicle was not covered by insurance, and no claim could be paid. Checking with the manager of the transportation section, the dispatcher discovered that this was indeed true. The company had a little known policy of not insuring any vehicles over four years old against collision damage, because the cost of the insurance was deemed excessive for a vehicle nearing the end of its service life. Upon learning this, the dispatcher notified Milltown Ford to stop any repair work on the truck.

The driver of the truck had been uninjured in the accident, but the investigating policeman charged him with failure to keep his vehicle under control. The same driver had been previously cited for driving at excessive speed, and his supervisor had warned him about speeding on two different occasions.

Nearly forty days have elapsed since the accident, and Milltown Ford notified the division ten days ago that, effective that date, a storage charge of $1.50 a day would be levied against the truck until all charges were paid and the vehicle removed. A quick check with Milltown Ford revealed that charges of $37.50 for wrecker service and $200 for labor already performed was due on the truck in addition to the storage charges.

The problem calls for early resolution, and your report will be the basis for deciding what action your company will take. Write a memorandum to the manager of the car-wash division reporting the situation and making your recommendations on what actions should be taken in regard to the truck and the truck driver.

14. *Recommending personnel action.*   The executives at Environmental Services, Inc., have examined their annual production report. They observed that in recent months there had been a slight but consistent decrease in output, particularly in the air pollution control devices department. Consequently, they decided it was time to modernize certain equipment and to initiate a new system of tighter inspection control.

In order to make the transition from the old to new equipment and to get the new inspection system operating on a smoother schedule, many employees were asked to make an effort to increase their productivity. Using the new procedures, a new schedule was set up with a goal of 12 percent increased output in the next four months.

Most workers were enthusiastic and anxious to see if they could meet the new goal. But Pete Idlewild, one of the chief inspectors, would have none of it. "This place is becoming a sweatshop," he griped. "They're never satisfied around here. We had plenty to do before this new mess and now they're trying to pile the load higher. I'm not going to work myself into a sweat for anybody!"

Pete Idlewild kept his word. He made no effort to increase his output, refused to try the new methods, and grumbled almost constantly. Pete became a nuisance to all those around him, because they had to wait until certain procedures passed through Pete before they could do their operations. Pete Idlewild knew he was slowing up the whole system and took a certain delight in his defiance.

The inspection foreman tolerated Pete's actions for only so long. Pete Idlewild had been given two written warnings and two short suspensions, but he refused to go along with the new system.

The inspection foreman kept the following written record of Pete Idlewild's work performance:

- August 4 — Left work to go to the phone booth on main floor, did not request permission, and resented criticism. Written warning issued.
- August 24 — Left tester console unattended and ruined two pollution control devices. Suspended for two days.
- September 7 — Came in 22 minutes late. When asked for a reason Pete said, "Don't be an old maid."
- September 27 — Loudly complained that the inspection foreman is "out to get me" when three devices were rejected. Rechecked and all three devices were out-of-tolerance. Issued written warning for poor work.
- October 22 — Asked permission to leave early for a Veterans Day long weekend trip. Permission refused because department was short of chief inspectors. Did not return from lunch. Suspended for three days.

You are the inspection foreman for Environmental Services, Inc. and must make your recommendation on Mr. Idlewild. Write your report to Harvard Forbes, the plant manager, supporting your recommendation with factual documentation. Use memorandum form.

15. *Writing a position paper to disagree with management's current policy of accounting.* You have recently joined the staff of a large public organization that raises money for charity. In your position as Director of Administrative Services you are responsible for purchasing and control of all support staff, including Word Processing, Duplicating Services, and Maintenance. One of your prime directives from the Executive Director was to cut the internal operating costs and increase efficiency.

Probably the greatest task ahead of you is the control of inventory and disbursement of supplies to the various departments within the organization. The current process is so complicated that one must requisition a requisition to receive supplies. That policy, you are told, was the brainchild of the Director of Accounting, who believes in charging each department for every item they use. The accounting clerks must spend a great deal of time each month processing the many forms being used and charging each department.

After taking a look at the process, you have decided that the organization is small enough (only thirty-five employees) that it does not need such an elaborate system. Further, you have determined through analysis that each department uses an average percentage of supplies and duplicating time which has held constant over the last several years. Your analysis shows the following figures for each of the departments:

No. of Department	Supplies	Printing
1 Administration	35%	30%
2 Budgeting	20%	23%
3 Campaign	25%	40%
4 Community Service	20%	7%

You did notice that the charges would vary from month to month, affected mostly by the timing of the campaign to raise funds. Yet, over the past three years, these percentages have been accurate.

You have now decided to write a memorandum to the Executive Director, Mr. Harry Goodsen, to whom you report. He is a man who requires details, presented in a personal tone. He will usually go along with his subordinates' recommendations if they are supported by a thorough analysis. You propose that the nitpicky accounting system be dropped for a percentage system, a plan that will save many hours of labor for both employees as well as those in accounting.

16. *Recommending action.*   You are the supervisor of the inventory control department at First Line Tire, Inc. Your department consists of three women clerks. (They do not belong to a union.) You report to the controller of the company. The entire accounting department consists of five department supervisors and fifteen clerks.

The personnel problem arose on a Thursday when the inventory control department was very busy. You were told by the controller that a major price change was to be effective the following Monday. So that prices could be changed in the computer, overtime for Friday and Saturday was scheduled and was considered mandatory for all accounting employees.

When you notified your employees, Carol Ruff, your senior employee, refused to work overtime for either of those days or in the future. Her reasoning was that since she was divorced and was raising her two small girls by herself, she could not leave them alone more than her normal working hours. As her supervisor, you know her feelings toward her job: she enjoys the work, but financially she is under no great burden. Carol had a strong will and an outgoing personality. Usually these would be assets to your department, but in this case she was setting the parameters of her employment instead of the company.

Write a memorandum report to the controller, Mrs. Ruth Jones. What will you recommend? Or do you wish to report the facts and ask to meet with her and Carol?

COMMUNICATION AND
EFFECTIVE BUSINESS
MANAGEMENT

Efficient and Economical
Communication Systems
and Procedures

19

Almost everything that occurs in a business office, as well as in plants and other areas of the business organization, consists of some facet of communication. Management techniques and knowledges are, for the most part, communication techniques. And, as all efficient managers know, systems and procedures — including communication systems and procedures — must be wisely planned and chosen if the organization is to prosper, or even continue to exist.

DICTATING BUSINESS MESSAGES

You may dictate to a secretary or to a machine. The secretary may be a person who works for you exclusively or one who works as departmental secretary or in a stenographic pool. If you dictate to a voice-writing machine, you may never see the person who transcribes the dictation, or even the machine itself. You may dictate through your telephone to a word-processing center, where your words are recorded to be transcribed by one of many typists.

If the services of a responsible, competent secretary are provided for your use alone, you are indeed fortunate. Many of your communication problems are over. But you are not sure to have a full-time secretary, or even a part-time one, especially in your early years in business — and that's the period when you need help the most.

If you are a good communicator — that is, if you are a good manager — you will communicate well with your secretary or with the other person or persons who transcribe your words. Communicate you must. If you do not know or see the transcriber, it is even more important that your instructions be clear on the tape or belt that is to be transcribed. Here, as in all other communication situations, the basic principles apply: courtesy, consideration, clearness, completeness, and all the rest.

Your secretary, like you, will have strengths and weaknesses and will make mistakes at times because of inaccurate perception, personal biases, and prejudices, along with all the other reasons for communication error. But you must work with this imperfect creature — who will also have certain misgivings about you.

Do not dictate unnecessarily. Many people in business do not delegate as many of their communication responsibilities as they should. Secretaries who are perfectly capable of writing business letters or other material are not given an opportunity to do so. Even though you have a private secretary, however, you will have some material that only you should write.

Some business persons, especially young ones, lack confidence in their dictating skills and are fearful of what the stenographer will think of their communication ability. If this is your problem, you know the answer: increase your communication ability. The best way to decrease frustration is to improve competence.

The first and most important factor of effective and efficient dictation is to be able to compose effectively and efficiently. If you cannot write a good letter with a pen or a typewriter, you surely cannot dictate one. This fact is the reason that this chapter on dictation is presented after the chapters covering the theory and techniques of business writing. Even if you are proficient in composing, however, you will need to develop skill and confidence in dictating practices and procedures in order to become an expert dictator of effective business messages.

Special Considerations When Dictating Business Messages

1. A secretary or a stenographer will probably be able to take dictation at the rate of 80 to 100 words a minute. An expert rate is 120 to 140 words a minute. In order to get some idea of what this rate means, time yourself for a minute or so as you read aloud from prepared material and count the words you have read. Although your rate will not be the same as that of a shorthand teacher who dictates at a predetermined rate from prepared copy, it is approximately the same. Your average speed in actual dictation will be considerably less, unless you are dictating routine, repetitive material, because you will need time to think. But it is not the average rate that bothers the person taking the dictation; it is the spurts of rapid speech, often followed by hesitations, pauses, or revisions.

Make sure to spell out unusual terms, especially if the secretary is not likely to be familiar with certain specialized words or phrases. Anticipate these terms, if you can, in order to prevent wasted time in the transcription process as the secretary ponders over a sentence or transcribes it incorrectly.   Or, if a secretary asks you how to spell or to use such a term (a wise procedure), do not look or act surprised at this lack of knowledge. All employees should be encouraged to ask questions in order to decrease the possibility of error, as well as to encourage an understanding of company terminology and procedures.

2. Some persons are reluctant to express their thought-in-progress to the ears of someone else.   As a result, the dictation, and thus the typewritten message, sounds strained and stilted.

3. Some persons want to impress secretaries or other typists transcribing the material, and thus tend to dictate too fast or to use unnecessarily long or unusual words.

4. The dictator does not have the advantage of immediate revision, which is easy to do when writing with a pen or a typewriter.   Dictation, especially by inexperienced persons, tends to be longer and less concise than material written with a pen or typewriter.   Because it is more like "talk language," however, it is likely to sound natural and conversational if the dictator is not making a conscious effort to impress.

5. Errors that would be immediately noted when we are writing, or that would not occur at all, can creep into dictated material.   When composing with a pen or typewriter, we look at the sentences as they are being recorded.   When dictating, especially if the sentence is long and involved, the wrong form of the verb or pronoun is likely to be used because the dictator has forgotten what was said in the earlier part of the sentence.   Part of the transcriber's responsibility is to correct obvious grammatical errors, but the transcriber may also overlook them.   The final responsibility is with the dictator.

6. As a general rule, dictated material will require more revision than personally composed material.   In most offices, however, time does not permit extensive revision of routine letters and memorandums.   These factors point again to the importance of the competence of the dictator as well as to the competence of the person who transcribes the material.

Pointers for Effective Dictation

1. Before you call the secretary in for a dictation period, or before you turn on the voice-writing machine or equipment, plan the content of each letter or other bit of writing to be dictated.   In preceding chapters you learned to make a brief outline of each message to be written or dictated.   A brief outline of each letter may consist of only a few words;

perhaps on the letter itself you may make a note of the contents of each paragraph. Less detailed planning will suffice after you have obtained considerable experience in writing and in dictating, but some planning will always be essential.

2. Speak clearly, at a fairly even pace. If you are dictating to a machine, make sure that it is adjusted properly and that you speak directly into the telephone or microphone. Make sure that no distracting noises detract from the clarity of your voice.

3. Give special instructions before you begin dictating the material to be transcribed. For example, specify the number of copies, unless you want only the usual file copy, and the persons to whom the copies are to be sent. If a particular letter is to be transcribed first, say so at the beginning of the dictation, most especially if you are using a machine. Give special mailing instructions.

Perhaps for a long, complicated letter or manuscript the first copy should be in the form of a rough draft for you to revise before the final copy is typewritten. If so, give this instruction at the beginning of the dictation, or the transcriber is likely to type a copy in mailable form. Making corrections and a carbon copy require more time than typewriting in rough draft form.

4. If you are dictating to a secretary, set aside a certain time of the day for this work. A morning hour is best. The secretary then has the rest of the day to complete the transcription process, return the letters for your signature, and put them in the mail. Do not dictate late in the day and ask that the work be completed before the secretary goes home unless the message is unexpected and urgent.

5. Make sure that a dictionary and other reference materials are available for use by the secretary or other person who transcribes the work.

6. Dictate paragraph endings. If you are an expert writer, you know more about where paragraphs should begin and end than does the transcriber. In addition, as you have learned in preceding chapters, paragraph construction is really a part of the composition; you can change emphasis and meaning by rearranging paragraphs.

7. Dictate unusual punctuation. Punctuation is also a part of the composition itself; and, as in the construction of paragraphs, punctuation comprises a portion of the meaning. If you are sure that the transcriber knows the rules for the ordinary and expected use of punctuation, to dictate each comma may indicate that you do not trust the ability of the person transcribing the work.

On the other hand, some persons prefer that all punctuation be dictated. This approach has an advantage in that your meaning as it comes through spoken words is more immediately clear, just as meaning through the written word is made more immediately clear through the use of punctuation.   Dictating all punctuation speeds up the transcription process.   If you follow this procedure, however, make sure that you are completely sure of the best punctuation for your work.

8. If you use a machine, always indicate the approximate length of the letter to be dictated.   This estimate enables the transcriber to set the margins of the letter so that it will be attractively centered on the page.

9. When dictating to a secretary, ask that the material be read back when desirable or necessary.   This reading-back process is one of the advantages of having an individual take your message in shorthand instead of using a voice-writing machine.

10. Provide the transcriber with the letter to be answered or any other related materials that will assist in the transcription process.

11. Spell out all proper names if they are not available in the letter being answered or in related materials.   Spell out all unusual terms.

12. Even though errors that occur in the transcription process are not your own, you are responsible for them.   You are responsible for all facets of your written communication, including the work of the person who transcribes your words and the person to whom you delegate writing assignments.   Check all work carefully and thoroughly, most especially until you are assured that the transcriber or writer is conscientious and accurate.   Even if you are confident of your assistant's ability and dedication, your checking of the copy is an extra safeguard.

Undetected errors can be costly and embarrassing.   If you feel that a transcript should be redone, ask the person who transcribed it to retype the material, but make sure that your instructions are clear and that your reasons are justified.   Time and money are wasted if the dictator of the message requires work to be redone if it is only slightly less than perfect.

Some persons read their finished letter and notice that the phrasing, although correct and clear, could be improved from the standpoint of graceful wording — and the letter is re-dictated and/or retyped.   Almost all written work could be improved by rewriting and rewriting again, but in the usual business office there is no time to construct literary masterpieces.   The efficient business writer is able to dictate good letters on the first trial, in most instances, although they may not be as good as they could be with endless time.

Under the best of circumstances, however, some letters and other communications must be dictated and transcribed more than once.   And, as mentioned earlier, a rough draft of complicated material may save time in the overall process.   But excessive duplication of effort is an expensive procedure.

13. Penwritten notes may be added to the typewritten message as long as they are used with judgment and discretion. In some types of letters these additions should be avoided, and some organizations frown upon this practice in any kind of letter. Sometimes penwritten notes are added deliberately, not because of an unintended omission but to add a personal touch. Penwritten notes serve as attention-getters if they are not overused. If they are overused, or used inappropriately, they appear as an inconsiderate shortcut to prevent retyping of the message.

14. When dictating to a machine, play back your voice occasionally. You may be surprised!

CUTTING THE COSTS OF COMMUNICATION

Business communications, both within and from the organization, are tremendously expensive. Their cost has been increasing for many years and is expected to continue to do so. Office managers and other persons concerned with cost control realize that much waste occurs in the management and procedures of office communications. Many companies have instituted programs to study the various items of expense and have taken steps to simplify and improve their entire communication systems.

Some progress has been made toward achieving economy, largely as a result of the recognition that it is possible to reduce costs and still maintain an effective, goodwill-building system of communication. Costs have been cut by the installation of automated processes of transcription, reproduction, and mailing. Because of extensive and intensive training programs in business writing, including company-sponsored courses within organizations and in colleges and universities, many business people now write more efficiently than in past years, and thus more economically.

Letters are improved from the standpoint of economy because, on the average, they are shorter than they were in previous years. This decrease in length has often been accomplished by eliminating wordy, trite phrases and unnecessary repetition, so that the letter is not only more economical, but also more interesting and readable.

Without this saving because of increased efficiency, communication costs would be very much higher than they are now, especially because of ever-increasing salaries. Other factors that make up the cost of a business letter have also risen. Only by a constantly watchful attitude can the costs of communication be controlled.

In the consideration of economy, we must not lose sight of the fact that our efforts to economize are unwise if they lower the quality of the correspondence. A poor letter, hastily written in order to save time, is no bargain at all if it requires another letter to explain what should have been included in the first one, or if the message does not build or maintain the goodwill of the reader.   A serious effort to improve communication, however, will result not only in more economical methods, but also in better quality communications.

The Cost of an Individually Dictated Letter

Various studies have been made over the years of the cost of an individually dictated letter.   The Dartnell study is made annually by the Dartnell Corporation.[1]   According to this study, in 1977 the average cost of an individually dictated letter was $4.47.   This amount is an increase of 30 cents from the reported cost in 1976.   This figure is based on a salary of $360 weekly for the person who dictates the letter and a salary of $168 a week for the secretary.   Because salaries, like other costs, are constantly rising, the present cost of an individually dictated letter is higher than the last reported figure.

Many dictators of business letters earn more than $360 a week, and their letters are proportionally more expensive.   If the dictator is slow and inefficient, then the letters cost more than $4.47 even if the weekly salary is less than average.   The amount of $1.05, shown by the Dartnell study to be the cost of the dictator's time, is based on the assumption that seven minutes are required to dictate an average-length letter.

The estimate of the cost of secretarial time ($1.26) is based upon the assumption that the secretary can take dictation, transcribe the letter, address the envelope, and do all the additional work — checking names, addresses, dates, and figures, and arranging for enclosures — in eighteen minutes.   A secretary must be fast and accurate to turn out letters at this rate consistently.   The actual cost of labor is higher than the figures shown, for the term "fixed charges" includes fringe benefits, which are really an added cost of personnel time.

This study is based upon "the traditional boss-secretary type of business letter.   The use of word processing is gaining momentum, but it is still generally accepted that most businesses use the secretary with steno pad and typewriter as their mode of business correspondence."[2]

The First Essential: Efficient Personnel

Whether or not the Dartnell Corporation is correct in the assumption that most businesses still use the secretary with a steno pad and a typewriter, other firms are even less progressive.

1. "Target Survey" (Chicago: The Dartnell Corporation, 1977), p. 1.
2. "Target Survey," p. 2.

Many persons write their letters in longhand to be copied on the typewriter by secretaries. This method is used because business people do not know how to dictate and/or because secretaries do not know how to write shorthand. In these offices, writers should learn to type their own letters or write the final copy in longhand. The cost of a 250-word letter written in longhand and copied by a typist is said to be $8.21.[3]

The most important element in saving time and money in the management of a business communications system is that everyone concerned be hard-working, conscientious, and highly proficient. Ideally, the executive can dictate top-quality messages in a minimum of time; the secretary can take dictation quickly and accurately and transcribe the letter into an excellent example of a perfect communication; the file clerk can quickly file and find all folders; the mail clerk knows the postal regulations and how to handle the processes of delivering and sending the mail.

From a practical standpoint, however, this ideal situation is far from the usual one. Even if the dictator of the message is extremely skillful, and the secretary can take dictation at the expert rate of 120 to 140 words a minute, much time can be lost if the secretary is slow or inaccurate in transcribing the shorthand notes or if the finished work is not carefully proofread and corrected. The dictator wastes time by requiring that acceptable but less than perfect work be redone.

Efficient personnel are the best "time-saving devices" to be found in any office. These employees deserve to be paid well, and, because of their ability, the employing organization can easily afford to do so. Less able persons, even if they are paid considerably less, would be more expensive.

The Choice of Equipment, Materials, and Procedures for Economical Communications

The *electric typewriter* should be chosen for economy because of the saving of secretarial time. The electric typewriter should be chosen even if it were not faster because it produces a more attractive letter.

Automatic typewriters or automated typewriting systems, although expensive to purchase, are useful if many copies of letters need to be made and if it is important that they have the appearance of personally typewritten letters.

A *"self-correcting" typewriter*, although more costly than a regular electric typewriter, may be less expensive because of the saving of secretarial time. It is almost certain to increase secretarial morale.

Good quality paper and typewriter ribbons can save time, in addition to

3. Gilbert J. Konkel and Phyllis J. Peck, "Traditional Secretarial Costs Compared to Word Processing," *The Office* (February 1976), p. 66.

producing more attractive work, because of the ease and speed of corrections.

Good quality carbon paper saves typewriting time and improves the appearance of carbon copies. Carbon paper comes in various weights and shades of darkness. A careful choice should be made according to the particular kind of work being done; the consideration should include the number of copies needed, the kind of paper, and the purpose for which the carbon copies will be used. Disposable carbons, purchased in "carbon sets" or "carbon packs," may add to the economy and efficiency of making multiple copies.

The *photocopy machine* has decreased the number of carbon copies used in the business office. For regular use, carbon paper is usually less expensive, although the saving of secretarial time may absorb the added cost. The use of a photocopy machine for copies of routine correspondence is more expensive than carbon paper if the secretary must walk some distance to the machine or stand in line to make the copies. In addition, the materials cost of photocopies is considerably higher.

A photocopy machine should be available in every office, for most certainly a photocopy is cheaper than a typewritten copy. A photocopy, not a carbon copy, should be made of tables, illustrations, graphs, or any such complicated material. A photocopy machine can be used to save the time and cost of dictating and typewriting a letter. This method of reply is not suitable for all correspondence and should not be used if there is a possibility that such an answer will offend the reader. It can be used for much routine correspondence, especially for communications between persons working in the same organization. This method of replying to correspondence is as follows.

The person who ordinarily dictates a reply to a letter merely jots a note or two on the letter being answered. Sometimes the answer can be only "Yes" or "No" in reply to a question from a correspondent. After the needed information is written on the original letter, a photocopy is made. Then the photocopy, which now is a copy of the incoming letter and a copy of the reply as shown by the handwritten notes, is mailed to the writer of the original letter. The original letter is filed. Or the process can be reversed, with the original letter being returned and the photocopy being filed.

This procedure saves dictating time, transcribing time, paper, and filing space. It also provides a concise record of the incoming letter and the outgoing reply.

Voice-writing machines save time, for while one person is dictating, the secretary can be busy at other tasks. Also, the voice-writing machines can be used when the executive is away from the office, or when the secretary is away. Portable machines are small enough to be carried with ease, and the cartridge or tape can be mailed to the office for transcription. In many offices, dictation should be given both to machines and to secretaries, depending upon the kind of materials involved, the particular office situation, and the other duties of the secretary and of the executive.

The *telephone* is often more economical than the business letter, even if the message is to be transmitted from one coast to the other. Telephone calls have the obvious advantage of gaining an immediate reply. They do not, however, provide the written record that may be necessary for future reference. Sometimes a confirming letter is necessary after a telephone agreement. But for routine matters that do not require a file copy, the telephone is often the most economical method of communication. Notes about the conversation can be made as soon as the conversation is over or as it proceeds in order to have a record of the communication, and these notes can be filed in the same way that a letter would be.

Special communications systems in use in many companies are leased telephone lines, Wide Area Telephone Service (WATS), and Wideband Data Service. When these systems are available, they often should be used instead of letters or regular telephone calls. Companies that have access to these systems should make sure that all employees with the responsibility of communicating to areas outside their own city know exactly how and when to use the equipment and services. Studies have shown that many organizations do not adequately inform their employees of the most suitable and economical methods of transmitting business messages. (For a more complete discussion of these communication systems, see a recent, complete book on office management.)

The wise choice of a *letter style*, to be used in all letters coming from an organization, saves time and money as well as assuring a uniform, attractive, appropriate appearance of business messages. The simplified and the full-block arrangement, in which all lines begin at the left margin, can be typewritten more quickly than arrangements that require indentions or other special formats. (See the section in Appendix B entitled "Choosing the Most Appropriate and Efficient Letter Style.")

Eliminating unnecessary correspondence and interoffice communications obviously decreases costs. It also seems obvious that if a message is not necessary, it will not be sent. The actual need for many business messages, however, is at least questionable. Memorandums are often used unnecessarily. This policy has probably developed because of the admirable desire to keep personnel informed. An open system of communication within an organization is preferable to an overly restrictive one, for all employees like to feel that they know what is going on and that they are important enough to be notified of everything that happens or is planned.

Overcommunication, though, is expensive and often otherwise undesirable. Memorandums of instructions or other information need be sent only to the particular persons concerned. For other people the communication is a waste of both the sender's and the receiver's time; it may also be confusing and result in additional communications. Moreover, even with the most open policy of communication, and with no desire whatsoever to misrepresent or to discriminate, some information should be distributed only to the individuals concerned.

Some letters are also unnecessary. If a letter requires no reply, either from the standpoint of giving information or building goodwill, then no reply should be sent.

Decreasing the length of business messages also decreases the cost, but leaving out necessary words, sentences, or paragraphs is false economy. Words can be necessary, although they do not convey information, for a courteous, considerate tone. "Please" and "thank you" are worth far more than their cost to dictate and transcribe. So are well-written and appropriately placed sales promotion paragraphs.

Delegating correspondence duties decreases the cost of business communications, especially those coming from the offices of highly paid executives. These persons should dictate only those messages that they alone can compose, and delegate all other material to competent, although lower paid, employees. All executives should delegate to their secretaries the messages that the secretaries can write. Studies have shown that executives dictate many letters that could be quickly and easily written by their secretaries.

Short handwritten messages are often more economical than dictated and transcribed ones. A memorandum of only a few lines can be handwritten while the secretary is being called to the employer's desk. Legibility must be considered, but a business executive who can't or won't write so that the message can be read cannot be described as being completely efficient, regardless of other sterling qualities.

The Use of Form Messages for Economical Communications

Form messages, if used wisely, can decrease the cost of business communications and retain the goodwill, customer–relations aspects of individually dictated messages. Form letters, along with other duplicated messages of varying kinds, are not only desirable but absolutely essential if the overall cost of an organization's communication system is to be held to any reasonable figure.

Because form letters are not always attractively reproduced, or wisely used, to some persons the term "form letter" carries an unfavorable connotation. Often the word "just" precedes the term — as "just another form letter." Although form letters can be used inappropriately, they certainly should not be, and, for the most part, they are not. If a form letter conveys the necessary information, if it is neat in appearance, and if it is promptly mailed, it can be just as effective in every aspect as an individually typewritten letter. It is certainly much less expensive.

To dictate letters over and over that say about the same thing is a complete waste of time; a form letter should be prepared for recurring situations. The greatest care, however, should be taken to make sure that the prepared form letter actually does meet all the needs of the individual situation. In form letters, effective writing of the original letter is even more important than when dictating or writing individual letters, as the form letter is sent to many persons.

Form letters are used as replies to requests for information about products or services, acknowledgment of orders, prompt replies before mailing more complicated letters that will be somewhat delayed, requests for additional information, early-stage collection letters, and many other kinds of communication.

Some letters are "fill-in" in that they are duplicated completely except for special items of information that apply to the particular individual. This information is inserted on a blank line in the letter, as

Your check for last month's purchases, totaling

_____, has not yet been received by our credit office.

When using forms that require fill-in information, the typist should make sure that the color of the typewriter ribbon closely matches the ink on the printed form.

The method of duplication will depend upon the number of copies needed and the purpose for which they are used. Whatever method is chosen, the messages should be attractive in appearance; many should resemble an individually typewritten letter.

The offset process provides an inexpensive method of excellent quality reproduction. The original letter can be typewritten on an offset master, and, if desired, copies can be run on letterhead stationery. Or masters may be made by the use of a photocopy process. Using good equipment, an experienced operator can produce copies that are almost indistinguishable from neatly typewritten copies.

Various printed forms have been prepared and are ready for sale by printers or companies that specialize in the design of business forms. Other forms can be designed and prepared to meet many other business needs.

Form paragraphs are used as a method of decreasing dictation when completely written form messages are not appropriate. A series of form paragraphs is written to be used in often-occurring business situations. These form paragraphs are numbered and inserted into business messages as they are needed. For example, an executive may say to the secretary: "Use paragraphs 27, 31, 19, 7, and 2."

Often the secretary can arrange such letters without any instruction at all. Such a series must be used with extreme care in order to make sure that the chosen paragraphs completely answer all the questions that were asked, and that everything in each of the paragraphs applies to the particular situation.

Some companies put form paragraphs on punched or magnetic tape for use on automatic typewriters. Entire form letters are also put on tape and typewritten automatically. Automatic typewriters, even the most sophisticated ones, are too slow and thus too expensive to be used for great quantities of duplicated letters. They are much faster than the fastest secretary, and they are economical to use when it is necessary that letters be typewritten. These letters are the same in appearance as letters typewritten by an individual, except that they are usually more nearly perfect. Automatic typewriters make perfect fill-in's because the machines are set to stop so that the special bits of information can be inserted.

Window envelopes are often used with form messages. They can be used with any kind of message, and they are economical in that they save the secretary's time in addressing the envelope.

Reducing Postage and Mailing Costs

The office manager or other person responsible for cost control should make sure that every person concerned with business communications take the following steps:

1. Use special delivery mail only when it is clearly needed. Regular first class mail is usually delivered as quickly as the expensive special delivery mail. Express mail can be less expensive, depending on the weight and distance, than first class mail with added special delivery charges.

2. Use registered mail only when something of insurable value is enclosed. Certified mail provides proof of mailing and is less expensive.

3. Plan for most first class mail to go at the one-stamp rate. If many letters exceed this weight, check the length of the messages. If they are so long as to require additional postage, they are most likely unnecessarily long; in addition to the increased postage, they are also excessively expensive because of their use of extra time. If many letters are necessarily longer than the average one, the weight of the paper may be reduced to the 16-pound from the 20- or 24-pound weight. If pica type is being used, consider changing to the smaller elite so that more words can be typed on a page. (Most offices already use elite type for this reason, although, to some persons, the pica type produces a more attractive letter.)

5. Make full use of the postage attached to each mailing, if appro-

priate. Sales promotion form letters or other envelope stuffers "ride free" with monthly statements or with other messages that weigh less than that allowed at the one-stamp rate.

6. Keep mailing lists up to date so as to decrease the amount of unproductive mailings.

7. Use business reply envelopes, whenever possible, instead of stamped return envelopes. By this method the company pays only for the envelopes that are returned. Although the post office adds a slight additional fee for this service, it results in economy unless there is an unusually high percentage of returns.

8. Use appropriate and adequate equipment, such as automatic mail openers, postage meters, postage scales, collators, sorting tables and racks, mail bags and holders, and date-time recorders. Consider the use of computerized mailing lists and a label applicator, or other automated addressing and mailing equipment.

SUMMARY ◆ 19

Organizations need effective management through communication, as well as the efficient and economical management of communication and communication systems.

Consideration of the cost of the overall communication system is essential for the financial well-being of any business organization. With careful planning and efficient personnel, economy can be achieved without lowering the quality of business messages or the effectiveness of the communication system.

Dictating skills affect the cost and quality of business communications. The most important factor of dictating ability is the ability to compose.

The person proficient in composing but inexperienced in dictating messages to be transcribed by other persons must develop confidence and ability in dictating practices and procedures.

As a general rule, dictated material will require more revision than personally written material. Much of this revision can be done by a competent transcriber.

Planning, which is essential in all composing efforts, is even more important when preparing to dictate business messages.

The dictator of the message should be aware of various techniques that can aid the process of getting words on paper.

The most expensive factor of business communications of any kind is the cost of personnel time.   Many organizations waste time and money because of inefficient personnel, poor, inadequate, or inappropriate equipment or materials, and unplanned or unwise procedures of handling communication tasks.

QUESTIONS AND PROBLEMS ◆ 19

1. Turn back to the letters assigned at the end of Chapters 6, 9, or 10.   Choose either those letters that you did not write when studying these chapters or those that you wrote at that time.   If you choose letters you have already written, do not refer to the original version at this time.

    Plan these letters to be dictated by making a short outline of what to include in each paragraph.   Remember to consider whether these letters are good-news, bad-news, or neutral messages; plan the sequence of ideas accordingly, either in the direct or the indirect arrangement.

2. Dictate to a tape recorder or other voice-writing machine the letters you planned in Problem 1.   At the beginning of the dictation, give any special instructions you feel the transcriber will need.

3. Listen to your recording of the dictation.   Evaluate your performance according to these criteria:

    a.   Have you given the necessary information?

    b.   Are all words distinctly pronounced?

    c.   Is your tone of voice pleasant and uniformly clear?   Make sure that your voice does not drop at the end of sentences so that it cannot be understood.

    d.   Could you tell immediately from the sound of your voice where the sentences end?   If you cannot, then remember to say "period" at the end of each sentence.

    e.   Is your rate of dictation fairly uniform, or is it marked by rapid spurts of dictation followed by long pauses and hesitation?

    f.   Have you spelled out all unusual words?

    g.   Have you indicated any punctuation of which the transcriber may be uncertain?

4. If someone in your class is able to take shorthand notes, or if another stenographer is available for your practice, dictate some or all of the letters from Chapters 6, 9, and 10 to this person.   Ask for the stenographer's comments about your dictating methods.   Ask for suggestions for improvement.

5. Discuss the advantages and disadvantages of dictating to a machine rather than to an individual private secretary, a part-time secretary, or to an individual in a stenographic pool.

6. Discuss the advantages and disadvantages of dictating to a machine that you keep in your own office versus dictating to a machine in a word-processing center.

FURTHER READING ◆ 19

Neuner, John J.; Keeling, B. Lewis; and Kallaus, Norman F. *Administrative Office Management.*   6th ed.   Cincinnati: South-Western Publishing Company, 1972.

Place, Irene; Hicks, Charles B.; and Wilkinson, Robin L. *Office Management.*   3d ed.   Boston: Allyn and Bacon, 1971.

Terry, George T. *Office Management and Control.*   7th ed.   Homewood, Ill.: Richard D. Irwin, 1975.

Oral Communication and Management

20

Effective oral communication was discussed in Chapter 5, including communication in interpersonal situations and effective listening. As mentioned in Chapter 5, oral communication, insofar as the amount of time spent is concerned, is far more important in business than is written communication. Business people, however, tend to communicate much better orally than in written form. This difference in ability is true especially of young college graduates.

Most of the aspects of effective communication that have been presented throughout this book apply to both oral and written communication. Precise use of language, a sincere concern for the reader or listener, a thorough knowledge of what you are trying to write or say, self-confidence — all these qualities are necessary for the transmission of the message, regardless of the method. In addition, throughout the course, if you are using this book as a text, you have been given problems, along with practice in written communication, in which you communicated orally to your instructor or to your classmates.

This chapter summarizes some of the aspects of rather formal oral communication in business. Although these kinds of communication experiences will not occur so often as day-to-day interaction with your co-workers, excellent oral presentations to groups display your thinking and ability. Outstanding oral presentations, as well as overall skill in oral communication, can be extremely helpful to your business career.

SPEAKING TO GROUPS

The following passage is taken from a book devoted entirely to oral communication, *Productive Speaking for Business and the Professions,* by James M. Holm.[1]

PUBLIC SPEAKING IS PLANNED
CONVERSATION WITH A GROUP
OF LISTENERS

Let's start by getting rid of any lingering misconceptions. When we talk about public speaking, we are not talking about high-flung arm-waving oratory. We are not interested in bombastic spellbinding on the one hand, nor in the dull reading of a "paper" on the other. We are not thinking about an address which is transferred from the speaker's manuscript to the listener's notes without going through anyone's mind. Nor are we thinking of "the speech" as an imperishable composition, ready to go down in history.

"Public speaking," said Victor Alvin Ketcham, a master teacher of the art, "is dignified, amplified conversation." It is in this sense that we shall consider it.

At what point does conversation stop and public speaking begin? When the size of the group increases from nine to ten? Or from nineteen to twenty? Obviously there is no identifiable point at which we can say, "You are now making a speech." As the crowd grew you may have spoken more loudly, you may have worked harder to invoke understanding in all your listeners, and you may have gestured more actively, but at all times you were conversing with those who attended you.

To be conversational in public speaking, then, means that the speaker has the same attitude in speaking to a group that he would have in talking to one or two friends. He thinks and understands his words as he utters them, fully aware of the idea he is trying to evoke and of the way in which his message is being received. At the moment of delivery he creates or recreates the thought, fully realizing the content of his message as he delivers it.

But public speaking is conversation at its best. This means that the speaker is not satisfied with commonplace ideas or mediocre utterance. His presentation is the finest of which he is capable, both in content and delivery. He avoids carelessness, apathy, slovenliness, and indifference. His conversation is therefore dignified in that it is worthy of both speaker and listener, and the degree of dignity is that which is appropriate to the subject, the place, and the occasion.

Furthermore, the conversation of public speaking is planned. It starts at a definite and prepared beginning, moves through a carefully thought-out development of the message, and ends crisply and with satisfaction to the listeners. This kind of conversation *goes* somewhere because it has been

1. James N. Holm, *Productive Speaking for Business and the Professions* (Boston: Allyn and Bacon, 1967), pp. 311–312. Reprinted by permission of the publisher.

planned that way to evoke a desired response from the listeners. This response can rarely be secured without great care in planning. The speaker who delights listeners by his ability to think on his feet can do so only because he has "thought on his seat" long before he rose to speak.

Finally, this conversation is with a *group* of listeners. It is not directed at a dimly-seen "audience" as a whole, because an audience is not a whole or a unit, but rather a *collection* of people. The listeners hear you individually, and they react individually. True, they sometimes do stimulate one another — when one laughs he arouses laughter in those about him, and when one unconsciously nods his head in agreement he encourages others to agree. But even this is an individual response to the situation as a whole. Therefore the knowledgeable speaker holds his conversation with a group of listening individuals, and to the best of his ability he directs his remarks to those he sees before him as discrete and particular persons.

Holm expresses the you-attitude as it pertains to public speaking in the following paragraphs.[2]

YOUR LISTENERS HAVE RIGHTS;
YOU HAVE OBLIGATIONS

You noted earlier that business and professional people attending conventions look forward to definite benefits from their experience. We also observed that listeners to a good will speech resent a speaker who uses their time to sell something instead of giving them the new ideas and information they were expecting. A crew of workers expects its foreman to have something to say when he calls them together, and many salesmen would be less apathetic about the weekly sales meeting if they could look forward to a productive investment of their time. All listeners, as a matter of fact, invest valuable time in a speaker. For this investment they have a right to expect certain returns. It is your obligation as a speaker to make sure the listener receives useful goods. Your obligation is four-fold.

Listeners Have a Right to a Message
Worth the Time and Effort Invested in
Listening

If you talk to thirty people for twenty minutes, the audience has collectively given you 10 hours of time. And while the value of no speech can be measured purely in dollars and cents, we can reach an approximation of value by supposing that this time represents a full eight-hour day, with two hours of overtime. Multiply this time by the hourly income of your average listener, and you will arrive at a figure which stands for their minimum investment. In addition, many may have traveled a distance to hear you, may have altered the day's schedule at some inconvenience, or otherwise made arrangements to be present. It is your obligation to see that what they hear from you is worthwhile.

Furthermore, these are people with business and professional problems.

2. Holm, pp. 320–323.

They may hope to learn something which will help them make a difficult decision, they may want technical or engineering information, they may need encouragement or hope, or they may simply be wishing for new insights into time-worn topics. At any rate, they look to you with an anticipation you cannot disappoint. Even a sales message must be presented for the benefit of the listener, for if a salesman cannot benefit his customers he should shut up shop. The listener is eager for an idea that will make a difference in his affairs.

Beyond these considerations is the fact that you or your company have something at stake in your talk. Your reputation may be increased or diminished. Future business may depend on the address. The efficiency of production, the safety of a group of workers, the cooperation of other organizations, the success of a new policy, or some other outcome may hinge on your ability to present a worthy message clearly and effectively.

All this means that your first obligation is to have a message for your listeners. You must give them some new ideas or must present a fresh approach to old ideas, for they will have a right to complain if they hear the same old message in the same old words. The audience, as a general rule, is eager to learn from *you;* it is not interested in the second-hand material you have appropriated from somebody else. This is not to say you shouldn't do research on your subject — you should. But the research should be to develop and to round out your own thinking, since the integrity of your message depends on its being essentially your own. This is the only way public address attains its best, and the only way you can give your listeners what they have a right to expect.

Listeners Have a Right to an Orderly
Presentation of Material

Even an important message can become almost repulsive to an audience if it is not presented in a clear and easy-to-follow way. When the listener is forced to submit to a confused jumble of words and ideas, when he would like to understand the speaker but is frustrated by hearing a hodge-podge of unassorted thoughts which do not merge into a clean-cut development of theme, the speaker has failed to meet his second basic obligation.

Your listeners have a right to expect that you will have taken the time and effort to plan what you have to say so they can follow you without trouble. They have a right to expect that you will be able to give them a complete message within the time limits which have been set for your talk, or within a reasonable length of time if no limit has been set. Your obligation, then, consists in so arranging your material, in so planning the order or sequence of your remarks, that your audience will be able to think with you without effort, from a specific conversational opening to an ending which wraps up the speech with satisfaction and completeness. And you are obliged to make certain that you do not overstep the bounds of courtesy and common sense by talking longer than you should.

Listeners Have a Right to Direct
Communication, Sparked with Enthusiasm

Your listeners are not at all unreasonable to insist that you talk *with* them. They have a right to sense that you seek mental and emotional rapport and that you do so because you have a high desire to communicate something of importance. . . . You may want notes at times, and rarely a manuscript, but under no conditions will your audience become a part of the communicative process with you if you are not free from all encumbrance and able to converse with directness.

Furthermore, your audience expects, and you have an obligation, to talk with verve, enthusiasm, and physical animation. This does not mean that you must be a table-thumping rabble-rouser, but that you must be alive with the excitement of your message and the opportunity to do something for the audience. . . .

Listeners Have a Right to Material Which
Is Specific and Factual and Therefore
Interesting

Unless your audience is captive, it will walk out on you if you insist on talking in generalities and abstractions. And if it is captive, it may sit before you but won't listen. It will go to sleep — and audiences can easily sleep with eyes wide open! You will have to pin your ideas down with illustrations, examples, instances, facts, and figures. You will have to express your thinking in specific words — in words which sparkle because they have meaning in the everyday life of the listener.

A quip on a five-cent card reads, "Your argument is sound. All sound." Unless you want the audience to make remarks like this about your speech, you must substitute facts for sound. You cannot interest or impress business and professional audiences with noise and fireworks, but you can do so with specific materials which show that you know what you're talking about and which make sense to the listener. This is your obligation.

If you can give your audiences these four things which they have a right to expect, they will appreciate you as a speaker, and you can reasonably anticipate success in achieving the results you are after. A solid message, clear arrangement of material, enthusiastic delivery, and specific content are the minimum satisfactory requirements. This is not to say that you should not aspire for greater virtues as a speaker, but that you cannot get by with less. The minimum requirements are based on the rights of the listeners.

The following discussion, "Talk to People," is also from Holm's book, *Productive Speaking for Business and the Professions*.[3] He expresses principles that apply to forms of communication, but here they are related particularly to public speaking. The specific principles emphasized are the consideration of the receiver of the message and the importance of a direct, personal, and conversational tone.

Talk to People

Do not make the mistake of talking *at* an audience or *toward* an audience as if it were a mysterious being somehow independent of the individuals who comprise it. True, there is often a social facilitation of response as listeners

3. Holm, p. 44.

affect one another, and you may find it possible to use such interaction to help achieve the response you seek.   However, you are always conversing with individuals who have gathered to hear you, and the focus of your attention should be on those people.   Only in this way will you naturally achieve the unaffected voice of good conversation rather than the stilted tones of some political orators.

Talking with people requires that you see them; your voice is quite likely to follow your gaze.   Therefore, in the pause just before you begin speaking, look to your audience and *see somebody*.   Let your gaze go to others, mentally noting what kinds of people they seem to be and whether they are attentive and ready to hear you.   When both you and they are ready, you may begin.   Start deliberately, as a rule speaking more slowly than normal, so that your opening words will not be lost while the hearers get accustomed to your unique speaking characteristics.   You will quicken your pace as you warm to the occasion.

As you talk, or even during your initial scanning of the audience, locate those on the far fringes of the group.   They are the ones most likely to have difficulty hearing and understanding you, and you must therefore devote special attention to reaching them.   Note if they seem to be getting your message, and adjust your volume and projection as necessary — do not assume that a public address system automatically makes you understandable.   If those along the outer edges can understand you comfortably, your speaking is probably satisfactory.

Your goal should be to speak conversationally with a relaxed voice, even though you will have to use more power than you would over a luncheon table.   If you give the effect of shouting or straining you are not conversational.   And if you speak with tension, your voice will tire easily.   Tension and power are not synonymous, for tension strikes the throat and jaws, while power generates at the abdomen.

ORAL REPORTING

Oral reporting — one of the purposes of speaking to groups — requires much of the same preparation as a written report.   An oral report must be preceded by careful and thorough research and by an objective analysis of the data.   And, as in other types of presentations to groups, you must consider the audience and their probable reaction to your conclusions as you plan the arrangement of the presentation of ideas.

An oral report, like a written one, may begin with the introduction, followed by a discussion of findings, and end with conclusions and recommendations.   The order or arrangement may be reversed, as in written reports, so that conclusions and recommendations are presented first, followed by supporting details.

Many people find oral reporting easier than preparing written reports. For others, however, facing an audience is terrifying. The best way to build confidence in yourself, as well as to make your report convincing and informative, is to know your subject thoroughly and completely, and to take the attitude that your purpose is to inform and to explain, not to impress.

If you are completely familiar with all aspects of the problem, even though you don't know all the answers, and if you sincerely wish to pass this knowledge on to your listeners, you should be able to express your ideas clearly and convincingly.

An advantage of oral communication over written communication is that you have immediate feedback. And you have the use of facial expressions, tone of voice, and gestures to help you make your meaning clear.

Your written report may become the basis of an oral report. The synopsis can be distributed as a basis for an oral presentation. Time should be allowed for questions and comments from the audience.

Audiovisual aids can be of help in an oral presentation of any kind. For example, graphic illustrations such as bar or line charts will express relationships much more quickly and accurately than spoken words. The same advantages that graphic aids bring to written reports apply to oral presentations; in many instances, these aids are even more necessary.

The opaque projector is the simplest and easiest way to project any written or pictorial material. No reproduction of the copy is necessary: the material to be shown is simply inserted into the projector and enlarged on the screen. If there is sufficient distance between the projector and the screen, the copy can be made large enough to be easily seen by all persons in a large group.

An overhead projector can also be used for displaying charts and other materials. The use of this type of projector, however, requires that a transparency be made from the original copy. Many photocopy machines, readily available in most offices, can in a few minutes make a transparency. Transparencies can also be prepared in color. Regular size typewriting, however, when transferred to a screen by an overhead projector, is too small to be easily read by all persons in a large room. The use of visual aids that cannot be easily seen is worse than using none at all.

Duplicated handouts also serve as a form of visual aid. Some speakers believe, though, that the use of such material distracts from the immediate proceedings and becomes a form of noise. Avoid distributing several pages at one time, some of which do not apply to what is being discussed at the moment. Members of the audience, instead of listening to the speaker or participating in the discussion, may spend their time reading the handouts. Such a distraction is often the reason that someone asks a question that has been answered only a few moments previously.

Oral reporting takes place at gatherings described as conferences, meetings, or committee meetings. Oral reporting may also consist of reporting to only one person. In fact, this we do every day, if only in response to a question from a supervisor or co-worker about the progress of our work.

PLANNING AND CONDUCTING MEETINGS AND CONFERENCES

The terms "conference" and "meeting" are often used interchangeably in business situations. And, if persons are to confer, they must meet together, although this meeting can be through the use of conference telephones or closed-circuit television.

The word conference is also used to mean a convention, as well as an interview, as in "I had a conference with the President." Usually the word conference — as distinguished from meeting — in business situations implies that the group as a whole is thinking together as a team, often working to solve a problem or problems. Thus many committee meetings could be described as conferences. Ideally, every person is an active participant throughout the entire conference:

> Although the conference is usually under the guidance of a competent leader, his function is not that of a master of ceremonies directing a program of arranged speeches. He can be thought of rather as a catalyst, in that he does not enter into the substance of a group reaction but is the prime means of effecting it.[4]

A conference, provided that it is sincerely for the purpose of management's obtaining the ideas of all participants, can be a way of implementing the philosophy of listening, of allowing employees to be heard. Active participation in decision making builds and strengthens positive relationships among employees and between employees and management, increases productivity and efficiency, and releases creative thinking.

Employees want to be heard, to be recognized as valuable members of the organization for which they work. Members of an organization have a right to participate in decision making because they are vitally affected by these decisions. The need to participate, to be heard, seems to be one of the basic human drives. In addition, all members of an organization can profit by obtaining the use of the ideas and creative ability of all other members.

4. Holm, pp. 262–263.

James Holm has this to say on this subject:[5]

Participation through conferences can offer a number of benefits to an organization.

1. It can improve morale in the group by satisfying the basic want to belong.
2. It can result in better decisions by drawing on the knowledge and experience of many, thus helping to avoid unwise judgment.
3. It can provide a communication medium by bringing into face-to-face relationship a group of people who must share information and ideas.
4. It can help to improve or modify the attitudes of participants as they gain insight into the attitudes and viewpoints of others.
5. It can help develop a more willing acceptance of change, the members having a sense of participation in the process of change.

Conferences are not an unmixed blessing, however, as anyone knows after sitting through a number of them, for as one businessman remarked in disgust, "You sit, and talk, and adjourn." Indeed, waste of time and slowness of decision often constitute good reasons for avoiding conferences. There are, though, other disadvantages even more considerable. One of these is the fact that because a group's judgment must be bland enough to be acceptable to everyone, a group decision will sometimes not be as good as one man alone could make. When the decision must please everyone it is often one which displeases no one and therefore it may be timid and inconclusive.

There are times, too, when a committee is given the responsibility for a decision only because no individual is willing to accept that responsibility or because the person who should make a decision is afraid. When responsibility is divided, no person feels fully accountable.

The conference method may in itself limit its own usefulness, for it is essentially a democratic procedure and therefore incongruent with the authoritarian structure of many organizations. Furthermore, some subjects and some decisions do not lend themselves to judgment by discussion, being more suitable to objective inquiry, measurement, or executive determination.

As we have seen before in various communication situations, aspects of different types of communication are quite similar. For example, an oral report is planned much like the written report, and an effective and pleasant conversation about business matters is similar to that of social and personal encounters. The same knowledges, skills, understandings, and techniques apply to most communication problems and situations, regardless of their purpose, provided sufficient and correct adaptations are made according to the material, the communicator, and the receiver of the message.

5. Holm, pp. 264–265.

Planning and participating in a conference or meeting, as described by James Holm, consists essentially of the same steps that you followed in planning a research study.[6]

The Conference Structure Follows the
Stages of Reflective Thinking

We have already noted that the process of creative thinking can be organized into a series of steps and it is the sequence of these steps which provides the structure of a conference. Ordinarily the conferees begin with the first step and arrive at an agreement on it, after which they go on to the next step, and so on. In practice, however, the steps are likely to overlap, and the conferees may find it necessary to retrace their path, returning to a step presumably settled earlier. There are digressions, too, as one or more men allow the talk to wander into by-paths. Yet the fundamental sequence remains, and provides the basic structure necessary to coordinate the thinking of all. We shall consider it as a series of six steps.

1. *What Is the Problem?* A conference gets off to a strong start only when the problem itself is clearly defined and understood. Some people even prefer to call the conference a "problem-stating, problem-solving" meeting, to emphasize the importance of knowing unmistakeably the character and dimensions of the difficulty before seeking a solution or decision.

Under normal conditions it is undoubtedly preferable to name the problem at the very outset, using a declarative statement to express the difficulty. A common practice, and one which can lead to poor thinking, is to begin by expressing the subject of the conference in the form of a question. The question opening tends to direct the conferees immediately into a consideration of solutions, causing them to neglect a thorough analysis of the problem itself, whereas a declarative statement invites appraisal and analysis before solution. Thus it would be better to start a conference with the statement, "Too many employees are jumping the clock at quitting time," than with the question, "How can we reduce clock jumping among our employees?" The following list illustrates typical problem-statements:

• The men in the shop are not utilizing waste materials.

• Rest room privileges are being abused.

• Trucks are forced to wait too long before unloading at our docks.

• Our customers are complaining about the high cost of service calls.

• Material on bulletin boards is not being read.

• Down-time on machines in Plant X is increasing.

• Noise in the building is distracting.

The simple declarative statement, however, is generally not more than a good beginning, for it is usually necessary to come to grips more fully with the problem. To do this the participants may find it helpful to size the difficulty up by objective measurement, to search for answers to such analytical questions as *Where? What? How? Who? When?*, or to inquire into the location, nature, extent, and significance of the problem. To return

6. Holm, pp. 274–278.

to the clock jumping problem, it would be useful to be more specific by at least determining that employees in the finishing department are losing an average of ten minutes a day by stopping work before the end of the shift, totalling a man-hour loss of sixty hours per month.

Good team-work in thinking, then, begins when all the members of a conference recognize that the problem to be solved affects each of them, when they can reach a common understanding of it, and when each sees that he will benefit in some way by helping find the best solution.

2. What Are the Causes of the Problem? The second step attempts to answer the question Why? There are times when the solution will be found by isolating and overcoming the significant causes of the difficulty, and even when the causes themselves cannot be overcome, knowing them will add insight to the deliberation. Ideally, all major causes should be listed, appraised, and agreed upon by the conferees.

Continuing with the clock jumping problem, we might find such items as these listed among the causes:

- Time card racks contain so many cards that men quit early to avoid standing in line.
- Time card racks are at a distance from work locations, so men get started toward them early to avoid waiting past the quitting time.
- Cards are printed in small type, making men look carefully for the right card; this takes time.
- Men avoid starting a new piece of work when they know the job will run past the quitting time.

3. What Are the Standards of a Desirable Solution? This third step may not always be necessary, but it is more frequently useful than not, and is apt to be overlooked. If the group can agree at this point on the criteria or specifications of the solution for which they are looking, they may eliminate later conflict when appraising the solutions themselves. For instance, if they can agree whether the solution must cost not more than a given amount, they have a handy measure for judging the desirability of solutions. Or if they decide whether the solution should have an immediate or a long-range effect, they are similarly in a better position to judge. . . .

A quality decision which is not acceptable to a number of people may be ineffective, whereas a decision of lesser quality but of greater acceptability may be quite effective. These two dimensions may not be mutually inconsistent in every case, but they are worthy of consideration as important guides to a productive solution.

4. What Are the Possible Solutions? In the fourth step, the conference becomes more creative, turning to the search for ways of solving the problem. This is the point at which a permissive climate is especially desirable. No potential solution should be overlooked because some member was unwilling to suggest it, being apprehensive about the consequences of his contribution.

There are two ways of proceeding at this juncture. One is to list in rapid succession as many potential solutions as can be thought of, with no attempt being made to evaluate or appraise each as it is suggested. This procedure divorces the creative from the judicial process, and is thought by some to be more productive.   The other is to weigh and evaluate each solution as it comes up, in effect combining this step with what is next listed as the fifth. Either way can be effective.

We should note that while I have been using the term "solution" throughout this section, either "policy" or "decision" could be equally applicable, since we are examining the conference as a way of solving problems, creating policy, or making group decisions.   The distinction lies only in the character of the outcome and not in the process by which it is produced.

Returning to the sample problem of clock jumping, we might list the following as potential solution:

- Eliminate the use of time cards altogether; make the foreman responsible for recording the presence of each worker, and assume that all work a full shift.
- Have new time cards printed, using large, easily-read numbers.
- Decentralize time-card racks and use smaller ones.
- Pay workers by piece-rates instead of hourly rates.
- Have foreman issue time-cards to workers just before the end of the shift, eliminating the need to search the rack.

Assuming that steps four and five have not been combined, the conference would then take up its judicial function.

5. *Which Is the Preferable Solution?*   If the standards of a desirable solution have been established, this step becomes a matter of measuring each suggested solution against those standards and choosing the one which best matches.   If, however, no standards have been determined, the judicial process becomes a matter of assessing the several solutions in general, comparing them, and using whatever evidence can be secured to predict the productivity of each.   During this process issues may emerge which must be deliberated by the conferees in order to arrive at the final decision.

The decision itself may be by consensus or by majority vote.   The former, involving a unanimous agreement among the conferees, is the more desirable method, especially if the degree of acceptability is a measure of the desired outcome.   Consensus is frequently more possible than commonly supposed, especially if the group is not under pressure to reach a decision.   Voting, the usual democratic procedure, is always an effective way of deciding, but it may leave an unsatisfied minority.   Decision by negotiation or compromise is always possible in strongly divided groups.

6. *What Shall Be Done with the Solution?*   A group may not have finished its work by having arrived at a solution, for often there remains the task of putting that solution to work.   Should the decision be reported?   If so, to whom and under what conditions?   Should the group take steps of its own to implement the solution?   How far does the group responsibility go?   If steps of implementation should be taken, what should be done, and who should make the effort?   These questions suggest the final actions possible if the work of the conference is to bear fruit.

While the foregoing six steps can form the working structure of any conference, it would be a mistake to assume that a group will, in any one meeting, invariably follow this precise pattern.   Many times the steps will form the pattern for a series of meetings, at each of which only parts of the structure will appear.   At other times a group will take up a number of problems in order, repeating the pattern, or parts of it, for each item of business.   There will be occasions, too, when for a variety of reasons, it is necessary to employ only certain of the steps.   In short, the conference structure for creative thinking is a tool to be used appropriately in the service of the group.   When it becomes a master, followed slavishly and mechanically, the vital spirit of inquiry and cooperation is notably missing.

Meetings that cannot be described as conferences in that all listeners do not have a chance to participate also require capable leadership and adequate planning.   The ultimate success or failure of any meeting or conference rests on the extent to which it has been planned — more so than upon any other factor.   Preparation must be made in several major areas, including the choice of persons who will attend; speakers, if any; the room; sound or visual equipment; other physical facilities; and the program or agenda.

An agenda is a plan of the flow of business or discussion.   The person planning the agenda can use the standard *Robert's Rules of Order* format, but it is usually best to use this format as a starting point from which to create an agenda tailored to the individual organization and to the type of meeting or conference.   Although many organizational meetings and conferences do not follow the strict parliamentary procedure presented in *Robert's Rules of Order,* some semblance of order and formality must be maintained to avoid wasting time and to ensure that all matters that need to be discussed by the group will receive recognition.

The leader of the group writes the agenda, as he or she is most familiar with all the concerns and issues of the group.   The leader must make a value judgment as to the relative importance of the various items and place these items on the agenda in order from the most important to the least important.   People's minds are fresh at the beginning of the meeting, and ordinarily important items should be considered first.   In addition, the leader should attempt to allocate the length of time to be spent in discussing each item.   If no time limit is imposed, many group members will continue talking endlessly so that some items on the agenda do not receive proper consideration.

Once the agenda has been formalized by the leader, it should be made available to all members of the group several days before the time of the meeting or conference.   In this way the members of the group will know the topics to be discussed and can come prepared to present ideas.   Many organizations include all material that will be covered at the meeting, such as budgets or lengthy reports, with the mailing of the agenda.   This procedure provides members with time to consider material and to make decisions.

Another area of concern is in considering the persons who will attend. The leader must ensure that persons attending the meeting will be prepared to bring up points and make motions.   If the leader isolates himself or herself from the members of the organization to the extent that no one knows what is going on, a dull and unproductive meeting is likely to follow.

The two main tasks of the chairperson, once the conference is underway, are dealing with the subject and dealing with the persons in attendance. All members must understand each issue and why they are discussing it. The leader has the responsibility to prevent misunderstanding and confusion. Group discussions should be encouraged in order to work out conflicts and to clarify goals. Perhaps one of the most common faults of a conference leader is failure to terminate the discussion early enough.

At the end of the discussion of each agenda item, the chairperson should give a brief and clear summary of what has been agreed upon. The chairperson can control the direction of the meeting by bringing opposing points of view out into the open where they can be discussed and pooled toward group agreement. Meetings and conferences, like other business endeavors, are only as successful and effective as the persons who plan and conduct them. These leaders must be efficient communicators.

SUMMARY ◆ 20

To be conversational in public speaking, the speaker takes the same attitude in speaking to a group as when talking to one or two friends. Public speaking is conversation at its best.

Listeners have a right to a message worth their time and effort; to an orderly presentation of material; to direct, enthusiastic communication; to specific, factual, and interesting material.

A public speaker should talk to people, not at or toward an audience.

Oral reporting requires much of the same preparation as written reports. The speaker who gives an effective oral report is knowledgeable about the subject, confident, and considerate of the audience. Audiovisual aids can be of help in oral reporting.

Meetings and conferences must be carefully planned. They can improve morale and encourage employee participation and creative thinking.

QUESTIONS AND PROBLEMS ◆ 20

1. Give an oral report to the class based on the formal analytical report you prepared as an assignment for Chapters 15 through 18. Adhere strictly to

your allotted time as assigned by your instructor or as agreed upon by you and your classmates. If appropriate and practical, use audiovisual aids to illustrate and emphasize. Allow time for questions from your audience.

2. Prepare an outline of a speech on a subject with which you are thoroughly familiar.

3. Prepare a short talk to be presented to your classmates. Plan the time according to your instructor's specifications as to the amount of time available. Choose some subject that is related to communication but preferably one that is not discussed in this book. For example, discuss the use of visual aids in oral presentations, perhaps limiting your talk to the use of one particular kind of visual aid. Other possible suggestions include recent developments in technology that speed the process of transcription; the choice of a voice-writing machine; differences between language usage in Great Britain and America; regional differences in pronunciation or word usage.

All these topics are broad enough for long presentations. If you attempt to cover them in a short talk, you will of necessity be giving a broad overview. Or perhaps you can limit your topic to some particular aspect of these subjects, for example, a few examples of extraordinary word usage in the Ozarks, or from any other section of the country that you know well. In addition to these suggested topics in communications, you can think of many more.

4. Tape record a speaker on television or on the radio. Evaluate the performance according to principles presented in this chapter.

5. Members of the class are to form into four- to six-person groups. Assume that the members make up a panel on a convention program. Each group is to select a topic similar to the one described in Problem 3. One member of the panel is to act as both chairperson and master of ceremonies. On the day of the class presentation, each member is to be allowed a specified time, according to the total time available, in which to present a report on one aspect of the overall subject. The chairperson is to introduce the panel members to the class before they make their presentations. After all presentations have been made, allow time for questions from the audience, which may be directed to any member of the panel.

FURTHER READING ◆ 20

Holm, James N. *Productive Speaking for Business and the Professions*. Boston: Allyn and Bacon, 1967.

Huseman, Richard C.; Lahiff, James M.; and Hatfield, John D. *Interpersonal Communication in Organizations*. Boston: Holbrook Press, 1976.

Huseman, Richard C.; Logue, Cal M.; and Freshley, Dwight L., eds. *Readings in Interpersonal and Organizational Communication*. 3d ed. Boston: Holbrook Press, 1969.

Keltner, John W. *Group Discussion Processes*. Rev. ed. New York: Longmans Green and Company, 1974.

Lee, Irving J. *How to Talk With People*. New York: Harper and Row, 1952.

Loney, Glenn M. *Briefing and Conference Techniques*. New York: McGraw-Hill Book Company, 1959.

Maier, Norman R. F. *Problem-Solving Discussions and Conferences*. New York: McGraw-Hill Book Company, 1963.

Markley, Kenneth A. *Our Speaker This Evening*. Grand Rapids, Mich.: Zondervan Publishing Company, 1974.

Morgan, John S. *Practical Guide to Conference Leadership*. New York: McGraw-Hill Book Company, 1966.

Shaw, Marvin, *Group Dynamics: The Psychology of Small Group Behavior*. New York: McGraw-Hill Book Company, 1971.

Snell, Frank. *How to Hold a Better Meeting*. New York: Harper & Row, 1974.

Wilcox, Roger P. *Oral Reporting in Business and Industry*. Englewood Cliffs, N.J.: Prentice-Hall, 1967.

Wilson, John F., and Arnold, Carroll C. *Public Speaking as a Liberal Art*. Boston: Allyn and Bacon, 1974.

A Summary of the Characteristics and Concepts of Effective Business Communication

Good writing or oral communication does not consist of one quality but of several qualities woven together. Writing or speaking cannot be completely effective if it is weak in any area, regardless of how strong it is in other areas. For example, a letter can be carefully planned and written with the reader in mind, using the positive approach, and still be less than effective if the writer does not know the principles of sentence construction or of correct language usage. On the other hand, correct language alone is far from enough.

This appendix is planned to be used as a partial glossary or for quick review. It is also useful as an overview of the basic techniques of communication. The terms used here are not exclusive in meaning, and some are very similar; for example, *courteous* and *considerate*. *Considerate* is the broader term, however, and *courteous* has more to do with phrasing, such as "thank you" and "please." We cannot really be considerate, though, without being courteous. *Readable* and *clear* are also approximately the same in meaning.

Appropriate in Tone and Approach

Communication differs in tone and approach according to the message, the listeners or readers, and the occasion.

Attractive in Appearance

Your business messages should be neatly typewritten and arranged attractively on the sheet. The typewriter keys must be clean. An electric typewriter and a carbon or nylon ribbon are best.   Choose an appropriate letter style and use the customary and accepted placement of parts of the letter.   Choose an attractive letterhead printed on good quality paper. Keep the paper free of smudges.   Fold the sheet neatly.

Businesslike

The term *businesslike* does not mean that the letter or other message is written in any specialized or particular language.   Good business language is the same kind that is correctly used in other aspects of life.   You are not being businesslike but rather old fashioned if you use such jargon as this: "Please find enclosed," or "With best wishes I remain."   On the other hand, your writing can go too far in the way of informality and casualness. It should not have an overly familiar tone but be polite and matter-of-fact, much as you would address associates in your office.

Clear

Business writing must be immediately clear.   Clearness is discussed in this book under the topic of *readability*.   Good sentence construction, the wise choice of words, and careful planning of the message as a whole are aids to clear writing.   Clear thinking must precede clear writing; if the writer does not know exactly what he or she wants to say, and forgets to keep the reader in mind, the message will be far from effective.

Coherent

Sentences and paragraphs should "hang together"; that is, the thought should flow naturally and freely from the beginning of the message to the end.   If a message is well organized and contains well-chosen words, it will be coherent.

Courteous

All business communication should be courteous.   Always take time to say "please" and "thank you."   Good manners will never go out of style.

Considerate

Consideration goes one step further than courtesy.   The terms are not exactly synonymous.   Courtesy has more to do with phrasing and word choice; it can be compared to a smile.   Consideration is a broader term and includes what you actually say in your message or your solution to the particular business problem.   Consideration is simply another name for one aspect of the you-attitude, which is mentioned below and discussed throughout the book.   Consideration is also similar in meaning to empathy; that is, looking at a situation through the reader's eyes.

Complete

The message must be complete in that it answers fully all the reader's questions and gives all the needed or desired information.   It must also include the necessary and appropriate psychological appeal and the goodwill approach.

Concise

Conciseness means that a message is no longer than it needs to be in order to accomplish its purpose.   Conciseness is not necessarily brevity.   A ten-page letter could be concise if every word is needed to convey the desired information, to be courteous, or to be convincing.   A writer should not work so hard for conciseness that the message lacks completeness or courtesy.

Constructive

Constructive writing is positive and pleasant.

Correct

A message should be correct in information given, in the form and approach chosen, and in English usage.   Being grammatically correct in every detail, as important as this feature is, is not enough for good business writing.   The letter that gives the wrong date or price causes more havoc than the misspelled word.

Cheerful

Not all business letters can bubble with happiness, but they should be cheerful from the standpoint that they are optimistic and stress the pleasant aspects of the situation rather than the unpleasant.   This writing style is discussed under the *positive approach*.

Conversational

A simple, natural writing style is similar to simple, natural conversation. You should not write exactly as you talk unless you are an unusually good conversationalist.   In writing we have the advantage of planning our words and of seeing them on paper.   Often revision is desirable.   We can thus make our writing better than our oral conversation, and we should try to do so.   The term *conversational* is used and emphasized because some business writers feel that their message must be formal and read like a textbook.   Others feel that good business writing must include such phrases as "This is to inform you," "We kindly thank you for," and other expressions they would not think of using in conversation.   Good writing is natural and usually informal.

Creative

Business writing is not generally referred to as "creative writing," a term most often used to describe novels, poetry, short stories, and, perhaps, some advertising copy.   All of our work, however, is creative, if we have put our best into it, if we have looked at the situation and tried to solve it in the best possible way, not necessarily in the way it has always been solved before.   Also, there is a place in business writing for the creative use of words and ideas, particularly in sales writing and in advertising.

Convincing and Effective

Convincing writing is sometimes described as persuasive writing, or bringing the reader to agree with us.   A sales letter must sell the product if it is to be effective; a collection letter must collect; an application letter must obtain an interview.   The best way to convince readers is to show them how they will benefit by buying the product, by paying the debt, or by granting the interview.

Emphatic

Emphasis should be used to call attention to the most important parts of the message or, at times, to emphasize the pleasant and to de-emphasize the unpleasant.   Emphasis is attained or can be attained by the proper use of position, space, word choice, and sentence construction.   Another method is by the use of the typewriter in underlining, writing in all capitals, indenting, or arranging in some attention-getting way.

Ethical

Business communication should be honest and sincere. It should be based on a sincere interest in the reader's well-being, as well as upon a loyalty to the employing company.

Forceful

Good writing is not forceful from the standpoint that it is dictatorial or demanding. It is forceful in that it is strong and vivid, written mostly in the active voice. Forceful writing is usually concise, for it is not weighted down with unnecessary, wordy phrases. Because it moves, it is likely to have good sentence construction. Forceful writing is also emphatic writing, and it is likely to be convincing.

Goodwill Building

Goodwill is one of the most valuable assets that a company can have, for without goodwill it cannot long exist and profit. The use of all these other attributes of effective communication will build goodwill. Some letters are written only for the purpose of building goodwill. An example is a Christmas greeting or a letter of congratulations. If this greeting or congratulations is not sincere — if the writer doesn't honestly care — then the messages violate another principle of good writing. For real goodwill, a company and its employees must *feel* goodwill toward its customers, instead of being motivated only by the profit motive.

Honest

This book is based on the premise that honesty is the most necessary quality of communication.

Interesting

Business messages will be interesting if they answer the readers' questions or show how your merchandise will meet their needs, provided that the writing is clear and concise. In some letters — especially sales or some collection letters — anecdotes, quotations, or jokes may be used with discretion. In most business writing, though, these are unnecessary or even undesirable.

Objective

Business writing should be objective, or nonbiased, in that it is based upon facts, not upon the writer's particular beliefs or prejudices. Objective writing is especially stressed in report writing, but it is important in all forms of communication. In reports, when opinions are stated, they should be clearly identified as opinion.

Original

Not every business letter can be completely different from every other business letter, for often the situations are the same or similar. They should be original, though, in that they are written in the writer's own words, not copied from some manual or handbook. Form letters are widely used in business, and they must be used for economy; but the letter from which the duplicate copies are made must be original and especially well written, since it goes to many readers.

Positive and Pleasant

The positive approach accents the pleasant aspects of a situation, not the unpleasant. It tells what can be done, not what cannot be done. Negative words such as "fail," "criticize," and "reject" are minimized, if not completely eliminated. Other terms used in this book that are similar to the positive approach or contribute to the positive approach are *cheerful, considerate, constructive,* and *conversational.* The several methods of emphasis and subordination can be used to construct the message in a positive, pleasant, and diplomatic way.

Planned and Organized for the Proper Psychological Appeal

Business messages may contain good news, bad news, or routine matter-of-fact news. They may ask a favor that may make a routine request that is likely to be granted. Letters and other messages should be arranged in different ways according to these differing situations. A good-news letter, which is also referred to as a "Yes" letter, should ordinarily begin with the good news and then follow with details or any other necessary information. Ordinarily, bad news should not be included in the beginning of a letter or memorandum, but necessary explanation should be given first.

If a request is likely to be refused, this request usually should be delayed until the writer has convinced the reader that the request is worthwhile and should be granted.   In a routine letter in which the request is likely to be granted, a good opening for the business message is the request itself so that the reader will know immediately what the letter is about.

These two basic plans are referred to as the direct, which gives the gist of the message first, and the indirect, which delays the most important part of the message.   Other names for the direct are the *deductive* and the *psychological*.   Other names for the indirect are the *inductive* and the *logical*.

Professional

A writer makes his work professional by his continuing study of the use of the English language, of business psychology, and of the art and skill of writing.

Persuasive

Persuasive writing is convincing and effective.

Readable

Readability is used to mean immediate clearness.   Readability is influenced by sentence and paragraph length, by word length and word choice, by the arrangement of the writing as a whole, by transitions, and by coherence so that the thought flows naturally from the beginning to the end.   The typewritten arrangement also affects readability.   Indentions, plenty of white space, listings and tabulations, and the use of underlining make writing easier to read.

The Service-Attitude or the Reader-Attitude

The *service-attitude* and the *reader-attitude* are other terms for the *you-attitude*.   Opposite terms are the *company-attitude,* the *writer-attitude,* and the *I-attitude*.

Sincere and Truthful

These concepts are discussed under the terms *ethical* and *honest*.

Specific

Specific writing is the opposite of vague, general writing. It is concrete, not abstract or general. Specific writing is more forceful and vivid than general, abstract writing. Specific writing is usually the better choice; however, at times, in order to be tactful and courteous, we cannot be completely specific. Sometimes the general term is to be preferred to the more specific term. This statement does not in any way mean that the message is less than sincere. It is merely making use of the positive approach.

Success Oriented

This term can also be referred to as the *yes-approach*. It is the opposite of what is referred to as the *doubtful tone*. The yes-approach is an aspect of the overall *positive-approach* in that it implies that the answer or action will be a favorable one. An example of the yes-approach versus the doubtful tone is this: "If you want to buy our product" includes the doubt that the reader may not want to buy the product. A sentence that is more *success oriented* reads like this: "To receive this valuable painting, just return the enclosed card." This implies that the reader will want to buy the product and does not suggest doubt.

Tactful

Tactlessness does not always occur because the writer is discourteous or inconsiderate. It is most likely to occur because of carelessness in wording or phrasing so that the reader gets a message other than the one intended. Real courtesy and consideration combined with careful writing should make all your messages tactful.

You-Approach

The you-approach is *empathy* — looking at the situation from the standpoint of the reader or the listener.

APPENDIX

B

The Appearance and Format of Business Letters

The overall appearance and the format of the letter affect the reception of the intended message. If the reader's attention is drawn to obvious erasures, poor centering, or a most unusual letter arrangement, rather than to the words themselves, the intended meaning is delayed or perhaps incomplete.

An even greater disadvantage of an unattractive letter is that it shows lack of consideration for the reader, as if the writer did not care enough to make sure that the letter was sent out in perfectly typewritten, well-arranged form.

An unattractive letter reflects adversely upon the business policies of the company from which the letter comes. It may cause the reader to wonder whether such sloppy practices are applied to other company activities.

PLANNING FOR AN ATTRACTIVE APPEARANCE

The first requirement for attractive letters is a good typist who does not make a great many errors and who can neatly correct the few errors that do occur. An acceptable correction is one that is not noticeable without direct scrutiny; if it can be seen immediately, it is not good enough. Poor corrections are often due to the pressure of time or to poor quality paper. The choice of an eraser or other correction aids will affect the speed and neatness with which the typist makes corrections.

The good secretary will keep in mind the importance of attractive letters and send out very few that could be considered less than perfect in appearance. However, the person who dictates or assigns the letter is not free from responsibility for appearance and format, but has final responsibility for all aspects of the letter.

In addition to stenographic skills, the equipment and materials used in a business office affect the appearance of the finished correspondence. Good quality paper is essential. Buying paper of less than excellent quality is false economy. Although top quality paper has a higher initial cost than inferior paper, it actually costs less in the long run because it can be erased more quickly and neatly, thus saving the most expensive element of a letter, the secretary's time. Regardless of the time spent, poor paper will never result in a really attractive letter.

The 20-pound paper is the one most used in business offices. The "20-pound" refers to the weight of four reams. The paper comes from the mill in a sheet four times as large as the regular sheet, which is 8½ by 11 inches. This large sheet is cut into fourths before it reaches the office supply store. The weight of this large sheet, multiplied by 500 sheets in a ream, determines the weight of the paper.

Other weights most likely to be found are the 16-pound and the 24-pound. The 16-pound is sometimes chosen in order to save postage, especially if many of a firm's mailings consist of several pages. Unless this factor is a consideration, the 20-pound paper is preferable for ordinary use. The 24-pound is chosen for some offices by persons who believe that it gives the finest appearance of all. Disadvantages of this heavier weight are that it is more difficult to fold and may require additional postage.

In addition to weight, paper is classified by the materials that make up its content. Good quality paper will contain at least some cotton fiber, which is sometimes described as "rag" content. Most papers are not made completely of fiber, but consist partly of wood pulp, which is also known as sulphite. It is not necessarily true that the higher the rag content the better the paper, for, as in most other materials, several factors enter into the quality of the finished product. Paper made entirely of sulphite or wood pulp is not usually the best choice for a business office.

The color of the paper should be considered when planning for the best appearance. White is by far the most popular color, as it has always been; but colored papers are being used to some extent, especially by specialized shops or departments. Any choice other than white should be thoroughly considered and tried on a small scale before being purchased for general office use. Colors have different emotional appeals. In addition, some colored papers may cause eyestrain. If possible, some expert in this field should be consulted before colored paper is adopted for general use.

Color is often used in the printing of the letterhead, although the traditional black is still the most popular, as well as being most conservative. The type of company and the impression (or image) that the company wishes to convey should be considered when choosing the letterhead. The ultraconservative organization would not choose brilliant colors or an unusual, flashy arrangement.

Color and decoration can be overused in the letterhead of any organization. In addition to an appearance that may seem garish, an unusual letterhead can be distracting in that the reader's attention is directed away from the message itself. Simplicity is the key in designing appropriate, effective letterheads, provided all needed information is included.

Information that should be shown on every letterhead is as follows:

1. The company name. The organization should always use the same method of presenting its name, wherever it is used. In some instances the company name, presented in a certain way, is its trademark, or part of the trademark.
2. Information about the product or services of the company, if this information is not apparent in the name of the organization. For example, if the company name is Smith's Hardware, no further mention that the company sells hardware is necessary. If Smith's Hardware is a wholesale supplier, however, this fact should be included on the letterhead, or perhaps the company name should be lengthened to include this information.
3. The complete address.
4. The telephone number.

The letterhead should take up no more than two inches at the top of the paper. A deeper letterhead will decrease the amount of space left for the typewritten message, causing some letters that could ordinarily be fitted on one page to require two pages. A two-page letter is more time consuming to type, to fold, to mail, and to read than is a one-page letter, provided the one-page letter is not crowded on the sheet. An unusually wide letterhead also interferes with the centering plan the typist ordinarily uses.

The typewriter and the typewriter ribbon affect the appearance of the finished letter. An electric typewriter is preferable, for several reasons, to a manual. In addition to the ease of operation and the added speed, an electric typewriter produces a better-looking letter than does the manual because of the evenness of touch.

The carbon or plastic film ribbon that turns through the typewriter and is used only once gives the best possible appearance because it cannot become worn or dim. If the typewriter is not equipped for a carbon or film ribbon, ribbons made of nylon or polyester are preferable to all-cotton ones. Cotton ribbons blur and quickly lose their ink.

The keys of the typewriter should always be kept completely clean.

Letters should be attractively arranged on the sheet with adequate top, bottom, and side margins. A well-centered letter is described as looking like a picture in a frame. Although the "long-line" length can be used for all letters (this method of centering is called the "standard-line" arrangement), the method described as the "picture-frame" arrangement ordinarily gives the best appearance. In the picture-frame arrangement, three line lengths are used according to the length of the letter.

Letters are classified as being short, average, or long, and a typist soon learns to estimate rather exactly the length of the letter to be arranged. The table below summarizes the centering plan to be used for the three lengths of letters, using the picture-frame arrangement. (In the standard-line arrangement, all letters are typewritten with the margins set for the six-inch line. Adjustments are made for letters varying in length by the amount of space left between the date and the inside address, or by other adjustments.)

Picture-Frame Centering Plan for Short, Medium, and Long Letters

1. Set margins according to the following plan:

Letter Length	Line Length in Inches	Line Length In Spaces
Short (fewer than 100 words)	4	40, pica; 50, elite
Medium (100–200 words)	5	50, pica; 60, elite
Long (over 200 words)	6	60, pica; 70, elite

2. Begin date on the fifteenth line from the top of the page or two spaces below the letterhead.

3. Leave three to eight blank line spaces between the date and the inside address. Use your judgment here. A very short letter of fifty words or so will need about eight lines between the date and the inside address, even if you are using the four-inch line length.

In summary, an attractive appearance of business communications is necessary in order to project an efficient, considerate, businesslike company image. Attractive appearance is achieved by:

- an accurate, conscientious typist;
- the wise choice of equipment and supplies;
- good quality paper;
- an appropriate, well-designed letterhead.

CHOOSING THE MOST APPROPRIATE AND
EFFICIENT LETTER STYLE

The choice of a letter style is important from the standpoints of appearance and efficiency. Differing letter styles convey different impressions of the company, or various company "images."

For example, the simplified letter is considered to be the most progressive and modern. If this style is used, it is likely to be chosen by a company that regards itself as young, at least in spirit, and always willing to change to meet changing conditions. The most traditional, conservative style is the indented. This old arrangement is still used by a few companies, but it is too time consuming to be a wise choice, for regular use, by any company of any kind.

The choice of a letter style may be left to the individual business writer, who may in turn delegate this responsibility to the secretary. In other instances, particular departments or offices of a company have a selected arrangement to be used throughout the departments or offices. Some companies pick a particular letter style to be used throughout the entire business organization.

The *indented style* is very seldom used in the United States, although it is still widely used in some foreign countries. For many years this especially time-consuming style was considered to be the only way to arrange a business letter. Look at the illustration of the indented letter (Figure B–1) and notice how time can be wasted by using this style.

The *semiblock* letter (see Figure B–2) was probably the second arrangement to become widely used, for it differs least from the indented style. This form eliminates the most time-consuming elements of the indented letter — the indented lines of the inside address and the closing section. Although paragraphs are still indented, these indentions take much less time than that needed for the indented letter style.

The semiblock letter is considered conservative, but businesslike. In the semiblock letter, as in the modified block, the date may be backspaced from the right margin point; it may be centered; or it may begin at the center. The most time-saving way to set up the date and closing lines is to begin them at the center.

Although not shown in the letter illustrated, special parts, such as the attention line, the subject line, and an enclosure notation, can be used in the semiblock style, as well as in all other letter arrangements. (See the section titled "Arranging the Usual and Special Parts of a Business Letter" in this appendix.)

The *modified-block* letter shown in Figure B–3 is a step further in the elimination of indentions in that paragraphs are not indented.

The *full-block letter* (see Figure B–4) is a continuation of the trend toward modernization and decreasing any unnecessary time spent in typ-

MEMPHIS STATE UNIVERSITY
MEMPHIS, TENNESSEE 38152

Office Administration Department

February 18, 1979

Mrs. Betty Claiborne, Office Manager
    Swallows Insurance Company
        5983 Maplewood Cove
            Memphis, TN 38117

Dear Mrs. Claiborne:

    As you requested, I am sending you a group of letters
that illustrate the various letter styles. I am glad to help
you in this way in the preparation of your new correspondence
handbook. You are wise to pick one particular arrangement to
be used by all offices and departments.

    The letters are numbered in the order of their approximate
development in the United States according to the general time
when they first came into widespread use. Like changing styles
in everything else, though, there is no exact time when one
style surpasses another. Except for the indented arrangement,
which is illustrated by this letter, all are now used in many
business offices.

    The indented style, as you can readily see, has reasons
for being used very little. Its major disadvantage is that
it is extremely time consuming compared to the more simple
letter arrangements. The only possible advantage of the
indented letter is that it is considered ultra-conservative
because it is the oldest arrangement. This description is
not necessarily true, at the present time, because this
format is seen so seldom that it may qualify as being an
unusual, "far-out" arrangement.

    I am sure you will not recommend this style for
general use at Swallows Insurance Company.

                    Sincerely yours,

                    Binford H. Peeples, Professor
                        Department of Office Administration

mh

Figure B-1. *Letter Showing the Indented Style. (A long letter, typed
on a 6-inch line.)*

MEMPHIS STATE UNIVERSITY
MEMPHIS, TENNESSEE 38152

Office Administration Department

February 18, 1979

Mrs. Betty Claiborne, Office Manager
Swallows Insurance Company
5983 Maplewood Cove
Memphis, TN 38117

Dear Mrs. Claiborne:

    This letter illustrates the semiblock style.
This arrangement is also called the modified block
with indented paragraphs.

    When referring to letter styles, remember that
the terminology differs widely. The basic formats,
however, are standard.

    This semiblock style differs from the indented
style only in that the opening and closing lines
are blocked. It differs from the modified-block,
the next letter shown in this series, only in that the
paragraphs are indented.

    This arrangement would be appropriate for use
at your insurance company, but I do not enthusiastically
recommend it. Although the paragraph indentions
effectively separate the paragraphs, they are not
really necessary, for there is always a blank line
space between paragraphs. This letter is certainly
more efficient than the indented, but not so efficient
as one with no indentions.

Sincerely,

Binford H. Peeples, Professor
Department of Office Administration

mh

Figure B-2. *Letter Showing the Semiblock Style. (Also described as
the modified block with indented paragraphs. This illustration is a
medium-length letter. Line length is 5 inches.)*

MEMPHIS STATE UNIVERSITY
MEMPHIS, TENNESSEE 38152

Office Administration Department

February 18, 1979

Mrs. Betty Claiborne, Office Manager
Swallows Insurance Company
5983 Maplewood Cove
Memphis, TN 38117

Dear Mrs. Claiborne:

This letter illustrates the use of the modified-block
letter. This arrangement is also described as the
modified-block with blocked paragraphs. In addition,
it is described simply as the block, or the blocked.

This modified-block letter, as I choose to call it, is
probably used more often than any other letter style.

If you should decide to adopt this style, or the
semiblock shown in the preceding letter, I believe
that you should recommend that the date and the
closing lines begin at center--that they not be
backspaced from the margin point. Although they
often are placed by the backspace method, beginning
them at the center or near the center is quicker and
just as correct and attractive.

In all the letters shown so far, "standard" punctuation
has been used. This term refers only to the colon
after the salutation and the comma after the complimentary close. The "open" style will be shown in the
next letter, the full-block. In open punctuation the
colon and the comma are omitted. Either style of
punctuation can be correctly used with any letter style.

As you may have decided by now, there is no exact
answer as to the best letter style for every office
and every situation.

Sincerely,

Binford H. Peeples, Professor
Department of Office
            Administration

mh

Figure B-3. *Letter Showing the Modified-block Style*

Office Administration Department

February 18, 1979

Mrs. Betty Claiborne, Office Manager
Swallows Insurance Company
5983 Maplewood Cove
Memphis, TN 38117

Dear Mrs. Claiborne

This letter illustrates the use of the full-block style.

Because of the efficiency with which this letter can be
typewritten, its use is growing in popularity.

Some persons object to this arrangement because everything
is at the left; they believe that the date and the closing
lines should be centered or backspaced from the right
margin in order to give balance to the letter. Other
persons prefer the crisp, businesslike appearance of the
full-block style.

Notice that the open style of punctuation is used in
this letter. Although open punctuation is not an
essential characteristic of the full-block arrangement,
the two styles are often used together.

You will notice that the simplified letter, shown next
in this series, is a modification of this full-block
style.

Sincerely

Binford H. Peeples, Professor
Department of Office Administration

mh

Figure B–4. *Letter Showing the Full-block Style*

ing a letter. In the full-block style, all lines begin at the left margin. The full-block letter seems to be a wise choice for almost all companies. It is easily typewritten and arranged, and it has a neat, orderly appearance. With costs increasing daily, using unnecessary time in typewriting letters is a violation of good business management.

The *simplified style* was originally referred to as the Noma Simplified Letter. The "Noma" comes from the organization that first advocated it (in 1947) especially for the purpose of efficiency. This organization, which was at that time the National Office Management Association, has since changed its name to the Administrative Management Society. The letter is now sometimes referred to as the "AMS Simplified," but, to avoid confusion, it is usually referred to merely as the simplified (see Figure B–5).

This letter style has never reached the popularity that its backers hoped. Its use does not seem to be increasing, and it is still used in perhaps less than 5 percent of the total number of business letters. According to its advocates, an advantage of the simplified style is that it eliminates the unnecessary and old-fashioned salutation and complimentary close. They say that the salutation and complimentary close serve no useful purpose, that they take extra typewriting time and thus increase the cost, and that they are only leftovers from the business writing of the last century, which included an abundance of flattering phrases and the humble, servile attitude.

Even these persons, though, believe that the reader's name is important and that it should be used in the letter, provided it is not used to excess. In the simplified style, usually the reader's name is put into the first paragraph, as in this sentence: "Thank you, Mrs. Brown, for your explanation — ."

All lines begin at the left margin. The simplified letter always includes a subject line, typewritten in all capitals. The signer's name and title are usually typed in all capitals. The subject line is not characteristic of only the simplified letter style; it can be and often is used in all other letter arrangements. It is a definite and expected part, though, of all letters arranged in the simplified style.

The simplified letter has certain disadvantages, at least in the opinion of some office managers and business writers. They object to the letter because to them it seems too impersonal, too cold and formal. They do not wish to give up the usual, conventional salutation and complimentary close. They say that their readers expect to see these letter parts because they have seen them in so many other business letters over the years — that even if the reader does not consider the omission of his name, along with "Dear Mr.," as being unfriendly, the omission may cause distraction, at least momentarily, and take attention away from the message. They prefer to have a letter sound somewhat old-fashioned rather than to give the impression of being unnecessarily abrupt and brusque. (Actually, the

MEMPHIS STATE UNIVERSITY
MEMPHIS, TENNESSEE 38152

Office Administration Department

February 18, 1979

Betty Claiborne, Office Manager
Swallows Insurance Company
5983 Maplewood Cove
Memphis, TN 38117

THE SIMPLIFIED LETTER

Betty, do you like this letter style? It has several
advantages, but possibly some disadvantages, too.

It is the easiest letter of all to set up and type. In
addition, it has a businesslike, no-nonsense look about
it.

Another advantage, at least in most letters, is the use
of the subject line, which is always a part of the
simplified style. Notice that the subject line is
preceded and followed by two blank line spaces.

Some persons feel that this letter arrangement is
unfriendly and impersonal because the customary salutation
and complimentary close are omitted. These lines are
unnecessary, though, for if the letter is written as
it should be, the reader will believe and understand
that it is "sincere," "cordial", and "very truly yours."
Besides, all the persons we address as "dear" are not
really dear to us, using the ordinary meaning of the word.

Perhaps you will choose this letter to be the standard
one for your office. If not, I think full-block would
be a good choice. Either the semiblock or the modified-
block could be your standard arrangement, if you prefer
their appearance--but your typists will lose some time
in setting them up.

The letters that follow this one are special purpose
letters only.

BINFORD H. PEEPLES, PROFESSOR
DEPARTMENT OF OFFICE ADMINISTRATION

mh

Figure B-5. *Letter Showing the Simplified Style*

overall tone and friendliness of the letter are determined not by the arrangement or style, but by the choice of words.)

The use of the simplified style, then, still remains a matter of opinion. But the consensus seems to be that it is not the best choice for all companies or for all kinds of letters.

The *hanging-indention style letter* shown in Figure B–6 is one of several unusual arrangements that should not be considered for everyday use. It may be used for special purposes, and it is especially adapted to sales letters.

The *official letter style* (see Figure B–7) is more formal than the usual business letter. Notice that the inside address is moved to the bottom of the letter. Reference initials are omitted.

Other letter styles, in addition to these shown, are occasionally used. The *square-block* is a variation of the modified-block. This arrangement allows the absolute maximum number of words to be typewritten on the sheet. The date is placed at the right on the same vertical line space as the first line of the inside address. The reference initials or other notations, such as the enclosure or carbon copy notations, are in the lower left corner, on the same vertical line space as the last line of the signature block.

The letter is described as square because all these items of information neatly form the four corners. This letter arrangement is suitable for special purposes, but it almost always looks crowded. It may also have the disadvantage of being distracting because of its unusual appearance.

A letter similar to the official style is being advocated by at least one large insurance company as the standard letter to be used for all purposes throughout their offices. Although the official letter is considered formal, this similar letter is designated as the *informal style*.

The inside address is placed at the bottom, as in the official style, but the salutation and complimentary close are omitted, as in the simplified style. Paragraphs and the date line are placed in the arrangement of the semiblock or the modified-block. Each letter is to begin something like this: "We agree with you, Mrs. Blair, that — " or "Your questions, Mrs. Blair, is especially interesting because — ." The purpose of such openings is to use the reader's name early in the letter in place of the omitted salutation.

In summary, the selection of a letter style should be made after considering the type of company or department and the kind of letters being mailed, as well as the readers of the letters. In all situations, the ease and efficiency of setting up the letters should be a vital factor in making a choice. In order to assure a standard and attractive appearance for all company correspondence, one style should be chosen for use throughout an organization, or at least for use throughout individual departments or branches.

The following is a summary on points in letter style:

MEMPHIS STATE UNIVERSITY
MEMPHIS, TENNESSEE 38152

Office Administration Department

February 18, 1979

Mrs. Betty Claiborne, Office Manager
Swallows Insurance Company
5983 Maplewood Cove
Memphis, TN 38117

Dear Mrs. Claiborne:

Attention may be gained by using, for special purposes,
          the hanging-indented letter, as illustrated
          here.

Interest is a factor that must be planned for, in some
          letters, and even the form of the letter is
          occasionally used to catch the reader's eye,
          with the hope that he will read the message.
          These messages are likely to be unsolicited
          sales letters.

Desire to be different, in letter arrangement as in
          other things, is not always completely desirable.
          In most letters, we should work for a conventional
          arrangement that will not distract from the
          message.

Action is the purpose of sales letters, as well as
          many other letters you will write. An
          unusual letter style alone will not obtain
          the desired action. What you say in a letter
          is far more important than the arrangement,
          although we should always make sure that all
          letters are planned for quick and easy reading.

                              Sincerely,

                              Binford H. Peeples, Professor
                              Department of Office
                                   Administration

mh

P. S. Mrs. Claiborne, notice that the first words in
        each paragraph spell out the old formula for
        writing sales letters.

Figure B-6. *Letter Showing the Hanging-indention Style*

MEMPHIS STATE UNIVERSITY
MEMPHIS, TENNESSEE 38152

Office Administration Department

February 18, 1979

Dear Mrs. Claiborne:

This letter illustrates the arrangement described as the official letter style.

The word "official" denotes that the letter is often sent to a public official, such as a governor or a senator. It can be addressed to any person. It is especially useful for letters of congratulation or similar personal messages.

This illustration is merely an adaptation of the semiblock style; the only change is that the inside address has been moved to the bottom. The modified-block style, too, becomes the official letter by moving the inside address to the bottom.

This is a rather formal letter. The complimentary close, "Respectfully yours," is especially appropriate; but "Sincerely" or "Sincerely yours" could also be used.

Mrs. Claiborne, I have enjoyed advising you about your letter selection. Will you let me know which one you choose for general office use?

Respectfully yours,

Binford H. Peeples, Professor
Department of Office
                Administration

Mrs. Betty Claiborne, Office Manager
Swallows Insurance Company
5983 Maplewood Cove
Memphis, TN 38117

An Equal Opportunity University

Figure B-7. *Letter Showing the Official Letter Style*

- The indented style is too time consuming and expensive to be chosen for ordinary use in any company.
- The semiblock arrangement is considered conservative. Paragraph indentions effectively separate the paragraphs and may be an aid to readability. This letter style, too, wastes time, but not nearly so much as the indented.
- The modified-block is also conservative. It is one of the most widely used styles, perhaps the one used most of all.
- The full-block style is the most efficient arrangement, except for the simplified. This arrangement is gaining in popularity, although it is already widely used.
- The simplified style is efficient and modernistic. It is not yet widely used.
- The hanging-indention style is used mostly in sales letters.

ARRANGING THE USUAL AND SPECIAL PARTS OF THE LETTER

Business letters, with the exception of the simplified style and the informal style, will almost always contain these parts: letterhead, date, inside address, salutation, complimentary closing, the signer's name and title, and the typist's reference initials, plus the paragraphs that make up the body of the letter. Other lines used on many letters are the subject line, attention line, enclosure notation, and carbon copy notations.

The simplified and the informal styles omit the salutation and the complimentary close.

Letters coming from a business office, written by a company representative about matters concerning the company, should be typewritten on letterhead stationery. Letters written by an individual about personal business matters should not be on company letterhead.

In personal business letters, *the return address* is typewritten just above the date:

1064 Estate Drive
Memphis, TN 38117
February 18, 1979

Personal business letters may be set up in any letter arrangement.

Dateline. The date should always be set up in this way: February 18, 1979. Do not abbreviate the month. Do not use an abbreviated form, such as 2-12-79.

Inside Address. The name, title, and complete mailing address make up the part of the letter described as the inside address. The individual's name should be preceded by a courtesy title, usually "Mr.," "Mrs.," "Miss," or "Dr." The use of "Ms." is increasing in popularity.

Mrs. Harry B. Billings 1187 Mockingbird Lane Yonkers, NY 10028	Mr. Bill Bond, Manager ABC Appliances, Inc. 95 State Street Camden, NJ 08108
Dr. L. M. McCormick 4646 Poplar Avenue Memphis, TN 38117	Mr. Bill Bond Personnel Manager Scott Manufacturing, Inc. 2637 Lamar Avenue
Ms. Mary Lynn Jackson 1048 Adams Street Blytheville, AR 74602	Austin, TX 76105

Notice that in all the above illustrations the two-letter abbreviations are used for state names. (A complete list is given in the table on page 553.) Do not abbreviate other words in the inside address, except for the courtesy title, and "Inc."

The *attention line,* when used, is usually placed a double space after the last line of the inside address and a double space before the salutation, as in the following illustrations:

Smith Manufacturing Company
2031 Hickory Ridge Road
Macon, GA 30567

Attention Mr. Ronald Duncan, Treasurer

Gentlemen:

Smith Manufacturing Company
2031 Hickory Ridge Road
Macon, GA 30567

Attention Sales Manager

Gentlemen:

The attention line is not necessary in most letters. When writing to an individual in a particular company, you should ordinarily address the letter to this person, not to the company (see page 553).

Two-Letter State Abbreviations

Alabama	AL	Nebraska	NB
Alaska	AK	Nevada	NV
Arizona	AZ	New Hampshire	NH
Arkansas	AR	New Jersey	NJ
		New Mexico	NM
California	CA	New York	NY
Colorado	CO	North Carolina	NC
Connecticut	CT	North Dakota	ND
Delaware	DE		
District of Columbia	DC	Ohio	OH
		Oklahoma	OK
Florida	FL	Oregon	OR
Georgia	GA		
Guam	GU	Pennsylvania	PA
		Puerto Rico	PR
Hawaii	HI		
		Rhode Island	RI
Idaho	ID		
Illinois	IL	South Carolina	SC
Indiana	IN	South Dakota	SD
Iowa	IA		
		Tennessee	TN
Kansas	KS	Texas	TX
Kentucky	KY		
Louisiana	LA	Utah	UT
Maine	ME	Vermont	VT
Maryland	MD	Virginia	VA
Massachusetts	MA	Virgin Islands	VI
Michigan	MI		
Minnesota	MN	Washington	WA
Mississippi	MS	West Virginia	WV
Missouri	MO	Wisconsin	WI
Montana	MT	Wyoming	WY

Mr. Ronald Duncan, Treasurer
Smith Manufacturing Company
2031 Hickory Ridge Road
Macon, GA 30567

Dear Mr. Duncan:

When, then, should the attention line be used? A possible use is on an occasion when you do not know the individual's name. For example, some application letters are addressed to the company with an attention line to the personnel manager. This is not the best choice, though, if you can obtain the personnel manager's name. Using the name is more personal and friendly, and it also shows more initiative on the part of the applicant because he used extra consideration in addressing the manager by name.

The effect of an attention line on the routing or forwarding of a letter is dependent on the mail policy of each company.

The *salutation* is the greeting to the reader, similar to the "hello" used in a conversation. In a letter addressed to an individual, as, for example, Mr. Harry B. Graham, the best salutation is "Dear Mr. Graham." The salutation "Dear Sir" is more formal and impersonal than "Dear Mr. Graham."

The salutation should agree with the inside address. Notice that when the letter is addressed to a company, the salutation is "Gentlemen" even though an attention line is used. (Some writers now use "Ladies/ Gentlemen.")

The salutation is usually followed by a colon, but the colon may be omitted if the usual comma after the complimentary close is also omitted. This style of punctuation is called open punctuation.

The *subject line* may be used in any style of letter; it is always used in the simplified arrangement. It must be worded with care to accurately describe the contents of the letter. A subject line, like a subhead, helps the reader to obtain quickly the gist of the letter. Use of the subject line also helps the writer to organize the message and write the letter more quickly and efficiently. A subject line is not always desirable, however, especially when the letter involves an unpleasant subject.

Vertically, the subject line is placed a double space below the salutation. Horizontally, it may be centered; it may begin at the left margin; or it may begin even with the paragraph indentions. In the full-block and the simplified arrangements, the subject line always begins at the left margin.

The complimentary close is placed a double space below the last line of the letter. A "Sincerely" closing is more informal than a "truly" closing. "Yours truly" is often considered old-fashioned and abrupt. "Respectfully" and "Respectfully yours" should be used to show special respect. "Cordially" and "Cordially yours" indicate personal or business friendship.

The *company name*, used in the signature block, appears like this:

Very sincerely yours,

SMITH MANUFACTURING COMPANY

Ronald Duncan, Treasurer

The *penwritten signature* is inserted in the space left for it between the complimentary close (or the company name) and the typewritten name of the person who signs the letter. Ordinarily, three blank line spaces are left for signature. Four or five lines may be left if it is desirable to "stretch" the letter so that it will end lower on the page.

The *typewritten name and title* may be placed on the same line or on separate lines. For example:

Mary Holt, Manager

or

Mary Holt
Manager

or

Henry Holt, Manager
Shipping Department

or

Hannibal Alexander Witherspoon, Jr.
Manager, Shipping Department

The form chosen should be the one that will be more balanced in appearance, and the choice will depend upon the length of the name and the title. This choice of arrangement will also be necessary in the inside address. If the individual's title and department are shown on the letterhead, they need not be repeated in the signature block.

A man should not use the courtesy title of "Mr." with his typewritten name or with his signature. A woman, however, may precede her typewritten name with a courtesy title in order to let the reader know how to address her in the responding letter. In a letter addressed to a woman, the writer should use the "Ms." title if the marital status is unknown.

The *reference initials* are usually placed two lines (a double space) below the last line of the signature block. If the person who signs the letter also dictates it, only the initials of the typist are necessary. An illustration:

Cordially yours,

Wayne Johnson

Wayne Johnson, President

rt
Enclosure

The carbon copy notation is usually placed a double space below the enclosures notation, or a double space below the reference initials if no enclosure notation is used. For example:

rt

Two enclosures

cc: Mrs. Harriet Jensen

A variation is:

Copies to: Mrs. Harriet Jensen
            Mr. James Harris

The *postscript*, if used, should be the last item of the letter. Ordinarily, the purpose of the postscript is to emphasize, not to include material that has been mistakenly left out of the letter.

The *heading of the second and succeeding pages* of a letter includes the name of the addressee, the page number, and the date. The heading may be set up in one of these ways:

Mrs. Harriet Jensen   2   February 18, 1979

Mrs. Harriet Jensen
February 18, 1979
Page 2

Mrs. Harriet Jensen, February 18, 1979, page 2

In summary, using the usual and special parts of the business letter in the conventional arrangement adds to the readability of the letter. All these parts serve a useful purpose (with the possible exception of the salutation and complimentary close) in that they present needed information in an easy-to-find and understandable form.

C

Memorandum and Report Format; Documentation

THE MEMORANDUM

As in all forms of written communication, the physical appearance of a memorandum or a report affects readability and the reception of the message. Neatness and consistency, as well as a conventional arrangement, add to a positive psychological approach and free the reader's mind to concentrate upon the message. The format and content of an interoffice memorandum are explained and illustrated in Figure C–1.

PHYSICAL PRESENTATION OF REPORTS

The format and arrangement of a report or manuscript of any kind will depend upon these factors:

1. The expected or required form and arrangement, according to organizational precedent or a specified handbook. Footnotes, headings, indentions, and other kinds of format and arrangement differ from "authority" to "authority." If you have no specified handbook or guide to follow, use readability, simplicity, and consistency as your guides.

2. The complexity of the material and the need for breakdown into various divisions. For example, if a report outline includes headings to correspond to *I, A, 1,* and *a,* the text of the report

TO: All Office Employees

FROM: Mary Wells, Office Manager

SUBJECT: Your Interoffice Memorandums

DATE: January 30, 1979

The following suggestions should help you plan and prepare your writing to other employees in this organization.

SPACING

Memorandums may be single or double spaced. If they are single spaced, leave a double space between paragraphs, as you should do when single spacing any typewritten material.

PARAGRAPHS

Paragraphs may be blocked or indented, as in letters. The blocked style saves time and, to many persons, presents a more modern appearance. Paragraphs in memorandums, as in letters, should be fairly short. Long, unbroken paragraphs are hard to read.

MARGINS

The long line length (6 inches, which is 60 spaces pica, 70 elite) is ordinarily used in all memorandums, even short ones. The writing need not be centered vertically.

SIDE HEADINGS

Although side headings as shown here are not the only type that can be used in the memorandum, this all-capital side heading is easy to see and, if properly worded, immediately tells the reader something of the content of the following section. As compared to centered headings, side headings are quicker to type.

Figure C-1. *An Interoffice Memorandum*

Figure C-1. *(Continued)*

Your Interoffice Memorandums   2   January 30, 1979

SECOND-PAGE IDENTIFICATION

The second page of a memorandum should be identified by subject, date, and page number. Instead of the illustration shown above, this identification may be shown in this order: subject, date, and page number.

SIGNATURE

No signature is required or expected on most memorandums, although they may be signed. They should be signed if the contents are of special importance or if the writer wants the reader to know that he or she personally wrote or dictated the message.

A complimentary close is never used on a memorandum.

The signature may consist only of the writer's initials, placed at the end of the memorandum or by the writer's typewritten name at the top. The complete signature may also be placed in one of these two positions.

TITLES

The writer should show his or her title or position unless the readers are already sure of it, as in Mary Wells, Office Manager. A woman does not usually show a Miss, Mrs., or Ms. before her name in a memorandum, although it is not considered incorrect to do so. A man never shows Mr. before his name in a memorandum or elsewhere. Often a courtesy title should appear before the name of the addressee, particularly if the addressee is in a position of higher authority than the writer. Although there is no rule to this effect, the writer is slightly discourteous to do otherwise.

NEATNESS

As in all written communications, an attractive appearance is psychologically conducive to the acceptance of ideas. In addition, neatness is a matter of common courtesy.

must include four types of headings. But if the report contains only the main heading, (the title) and one level of division, only one form of heading is necessary, in addition to the title.

3. The readers of the material, with their known or likely preferences.

Headings

Headings should be consistent and indicate the order of importance, or "weight," of each section. Headings in the table of contents are repeated exactly in the text. Placement and capitalization indicate the relationship of each heading to all the rest.

The traditional outline arrangement includes headings preceded by roman and arabic numerals and by alphabetic letters in capitals and lower case, as shown below.

FIRST-DEGREE HEADING (TITLE)

I. Second-Degree Heading

   A. Third-Degree Heading

   B. Third-Degree Heading

      1. Fourth-Degree Heading

      2. Fourth-Degree Heading

         a. Fifth-Degree Heading

         b. Fifth-Degree Heading

II. Second-Degree Heading

These divisions of the report outline, which are also shown on the table of contents (often in revised form), can be shown in the report according to the method shown below.

FIRST-DEGREE HEADING

The first-degree heading (title) is centered and typed in all capitals. When the title consists of more than one line, usually these lines are double spaced; the first line is longer than the second, and the second is longer than the third. (Titles should be as short as possible, but they should also be exact and descriptive.)

Second-Degree Headings

Second-degree headings, using the arrangement shown here, are centered and underlined. They describe the major sections of the report and correspond to the headings preceded by roman numerals, as shown in the report outline.

Third-Degree Headings

Third-degree headings correspond to A, B, C, and following letters, as shown in the report outline. In this plan of arrangement, they are placed at the left margin, typed in capitals and lower case, and underscored.

Fourth-degree headings — Placement at the paragraph indention on the same line with the text distinguishes fourth-degree headings from third-degree ones. The underscore and the dash separate the heading from the remainder of the paragraph.

Fifth-degree headings are also placed at the paragraph indention, on the same line as the text. These headings, however, are integral parts of beginning sentences.

The alternate plan described below, as well as other variations, may be used for headings within the text of a report.

Type the title as a spread heading, like this:

TITLE OF REPORT

One space is left between each two letters, and three spaces are left between words. Thus the first-degree heading is a spread heading, second-degree headings are centered in all-capitals, third-degree headings are centered and underscored, and following headings of decreasing importance are moved up one level throughout the report.

Ordinarily you will not need all these divisions, even for long reports. Although the wise use of exactly worded headings increases readability, an overly complicated system with unnecessary divisions may be confusing or even annoying to the reader.

When you need fewer divisions than those shown here, you need not exactly follow this suggested order of arrangement — unless a variation would consist of a departure from instructions in the handbook you are using as a guide. For example, if your report requires only one level of division, you might choose to use side headings instead of the centered ones described here as second-degree headings. And, as in the preceding example of a well-designed memorandum, these side headings may be displayed in all capitals.

An example of a complete report, including a table of contents with corresponding headings within the text, is shown in Chapter 18. In addition, wording of headings is considered with report organization in Chapter 17.

Margins

If the manuscript is to remain unbound, use a six-inch line (60 spaces pica, 70 spaces elite). Exceptions to this general rule include material to be published, for which you ordinarily should leave an additional half inch on each side. Another exception is that in some situations you should consider using a longer line in order to save duplicating expense, filing space, and paper.

For manuscripts to be bound on the left, move side margins an additional half an inch to the right.

On the first page of a report manuscript, leave a two-inch top margin. On following pages, leave a top margin of approximately one inch. On all pages, leave a bottom margin of one to one and one-half inches.

Spacing

Formal reports are traditionally double spaced, as are many, if not most, informal reports. Some organizations are now preparing all typewritten work in single-space form in order to economize.

Pagination

The first page of the report itself (the "report proper") is considered as page 1. This page number is placed at the bottom of the page, centered, or omitted. Page numbers of following pages are placed in the upper right-hand corner, on line 5 to 7 from the top. Thus the "approximately one inch" top margin refers to the "white space" above the page number. Triple space after the page number before beginning the first line of type.

Preliminary parts of a formal report are numbered with small roman numerals (see the illustration in Chapter 18). Supplementary parts are numbered with arabic numerals continued in the regular sequence from page 1 of the report proper through the last page of the final supplementary part.

A Short Informal Report (First Page)

An illustration of the first page of a short, informal report is given in Figure C–2. An illustration of a complete, formal report is given in Chapter 18.

AN INFORMAL REPORT

The format illustrated here is a good choice for informal reports, term papers, and other similar manuscripts unless you are expected to follow differing instructions because of company precedent or a specified style manual.

Headings

As mentioned in the preceding section of this appendix, when you need only one or two levels of division, you need not take them in the order that would be necessary if your work required greater division. Other variations of the underlined side heading shown here are centered underlined headings, and headings in ALL CAPITALS.

Spacing

Double-space the body of the manuscript unless cost and time considerations indicate that it should be single spaced, or unless the format you are expected to follow is in the single-space arrangement. Triple-space (leave two blank lines) after the main title and before each side heading.

Paragraph Division

Leave at least two lines of a paragraph at the bottom of the page and carry over at least two lines.

Figure C–2.   *First Page of a Short, Informal Report*

DOCUMENTATION

When to Footnote

Use footnotes to give credit for all material written by other persons, whether this material is quoted exactly or paraphrased. An exception to this general rule is that information of general knowledge paraphrased from another work need not be footnoted. For example, if you should state that the computer has brought vast changes to the business world, you need not quote the author (or the multitude of authors) who also made this statement, unless you use the exact words or some particular idea or mode of expression of an author other than yourself.

Placement of Quoted or Paraphrased Material

Short quotations (four lines or fewer) are typed within the text of the report and enclosed by quotation marks. Longer quotations are set in from both the right and left margins; no quotation marks are used. If the manuscript is double-spaced, use single-spacing for the long quoted passage. (Paraphrased material, although footnoted, is not distinguished from the remainder of the report text.)

If you leave omissions within a quoted passage, indicate this by use of the ellipsis, a series of three periods typed with intervening spaces. The omission of a paragraph or more is indicated by a full line of periods.

A Suggested Footnote Form

A suggested form to use for footnotes of varied material is as follows:[1]

For a book with one author:
1. Carl G. Gustavson, *Europe in the World Community since 1939* (Boston: Allyn and Bacon, 1971), pp. 322–30.

For a book with two or three authors:
2. William C. Resnick and Herbert L. Sachs, *Dynamic General Psychology: An Introduction* (Boston: Holbrook Press, 1971), p. 112.

For a book with more than three authors:
3. Henkel et al., *Foundations of Health Science*, 2d ed. (Boston: Allyn and Bacon, 1971). [All authors should be listed in a bibliography.]

For a book with no author given:
4. *A Manual of Style*, 12th ed. rev. (Chicago: University of Chicago Press, 1969), pp. 42–44.

1. "Footnotes," *Author's Guide* (Boston: Allyn and Bacon, 1973), pp. 18–19. Used by permission of the publisher.

For an edited book or one revised by a person other than the original author:

5. H. W. Fowler, *A Dictionary of Modern English Usage,* 2d ed., rev. and ed. Sir Ernest Gowers (Oxford: Clarendon Press, 1965), p. 157.

or

6. W. S. Lewis and A. Dayle Wallace, eds., *Horace Walpole's Correspondence with the Rev. William Cole* (New Haven: Yale University Press, 1937), 1:74–76.

For a translated book:

7. Thomas Mann, *Joseph in Egypt,* trans. H. T. Lowe-Porter (New York: Alfred A. Knopf, 1944), p. ix.

or

8. Guy Lee, trans., *Ovid's Amores* (New York: Viking Press, 1968), p. 11.

For a chapter of a collective work:

9. Mildred C. Robeck, "An Ounce of Prevention," in *Remedial Reading: Classroom and Clinic,* ed. Leo M. Schell and Paul C. Burns (Boston: Allyn and Bacon, 1972), pp. 513–21.

For a book in a series:

10. James A. Smith, *Creative Teaching of the Language Arts in the Elementary School,* Allyn and Bacon Series in Creative Teaching, vol. 2 (Boston, 1967), p. 30.

For an unpublished work:

11. M. M. Bayne, "Sir Thomas Browne and the Metaphysicals" (Master's thesis, Harvard University, 1945), p. 30.

12. Sidney Colvin to R.L.S., 26 April 1880, Stevenson Papers, Yale University, New Haven.

For a legal treatise:

13. Plucknett, *Concise History of the Common Law* (4th ed., 1948) 29.

For an article in a periodical:

14. S. K. Norton, "Student Problems Met by the Teacher," *School Review* 51 (1948): 404.

15. "Training Probation and Parole Personnel," *Focus,* March 1948, pp. 44–48.

16. Alan Grob, "Tennyson's *The Lotos Eaters*: Two Versions of Art," *Modern Philology* 62 (1964): 119.

For an article in a well-known reference book:

17. *Encyclopaedia Britannica,* 1966, s.v. "Descriptive Geometry."

18. *The Concise Oxford Dictionary of Current English,* 5th ed., s.v. "evolution."

For a newspaper article:

19. *New York Times,* 20 August 1972, sec. 2, p. 19.

20. *Boston Globe,* 25 August 1972, p. 1.

For an article in a legal journal:

21. 39 *Harv. L. Rev.* 725 (1926).

Miscellaneous:

22. U.S., Congress, House, Committee on Business, *Operating Small Businesses*, 79th Cong., 2d sess., 1946, H. Rep. 1888, p. 63.

23. U.S., Congress, House, *Hearings on H.R. 6492*, 66th Cong., 2d. sess., 1920, pp. 1023–26.

24. U.S., Treasury Department, Federal Specifications Board, *Federal Specifications for Chambray*, Federal Stock Catalogue, Sec. 4, Part 5, CCC-C-231a (Washington, D.C.: Government Printing Office, 1942), p. xi.

25. Mary Ruth Colby, *Problems and Procedures in Adoption*, U.S. Department of Labor Bulletin 262 (Washington, D.C.: Government Printing Office, 1941), p. 111.

26. Social Science Research Council, *Labor Force Definition and Measurement*, Bulletin 56 (Washington, D.C., 1947), pp. 10–11.

27. The Brookings Institution, *Essays on Research in the Social Sciences* (Washington, D.C., 1931), p. 5.

28. Shakespeare, *Hamlet*, Act 1, sc. 3, lines 5–6.

29. James Madison, *The Federalist*, no. 10.

For subsequent references to previously quoted works, a simplified footnote is preferable to the older, hard-to-remember Latin terms. For example, in a subsequent reference to a book by Edward T. Hall, you may use this footnote:

Hall, p. 217.

If you refer in the same paper to two or more works by the same author, the title must be included in all footnotes:

Hall, The Silent Language, p. 217.

Or, if you use materials written, for example, by both Jon Hall and Edward T. Hall, complete names must be included in all footnotes.

Footnotes may be placed at the bottom of the page to which they apply or grouped together at the end of the manuscript. Although they are more easily typewritten when placed at the end of the manuscript, they are more easily read when they appear at the bottom of the page to which they refer. And, as in all communication situations, consider your reader.

The Bibliography

The bibliography is considered as a supplement to a formal report. It may come before or after appendix sections, depending upon the materials included as appendixes. (Page numbering is often simplified by placing the bibliography first. The arabic numerals used in the report proper continue in sequence throughout all supplementary parts.)

Like footnotes, bibliographical references differ in format. Regardless of the handbook you are using as a guide, however, these instructions apply:

1. List the authors' names in reverse order.
2. Use a hanging indention form to make the entries easy to read.
3. Arrange in alphabetical order according to the surname of the author. If no author is given, alphabetize according to title.
4. All entries may be grouped together and alphabetized accordingly, or entries may be subdivided into such groupings as "Books," "Periodicals," or "Government Publications."

A suggested form of a bibliography suitable for business reports is shown in Figure C-3.

13

BIBLIOGRAPHY

Anderson, Leo, ed. New Techniques in Office Operations. Elmhurst, IL: Business Press, 1968.

Anderson, Thomas J., and Trotter, William R. Word Processing. New York: AMACOM, 1974.

Aspley, J. C., ed. Office Administration Handbook. Chicago: Dartnell Corporation, 1967.

Kleinschrod, Walter A. Word Processing. New York: AMACOM, 1974.

Konkel, Gilbert J., and Peck, Phyllis J. "Traditional Secretarial Costs Compared to Word Processing." The Office (February 1976), pp. 66–67.

Law, Donald E., and Pereira, Cesar L. "Word Processing: How to Cut Secretarial Administrative Costs." Management Review (March 1976), pp. 28–35.

Nardiello, Virginia M. "Word Processing Aids Secretaries' Careers." The Office (February 1976), pp. 82, 84, 87.

O'Neal, Jeffrey D. "We Increased Typing Productivity 340%." The Office (February 1976), pp. 95–100.

Figure C-3. *Suggested Form for a Bibliography for Business Reports*

Figure C–3.   *(Continued)*

Ornelas, Mary Jane. "Humanizing Word Processing Mechanization."
    The Office (January 1976), pp. 95, 97.

Place, Irene; Hicks, Charles B.; and Wilkinson, Robin L.
    Office Management.   3d ed.   Boston: Allyn and Bacon, 1971.

Wylie, Harry L., ed.   Office Management Handbook.   2d ed.   New York:
    Ronald Press Company, 1958.

An annotated bibliography briefly describes each listed reference, as in these examples:

Gunning, Robert.   New Guides to More Effective Writing in

Business and Industry.   Boston: Industrial Education

Institute, 1964.

Gunning, best known for the development of a

readability formula, offers help to the technical writer

toward the clear expression of ideas.   The theme is that

clear expression is based upon exact thinking and

understanding.

Hamburger, Edward.   A Business Dictionary.   Englewood

Cliffs, NJ: Prentice-Hall, 1967.

A brief listing of business and economic terms with

definitions.

APPENDIX **D**

A Brief Guide to English Usage

This appendix section is of necessity an incomplete guide to the use of the English language. A "completely complete" handbook, even if one could exist, would fill many large books. Moreover, many handbooks, some of them excellent, are available for your use through school and public libraries. And, as discussed in Chapter 8, every business writer should own one or more reliable and comprehensive handbooks, as well as a large, up-to-date dictionary.

The material chosen for Appendix D includes the most usual areas of difficulty for college students and business writers. As you look over the illustrations, no doubt you will find that you are already completely sure of most of the points discussed. But you are likely to find at least a few examples of weaknesses that occur in your own writing or speech, or points about which you may be uncertain.

PUNCTUATION AS AN AID TO READABILITY

The Apostrophe

②. **Use an apostrophe in contractions.**

- won't
- it's (it is)
- couldn't
- you're (you are)

(Avoid contractions in formal writing.)

2. Use an apostrophe to indicate the possessive case of nouns and indefinite pronouns.

- Mary's cat
- anybody's guess
- a stone's throw
- a year's experience
- children's clothing
- the student's paper (one student)
- the students' papers (more than one student)
- Mr. Ross's automobile
- The Rosses' automobile (an automobile owned by more than one person named Ross)
- Jefferson Davis's home
- Bob and Mary's house (joint ownership)
- Bob's and Mary's shoes (individual ownership)

(Singular nouns ending in *s* may be followed by the apostrophe alone, as: Dr. Jennings' office.)

3. Use an apostrophe in plurals of lower-case letters and abbreviations followed by periods and — optional — in plurals of capital letters, figures, abbreviations not followed by periods, and words referred to as words.

- c's
- Ph.D's
- B's or Bs
- CPA's or CPAs
- 8's or 8s
- the 1940's or 1940s
- and's or ands
- %'s or %s

(Be consistent in your use of the apostrophe. For example, use *and's* or *ands,* but do not use both in the same paper. According to some English handbooks, *and's* is preferred.)

Note: The use of the apostrophe is sometimes described as being an aspect of spelling, not punctuation.

The Comma

1. Use a comma to set off an introductory subordinate clause from the independent statement.

- If Johnny can't write, one of the reasons may be a conditioning based on speed rather than respect for the creative process.
- If you don't like the weather in New England, wait a few minutes.
- Although the ability to type is a requisite to many jobs, it should no more be considered purely vocational than the ability to read or write the English language.
- When in doubt, tell the truth. [Mark Twain] (Introductory element with "you are" understood.)

2. Use a comma after introductory participial phrases.

- Thinking that he could complete the work in an hour, he left it until the afternoon.
- Having received the notice of cancellation, we tried to stop shipment.
- Elated over the news of his promotion, he kissed everyone on the third floor.

Distinguish between a participle, which is a verb form used as an adjective, and a gerund, which is a verb form used as a noun. A gerund is also referred to as a verbal noun. In the following sentences the gerund acts as the subject; it should not be followed by a comma:

- Seeing is believing.
- Driving along the Natchez Trace is a memorable experience.

3. Use a comma after introductory infinitive phrases.

- To enter the stacks, go to the admission desk and present your identification card.

An infinitive, like a gerund, is not followed by a comma when it is used as the subject. In the following sentence, both clauses of the compound sentence contain an infinitive used as the subject:

- To err is human; to blame it on someone else is even more human.

4. Use a comma after an introductory sentence element consisting of a long prepositional phrase or of two or more phrases.

- In addition to all the books in the general library, many others are shelved in specialized collections.

5. Use a comma after introductory words and phrases.

- Confidentially, this policy is to be changed.
- Nevertheless, we must continue the usual procedure throughout this month.

6. Use a comma to separate words, phrases, or clauses in a series.

- Today I made errors, mistakes, blunders, and goof-ups.
- His morning consists of eating breakfast, reading the newspaper, and sitting in the sunshine.
- Go to the end of the hall, turn left, and follow the arrows on the wall.

7. Use a comma to separate coordinate clauses joined by and, but, for, or, nor, yet.

- There is a lot to say in her favor, but the other is more interesting. [Mark Twain]
- All would live long, but none would be old. [Benjamin Franklin]
- Life is too short, and the time we waste in yawning never can be regained. [Stendhal]
- To be good is noble, but to teach others how to be good is nobler — and less trouble. [Mark Twain]
- The show had no chronological order, nor did it have an intelligent narration.

In short sentences the comma is sometimes omitted, as in:

- I came late and you left early.

8. Use a comma to set off nonrestrictive (nonessential) clauses; do not set off restrictive clauses that come within or at the end of a sentence.

- Our salesmen, who are paid a salary plus commissions, earn from $900 to $2,000 a month. (nonrestrictive)
- Salesmen who exceed their quotas receive an extra bonus. (restrictive)

9. Use a comma to set off parenthetical (nonrestrictive, nonessential) words or phrases.

- He said that, in the first place, he was not interested in our product.
- The sales manager, Mr. Harvey L. Wells, is a friend of the customer's sister.
- The store first opened its doors on Monday, May 13, 1904, in St. Louis, Missouri, on the bank of the Mississippi River.
- The statement is true, perhaps, that our prices could be reduced.

Words that are at times used parenthetically are at other times used adverbially. If a word or phrase can be considered supplemental, interrupting, or explanatory, precede and follow the word or phrase with commas. In the following sentences, *perhaps, however,* and *also* are used as adverbs, and, because of their placement in the sentence, should not be set off by commas:

- It is perhaps true that our prices could be reduced.
- However it happened, it was not according to customary office procedures.
- The second statement is also false.

10. Use a comma to separate adjectives of equal rank if the conjunction is omitted.

- She is an efficient, considerate teacher.

Do not use commas between adjectives of unequal rank, as in:

- The cold late autumn days are here again.

To check whether a comma is needed, try inserting the word *and*. If the expression now makes sense, use a comma.

11. Use a comma to set off contrasting expressions.

- The world is becoming warmer, not colder.

The Semicolon

1. Use a semicolon between main clauses that are not joined by one of the coordinate conjunctions (<u>and</u>, <u>but</u>, <u>for</u>, <u>or</u>, <u>nor</u>, <u>yet</u>).

- Punctuation is more than little marks to be sprinkled like salt and pepper through written words; punctuation determines emphasis and meaning.

2. Use a semicolon between main clauses joined with a conjunctive adverb.

- A readable writing style is simple and direct; consequently, it requires less punctuation than a more formal, complicated style.
- Semicolons are a useful means of expressing meaning through punctuation; nevertheless, a great many long compound sentences such as this one, with the main clauses joined by a semicolon and a conjunctive adverb (*nevertheless*), tend to suggest a rather heavy and formal writing style.

Important Note! The substitution of a comma for a semicolon to separate main clauses, as in sentences constructed like the preceding ones that contain no coordinating conjunction, is considered a serious error in punctuation and sentence construction. (See the section below titled "Basic Errors in Sentence Construction.")

3. Use a semicolon to separate items in a series if they are parallel subordinate clauses, or if they are long or contain internal punctuation.

- Those attending included Susan Smith, a college professor; Mark David, a field engineer; Diana Watson, an executive secretary; and Leonard Watson, a credit manager.
- We use language to talk about language; we make statements about statements; and we sing songs about songs.

4. Use a semicolon to separate complete clauses joined by a coordinate conjunction if the semicolon will increase readability when clauses are long or contain internal punctuation.

- The semicolon, which is sometimes overused, indicates a stronger break in thought than that indicated by a comma; but it is not so strong as that indicated by a period and is somewhat different in usage from a colon.

The Colon

1. Use a colon to introduce a series of items.

- The factors to be considered are these: cost, speed, and simplicity.
- Three possible areas of operation could be the source of the loss: shipping, advertising, and collections.

2. Use a colon to introduce long quotations or descriptions.

3. Use a colon after such words as "the following" or "as follows."

The Dash

1. Use a dash to show a sudden change in the structure of a sentence or to indicate emphasis.

- Indeed, it was a long leap from the jungle home of the chimpanzee to our modern civilization — and apparently we didn't quite make it.[1]

1. Wendall Johnson, *People in Quandries* (New York: Harper and Bros., 1946), p. 268.

- Several items — a stapler, two calendars, and three or more chairs — were lost by the movers.

Do not overuse the dash, especially in formal writing, as it may give a "scatterbrained" appearance.

The Hyphen

1. Use a hyphen to join a compound expression used as a single modifier before a noun.

- Is this an interest-bearing note?
- We need up-to-date equipment.

Omit the hyphen when the first word of the compound is an adverb ending in *ly*.   Omit the hyphen when the modifier comes after the noun:

- Is this note interest bearing?

2. Use a hyphen in some compound words in which the hyphen is considered part of the spelling, such as self-control and sister-in-law.

3. Use a hyphen to divide words at the end of a line.

Do not divide words unnecessarily, as many lines ending with hyphens can be distracting.   When you must divide to avoid extreme unevenness of typewritten lines, follow these guides:

- Divide only between syllables.
- Do not divide a word with fewer than seven letters.
- Do not separate the following syllables from the remainder of the word:
      a syllable that does not contain a vowel (couldn't)
      a first syllable of only one letter (ecology)
      a last syllable of one or two letters (extremely)
- Do not divide hyphenated words at any place other than at the hyphen. (well-being)
- Divide after a one-letter syllable within a word unless the word contains successive single-letter syllables. (congratu-lations)

- Try to avoid dividing proper names and numbers.
- Do not divide the last word of a paragraph or the last word on a page.

Parentheses

1. Use parentheses to set off explanatory or nonessential material.

- A choice of commas, dashes, or parentheses (used in pairs) can be used to set off parenthetical material.

You can change the meaning slightly according to your choice of punctuation. Dashes are more emphatic than commas. Parentheses indicate a more definite separation in meaning from the rest of the sentence than commas imply.

Quotation Marks

1. Use quotation marks to enclose the exact words of a writer or speaker.

2. Use quotation marks to enclose titles of songs, magazine and newspaper articles, poems, reports, and other short written works.

3. Use quotation marks to define terms.

4. Use quotation marks to enclose slang expressions.

5. Use quotation marks to enclose words used in an unusual way.

Quotation marks are used with other marks of punctuation in this way:

- Place commas and periods inside quotation marks.
- Place colons and semicolons outside quotation marks.
- Place question and exclamation marks inside the quotation marks when they refer to the quoted material, outside when they refer to the sentence as a whole.

WRITING NUMBERS

1. Spell out numbers one through ten if no larger number appears in the same sentence.

(Another rule for spelling out numbers is to write in words any number that can be expressed in no more than two words — which is, in effect, numbers one through one hundred. In business writing, however, the "through ten" rule is more readable and saves time.)

2. Spell out numbers that represent time when they are used with "o'clock." Use figures with a.m. and p.m.

3. Spell out the smaller number when two numbers come together.

- We ordered sixteen 24-inch mirrors.

4. Spell out amounts of money shown in legal documents; follow with the amount shown in figures.

(Do not use this method of expressing numbers in ordinary business writing.)

5. Use figures, regardless of the expressed quantity, to state:

- dates: April 15, 1978 — *not* April 15th
- money: $5, $17.20, 5 cents
- dimensions: 5 feet, 2 inches
- percentages: 5 percent
- page numbers: page 7

6. Spell out numbers at the beginning of sentences.

FREQUENTLY MISSPELLED WORDS

accommodate	efficient	occurrence
accompanying	embarrassing	pamphlet
acknowledging	enclosed	parallel
acknowledgment	equipped	permanent
across	exceed	personnel
advisable	excellent	precede
all right	existence	preceding
attorneys	familiar	preferred
bargain	feasible	prevalent
beginning	February	privilege
believe	forcible	procedure
beneficial	guaranteed	proceed
benefited	handling	quantity
bulletin	incidentally	questionnaire
calendar	indispensable	receive
chargeable	interfered	recipient
competent	introducing	referred
congratulations	journeys	separate
controlled	legible	similar
convenience	leisure	sincerely
deficiency	management	surprise
definite	noticeable	transferring
desirable	occasion	traveling
discrepancy	occurred	truly

FREQUENTLY CONFUSED OR MISUSED WORDS

accept, except

- *Accept* means "to receive with approval."
- *Except* means "excluding."
- All the employees *except* Mr. Jones *accepted* the small gifts.

adapt, adept, adopt

- *Adapt* means "to make suitable or fit," as for a particular use, purpose, or situation.

- *Adept* means "highly skilled, well trained, thoroughly proficient."
- *Adopt* means "to take by free choice into a close relationship, previously not existing."

- With a few minor changes we can *adapt* this room for use as a study.
- Because of his many years of experience, Bill is quite *adept* at newspaper writing.
- The young couple has plans to *adopt* a child within the next year.

advice, advise

- *Advice* is a noun that means a "view, opinion, judgment."
- *Advise* is a verb that means "to give an opinion, inform, consider."

- His *advice* was to think first, then respond with an answer.
- The captain will *advise* the tourists of the risk involved as they board his vessel.

affect, effect

- *Affect* is a verb meaning "to influence."
- *Effect,* used as a verb, means "to bring about." Effect is also a noun, meaning "result."

- The weather *affects* our moods.
- Do you think we could *effect* a change in working hours?
- What will be the *effect* of the change?

all together, altogether

- *All together* means "in one group."
- *Altogether* means "entirely."

- The committee members were *all together* when the vote was taken.
- The committee members were *altogether* in agreement.

already, all ready

- *Already* means "previously."
- *All ready* means "entirely ready."

- The secretary had *already* opened the office.
- She had the conference room *all ready* for the meeting.

appraise, apprise

- *Appraise* means "to estimate value."
- *Apprise* means "to inform" or "to advise."

anxious, eager

- *Anxious* ordinarily denotes anxiety or apprehension.
- *Eager* means "looking forward" or "enthusiastic."

biannual, biennial

- *Biannual* means "occurring twice a year"; "semiannual."
- *Biennial* means "happening every two years."

capital, capitol

- *Capital* means the city or town that is the official seat of government.
- *Capitol* is the building that contains the governmental offices. (Often not capitalized when referring to state capitol buildings.)

cite, sight, site

- *Cite* means "to quote."
- *Sight* means "something seen."
- *Site* means "position or location."

complement, compliment

- *Complement* means "to complete."
- *Compliment* means "to praise."

continual, continuous

- A *continual* action implies that the action is often occurring, but is not *continuous*, which means "uninterrupted."

council, counsel

- *Council* is a noun meaning "a group of persons delegated to give advice."
- *Counsel* used as a noun means "advice"; used as a verb, counsel means "to give advice."

credible, creditable

- *Credible* means "believable."
- *Creditable* means "worthy of credit."

flaunt, flout

- *Flaunt* means "to parade" or "to display boldly."
- *Flout* means "to treat with scorn."

formally, formerly

- *Formally* means "in a formal manner."
- *Formerly* means "previously."

its, it's

- *Its* is a possessive pronoun.
- *It's* is the contraction of "it is" or "it has."

- The horse lost *its* saddle.
- *It's* difficult to study before breakfast.

lose, loose

- *Lose* is a verb, the opposite of "find."
- *Loose* is an adjective, the opposite of "tight."

moral, morale

- *Moral* pertains to right conduct.
- *Morale* means a mental condition with respect to cheerfulness, confidence, and zeal.

passed, past

- *Passed* is the past tense of pass, as "The two ships passed in the night."
- *Past* means "gone by or elapsed in time," as "in past times," or "in the past."

personal, personnel

- *Personal* means "individual" or "private," as in "my personal opinion."
- *Personnel* means "the persons employed in an organization."

precede, proceed

- *Precede* means "to come before."
- *Proceed* means "to go ahead" or "to continue."

principal, principle

- *Principal* means "the most important." It is also "the amount of a loan."
- *Principle* means "a rule or basic truth."

quiet, quite

- *Quiet* means "not noisy."
- *Quite* means "entirely."
- This room is not *quite quiet.*

sometime, some time

- *Sometime* is a point in time, as "The work will be completed sometime soon."
- *Some time* means "an amount of time," as "This method has not been in effect for some time."

stationary, stationery

- *Stationary* means "not moving."
- *Stationery* is writing paper.

who's, whose

- *Who's* means "who is."
- *Whose* means "of or belonging to a person or persons as possessor or possessors."

- *Who's* going to travel by train?
- *Whose* little black puppy is this?

your, you're

- *Your* means "of or belonging to you or yourself."
- *You're* is the contraction for "you are."

- *Your* talent in musical performance is superb.
- *You're* not to pass another vehicle in this lane.

FREQUENTLY OCCURRING GRAMMATICAL ERRORS

Subject-Verb Disagreement

This commonly occurring error is particularly troublesome when dictating. Because words or phrases often come between the subject and the verb, the wrong form of the verb is dictated unthinkingly. Using the wrong form of the verb — as in "the boys is" or "the girl are — " is a serious error, a real error, according to all authorities and handbooks, and to almost everyone who will read your message. In simple constructions like these, the mistake is not likely to occur. In slightly more complicated sentences, it often does occur, as in:

The logic of good communicators seem to be —

Because the plural word *communicators* immediately precedes the verb, *seem* may creep into the sentence, although in a sentence no more involved than this one there is little reason for the wrong verb form, even when dictating. As more words intervene, the subject "gets lost" so that the wrong verb seems to be the appropriate one. One of the principles of good writing, however, is that it be simple and direct; another guide is that the subject and verb be close together. Sentences constructed in this way are likely to include the correct form of the verb.

In the sentence below, the verb is singular to agree with the subject *box:*

The box, together with the baskets, was sent to the shipping room.

The word *baskets* is not part of the subject, but because *baskets* immediately precedes the verb, it seems natural to use *were.*

In the following sentence, *were* is the correct verb:

The box and the baskets were sent to the shipping room.

Compare the above sentences with the following:

Neither the box nor the basket was sent to the shipping room.

Neither the box nor the baskets were sent to the shipping room.

The following guideline applies to sentences like the preceding ones: When one subject is singular and the other is plural, the verb agrees with the subject closer to the verb.

The Wrong Case of the Pronoun

Using the wrong case of the pronoun is an error that seems to occur more in speech than in writing. It is especially likely to occur in sentences in which *I* is used incorrectly (instead of *me*) as the object of a verb or preposition. Few persons, regardless of their position or educational background, say something like this:

Me and Jim are friends.

However, many persons say or write:

Jim and he are good friends of Mary and I.

In the preceding sentence, "Mary and *me*" should be used because the pronoun is the object of the preposition *of.* The *I* is just as incorrect as the *me* in "me and Jim," but for some reason the *I* seems to many persons to be more "cultured," more "elegant," more correct.

Remember these cases of pronouns:

Subjective:	I	you	he	she	it	we	they	who	whoever
Possessive:	my	your	his	her	its	our	their	whose	whosoever
Objective:	me	you	him	her	it	us	them	whom	whomever

A pronoun in the subjective case is used

• as the subject of a main or a subordinate clause;
• as a predicate nominative (as in "it is I," although "it is me" is more frequently heard in conversation) and;
• as a word that is in apposition with another word in the subjective case, as "only three persons attended — Jim, Jeannie, and I." (*I*, as well as *Jim* and *Jeannie*, is in apposition with *persons*, which is the subject of the sentence.)

A pronoun in the objective case is used when it is the object of a verb or a preposition or when it is used as an indirect object.

A pronoun modifying a gerund (a verb form used as a noun) is in the possessive case, as in:

We will appreciate your writing us immediately.

The use of *who* and *whom* confuses many persons, even to the extent that some have given up altogether and use only *who*. Some grammarians say that *whom* is in the process of passing from the language, although it has not yet done so. When these words are used, however, the choice of which to use should be according to the established rules — at least in formal writing and in most business writing of all kinds.

Languages change constantly in many ways, including what is considered to be correct. At some future time, the word "whom" may become obsolete. (Its passing will certainly eliminate many headaches for English teachers.) Most readers and listeners at the present time expect the more formal usage, with the possible exception of questions that start in this way:

Whom are you expecting?

In conversation among persons of all educational backgrounds, it is now much more usual to hear *who* used in questions of this kind. This use of *who* is not of recent origin, at least in colloquial speech, but goes back for many years, perhaps for as long as the words have been in existence. Some persons still object to this *who* usage, though, especially in writing; perhaps we as business writers should recast such sentences so that the problem does not arise.

Some persons approach the *who* and *whom* distinction as they do the *I* and *me* usages, seemingly with the idea that if one *whom* (or *I*) is good, a great number is better. *Whom* used incorrectly for *who* is no worse, from a grammatical standpoint, than using *who* in place of *whom;* but to most of us, somehow it sounds worse — as if the speaker has made an effort to be "proper," and failed.

Lydel Sims comments in this way in his column in *Mid-South Magazine,* "Watch Your Language." In answer to the following question:

> Sir: I keep reading phrases like "the men whom he thought were going" or "to whomever was interested." Surely such constructions can't be right. M.G.

Mr. Sims replies:

> Of course they can't. What's worse, they aren't even natural; people simply don't talk that way. But when they write, they fling out sacrificial *whoms* and *whomevers* like terrified worshippers appeasing the Great God Whom.
>
> Your first example should read "the men who he thought were going" because *who* is the subject of *were going*. There's no reason to be panicked by the parenthetical "he thought." The second example should read "to whoever was interested" because the clause "whoever was interested" is the object of the preposition *to*.
>
> There's some excuse for making errors that come naturally. But ingeniously cruel punishments should be devised for people who goof up the language with words they think must be right just because they sound wrong.[2]

In Mr. Sims's second example, *whoever* is the subject of the verb *was interested*. The entire clause is the object of the preposition *to*.

Notice the reasons for the choice of words in the following sentences:

- Who is to be the new president? (subject)
- Who do you think will be the new president? (Still the subject of the sentence, not the object of *think*.)
- John Jackson, who is our new president, will be at the meeting. (*Who* is the subject of the subordinate clause. A more concise way to word this sentence is to omit *who is* so that *our new president* is used in apposition with *John Jackson*.)
- *For Whom the Bell Tolls*. (*Whom* is the object of the preposition *for*.)

2. Lydel Sims, "Watch Your Language," *Mid-South Magazine*, November 23, 1975, p. 22. Used by permission of Lydel Sims and Columbia Features, Inc.

You will have many other decisions to make during your business career in addition to pondering over the question of whether to use *who* or *whom*.   Master the expected usage now and stop worrying about it.   (Yes, no doubt you already have more important things to worry about.   But this is one problem you can solve with very little effort.)

BASIC ERRORS IN SENTENCE CONSTRUCTION

Most conspicuous weaknesses in sentence construction are the following:

1.   Fragmentary sentences, although these can at times be used effectively
2.   The comma fault, also called a comma blunder, a comma splice, and a baby comma
3.   A fused sentence, also called a run-on sentence
4.   Nonparallel sentences, or sentences of mixed construction
5.   Sentences with dangling or misplaced modifiers

A fragmentary sentence, the comma fault, and the fused sentence can also be considered as errors in punctuation.   These weak constructions occur, however, because the writer is not sure of what constitutes a sentence.   The lack of necessary and wisely chosen punctuation results in these sentence weaknesses.

A fragmentary sentence is incomplete in itself; it is usually a phrase or a dependent clause.   Ordinarily it should not be punctuated as a complete sentence, as in the following examples:

This information is presented here.   Because it is necessary to the understanding of the following pages.

Improve by eliminating the period:

This information is presented here because it is necessary to the understanding of the following pages.

Aristotle's position on the subjugation of women contributed to their inferior status.   Which has continued to the present time.

Improve by eliminating period and making the "which" clause part of the sentence.   This would be better:

Aristotle's position on the subjugation of women contributed to their inferior status, which has continued to the present time.

Notice that in the first of the two correct sentences above no comma is necessary because the ending clause is restrictive, or necessary to continue the idea begun in the main clause. In the second example, the clause beginning with *which* is nonrestrictive. (See Item 8, in the section on use of the comma.)

The comma fault occurs when two sentences that are definitely separate have been joined together with a comma. They should be punctuated as two separate sentences, joined with a conjunction, or joined with a semicolon. The choice of the method of connection depends, to a certain extent, upon the desired meaning and emphasis. If the ideas are not related to the degree that they belong in the same sentence, they should be expressed in separate sentences. Avoid using a great many semicolons, as they can result in a choppy effect, just as a great number of short, simple sentences can. Usually one idea is more important than another; in this case, a complex sentence should be used.

Notice the following example of a comma fault:

> Children in all cultures are taught to become a part of that culture and to transmit it, perhaps it has been considered dangerous to allow excessive questioning of any particular culture. (Improve by starting a new sentence with *perhaps* or by using a semicolon before *perhaps*.)

This sentence could also be revised in the following way, although the meaning and emphasis are slightly changed:

> Because it has been considered dangerous to allow excessive questioning, children in all cultures are taught to become a part of that culture and to transmit it.

In short and closely related sentences, commas may at times be effectively used to join the clauses of compound sentences, as:

> I came, I saw, I conquered.

This construction, however, should be used with discretion and extreme caution, especially by the inexperienced writer. (See the discussion of the use of the semicolon under "Punctuation as an Aid to Readability," earlier in this appendix.)

A *fused sentence* occurs when two sentences are "run-on" with no separation at all. The sentences should be separated by a period, a semicolon, or a comma and a conjunction.

Nonparallel sentences occur when parallel ideas are not expressed in parallel form. An orderly arrangement is necessary for the immediate recognition of relationships of ideas.

The following sentences are not parallel because of unnecessary shifts from active to passive voice.

Jane wrote the music, and the lyrics were written by Mary Hicks.

The play was well written, and the director did a capable job.

Improved versions of these sentences are:

Jane wrote the music, and Mary Hicks wrote the lyrics.

The play was well written and capably directed.

The following sentence is nonparallel because similar ideas are expressed in differing ways, by use of the infinitive and of the gerund:

Taking the elevator is not so healthful as to climb the stairs. (Improve by changing "to climb" to "climbing.")

The following sentence is nonparallel because a relative clause and an infinitive phrase are used to express similar ideas:

We want a personnel manager who can motivate all workers and to recruit experienced salesmen.

An improved version of this sentence is:

We want a personnel manager who can motivate workers and who can recruit experienced salesmen.

A more concise version is:

We want a personnel manager who can motivate workers and recruit experienced salesmen.

The following phrases are not parallel because two gerunds and one infinitive are used in a sentence in which similar expressions should be of the same form:

Buying supplies, keeping the books, and to answer the telephone —

An improved version is:

Buying supplies, keeping the books, and answering the telephone —

The following sentence beginning is not parallel because two phrases are used with a clause:

Government of the people, by the people, and that is for the people —

The following sentences are nonparallel because of a misplaced correlative. (Correlatives are pairs of joining words, such as *either, or; neither, nor; both, and; not only, but also.*)

Either to make a living or a life is not an easy task, if it is done well.

Not only must we be concerned with the initial cost but also with the upkeep.

These sentences can be improved in this way:

To make either a living or a life is not an easy task, if it is done well.

We must be concerned not only with the initial cost but also with the upkeep.

Dangling or misplaced modifiers may consist of adjectives or adverbs; phrases, including participial, infinitive, or prepositional; and clauses. Any modifier is misplaced if it does not exactly and logically qualify (restrict, limit, describe) the word or words that it is intended to qualify.

A modifier is said to dangle when it has no reasonable or logical word to modify, as in this sentence:

Working without a coffee break, the telephone calls were completed before noon.

As this sentence is constructed, the participle *working* seems to modify telephone calls, when obviously it cannot. The modifier here could also be described as all the words that come before the main part of the sentence, "working without a coffee break." The sentence should be improved in this way:

Working without a coffee break, I completed the telephone calls before noon.

Dangling participles sometimes occur because the writer is too much concerned with avoiding the word *I*. *I* and *we* should be used when they are natural and necessary to the sentence, except for the few kinds of business writing that use only the impersonal tone.

Here are more examples of dangling modifiers:

When stewed until mushy, put the fruit into the blender.

Rapping with the dean, every problem in the college was mentioned by some student or other.

(Do you suppose that they got around to mentioning the need for further study in sentence structure?)

Being dark and winding, she could barely see the road.

Completely renovated two years ago, I was most impressed by the old building.

Many misplaced or dangling modifiers do not distort the meaning, at least upon a second reading. But clarity, even immediate clarity, is not our only goal in writing or speaking. We also want to communicate exactly, precisely, and professionally. Even if an imperfect sentence does not result in an unintentional humorous or preposterous statement, like (or worse than) those above, it is still an inexact, amateurish expression.

Avoid using a great many participial openings, even if they do not dangle. Usually the sentence is more direct and forceful when it opens with the subject-verb combination.

Misplaced modifiers may be in sentence positions other than the beginning, as in the following sentence:

> The woman driving the Thunderbird in a red pantsuit is my grandmother. (misplaced prepositional phrase)

> In the downtown section, with sirens screaming, we saw the fire truck skid to a stop. (misplaced prepositional phrase)

Modifiers, sometimes placed so they could refer to either one of two elements, are called "squinting modifiers." In the following sentence, what does *somehow* modify?

> Although it was yearly said that the old boat would sink somehow it seemed blessed with unsinkability.[3]

If the introductory clause had been followed with a comma, the adverb *somehow* would unmistakenly modify the clause following. With the comma after *somehow,* it would modify *sink.* Without a comma, two different meanings could be interpreted. This example illustrates the wisdom of punctuating according to accepted conventions.

The word *only* is easily misplaced. *Rarely, merely, hardly, just, even,* and other words are also located in various places in the sentence, often not in the best location to refer to the exact word or group of words that it modifies. As a general rule, put closely related words together.

The following sentence contains a misplaced *only,* although this particular construction is often used in conversation and sometimes in writing.

He only received a few dollars for his poem.

In formal writing, and preferably on all occasions, the following construction should be used:

He received only a few dollars for his poem.

Regardless of the formality of the writing, the expression is more exact if the modifier is in the best possible location in relationship to the rest of the sentence. In addition, the placement of *only* or similar words can affect the meaning of the sentence.

3. Porter G. Perrin and George H. Smith, *Handbook of Current English* 3d ed. (Glenview, Ill.: Scott Foresman and Company, 1968), p. 132.

Notice how the meaning changes, according to the placement of *only*, in the following sentences:

> Only MacArthur said that he would return.
> MacArthur only said that he would return.
> MacArthur said only that he would return.
> MacArthur said that only he would return.
> MacArthur said that he only would return.
> MacArthur said that he would only return.

In the next to the last sentence, the *only* is squinting in that it could modify either *he* or *would return*.

QUESTIONS AND PROBLEMS ◆ APPENDIX D

Exercise 1: Apostrophes

Choose the correct word. (*Review pages 569–570.*)

1. (That's, Thats) (someone else's, someone elses) problem.   1. _____
2.   2. _____
3. (You're, your) not going alone, are you?   3. _____
4. (Your, You're) sister knows my brother.   4. _____
5. (John's, Johns) car is now paid for.   5. _____
6. Mr. Jones has one (year's, years', years) experience; Miss   6. _____
7. Black has three (year's, years', years) experience.   7. _____
8. This (boy's, boys') bicycle is in the shop.   8. _____
9. These (boy's, boys') bikes are here.   9. _____
10. Mr. (Johnson's, Johnsons') house is on the corner.   10. _____
11. The clinic is owned by two (M.D.s, M.D.'s).   11. _____
12. Is the past tense of travel spelled with one or two (1s, 1's)?   12. _____
13. The (Davises', Davis's) automobile, which belongs to the   13. _____
    entire family of nine persons, is quite battered by now.
14. (Jim's and Mary's, Jim and Mary's) family consists of   14. _____
    three boys.
15. (Jim's and Mary's, Jim and Mary's) personalities are very   15. _____
    different.

Exercise 2: Commas, Semicolons, and Colons

Insert necessary commas, semicolons, and colons. Some sentences need more than one mark of punctuation, and some are correct as given. Do not use additional periods. If you believe a sentence needs no further punctuation, write "correct" by the sentence. (*Review pages 571–575.*)

1. Nonverbal communication includes all messages except written and spoken ones.
2. Nonverbal communication which consists of many forms permeates all speech and much of written communication.
3. We can never learn to read a person like a book fortunately for we are all too complicated for that.
4. Many people take an overly simplified view of the subject.
5. As we all know perfect communication cannot be achieved by reading a book.
6. Ruesch and Kees classify human nonverbal communication into three broad categories sign language object language and action language.
7. We also communicate by tone of voice which differs according to our mood and the person with whom we are talking.
8. Much of nonverbal communication is not silent however regardless of Hall's title *The Silent Language*.
9. The slamming of a door is not silent and it is most expressive.
10. Some communication is silent nevertheless it is at times most expressive.
11. We all want to express ourselves and to receive the messages of others.
12. We communicate nonverbally to machines and they communicate nonverbally to us.
13. We push a button to receive black coffee the machine responds by supplying the coffee.
14. If it doesn't we kick it.
15. To test the theory that humans will fight for their territorial rights try giving your husband's favorite chair to Goodwill.
16. In the United States and the Western European countries personal distance zones are greater than in Arab countries.
17. Believing that height adds status a businessman put his desk and chair on a raised platform.
18. We carry with us a kind of invisible bubble that we consider to be our own space.
19. As you interview persons or talk with visitors your desk becomes a barrier between you.
20. Looking over glasses at someone results in a condescending scrutinizing look.
21. The pupils of our eyes enlarge when we are looking at something that pleases us they contract when we are displeased.
22. There are regional differences as well as national differences in nonverbal

communication and people in the South especially in Georgia smile more often than those in Maine or New York.

23. Millions of frames are chewed up each year but people tell the ophthalmologists that the dog chewed them up.

24. Because it is mostly unplanned it is one of the most sincere forms of communication.

25. The four zones of personal distance are these intimate personal social and public.

26. All communication is imperfect not entirely accurate or complete.

27. We can improve our communication by becoming aware of what other people are trying to tell us through nonverbal communication.

28. Nonverbal communication should not be taken out of context the spoken message the environment and previously established relationships.

29. Authors in the field include Edward T. Hall who wrote *The Silent Language* and *The Hidden Dimension* Ray Birdwhistell author of *Kinesics and Context* and Flora Davis who wrote *Inside Intuition*.

30. Perhaps communication can bring us all closer together and actually make possible the often meaningless "Have a nice day."

Exercise 3: Hyphens and Quotation Marks

Use hyphens and quotation marks as needed in the following sentences. All other marks of punctuation are used correctly. (*Review pages 576– 577.*)

1. A well written refusal letter does not present the refusal in the last sentence.
2. Is this letter well written?
3. Preparations are now being made is an example of the use of the passive voice.
4. The blocked arrangement is one of the most widely used letter styles.
5. The time saving factor must be kept in mind when choosing a letter style.
6. The new production manager displayed admirable self control when he was referred to as old fashioned.
7. The expression buzz off was not understood by the teacher.
8. The poem entitled A Note to Queen Elizabeth won an award.
9. The best sales messages do not use high pressure techniques.
10. Have you read the poem, The Professor's Funeral?
11. Other poems by the same author include A Ride to the Airport.
12. The student said, I do not understand.
13. Phrases such as Act today! and Hurry! are not usually effective in the action section of a sales letter.
14. The term resale is not an exact synonym for the term sales promotion.

15. The teacher made this statement: Personalize the favorable and impersonalize the unfavorable is good letter writing advice.

Show where each of the following words can be correctly divided at the end of a typewritten line. Some cannot be correctly divided.

16. compound		21. no-hitter
17. alone		22. shouldn't
18. elopement		23. drollery
19. stopping		24. pizzazz
20. stopped		25. plight

Exercise 4: Writing Numbers

Choose the correct word. (*Review page 578.*)

1. The graduation was (two, 2) weeks ago on (May 8, May   1. _____
2. 8th) 1978.   2. _____
3. (Seventeen, 17) books are now overdue.   3. _____
4. The cost is only ($5, five dollars, 5 dollars, $5.00).   4. _____
5. The wedding is to be at (5, five) o'clock.   5. _____
6. The wedding is to be at (5, five) p.m.   6. _____
7. Place an order for (11, eleven) (25, twenty-five) pound bags of 7. _____
8. flour.   8. _____
9. The interest rate of (7, seven) percent is stated on page   9. _____
10. (4, four) of the sales contract.   10. _____
11. We brought (thirteen, 13) suitcases, (5, five) garment   11. _____
12. bags, and 172 boxes of books.   12. _____
13. The hall is (19, nineteen) feet, (2, two) inches wide.   13. _____
                                                                 14. _____
15. The copies cost (5¢, 5 cents, five cents) each.   15. _____

Exercise 5: Spelling

Check *a*, *b*, *c*, or *d* to indicate a misspelled word. If all four words are correct, check *e*. No group has more than one misspelled word. (*Review page 579.*)

1. ____a. accommodate
   ____b. truely
   ____c. occurred
   ____d. discrepancy
   ____e. all are correct
2. ____a. accompanying
   ____b. traveling
   ____c. occassion
   ____d. desirable
   ____e. all are correct

3. ____a. definate
   ____b. acknowledgment
   ____c. traveling
   ____d. noticeable
   ____e. all are correct
4. ____a. sincerely
   ____b. accross
   ____c. management
   ____d. leisure
   ____e. all are correct

5. ____a. similar
   ____b. efficient
   ____c. embarrassing
   ____d. questionnaire
   ____e. all are correct

6. ____a. seperate
   ____b. deficiency
   ____c. convenience
   ____d. introducing
   ____e. all are correct

7. ____a. controlled
   ____b. congradulations
   ____c. interfered
   ____d. recipient
   ____e. all are correct

8. ____a. quantity
   ____b. procede
   ____c. procedure
   ____d. precede
   ____e. all are correct

9. ____a. advisable
   ____b. bargain
   ____c. all right
   ____d. attorneys
   ____e. all are correct

10. ____a. believe
    ____b. beginning
    ____c. February
    ____d. recieve
    ____e. all are correct

11. ____a. guaranteed
    ____b. handling
    ____c. incidentally
    ____d. feasable
    ____e. all are correct

12. ____a. priviledge
    ____b. journeys
    ____c. companies
    ____d. existence
    ____e. all are correct

13. ____a. efficient
    ____b. bulletin
    ____c. handling
    ____d. guaranteed
    ____e. all are correct

14. ____a. excellent
    ____b. equipped
    ____c. exceed
    ____d. personel
    ____e. all are correct

15. ____a. pamphlet
    ____b. familar
    ____c. excellent
    ____d. enclosed
    ____e. all are correct

16. ____a. benefical
    ____b. preferred
    ____c. parallel
    ____d. occurrence
    ____e. all are correct

17. ____a. chargeable
    ____b. acknowledging
    ____c. benefited
    ____d. bulletin
    ____e. all are correct

18. ____a. permanent
    ____b. surprise
    ____c. calender
    ____d. competent
    ____e. all are correct

19. ____a. discrepancy
    ____b. desirable
    ____c. indispensible
    ____d. referred
    ____e. all are correct

20. ____a. legible
    ____b. deficiency
    ____c. preferred
    ____d. similiar
    ____e. all are correct

Exercise 6: Word Choice

Choose the correct word.   (*Review pages 579–584.*)

1. All the salesmen (except, accept) Mr. Barnes voted to
2. (except, accept) the proposed schedule changes.

1. _____
2. _____

3. Employees are not permitted to (except, accept) gifts   3. _____
   from suppliers.

4. Can we (adapt, adopt) the suggested course outline for   4. _____

5. use with the newly (adopted, adapted, adept) textbook?   5. _____

6. Free (advice, advise) is said to be worth as much as it   6. _____
   costs.

7. What do you (advice, advise) me to do about the   7. _____
   situation?

8. What do you believe will be the (affect, effect) of the tax   8. _____
   increase on inflation?

9. To (effect, affect) improvements in employee morale, we   9. _____
   should communicate more openly and completely.

10. Our emotions are often (affected, effected) adversely by   10. _____
    physical or mental fatigue.

11. That statement is not (all together, altogether) correct.   11. _____

12. The family will be (all together, altogether) for   12. _____
    Christmas.

13. We have (already, all ready) made plans for our vacation.   13. _____

14. On Friday, June 1, we will be (already, all ready) to   14. _____
    leave for Spain.

15. She had the diamond (appraised, apprised).   15. _____

16. I was not (apprised, appraised) of the transfer of the   16. _____
    manager.

17. Try not to be (eager, anxious); remember the   17. _____
    admonition, "Sufficient unto the day is the evil thereof."

18. I am (eager, anxious) to meet my new in-laws, although   18. _____

19. I'll admit I feel somewhat (eager, anxious) about making   19. _____
    a good impression.

20. The word (*biannual, biennial*), meaning half-yearly, is   20. _____
    about one hundred years old.

21. (*Biannual, Biennial*), meaning "every two years," is an   21. _____
    older word.

22. My ring is too (lose, loose); I fear I shall (lose, loose) it. 22. _____
                                                                  23. _____

24. Communication systems that conform to (moral, morale)   24. _____

25. (principles, principals) increase employee (moral,   25. _____

26. morale.)   26. _____

27. In (passed, past) years, the test was (passed, past) by a   27. _____

28. higher percentage of high school graduates.   28. _____

29. The (personal, personnel) manager does not discuss her   29. _____

30. family or any other aspect of her (personal, personnel)   30. _____
    life.

31. The speaker was asked to (precede, proceed) with his   31. _____

32. presentation without delay, as the (preceding,   32. _____
    proceeding) speaker had exceeded the time limit.

33. (Sometime, Some time) in the future, I hope to spend   33. _____
34. (sometime, some time) in Australia.   34. _____
35. The writing paper (stationary, stationery) is weighted   35. _____
36. down with a brick. It is now (stationary, stationery).   36. _____
37. (Who's Whose) the new man in the group?   37. _____
38. (Who's, Whose) yellow sports car is in my parking space?   38. _____
39. (Your, You're) too unsure of (your, you're) ability.   39. _____
                                                                  _____

40. "With our (compliments, complements)" means in less   40. _____
    gracious language that whatever is offered is free.
41. The artist was most (complimentary, complementary)   41. _____
42. about our use of (complimentary, complementary) colors.   42. _____
43. The (continual, continuous) interruptions seemed to   43. _____
    annoy the speaker.
44. After working (continually, continuously) throughout the   44. _____
    morning, we spent two hours at lunch.
45. The Student (Council, Counsel) includes a few   45. _____
    representatives from the Graduate School.
46. Faculty (councilors, counselors) advise students about the   46. _____
    preparation of class schedules.
47. The data should create a (creditable, credible) impression   47. _____
48. if the readers are to be convinced of its (creditability,   48. _____
    credibility).
49. A bit of rather cynical (council, counsel) is: "If you've   49. _____
50. got it, (flaunt, flout) it."   50. _____
51. (Formerly, Formally), the ceremony was conducted quite   51. _____
52. (formerly, formally); it is now much more casual.   52. _____
53. (Its, It's) a lovely day.   53. _____
54. You can't judge a book by (its, it's) cover.   54. _____

Exercise 7: Word Choice

Choose the correct word. (*Review pages 584–588.*)

1. Various estimates from recognized authorities (indicate,   1. _____
2. indicates) that forms of nonverbal communication (make,   2. _____
   makes) up as much as 75 percent of the transfer of
   meaning and emotion in face-to-face interaction.

3. A business letter or a report (communicate,   3. _____
   communicates) through appearance.
4. Business letters and reports (communicate,   4. _____
   communicates) through appearance.
5. Nonverbal communication, as well as written or spoken   5. _____
   words, (is, are) sometimes misinterpreted.

6. Care and judgment in classifying and assigning types of letters (is, are) highly desirable.

                    6. _____

7. A cleverly phrased sentence or vivid, descriptive words (is, are) of little value if the message is not based on accurate knowledge.

                    7. _____

8. The invitation was sent to my husband and (I, me).

                    8. _____

9. Three members arrived early—Mr. Hames, Mr. Baker, and (I, me).

                    9. _____

10. It was John and (I, me) who presented the skit.

                    10. _____

11. (Who, Whom) is the new salesman?

                    11. _____

12. (Who, Whom) telephoned about the contract?

                    12. _____

13. (Who, Whom) did you say called?

                    13. _____

14. Miss Brown, (who, whom) you met in St. Louis, is the new sales representative in Maine.

                    14. _____

15. Mr. Wilson, (who, whom) I thought would go to Maine, has left our organization.

                    15. _____

16. Miss Jones taught my sister and (I, me) when we were in the first grade.

                    16. _____

Exercise 8: Sentence Structure

Improve each sentence and state its weakness. (*Review pages 588–593.*)

1. This statement is only one illustration of the ways in which words can have several meanings.   As I shall discuss later.

2. I shall also speak of barriers to communication many of these barriers are of our own making.

3. Even secretarial work was not acceptable for many years, women were said to be too weak, physically, for office work.

4. Knowing that words have differing meanings to various individuals, the word "tree" may remind you of a magnolia, an oak, or a pine.

5. Meaning is in the mind therefore all communication is imperfect.

6. The expression "walking on air" would not apply either when you are tired or depressed.

7. Verbal communication only transfers about 25 percent of our meaning.

8. Believing the subject to be important, the book was written in a year.

9. The writer only slept for five hours a night.

10. Women's duties previously consisted of plowing fields, raising children, and to do heavy housework.

11. I shall relate this discussion of communication to management. And especially toward management by women.

12. Women typists were known as "typewriters" in the early years of office work, in addition, they "manned" the heavy machines.

13. The woman at the computer smoking a cigarette is breaking office rules.

14. Sleeping is better than to get up, at least at times.

Index